MY SECRET LIFE

ABRIDGED BUT UNEXPURGATED

INTRODUCTION BY
G. LEGMAN

GROVE PRESS, INC.
NEW YORK

Sixteenth Printing

Manufactured in the United States of America

DISTRIBUTED BY RANDOM HOUSE, INC., NEW YORK

GROVE PRESS, INC., 53 EAST 11TH STREET,
NEW YORK, NEW YORK 10003

A NOTE ON THIS ABRIDGMENT
OF *MY SECRET LIFE*

As the reader will see from the descriptions in the Publisher's Preface and Introduction that follow, the underground classic *My Secret Life* is an enormous work. As originally printed privately for its anonymous author, it consisted of eleven volumes of approximately 380 pages each. The first public edition, prepared by Grove Press in 1966, uses a much larger page size, but the text still occupies some 2,400 pages bound in two volumes and sold as a boxed set for $30.

This abridgment was found necessary because it proved impossible to produce a single-volume paperback edition containing the entire work in readable form and at a reasonable price. Every effort has been made, however, to make the abridgment as representative of the full text as possible. Episodes from childhood and youth, maturity and later years are included, as well as selections reflecting the author's experiences in various social milieus and European countries. Sections describing his relations with the three most important women of his life have been retained, as well as his reflections on sex. Therefore, while this is an abridgment it is not an expurgation, and represents the entire text as faithfully as could be done without including all of it.

The Publisher's Preface and the Introduction to the full Grove Press two-volume edition are included here as they originally appeared, because they contain much that is indispensable to an understanding of *My Secret Life*. The reader will understand, however, that where they describe the edition as "complete" or "integral," they refer not to this paperback edition but to the cloth-bound boxed set described above.

5

PUBLISHER'S PREFACE

My Secret Life is one of the longest erotic autobiographies ever written. As such memoirs go, it has no equal, both for the variety of sexual experiences described and for the frankness of the language employed. Not even Frank Harris' near-legendary exercise in frankness and fantasy — which, some scholar may one day prove, might well owe more of a debt to *My Secret Life* than its author ever acknowledged — can vie with it.

Despite considerable speculation concerning the authorship of this work, including an interesting attempt by G. Legman in the Introduction to the present edition to make a convincing case for the famous Victorian bibliographer and collector of erotica, H. Spencer Ashbee, concrete proof of authorship remains to be discovered. Whatever his name, he was a well-to-do English gentleman who, judging from the internal evidence of the work itself, must have been born some time between 1820 and 1825. From his account, he was one of several children, and some indication of the family's wealth and social position can be had by an enumeration of the maidservants living in the household at various times during the author's youth, and also from the fact that at one point he remarks that, when he was a boy, he "was carefully kept from the grooms and the other man servants." As the future author moved from childhood to adolescence, however, the family fortunes seem to have taken a turn for the worse: he relates how his father "got into difficulties, we moved to a smaller house, [and] I was sent to another school." Shortly thereafter his father went abroad for a year, presumably to some English colony to try and recoup his waning fortune, for the author refers to his having to "look after some plantations." After a year away, however, his father returned home, "broken hearted, I have heard, and ill," and, two or three years later, died, "nearly bankrupt." These monetary considerations are not without their bearing upon the author and his work-to-come, for the life he describes could never have been lived, and the work he penned could never have been written, by a man without money.

At the time of his father's death, the author, who refers to himself throughout *My Secret Life* as Walter, was sixteen years old. In true Victorian-novel tradition, however, the threat of poverty, at this juncture of his life as later, was staved off by the timely intervention of a wealthy relative or family friend, in this instance by a god-father, who died and bequeathed him "a fortune" when he was twenty-one. Young Walter succeeded in dissipating this fortune with amazing speed even for a young man of his obvious gifts for dissolu-tion. Although he admits to squandering a good deal of his fortune on women, in the company of an equally profligate cousin who shared his tastes and amatory escapades, he apparently spent even more on gambling and other frivolities, for he states enigmatically: "Had I spent it [his godfather's fortune] only on women, it would have lasted much longer."

By the time he had reached his mid-twenties, Walter was pen-niless and once again obliged to resort to the meager allowance which his mother doled out to him, each time with a futile admon-ishment for the young man to mend his ways. It was about this same period apparently — some time between the author's twenty-third and twenty-fifth year — that he began to record his memoirs, de-tailed accounts of his erotic encounters. Earlier in his life, like many another Englishman of the Victorian era, he had "kept a diary of some sort," but the journals he began in his mid-twenties seem to have been the initial recording of those events which were ulti-mately to become *My Secret Life*. The full details of the subsequent chronology and methods of composition are related in the author's Preface to the first volume, which description can probably be taken at face value. Suffice it to say here that after pursuing his more serious efforts to record his experiences for a number of years, he eventually "tired of it and ceased." Then, when he was about thirty-five, he met a woman with whose help, and the help of those to whom she introduced him, he "did, said, saw, and heard well nigh everything a man and a woman could do with their genitals." These experiences impelled him once again to begin recording "those events, when quite fresh in my memory, a great variety of incidents extending over four years."

When he was in his early forties, he was stricken by the first of two unnamed but apparently serious illnesses which kept him con-fined, and during this time, he notes, "I amused myself by reading, sorting, and arranging these memoirs. I referred to them by dates in my diary, and made them in their order pretty complete." Two years later, during his second illness, he once again turned to the manuscript, reread it, "and filled in some occurrences which I had forgotten, but which my diary enabled me to place in their proper order."

Professor Steven Marcus, in his recently published study of what he called the "underbelly" of Victorian England, entitled *The Other Victorians*, comments judiciously on the author's methods of composition at this point in his career:

What can be observed, then, is that by about the time the author had reached the midpoint of his career as a memoirist, a rough paradigm of a method of composition had emerged and stabilized itself. It emerged out of a complicated and regular series of interchanges between diary notes, notes in the form of copious memoranda, and fully written out episodes, and may be typified as follows. The author would have a sexual experience and would make a diary notation of it. Shortly thereafter, most usually within a couple of days, he would sit down and write out the episode in as much detail as he could. Over a period of time, quantities of manuscript would accumulate, and at uncertain though increasingly frequent intervals the author would reread, rearrange, sort, order, revise, abbreviate, edit, and add comment to portions of the ever enlarging mass. When the author arrived at the decision to commit himself to print, a final further rereading and revision of the manuscript was undertaken. It was at this moment that he began to change names and suppress dates and places; he also decided to change and unify the tense of the narrative throughout—replacing the present tense, in which a good deal of the original manuscript was written, with the past. In the course of his rereadings, he would often add passages of critical or ideological reflection on the episode described, on his own attitudes, on changes that had since occurred in him; and during the final rereading and editing, he sometimes added comments to the comments. On some occasions he would insert these comments in square brackets; on others he would recast an entire passage. . . .

In certain ways, therefore, the text of *My Secret Life* has something of the quality of a palimpsest—particularly since the author was not always concerned to indicate his revisions. But it should in addition be emphasized that the author in no way followed this procedure with any kind of regularity, tenacity of purpose, or organizing conception. He did not hesitate to print unrevised passages, dislocated jottings, repetitive episodes or adventures. He had little interest in formal or internal consistency, and no interest in formal structure. Like Ashbee's bibliography,[1] *My Secret Life* is not to be thought of as primarily a triumph of intellect—of insight shaped by discipline and method—over tabooed and refractory material. But it is something equally interesting, for it reveals to us the workings and broodings of a mind that had for an entire lifetime been possessed by a single subject or interest. It further reveals to us how that interest had shaped the mind and person which it possessed; how the mind which was possessed attempted in turn to cope with the forces which possessed it; and how, during the Victorian period, a man who tried to deal directly with the demons of sexuality lived and felt and thought. That in itself, we shall see, is triumph enough.[2]

It was at this period of the author's life, that is, some time in the 1860's, that the thought of printing the work privately first occurred to him. He was, he relates, then torn between the temptation to burn it and the desire to see it in print. But reason — or pride — finally prevailed. In his Second Preface, the author notes:

> It would be a sin to burn all this, whatever society may say, it is but a narrative of human life, perhaps the every day life of thousands, if the confession could be had. . . . Shall it be burnt or printed? How many years have passed in this indecision? why fear? it is for others' good and not my own if preserved.

The fact was that more than twenty years were to pass "in this indecision" before *My Secret Life* actually moved from "unmanageable manuscript" to bulky book. Some time in the neighborhood of 1882,[3] the author summoned a well-known printer of erotica from Amsterdam to England, to discuss the possible terms and conditions for printing the work. The author had determined that only six copies were to be printed, and that the type would then be broken up and destroyed. The price agreed upon was presumably 100 guin-

---

[1] Mr. Marcus is referring of course to the bibliographical trilogy published by Henry Spencer Ashbee, the man whom Mr. Legman judges the likeliest candidate for the authorship of *My Secret Life*. The three volumes published by Ashbee, under the pseudonym of Pisanus Fraxi, are: *Index Librorum Prohibitorum: being Notes Bio-Biblio-Icono-graphical and Critical, on Curious and Uncommon Books* (1877); *Centuria Librorum Absconditorum* (1879); *Catena Librorum Tacendorum* (1885).

[2] *The Other Victorians*, (New York: Basic Books, 1966), pp. 84–87.

[3] In his Introduction to the present edition, G. Legman quotes the Paris bookseller Carrington as noting in his 1902 catalogue, which describes *My Secret Life*, that it was only in 1888 that the Amsterdam printer was called to London. Be that as it may, it appears that the printing was completed no later than 1894.

eas a volume since the total cost was 1,100 guineas and, as it turned out, there were eleven volumes. From the various errors and incon-sistencies from one volume to the next, it is evident that different volumes were set by different compositors, probably over a period of years. According to Legman and others, it was not until 1894 that the eleventh and final volume — with its extraordinary, and perhaps unique, index — was finally completed. By then the author would have been in his late sixties or mid-seventies, depending on what precise date of birth one assigns him.

Professor Marcus' description of this Amsterdam edition is worthy of note:

> *My Secret Life* consists of eleven uniform volumes, the whole coming to some 4,200 pages.[4] It is in small crown octavo and is printed on handmade ribbed paper. The title page of each volume bears the imprint "Amsterdam. Not for publication." There is no date, but we can be reasonably certain that it was printed over a period of time in which 1890 can stand as a mid-point. . . . The manuscript seems to have been presented in large-sized batches to the printer, who would then run them up, hand over the printed volumes to the author, and receive in turn additional manuscript.[5]

So much for the historical data, or as much as is presently known, concerning the author himself, the details of the work's composition, and the methods and dates of its six-copy printing.

What of the work itself? What is its value, as literature, as social history, or, simply, as a revealing human document? Is it an authentic autobiography, an attempt to portray the truth as the author lived it, or does it contain portions, and perhaps even gen-erous portions of fantasy and wish-fulfillment?

Despite the limitations and crudities of the author's style, one is constantly amazed by a certain freshness in the writing and im-pressed by scene after scene which strike home as authentic and unsentimentalized portraits, alive and unforgettable. Critics may, if they wish, carp at the stylistic awkwardnesses which dot the work from start to finish. Yet, as the author notes in his Preface, "This is intended to be a true history, and not a lie," and, throughout, the ring of truth and authenticity are present, to a degree often lacking

---

[4] The present edition includes the complete and unexpurgated Amsterdam work. The small crown octavo format of the private printing allowed only about half as much text per page as is contained in this, the first public printing of the work.

[5] Marcus, *op. cit.*, p. 82.

in works of greater literary merit. There can be no question but that
My Secret Life, as Professor Marcus declares, is "a unique docu-
ment . . . the most important document of its kind about Victorian
England."[6]

Considering it as a work valuable as social history, for the in-
sights it can give us into the methods and mores of a particular era,
Mr. Marcus has this to say:

> As simple social history, then, the facts and details of *My Secret Life*
> are interesting and useful, and there can be no question that we
> should know them. They add to and thicken our sense of the Victorian
> reality, and they move it further ahead in the direction toward which
> much modern historical research has already tended. . . . [It] shows
> us that amid and underneath the world of Victorian England as we
> know it—and as it tended to represent itself to itself—a real, secret
> social life was being conducted, the secret life of sexuality. Every day,
> everywhere, people were meeting, encountering one another, coming
> together, and moving on. And although it is true that the Victorians
> could not help but know of this, almost no one was reporting on it;
> the social history of their own sexual experiences was not part of the
> Victorians' official consciousness of themselves or of their society.[7]

One of the most interesting aspects of *My Secret Life* is the
way in which it relates, and adds a new dimension, to the Victorian
novel. "Its material," says Marcus, "bears directly on both the con-
cerns or interests of the great Victorian novelists and on their ways
of representing those interests. . . . It adds considerably to our un-
derstanding of the Victorian novel if we read it against such scenes
as those represented in *My Secret Life*, if we understand that the
Victorian novelists were aware of such scenes, and that their great
project, taken as a whole, was directed dialectically against what
such scenes meant. There is no doubt that the Victorian conventions
of censorship had a severely limiting effect on the range of the
novel."[8] In a fascinating section of *The Other Victorians*, Professor
Marcus goes on to cite roughly parallel passages from both *My
Secret Life* and, say, Dickens, showing the similarities of subject
and demonstrating how one complements the other.

In most memoirs, and indeed especially in those where candor
is emphasized, as in this work or in Frank Harris' *My Life and*

6 *Ibid.*, p. 97.
7 *Ibid.*, pp. 101–3.
8 *Ibid.*, pp. 103, 109.

Loves, the differentiation between fact and fancy is often extremely difficult and tenuous. "A work such as *My Secret Life*," notes Mr. Marcus, who has studied the work as closely as any contemporary scholar,

> falls within the scope of G. M. Young's statement that "the real, central theme of History is not what happened, but what people felt about it when it was happening." That is to say, *My Secret Life* is important by virtue of its authenticity. It is the authentic record of what one man perceived, felt, saw, believed, and wanted to believe.[9]

One clear proof of the work's authenticity, Mr. Marcus believes, is the very fact that it contains certain distortions and is often informed by a typically Victorian ignorance on certain subjects, especially on sexual matters. Nor does it matter essentially, in his opinion, whether fantasy and falsehood creep in occasionally, or even more than occasionally:

> To what degree, then, is the credibility of the author's account impaired by such distortions, by these fantasies and falsehoods? The answer to this question is altogether evident. Its credibility is not impaired in the least; indeed it is, if anything, enhanced by them. They are an important part of its authenticity, an authenticity which is subjective, historical, and profoundly conditioned, and which is considerably more complex, interesting, and problematical than an authenticity which confines itself to "fact" alone. These fantasies, we should remember, are also facts. And even if it were to be proved that the whole eleven volumes of *My Secret Life* were nothing but fantasy, such a discovery could not, in this context, radically alter the circumstances or our attitude toward them. . . . Since it has been demonstrated that, when it comes to matters of reporting about sexual experience, there is always an intermixture of fact and fantasy, that the fantasies are at least equally important as the "facts," and that they have as much if not more meaning to them, we must in our examination of these documents pay as much respect to their errors and falsifications as we do to those parts of the account which seem, in the usual sense of the expression, to have actually happened.[10]

In a recent review of Professor Marcus' *The Other Victorians*, critic Robert Phelps refers to "the long central section describing 'the most important document of its kind about Victorian England.'" He says:

---

[9] *Ibid.*, p. 111.
[10] *Ibid.*, pp. 113–14.

This is the near-legendary autobiography known as *My Secret Life*. . . . [It] is the other side of the Victorian novel, what Dickens and Meredith and George Eliot and Thomas Hardy were obliged to leave out. And if only for this reason (though, in the passages Mr. Marcus quotes, it is immensely readable for its own sake), it should be published as soon as possible.[11]

Of the six copies of the author's original, private printing only three apparently are extant today. One of these is in the Kinsey Institute, another is in the possession of the British Museum, and a third is in a private collection in Europe. The present edition was taken from the third of these three known copies. There is, of course, scholarly speculation as to the size of the original printing. Legman contends (see Introduction) that the printer undoubtedly struck off additional copies, and that more than three copies are extant today. Marcus, on the other hand, holds that the three copies listed above exist, and to our own knowledge they are indeed the only copies extant; however, it is certain that the author never authorized the sale of the work.

In preparing this work for publication, the editors have made every effort to keep to the original as closely as possible. A great number of outright errors — all obvious and clearly due to the circumstances of the work's composition by typesetters who knew little or no English and whose work had apparently never been proofread — have been corrected. The author's many grammatical lapses, errors, and inconsistencies of all sorts, have generally not been corrected, except where they tended to make the author's meaning unduly ambiguous or obscure. Further, a number of his quaint spellings have also been expressly retained. In the original edition the Table of Contents which precedes each volume was repeated at the end of Volume XI, following the index; in this edition the duplication has been omitted. In the interest of preserving the authenticity of a document of great importance, which until now has been available only to a very few scholars, it was deemed best to make as few changes as possible.

It should be noted, too, that the complete index, which appears in the last part of Volume XI, has been included, but that page references have been changed to refer to the pagination of the present edition.

[11] *Book Find News*, No. 357 (published by Basic Books).

INTRODUCTION

I

Bibliography is the poor man's book collecting. The rich who collect books — a minority, nowadays — do not in general write bibliographies, though they do sometimes hire librarians to do this work for them. This Introduction is about a man who wrote his own. The bibliographies, or rather the collection catalogues, of rich collectors are a harmless ostentation, and an honorable one. They clearly represent the urge to display the rarities of one's own library, just as autobiography satisfies the urge — however denied, and under whatever disguise — to display the realities of one's own life. Just as the autobiographies are invariably fascinating psychological documents (when honest), the bibliographies are almost always useful tools, being essentially more or less complete subject catalogues of the collectors' interests. As such, they form a partial key to these subjects, when the collections have been dispersed forever at public sale or auction, or spread out irrecoverably among the over-large holdings of modern public and university libraries many of which, as in Great Britain, have no satisfactory subject catalogues and seem unaware that these are an indispensable tool.

Erotic literature is one of the few exceptions to this danger of dispersion. It should be noted, however, that most private collections of erotica do not survive their collectors. Though seldom burnt nowadays, as was once almost the rule, they are generally sold off immediately to trusted bookdealers. But in the exceptional cases, where erotic collections are made part of a posthumous gift to a great public or university library, the usual prudery will assist in preserving such collections intact, rather than dispersing them among the general library stock. They still commonly take their place among the other "hell" books, or secret collection of erotica and sexualia, in the repository libraries (not one of which, so far as I know, puts any similar restriction on books about murder). The Enfer of the Bibliothèque Nationale in Paris, which is the only great library that straightforwardly lists its erotic holdings in the printed

15

catalogue, was itself only separately catalogued for the first time in 1913, *more* than a century after the creation of this collection, under Napoleon. Almost invariably, the catalogues of the libraries' erotica are also kept secret. Nevertheless, the prize beauties have an embarrassing habit of being regularly stolen — by the trusted readers or trusted library staff — from all these "Private Cases" and "Cherry Cabinets," these "Librarians' Offices" and "Special Reserves."

What little we know of collections and collectors outside this handful comes to us, often with dubious correctness, from the few auction catalogues, mostly of the nineteenth century, in which erotic books have been allowed to figure. One of the first of these was the *Verzeichniss einer Sammlung . . .* of C. G. Guenther (Dresden, 1834: reprinted in 1862 for its bibliographical interest), largely composed of erotic and "sotadic" books — so called after Sotades, the earliest Greek author of erotica of whom any record still exists. Others are those of the George Daniel collection, auctioned off by Sotheby in London, 1864, the George Holliday library, sold by Bouton, in New York, 1870, and the *Bibliotheca Curiosa*, or library of Andrew Odell, sold by Bangs, 1878. Among the last such catalogues published in France was the *Catalogue . . . composant le cabinet de M. L.C.* (*i.e.*, Constantin), 1876. The *Catalogue du cabinet secret du Prince G°°°* (*i.e.*, Augustin Galitzin), Bruxelles, 1887, was stopped after only the first half of the alphabet had been published. The only known copy of it seems to be my own. Few or no such wholly erotic sales catalogues have been published since, except an eighty-four-page item, apparently issued about 1905 in Paris by Albin-Michel. Of this catalogue, too, only a single copy is now known, in Paris.

As to private erotica collections, though several very important ones now exist in various European countries, the United States, and Japan, the catalogues of almost none have been published since that of Charles Cousin (Paris, 1891) Section IX, "Dissertations Singulières," pp. 163–78. This part of the Cousin catalogue was also issued separately as *Enfer du Grenier*, without Cousin's name (a copy is in the British Museum). The most recent is the *Curiosa*, volume III of the *Bibliothèque "La Leonina"* (Monte Carlo, 1955), prepared for the collector M. Arpad Plesch by M. Jacques Pley; the first two volumes being the catalogue of the world-famous botanical library of M. Plesch, the finest ever collected by a single person.

It was on the basis of such listings, public and private, of great collections about to be broken up by sale or auction, that the first published bibliography of erotic and facetious literature was undertaken, in the 1860's. This was the *Bibliographie des ouvrages relatifs à l'amour,* by "le Comte d'I°°°" (actually the publisher of erotica Jules Gay), with the help of many collectors; a work later enlarged to four heavy volumes by J. Lemonnyer, 1894–1900, which remains the principal bibliography of French and Italian erotica. No equivalent work has ever been published wholly devoted to the erotic literature of the English language — the only major language of which this is true.

The "Notes on Curious and Uncommon Books" of the British author calling himself Pisanus Fraxi, printed originally in private quarto editions, in red and black, under the elegant disguise of forbidding Latin titles to the three volumes: *Index Librorum Prohibitorum* (1877), *Centuria Librorum Absconditorum* (1879), and *Catena Librorum Tacendorum* (1885), a set recently reprinted three times by photo-facsimile (London, 1960, and New York, 1962 and 1963), are a principal exception to the modern rule of journalistic smattering and superficiality on the one hand, and bibliological over-precision and futilitarianism on the other.

II

Henry Spencer Ashbee — to call "Pisanus Fraxi" by his real name — set out to do only a very limited thing, but in a thorough and profound way. He proposed simply to describe, and copiously to quote, some of the many hundreds of erotic books in various languages that had passed through his hands, and through the hands of some of his friends, during a long and assiduous career as a collector of erotica. His striking success rises clearly from the limitations within which he was satisfied to work, without any megalomaniacal vaunting and flaunting of his interests and his evident erudition to cover everything in the world in a pretended "system" or history.

Ashbee's work is modeled on three main annotated bibliographies of the early nineteenth century, which are the masterpieces of the form: Charles Nodier's *Mélanges tirés d'une petite bibliothèque* (Paris, 1829; importantly supplemented in the catalogue of the Nodier auction, *Description raisonnée . . .* , 1844), of which the title politely mocks the "Mélanges tirés d'une *grande* bibliothèque"

of a predecessor; likewise the *Analectabiblion, ou Extraits critiques
de divers livres rares, oubliés ou peu connus,* by the Marquis D.
R.*** (*i.e.,* Du Roure; 2 volumes, Paris, 1836–37; also supplemented
in his auction catalogue, under the initials M. L. M. D. R., Paris:
Jannet, 1848); and in particular, the *Medical Bibliography: A. and
B.,* of James Atkinson (London, 1834), which, being delayed until
the author's seventy-fifth year, never proceeded beyond the first two
letters of the alphabet, but which is a truly remarkable production,
to which Ashbee gives full appreciation (*Centuria,* pp. 502–3).

What is so exceptional about all these works — in particular
those of Nodier and Atkinson — is their *personalness* of approach, and
fullness of quotation, at a time when bibliography was already turn-
ing into what it has almost entirely become today: a soulless and
endless cataloguing of titles, publishers, dates, and (sometimes)
paginations, and nothing more, owing to the pressure of increasingly
enormous international book production, requiring at the very least
this cold and meager indexing. Nodier and Atkinson — and Ashbee
like them — do not hesitate to devote ten or a score of pages to a
single work that they consider to be typical or crucial. All of them
work on the unspoken principle of the discoverers of dinosaurs'
bones in Chinese pharmacy shops: *Ab uno disce omnes*; from this
one guess all the rest. (Virgil, *Æneid* II. 65.) Ashbee in particular
quotes lavishly from the texts before him, partly because he was a
rich man publishing his bibliographies himself, and could afford to
quote as he pleased, but also clearly because he was aware that
he was dealing with books of exceptional rarity, far more so than
the merely medical rarities or bibliographical curios under the atten-
tion of Atkinson and Nodier. In very many cases nothing more is
known today, or will probably ever be known, of certain works
quoted by Ashbee, than the passages he quotes; the books them-
selves having disappeared since.

It is not well known, and is worth underlining here, that *most
erotic books of earlier centuries have disappeared almost completely,
or are in the process of doing so.* An extraordinarily large number of
erotica, in all languages, are known only by their titles or else by an
occasional and very often unique printed copy — a reprint of some
later century, as often as not — preserved by accident in some great
public or university library. Any collection of erotica (or, for that
matter, of any other type of literary ephemera, such as jokebooks,

songbooks, or humorous magazines) composed of materials published even so recently as the 1900's or 1930's, will invariably contain an astonishing proportion of absolutely unique items, unknown in any other collection after even so short a time as twenty years. Gutenberg Bibles and other incunabula are not rare, and Shakespeare folios even less so; anyone who cares to put up the money can buy one today. But of so famous or infamous an erotic chapbook as the *Sonetti lussuriosi* of Aretino (if their original title was not, more likely, *La Corona di Cazzi*), with woodcut illustrations after the drawings by Giulio Romano, printed in Venice, possibly for Francesco Marcolini, in 1527, not a single copy has been recorded in over four hundred years; and this slender pamphlet was utterly despaired of as lost forever, until, by an incredible stroke of good luck, a copy containing fourteen of the original sixteen woodcuts was discovered only a few years back, in Milan.

The social historian of the eighteenth and early nineteenth centuries in England will, in particular, have much to thank Ashbee for. The only large-scale social history of this nature as yet written, *Englische Sittengeschichte* (2d ed., 1912, in two volumes; the English translation in the 1930's is much abridged), was, in fact, written by one of Ashbee's co-collectors, and his main biographer, Iwan Bloch — writing under the pseudonym of "Eugen Duehren" — who was given access to Ashbee's library (his own collection of modern Spanish erotica and other unique materials was broken up by public sale after his death, with several of the further collections into which it went being seized and destroyed by the Nazis). There is still a great deal to be mined, both in Ashbee's bibliographies and in that part of the collection described which has been preserved in the British Museum, especially in connection with the period from 1700 to about 1860, the period of Dr. William King's *The Toast* (see *Centuria*, pp. 301–25), of Wilkes' and Potter's *Essay on Woman* (see *Index*, pp. 198–236, and *Centuria*, pp. xiv–xv), and of John Cleland's *Memoirs of a Woman of Pleasure*, better known as *Fanny Hill* (see *Catena*, pp. 60–95). This is the period which is now becoming the principal and most desperately hasty area of library collecting, now that most of the desirable books in English, of earlier centuries, have been thoroughly bought up, locked up, and docketed in the *Short-Title Catalogue* (to 1640, of which a revised edition is now announced in preparation), and its continuation to 1700 by Mr. Donald

G. Wing, the indefatigable associate librarian of Yale University. Unfortunately, the only *subject*-indexing to all this enormous mass of books, from 1475 to 1700, so far attempted, is the magnificent but evidently insufficient *Cambridge Bibliography of English Literature* (5 volumes, 1940–55), and it goes without saying that little will be learned from the *C.B.E.L.*, or from its collateral text-volumes, the *Cambridge History of English Literature*, as to even the English-language erotica.

Ashbee remains — with a few recent minor works, such as Ralph Straus' biography of the erotica publisher Curll (of whose books one of the best collections, that made by the late Peter Murray Hill, is now in the University of Kansas Library), and the bibliographies by Case and Bond of poetic miscellanies and burlesque verse of the eighteenth century — remains, I say, the principal guidebook and source work for the future moral historian of England in the eighteenth century, and has a great deal to tell any similar historian of England and the rest of Europe, as well as America, to nearly the end of the nineteenth century as well. A number of attempts at such a social history have appeared since the 1920's. All of them almost without exception have the curious feature — a hallmark of modern hurry-up research, and a clear result of the gross inadequacy of modern subject-indexing of published books — of being written in total ignorance of the existence of their predecessors, and they naturally limp badly as a result of this superficiality. The best, after the work by Iwan Bloch cited above, is probably that of Victor F. Calverton (George Goetz) in the 1920's; along with the more recent works — principally on the Victorian age — by Maurice Quinlan, Clarence R. Decker, and, in England, Cyril Pearl (a mere journalist), and G. Rattray Taylor; of which latter only the volumes by Quinlan and Taylor are anchored, with any real erudition or perception, in the subterranean literature to which Ashbee is still the principal key.

III

The few known facts of Ashbee's public life are simply the stiff British externals. These are fully reviewed by Iwan Bloch, in *Englische Sittengeschichte* (1912) II, 498–510, following an exceedingly valuable chapter on English publishers and collectors of erotica, and with a long appreciation, well worth consulting, of Ashbee's bibliographical method and achievements. The biographical materials are again presented briefly, by Dr. Paul Englisch, with a handsome ex-libris portrait of Ashbee (*"ein auffallend schöner Mann,"* as Bloch says, II, 502; *"mit einem sehr sympathischen Gesicht"*), in the finest, and first illustrated, erotic bibliography in existence, volumes II and IV of the fabulous *Bilder-Lexikon der Erotik* (Vienna, 1928–31), now republished in Hamburg with a new and important supplement edited by Armand Mergen, though announced as under the editorship of Dr. Hans Giese. Almost nothing had earlier been divulged, other than Ashbee's pseudonym of "Pisanus Fraxi," in the excessively discreet notice of his death appearing in the *Annuaire de la Société des Amis des Livres* (Paris, 1901) XXII, 45–52, a society of which Ashbee had been the principal foreign member, and whose secretary was Alfred Bégis — part-author with Duponchel and Hankey of *L'École des biches* (1868) — whose private library of erotica had been added, by police seizure, to the Enfer of the Bibliothèque Nationale, and is still there.

To state very briefly what is known: Henry Spencer Ashbee was born on April 21, 1834. He was a businessman by profession, becoming head of the international firm of Charles Lavy & Co., Coleman Street, London, dealers in "essential oils" according to one source. His library was, until 1895, shelved in his London home, at 53 Bedford Square, where he was always willing generously to display its treasures to visiting European book collectors and bibliographers, by all of whom he was extremely well liked and respected. Ashbee traveled extensively, everywhere in the world — Asia, Africa, America, China, and Japan (this is an age long before airplanes) — and his book *Travels in Tunisia* is still of value. He spent most of his winters in Spain, where he accumulated one of the world's best private collections of editions of Cervantes' *Don Quixote*, of which he published an elegant catalogue. More importantly, Ashbee also made, and continued with its collecting right up to the last month of his life, what is still the finest private collection of erotic books in all European languages; though his three volumes of erotic bibliography under the pseudonym "Pisanus Fraxi" are *not* the catalogue of that collection, a point well worth underscoring. On a final voyage to Spain and Morocco, at the age of sixty-seven, Ashbee had a serious heart attack while at Burgos, following a case of influenza, but managed to regain England, where he died at his country estate, Fowlers

Park, in Hawkhurst, Kent, on the twenty-ninth of July, 1900. In Apollinaire, Fleuret, and Perceau's *L'Enfer de la Bibliothèque Nationale*, the Paris erotica publisher Hirsch tells the end of the story, at No. 21, *L'École des Biches:*

> The erotic library of Mr. Ashbee, who died a few years ago, was given to the British Museum, which at first considered refusing the gift, but finally accepted it because Mr. Ashbee, who had similarly bequeathed his collection of all the editions and translations of *Don Quixote*, had made it a condition of this bequest, that the British Museum also conserve his erotic library. It will be found there today.

The Ashbee Bequest forms, in fact, the nucleus of the Private Case, or "Enfer" of the British Museum, to this day, with an important group of manuscript bibliographies of erotica (in particular those of James Campbell Reddie and of Bérard) and similar works kept separately in the Department of Manuscripts. As opposed to the Enfer of the Bibliothèque Nationale in Paris, of which the full contents are described in their alphabetical place in the general printed catalogue; the Private Case books of the British Museum are still rigidly excluded from the printed catalogue of that institution, and the only available key to them is the *Registrum Librorum Eroticorum* (1936) of Alfred Rose, published posthumously under the anagram of "Rolf S. Reade."

A final word of warning will not be out of place here as to the Ashbee Bequest in the Private Case of the British Museum. The three Ashbee volumes have long been misunderstood as the *catalogue* of Ashbee's own collection, with the further erroneous belief that the books here described will be found *in toto* in the British Museum. This is unfortunately not the case. These volumes constitute simply, though superbly, a select and annotated bibliography of erotic works in many languages, on the basis of notes taken from the books themselves in almost all cases. That is a very different thing from being the catalogue of an existing collection, and this point is again insisted upon here to help other researchers avoid the intense disappointment that awaited the present writer when he made a special voyage to England, with the expectation of finding all the books described in the three volumes neatly preserved — under lock and key, to be sure — in the British Museum. They are not there, not half!

The explanation of this contretemps is, in part, as follows: Ashbee's bibliographies were inspired by his receiving from his dying friend, James Campbell Reddie (whose biography is given in *Catena*, p. xlvii, with portrait facing in the original edition — the New York reprint unfortunately omits all the fascinating frontispieces and plates, throughout the set), an exceedingly full and fine manuscript bibliography of erotic works that had passed through Reddie's hands, but which, not being as rich as Ashbee, he had not always been able to buy, and had preserved only in the form of bibliographical notes and excerpts, later quoted — without actual access to the books themselves — in Ashbee's three printed volumes. Campbell Reddie's "Bibliographical Notes," as the manuscript is called (fully described in *Catena*, pp. xlviii–xlix, and 493–94), are well worth separate publication.

To give one striking example of the misconceptions these notes in Ashbee can lead to: there will be found in his first volume (*Index Librorum Prohibitorum*, pp. 133–37), a list of nearly fifty bawdy "songsters and reciters" published in London during the "coal-hole and cider-cellar" period of the early and mid-nineteenth century, when the singing of such songs was a principal feature of the early music halls, as described by Ashbee. The titles of these songsters are apparently among the material supplied to Ashbee by Reddie. Far from all fifty of these priceless chapbook songsters being preserved in Ashbee's collection in the British Museum, only *four* will be found there, bound up into a single volumelet as a curiosity, perhaps (under the call-mark P.C. 31 g 20, and including *The Cuckold's Nest of Choice Songs*, among others). Among these four is not even included *The Blowen's Cabinet of Choice Songs*, of which the amusing full title is transcribed to the tune of twenty lines, by Ashbee, *Index*, p. 133. As to the others, no one knows; though a further group of such songsters — probably rather extensive — is still preserved in the important Harding collection of songbooks of all kinds, originally made by Sir John Stainer and now in Chicago. (Another such item, *The Bang-Up Reciter*, probably dating from the 1870's or 1880's, but not mentioned by Ashbee, is in my own collection; its full title is given in my article, "The Bawdy Song . . . in Fact and in Print," in *The Horn Book: Studies in Erotic Folklore and Bibliography*, 1964, p. 380).

Since these lines were written, the unerring bibliographical flair of David Foxon, Esq., whose series of articles on lost and early English erotica, appearing in *The Book Collector*, London, and recently reissued in America as *Libertine Literature in England, 1660–1745*, pile discovery upon flabbergasting discovery, has turned up no less than fifty further bawdy songsters of the period — all in the same 24to size, but entirely different from Ashbee's untraceable fifty except for two items — slumbering peacefully for the last thirty years in the British Museum, under the call-mark C. 116 *a* 6–55, not ten feet across the aisle from the Private Case incorporating Ashbee's collection, but not included even in its secret catalogue. Let it be understood, therefore, that Ashbee's three great bibliographical volumes are strictly a bibliography, not a collection catalogue, and must be accepted as such — the poor man's book collecting, as the reader has already been warned.

IV

The hidden world of erotic literature offers a challenge to the bibliographer, far more difficult than the incunabula of the fifteenth century and the secret publications of religious and political controversy. All of these share to some degree the same curious anonymity, appearing originally without any printed place or date of publication — or with place and date disguised and falsified — and without any satisfactory indication of the real names of the authors, publishers, and printers. But with this difference: the early incunabula, and the religious and political tracts, can generally be identified by the internal typographical evidence of printing types and styles, or when, eventually, the authors and publishers of the polemic tracts win the day and come out of hiding, to sign their later productions and even to brag of the earlier. The authors and publishers of erotic literature have never come out of hiding, so far as the Western civilizations are concerned, until barely yesterday.

The last erotic writings — actually only good-natured folk facetiæ — ever published openly in the West, without the slightest thought on anyone's part that they might be considered morally "wrong," were the jestbooks in all European countries, beginning with Poggio's *Facetiarum liber* (written in 1451, first published about 1470, and first translated into English for Liseux, Paris, 1879); and a semi-folkloristic work, the *Origine delle volgari proverbi* of

Cynthio degli Fabritii, published by Bernardino Vitali in Venice, 1526, with the author's and publisher's names plainly given, along with a dedication to Pope Clement VII. A brief analysis of Cynthio's forty-five proverbs will be found in the introduction to Aretino's *Sept petites nouvelles* (Paris: Jules Gay, 1861, pp. 52–68). Exception was taken by the Catholic hierarchy of the Inquisition — particularly by the Franciscans, satirized in some of Cynthio's proverbial "explanations" — to the unexpurgated tone of his work, especially in view of its being dedicated to the Pope, whose "privilege" it bore, as well as that of the Seigneurie of Venice, for ten years. The work was seized and destroyed in large part, and the licensing and censoring of books, both before and after publication, was undertaken as of that year, 1526 (Old Style), in Italy, by the following deliberation of the Council of Ten (Consiglio dei Dieci) of Venice, the printing capital, on January 29, 1527:

> That from this day onward there may not be printed, nor, after having been printed, be published any work or book newly composed and not formerly printed . . . unless there has first been obtained the permission of the heads of this Council, by a *termination* signed by their hand. [Italian text quoted by Giuseppe Fumagalli, *Dictionnaire géographique d'Italie, pour servir à l'histoire de l'imprimerie dans ce pays*; Florence: Olschki, 1905, chap. xiii, p. 494. See also G. I. Arneudo, *Dizionario esegetico per le arti grafiche*, p. 2123, under Vitali; both these references from an unpublished article on Aretino by Albini and Toscanini.]

Behind the pretext of Cynthio's proverbs, there was, to be sure, the real alarm of the Church concerning the rapidly spreading doctrines of Luther, which would probably never have converted half of Europe had it not been for the assistance of the printing press. The real intention behind the new censorship is made clear by the fact that the Venetian edict of January 29, 1527, was applied rigorously only against works of an anti-religious or anti-governmental tone, leaving quite free the bawdy satire of Aretino's *Ragionamenti* and those of his school of secretaries, Franco and Veniero, as well as the fabulous bawdry of the burlesque academicians such as Vignale, appearing with tacit permission under obviously false rubrics of publication (such as "Lugano"), and false predatings. With the organization of the Inquisition in Spain showing the way in repressive religious control, this led immediately, on the one hand, to the

modern laws of printers' "privilege" and copyright, and on the other
hand to the institution several decades later of the thus easily op-
erated Roman Catholic censorship and its *Index Librorum Prohibi-
torum* (1559) — whose title Ashbee appropriated, in delicate jest.

The open publication of erotic and facetious works having be-
come forbidden, their secret publication immediately began, within
a year, in the *Sonetti lussuriosi* of Pietro Aretino, written to fit the
sixteen earlier engravings by Marc-Antonio Raimondi of Giulio
Romano's drawings, a set of engravings already prohibited and
almost entirely destroyed. The secret publisher of Aretino's *Sonnets*
in 1527 was perhaps Marcolini, if not Bindoni & Pasini, or even the
same Vitali whose open publication of Cynthio's work had been
reprimanded the year before; but now neither printer's name nor
that of the author appeared anywhere on the book, which was sold
surreptitiously (according to a contemporary libel on Aretino, prob-
ably by his disaffected secretary, Niccolò Franco, under the name of
Fr. Berni) to passers-by on the Rialto bridge, the most public place
in Venice.

By the early 1530's, the secret and occasionally the semi-open
printing of erotic and facetious prose and verse had become a matter
of course: by Aretino and his imitators, in particular Niccolò Franco
(who set out to double Aretino's sixteen "postures" in the *Sonnets*
to the now classic thirty-two, in the prose *Puttana errante* — the first
work described in Ashbee's first volume — which he cannily signed
with Aretino's name!); by the tellers of erotic folktales in the style
of Boccaccio and the *Arabian Nights*; and by the burlesque acade-
micians of Siena and elsewhere, among whom Antonio Vignale, in
his *Cazzaria* (1531), or "Book of the Prick," stands out as the most
astonishing collector of erotic folk beliefs and just-so stories in the
literature of the world. (A manuscript translation into English, by
the late Samuel Putnam, is in my possession, but has never been
printed.)

Only one real help exists for the bibliographer of erotic litera-
ture, and that is the raw necessity for the publishers of erotica to
advertise their wares, usually by the publication of semi-erotic,
sexual scientific, or merely gallant works (nowadays called in French
slang the *officiel*, or cover-up, of the publisher), intended as window
dressing, or for open display to prospective customers, and also to
explain to the authorities. if necessary, the publisher's otherwise

inexplicable activity. There is a whole chapter on this subject, with very amusing facsimiles, in Michael Sadleir's *Forlorn Sunset* (London, 1947) pp. 412–20. These semi-erotic or "official" wares naturally give the publishers' real names and addresses, often very conspicuously displayed, and by the study of the distinctive typographical *style* of this sort of signed and dated merchandise, it is generally not too difficult to distinguish, to place, and to date the secret publications of the same publishers, operating simultaneously *sous le manteau*, as — to take a group of publishers now all safely dead — Poulet-Malassis, Gay (father and son), Vital-Puissant, and Kistemaeckers, toward the end of the nineteenth century in Brussels; and by Carrington, Hirsch, Fort, the brothers Briffaut, and later Duflou, Seheur, Pia, and many others, at the beginning of the twentieth century in Paris.

A few erotic books escape even the method of identification by typographical style. These are, in particular, the erotic autobiographies and private poetic ejaculations of amateurs, which are printed privately by or for the authors themselves, usually in very small editions — as opposed to the only pretendedly small editions, fraudulently "numbered," of many erotica and other *faux-luxe* publications. Such amateur works are seldom paralleled by any typographically similar group of openly published gallantiana, intended as advertising, and only by the discovery of indiscreetly inscribed presentation copies, or by the chance divulgation's of contemporary collectors, bibliographers, and friends — and sometimes of enemies — can the authors and origins of such works be determined at all. Ashbee's bibliographies are of extraordinary value here, as he seldom hesitated, except in the case of living authors and publishers, to divulge what he knew (which was just about everything) of the hidden literary history of his time.

In France, the literary reputations of great authors such as Alfred de Musset, Théophile Gautier, Henry Monnier, Maupassant, Verlaine, Pierre Louÿs, and many others, have never really been seriously prejudiced, among readers of any pretention to culture, by the knowledge that the erotic romances, playlets, sketches, and poems circulated privately and in very limited editions under these famous names are, in all probability, the authentic juvenilia, or bagatelles of later hours of distraction, of these writers famous for more serious work.

In the Anglo-Saxon countries the opposite is true: any identification with erotic literature would invariably have spelled total disaster for any famous writer, or person in public or professional life, until the advent recently of James Joyce, D. H. Lawrence, and Henry Miller; all of whom, in any case, suffered every sort of indignity for the "obscenity" of their work. The classic case is that of the English liberal Parliamentarian in the eighteenth century, John Wilkes, whose enemies planned to ruin him by reading before the Houses of Parliament the *Essay on Woman* — written, in fact, by Thomas Potter, the son of an archbishop, as an erotic parody of Pope's *Essay on Man* — which had been printed on Wilkes' private press. (See the whole story, in Ashbee's *Index Librorum Prohibitorum*, pp. 202–10.) A bit, but not much more, leeway is allowed to humorists, such as Mark Twain and Eugene Field, and no one makes much secret any more of the bawdy skits and erotic poems that both these writers were pleased to issue privately for the delectation of their friends, for instance Twain's "1601," and Field's many poems (with the exception of "The Boastful Yak," all printed in *Immortalia*, 1927), and his *Only a Boy*. In their lifetimes, however, no such open jesting could be permitted, as is shown by the famous case of the first edition of Twain's *Huckleberry Finn*, with the phallic addition to one of the illustrations (surreptitiously engraved on the cut by a disgruntled printer's assistant), which is removed and replaced with a properly sedate illustration in almost all copies.

It is hardly to be wondered at, therefore, that the principal erotic autobiographies and autobiographical fantasies in English have been published only in the most restricted editions, and are already among the most difficult books to procure in this language. The only exceptions are the autobiographical writings of Henry Miller, but the first and original editions of the few other such autobiographies in English are absolutely no longer to be found: Frank Harris' *My Life and Loves* (Germany, 1922–27, four volumes); *The Confessions of Nemesis Hunt* (1902–3, three volumes, apparently written by an Englishwoman connected with the theater); *Suburban Souls* (1901, three volumes, probably a mere work of fiction); and, above all, *My Secret Life*, in eleven volumes, of which the present edition constitutes the first open publication anywhere in the world.

V

Let it be frankly stated, before going any further, that every-thing connected with the mysterious *My Secret Life* is based on supposition and deduction, and on hearsay testimony, such as that of the interested publisher "Charles Carrington," with the exception of the purely bibliographical descriptions taken from the printed volumes themselves. The first reference ever made to *My Secret Life* appears in Carrington's most ambitious catalogue, for 1902, issued anonymously under the transparent disguise of being the catalogue of a private library, and grotesquely aping the great erotic bibliographies of "Pisanus Fraxi," under the title *Forbidden Books: Notes and Gossip on Tabooed Literature,* "by An Old Bibliophile, Paris: For the Author and his Friends, 1902." There is a copy of the original in the Bibliothèque Nationale, catalogued as 8° Q. 4665.

My Secret Life is the fifth work described, and it is evident, from Carrington's way of puffing it, that he had come into posses-sion of the remainder of the edition, and was trying to sell it off at £60 sterling per set, an astronomical sum at that time. Here is the opening of his notice, on which all the legends connected with this work are based:

My Secret Life. Amsterdam (n.d.) Not for publication. — 11 vols. crown 8vo, of 378, 373, 379, 380, 388, 384, 369, 383, 396, 376, and 394 pp. (The first volume contains an introduction, a preface, and a second preface. The last volume has only 255 pp. of text, and the rest to page 394 is made up of an exhaustive alphabetical index.)

About the year 1888, a well-known bookseller and publisher of Amsterdam, whose specialty was literature of an incandescent kind [Auguste Brancart?] was summoned to London by one of his cus-tomers, a rich old Englishman, who desired to have privately printed for his own enjoyment an enormous MSS., containing in the fullest detail all the secret venereal thoughts of his existence. He defrayed all costs of printing, on condition that no more than six copies should be struck off. A few years afterwards, this eccentric amateur shuffled off the mortal coil; and a few copies of the extraordinary work made a timid appearance on the market, being quoted at the high figure of £100!

It is evident that many more than the half-dozen copies stipulated must have been printed ...

The remainder of Carrington's notice consists of an excerpt from the remarkable alphabetical index to *My Secret Life* and a long quotation (intended, as he says, "to whet the curiosity of collectors"), giving one of the author's affairs "differing entirely from any other in all the eleven volumes." This is the story of a French woman — told in her own words to the author — who, while visiting her sister in Italy in 1859, is gang-raped by twelve Austrian soldiers, in the course of a single *hour*, on the eve of the Battle of Solferino. When she attempts to struggle she is told by the Austrians: "If you're not quiet we'll fuck you and your sister too, then kill you both, and set fire to the house — they will think the French did it." Another soldier adds, even more cynically, that she is lucky to be raped by Austrian soldiers and not by the French, because: "If the French catch you, they will bugger you, as well as fuck you, and certainly cut your throats afterwards." The whole scene, and its emotional aftermath, is described with unusual incisiveness and depth, from the woman's point of view, and is clearly authentic.

My Secret Life is unusual among erotic autobiographies in many ways, of which not the least is the didactic tone into which the author falls on occasion, actually giving in one place a short but complete treatise on the art of sexual intercourse, which makes rather absurd any pretense that he is writing without the hope of an audience, or of any audience further than six other erotica collectors (who would presumably know something about the art of intercourse already). The most unusual aspect of *My Secret Life*, among erotic autobiographies, is that it is concerned almost exclusively with the author's physical erotic experiences, and purposely omits any discussion of his emotional relationships.

This is not accidental, nor a "pornographic" conventionalism on the part of the writer, nor even altogether a matter of reserve about those parts of his life at a deeper level of intimacy than the "Secret" life he is here unveiling. In the first serious discussion of this work that has yet appeared — in the Drs. Eberhard and Phyllis Kronhausen's *Pornography and the Law*, revised edition (1964) pp. 106–11 — the important socio-analytic point is made by the psychologist-authors:

We have placed less emphasis on the sexual pathology that was, in certain respects, quite obviously involved in this case. Instead, we have taken the existentialist approach to the problem of evaluating so absolutely unique and — to our common ways of thinking — unsettling a life and personality as that of the English Casanova. For here was a man who, unlike most of his fellow men, did not place family, business, profession, security or "future" first, that is, the commonly accepted values and goals to be striven for in our kind of society. Instead, he reversed the normal order of things by placing all such considerations second, and his sexual happiness first and foremost in his life.

What the pathology "quite obviously involved" may have been, the Kronhausens do not say, but they return to the matter on pages 314–15, in connection with a scene of voyeurism, to note that the author of *My Secret Life* was probably not homosexual [!] but was engaging in the usual "attempts to abreact a genital trauma and inferiority feelings about his own sex organs," meaning that he thought — as most of us do, when young — that they were too small. More important, certainly, is the author's evident Don Juan complex: his *inability* to maintain any deep emotional relationship with the women he makes love to. That is to say, he is searching for something in his sexual life with many women which he is fated never to find, because what he is searching for — what he is dissatisfied with — is in himself.

There is more than a little validity to the suspicion invariably voiced as to such men by psychoanalysis (it is to this that the Kronhausens are alluding) that a profound undercurrent of homosexuality does exist in them, or, at the least, an unconscious fear and hatred of the female genitals as being "castrated," because lacking the penis, of whose satisfactory existence in himself the Don Juan is basically unsure. He therefore moves endlessly from one woman to the next, never really able to accept any of them, nor to be sure that they accept him, or *would* accept him — that is, his penis — except for the irrelevant handsomeness, glamour, or sordid money which he offers them. Popular folklore arrives at the same conclusion as psychoanalysis, and the same suspicion as to the unconscious element in Don Juanism, in the line: "*Any man that can't find what he's looking for in a thousand women is really look-*

ing for a boy!" The same is also true, of course, of the unconscious lesbianism of women who can't find what they're looking for in a thousand men.

As to the actual figures involved in *My Secret Life*, the Albin-Michel (?) sales catalogue of 1905 cited earlier, in offering *My Secret Life* (at No. 783), at the very high price of 1,250 pre-war francs — the same catalogue estimated that the private printing of thirty copies had cost the author no less than 1,100 guineas — notes flatly that this is: "The most extraordinary of all modern works. It is the autobiography of an English captain who, day by day, noted his gallant prowesses since his youth. In his amorous career he had over two thousand women, and that *in all countries* except Lapland." A later catalogue cited in the bibliography of French erotica by Louis Perceau (at No. 322), drops the price to 800 francs, but raises the count of "gallant prowesses" to twenty-five hundred. The Kronhausens, p. 106, resolutely cut this figure to half, calculating that the author, "if we may trust his own estimate . . . made love to a record number of some twelve hundred women (not counting those with whom he had other sexual contacts short of intercourse)."

One of the most striking peculiarities about *My Secret Life* is its style, not only in the unassuming and non-literary matter-of-factness of the way it is written, except for a few self-consciously didactic passages, but also in the sudden and abrupt jumps in the narrative, within the body of the chapters themselves, without any more warning than the beginning of a new paragraph, and sometimes not even that: rather like the fast "cutting" of a motion picture. This is unquestionably the result of the book's having been written — as the author specifically observes in one of his Prefaces — from an erotic diary kept since his early youth. He has simply strung together his diary entries, in re-editing them for secret publication, adding the remembered dialogue and taking care to disguise all names, places, and professions. The author himself is given as "Walter" (no surname), a sometime employee of the War Ministry. Though admittedly a disguise, and not his true profession at all, this is doubtless the source of the booksellers' catalogues' referring to him as an English "captain" or "colonel." That everything else *but* these disguised details are true, he insists:

I had from my youth an excellent memory, but about sexual matters, a wonderful one. I recollect even now to a degree which astonishes me, the face, colour, stature, thighs, backside, and vagina of well nigh every woman I have had, who was not a mere casual, and even of some who were. I had before me mentally as I wrote, the clothes they wore, the houses and rooms in which I had them, the way the bed and furniture were placed, on what side of the room the windows had been, and so forth. Besides, I was able to fix by reference to my diary, in which the contemporaneous circumstances of my life were recorded, just about every incident sufficiently nearly with regard to time.

I also recollect by and large not only what was done, but also what was said between the women and myself, and in those few instances where my memory did fail me, I have preferred to leave out details of our conversation or bawdy amusements, rather than attempting to make the story more coherent by inserting that which was merely probable. . . .

I may occasionally have been in error where I have mentioned the number of times that I made love to one or the other woman in my youth: it is difficult to be quite accurate on such points after a lapse of time. But, as before said, in many cases the incidents were, during that period, written down a few weeks, and often within a few days, after they occurred, and in these instances are quite reliable. Still, I do not attempt to pose as a Hercules in copulation. There are quite sufficient braggarts on that head, though much conversation with gay women [prostitutes] and doctors makes me doubt the wonderful feats in coition that some men like to tell of.

So solemn a statement of one's own sexual veracity is, of course, rather humorous, in a way of which the author is entirely uncon= scious. He has "had," according to his own records, over a thousand women, and does not wish to be written off as a braggart, such as "gay women and doctors" have told him about, simply because he can no longer remember, in his mature age, the exact "number of times [he] made love to one or the other woman" in the fire and folly of his youth. Meanwhile, his memory is self-admittedly almost perfect and complete for every detail of these thousand women's bodies and underclothing, and even the placing of their beds and windows, thirty or more years before; not to mention his remember-ing "not only what was done, but also what was said," in all but a "few instances" of these thousands of times, and to such a degree that he has no intention of unreliably "attempting to make the story more coherent by inserting that which was merely probable." What is even more incredible is that he may be telling the truth!

That the author has assimilated to his sexual potency the potency of his *memory* (probably in his fifties) is clear, as also that he is tempted to brag of his fabulous feats of memory in exactly the same way — and for exactly the same reason — that other men, suffering from similar feelings of sexual if not social inferiority, or both combined, like to tell of their "wonderful feats in coition." This type of sexually displaced bragging, as to the power of one's memory (or the steely glance of one's eye, aim with a gun, or ability at driving a fast car), is all the more common in that the failure of memory (and coordination) is one of the commonest signs of advancing age in men, next after sexual impotence. Yet it is also clear that we have before us here the record of the erotic life of a profoundly compulsive person of precisely the kind who not only did write down in a diary all the salient details of that erotic life, for decades, but might well have remembered the rest. The basic compulsiveness involved is, after all, implicit in the keeping of the diary and in the author's attempting to leave behind so intimate a record in printed form, for others to read.

He maintains throughout a gallant British reserve about every woman he really loved, and in particular about his own wife. The style of *My Secret Life* is undistinguished and matter-of-fact, yet in a way which authenticates even further the self-evident intention of the author to tell the simple autobiographical truth about his hidden sexual history, "a plain narrative of facts," as he puts it, "and not a psychological analysis." His work is therefore, in almost every way — and not solely on the question of literal truth — the exact opposite of the *Mémoires* of Casanova, published for the first time, in 1960–62, by Brockhaus, in Wiesbaden and Paris, from the original manuscript in Casanova's racy and idiomatic French, to replace the high-falutin' and academic expurgated text (by a university professor) in which Casanova has hitherto been known.

Even in his own words, however, Casanova is eternally concerned not with his sexual activity, but with his emotions about it; with his ideas of self-importance, with what he thought about his women and what they seemed to think of him, etc., etc. . . . the typical Latin egocentrism, even in the midst of the emotion of love, which is supposed to be — as Stendhal indicates — an enormous overevaluation and crystallization of the virtues of the *other* person. This emphasis on himself is also very much heightened by Casanova's clear need for emotional reassurance, obviously difficult for him to find anywhere else in his miserable career as an international adventurer and swindler, as a failed dramatist (he collaborated with DaPonte on Mozart's *Don Juan*, surely never imagining for an instant that history would identify him with this hero), also as card-sharp and spy, who finally managed to get himself thrown out of his beloved Venice forever by "revealing" in *Nè amori, nè donne*, in 1782 (written as a work of revenge, after having apparently been caught cheating at cards), that he was the illegitimate son of the nobleman Michel Grimani, and as such the rightful heir of the Grimani fortune!

The author of *My Secret Life* writes, per contra, from a completely assured social position, and does not concern himself in the slightest with any such attempts to bolster up his self-esteem, which is clearly under no strain whatever. He does not seek women, as does Casanova, to love them briefly and abandon them promptly; but rather for the simple and direct purpose of sexual pleasure. When he finds this pleasure with a woman — and everyone is aware that this is by no means so simple or so common as the anatomy of the matter would lead one to believe — he makes every effort to continue the pleasant relationship as long as possible, and to renew it whenever he can. This again is the precise opposite of the character of Casanova, who spends half his time traveling; that is to say, getting away from his last sexual failure, and on to his next "victory," and whose real emotions seem never to be involved with any woman whatsoever except in the one profoundly masochistic affair with La Charpillon. This is the incident on which, as is well known, Pierre Louÿs based *La Femme et le pantin* (translated as *Woman and Puppet*) as also his erotic rewriting of the same theme, under the title *Trois filles de leur mère*, the most extraordinary work of erotic fiction in modern French; with a liberal dose taken from Mérimée's *Carmen*, or, rather, from Halévy's operatic revision of her character — to Bizet's passionate music — dramatically heightening all the sado-masochistic overtones of the original story.

The motives of the author of *My Secret Life* in keeping the diaries on which it is based, and the first draft of the memoirs themselves begun "when about twenty-five years old," are of course no one's affair but his own. One has a perfect right to so perhaps excessive an interest in all the incidents of one's own life, just as one has the right, if one wishes, to examine one's body naked, however strange or strained a position it is necessary to get into. *Ton corps est à toi!* But his eventual rewriting of these diaries and memoirs for actual publication seems to have been a rather curious and ambivalent affair. On the one hand, the author is meticulously careful as to concealment and disguise, not only for himself but for every man, woman, and geographical place (except, perhaps, London) that he has ever been in or known. On the other hand, he clearly wanted an audience, and well knew he had a "story," as he calls it, worth committing to print.

He had sat himself down, as it appears, well after the midpoint of his life, to write his erotic memoirs from his diaries and his perfect verbal recollections — exactly as did Casanova, nearly a century earlier, in a somber little room in the Château of Dux, Czechoslovakia, when all his splendid rogueries had landed him at last nothing better than a revolting job as a police spy (spying as *voyeurism*, often in disguise, and always sexually toned), and the final small sinecure as ducal librarian. But where Casanova's *Mémoires* were never printed at all during his lifetime, except for his favorite story about his escape from prison in Venice, the author of *My Secret Life* very specifically wants six copies of his memoirs — but only six copies — to exist. That is why he paid his 1,100 guineas, a young fortune then and now, almost certainly to the shady erotica publisher Auguste Brancart (a Belgian, in refuge at that time in Holland), who might otherwise have paid *him* for the right to publish these memoirs "for the trade." Who these six copies were to have been presented to, we do not know of course, nor whether they were perhaps simply to be left behind, after the act of authorship and private publication, as the ostrich is said to leave its eggs in the desert sands to be hatched by the hot desert sun.

Again, contradictorily, the author purposely rejects the possibility of any large audience, but he is nevertheless anxious to transmit his sexual wisdom to his eventual readers — all six of them — and thus, eventually, the world, if these literary heirs will do their job, in a sort of chain-letter arrangement perhaps. Thus he even goes to the length of the little treatise or disquisition on the art of intercourse, already mentioned, which, as will be seen, is really not terribly advanced. The author is and remains a Victorian gentleman, and though he certainly understands sexual intercourse in a workmanlike fashion, one is tempted to believe that he would find much to be surprised by in some of the more advanced *fin-de-siècle* "clowneries" of such a work as *Les Paradis Charnels* (1903) by "Dr. A. S. Lagail" (i.e., the French littérateur Alphonse Gallais), or in such sub-flagellational manipulations as the "Ice-Spurred Special" in chapter 6 of the current American handbook by Dr. John Eichenlaub, *The Marriage Art* (1961), which is peacefully sold to non-promiscuous housewives and college girls in among the soap chips in the supermarkets, at 60¢. It is a final contradiction that the author of *My Secret Life* often teaches a great deal more where he least expects to, and possibly quite unconsciously, as in the early chapter describing his shock and revulsion when a French girl tries to please him specially by adding the "luxury" of anal digitation to fellation, about which he also has his youthful doubts.

His principal form of sexual experimentation or search for novelty is not in sex technique at all — as it must be, with monogamists — but, as with almost all Don Juans, in *varietism*. In his youth, in particular, he is all of a jumble, in a sort of massive Oedipal search for incest substitutes: aunts, cousins, nursing women's legs, old women, young girls, fat girls, thin girls, women of all other countries (except Lapland), and the like. He also suffers from one very important peculiarity, and though he is quite conscious of it, he does not at all see the ruinous effect it has on any possibility of real emotional relations with the women and girls he frequents: HE IS TOO RICH, too prone to cut impatiently through the delay about seducing a woman by simply buying her. It is for this reason that the roll-call of his "conquests" shows the same rather high percentage of women of low social caste as do the *Mémoires* of Casanova. Too many of them have been bought. That is also perhaps why he so seldom speaks of love.

In observing, in the first crack in the Establishment dike concerning the present work, in the London *Times Literary Supplement* (February 16, 1964), that *My Secret Life* is a "treasure house of information about nineteenth-century sexual mores," the *Times*

writer did not perhaps mean to allude to the terrible insight one is
given by it into the raw sexual exploitation of the poor by the rich
in Victorian England, but it is there to be had. The author does
evidently have certain second thoughts about some of the incidents
of his sexual life. He remarks prefatorily, for instance:

> I have one fear about publishing my memoirs, and that is of having
> done a few things by curiosity and impulse which even professed
> libertines may cry fie on. Yes, I know they will cast stones at me, even
> though they themselves may habitually have done all that I have
> done, and worse. But crying out at the sins of others has always been
> a way of hiding one's own iniquities.

But he certainly does not mean, by this, that the "professed liber-
tines" (who are somehow going to get hold of his book despite its
limitation) will "cry fie" on his self-complacently greasing his sexual
pleasures with cash. That they would approve of. And one is left
to understand that that is simply the way things were then being
done. It is also not beyond the limits of probability that it is still
being done the same way. At any rate, that is the impression one
is left with by the current crop of earn-while-you-learn manuals
and "guides" for modern American business girls anxious to screw
their way to the top.

What is basic in the fascination of other people's private lives,
essentially, is not what they *do* — since all of us do more or less
the same things privately, especially in bed. It is, rather, the punc-
turing of the mystery that is the heart of the fascination: the un-
veiling of the names and faces that go with these otherwise rather
ordinary acts. It seems clear that this is the not-very-well-hidden
urge to witness what Freud calls the "primal scene" of parental
intercourse, and to learn at last what the great mystery is all about.
But in the last analysis, the fascination of autobiography is not
only in how much it reveals but in how true we believe it to be, and
we generally believe it to be true in direct proportion as to how
much it reveals. The true future direction of Western literature
has therefore already been shown in the fantasy autobiographies
disguised as fiction at the turn of the present century, and in the
shadow art of fiction disguised as autobiography that everyone
seems to have been writing since, on the unavowed model of Louis-
Ferdinand Céline and in the say-the-first-damn-thing-that-comes-

into-your-head free-association style that he, in turn, learned from
James Joyce — which is also a kind of truth-telling. The best and
most prophetic summing-up is that of Ralph Waldo Emerson over
a century ago, quoted as motto, and doubtless the inspiration, of
Henry Miller's *Tropic of Cancer*:

> The novels will give way, by and by, to diaries or autobiographies
> — captivating books, if only a man knew how to choose among what
> he calls his experience that which is really his experience, and how
> to record truth truly.

VI

It would evidently be of great interest to discover the name of
the author of *My Secret Life*. I have a theory on this subject, which
is bound up closely with the later bibliographical history of the
book, and in particular with the publisher calling himself "Charles
Carrington." This Paris erotica-and-flagellantiana dealer, who domi-
nated the English-language field from about 1895 to 1917, was, in
fact, a Portuguese of the real name of Paul Ferdinando, to which
he returned only once in his long career, so far as I know, on the
title page of an eccentric work on the so-called Shakespeare con-
troversy, vanity-published for one Célestin Demblon, and entitled
Lord Rutland est Shakespeare (1912), which — though telling us
precious little worth knowing about Shakespeare — does give at
least the publisher's identity in full, in the imprint: "Paul Ferdi-
nando, libraire-éditeur, Ancienne Maison Charles Carrington, 11,
rue de Châteaudun." This was his real address and main store,
under his true name; the official "Maison d'Éditions Scientifiques"
under the Carrington name, at 13 Faubourg Montmartre — the
address continually mentioned in the transcripts of title pages in
Forbidden Books, as a help to prospective customers — was only
a cover address or front, where his "Medical, Folklore and Historical
Works," or official cover items, were displayed.

Further details as to Carrington's career, from his beginnings
with a barrowload of cheapjack books in the street markets of Lon-
don, to his repellent end, will be found in the new and enlarged
edition of *The Banned Books of England* (London, 1962) by Alec
Craig, the principal fighter for and historian of the "limited freedom
of speech and press" one can hope for, at best, in Britain. Mr. Craig
notes, p. 74, that the minutes of the Joint Select Committee on Lot-

teries and Indecent Advertisements of 1908, in England, contain "evidence about the trade in pornography going on at the time, including details of the activities of Roland de Villiers [the original publisher of Havelock Ellis' *Studies in the Psychology of Sex*] and Charles Carrington." These details, however, are not quoted in Mr. Craig's work, and I have not been able to have access to the minutes of this Committee. Of Carrington's personal career the following details were supplied to Craig, p. 71, by Vernon Symonds:

> Carrington started life as an errand boy, vanboy, and then lavatory attendant. At sixteen he was keeping a book barrow in Farringdon Market. By reading his wares he graduated into the company of men like Dowson, Beardsley, and Wilde. In the Paris of the early twenties he was a pathetic figure not without a little dignity of tragedy. Blind as the result of syphilis, he was no match for his predatory mistress and was helpless before the follies of his five children. They and their hangers-on swarmed over his house and stole his books. A shop was even opened specially to dispose of the thefts. He endured five years of this misery before perishing in a lunatic asylum at the age of sixty-five. His mistress provided a magnificent funeral and his tortured body was consigned to earth by the Catholic Church.

A very striking description of Carrington is given, somewhat resembling a drug-addicted satyr surging up out of one of his own publications, in Gaston LeRouge's *Verlainiens et décadents* (Paris: Marcel Seheur, 1928), in connection with the writer Hugues Rebell who, having lost all his money, lived by writing works on erotic flagellation for Carrington, in particular a curious novel on the background of the American Civil War and slavery, *The Memoirs of Dolly Morton*, of which the cover item — omitting all the erotic passages, but retaining the perfectly legal sadistic flagellation! — is entitled *En Virginie*, and is signed "Jean de Villiot." (The erotic form of the French text, entitled *Dolly Morton*, which is unknown to Perceau's bibliography of erotica, gives as author "Donovan Kipps," at least on the prospectus.) A *bibliographie raisonnée* of other works on erotic flagellation, pp. 187–343, takes up nearly half of Rebell's and Carrington's cover volume, to replace the missing erotic passages.

Observing that Carrington implies, in *Forbidden Books*, that he had access to some twenty-five sets, at least, and that he states directly that the wily Dutch publisher had "struck off" far more copies than the author had specified, I tried to find out from Best how many sets of the original edition he himself had actually handled for Carrington. Six sets have since been independently traced, of which three are at present in the United States — one in the Kinsey Institute, and another erroneously reported at Yale. The fourth complete set was until recently languishing on a dealer's shelves in Paris (being ruthlessly overpriced), and has since moved on to another dealer — this time in Athens, as it appears — and thence to an important Swedish collector. The fifth set was formerly in the particularly fine private collection, in England, of the late C. R. Dawes, biographer of Restif de la Bretonne, and is now willed to the British Museum's Private Case. The sixth and final set known, is in a very important private collection in Hamburg, Germany. As to the others ... ?

VII

It will easily be understood that I accepted with every possible reserve the revelation made by St. George Best, as to *My Secret Life*; that he had always been told by Carrington that the author was the great bibliographer of erotica "Pisanus Fraxi," otherwise known as H. Spencer Ashbee. (As is common among bookdealers, Best always referred to Ashbee by his pseudonym, as "Fraxi," thus avoiding the embarrassment of the forename, which seems always to come out scatologically whether pronounced with the accent on the first syllable or the second! The same problem has been observed by philologists as to the planet Uranus.) This attribution of *My Secret Life* to Ashbee has occasionally been heard since, from bookdealers, but I assume that in all cases the proximate source must have been St. George Best, who "drummed" the better booksellers of England and America year after year. The attribution carries with it, however, a striking air of verisimilitude, as Ashbee fits perfectly into every portion of the picture of the rich old English amateur described in *Forbidden Books*, which is, as noted, itself only a parody of Ashbee's three great bibliographical volumes.

Three elements in particular make Ashbee the absolutely right choice as probable author of *My Secret Life*, and these are: first, his total and lifelong immersion in the field of erotic literature (the collecting of editions of *Don Quixote* was hardly more than a front); second, his having the money to undertake the private publication of such an eleven-volume autobiography — which is not only the most erotic but also, I believe, the *largest* autobiography ever published for an author — plus the almost-eccentric yearning for secrecy and exclusiveness leading to the absurd underprinting of six copies for the very private edition; and third, his lifetime of travel in all parts of the world, exactly as with the author of *My Secret Life*.

Not one of these elements is perhaps conclusive in itself. Many other nineteenth-century author-collectors of erotica existed in Britain, notably Edward Sellon, James Campbell Reddie, Frederick Hankey, G. A. Sala, and probably Swinburne. Many rich book collectors exist and have always existed; in fact you *have* to be rich to collect books — and especially erotica — successfully (let it be said that I speak from long and bitter experience). And most of them are equally gnarled and knotted with this jealous, wasting disease of "exclusiveness," limited editions, and all that fake-bibliophile foppery and snobbishness, as though an important part of the pleasure in collecting (collecting anything) is not just in having the rarities and luxuries oneself, but in arranging and gloating over the fact that *nobody else* can have them, or even see them! And, finally, many British businessmen and idle rich of the past century naturally spent a part of their money and leisure in travel — the Holy Land was, I believe, particularly frequented. But taken altogether, there is really no one else who offers all three of these particularities at once. Their necessary combination — that is the essential point: their *necessary* combination in the author of *My Secret Life* is too closely paralleled by their known combination, uniquely, in Henry Spencer Ashbee, for there to be any mistake here.

Let us consider the elements separately, before moving on to the question of "internal evidence" so dear to bibliographers and collectors who prefer to deal with the dead simplicity of books (which are not always either so dead or so simple) rather than with the living complexity of the authors who wrote them. Ashbee, of course, knew and owned the erotic memoirs and many of the other writings and erotic drawings of his predecessor, Edward Sellon (*d.* 1866), who will be discussed in somewhat more detail below. He was also allied very closely with the older Scottish bibliographer-collector, James Campbell Reddie, who had left his books and bibliographical notes to Ashbee on his death in 1872, and had earlier doubled as editor of the erotic Holywell Street magazine,

The Exquisite, in 1842–44. Reddie's own erotic novel, the *Amorous Experiences of a Surgeon,* is also cast in the form of an autobiography, and was published only the year before his death, under the obviously false but curiously significant rubric: "Printed for the Nihilists, Moscow, 1871," an allusion — perhaps unconscious — to the important social-revolutionary impact of the underground movement toward sexual freedom throughout the nineteenth century and still.

Enough has been said, earlier, about Ashbee as a bibliographer. A word should perhaps be added here on Ashbee as an erotica collector, a subject on which more will be found in my article "Great Collectors of Erotica," in *The Horn Book,* pp. 71–128. It must not be lost sight of that Ashbee was a member of a numerically rather small group — the rich — and that his success as a collector is strictly assimilable to his private fortune, without which all the special knowledge and assiduity in the world could not have created his collection. This is plainly shown by the more particularly bibliographical, rather than collecting, activity of Ashbee's less fortunate friend and predecessor Reddie, on whose materials the Ashbee collection and sumptuously printed bibliographies so importantly draw, as Ashbee gratefully acknowledged. I have tried to express this as a joke: that "bibliography is the poor man's book collecting." But it is not a joke. The day of the little collector is nearly over, and was already becoming untenable a century ago, as seen clearly in the relations between the rich collector and amateur Ashbee, and the poor bibliographer and literary hack Reddie, who aspired to collect in the difficult erotic field.

Ashbee's wholesale, or money-implemented, approach is far more visible in the "gallantiana" he collected — what is nowadays irreverently known in the book trade as "semi-stuff," meaning semi-erotica, anthropologica, etc. — than in his collection of erotica. The former have not been retained as a separate group in the Ashbee Bequest to the British Museum, of some 15,299 books in all; but he had, however, "everything" in the gallant or semi-erotic field. This collection of Ashbee's can still be traced in the shelf lists (the so-called "4th copy cards") of certain of the British Museum presses, quite other than the Private Case. For example, Presses 1080–81, 1093–94, and 1102 — and probably others, not traced — and Tables 603–604–605 in the Royal Library hall, principally concentrating on eighteenth-century semi-erotic works in English and French, including an unparalleled collection of the works of Restif de La Bretonne.

Wholesale sweepings-up of this kind, of entire slices of literature (except for the most inexpensive kind of colportage literature, such as jestbooks, scandal news sheets and tabloids, and semi-erotic "men's" magazines, which will be the fought-for rarities of the future among collectors wise enough to gather them *now*), can no longer be undertaken by private individuals other than million-naires, as the amounts of money necessary to be spent can easily and very rapidly pass what is, in effect, the interest on more than several million dollars per year. At an average of even so little as $20 per book, five thousand books bought involve the expenditure now of $100,000. Compare with these figures the total of 15,299 books left by Ashbee to the British Museum; though obviously he did not pay so much as an average of £7 for each of these fifteen thousand books — or did he?

Ashbee came into his money early, having, according to *Dictionary of National Biography, Supplement* (1903) i, 79, "founded and become senior partner in the firm of Charles Lavy & Co., of Coleman Street, merchants, the parent house of which was in Hamburg," for which he "organized an important branch of the business at Paris" toward the end of the 1860's, when still some thirty years old. He also married Miss Lavy. Ashbee lived handsomely. Aside from his London home, where his collection was shelved and proudly shown to other collectors, and the country estate in Kent, he also kept an apartment in Paris, at 38 rue des Jeûneurs. We are told, for instance, that the ultimate meeting between the journalist-bibliophile Octave Uzanne and the neo-Sade collector Hankey was arranged by Ashbee one evening in Paris, after dining out with Uzanne and the Belgian erotico-exotic artist Félicien Rops. The necrology of Ashbee by Eugène Paillet, in the *Annuaire* of the Société des Amis des Livres (1901) xxii, 45–52 pointedly notes in closing: "It often arrived for him to cross the Channel and come to Paris solely for our meetings [the second Tuesday of each month] and to pass a pleasant evening with us. There was no other English-man capable of similar heroism, and its memory deserves to be retained."

It is only in the erotic side of his collecting that Ashbee shows himself secretive, as in his rebus bookplate of an ash-tree and bee; nor was a word of this ever breathed in public — as was wise in those days, and perhaps even now — until after his death. Even the clarification of the pseudonym "Pisanus Fraxi," signed to his elegant bibliographies (themselves disguised, to all intents and purposes, under Latin titles), was only given for the first time in the obituary by Paillet just cited. Writing late in life to the German sexologist Iwan Bloch, then preparing his massive *Sexual Life in England* — which, as mentioned, appeared under the pseudonym "Eugen Duehren" — Ashbee states: "That you have no intention of associating my name with that of P. F., I am thankful. *That must never be done* [his italics]." This so much impressed Bloch that he continued to use Ashbee's pseudonym even a dozen years after Ashbee's death, referring to him solely as "Fraxi" in the second edition of his work, *Englische Sittengeschichte* (Berlin, 1912), but adding, however, the note (II, 498, n. 1) that anyone who might seriously want to learn the real names of either "Fraxi" or "Duehren" would now have no difficulty.

A final example of Ashbee's lavishness with his money when it came to his collection of erotica is to be seen not only in the collection itself, and however much it must have cost, but in the typographical get-up of his three bibliographical ·volumes. These are taken to every possible excess in the printing, with the use of five faces of type — all handset of course — and two-color printing on almost every page, for the titles of the books quoted in half-a-dozen languages, even in the bibliography to each bibliography! I do not know of any other bibliographical work in any language allowing itself this florid wastefulness or "conspicuous consumption" of printing all the cited titles *in red*. It is also a fact that the entire edition of two hundred and fifty copies was bound at the author's expense in half-leather: "a roxburghe binding of dark red morocco, red cloth sides marbled with black, uncut edges, top gilt. It is in this state that they are *always* (not usually) found, unless they have encountered the Philistine Binder."

These specifications are quoted from an interleaved and annotated copy of an imitation, and partial plagiarism, of Ashbee's bibliographies, *Bibliotheca Arcana*, pseudonymously prepared in a hopelessly amateur omnium-gatherum style by Sir William Laird Clowes, and published in 1885. The annotations are by an unknown

British bookseller, and are dated New Year's Eve, 1900. The information is also given that Ashbee's bibliographies — his name is given — were "put into circulation by (chiefly) E. Avery," a London bookseller. Avery is noted further at No. 136, concerning John Camden Hotten's fake "1827" edition of Burns' *Merry Muses of Caledonia*, as being the distributor of a reprint of this work — apparently the reprint noted in my type-facsimile edition of Burns' *Merry Muses* (New Hyde Park, 1966), bibliography, p. 281, at date 1903 — "in a pretty half-morocco jacket by the french [sic] binder, Chatelain," whom one may suspect, therefore, of having been the binder of the whole edition of Ashbee's bibliographies as well.

The anonymous bookseller finishes his note on the *Merry Muses* rather amusingly: "I don't think the impression was limited to a few copies, as it may always be had, for the seeking . . . Blanks are left for the obscenities, in the manner of Rochester's *Cabinet of Love*, which every reader is supposed to have at his or her tongue's end." So much — and from the horse's mouth — for the "strictly limited" nonsense usually put on erotic or other undercover works (and on not a few perfectly legal "bibliophile" editions, *n.b.*) as bait for suckers. The limitation notes on the Ashbee bibliographies are, however, certainly true, as they have always been very rare books indeed and very expensive, despite the *three* recent offset reprints.

Ashbee must have taken very early the habit of travel, having begun as a commercial traveler or salesman. As the *D.N.B.* puts it, he was "apprenticed in youth to the large of firm of Copestake's, Manchester warehousemen . . . for whom he travelled for many years," before branching out, on his own, for the Hamburg firm of Lavy & Co. Except for his favorite country, Spain, the places to which Ashbee traveled are veiled in his usual mystery except where he wrote books or articles about them. The best list of Ashbee's travels is given in Iwan Bloch's *Englische Sittengeschichte*, II, 499, to wit: "He knew all the main countries of Europe, and undertook long journeys in India, China, Japan, Tunis, Cyprus, Egypt, North and South America and in many other lands." His Chinese journey is written up in "A Ride to Peking" and "The Metropolis of the Manchus," published in 1881–82; and the visits to Tunis with Alexander Graham developed into the published *Travels in Tunisia* and *A Bibliography of Tunisia* (1887, and 1889). There is also Ashbee's interesting, if somewhat unexpected, "A Sunday at Coney Island" in *Temple Bar Magazine*, 1882.

One observes in Bloch's list of the countries Ashbee visited that, outside of Europe, his first long journey seems to have been to India, and one wonders whether this choice was perhaps influenced by Ashbee's knowledge of the Indian adventures, and his collection of the erotic works, of his departed friend Edward Sellon. We come here very close again to the question of the authorship of *My Secret Life*, since Sellon is, with Casanova, the only positively identifiable author of an unblushingly erotic autobiography published in the nineteenth century, and is also, except for Ashbee himself, the only other possible candidate for the authorship of *My Secret Life*.

There is really not the space here to discuss the remarkable life and truculent character of Captain Edward Sellon, who deserves a whole monograph to himself, a monograph for which all the primary points of departure will be found in Ashbee's bibliographies and in Bloch's *Englische Sittengeschichte*, II, 444–56. The essential point here is that before his suicide in 1866, Sellon had written a most interesting erotic autobiography, *The Ups and Downs of Life*, with erotic illustrations by himself, secretly published by the shadiest of all the nineteenth-century British erotica publishers, William Dugdale, in London, 1867, the publisher dying a year later in jail.

Sellon discusses in his autobiography, among other matters of relevance here, his life in India, on the basis of which he also wrote his valuable study of Hindu eroticism, *Annotations on the Secret Writings of the Hindus* (London: Printed for Private Circulation, 1865), not forgetting to extasiate over the charms of the women of India, those "salacious, succulent houris of the far East" (p. 42), which is a fairly good sample of his overcharged prose, dripping with intentionally gross symbols and puns, as is the title itself, *The Ups and Downs of Life*. Sellon also interestingly compares the Indian women as to their sexual charms with English, French, German, and Polish women of all social classes, in a way that suggests very clearly that he knew what he was talking about.

Sellon's whole approach, his evident erotomania, his travels in many countries, his known erotic and autobiographical writings — even the title of "Captain" — bring him very close indeed to the author of *My Secret Life;* but their dates are parallel only for the first part of the narrative. Were it necessary to offer any other possible candidate for the authorship of *My Secret Life*, Sellon would be the likeliest choice, both on the grounds of erotic interest and travel in many countries. But he died a suicide in 1866, and so could not have seen these memoirs through the press in Holland in 1888. It would therefore be necessary to add another character to the theory: the wealthy friend and editor — Ashbee again! — publishing at his own expense, more than twenty years after Sellon's death (and why the delay?) the now-complete memoirs of the dead voluptuary. The writer of *My Secret Life* does, by the way, claim that he is not its author, but only the editor and publisher. I do not think this disclaimer is serious, or that the Sellon theory will hold water. What is important in it is, again, that all the lines seem to be pointing to Ashbee, to his friends, his collections of the erotic manuscripts left behind at their deaths, and to his ability and penchant, alone of the whole group, to pay for expensive private publications. Sellon had, in any case, written his own superb epitaph — summing up any erotic autobiography in four words of Sanskritized Latin:

VIVAT LINGAM

NON RESURGAM

The most singular feature of Ashbee's erotic bibliographies must surely be the enormous Alphabetical and Analytical Index, appended to each volume and printed in five different kinds of type, mercilessly subdividing to infinity every subject touched upon, even in passing (with, for instance, nine full columns of page references to the *general* subject of "Bibliography" in the first volume only), on the stated principle that "a good book cannot be too concise — a good index can hardly be too prolix." (*Index*, p. 478.) This is of course nonsense, and would end in putting Cruden's *Concordance* above the Bible, not to mention Shakespeare and his indexers; but it is the principle on which Ashbee was pleased to work.

The resultant indexes have a striking stylistic similarity, particularly as to the subject of "Copulation," to the extraordinary subject index appended to *My Secret Life*, which is surely the only autobiography — erotic or otherwise — ever to have such an index printed for it at the author's expense, let alone one extending to a total of eighty-seven pages (XI, 307–94), in addition to a detailed forty-six-page Table of Contents for all the eleven volumes preceding (XI, 257–303). One almost suspects that the purpose of such an index is not to be useful to the reader, but to allow the aging author

to turn over and classify his erotic materials and writing in a long-
drawn-out *delectatio morbosa*. The matching concentration in both
the bibliographies and the autobiography on the equally protracted
foreplay of prefaces, introductions, epigraphs, and the like (see, in
particular, Ashbee's opening volume), is perhaps to be discounted
as only the literary formulae of the time. But there is something
more than that in the similarity of the indexes, which are certainly
not the result of any formula. Even Wheatley's edition of Pepys'
Diary — and Wheatley one of the principal index enthusiasts of his
time (see *Centuria*, p. 520) — does not go to any such extreme.

Here, in parallel columns, are the first and last few subject
listings under the head of "Copulation" from both works: The full
listing, from *My Secret Life*, will be found in *Forbidden Books*,
(six columns!) with the pious note that "The common, vulgar word
is used in the original."*

INDEX LIBRORUM PROHIBITORUM	MY SECRET LIFE
Copulation:	Copulating and Copulative organs:
The two most natural modes are the best.	— Essay on.
A woman may be enjoyed by two men at the same time.	— the nature of.
The woman should not be quite naked.	— described fully.
The woman has more pleasure than the man . . .	— æsthetic aspects of.
Pleasures of rape.	— is not obscene or filthy.
Time when a virgin should be enjoyed . . .	— is obedience to the Divine command "Increase and multiply."
Preliminaries described.	[*ending:*] Eccentric postures:
Various postures enumerated.	— against field gates.
Monotony condemned.	— against railings.
	— against trees.
	— against windows.
	— against a bed.
	— against a kitchen dresser.

One must imagine Ashbee sitting down to write his erotic
memoirs — if that is what *My Secret Life* may correctly be consid-

* The index as reproduced in *Forbidden Books* does not correspond in
every detail to the index of the original, which is fully printed in this edition.
—*Publisher's note.*

ered to be — after having finished his more scholarly erotic lifework with the publication of *Catena Librorum Tacendorum* ("of books about which one is silent") in 1885. Or, rather, simply indexing and arranging them for publication, with a second preface and a second disguising of names and places undertaken, a sort of erotic diary much more frequently kept by Don Juans of all three sexes than is commonly realized, especially not by their conquests. Judged by its typography, *My Secret Life* was visibly and certainly printed somewhere about the time of the last of Ashbee's main bibliographical volumes. The date that Carrington gives, 1888, could of course be extended to about 1894 to finish the eleven volumes; and we are told — again by Carrington — that the first prospectus, by the original publisher (if not by Carrington himself), attempting to sell off the surreptitious copies, was issued in July, 1894. In the only bibliographical work which gives a correct notice of it, *Registrum Librorum Eroticorum* (London, 1936) by "Rolf S. Reade" (*i.e.*, Alfred Rose) at No. 3136, *My Secret Life* is dated as *circa* 1890.

It is to be observed that Carrington's prospectus volume *The Dawn of Sensuality* in 1901, and *Forbidden Books* in 1902, followed almost immediately after Ashbee's death in 1900; offering *My Secret Life* for sale at the "bargain" price of £60, instead of the Dutch dealer's £100. Ashbee's correspondence, and his collection of booksellers' catalogues and prospectuses, if he made such a collection, have not survived (his article "The Distributor of Prospectuses" appears in *Paris qui crie*, 1890), but he would clearly have been acquainted with Carrington's early publications. As the most important collector in the erotic field, Ashbee was certainly not a man for Carrington to offend, and it would hardly have been diplomatic to discuss *My Secret Life*, if it stemmed in any way from Ashbee, until after his death. This is, of course, arguing from a negative ("Wireless telegraphy must have been invented in ancient Greece, since *no* telegraph wires have been excavated there"), but I believe it has a certain force. In any case, the ignorant and impertinent parody of his bibliographical masterpiece that *Forbidden Books* itself constitutes would certainly not have been appreciated by Ashbee.

I would be less than candid were I to omit the evidence, or at least the contra-indications that seem to oppose this theory — it is only a theory — ascribing *My Secret Life* to Ashbee. In a never-cited and utterly unknown, yet highly informative catalogue list of erotic books for sale, during the most open period of Paris erotica pub-

lishing, about 1910, listing the remainder of this work, the author
is identified by his presumed initial, and that initial is not "A." This
list appeared serially as "Bibliographie galante," covering ten to
twenty pages at the end of each annual issue, 1908–13, of *Paris-
Galant*, an illustrated yearbook specializing in gallant and humorous
illustrations of the eighteenth and nineteenth centuries, and issued
by the Paris bookseller and publisher, specializing in semi-erotic
works, H. Daragon. It was apparently edited, in continuation of an
earlier gallant almanac of 1906–7, *Rire et Galanterie*, by John Grand-
Carteret, the Franco-Swiss picture editor whose very successful for-
mula of *"tout par l'image"* so signally influenced modern magazine,
and now book, publication, in the new anti-cultural return to pre-
cisely that preliterary pictorialism the world has been struggling out
of since the cave drawings, the *Biblia Pauperum* before Gutenberg,
and the grossly colored *imagerie populaire* since, only to find itself
now slid completely back to the even more total illiteracy of the
picture magazines, glossy "art"-books and other pop-culch, and the
even grosser coloring of the comics.

.The so-called "Bibliographie galante" of *Paris-Galant* is of course
only a catalogue of highly erotic and flagellational books offered for
sale, at marked prices, by Daragon. It is particularly strong in other
publishers' ends-of-stocks and remainders, often with their dates of
publication, as far back as the 1870's, frankly stated. It is the only
such publicly issued catalogue known to exist, until recently in cer-
tain Mexican towns on the U.S. border; all others — from that day
to this — being available only "in plain sealed wrapper, client must
be above 18 years of age," etc., mailed from drop addresses in Paris,
Germany, Spain, and formerly Cuba. In the issues for 1910 and
1912, only, *Paris-Galant* made the following offer, in its alphabetical
place, reprinted literally here:

My SECRET LIFE, or the Modern Casanova
Memoirs of the well. Knonn celebrates Colo-
nel W. Eleven, volumes of 358 pages each.
printed on dutch paper . . . . 2.500 fr.
　　*Ouvrage de la plus grande rareté tiré seu-
lement à 40 ex. pour l'auteur et ses amis.
Les exemplaires qui restaient dans sa biblio-
thèque lors de sa mort ont été* DÉTRUITS.

As repeated in 1912, with all the same typographical errors, except that Colonel W. has been sorted out from the "Eleven, volumes" (which are now down to 10, in figures, at the same enormous price), the interesting statement as to the destruction of the copies found in the author's library at his death is abbreviated, and the bold puff is added that the work is an "Excellent bargain at this price." (2,500 pre-war francs were worth a great deal more than their translation as $500 would imply. Compare the printing of a whole book on rag paper, the entire edition, for so little as £100, at that period, noted above.) Whether or not the "well. Knonn celebrates Colonel W." was intended to point to some British celebrity then in the news, but now unidentifiable, or was simply a name taken by the bookseller out of the air, à la bonne heure, to make the mystery more piquant, it is impossible to say. At any rate, and for what it is worth, this is the only other ascription of authorship ever made as to My Secret Life. The initial "W" refers, of course, to the author's self-applied pseudonymous given name, "Walter," possibly chosen for its assonance with Spencer.

The principal opponent of the ascription of authorship to Ashbee is Dr. E. J. Dingwall, whose opinion on such matters is of particular weight, not only as the biographer, in his Very Peculiar People (1949), of one of the most curious erotico-mystic eccentrics of all time, Adriaan Beverland (to whom the "heresy" is credited identifying the Original Sin of Adam and Eve as sexual intercourse, and the serpent as the penis), but also as Honorary Curator of the Private Case of the British Museum, and the one person in the world best acquainted with the Ashbee Bequest as it stands today. Dr. Dingwall has also generously and courageously instituted a testamentary fund for the purchase of appropriate works for the Private Case of the British Museum, which is otherwise able only with difficulty so to allocate funds.

In a letter of August 14, 1962, Dr. Dingwall makes the considerable point that "Ashbee would have had a copy [of My Secret Life] himself, and would have had it passed on as he did with the extra illustrated and annotated copies of two of his great bibliographies." That is to say, would have had this passed on to the British Museum, which, in fact, did not receive any such copy with the Ashbee Bequest. At first sight the idea seems very probable, yet on reflection, it is exactly what no erotic autobiographer would have done, after having gone to so much trouble, as that visible in

My Secret Life, to disguise himself from any personal recognition or connection with the autobiographical truth there told, along with every other real personal and perhaps even place name given.

There is also the author's attempted restriction of the number of copies to the fantastic few which makes the original private printing of *My Secret Life* the highest priced of all erotic books actually available for sale. (The price at which the last copy sold is known to have gone, $1,000, is, however, piddlingly small compared with the inflated figures reached by certain well-touted modern rarities in the auction rooms, actually nowhere near as rare.) The really suspicious point is precisely its *absence* from Ashbee's great contemporary collection, an absence which really cannot otherwise be explained than as a purposeful omission or withdrawal.

Whoever the author may have been, if he did actually extra-illustrate and annotate his own copy, this would in all probability have been the one erotic book in his collection (and such an auto-biographer would certainly have had some such collection) that he would have forced himself back, a dying man, from Burgos in Spain, were he to have been stricken there, to get to his library *and burn!* This is implicit in the whole search for anonymity, struggling ambivalently against the desire for sexual publicity and immortality, in the secret publication of such a work. One may interestingly compare Sir Richard Burton's last effort on his deathbed to complete his homosexually oriented edition or "translation" of the *Perfumed Garden* of al-Nafzawi, in the same decade; and Lady Burton's burning the manuscript, for the same reason, before her husband's body was cold.

"Again," Dr. Dingwall concludes, "I hardly think that Ashbee was the sort of person to engage in these manifold activities either in London or abroad, and if we put it down to fantasy I don't think Ashbee had that much imagination." Discounting the last part of this statement, which the examination of Ashbee's bibliographies shows to be only too true, there is a profound insight expressed here, from the point of view of a specialist, as to the *distance* between erotic literature and erotic life. Ashbee, certainly the greatest erotic collector of all time, is hardly to be thought "the sort of person" to engage in the "manifold activities" — even the normal and utterly non-sadistic ones of *My Secret Life* — that are the principal matter of precisely the collection of books he left behind. And yet . . .

VIII

What there is left to tell of the story has taken place in France. The *Bibliographie du roman érotique* (1930) of Louis Perceau, II, 154–55, quotes a French bookseller's cataloguing of the original edition in English — the price demanded being 800 pre-war francs, still a sizable sum — with the remark that the author "gives the description of the morals, the habits, and the customs of 2,500 women of all the countries of the world (except Lapland), whom he had known, and with whom he had sexual relations." This squares in a striking fashion with the known fact of Ashbee's lifetime of travel, everywhere in the world. Unfortunately, the author's care in disguising dates and places in *My Secret Life* makes it difficult to work out any parallels of chronology or itinerary in the life of Ashbee (on which see further the "official" life in the *Dictionary of National Biography, Supplement*, 1903, I, 79). One wonders what was the matter with Lapland.

Perceau's *Bibliographie du roman érotique*, at this same item (No. 322), notes the original edition of a translation into French: *Ma Vie Secrète* (My Secret Life). *Mon enfance et mon adolescence amoureuses. Traduit pour la première fois de l'anglais sur l'un des 10 exemplaires [sic] de l'édition originale et unique.* Paris: Collection de l'Académie des Dames, 1923, two volumes, 12mo, of 183 and 175 pages. The only copy that Perceau notes is his own, but its present location is not certain, owing to the following unfortunate, and only too typical, contretemps. Perceau states, in the "Avertissement" prefacing his *Bibliographie* (I, 17), concerning his own "collection, perhaps unique, and which it would certainly be impossible to reconstitute now. . . . It is my desire to see it united one day to that of the Bibliothèque Nationale." His wish, however, has not been followed, and the collection has continued to remain in the possession of his family since Perceau's death at the end of World War II. For the last ten years the present writer has attempted, without success, to organize a fund among French and foreign bibliophiles, to buy this irreplaceable collection *en bloc* for the Bibliothèque Nationale, before it is accidentally broken up, owing to the continual monetary temptations set before the legatees of such collections by egoistic booksellers. So far, it has not been possible to make the bibliophiles understand the clear necessity, the historical value, and the evident correctness of this very inexpensive gesture, which would not cost any of them more than the price of one moderately well-bound erotic work, each.

A later reprint is ornamented with a *"suite libre"* of twenty-six erotic plates in color, and forty head- and tailpieces in sanguine, also erotic, attributed to Berthommé Saint-André, in which all the actors are charmingly dressed in the clothing of the 1880's. Seheur's edition is in the small square format and pink paper wrappers that are the typographical "key" to many of his clandestine publications, as for instance *Eveline* ("Londres, 1911," also published about 1930, on which see Pley, p. 59), which is likewise translated from the English, with an extremely spirited *suite libre* in color. Identical in format is the Seheur reprint of *Alcibiade enfant à l'école* — a classic of homosexual literature of which the oldest existing edition is that of "Oranges, Juann Wart," 1652 — in the translation first published by Poulet-Malassis in 1866; with cover imprint giving at least the correct date, "Amsterdam et Paris, 1936," and a suite of five (?) homosexual illustrations, almost the only such existing in modern French erotica except for editions of Verlaine's *Hombres*, written in 1891 and first published by Messein in 1904.

Attempting to complicate even worse the already tangled problem of the *Alcibiade*, Seheur's title page gives his usual false date, in the imprint "Amsterdam, chez l'ancien Pierre Marteau, 1862," and credits the work to Ferrante Pallavicino, as is invariably done in all erotic bibliographies, including Ashbee's *Index*, pp. 23–29. This work is important enough, in the history of literature and morals, to correct this invariable but erroneous ascription of authorship. Two contemporary letters have been discovered, from Gian-Francesco Loredano, founder of the Accademia degli Incogniti, to the paradoxal Father Angelico Aprosio ("Scipio Glareano," author of *La Grillaia curiosità erudite*, Napoli, 1668), now preserved in the library of the University of Genoa (Cod. E.V. 19), indicating that the real author of *Alcibiade fanciullo a scola*, D.P.A. (*i.e.,* "di Pietro Aretino," the inevitable false ascription on the title page) was not Pallavicino but a somewhat older contemporary of his, Antonio Rocco, professor of philosophy at Venice; and further that the original edition — now lost — was published in Venice by Ginammi early in 1651, from a manuscript that had been in Loredano's possession for some twenty years; that is, since about 1630. This puts

Pallavicino, who had made the mistake of writing an attack on the Pope, and was executed in 1644 at the age of twenty-six, and who was thus only about twelve years old in 1630 when Loredano received the manuscript, quite out of the question. (I am indebted to Mr. Joseph Wallfield for this clarification, and for reference to the articles by the historian Achille Neri, in the *Giornale storico della letteratura Italiana*, 1888, XII, 219–27; and in the *Bolletino storico piacentino*, 1918, XIII, 25–29, first making this corrected attribution, now accepted by Giorgio Spini in his *Ricerca dei libertini*, Rome, 1950, pp. 155–57.)

Perceau observes that further volumes of the French translation of *Ma Vie Secrète* were intended to be translated from the English, as a sequel to the 1923 edition, but that "the sequel never appeared." This is a pity, since the existing French translation, which is the most easily available text, gives hardly more than a tenth of the 4,200 pages of the English original. The same translation has recently been published openly, for the first time (Paris: Cercle du Livre Précieux, 1961), with an abridgment of the closing sections of the present essay serving as preface. Perceau adds: "I was able to obtain certain details as to this translation. It had first been made — for the only two volumes published — with very definite attenuations, by a professor of letters. The publisher demanded of another writer to review this translation, made *currente calamo*, and to give it body [!] by restoring the crude words that had been replaced by more decent terms." This is the same fate, more or less, that overtook Casanova's *Mémoires*, "professor of letters" and all. Whether the writer entrusted with the revision of *My Secret Life* worked with the English text before him, or simply after his own fancy, we are not told.

It is a matter of congratulation that the present integral reprint of *My Secret Life* has now been undertaken. *My Secret Life* is admittedly electrifyingly frank, and utterly outside the usual line of expurgated autobiographical ditherings. Now that Joyce's *Ulysses*, D. H. Lawrence's *Lady Chatterley's Lover*, and Miller's *Tropic of Cancer* have openly appeared in America without the utter collapse of public morality once hysterically foretold by the Comstocks, the Sumners, and other bluenoses, if "such things" were to see the open light of day, it does seem that the eleven volumes of *My Secret Life* should also be reprinted. They are a document worthy of publication. The evolution of the world to an adult sexual sensibility is not going to be achieved on the basis of fictitious autobiographies — whether sexually expurgated or bragging — and other balderdash and lies. Very few authentic erotic autobiographies have ever been published. With the possible exception of Casanova's *Mémoires*, now at last available as he wrote them (Wiesbaden: Brockhaus, 1960–62, but never as yet integrally translated into English), and the *Confessions* of Jean-Jacques Bouchard, written in 1630 but only first printed in 1881 by the erudite ex-priest and bibliophile Isidore Liseux, *My Secret Life* may be the only one. As far as the attribution of authorship to Henry Spencer Ashbee is concerned, *se non è vero, è ben trovato*. A more likely candidate will not easily be found.

G. LEGMAN

MY SECRET LIFE

INTRODUCTION

In 18 — my oldest friend died. We had been at school and college together, and our intimacy had never been broken. I was trustee for his wife and executor at his death. He died of a lingering illness, during which his hopes of living were alternately raised, and depressed. Two years before he died, he gave me a huge parcel carefully tied up and sealed. "Take care of but don't open this," he said; "if I get better, return it to me, if I die, let no mortal eye but yours see it, and burn it."

His widow died a year after him. I had well nigh forgotten this packet, which I had had full three years, when, looking for some title deeds, I came across it, and opened it, as it was my duty to do. Its contents astonished me. The more I read it, the more marvellous it seemed. I pondered long on the meaning of his instructions when he gave it to me, and kept the manuscript some years, hesitating what to do with it.

At length I came to the conclusion, knowing his idiosyncrasy well, that his fear was only lest any one should know who the writer was; and feeling that it would be sinful to destroy such a history, I copied the manuscript and destroyed the original. He died relationless. No one now can trace the author; no names are mentioned in the book, though they were given freely in the margin of his manuscript, and I alone know to whom the initials refer. If I have done harm in printing it, I have done none to him, have indeed only carried out his evident intention, and given to a few a secret history, which bears the impress of truth on every page, a contribution to psychology.

PREFACE

I began these memoirs when about twenty-five years old, having from youth kept a diary of some sort, which perhaps from habit made me think of recording my inner and secret life.

When I began it, had scarcely read a baudy book, none of which, excepting *Fanny Hill*, appeared to me to be truthful: that did, and it does so still; the others telling of recherché eroticisms or of inordinate copulative powers, of the strange twists, tricks, and fancies of matured voluptuousness and philosophical lewedness, seemed to my comparative ignorance as baudy imaginings or lying inventions, not worthy of belief; although I now know, by experience, that they may be true enough, however eccentric and improbable, they may appear to the uninitiated.

Fanny Hill's was a woman's experience. Written perhaps by a woman, where was a man's written with equal truth? That book has no baudy word in it; but baudy acts need the baudy ejaculations; the erotic, full-flavored expressions, which even the chastest indulge in when lust, or love, is in its full tide of performance. So I determined to write my private life freely as to fact, and in the spirit of the lustful acts done by me, or witnessed; it is written therefore with absolute truth and without any regard whatever for what the world calls decency. Decency and voluptuousness in its fullest acceptance cannot exist together, one would kill the other; the poetry of copulation I have only experienced with a few women, which however neither prevented them nor me from calling a spade a spade.

I began it for my amusement; when many years had been chronicled I tired of it and ceased. Some ten years afterwards I met a woman, with whom, or with those she helped me to, I did, said, saw, and heard well nigh everything a man and woman could do with their genitals, and began to narrate those events, when quite fresh in my memory, a great variety of incidents extending over four years or more. Then I lost sight of her, and my amorous amusements for a while were simpler, but that part of my history was complete.

After a little while, I set to work to describe the events of the intervening years of my youth and early middle age, which included most of my gallant intrigues and adventures of a frisky order; but not the more lascivious ones of later years. Then an illness caused me to think seriously of burning the whole. But not liking to destroy my labor, I laid it aside again for a couple of years. Then another illness gave me long uninterrupted leisure; I read my manuscript and filled in some occurrences which I had forgotten but which my diary enabled me to place in their proper order. This will account for the difference in style in places, which I now observe; and a very needless repetition of voluptuous descriptions, which I had forgotten and had been before described; that however is inevitable, for human copulation, vary the incidents leading up to it as you may, is, and must be, at all times much the same affair.

Then, for the first time, I thought I would print my work that had been commenced more than twenty years before, but hesitated. I then had entered my maturity, and on to the most lascivious portion of my life, the events were disjointed, and fragmentary and my amusement was to describe them just after they occurred. Most frequently the next day I wrote all down with much prolixity; since, I have much abbreviated it.

I had from youth an excellent memory, but about sexual matters a wonderful one. Women were the pleasure of my life. I loved cunt, but also who had it; I like the woman I fucked and not simply the cunt I fucked, and therein is a great difference. I recollect even now in a degree which astonishes me, the face, colour, stature, thighs, backside, and cunt, of well nigh every woman I have had, who was not a mere casual, and even of some who were. The clothes they wore, the houses and rooms in which I had them, were before me mentally as I wrote, the way the bed and furniture were placed, the side of the room the windows were on, I remembered perfectly; and all the important events I can fix as to time, sufficiently nearly by reference to my diary, in which the contemporaneous circumstances of my life are recorded.

I recollect also largely what we said and did, and generally our baudy amusements. Where I fail to have done so, I have left description blank, rather than attempt to make a story coherent by inserting what was merely probable. I could not now account for my course of action, or why I did this, or said that, my conduct seems strange, foolish, absurd, very frequently, that of some women equally so, but I can but state what did occur.

In a few cases, I have, for what even seems to me very strange, suggested reasons or causes, but only where the facts seem by themselves to be very improbable, but have not exaggerated anything willingly. When I have named the number of times I have fucked a woman in my youth, I may occasionally be in error, it is difficult to be quite accurate on such points after a lapse of time. But as before said, in many cases the incidents were written down a few weeks and often within a few days after they occurred. I do not attempt to pose as a Hercules in copulation, there are quite sufficient braggarts on that head, much intercourse with gay women, and doctors, makes me doubt the wonderful feats in coition some men tell of.

I have one fear about publicity, it is that of having done a few things by curiosity and impulse (temporary aberrations) which even professed libertines may cry fie on. There are plenty who will cry fie who have done all and worse than I have and habitually, but crying out at the sins of others was always a way of hiding one's own iniquity. Yet from that cause perhaps no mortal eye but mine will see this history.

The Christian name of the servants mentioned are generally the true ones, the other names mostly false, tho phonetically resembling the true ones. Initials nearly always the true ones. In most cases the women they represent are dead or lost to me. Streets and baudy houses named are nearly always correct. Most of the houses named are now closed or pulled down; but any middle-aged man about town would recognize them. Where a road, house, room, or garden is described, the description is exactly true, even to the situation of a tree, chair, bed, sofa, pisspot. The district is sometimes given wrongly; but it matters little whether Brompton be substituted for Hackney, or Camden Town for Walworth. Where however, owing to the incidents, it is needful, the places of amusement are given correctly. The Tower, and Argyle rooms, for example. All this is done to prevent giving pain to some, perhaps still living, for I have no malice to gratify.

I have mystified family affairs, but if I say I had ten cousins when I had but six, or that one aunt's house was in Surrey instead of Kent, or in Lancashire, it breaks the clue and cannot matter to the reader. But my doings with man and woman are as true as gospel. If I say that I saw, or did, that with a cousin, male or female, it was with a cousin and no mere acquaintance; if with a servant, it was with a servant; if with a casual acquaintance, it is equally true. Nor if I say I had that woman, and did this or that with her, or felt or did aught else with a man, is there a word of untruth, excepting as to the place at which the incidents occurred. But even those are mostly correctly given; this is intended to be a true history, and not a lie.

SECOND PREFACE

Some years have passed away since I penned the foregoing, and it is not printed. I have since gone through abnormal phases of amatory life, have done and seen things, had tastes and letches which years ago I thought were the dreams of erotic mad-men; these are all described, the manuscript has grown into unmanageable bulk; shall it, can it, be printed? What will be said or thought of me, what became of the manuscript if found when I am dead? Better to destroy the whole, it has fulfilled its purpose in amusing me, now let it go to the flames!

I have read my manuscript through; what reminiscences! I had actually forgotten some of the early ones; how true the detail strikes me as I read of my early experiences; had it not been written then it never could have been written now; has anybody but myself faithfully made such a record? It would be a sin to burn all this, whatever society may say, it is but a narrative of human life, perhaps the every day life of thousands, if the confession could be had.

What strikes me as curious in reading it is the monotony of the course I have pursued towards women who were not of the gay class; it has been as similar and repetitive as fucking itself; do all men act so, does every man kiss, coax, hint smuttily, then talk baudily, snatch a feel, smell his fingers, assault, and win, exactly as I have done? Is every woman offended, say "no," then "oh!" blush, be angry, refuse, close her thighs, after a struggle open them, and yield to her lust as mine have done? A conclave of whores telling the truth, and of Romish Priests, could alone settle the point. Have all men had the strange letches which late in life have enraptured me, though in early days the idea of them revolted me? I can never know this; my experience, if printed, may enable others to compare as I cannot.

Shall it be burnt or printed? How many years have passed in this indecision? why fear? it is for others' good and not my own if preserved.

Earliest recollections. — An erotic nursemaid. — Ladies abed. — My cock. — A frisky governess. — Cousin Fred. — Thoughts on pudenda. — A female pedlar. — Baudy pictures. — A naked baby.

My earliest recollections of things sexual are of what I think must have occurred some time between my age of five and eight years. I tell of them just as I recollect them, without attempt to fill in what seems probable.

She was I suppose my nursemaid. I recollect that she sometimes held my little prick when I piddled, was it needful to do so? I don't know. She attempted to pull my prepuce back, when, and how often, I know not. But I am clear about seeing the prick tip show, of feeling pain, of yelling out, of her soothing me, and of this occurring more than once. She comes to my memory as a shortish, fattish, young female, and that she often felt my prick.

One day, it must have been late in the afternoon for the sun was low but shining — how strange I should recollect that so clearly — but I have always recollected sunshine, — I had been walking out with her, toys had been bought me, we were both carrying them, she stopped and talked to some men, one caught hold of her and kissed her, I felt frightened, it was near a coach stand, for hackney coaches were there, cabs were not then known, she put what toys she had on to my hands and went into a house with a man. What house? I don't know. Probably a public-house, for there was one not far from a coach stand, and not far from our house. She came out and we went home.

Then I was in our house in a carpeted room with her; it could not have been the nursery I know, sitting on the floor with my toys; so was she; she played with me and the toys, we rolled over each other on the floor in fun, I have a recollection of having done that with others, and of my father and mother being in that room at times with me playing.

She kissed me, got out my cock, and played with it, took one of my hands and put it underneath her clothes. It felt rough there, that's all, she moved my little hand violently there, then she felt my cock and again hurt me, I recollect seeing the red tip appear as she pulled down the prepuce, and my crying out, and her quieting me.

Then of her being on her back, of my striding across or between her legs, and her heaving me up and down, and my riding cock-horse and that it was not the first time I had done so; then I fell flat on her, she heaved me up and down and squeezed me till I cried. I scrambled off of her, and in doing so my hand, or foot, went through a drum I had been drumming on, at which I cried.

As I sat crying on the floor beside her, I recollect her naked legs, and one of her hands shaking violently beneath her petticoats, and of my having some vague notion that the woman was ill; I felt timid. All was for a moment quiet, her hand ceased, still she lay on her back, and I saw her thighs, then turning round she drew me to her, kissed me and tranquillised me. As she turned round I saw one side of her backside, I leant over it and laid my face on it crying about my broken drum, the evening sunbeams made it all bright, it had at some time been raining, I recollect.

I expect I must have seen her cunt, as I sat beside her naked thigh. Looking towards her and crying about my broken drum, and when I saw her hand moving no doubt she was frigging. Yet I have not the slightest recollection of her cunt, nor of anything more than I have told. But of having seen her naked thighs I am certain, I seem often to have seen them, but cannot feel certain of that.

The oddest thing is that whilst I early recollected more or less clearly what took place two or three years later on, and ever afterwards, on sexual matters, and what I said, heard, and did, nearly consecutively, this, my first recollection of cock and cunt, escaped my memory for full twenty years.

Then one day, talking with the husband of one of my cousins, about infantine incidents, he told me some thing which had occurred to him in his childhood; and suddenly, almost as quickly as a magic lantern throws a picture on to a wall, this which had occurred to me came into my mind. I have since thought over it a hundred times, but cannot recollect one circumstance relating to the adventure more than I have told.

My mother had been giving advice to my cousin about nursemaids. They were not to be trusted. "When Walter was a little fellow, she had dismissed a filthy creature, whom she had detected in abominable practices with one of her children"; what they were my mother never disclosed. She hated indelicacies of any sort, and usually cut short allusion to them by saying, "It's not a subject to talk about, let's talk of some thing else." My cousin told her husband, and when we were together he told me, and his own experiences, and then all the circumstances, came into my mind, just as I have told here.

I could not, as the reader will hear, thoroughly uncover my prick tip without pain till I was sixteen years old, nor well then when quite stiff unless it went up a cunt. My nursemaid I expect thought this curious, and tried to remedy the error in my make, and hurt me. My mother, by her extremely delicate feeling, shut herself off from much knowledge of the world, which was the reason why she had such implicit belief in my virtue, until I had seen twenty-two years, and kept, or nearly so, a French harlot.

I imagine I must have slept with this nursemaid, and certainly I did with some female, in a room called the Chinese room, on account of the color of the wall papers. I recollect a female being there in bed with me, that I awoke one morning feeling very hot and stifled, and that my head was against flesh; that flesh was all about me, my mouth and nose being embedded in hair, or some thing scrubby, which had a hot peculiar odour. I have a recollection of a pair of hands suddenly clutching and dragging me up on to the pillow, and of daylight then. I have no recollection of a word being uttered. This incident I could not long have forgotten, having told my cousin Fred of it before my father did. He used to say it was the governess. I suppose I must have slipped down in my sleep, till my head laid against her belly and cunt.

Some years afterwards, when I got the smell of another woman's cunt on my fingers, it at once reminded me of the smell I had under my nose in the bed; and I knew at a flash that I had smelt cunt before, and recollected where, but no more.

How long after I have no idea, but it seems like two or three years, there was a dance in our house, several relations were to stop

the night with us, the house was full, there was bustle, the shifting
of beds, the governess going into a servant's room to sleep, and so
on. Some female cousins were amongst those stopping with us; going
into the drawing-room suddenly, I heard my mother saying to one
of my aunts, "Walter is after all but a child, and it's only for one
night." "Hish-hish," both said as they saw me, then my mother
sent me out of the room, wondering why they were talking about
me, and feeling curious and annoyed at being sent away.

I had been in the habit then of sleeping in a room either with
another bed in it or close to a room leading out of it, with another
bed, I cannot recollect which; I used to call out to whoever might
have been there when I was in bed: for being timid, the door was
kept open for me. It could not have been a man who slept there, for
the men-servants slept on the ground-floor, I have seen their beds
there.

The night I speak of, my bed was taken out, and put into the
Chinese-paper room, one of the maids who helped to move it sat on
the pot and piddled; I heard the rattle, and as far as I can recollect
it was the first time I noticed anything of the sort, tho I recollect
well seeing women putting on their stockings and feeling the thigh
of one of them just above her knee. I was kneeling on the floor at the
time and had a trumpet, which she took angrily out of my hand
soon afterwards, because I made a noise.

I recollect the dance, that I danced with a tall lady, that my
mother, contrary to custom as it seems to me, put me to bed her-
self, and that it was before the dance was over, for I felt angry and
tearful at being put to bed so early. My mother closed the curtains
quite tightly all round a small four post bed, and told me I was to
lie quietly and not get up till she came to me in the morning; not to
speak, nor undo my curtains, nor to get out of bed, or I should dis-
turb Mr. and Mrs. *** who were to sleep in the big bed; that it
would make them angry if I did. I am almost certain she named a
lady and her husband who were going to stay with us; but can't be
sure. A man then frightened me more than a woman, my mother
I dare say knew that.

I dare say, for it was the same the greater part of my early life
that I went to sleep directly I laid down, usually never awaking till
the morning. Certainly I must have gone fast asleep that night;
perhaps I had had a little wine given me, who knows; I have a sud-

den consciousness of a light, and hear someone say, "He is fast asleep, don't make a noise"; it seemed like my mother's voice. I rouse myself and listen, the circumstances are strange, the room strange, it excites me, and I rise on my knees, I don't know whether naturally, or cautiously, or how; perhaps cautiously, because I fear angering my mother, and the gentleman; perhaps a sexual instinct makes me curious, though that is not probable. I have not in fact the slightest conception of the actuating motive, but I sat up and listened. There were two females talking, laughing quietly and moving about, I heard a rattling in the pot, then a rest, then again a rattle and knew the sound of piddling. How long I listened I don't know, I might have dozed and awakened again, I saw lights moved about; then I crawled on my knees, with fear that I was doing wrong, and pushed a little aside the curtains where they met at the bottom of the bed. I recollect their being quite tight by the tucking in, and that I could not easily make an opening to peep through.

There was a girl, or young woman, with her back to me, brushing her hair, another was standing by her, one took a night gown off the chair, shook it out, and dropped it over her head, after drawing off her chemise. As this was done I saw some black at the bottom of her belly, a fear came over me that I was doing wrong and should be punished if found looking, and I laid down wondering at it all; I fancy I again slept.

Then there was a shuffling about, and again it seems as if I heard a noise like piddling, the light was put out, I felt agitated, I heard the women kiss, one say "Hish! you will wake that brat," then one said, "Listen" then I heard kisses and breathing like some one sighing, I thought some one must be ill and felt alarmed and must then have fallen asleep. I do not know who the women were, they must have been my cousins, or young ladies who had come to the dance. That was the first time I recollect seeing the hair of a cunt, though I must have seen it before, for I recollect at times a female (most likely a nursemaid) stand naked, but don't recollect noticing anything black between her thighs, nor did I think about it at all afterwards.

In the morning my mother came and took me up to her room, where she dressed me; as she left the room, she said to the females in bed they were not to hurry up, she had only fetched Wattie.

But all this only came vividly to my mind when, a few years

after, I began to talk about women with my cousin, and we told each other all we had seen, and heard, about females.

Until I was about twelve years old. I never went to school, there was a governess in the house who instructed me and the other children, my father was nearly always at home. I was carefully kept from the grooms and other men servants; once I recollect getting to the stable yard and seeing a stallion mount a mare, his prick go right out of sight in what appeared to me to be the mare's bottom of father appearing and calling out, "What does that boy do there?" and my being hustled away. I had scarcely a boy acquaintance, excepting among my cousins, and therefore did not learn as much about sexual matters as boys early do at schools. I did not know what the stallion was doing, I could have had no notion of it then, nor did I think about it.

The next thing I clearly recollect, was one of my male cousins stopping with us, we walked out, and when piddling together against a hedge, his saying, "Shew me your cock, Walter, and I will shew you mine." We stood and examined each other's cocks, and for the first time I became conscious that I could not get my foreskin easily back like other boys. I pulled his backwards and forwards. He hurt me, laughed and sneered at me, another boy came and I think another, we all compared cocks, and mine was the only one which would not unskin, they jeered me, I burst into tears, and went away thinking there was some thing wrong with me, and was ashamed to shew my cock again, tho I set to work earnestly to try to pull the foreskin back, but always desisted, fearing the pain, for I was very sensitive.

My cousin then told me that girls had no cock, but only a hole they piddled out of, we were always talking about them, but I don't recollect the word cunt, nor that I attached any lewed idea to a girl's pidding hole, or to their cocks being flat, an expression heard I think at the same period. It remained only in my mind that my cock and the girl's hole were to piddle out of, and nothing more, I cannot be certain about my age at this time.

Afterwards I went to that uncle's house often, my cousin Fred was to be put to school, and we talked a great deal more about girls' cocks, which began to interest me much. He had never seen one, he said, but he knew that they had two holes, one for bogging and the other to piddle from. They sit down to piddle said he, they don't piddle against a wall as we do, but that I must have known already, afterwards I felt very curious about the matter.

One day, one of his sisters left the room where we were sitting. "She is going to piddle," he said to me. We sneaked into a bed-room of one of them one day and gravely looked into the pot to see what piddle was in it. Whether we expected to find any thing different from what there was in our own chamber pot I do not know. When talking about these things my cousin would twiddle his cock. We wondered how the piddle came out, if they wetted their legs and if the hole was near the bum hole, or where; one day Fred and I pissed against each other's cocks, and thought it excellent fun.

I recollect being very curious indeed about the way girls pid-dled after this, and seeing them piddle became a taste I have kept all my life. I would listen at the bed room doors, if I could get near them unobserved, when my mother, sister, the governess, or a serv-ant went in, hoping to hear the rattle and often succeeded. It was accompanied by no sexual desire or idea, as far as I can recollect; I had no cock-stand, and am sure that I then did not know that the woman had a hole called a cunt and used it for fucking. I can recall no idea of the sort, it was simple curiosity to know something about those whom I instinctively felt were made different from my-self. What sort of a hole could it be, I wondered? Was it large? Was it round? Why did they squat instead of stand up like men? My curiosity became intense.

How long after this the following took place I can't say, but my cock was bigger. I have that impression very distinctly.

One day, there were people in one of the sitting rooms; where my mother and father were I don't know; they were not in the room, and were most likely out. There were one or two of my cousins, some youths, my big sister and one brother, besides others, our gov-erness, and her sister, who was stopping with us, and sleeping in the same room with her. I recollect both going into the bed room to-gether, it was next to mine. It was evening, we had sweet wine, cake, and snap-dragon, and played at something at which all sat in a circle on the floor. I was very ticklish, it nearly sent me into fits, we tickled each other on the floor. There was much fun, and noise, the governess tickled me, and I tickled her. She said as I was taken to

bed, or rather went, as I then did by myself, "I'll go and tickle you."
Now at that time, when I was in bed, a servant, or my mother, or the
governess took away the light and closed the door; for I was still
frightened to get into bed in the dark, and used to call out, "Mam-
ma. I'm going to get into bed." Then they fetched the light, they
wished to stop this timidity, often scolded me about it, and made
me undress myself, by myself, to cure me of it.

I expect the other children had been put to bed. My mother
keeping all the younger ones in the room near her. The nursery was
also upstairs; my room, as said, was next to the governess.

When in bed, I called out for some one to put out the light, up
came the governess and her sister. She began to tickle me, so did her
sister; I laughed, screeched, and tried to tickle them. One of them
closed the door and then came back to tickle me. I kicked all the
clothes off and was nearly naked, I begged them to desist, felt their
hands on my naked flesh, and am quite sure that one of them
touched my prick more than once, though it might have been done
accidentally. At last I wriggled off bed, my night-gown up to my
armpits, and dropped with my naked bum on to the floor, whilst
they tickled me still, and laughed at my wriggling about and yelling.

Then what induced me heaven alone knows; it may have been
what I had heard about the piddling-hole of a woman, or curiosity,
or instinct, I don't know; but I caught hold of the governess' leg
as she was trying to get me up on to the bed again, saying, "That
will do, my dear boy, get into bed, and let me take away the light."
I would not; the other lady helped to lift me, I pushed my hands up
the petticoats of the governess, felt the hair of her cunt, and that
there was something warm, and moist, between her thighs. She let
me drop on to the floor, and jumped away from me. I must have
been clinging to her thigh, with both hands up her petticoats, and
one between her thighs, she cried out loudly — "Oh!"

Then slap-slap-slap, in quick succession, came her hand against
my head. "You . . . rude . . . bad . . . boy," said she, slapping me at
each word. "I've a good mind to tell your mamma, get into bed this
instant," and into bed I got without a word. She blew out the light
and left the room with her sister, leaving me in a dreadful funk. I
scarcely knew that I had done wrong, yet had some vague notion
that feeling about her thighs was punishable. The soft hairy place

my hand had touched, impressed me with wonder, I kept thinking there was no cock there, and felt a sort of delight at what I had done.

I heard them then talking and laughing loudly thro the partition. "They are talking about me; oh, if they tell mamma, oh! what did I do it for?" Trembling with fear, I jumped out of bed, opened my door, and went to theirs, listening; theirs was ajar; I heard: "Right up between my thighs. I felt it! He must have felt it; ah! ah! ha! would you ever have thought the little beast would have done such a thing!" They both laughed heartily. "Did you see his little thing?" said one. "Shut the door, it's not shut"; — breathless I got back to my room and into bed, and laying there heard them through the partition roaring with laughter again.

That is the first time in my life I recollect passing an all but sleepless night. The dread of being told about, and dread at what I had done, kept me awake. I heard the two women talking for a long time. Mixed with my dread was a wonder at the hair, and the soft, moist feel I had had for an instant on some part of my hand. I knew I had felt the hidden part of a female, where the piddle came from, and that is all I did think about it, that I know of, I have no recollection of a lewed sensation, but of a curious sort of delight only.

It must have been from this time, that my curiosity about the female form strengthened, but there was nothing sensual in it. I was fond of kissing, for my mother remarked it; when a female cousin, or any female, kissed me, I would throw my arms round her and keep on kissing. My aunts used to laugh, my mother corrected me and told me it was rude. I used to say to the servants, "Kiss me." One day I heard my godfather say: "Walter knows a pretty girl from an ugly one doesn't he?"

I had a dread of meeting the governess at breakfast, watched her and saw her laugh at her sister, I watched my mother for some days after, and at length said to the governess, who had punished me for something, "Don't tell mamma." "I have nothing to tell about, Walter," she replied, "and don't know what you mean." I began to tell her what was on my mind. "What's the child talking about? You are dreaming, some stupid boy has been putting things into your head, your papa will thrash you, if you talk like that." "Why, you came and tickled me," said I. "I tickled you a little when

I put your light out," said she, "be quiet." I felt stupefied, and suppose the affair must have passed away from my mind for a time, but I told my cousin Fred about it afterwards. He thought I must have been dreaming, and I began to wonder if it really had occurred, I never thought much about it until I began to recall my childhood for this history.

I must have been twelve years old when I went to an uncle's in Surrey and became a close friend of my cousin Fred, a very devil from his cradle, and of whom much more will be told: before then I had only seen him at intervals. We were then allowed, and it seems to me not before that time, to go out by ourselves. We talked boyish baudiness. "Ain't you green," said he, "a girl's hole isn't called a cock, it's a cunt, they fuck with it," and then he told me all he knew. I don't think I had heard that before, but can't be sure.

From that time a new train of ideas came into my head. I had a vague idea, though not a belief, that a cock and cunt were not made for pissing only. Fred treated me as a simpleton in these matters and was always calling me an ass; I have quite a painful recollection of my inferiority to him in such things, and of begging him to instruct me. "They make children that way," said Fred. "You come up and we will ask the old nurse where children come from, and she'll say 'out of the parsley-bed,' but it's all a lie." We went and asked her in a casual sort of way. She replied, "The parsley-bed," and laughed. The nurse at my house told me the same when I asked her afterwards about my mother's last baby. "Ain't they liars?" Fred remarked to me. "It comes out of their cunts, and it's made by fucking."

We both desired to see women piddling, though both must have before seen them at it often enough. Walking near the market-town with him, just at the outskirts, and looking up a side-road, we saw a pedlar woman squat down and piss. We stopped short and looked at her: she was a short-petticoated, thick-legged, middle-aged woman; the piss ran off in a copious stream, and there we stood, grinning. "Be off, be off, what are you standing grinning at, yer damned young fools," cried the woman. "Be off, or I'll heave a stone at yer," and she pissed on. We moved a few steps back, but, keeping our faces toward her, Fred stooped and put his head down. "I can see it coming," said he jeeringly. He was rude from his infancy, bold in baudiness to the utmost, had the impudence of the Devil. The stream ceased, the woman rose up swearing, took up a big flint and threw it at us. "I'll tell on yer," she cried. "I knows yer, wait till I see yer again." She had a large basket of crockery for sale, it was put down in the main-road at the angle; she had just turned round into the side lane to piss. We ran off, and, when well away, turned round and shouted at her. "I saw your cunt," Fred bawled out; — she flung another stone. Fred took up one, threw it, and it crashed into the crockery, the woman began to chase us, off we bolted across the fields home. She could not follow us that way; it was an eventful day for us. I recollect feeling full of envy at Fred's having seen her cunt. Though writing now, and having in my mind's eye exactly how the woman squatted, and the way her petticoats hung, I am sure he never did see it; it was brag when he said he had, but we were always talking about girls' cunts, the desire to see one was great, and I then believed that he had seen the pedlar woman's.

Then one of Fred's companions shewed us a baudy picture, it was coloured. I wondered at the cunt being a long sort of gash. I had an idea that it was round, like an arse-hole. Fred told his friend I was an ass, but I could not get the idea of a cunt not being a round hole quite out of my head, until I had fucked a woman. We were all anxious to get the picture, and tossed up for it, but neither I nor Fred got it, some other boy did.

Soon after that, Fred came to stop with us and our talk was always about women's privates, our curiosity became intense. I had a little sister about nine months old, who was in the nursery. Fred incited me to look at her cunt, if I could manage it. The two nurses came down in turns, to the servants' dinner, I was often in the nursery, and, soon after Fred's suggestion, was there one day when the oldest nurse said: "Stop here, master Walter, while I go downstairs for a couple of minutes. Mary (the other nurse) will be up directly, and don't make a noise." My little sister was lying on the bed asleep. "Yes, I'll wait." Down went nurse, leaving the door open; quick as lightning, I threw up the infant's clothes, saw her little slit, and put my finger quite gently on it, she was laying on her back most conveniently. I pulled one leg away to see better, the child awakened and began crying, I heard footsteps and had barely

time to pull down her clothes, when the under nursemaid came in,
I only had had a momentary glimpse of the outside of the little
quim, for I was not a minute in the room with the child by myself
altogether and was fearful of being caught all the time I was look-
ing.

There must have been something in my face, for the nursemaid
said, "What is the matter, what have you been doing to the baby?"
"Nothing." "Yes, you are colouring up, now tell me." "Nothing, I
have done nothing." "You wakened your sister." "No, I have not."
The girl laid hold of me and gave me a little shake. "I'll tell your
mamma if you don't tell me, what is it now?" "No, I have done
nothing, I was looking out of the window when she began to cry."
"You're telling a story, I see you are," said the nursemaid; and off
I went, after being impudent to her.

I told Fred, and he tried the same dodge, but don't recollect
whether he succeeded or not. His sisters were some of them older,
and we began to scheme how to see their cunts, when I was on a
visit to his mother's (my aunt), which was to come off in the holi-
days. The look of the little child's cunt, as I described it, convinced
him that the picture was correct, and that a cunt was a long slit
and not a round hole. That cast doubt on males putting their pricks
into them, and we clung somehow to the idea of the round hole,
and we quarrelled about it.

It must have been about this time that I was walking with my
father and read something that was written in chalk on the walls.
I asked him what it meant. He said he did not know, that none but
low people, and blackguards wrote on walls; and it was not worth
while noticing such things. I was conscious that I had done wrong
somehow, but did not know exactly what. When I went out, which
I was now allowed to do for short distances by myself, I copied
what was on the walls, to tell Fred, it was foul, baudy language of
some sort, but the only thing we understood at all, was the word
cunt.

Just then being out with some boys, we saw two dogs fucking.
I have no recollection of seeing dogs doing that before. We closed
round them, yelling with delight as they stuck rump to rump, then
one boy said that was what men and women did, and I asked, did
they stick together so, a boy replied that they did; others denied it,
and, all the remainder of the day, some of us discussed this; the

impression left on my mind is that it appeared to me very nasty; but it seemed at the same time to confirm me in the belief that men put their pricks up into women's holes, about which I seem at that time to have had grave doubts.

After this time my recollection of events is clearer, and I can tell not only what took place, but better what I heard, said, and thought.

My godfather. — At Hampton-Court. — My aunt's backside. — Public baths. — My cousins' cunts. — Haymaking frolics. — Family difficulties. — School amusements. — A masturbating relative. — Romance and sentiment.

My godfather (whose fortune I afterwards inherited) was very fond of me; somewhere about this time he used perpetually to be saying, "When you get to school, don't you follow any of the tricks yourself that other boys do, or you will die in a mad-house; lots of boys do." And he told me some horrible tales; it was done in a mysterious way. I felt there was a hidden meaning and, not having knowledge of what it was, asked him. I should know fast enough, said he, but mark his words. He repeated this so often that it sunk deeply into my mind, and made me uneasy, something was to happen to me, if I did something — I did not know what — it was intended as a caution against frigging, and it had good effect on me I am sure in various ways in the after time.

One day talking with Fred, I recollected what I had done to the governess. I had kept it to myself all along for fear. "What a lie," said he. "I did really." "Oh! ain't you a liar," he reiterated, "I'll ask Miss Granger." The same governess was with us then.

At this remark of his, an absolute terror came over me, the dread was something so terrible that the recollection of it is now painful. "Oh don't, pray, don't, Fred," I said, "oh, if Papa should hear!" He kept on saying he would. I was too young to see the improbability of his doing anything of the sort. "If you do, I'll tell him what we did when the pedlar woman piddled." He did not care. "Now, it's a lie, isn't it, you did not feel her cunt?" In fear, I confessed it was a lie. "I knew it was," said Fred. He had kept me in a state of terror about the affair for days, till I told a lie to get quit of the subject.

I was evidently always secret, even then, about anything amorous, excepting with Fred (as will be seen), and have continued so all my life. I rarely bragged or told anyone of my doings; perhaps this little affair with the governess was a lesson to me, and confirmed me in a habit natural to me from my infancy. I have kept to myself everything I did with the opposite sex.

We now frequently examined our pricks, and Fred jeered me so about my prepuce being tight that I resolved no other boy should see it; and though I did not keep strictly to that intention, it left a deep-seated mortification on me. I used to look at my prick with a sense of shame and pull the prepuce up and down, as far as I could, constantly, to loosen it, and would treat other boys' cocks in the same way, if they would let me, without expecting me to make a return; but the time was approaching when I was to learn much more.

One of my uncles, who lived in London, took a house in the country for the summer near Hampton-Court Palace. Fred and I went to stay there with him. There were several daughters and sons, the sons quite young. People then came down from London in vans, carts, and carriages of all sorts, to see the Palace and grounds (there was no railway), they were principally of the small middle classes, and used to picnic, or else dine, at the taverns when they arrived; then full, and frisky, after their early meal, go into the parks and gardens. They do so still, but times were different then, so few people went there comparatively, fewer park-keepers to look after them, and less of what is called delicacy amongst visitors of the class named.

Our family party used to go into the grounds daily, and all day long nearly, if we were not on the river banks. Fred winked at me one day, "Let's lose Bob," said he, "and we'll have such a lark." Bob was one of our little cousins, generally given into our charge. We lost Bob purposely. Said Fred, "If you dodge the gardeners, creep up there, and lay on your belly quietly, some girls will be sure to come and piss, you'll see them pull their clothes up as they turn round, I saw some before you came to stay with us." So we went, pushing our way among shrubs and evergreens, till a gardener, who had seen us, called out, "You there, come back, if I catch you

going off the walks, you'll be put outside." We were in such a funk,
Fred cut off one way, I another, but it only stopped us for that day.
Fred so excited me about the girls' arses, as he called them, that we
never lost an opportunity of trying for a sight, but were generally
baulked. Once or twice only we saw a female squat down, but
nothing more, till my mother and Fred's came to stop with us.

Fred's mother, mine, the girls, Fred and I went into the park
gardens, one day after luncheon. A very hot day, for we kept on the
shady walks, one of which led to the place where women hid them-
selves to piss. My aunt said, "Why don't you boys go and play, you
don't mind the sun," so off we went, but when about to leave the
walk, turned round and saw the women had turned back. Said
Fred, "I'm sure they are going to piss, that's why they want to get
rid of us." We evaded the gardeners, scrambled through shrubs, on
our knees, and at last on our bellies, up a little bank, on the other
side of which was the vacant place on which dead leaves and sweep-
ings were shot down. As we got there, pushing aside the leaves,
we saw the big backside of a woman, who was half standing, half
squatting, a stream of piss falling in front of her, and a big hairy
gash, as it seemed, under her arse; but only for a second, she had
just finished as we got the peep, let her clothes fall, tucked them
between her legs, and half turning round. We saw it was Fred's
mother, my aunt. Off aunt went. "Isn't it a wopper," said Fred,
"lay still, more of them will come."

Two or three did; one said, "You watch if anyone is coming,"
squatted and piddled, we could not see her cunt, but only part of
her legs, and the piddle splashing in front of her. Then came the
second, she had her arse towards us, sat so low that we could not
even see the tips of her buttocks. Fred thought it a pity they did
not stand half up like his mother. On other occasions, we went to
the same place, but though I recollect seeing some females' legs,
don't recollect seeing any more. Nevertheless the sights were very
delightful to us, and we used to discuss his mother's "wopper" and
the hair, and the look of the gash, but I thought there must be some
mistake, for it was not the idea I had formed of a cunt.

Fred soon after stopped with us in town, we had been forbid-
den to go out together without permission, but we did, and met a
boy bigger than either of us, who was going to bathe. "Come and
see them bathing," he said. My father had refused to take me to the

public baths. Disregarding this, Fred and I paid our six pence each, and in we went with our friend; we did not bathe, but amused ourselves with seeing others, and the pricks of the men. None, as far as I can recollect, wore drawers in those days, they used to walk about hiding their pricks generally with their hands, but not always. I was astonished at the size of some of them, and at the dark hair about them and on other parts of their bodies. I wondered also at seeing one or two, with the red tip shewing fully, so different from mine. All this was much talked over by us afterwards, it was to me an insight into the male make and form. Fred told me he had often seen men's pricks in their fields, and in those days, living in the country as he did, I dare say it was true, but I don't recollect ever having seen the pricks of full grown men, or a naked man, before in my life.

It must have been in the summer of that same year that I went after this to spend some days at my aunt's at H***dfs***l***, Fred's mother. We slept in the same room and sometimes got up quite at daybreak to go fishing. One morning Fred had left something in one of his sisters' rooms, and went to fetch it, though forbidden to go into the girls' bed-rooms. The room in question was opposite to ours. He was only partly dressed, and came back in a second, his face grinning. "Oh! come Wat, come softly, Lucy and Mary are quite naked, you can see their cunts, Lucy has some black hair on hers." I was only half dressed, and much excited by the idea of seeing my cousins' nudity. We both took off our slippers and crept along through the door half open, then went on our knees! but why we did so, to this day I don't understand, and so crept to the foot of the bed, then raising ourselves, we both looked over the footboard.

Lucy, fifteen years old, was laying half on her side, naked from her knees to her waist, the bed-clothes kicked off (I suppose through heat), were dragging across her feet and partly laying on the floor; we saw her split, till lost in the closed thighs, she had a little dark short hair over the top of her cunt, and that is all I can recollect about it.

Mary-Ann by the side of her, a year younger only, laid on her back, naked up to her navel, just above which was her night-gown in a heap and ruck; she had scarcely a sign of hair on her cunt, but a vermillion line lay right through her crack. Projecting more to-

wards the top, where her cunt began, she had what I now know
was a strongly developed clitoris; she was a lovely girl and had long
chestnut hair.

Whilst we looked she moved one leg up in a restless manner,
and we bobbed down, thinking she was awaking; when we looked
again, her limbs were more open, and we saw the cunt till it was
pinched up, by the closing of her buttocks. In fear of being caught,
we soon crept out, closed the door ajar, and regained our bed-room,
so delighted that we danced with joy as we talked about the look of
the two cunts; of which after all we had only had a most partial,
rapid glimpse.

Lucy was a very plain girl, and was so as a woman. She had,
I recollect, a very red bloated looking face as she lay (it was so hot);
she it was, who in after-life my mother cautioned about leaving her
infant son to a nursemaid.

Mary-Ann was lovely. I used afterwards to look and talk with
her, thinking to myself: "Ah! you have but little idea, that I have
seen your cunt." She was unfortunate; married a cavalry officer,
went to India with him, was left at a station unavoidably by her
husband, who was sent on a campaign, for a whole year; could not
bear being deprived of cock, and was caught in the act of fucking
with a drummer boy, a mere lad. She was separated from him, came
back to England, and drank herself to death. She was a salacious
young woman, I think, from what I recollect of her, and am told
was afterwards fucked by a lot of men; but it was a sore point with
the family, and all about her was kept quiet.

One of Lucy's sons, in after years, I saw fucking a maid in a
summer-house: both standing up against a big table; I was on the
roof. Many years before that I fucked a nursemaid, she laying on
that table in the very same summer-house, as I shall presently tell.

Fred and I used to discuss the look of his sisters' and mother's
cunts, as if they had belonged to strangers. The redness of the line
in Mary-Ann's quim astonished us. I do not recollect having even
then formed any definite notion of what a girl's cunt was, though
we had seen the splits, but had still, and till much further on, the
notion that the hole was round, and close to where the clitoris is,
having no idea then of what a clitoris was, though we had got an
Aristotle and used to read it greedily; the glimpses of the two cunts

were but momentary, and our excitement confused our recollections.

Fred and I then formed a plot to look at another girl's cunt; who the girl was I don't know, it may have been another of Fred's sisters, or a cousin by another of my aunts, but I think not; at all events, she was stopping in aunt's house, and from her height, which was less than that of Fred and myself, I should think a girl of about eleven or twelve years of age. I scrupulously avoid stating anything positively unless quite certain. Some years afterwards when we were very young men, we did the same thing with a female cousin (but not his sister), as I shall tell.

There was haymaking. We romped with the girl, buried each other in hay, pulled each other out, and so on. I was buried in the hay and dragged out by my legs by Fred and the girl. Then Fred was; then we buried the girl, and as Fred pulled her out he threw up her clothes, I lay over her head, which was covered with hay. Fred saw, winked, and nodded. It came to my turn again to be buried, and then hers; I laid hold of her legs and pulling them from under the hay, saw her thighs, I pushed her knees up, and had a glimpse of the slit, which was quite hairless. My aunt and others were in the very field, but had no idea of the game we were playing, the girl romping with us had no idea that we were looking at her cunt, and an instantaneous peep only it was.

What effect sensuously these glimpses of cunt had on me, I don't know; but have no recollection of sexual desire, nor of mine nor Fred's cock being stiff. I expect that what with games and our studies, that, after all, the time we devoted to thinking about women was not long, and curiosity our sole motive in doing what we did. I clearly recollect our talking at that time about fucking, and wondering if it were true or a lie. We could repeat what we had read and heard, but it still seemed improbable to me that a cock should go up a cunt, and the result be a child.

Then a passionate liking for females came over me; I fell in a sort of love with a lady who must have been forty, and had a sad feeling about her, that is all I recollect. Then I began to follow servants about, in the hope of seeing their legs or seeing them piddle, or for some undefined object: but that I was always looking after them I know very well.

Then (I know now) my father got into difficulties, we moved into a smaller house, the governess went away, I was sent to another school, one of my brothers and sisters died; my father went abroad to look after some plantations, and after a year's absence came back and died, leaving my mother in what, compared with our former condition, were poor circumstances, but this in due course will be more fully told.

I think I went to school, though not long before what I am going to tell of happened, but am not certain; if so, I must have seen boys frigging; yet as far as I can arrange in my mind the order of events, I first saw a boy doing that, in my own bed-room at home.

I was somewhere, I suppose, about thirteen years of age when a distant relative came from the country to stay with us, until he was put to some great school. He was the son of a clergyman, and must have been fifteen, or perhaps sixteen, years old, and was strongly pitted with the small-pox. I had never seen him before and took a strong dislike to him; the family were poor, this boy was intended for a clergyman. I was excessively annoyed, that he was to sleep with me, but in our small house there was just then no other place for him.

How many nights he slept in my bed I don't recollect, it can have been but few. One evening in bed he felt my prick; repulsing him at first, I nevertheless afterwards felt his, and recollect our hands crossing each other and our thighs being close together. Awakening one morning, I felt his belly up against my rump, and his feeling or pushing his prick against my arse, putting my hand back, I pushed him away; then I found it pushing quickly backwards and forwards between my thighs, and his hand, passed over my hips, was grasping my cock. Turning round, I faced him; he asked me to turn round again, and said I might do it to him afterwards, but nothing more was done. An unpleasant feeling about sleeping with him is in my memory, but as said, I disliked him.

The next night, undressing, he showed me his prick stiff, as he sat naked on a chair; it was an exceedingly long but thin article; he told me about frigging, and said he would frig me, if I would frig him. He commenced moving his hand quickly up and down on his prick, which got stiffer and stiffer, he jerked up one leg, then the other, shut his eyes, and altogether looked so strange that I thought he was going to have a fit, then out spurted little pasty lumps, whilst he snorted, as some people do in their sleep, and fell back in the chair with his eyes closed; then I saw stuff running thinner over his knuckles. I was strangely fascinated as I looked at him, and at what was on the carpet, but half thought he was ill; he then told me it was great pleasure, and was eloquent about it. Even now, as it did then, the evening seemed to me a nasty, unpleasant one, yet I let him get hold of my prick and frig it, but had no sensation of pleasure, He said, "Your skin won't come off, what a funny prick"; that annoyed me, and I would not let him do more, we talked till our candle burnt out; he stamped out the sperm on the carpet, saying the servants would think we had been spitting. Then we got into bed.

Afterwards he frigged himself several times before me, and at his request I frigged him, wondering at the result, and amused, yet at the same time much disgusted. When frigging him one day, he said it was lovely to do it in an arse-hole, that he and his brother took it in turns that way: it was lovely, heavenly! would I let him do it to me. In my innocence I told him it was impossible, and that I thought him a liar. He soon left us and went to college. I saw him once or twice after this, in later years, but at a very early age he drowned himself. I told my cousin Fred about this when I saw him; Fred believed in the frigging, but thought him a liar about the arse-hole business, just as I did. This was the first time I ever saw frigging and male semen, and it opened my eyes.

Though now at a public school, I was shy and reserved, but greedily listened to all the lewed talk, of which I did not believe a great deal. I became one of a group of boys of the same tastes as myself. One day some of them coaxed me into a privy, and there, in spite of me, pulled out my cock, threw me down, held me, and each one spat upon it, and that initiated me into their society. They had what they called cocks-all-round: anyone admitted to the set was entitled to feel the others' cocks. I felt theirs, but again, to my mortification, the tightness of my prepuce caused jeering at me; I was glad to hear that there was another boy at the school in the same predicament, though I never saw his. This confirmed me in avoiding my companions, when they were playing at cocks-all-round; being a day scholar only, I was not forced at all times into their intimacy, as I should have been had I been a boarder.

We had a very large playground; beyond it were fields, orchards, and walks of large extent reserved for the use of the two head-masters' families, many of whom were girls. On Saturday half-holidays only, if the fruit was not ripe, we were allowed to range certain fields, and the long bough-covered paths which surrounded them. Two or three boys of my set told me mysteriously one afternoon that when the others had gone ahead we were to meet in the playground privy, in which were seats for three boys of a row, and I was to be initiated into a secret without my asking. I was surprised at what took place, there was usually an usher in the playground in play-hours, and if boys were too long at the privy, he went there, and made them come out. On the Saturdays, he went out with the boys into the fields: there was no door to the privy; I should add, it was a largish building.

One by one, from different directions, some dodging among trees which bordered one side of the playground, appeared boys. I think there were five or six together in the privy, then it was cocks-all-round, and every boy frigged himself. I would not, at first. Why? I don't know. At length incited, I tried, my cock would not stand, and vexed and mortified, I withdrew, after swearing not to split on them, on pain of being kicked and cut. I don't think I was one of the party again, though I saw each of the same boys frig himself in the privy when alone with me, at some time or another.

After this a boy asked me to come to a privy with him in school time, and he would show me how to do it. Only two boys were allowed to go to those closets at the same time, during school time. There were two wooden logs with keys hung up on the wall by string: A boy, if he wanted to ease himself, looked to see if a log and key was hanging up, and if there was, stood out in the centre of the room; by that the master understood what he wanted. If he nodded, the boy took the key and went to the bog-house (no water-closets then), and when he returned, he hung up the log in its place. Those privies were close together, and separate, there were but two of them.

You wait till there are two logs hanging up, and directly I get one, you get up and come after me. Soon we were both in one privy together. "Let's frig," said he; we were only allowed to be away five minutes. Out he pulled his prick, then out I pulled mine; he tried to pull my skin back, and could only half do it, he frigged himself successfully, but I could not. He had a very small prick compared with mine. How I envied him the ease with which he covered and uncovered the red tip. I frigged that boy one day, but finding my cock was becoming a talk among our set, I shrunk from going to their frigging parties, which I have seen even take place in a field, boys sitting at the edge of a ditch whilst one stood up to watch if anyone approached. When they were frigging in the privy, a boy always stood in the open door on the watch, and his time for frigging came afterwards. With this set I began to look through the Bible and study all the carnal passages; no book ever gave us perhaps such prolonged, studious, baudy amusement; we could not understand much, but guessed a good deal.

Before I had seen anyone frig, I had been permitted to read novels, not a moment of my time when not at studies was I without one. My father used to select them for me at first, but soon left me to myself, and, now he was dead, I devoured what books I liked, hunting for the love passages, thinking of the beauty of the women, reading over and over again the description of their charms, and envying their lovers' meetings. I used to stop at print-shop windows and gaze with delight at the portraits of pretty women, and bought some at six pence each, and stuck them into a scrapbook. Although a big fellow for my age, I would sit on the lap of any woman who would let me, and kiss her. My mother in her innocence called me a great girl, but she nevertheless forbade it. I was passionately fond of dancing and annoyed when they indicated a girl of my own age, or younger, to dance with.

These feelings got intensified when I thought of my aunt's backside, and the cunts of my cousins, but when I thought of the heroines, it seemed strange that such beautiful creatures should have any. The cunt which seemed to have affected my imagination was that of my aunt, which appeared more like a great parting, or division of her body, than a cunt as I then understood it; as if her buttock parting was continued round towards her belly, and as unlike the young cunts I had seen as possible. Those seemed to me but little indents. That the delicate ladies of the novels should have such divisions seemed curious, ugly, and unromantic. My sensuous temperament was developing, I saw females in all their poetry and beauty, but suppose that my physical forces had not kept pace with my brain, for I have no recollection of a cock-stand when thinking about ladies; and fucking never entered into my mind, either when I read novels or kissed women, though the pleasure I had when my lips met theirs, or touched their smooth, soft cheeks, was great. I recollect the delight it gave me perfectly.

After having seen frigging, it set me reflecting, but it still seemed to me impossible, that delicate, handsome ladies, should allow pricks to be thrust up them, and nasty stuff ejected into them. I read Aristotle, tried to understand it, and thought I did, with the help of much talk with my schoolfellows; yet I only half believed it. Dogs fucking were pointed out to me; then cocks treading hens, and at last a fuller belief came.

I began then, I recollect, to think of their cunts when I kissed women, and then of my aunt's; I could not keep my eyes off of her, for thinking of her large backside and the gap between her thighs; it was the same with my cousins. Then I began to have cock-stands and suppose a pleasurable feeling about the machine, though I do not recollect that. I then found out that servants were fair game, and soon there was not one in the house whom I had not kissed. I had a soft voice and have heard an insinuating way, was timorous, feared repulse, and above all being found out; yet I succeeded. Some of the servants must have liked it, who called me a foolish boy at first; for they would stop with me on a landing, or in a room, when we were alone, and let me kiss them for a minute together. There was one, I recollect, who rubbed her lips into mine, till I felt them on my teeth, but of what she was like I have no recollection, and I did not like her doing that to me.

My curiosity became stronger, I got bolder, told servants I meant to see them wash themselves, and used to wait inside my bed-room till I heard one of them come up to dress. I knew the time each usually went to her bed-room for that purpose, the person most in my way was the nurse: she after a time left, and mother nursed her own children. "Let's see your neck; do, there is a dear," I would say. "Nonsense, what next?" "Do, dear, there is no harm; I only want to see as much as ladies show at balls." I wheedled one to stand at the door in her petticoats and show her neck across the bed-room lobby. The stays were high and queerly made in those days, the chemises pulled over the top of them like flaps. One or two let me kiss their necks, a girl one day said to my entreaties,

"Well, only for a minute"; and easing up one breast, she showed me the nipple, I threw my arms round her, buried my face in her neck and kissed it. "I like the smell of your breast and flesh," said I. She was a biggish woman, and I dare say I smelt breasts and armpits together; but whatever the compound, it was delicious to me, it seemed to enervate me. The same woman, when I kissed her on the sly afterwards, let me put my nose down her neck to smell her. We were interrupted, "Here is some one coming," said she, moving away.

"What makes ladies smell so nice?" said I to my mother one day. My mother put down her work and laughed to herself. "I don't know that they smell nice." "Yes, they do, and particularly when they have low dresses on." "Ladies," said mother, "use patchouli and other perfumes." I supposed so, but felt convinced from mother's manner that I had asked a question which embarrassed her.

I used to lean over the backs of the chairs of ladies, get my face as near to their necks as I could, quietly inhale their odours, and talk all the time. Not every woman smelt nice to me, and when they did, it was not patchouli, for I got patchouli, which I liked, and perfumed myself with it. This delicate sense of the smell of a woman I have had throughout life, it was ravishing to me afterwards when I embraced the naked body of a fresh, healthy young woman.

From about this time of my life I recollect striking events much more clearly, yet the circumstances which led up to them or succeeded them I often cannot. One day Miss Granger, our former governess, came to see us. I kissed her. Mother said: "Wattie, you must not kiss ladies in that way, you are too big." I sat Miss Granger on my lap in fun (my mother then in the room), and romped with her. Mother left us in the room, and then, seating Miss Granger on my lap again, I pulled her closely to me. "Kiss me, she's gone," I said. "Oh! what a boy," and she kissed me, saying, "Let me — go — now — your mamma is coming." It came into my mind that I had had my hand up her clothes, and had felt hair between her legs. My prick stiffened; it is the first distinct recollection of its stiffening in thinking of a woman. I clutched her hard, put one hand on to her and did something, I know not what. She said: "You are rude, Wattie." Then I pinched her and said: "Oh! what a big bosom you have." "Hish! hish!" said she. She was a tallish woman with brown hair; I have heard my mother say she was about thirty years of age.

A memorable episode then occurred. There were two sisters, with other female servants, in our house. My father was abroad at that time; I was growing so rapidly that every month they could see a difference in my height, but was very weak. My godfather used to look at me and severely ask if I was up to tricks with the boys. I guessed then what he meant, but always said I did not know what he meant. "Yes, you do; yes, you do," he would say, staring hard at me, "you take care, or you'll die in a mad-house, if you do, and I shall know by your face, not a farthing more will I give you." He had been a surgeon-major in the Army, and gave me much pocket-money. I could not bear his looking at me so; he would ask me why I turned down my eyes.

About this time, I had had a fever, had not been to school for a long time, and used to lie on the sofa reading novels all day. Miss Granger had come to stop with my mother. One day I put my hand up her clothes, nearly to her knees; that offended her, and she left off kissing me. One of my little sisters slept with her, in a room adjoining my mother's room; I slept now on the servants' floor, at the top of the house. Again I recollect my cock standing when near Miss Granger, but recollect nothing else.

I was then ordered by my mother to cease speaking to the servants, excepting when I wanted anything, though I am sure my mother never suspected my kissing one. I obeyed her hypocritically, and was even at times reprimanded for speaking to them in too imperious a tone. She told me to speak to servants respectfully. For all that, I was after them, my curiosity was unsatiable, I knew the time each went up to dress, or for other purposes, and if at home, would get into the lobby, or near the staircase, to see their legs, as they went upstairs. I would listen at their door, trying to hear them piss, and began for the first time to peep through keyholes at them.

A big servant. — Two sisters. — Armpits. — A quiet feel. — Baudy reveries. — Felt by a woman. — Erections. — My prepuce. — Seeing and feeling. — Aunt and cousin. — A servant's thighs. — Not man enough.

A big servant, of whom I shall say much, had most of my attention; she went to her room usually when my mother was taking a nap in the afternoon; or when out with my sisters and brother. When I was ill in bed, this big woman usually brought me beef-tea; I used to make her kiss me, and felt so fond of her, would throw my arms round her, and hold her to me, keeping my lips to hers and saying how I should like to see her breasts; to all which she replied in the softest voice, as if I were a baby. I wonder now if my homage gave the big woman pleasure, or my amatory pressures made her ever feel randy. She was engaged to be married, but I only heard that at a later day, when my mother talked about her; her sister was also with us, as already said.

The sister was handsome, according to my notions then (I now begin to remember faces clearly); both had bright, clear complexions. I kissed both, each used to say, "Don't tell my sister," and ask, "Have you kissed my sister?" I was naturally cunning about women, and always said I had done nothing of the sort. The two were always quarrelling, and my mother said she must get rid of one of them.

The youngest was often dancing my little sister round in the room, then swinging herself round, and making cheeses with her petticoats. As I got better, I would lay on the rug with a pillow, and my back to the light reading, and say it rested me better to be on the floor, but in hope of seeing her legs as she made cheeses. I often

95

did, and have no doubt now that she meant me to do so, for she would swing round, quite close to my head so that I could see to her knees, and make her petticoat's edge, as she squatted, just cover my head, immediately snatching her petticoats back and saying: "Oh! you'll see more than is good for you."

It used to excite me. One day as she did it, and squatted, I put out my hand and pulled her clothes, she rolled on to her back, threw up her legs quite high, and for a second I saw her thighs; she recovered herself, laughing. "I saw your thighs," said I. "That you didn't." One day she let me put my hand into her bosom; I sniffed. "What's there to smell?" said she. I have some idea that she used to watch me closely when I was with her sister, as she was always looking after her, and before she kissed me would open the door suddenly or go out of the room and then return. I've seen the other sister just outside the door of the room, when suddenly opened.

The big sister must have been five feet nine high, and large in proportion; the impression on my mind is that she was two and twenty: that age dwells in my recollection, and that my mother remarked it. She had brown hair and eyes, I recollect well the features of the woman. Her lower lip was like a cherry, having a distinct cut down the middle, caused she said by the bite of a parrot, which nearly severed her lip when a girl. This feature I recollect more clearly than anything else. My mother remarked that, though so big, she was lighter in tread than anyone in the house, her voice was so soft; it was like a whisper or a flute, her name was I think Betsy.

I had none of the dash, and determination towards females, which I had in after life; was hesitating, fearful of being repulsed or found out, but was coaxing and wheedling. Betsy used to take charge of my two little sisters (there was no regular nursery then), and used to sit with them in a room adjoining our dining room; it had a settee and a large sofa in it, we usually breakfasted there. She waited also at table, and did miscellaneous work. I am pretty certain that we had then no man in the house. I used to lie down on the sofa in this room. One day I talked with her about her lip, put my head up and said: "Do let me kiss it." She put her lips to mine, and soon after, if I was not kissing her sister, I was kissing her regularly, when my mother was out of the way.

One day when she went up to her bed-room, I went softly after her, as I often did, hoping to hear her piddling. Her door was ajar, one of my little sisters was in the room with her, I expect I must have had incipient randiness on me. She taught the child to walk up stairs in front of her, holding her up, and in stooping to do so, I had glimpses of her fat calves. At the door, I could not see her wash, that was done at the other side of the room, but I heard the splash of water and, to my delight, the pot moved, and her piddle rattle. The looking-glass was near the window. Then she moved to the glass and brushed her hair, her gown off, and now I saw her legs, and most of her breast, which looked to me enormous.

Then I noticed hair in her armpits; it must have been the first time I noticed any thing of the sort, for I told a boy afterwards, that brown women had hair under their armpits; he said every fool knew that. When she had done brushing, she turned round, and passing the door, shut it: she had not seen me.

I fell in love with this woman, an undefined want took possession of me, I was always kissing her, and she returned it without hesitation. "Hush! your mamma's coming"; then she would work, or do something with the children if there, as demurely as possible. I declare positively as I write this that I believe I gave that woman a lewed pleasure in kissing me, her kisses were so much like those I have had from women I have fucked in after years, so long, and soft, and squeezing.

One day I was in the sitting-room laying on the sofa reading, she sitting and working; where the children were, where my mother was, I can't say: they must have been out; why this servant was in the room with me alone, I don't know. On a table was something the doctor had ordered me to sip from time to time. "Come and sit near me, I like to touch you, dear" (I used to say "dear" to her). She drew her chair to the sofa, so that her thighs were near my head, she handed me my medicine, I turned on one side, put my head on her lap, and then my hand on her knee. "Kiss me." "I can't." I moved my head up and she bent forward and kissed. "Keep your face to mine, I want to tell you something." Then I told her I had seen her brushing her hair, her breasts, her armpits. "Oh! you sly boy! you naughty boy! you must not do it again, will you?" "Won't I, if I get the chance; put your head down, I've something more to tell you." "What?" "I can't if you look at me; put your ear to my mouth." I was longing to tell her, and could not do it whilst she looked at me. I recollect my bashfulness perfectly, and more than that, my fear of saying what I wanted to say.

She bent her ear to my mouth. "I heard you piddle." "Oh! you naughty!" and she burst into a quiet laugh. "I'll take care to shut the door in future." I let my hand drop by the side of the sofa, laid hold of her ankle, then the calf of her leg (without resistance); then up I slid it gently, and gradually above her garter, and felt the flesh; she was threading a needle. As I touched the thigh, she pressed both hands down on to her thighs, barring further investigation. "Now, Wattie, you're taking too much liberty, because I've let you feel my ankles." I whined, I moaned. "Oh, do, dear, do, kiss me dear; only for a minute." I tried very gently to push my hand (it was my left hand) further. "What do you want?" "I want to feel it, oh! kiss me — let me, — do, — Betsy, do," and I raised my head.

Sitting bent forward towards me as I lay, until she was nearly double, she put her lips to mine and, kissing me, said: "What a rude boy you are, what do you expect to find?" "I know what it's called, and it's hairy, isn't it, dear?" Her hands relaxed, she laughed, my left hand slid up, until I felt the bottom of her belly. I could only twiddle my fingers in the hair, could feel no split, or hole, was too excited to think, too ignorant of the nature of the female article; but of the intense delight I felt at the touch of the warm thighs, and the hair, which now I knew was outside the cunt, somewhere, I recollect my delight perfectly.

She kept on kissing me, saying in a whisper, "What a rude boy you are." Then I whispered modestly, all I had read, told of the Aristotle I had hidden in my cupboard, and she asked me to lend her the book. I touched nothing but hair, her thighs must have been quite closed, and a big stay-bone dug into my hand and hurt it, as I moved it about. I have felt that obstacle to my enterprise in years later on, with other women.

Then came over me a voluptuous sensation, as if I was fainting with pleasure, I seem to have a dream of her lips meeting mine, of her saying oh! for shame! of the tips of my fingers entangling in hair, of the warmth of the flesh of her thighs upon my hand, of a sense of moisture on it, but I recollect nothing more distinctly.

Afterwards she seems to have absorbed me. I ceased speaking to her sister, and could think of nothing but her neck, legs and the

hair at the bottom of her belly. I was several times in the same room
with her, and was permitted the same liberties, but no others. I lent
her Aristotle, which I had borrowed, and one day recollect my
prick stiffening, and a strange overwhelming, utterly indescribable
feeling coming over me, of my desire to say to her "cunt," and to
make her feel me, and at the same time a fear and a dread overtook
me, that my cock was not like other cocks, and that she might laugh
at me. After that, I used to pull the skin down violently every day,
I bled, but succeeded; it became slightly easier to do so, yet I have
no recollection of having a desire to fuck that woman, all that I
recollect of my sensations I have here described.

I was still ill, for there was brought me to my bed at nights a
cup of arrowroot. My mother usually did this, but sometimes the
big woman did; I was so glad when my mother did not. Then I
would kiss her as if I never wanted to part with her, but my hand out
of bed, scramble it up her clothes, till I could feel the hair. Then she
would jut her bum back, so that I could not touch more. One night
my prick stood, "Take the light outside," I said, "I've something to
say to you." The door was half open when she had complied; the
gleam of the light struck across the room, my bed was in the shade,
"Do let me feel you further, dear and kiss me." "You naughty boy!"
but we kissed. Again I felt her thighs, belly, and hair. "What good
does it do you, doing that," she said. I took hold of her hand, and
put it under the bed-clothes on to my prick. She bent over me,
kissing and saying, "Naughty boy," but feeling the cock, and all
around it, how long, I can't say, "Oh! I'd like to feel your hole," I
said. "Hish!" said she, going out of the room, and closing the door.

She felt me several times afterwards. When my mother brought
me the arrowroot, she having an idea that I liked her to do so, I
would not take it, saying it was too hot. She said, "I can't wait,
Wattie, while it cools." "Don't care, mamma, I don't want it." "But
you must take it." "Put it down then." "Well, don't go to sleep, and
I'll send Betsy up with it in a few minutes." Up Betsy would come,
and quickly and voluptuously kissing, keeping her lips on mine for
two or three minutes at a time, she would glide her hand down and
feel my cock, whilst my fingers were on her motte, her thighs closed,
then she would glide out of the room. I never got my hand between
her thighs, I am sure.

I used to long to talk to her about all I had heard, but don't think I ever did more than I have told, for I had a fear about using baudy words to a woman, though I already used them freely enough among boys. I used to talk only of her hole, my thing, of doing it, and so forth; but what made her laugh was my calling it pudendum, a word I had got out of Aristotle and my Latin dictionary. In spite of all this, and of the voluptuous sensations which used to creep over me, I have no clear, defined, recollection of wishing to fuck her, nor did I ever say anything smutty, if I could see her face.

I got better. Then she refused either to feel me, or let me feel her, on account of my boldness. One day, just at dusk, she was closing the dining-room shutters, I went behind her, and after pulling her head back to kiss me, stooped and pulled up her clothes to her waist; it exposed her entire backside. Oh how white and huge it seemed to me. She moved quickly round not hollering out but saying quietly: "What are you doing? Don't, now!" As she turned round, so did I, gloating over her bum, then laid both hands on it, slid them round her thighs, and rapidly kneeling down, put my lips on to the flesh, her petticoats fell over my head. She dislodged me, saying she would never speak with me again. She never either felt me or permitted me any liberties afterwards, and soon left. One or two years after that, she came to see my mother with her baby. She smiled at me. I don't recollect what became of her sister, but think she soon left us also.

My physique could not then have been strong, nor my sexual organs in finished condition, because I am sure that up to that time, I had not had a spend; perhaps my growing fast and the fever may have had something to do with it. My father came home broken-hearted I have heard, and ill. Soon after we only kept two female servants, a man outside the house, and a gardener. Father was ordered to the sea-side, my mother went with him, taking the children and one servant (all went by coach then). One of father's sisters, my aunt, a widow, came to take charge of our new house, and brought her daughter, a fair, slim girl, about sixteen years old.

I remained at home, so as to go to school; the servant left in the house was a pleasant, plump young woman, dark haired, and was always laughing; she was to do all the work. My godfather, who lived a mile or two away from us and whose maiden sister kept house for him, was to see me frequently, and did so till I was sick of him. Every half-holiday, he made me spend with him in walking, and riding; he insisted on my boating, cricketting, and keeping at athletic games when not at my studies. The old doctor I expect guessed my temperament, and thought, by thoroughly occupying and fatiguing me, to prevent erotic thoughts. He wanted me to stay at his house, but I refused, and it being a longer way from school, it was not persisted in.

My aunt slept in my parents' bed-room, my cousin in the next room. I was taken down, during my parents' absence, from the upper floor to sleep on the same floor as my aunt. They had not been in the house a week before I had heard my cousin piddle, and stood listening outside her bed-room door, night after night, in my bed-gown, trying to get a glimpse of her charms through the key-hole, but was not successful.

I made up to the servant, beginning when she was kneeling, by putting myself astride on her back. It made her laugh, she gave her back a buck up, and threw me over; then I kissed her, and she kissed me. She and my aunt quarrelled, my aunt was very poor and proud, and wanted a hot dinner at seven o'clock; I my dinner in the middle of the day. The servant said she could not do it all. The girl said quietly to me, "I'll cook for you, don't you go without, let her do without anything hot at night." She did not like her. My aunt said she was saucy and would write to my mother and complain that she wasted her time with the gardener. Godfather then re-newed his offer for me to stay with him, but I would not, for I was getting on very comfortably with the servant in kissing, and things settled themselves somehow. I learnt the ways of my aunt, and tried to get home when she was out, so as to be alone with the servant; but to escape both aunt and godfather was difficult. I did so at times by saying I was going out with the boys somewhere, on my half-holidays, or something of the sort, but was rarely successful.

The servant went to her bed-room, one afternoon; with palpitating heart I followed her, and pushed her on to the bed. She was a cheeky, chaffing, woman, and I guess knew better than I did, what I was about. I recollect her falling back on to the bed, and showing to her knees. "Oh! what legs!" said I, "Nothing to be ashamed of," said she. Whatever my wishes or intentions might have been, I went no further. My relations were of course out.

Another day we romped, and pelted each other with the pillows from her bed, she stood on the landing, I half way down the stairs, and kept when I could, my head just level with the top of the landing on which she was, so that as she whisked backwards and forwards, picking up the pillows to heave at me, I saw up to her knees. She knew what she was about, though I thought myself very cunning to manage to get such glimpses. On the landing I grappled with her for a pillow, and we rolled on the floor. I got my hand up her clothes, to her thighs, and felt the hair. "That's your thing," said I with a burst of courage. "Oh! oh!" she laughed, "what did you say?" "Your thing!" "My thing! what's that?" "The hole at the bottom of your belly," said I, ashamed at what uttered. "What do you mean? who told you that? I've no hole." It is strange, but a fact, that I had no courage to say more, but left off playing, and went down stairs.

On occasions afterwards, I played more roughly with her and felt her thighs; but fear prevented me from going further up. She gave me lots of opportunities, which my timidity prevented me from availing myself of. One day she said, "You are not game for much, although you are so big," and then kissed me long and furiously, but I never saw her wants, nor my chances that I know of, though I see now plainly enough that, boy as I was, she wanted me to mount her.

About that time, — how I got it, I know not, — I had a book describing the diseases caused by sacrificing to Venus. The illustrations in the book, of faces covered with scabs, blotches, and eruptions, took such hold of my mind, that for twenty years afterwards, the fear was not quite eradicated. I showed them to some friends, and we all got scared. I had no definite idea of what syphilis, and gonorrhea were, but that both were something awful we all made up our minds. My godfather also used to hint now to me about ailments men got, by acquaintance with loose, bad, women; perhaps he put the book in my way. Frigging also was treated of, and the terrible accounts of people dying through it, and being put into straight waistcoats, etc., I have no doubt were useful to me. Several of us boys were days in finding out what the book meant by masturbation, onanism, or whatever the language may have been. We used dictionaries and other books to help us, and at last one of the biggest boys explained the meaning to us.

One evening, my aunt being out (it was not I think any plan on my part), I had something to eat and then went into the kitchen, where the servant was sitting at needle-work by candle-light. I talked, kissed, coaxed her, began to pull up her clothes, and it ended in her running round the kitchen, and my chasing her; both laughing, stopping at intervals, to hear if my aunt knocked. "I'll go and lock the outer gate," said she, "then your aunt must ring, if she comes up to the door, she will hear us, for you make such a noise." She locked it and came back again.

The kitchen was on the ground-floor, separated from the body of the house by a short passage. I got her on to my knees, I was now a big fellow, and though but a boy, my voice was changing, she chaffed me about that; then my hand went up her petticoats, and she gave me such a violent pinch on my cock (outside the clothes), that I hollowed. Whenever I was getting the better of her in our amatory struggles, she said, "Oh! hush! there is your aunt knocking," and frightened me away, but at last she was sitting on my knees, my hand touching her thighs, she feeling my prick, she felt all round it and under. "You have no hair," she said. That annoyed me, for I had just a little growing. Then how it came about I don't recollect, but she consented to go into the parlor with me, after we had sat together feeling each other for a time, if mine could be called feeling, when my fingers only touched the top of the notch. I took up the candle. "I won't go if you bring a light," said she, so I put down the candle, and, holding her by the arm, we walked through the passage across the little hall to the front parlour; she closed the door, and we were in the dark. And now I only recollect generally what took place, it seems as if it all could but have occupied a minute, or two, though experience tells me it must have been longer.

We sat on a settee or sofa, she had hold of my prick, and I her cunt, for she now sat with thighs quite wide open. It was my first real feel of a woman, and she meant me to feel well. How large and hairy and wet it seemed; its size overwhelmed me with astonishment, I did not find the hole, don't recollect feeling for that, am sure I never put my finger in it, all seemed cunt below her belly, wet, and warm, and slippery. "Make haste, your aunt will be in soon," said she softly, but I was engrossed with the cunt, in twiddling it and feeling it in delighted wonder at its size and other qualities. "Your aunt will be in," and leaving off feeling my cock, she laid half on, half off the settee. "No, no, not so," I recollect the

words, but what I was doing, know not; then I was standing by her
side, my cock stiff, and still feeling her cunt in bewilderment. "I
can't . . . stop . . . get on to the sofa." I laid half over her, my prick
touched something — her cunt of course. Whether it went in or not,
God knows, I pushed, it felt smooth to my prick, then suddenly
came over me, a fear of some horrible disease, and I ceased what-
ever I was doing. "Go on, go on," said she, moving her belly up. I
could not, said nothing, but sat down by her side, she rose up, "You're
not man enough," said she, laying hold of my prick. It was not stiff,
I put my hand down, and again the great size — as it seemed to
me — of her cunt, made me wonder.

What then she did with me, I know not, she may have frigged
it, I think she did, but can't say, a sense of disgrace had come over
me as she said I was not man enough, disgrace mixed with fear of
disease. "Let me try," said I; again she laid back, I have a faint
recollection of my finger going in somewhere deep, again of my
prick touching her thighs and rubbing in something smooth, but
nothing more. "You're not man enough," said she again. A ring . . .
"Hark! it's your aunt, go!" and it was.

I went into the adjoining room, where my books were and a
lamp, she went to the street-door. My aunt and cousin came in and
went up to their bed-rooms, I sat smelling my fingers; the full smell
of cunt that I had for the first time. I smelt and smelt almost out of
my senses, sat poring over a book, seeming to read, but with my
fingers to my nose and thinking of cunt, its wonderful size and
smell. Aunt came down. "Have you got a cold, Wattie?" "No, aunt."
"Your eyes look quite inflamed, child." Soon after again, she said:
"You have a cold?" "No, aunt." "Why are you sniffing so, and hold-
ing your hand to your mouth?" Suddenly the fear of the pox came
over me, I went up to the bed-room, soaped and washed my prick,
and had a terrible fear on me.

I was overwhelmed with a mixed feeling of pride, at having
had my prick either touch or go up a cunt, fear that I had caught
disease, and shame at not being man enough. Instinct told me I
had lost, in the eyes of the woman, and my pride was hurt in a woe-
ful manner. I tried to avoid seeing her, instead of as before getting
excitedly into a room where she was likely to be alone for a minute.
I did that for three days, then fear of disease vanished, and my

hopes of feeling her cunt again, or of poking — I don't know which — impelled me towards her.

During those three days I washed my prick at every possible opportunity, and thought of nothing else but the incident; all seemed to me hurry, confusion, impossible; I wondered, and wonder still, whether my prick went into her or not; but above all, the largeness of the cunt filled me with wonder; for though I had had rapid glimpses of cunts as told, and had now seen a few pictures of the long slit, I never could realise that that was only the outside of the cunt, until I had had a woman. My fingers had no doubt slipped over the surface of hers, from clitoris to arse-hole; the space my hand covered filled me with astonishment, as well as the smell it left on my fingers, I thought of that more than anything else. This seems to me now laughable, but it was a marvel to me then.

When I sneaked into the kitchen again, I v. as ashamed to look at her, and left almost directly, but one day I felt her again. Laughing she put her hand outside my trowsers, gave my doodle a gentle pinch and kissed me. "Let's do it!" I said. "Lor! you ain't man enough," and again I slunk away ashamed.

My first frig. — My godfather. — Meditations on copulation. — Male and female aromas. — Maid and gardener. — My father dies. — A wet dream. — Bilked by a whore.

The frequency of my cock-stands up to this time I don't know. Voluptuous sensation I have no clear recollection of; but no doubt during that half swooning delight, which I had when big Betsy allowed me to lay my head on her lap and feel her limbs, that impulse towards the woman was accompanied by sensuous pleasure, though I don't recollect the fact, but soon my manhood was to declare itself.

Some time after I had felt this servant's quim, I noticed a strong smelling, whitish stuff, inside my foreskin, making the underside of the tip of the prick sore. At first I thought it disease, then pulling the foreskin up, I made it into a short of cup, dropped warm water into it, and working it about, washed all round the nut, and let the randy smelling infusion escape. This marked my need for a woman, I did not know what the exudation was, it made me in a funk at first. One day I had been toying with the girl, had a cock-stand, and felt again my prick sore, and was washing it with warm water, when it swelled up. I rubbed it through my hand, which gave me unusual pleasure, then a voluptuous sensation came over me quickly so thrilling and all pervading that I shall never forget it. I sunk on to a chair, feeling my cock gently, the next instant spunk jetted out in large drops, a full yard in front of me, and a thinner liquid rolled over my knuckles. I had frigged myself, without intending it.

Then came astonishment, mingled with disgust, I examined the viscid, gruelly fluid with the greatest curiosity, smelt it, and I think tasted it. Then came fear of my godfather, and of being found

106

out; for all that, after wiping up my sperm from the floor, I went up to my bed-room and, locking the door, frigged myself until I could do it no more from exhaustion.

I wanted a confidant and told two schoolfellows who were brothers, I could not keep it to myself, and was indeed proud though ashamed to speak of the pleasure. They both had bigger pricks than mine, and never had jeered at me because I could not retract my prepuce easily. Soon after they came to see me, we all went into the garden, each pulled my prepuce back, I theirs, and then we all frigged ourselves in an out-house.

Then I wrote to Fred, who was at a large public school, about my frigging. He replied that some fellows at his school had been caught at it and flogged; that a big boy just going to Oxford had had a woman and got the pox badly. He begged me to burn his letter, or throw it down the shit-house directly I had read it, adding that he was in such a funk for he had lost mine; and that I was never to write to him such things at the school, because the master opened every day indiscriminately one or two letters of the boys. He knew my mother was away and so did not mind writing to me. When I heard that he had lost my letter, I also was in a funk; the letter never was found. Whether the master got it, or sent it to my god-father or not, I can't say, but it is certain that just after I had one night exhausted myself by masturbation, my godfather came to see me.

He stared hard at me. "You look ill." "No, I am not." "Yes, you are, look me full in the face, you've been frigging yourself," said he just in so many words. He had never used an improper word to me before. I denied it. He raved out "No denial, sir, no lies, you have, sir; don't add lying to your bestiality, you've been at that filthy trick, I can see it in your face, you'll die in a mad-house, or of consumption, you shall never have a farthing more pocket-money from me, and I won't buy your commission, nor leave you any money at my death." I kept denying it, brazening it out. "Hold your tongue, you young beast, or I'll write to your mother." That reduced me to a sullen state, only at times jerking out: "I haven't!" He put on his hat angrily, and left me in a very uncomfortable state of mind.

I knew that my father was not so well off as he had been, my mother always impressed upon me not to offend my godfather, and now I had done it. I wrote Fred all about it, he said the old beggar

was a doctor, and it was very unfortunate; he wondered if he really
did see any signs in my face, or whether it was bounce; that I was
not to be a fool and give in, and still say I hadn't, but had better
leave off frigging.

From that time my godfather was always at my heels, he wait-
ed for me at the school-door, spent my half-holidays with me, sat
with me and my aunt of an evening till bed-time, made me ride and
drive out with him, stopped giving me pocket-money altogether,
and no one else did; so that I was not very happy.

The pleasure of frigging, now I had tasted it (and not before),
opened my eyes more fully to the mystery of the sexes, I seemed
at once to understand why women and men got together, and yet
was full of wonder about it. Spunking seemed a nasty business, the
smell of cunt an extraordinary thing in a woman, whose odour gen-
erally to me was so sweet and intoxicating. I read novels harder
than ever, liked being near females and to look at them more than
ever, and whether young or old, common or gentle, was always
looking at them and thinking that they had cunts which had a
strong odour, and wondering if they had been fucked; I used to
stare at aunt and cousins, and wonder the same. It seemed to me
scarcely possible, that the sweet, well dressed, smooth-spoken la-
dies who came to our house, could let men put the spunk up their
cunts. Then came the wonder if, and how, women spent; what
pleasure they had in fucking, and so on; in all ways was I wondering
about copulation, the oddity of the gruelly, close-smelling sperm
being ejected into the hole between a woman's thighs so astonished
me. I often thought the whole business must be a dream of mine;
then that there could be no doubt about it. Among other doubts,
was whether the servant's quim, which had made my fingers smell,
was diseased, or not.

Fear of detection perhaps kept me from frigging, but I was
weak and growing fast, and have no recollection of much desire,
though mad to better understand a cunt. It does not dwell in my
mind now that I had a desire to fuck one, but to see it, and above
all, to smell it; the recollection of its aroma seems to have had a
strange effect on me. I did not like it much, yet yearned to smell it
again. Watching my opportunity one day, I managed to feel the
servant; it was dusk, she stood with her back up against the wall,
and felt my prick whilst I felt her; it was an affair of a second or

two, and again we were scared. I went to the sitting-room, and passed the evening in smelling my fingers and looking at my cousin. This occurred once again, and I think now, that the servant must just have been on the point of letting me fuck her, for she had been feeling my prick and in a jeering way saying, "You are not man enough if I let you," I emboldened, blurted out that I had spent, I recollect her saying, "Oh! your story," and then something put us to flight, I don't now know what. I certainly was not up to my opportunities, that I see now plainly.

I had a taste for chemistry, which served my purpose, as will be seen further on, and used to experimentalise in what was called a wash-house, just outside the kitchen, with my acids and alkalis; that enabled me to slip into the kitchen on the sly, but the plan of the house rendered it easy for my aunt to come suddenly into the kitchen.

My bed-room window overlooked the kitchen yard, in which was this wash-house, a knife-house, and a servant's privy, etc., etc., the whole surrounded by a wall, with a door in it, leading into the garden. Just outside on the garden side, was a gardener's shed; the servant in the morning used to let the gardener in at the kitchen entrance; and he passed through this kitchen yard into the garden. I was pissing in the pot in my bed-room early one morning, and peeping through the blind, when I saw the servant's head just coming out of the gardener's shed, she passed through the kitchen yard into the kitchen in great haste, looking up at the house, as if to see if anyone was at the windows. Then it occurred to me, that if I got quite early to the kitchen, I could play my little baudy tricks without fear, for my relatives never went down till half-past eight to breakfast, whilst the servant went down at six.

The next morning, I went down early to the kitchen, did not see the wench, and thinking she might be in the privy in the kitchen yard, waited. The shutters were not down, after some minutes delay, in she came; she started. "Hulloh! what are you up for?" I don't think I spoke, but making a dash, got my hand up her clothes and on to her cunt. She pushed me away, then caught hold of the hand with which I had touched her cunt, and squeezed it hard with a rubbing motion, looking at me as I recollected (but long afterwards), in a funny way. "Hish! hish! here is the old woman," said she. "It is not." "I'm sure I heard the wires of her bell," and

sure enough there came a ring. Up I went without shoes, like a
shot to my bed-room, began to smell my fingers, found they were
sticky, and the smell not the same. I recollect thinking it strange
that her cunt should be so sticky, I had heard of dirty cunts, — it
was a joke among us boys — and thought hers must have been so,
which was the cause that the smell and feel were different.

Two or three days afterwards my mother came to town by her-
self, there was a row with the servant, I was told to leave the room;
the servant and gardener were both turned off that day and hour,
a char-woman was had in, a temporary gardener got, and my
mother went back to my sick father. Years passed away, and when
I had greater experience and thought of all this, concluded that my
aunt had found the gardener and the servant amusing themselves
too freely, had had them dismissed, and that the morning I found
my fingers sticky the girl had just come in from fucking in the
gardener's shed.

With all the opportunities I had, both with big Betsy and with
this woman, I was still virgin.

When I saw Fred next, he told me he had felt the cunt of one
of their servants. I told him partly what I had done, but kept to
myself how I had failed to poke when I had the opportunity, fear-
ing his jeers; and as I was obliged to name some woman, mentioned
one of my godfather's servants. He went there to try his chances of
groping her as well, but got his head slapped. We talked much
about the smell of cunt, and he told me that one day after he had
felt their servant, he went into the room where his sisters were, and
said, "Oh, what a funny smell there is on my fingers, what can it
be? Smell them." Two of his sisters smelt, said they could not tell
what it was, but it was not nice. Fred used to say that he thought
they knew it was like the smell of cunt, because they colored up so.

I had noticed a strong smell on my prick, whenever the curdy
exudation had to be washed out. Fred's talk made me imitative, so
I saturated my fingers with the masculine essence one evening, and,
going to my female cousin, "Oh, what a queer smell there is on my
fingers," said I, "smell them." The girl did. "It's nasty, you've got it
from your chemicals," said she. "I don't think I have, smell them
again, I can't think what it can be, what's it like?" "I don't think it's
like anything I ever smelt, but it is not so nasty, if you smell
it close, it's like southern wood," she replied. I wonder if that young

lady when she married, ever smelt it afterwards, and recognized it. I did this more than once, it gave me great delight to think my slim cousin had smelt my prick, through smelling my fingers; what innate lubricity comes out early in the male.

Misfortunes of all sort came upon us, the family came back to town, another brother died, then my father, who had been long ill, died, and was found to be nearly bankrupt; then my godfather died, and left me a fortune, all was trouble and change, but I only mention these family matters briefly.

My physique still could not have been strong, for though more than ever intensely romantic, and passionately fond of female society, I don't recollect being much troubled with cock-standings, and think I should, had I been so. My two intimate school-friends left off frigging, the elder brother, who had a very long red nose, having come to the conclusion with me that frigging made people mad, and worse, prevented them afterwards from fucking and having a family. Fred, my favorite cousin, arrived at the same conclusion — by what mental process we all arrived at it I don't know.

When I was approaching my sixteenth year, I awakened one night with a voluptuous dream, and found my night-shirt saturated with semen, it was my first wet dream; that set me frigging again for a time, but I either restrained myself or did not naturally require much spending at that time, for I certainly did not often do so.

But our talk was always about cunt and women, I was always trying to smell their flesh, look up their petticoats, watch to see them going to piddle; and the wonder to me now is that I did not frig myself incessantly; and can only account for it on the grounds, that though my imagination was very ripe, my body was not. The fact of hair under the arms of women had a secret charm for me about that time. I don't recollect thinking much about it before, though it had astonished me when I first saw it; and why it came to my imagination so much now I do not know, but it did. I have told of the woman under whose arms I first saw hair.

One afternoon after my father's death, and that of my god-father, Fred was with me, we went to the house of a friend, and were to return home about nine o'clock. It was dark, we saw a woman standing by a wall. "She is a whore," said Fred, "and will let us feel her if we pay her." "You go and ask her." "No, you." "I don't

like." "How much money have you got?" We ascertained what we
had, and after a little hesitation, walked on, passed her, then turned
round and stopped. "What are you staring at, kiddy," said the
woman. I was timid and walked away; Fred stopped with her.
"Wattie, come here," said he in a half whisper. I walked back. "How
much have you got?" the woman said. We both gave her money.
"You'll let us both feel?" said Fred. "Why of course, have you felt
a woman before?" Both of us said we had, feeling bolder. "Was it
a woman about here?" "No." "Did you both feel the same woman?"
"No." "Give me another shilling then, you shall both feel my cunt
well, I've such a lot of hair on it." We gave what we had, and then
she walked off without letting us. "I'll tell your mothers, if you
come after me," she cried out. We were sold; I was once sold again
in a similar manner afterwards, when by myself.

These are the principal baudy incidents of my early youth,
which I recollect, and have not told to friends; many other amusing
incidents told them are omitted here, for the authorship would be
disclosed if I did. One or two were peculiar and most amusing, yet
I dare not narrate them; but all show how soon sexual desires de-
veloped in me, and what pleasure early in life even these gave me
and others.

I now had arrived at the age of puberty, when male nature
asserts itself in the most timid and finds means of getting its legiti-
mate pleasure with women. I did, and then my recollection of
things became more perfect, not only as to the consummations, but
of what led to them; yet nothing seems to me so remarkable as the
way I recollect matters which occurred when I was almost an infant.

Our house. — Charlotte and brother Tom. — Kissing and groping.
— Both in rut. — My first fuck. — A virginity taken. — At a baudy
house. — In a privy. — Tribulations. — Charlotte leaves. — My de-
spair.

After father's death, our circumstances were further reduced.
At the time I am going to speak of, we had come to a small house
nearer London; one sister went to boarding-school, an aunt (I had
many) took another, I went to a neighboring great school or college,
as it was termed, my little brother Tom was at home; but reference
henceforth to members of my family will be but slight, for they had
but little to do with the incidents of this private life, and unless they
were part actors in it, none will be mentioned.

Our house had on the ground-floor a dining-room, a drawing-
room, and a small room called the garden parlour, with steps lead-
ing into a large garden. On the first floor, my mother's bed-room and
two others; above were the servants' room, mine, and another much
used as a lumber-room; the kitchens were in the basement, outside
them a long covered way led to a servants' privy, and close to it a
flight of stairs leading up into the garden; at the top of the stairs
was a garden-door leading into the fore-court, on to which opened
the street-door of the house. This description of plan is needful to
understand what follows.

I was about sixteen years old, tall, with slight whiskers and
moustache, altogether manly and looking seventeen or eighteen, yet
my mother thought me a mere child, and most innocent; she told
our friends so. I had developed, without her having noticed it, love
of women, and the intensest desire to understand the secrets of
their nature had taken possession of me; the incessant talk of fuck-

ing with which the youths I knew beguiled their leisure, the stories they told of having seen their servants or other girls half, or quite, naked, the tricks by which they managed this, the dodges they were up to, inflamed me, sharpened my instinctive acuteness in such matters, and set me seeking every opportunity to know women naked, and sexually. Frigging was now hateful to me; I had never done so more than the times related, that is as far as I now can recollect, frightened, as said, by my godfather telling me that it sent men mad and made them hateful to women. So although boiling with sensuality, I was still all but a virgin, and actually so in fucking.

A housemaid arrived just as I came home from college; the cook stood at the door, she was a lovely woman about twenty-five or -six years old, fresh as a daisy, her name was Mary. The housemaid was in a cart, driven by her father, a small market gardener living a few miles from us. I saw a fresh, comely girl about seventeen years old in the cart as I passed, and when I got inside our fore-court, turned round to look, she was getting down, the horse moved, she hesitated. "Get down," said her father angrily. Down she stepped, her clothes caught on the edge of the cart, or step, or somehow; and I saw rapidly appear white stockings, garters, thighs, and a patch of dark hair between them by her belly; it was instantaneous, and down the clothes came, hiding all. I stood fascinated, knowing I had seen her cunt hair. She, without any idea of having been exposed, helped down with her box, I went into the parlour ashamed of having, as I thought, been seen looking.

I could think of nothing else, and when she brought in tea, could not take my eyes off her, it was the same at supper (we led a simple life, dining early and having supper). In the evening my mother remarked, "That girl will do," I recollect feeling glad at that.

I went to bed, thinking of what I had seen, and stared whenever I saw her the next day, until, by a sort of fascination, she used to stare at me; in a day or two I fancied myself desperately in love with her, and indeed was. I recollect now her features, as if I had only seen her yesterday, and, after the scores and scores of women I have fucked since, recollect every circumstance attending my having her, as distinctly as if it only occurred last week; yet very many years have passed away.

She was a little over seventeen years, had ruddy lips, beautiful teeth, darkish hair, hazel eyes, and a slightly turn-up nose, large shoulders and breasts, was plump, generally of fair height, and looked eighteen or nineteen; her name was Charlotte.

I soon spoke to her kindly, by degrees became free in manner, at length chucked her under her chin, pinched her arm, and used the familiarities which nature teaches a man to use towards a woman. It was her business to open the door, and help me off with my coat and boots if needful; one day as she did so, her bum projecting upset me so that as she rose from stooping I caught and pinched her. All this was done with risk, for my mother then was nearly always at home, and the house being small, a noise was easily heard.

I was soon kissing her constantly. In a few days got a kiss in return, that drove me wild, her cunt came constantly into my mind, all sorts of wants, notions, and vague possibilities came across me; girls do let fellows feel them, I said to myself, I had already succeeded in that. What if I tell that I have seen it outside? will she tell my mother? will she let me feel her? what madness! yet girls do let men, girls like it, so all my friends say. Wild with hopes and anticipations, coming indoors one day, I caught her tightly in my arms, pulled her belly close to mine, rubbed up against hers saying, "Charlotte, what would I give, if you would . . ." it was all I dared say. Then I heard my mother's bed-room door open, and I stopped.

Hugging and kissing a woman never stopped there, I told her I loved her, which she said was nonsense. We now used regularly to kiss each other when we got the chance; little by little I grasped her closer to me, put my hands round her waist, then cunningly round to her bum, then my prick used to stand and I was mad to say more to her, but had not the courage. I knew not how to set to work, indeed scarce knew what my desires led me to hope, and think at that time, putting my hand on to her cunt, and seeing it, was perhaps the utmost; fucking her seemed a hopelessly mad idea, if I had the expectation of doing so at all very clearly.

I told a friend one or two years older than myself how matters stood, carefully avoiding telling him who the girl was. His advice was short. Tell her you have seen her cunt, and make a snatch up her petticoats when no one is near; keep at it, and you will be sure to get a feel, and some day, pull out your prick, say straight you want to fuck her, girls like to see a prick, she will look, even if she turns her head away. This advice he dinned into my ears continually, but for a long time I was not bold enough to put his advice into practice.

One day, my mother was out, the cook upstairs dressing, we had kissed in the garden parlour, I put my hand round her bum, and sliding my face over her shoulder half ashamed, said, "I wish my prick was against your naked belly, instead of outside your clothes." She with an effort disengaged herself, stood amazed, and said, "I never will speak to you again."

I had committed myself, but went on, though in fear, prompted by love or lust. My friend's advice was in my ears. "I saw your cunt as you got down from your father's cart," said I, "look at my prick (pulling it out), how stiff it is, it's longing to go into you, 'cock and cunt will come together.'" It was part of a smutty chorus the fellows sang at my college; she stared, turned round, went out of the room, through the garden, and down to the kitchen by the garden stairs, without uttering a word.

The cook was at the top of the house, I went into the kitchen reckless, and repeated all I had said. She threatened to call the cook. "She must have seen your cunt, as well as me," said I; then she began to cry. Just as I was begging pardon, my friend's advice again rang in my ears, I stooped and swiftly ran both hands up her clothes, got one full on to her bum, the other on her motte; she gave a loud scream, and I rushed off upstairs in a fright.

The cook did not hear her, being up three pairs of stairs; down I went again, and found Charlotte crying, told her again all I had seen in the court yard, which made her cry more. She would ask the cook, and would tell my mother — then hearing the cook coming downstairs, I cut off through the passage up into the garden.

The ice was quite broken now, she could not avoid me, I promised not to repeat what I had said and done, was forgiven, we kissed, and the same day I broke my promise; this went on day after day, making promises and breaking them, talking smuttily as well as I knew how, getting a slap on my head, but no further, my chances were few. My friend, whom I made a half confidant of, was always taunting me with my want of success and boasting of what he would have done had he had my opportunities.

My mother just at that time began to resume her former habits, leaving the house frequently for walks and visits. One afternoon she being out for the remainder of the day, I went home unexpectedly; the cook was going out, I was to fetch my mother home in the evening; Charlotte laid the dinner for me; we had the usual kissing, I was unusually bold and smutty. Charlotte finding me not to be going out, seemed anxious. All the dinner things had been taken away, when out went the cook; and there were Charlotte, my little brother and I alone. It was her business to sit with him in the garden parlour when mother was out, so as to be able to open the street-door readily, as well as go into the garden if the weather was fine. It was a fine day of autumn, she went into the parlour and was sitting on the huge old sofa, Tom playing on the floor, when I sat myself down by her side; we kissed and toyed, and then with heart beating, I began my talk and waited my opportunity.

The cook would be back in a few minutes, said she. I knew better, having heard mother tell cook she need not be home until eight o'clock. Although I knew this, I was fearful, but at length mustered courage to sing my cock and cunt song. She was angry, but it was made up. She went to give something to Tom, and stepping back put her foot on the lace of one boot which was loose, sat down on the sofa and put up one leg over the other, to relace it. I undertook to do it for her, saw her neat ankle, and a bit of a white stocking. "Snatch at her cunt," rang in my ears, I had never attempted it since the afternoon in the kitchen.

Lacing the boot, I managed to push the clothes up so as to see more of the leg, but resting as the foot did on one knee, the clothes tightly between, a snatch was useless: lust made me cunning, I praised the foot (though I knew not at that time how vain some women are of their feet). "What a nice ankle," I said, putting my hand further on. She was off her guard; with my left arm, I pushed her violently back on to the large sofa, her foot came off her knee, at the same moment, my right hand went up between her thighs, on to her cunt; I felt the slit, the hair, and moisture.

She got up to a sitting posture, crying, "You wretch, you beast, you blackguard," but still I kept my fingers on the cunt; she closed her legs, so as to shut my hand between her thighs and keep it motionless, and tried to push me off; but I clung round her. "Take your hand away," said she, "or I will scream." "I shan't!" Then followed two or three loud, very loud screams. "No one can hear," said I, which brought her to supplication. My friend's advice came again to me: pushing my right hand still between her thighs, with my left I pulled out my prick, as stiff as a poker. She could not do otherwise than see it; and then I drew my left hand round her neck, pulled her head to me, and covered it with kisses.

She tried to get up and nearly dislodged my right hand, but I pushed her back, and got my hand still further on to the cunt. I never thought of pressing under towards the bum, was in fact too ignorant of female anatomy to do it, but managed to get one of the lips with the hair between my fingers and pinch it; then dropped on to my knees in front of her and remained kneeling, preventing her getting back further on the sofa, as well as I could by holding her waist, or her clothes.

There was a pause from our struggles, then more entreaties, then more attempts to get my right hand away; suddenly she put out one hand, seized me by the hair of my head, and pushed me backwards by it. I thought my skull was coming off, but kept my hold and pinched or pulled the cunt lip till she hollowed and called me a brute. I told her I would hurt her as much as I could, if she hurt me; so that game she gave up; the pain of pulling my hair made me savage, and more determined and brutal, than before.

We went on struggling at intervals, I kneeling with prick out, she crying, begging me to desist; I entreating her to let me see and feel her cunt, using all the persuasion and all the baudy talk I could, little Tom sitting on the floor playing contentedly. I must have been half an hour on my knees, which became so painful that I could scarcely bear it; we were both panting, I was sweating; an experienced man would perhaps have had her then; I was a boy inexperienced, and without her consent almost in words would not have thought of attempting it; the novelty, the voluptuousness of my game was perhaps sufficient delight to me; at last I became conscious that my fingers on her cunt were getting wet; telling her so, she became furious and burst into such a flood of tears that it alarmed me. It was impossible to remain on my knees longer; in rising, I knew I should be obliged to take my hand from her cunt, so withdrawing my left hand from her waist, I put it also suddenly up her clothes, and round her bum, and lifted them up, showing both her thighs, whilst I attempted to rise. She got up at the same instant, pushing down her clothes, I fell over on one side, — my knees were so stiff and painful — and she rushed out of the room upstairs.

It was getting dusk, I sat on the sofa in a state of pleasure, smelling my fingers. Tom began to howl, she came down and took him up to pacify him, I followed her down to the kitchen, she called me an insolent boy (an awful taunt to me then), threatened to tell my mother, to give notice and leave, and left the kitchen, followed by me about the house; talking baudily, telling her how I liked the smell of my fingers, attempting to put my hand up her clothes, sometimes succeeding, pulling out my ballocks, and never ceasing until the cook came home, having been at this game for hours. In a sudden funk, I begged Charlotte to tell my mother that I had only come home just before the cook, and had gone to bed unwell; she replying she would tell my mother the truth, and nothing else. I was in my bed-room before cook was let in.

Mother came home later, I was in a fright, having laid in bed cooling down and thinking of possible consequences; heard the street-door knocker, got out of bed, and in my night-shirt went half way downstairs listening. To my relief, I heard Charlotte, in answer to my mother's enquiry, say I had come home about an hour before and had gone to bed unwell. My mother came to my room, saying how sorry she was.

For a few days I was in fear, but it gradually wore off, as I found she had not told; our kissing recommenced, my boldness increased, my talk ran now freely on her legs, her bum, and her cunt, she ceased to notice it, beyond saying she hated such talk, and at length she smiled spite of herself. Our kissing grew more fervid, she resisted improper action of my hand, but we used to stand with our lips close together for minutes at a time when we got the chance, I holding her to me as close as wax. One day cook was upstairs, mother in her bed-room, I pushed Charlotte up against the wall in the kitchen, and pulled up her clothes, scarcely with resistance; just then my mother rang, I skipped up into the garden and got into the parlour that way, soon heard my mother calling to me to fetch water, Charlotte was in hysterics at the foot of the stairs — after that, she frequently had hysterics, till a certain event occurred.

My chances were chiefly on Saturdays, a day I did not go to college; soon I was to cease going there and was to prepare for the army.

I came home one day, when I knew Charlotte would be alone — the cook was upstairs — I got her on to the sofa in the garden parlour, knelt and put my hands between her thighs, with less resistance than before, she struggled slightly but made no noise. She kissed me as she asked me to take away my hand; I could move it more easily on her quim, which I did not fail to do; she was wonderfully quiet. Suddenly I became conscious that she was looking me full in the face, with a peculiar expression, her eyes very wide open, then shutting them "Oho — oho," she said with a prolonged sigh, "do — oh, take away — oh — your hand, Walter dear, — oh I shall be ill, — oho, — oho," then her head dropped down over my shoulder as I knelt in front of her; at the same moment, her thighs seemed to open slightly, then shut, then open with a quivering, shuddering motion, as it then seemed to me, and then she was quite quiet.

I pushed my hand further in, or rather on, for although I thought I had it up the cunt, I really was only between the lips — I know that now. With a sudden start she rose up, pushed me off, snatched up Tom from the floor, and rushed upstairs. My fingers were quite wet. For two or three days afterwards, she avoided my eyes and looked bashful, I could not make it out, and it was only months afterwards, that I knew, that the movement of my fingers on her clitoris had made her spend. Without knowing indeed then that such a thing was possible, I had frigged her.

Although for about three months I had been thus deliciously amusing myself, anxious to feel and see her cunt, and though I had at last asked her to let me fuck her, I really don't think I had any definite expectation of doing it to her. I guessed now at its mutual pleasures, and so forth, yet my doing it to her appeared beyond me; but urged on by my love for the girl — for I did love her — as well as by sexual instinct, I determined to try. I also was quickened by my college friend, who had seen Charlotte at our house and not knowing it was the girl I had spoken to him about, said to me, "What a nice girl that maid of yours is, I mean to get over her, I shall wait for her after church next Sunday, she sits in your pew, I know." I asked him some questions, — his opinion was that most

girls would let a young fellow fuck them, if pressed, and that she would (this youth was but about eighteen years old), and I left him fearing what he said was true, hating and jealous of him to excess. He set me thinking, why should not I do it if he could, and if what he said about girls was true? — so I determined to try it on, and by luck did so earlier than I expected.

About one hour's walk from us was the town house of an aunt, the richest of our family and one of my mother's sisters. She alone now supplied me with what money I had, my mother gave me next to nothing. I went to see aunt, who asked me to tell my mother to go and spend a day with her, the next week, and named the day. I forgot this until three days afterwards, when hearing my mother tell the cook, she could go out for a whole holiday; I said, that my aunt particularly wished to see mother on that day. My mother scolded me for not having told her sooner, but wrote and arranged to go, forgetting the cook's holiday. To my intense joy, on that day she took brother Tom with her, saying to Charlotte, "You will have nothing to think of, but the house, shut it up early, and do not be frightened." I was as usual to fetch my mother home.

In what an agitated state I passed that morning at school, and in the afternoon went home, trembling at my own intentions. Charlotte's eyes opened with astonishment at seeing me. Was I not going to fetch my mother? I was not going till night. There was no food in the house, and I had better go to my aunt's for dinner. I knew there was cold meat, and made her lay the cloth in the kitchen. To make sure, I asked if the cook was out, — yes, she was, but would be home soon. I knew that she stopped out till ten o'clock on her holidays. The girl was agitated with some undefined idea of what might take place, we kissed and hugged, but she did not like even that, I saw.

I restrained myself whilst eating, she sat quietly besides me; when I had finished she began to remove the things, the food gave me courage, her moving about stimulated me, I began to feel her breasts, then got my hands on to her thighs, we had the usual struggles, but it seems to me as I now think of it that her resistance was less and that she prayed me to desist more lovingly than was usual. We had toyed for an hour, she had let a dish fall and smashed it, the baker rang, she took in the bread, and declared she would not shut the door unless I promised to leave off. I promised, and so soon as she had closed it, pulled her into the garden parlour, having been thinking when in the kitchen how I could get her upstairs. Down tumbled the bread on the floor, on to the sofa, I pushed her, and after a struggle she was sitting down, I kissing her, one arm round her waist, one hand between her thighs, close up to her cunt. Then I told her I wanted to fuck her, said all in favour of it I knew, half ashamed, half frightened, as I said it. She said she did not know what I meant, resisted less and less as I tried to pull her back on the sofa, when another ring came: it was the milkman.

I was obliged to let her go, and she ran down stairs with the milk. I followed, she went out, and slammed the door, which led to the garden, in my face; for the instant, I thought she was going to the privy, but opened and followed on; she ran up the steps, into the garden, through the garden parlour, and upstairs to her bed-room just opposite to mine, closed and locked the door in my face, I begged her to let me in.

She said she would not come out till she heard the knocker or bell ring; there was no one called usually after the milkman, so my game was up, but nothing makes man or woman so crafty as lust. In half an hour or so, in anger, I said I should go to my aunt's, went downstairs, moved noisily about, opened and slammed the street-door violently, as if I had gone out, then pulled off my boots, and crept quietly up to my bed-room.

There I sat expectantly a long time, had almost given up hope, began to think about consequences if she told my mother, when I heard the door softly open and she came to the edge of the stairs. "Wattie!" she said loudly, "Wattie!" much louder, "he has," said she in a subdued tone to herself, as much as to say that worry is over. I opened my door, she gave a loud shriek and retreated to her room, I close to her; in a few minutes more, hugging, kissing, begging, threatening, I know not how; she was partly on the bed, her clothes up in a heap, I on her with my prick in my hand, I saw the hair, I felt the slit, and not knowing then where the hole was or much about it, excepting that it was between her legs, shoved my prick there with all my might. "Oh! you hurt, I shall be ill," said she, "pray don't." Had she said she was dying I should not have stopped. The next instant a delirium of my senses came, my prick throbbing and as if hot lead was jetting from it, at each throb; pleasure mingled with light pain in it, and my whole frame quiver-

ing with emotion; my sperm left me for a virgin cunt, but fell outside it, though on to it.

How long I was quiet I don't know; probably but a short time; for a first pleasure does not tranquillise at that age; I became conscious that she was pushing me off of her, and rose up, she with me, to a half-sitting posture; she began to laugh, then to cry, and fell back in hysterics, as I had seen her before.

I had seen my mother attend to her in those fits, but little did I then know that sexual excitement causes them in women and that probably in her I had been the cause. I got brandy and water and made her drink a lot, helping myself at the same time, for I was frightened, and made her lay on the bed. Then, ill as she was, frightened as I was, I yet took the opportunity her partial insensibility gave me, lifted her clothes quietly, and saw her cunt and my spunk on it. Roused by that, she pushed her clothes half down feebly and got to the side of the bed. I loving, begging pardon, kissing her, told her of my pleasure, and asked about hers, all in snatches, for I thought I had done her. Not a word could I get, but she looked me in the face beseechingly, begging me to go. I had no such intention, my prick was again stiffening, I pulled it out, the sight of her cunt had stimulated me, she looked with languid eyes at me, her cap was off, her hair hanging about her head, her dress torn near her breast. More so than she had ever looked was she beautiful to me, success made me bold, on I went insisting, she seemed too weak to withstand me. "Don't, oh pray, don't," was all she said as, pushing her well on the bed, I threw myself on her and again put my doodle on to the slit now wet with my sperm. I was, though cooler, stiff as a poker, but my sperm was not so ready to flow, as it was in after days, at a second poke, for I was very young; but nature did all for me; my prick went to the proper channel, there stopped by something it battered furiously. "Oh, you hurt, oh!" she cried aloud. The next instant something seemed to tighten round its knob, another furious thrust, — another, — a sharp cry of pain (resistance was gone), and my prick was buried up her, I felt that it was done, and that before I had spent outside her. I looked at her, she was quiet, her cunt seemed to close on my prick, I put my hand down, and felt round. What rapture to find my machine buried! nothing but the balls to be touched, and her cunt hair wetted with my sperm, mingling and clinging to mine; in another minute nature urged a crisis, and I spent in a virgin cunt, my prick virgin also. Thus ended my first fuck.

My prick was still up her, when we heard a loud knock; both started up in terror, I was speechless. "My God, it is your mamma!" Another loud knock. What a relief, it was the postman. To rush downstairs, and open the door was the work of a minute. "I thought you were all out," said he angrily, "I have knocked three times." "We were in the garden," said I. He looked queerly at me and said, "With your boots off!" and grinning went away. I went up again, found her sitting on the side of the bed, and there we sat together. I told her what the postman had said, she was sure he would tell her mistress. For a short time, there never was a couple who had just fucked, in more of a foolish funk then we were; I have often thought of our not hearing the thundering knocks of a postman, whilst we were fucking, though the bed-room door was wide open; what engrossing work it is so to deafen people. Then after unsuccessfully struggling to see her cunt, and kissing, and feeling each other's genitals, and talking of our doings and our sensations for an hour, we fucked again.

It was getting dark, which brought us to reason; we both helped remake the bed, went downstairs, shut the shutters, lighted the fire which was out, and got lights. I then, having nothing to do, began thinking of my doodle, which was sticking to my shirt, and pulling it out to see its condition, found my shirt covered with sperm smears, and spots of blood; my prick was dreadfully sore. I said to her that she had been bleeding, she begged me to go out of the kitchen for a minute, I did, and almost directly she came out and passed me, saying she must change her things before the cook came home. She would not let me stay in the room whilst she did it, nor did I see her chemise, though I had followed her upstairs; then the idea flashed across me that. I had taken a virginity; that had never occurred to me before. She got hot water to wash herself. I did not know what to do with my shirt; we arranged I should wash it before I went to bed. We thought it best to say I had not been home at all, and that I should go and fetch my mother. After much kissing, hugging, and tears on her part, off I went, hatching an excuse for not having fetched mother earlier, and we came home with Tom in my aunt's carriage, I recollect.

Before going to bed, I ordered hot water for a footbath. How we looked at each other as I ordered it. I washed my shirt as well as I could, and looked sadly at my sore prick, I could not pull the skin back so much as usual, it was torn, raw, and slightly bleeding.

Awake nearly all night, thinking of my pleasure and proud of my success, I rose early and, looking at my shirt, found stains still visible, and that I had so mucked it in washing that an infant could have guessed what I had been doing. I knew that my mother, who now did household duties herself, selected the things for the laundress; and in despair hit on a plan: I filled the chamber-pot with piss and soap-suds, making it as dirty as I could, put it near a chair and my shirt hanging over it carelessly, so as to look as if it had dropped into the pot by accident; left it there, and put on a clean shirt. After breakfast my mother, who usually helped to make my bed and her own as well, called out to me; up I went with my heart in my mouth, to hear her say she hoped I would be a little more careful and remember that we had no longer my poor father's purse. "Look," said she, "a disgraceful state you left your shirt in, I am ashamed to have it sent to the laundress, have been obliged to tell the housemaid to partly wash it first, you are getting very careless." Charlotte afterwards told me that, when mother gave her the shirt to rough wash, she felt as if she should faint.

I need not repeat about my prepuce, which as said I could now pull down with a little less difficulty. Lacerated and painful over night, it was much more swollen and sore the next morning, when I pissed it smarted, the thinking and smarting made me randy: risking all, whilst my mother was actually in the adjoining room, the poor girl in horrid fear and looking shockingly ill, I thrust my hand up her clothes and on to her split. She whispered, "What a wretch you are!" I went to college, came back at three o'clock, thinking always on the same subject; my prick got worse, I took it into my head, that Charlotte had given me some disease, and was in a dreadful state of mind. I washed it with warm water and greased it, having eased it thus a little, got the skin down, then could not get it back again; it got stiff; as it did so, sexual pleasures came into my mind, and worse got the pain. I greased it more, my pain grew less, I touched the tip with my greasy finger, it gave a throb of pleasure, I went on without meaning, almost without knowing, the pleasure came, and spunk shot out. I had frigged myself unintentionally again.

I watched my penis shrink, its tension lessen, its high colour go, then came the feeling of disgust at myself that I have always felt after frigging, a disgust not quite absent even when done by the little hands of fair friends, to whose quims I was paying similar delicate attentions. I was able to pull up the skin again, but the soreness got worse, I told the poor girl that my prick was very sore, and that I thought it strange. It did not wound her feelings, for she did not know my suspicions. The next morning being no better, I with much hesitation told a college friend, he looked at my prick, and thought it either clap or pox. Frightened to go to our own doctor, I at his advice went to a chemist, who did a little business in such matters; we dealt there, but my friend assured me that the man never opened his mouth to any one, if youths consulted him, and many he knew had.

With quaking I said to the chemist, that I had something the matter with my thing. "What?" said he. "I don't know." "Let me see it." I began to beg him not to mention it to my mother, or any-one. "Don't waste my time," said he, "show it to me, if you want my advice." Out I pulled it as small as could be, but still with the skin over it. "Have you been with a woman?" said he. "Yes." He looked at my shirt, there was no discharge, then he laid hold of my prick with both hands, and with force pulled the skin right down, I howled. He told me there was nothing the matter with me, that the skin was too tight, that a snip would set me to rights, and ad-vised me soon to have it done, saying, "It will save you trouble and money if you do, and add to your pleasure." I declined. "Another day, then." "No." He laughed and said, "Well, time will cure you, if you go on as you have begun," gave me a lotion, and in three days I was pretty right: warm water I expect would have had the same effect. I had simply torn the skin in taking the virginity.

Of course I wanted Charlotte again, she seemed in no way to help me, and used to cry, still there was a wonderful difference be-tween then and before the happy consummation: she tried to pre-vent my hands going up her petticoats, but, once up, objection ceased, and my hands would rove about on the outside and inside of all, we stood and kissed at every opportunity. "When shall we do it again?" She replied, "Never!" for she was sure it would bring punishment on us both.

I neglected my studies absolutely; all I thought about was her, and how to get at her, it must have been a week or more before I did. Ready for any risk, that day my mother was out, I came home, had the early dinner; the cook after that always went up to dress, or, as she said, clean herself, and there she always was an hour. Waiting till I heard her go up, I went into the garden parlour, where as usual Charlotte was with my little brother. Going at her directly, I was refused, but now how different, once she would not rest until my hand was altogether away from her. Now I begged and besought her, with my hand up her clothes, my fingers on her quim. No — if we had not been found out, we were fortunate, but never, never, would she do it again; was I mad, did I wish to ruin her, was not the cook upstairs, might she not come down, whilst we did it? How light the room was, the sun was coming in. I dropped the blinds, her resistance grew less, as her cunt felt my twiddling. "No — now no — oh, what a plague you are; hush! it is the cook." I open the door, listen, there is no one stirring. "What will she think if she finds you here?" "What does it matter? Now do — let me, — I'll bolt the door, if she comes I will get under the sofa, you say you don't know how it got bolted." Such was my innocent device, but it sufficed, for both were hot in lust. I bolted it. My prick is out, I pull her reluctant hand on to it, my hands are groping now, but too impatient for dallying, I push her down on the sofa — that dear cunt. "Don't hurt me so much again, oh, don't push so hard." Oh! what delight! in a minute we are spending, together this time.

I unlock the door, go back to the dining-room, she strolls out into the garden, cook speaks to her out of the window. "Where is master Wattie?" "In the dining-room, I suppose." Soon out I stroll into the garden, play with Tommy of course, she can scarcely look me in the face, she is blushing like a rose. "Was it not lovely, Charlotte, is not your thing wet?" In she rushes with Tom, soon I follow, cook is still upstairs. "Come, be quick." Again the bolt, again we fuck, she walks off into the garden with Tommy, her cunt full, and cook and she chat from the window. How we laughed about it afterwards.

Modesty retired after this, we gave way to our inclinations, she refusing but always letting me if we got a chance! We were still green and timid, at the end of three weeks we only had done it a dozen times or so, always with the cook in the house, always with fear. I was longing for complete enjoyment of all my senses, had

never yet seen her cunt, except for a minute at a time, was mad
for "the naked limb entwined with limb," and all I had read of in
amatory poetry. I had gained years in boldness and manhood, and,
although nervous, began to practice what I had heard.

I heard of accommodation houses, where people could have
bed-rooms and no questions were asked; and found one not far
from my aunt's, although she lived in the best quarter of London.
Just before Charlotte's day out, I went to my aunt, complained of
my mother's meanness, and she gave me a sovereign. On my way
home, I loitered a full hour in the street with the baudy house,
marked it so as to know it in the day, and saw couples go in, as
my knowing friend who had told said I should. The next day, in-
stead of going to college and risking discovery, I waited till Char-
lotte joined me, took a hackney coach to the street, and, telling
Charlotte it was a tavern, walked to the door with her; to my aston-
ishment it was closed. Disconcerted, I nearly turned back, but rang
the bell. Charlotte said she would not go in. The door opened, a
woman said, "Why did you not push the door?" Oh! the shame I
felt as I went into that baudy house with Charlotte; the woman
seemed to hesitate, or so I fancied, before she gave us a room.

It was a gentleman's house, although the room cost but five
shillings: red curtains, looking-glasses, wax lights, clean linen, a
huge chair, a large bed, and a cheval-glass, large enough for the
biggest couple to be reflected in, were all there. I examined all with
the greatest curiosity, but my curiosity was greater for other things;
of all the delicious, voluptuous recollections, that day stands among
the brightest; for the first time in my life I saw all a woman's
charms, and exposed my own manhood to one; both of us knew but
little of the opposite sex. With difficulty I got her to undress to her
chemise, then with but my shirt on, how I revelled in her naked-
ness, feeling from her neck to her ankles, lingering with my fingers
in every crack and cranny of her body; from armpits to cunt, all
was new to me. With what fierce eyes, after modest struggles, and
objections to prevent, and I had forced open her reluctant thighs,
did I gloat on her cunt; wondering at its hairy outer covering and
lips, its red inner flaps, at the hole so closed up, and so much lower
down and hidden than I thought it to be; soon, at its look and feel,
impatience got the better of me; hurriedly I covered it with my
body and shed my sperm in it. Then with what curiosity I paddled

my fingers in it afterwards, again to stiffen, thrust, wriggle, and spend. All this I recollect as if it occurred but yesterday, I shall recollect it to the last day of my life, for it was a honey-moon of novelty; years afterwards I often thought of it when fucking other women.

We fell asleep, and must have been in the room some hours, when we awakened about three o'clock. We had eaten nothing that day, and both were hungry, she objected to wash before me, or to piddle; how charming it was to overcome that needless modesty, what a treat to me to see that simple operation. We dressed and left, went to a quietish public-house, and had some simple food and beer, which set me up, I was ready to do all over again, and so was she. We went back to the house and again to bed; the woman smiled when she saw us; the feeling, looking, titillating, baudy inciting, and kissing recommenced. With what pleasure she felt and handled my prick, nor did she make objection to my investigations into her privates, though saying she would not let me. Her thighs opened, showing the red-lipped, hairy slit; I kissed it, she kissed my cock, nature taught us both what to do. Again we fucked, I found it a longish operation, and when I tried later again, was surprised to find that it would not stiffen for more than a minute, and an insertion failed. I found out that day that there were limits to my powers. Both tired out, our day's pleasure over, we rose and took a hackney coach towards home. I went in first, she a quarter of an hour afterwards, and everything passed off as I could have wished.

From that day, lust seized us both; we laid our plans to have each other frequently, but it was difficult: my mother was mostly at home, the cook nearly always at home if mother was out; but quite twice a week we managed to copulate, and sometimes oftener. We arranged signals. If, when she opened the door, she gave a shake of the head, I knew mother was in; if she smiled and pointed down with her finger, mother was out, but cook downstairs; if it pointed up, cook was upstairs; in the latter case, to go into the garden parlour and fuck was done off hand. If cook was known to be going out, Charlotte told me beforehand, and if mother was to be out, I got home, letting college and tutors go to the devil. Then there was lip kissing, cunt kissing, feeling and looking, tickling and rubbing each other's articles, all the preliminary delights of copulation, and but one danger in the way: my little brother could talk in-a broken way; we used to give him some favorite toy and put him on the floor, whilst we indulged voluptuously. On the sofa one day, I had just spent in her when I felt a little hand tickling between our bellies, and Tommy, who had tottered up to us, said, "Don't hurt Lotty, der's a good Wattie." We settled that Tom was too young to notice or recollect what he saw, but I now think differently.

Winter was coming on, she used to be sent to a circulating library to fetch books, the shop was some distance off; a few houses, long garden-walls, and hedges were on the road. I used to keep out, or go out just before she went, and we fucked up against the walls. I took to going to church in the evening also, to the intense delight of my mother, but it was to fuck on the road home. One day, hot in lust, we fucked standing on the lobby near my bed-room, my mother being in the room below, the cook in the kitchen. We got bold, reckless, and whenever we met alone, if only for an instant, we felt each other's genitals.

At last we found the servant's privy one of the best places. I have described its situation near to a flight of steps, at the end of a covered passage which could be seen from one point only in the garden; down there, anyone standing was out of sight. If all was clear, I used to ring the parlour bell, ask for something, and make a sign; when she thought it safe, there she would go, I into the garden, to where I could see into the passage by the side of the garden stairs. If I saw her, or heard "ahem," down I went into the privy and was up her cunt in a second, standing against the wall and shoving to get our spend over, as if my life depended on it; this was uncomfortable, but it had its charm. We left off doing it in the privy, being nearly caught one day there.

We thought cook was upstairs, mother was out, I was fucking her, when the cook knocked saying, "Make haste, Charlotte, I want to come." We had just spent, she was so frightened I thought she was fainting, but she managed to say "I cannot." "Do," said cook, "I am ill." "So am I," said Charlotte. Said cook, "I can sit on the little seat." "Go to misses' closet, she's out." Off cook went, out we came, and never fucked in that place again; one day I did her on the kitchen table, and several times on the dining-room table.

We in fact did it everywhere else, and often enough for my health, for I was young, weak, and growing, and it was the same with her. The risks we ran were awful, but we loved each other with all our souls. Both young, both new at the work, both liking it, it was rarely we got more than just time to get our fucking over and clothes arranged before we had to separate, for her to get to her duties. Many times I have seen her about the house, cunt full and with the heightened colour and brilliant eyes of a woman who had just been satisfied. I used to feel pleasure in knowing she was bringing in the dinner, or tea, with my spunk in her cunt; not having had the opportunity to wash or piddle it out.

When she had another holiday, we went to the baudy house, and stayed so long in it that we had a scare; just asleep, we heard a knocking at the door. My first idea was that my mother had found me out, and, although I ruled her in one way, I was in great subjection to her, from not having any money. She thought her father was after her. What a relief it was to hear a voice say: "Shall you be long, sir, we want the room?" I was having too much accommodation for my money. That night we walked home, for I had no money for a coach, and barely enough to get us a glass of beer and a biscuit; we were famished and fucked out; my mother had refused to give me money, and another aunt whom I had asked said I was asking too often, and refused also.

Although we went to this baudy house, I always felt as if I was going to be hanged when I did, and it was with difficulty I could make her go: she called it a bad house, and it cost money. Something then occurred which helped me, penniless as I was.

At the extreme end of our village were a few little houses; one stood with its side entrance up a road only partially formed, and without thoroughfare; its owner was a pew-opener, her daughter a dressmaker, who worked for servants and such like; they cut out things for servants, who in those days largely made their own dresses. Charlotte had things made there. At a fair held every year near us, of which I shall have to tell more, my fast friend, who had put me up to so much and who, I forgot to say, tried to get hold of Charlotte, I saw with the dressmaker's daughter. Said he, talking to me next day, "She is jolly ugly, but she's good enough for a feel. I felt her cunt last night and think she has been fucked (he thought that of every girl); her mother's a rum old gal too, she will let you meet a girl at her cottage, not whores, you know, but if they are respectable." "Is it a baudy house?" I asked. "Oh, no, it's quite

respectable, but if you walk in with a lady, she leaves you in the
room together, and, when you come out, if you just give her half a
crown, she drops a curtsy, just as she does when she opens the pew-
doors and anyone gives her six pence, but she is quite respectable —
the clergyman goes to see her sometimes."

Charlotte asked to go out to a dressmaker, I met her as if by
chance at the door, the old pew-opener asked if I would like to
walk in and wait. I did. Charlotte came in after she had arranged
about her dress. There was a sofa in the room, and she was soon on
it; we left together, I gave two or three shillings (money went
much further then), and the pew-opener said, "You can always
wait here when your young lady comes to see my daughter."

When we went a second time, she asked me if I went to St.
Mary's Chapel (her chapel). We went to her house in the day that
time. When we were going away, she said, "Perhaps you won't
mind always going out first, for neighbours are so ill-natured." The
old woman was really a pew-opener, her daughter really a dress-
maker, but she was glad to earn a few shillings by letting her house
be used for assignations of a quiet sort; she would not have let gay
women in, from what I heard. She had lived for years in the parish
and was thought respectable. She had not much use of her house in
that way, wealthy people going to town for their frolics, — town
only being an hour's journey — and no gay women being in the
village that I knew of.

At this house, I spent Charlotte's third holiday with her, in a
comfortable bed-room. We stopped from eleven in the morning, till
nine at night, having mutton chops and ale, and being as jolly as
we could be. We did nothing the whole day long but look at each
other's privates, kiss, fuck, and sleep outside the bed. It was there
she expressed curiosity about male emissions. I told her how the
sperm spurted out, then discussing women's, she told me of the
pleasure I had given her when fingering her in the manner de-
scribed already; we completed our explanations by my frigging my-
self to show her, and then my doing the same to her with my finger.
I bungled at that, and think I hear her now saying, "No, just where
you were is nicest." "Does it give you pleasure?" "Oh, yes, but I
don't like it that way, oh! — oh! — I am doing it — oh!" I had no
money that day, Charlotte had her wages, and paid for everything,
giving me her money to do so.

One day we laughed at having nearly been caught fucking in the privy. "She must have a big bum, must Mary," said I, "to sit on that little seat at the privy." Said Charlotte, "She is a big woman, twice as big as me, her bottom would cover the whole seat." This set us talking about the cook, and as what I then heard affected me much at a future day, I will tell all Charlotte said, as nearly as I can recollect.

"Of course I have seen her naked bit by bit — when two women are together they can't help it, why should they mind — if you sit down to pee, you show your legs, and if you put on your stockings you show your thighs, then we both wash down to our waists, and if you slip off your chemise or night-gown you show yourself all over. Mary's beautiful from head to foot; one morning in the summer, we sleeping in the same bed, were very hot. I got out to pee, we had kicked all the clothes off, Mary was laying on her back with night-clothes above her waist fast asleep, I could not help looking at her thighs, which were so large and white — white as snow." "Had she much hair on her cunt?" said I. "What's that to you?" said she, laughing, but went on: "Oh! twice as much as I have, and of a light brown." "I suppose her cunt is bigger than yours?" said I reflectively. "Well, perhaps it is," said Charlotte, "she is a much bigger woman than me, what do you think?" I inclined to the opinion it must be, but had no experience to guide me; on the whole we agreed that it was likely to be bigger.

"Then," said she, "I suppose some men have smaller things than yours?" I told her that as far as I knew they varied slightly, but only had knowledge of youthful pricks, and could not be certain whether they varied much when full grown or not. We went on about Mary. "I know I should like to be such a big, fine woman." "But," said I, "I don't like light hair, I like dark hair on a cunt, light hair can't look well, I should think." "I like her," said Charlotte, "she is a nice woman, but often dull, she has no relatives in London, never says anything about them or herself, she used to have letters, and then often cried; she has none now; the other night she took me in her arms, gave me a squeeze and said, 'Oh! if you were a nice young man now,' then laughed and said, 'perhaps we would put our things together and make babies.' I was frightened to say anything, for fear she should find out I knew too much; I think she has been crossed in love."

I was twiddling Charlotte's quim, as I was never tired of doing, something in the sensation I suppose reminded her, for, laughing, she went on: "You know what you did to me the other night?" "What?" said I, not recollecting. "You know, with your finger." "Oh! frig." "Yes, well, Mary does that; I was awake one night, and was quite quiet, when I heard Mary breathing hard, and felt her elbow go jog, jog, just touching my side, then she gave a sigh, and all was quiet. I went to sleep, and have only just thought of it." She had heard or felt this jog from the cook before, so we both concluded that she frigged herself; Charlotte knew what frigging was.

"Do you recollect your mamma's birthday?" said Charlotte. "She sent us down a bottle of sherry, the gardener was to have some, but did not; so we were both a little fuddled when we went to bed. When Mary was undressed she pulled up her clothes to her hips, and looking at herself said, 'My legs are twice as big as yours.' Then we made a bet on it and measured; she lost, but her thigh was half as big again round as mine; then she threw herself on her back and cocked up her legs, opening them for a minute. I said 'Lord, Mary, what ever are you doing?' 'Ah!' said she, 'women's legs were made to open,' and there it ended. I never heard her before say or do anything improper, she is most particular." If Charlotte had been older or wiser, she would not have extolled the naked beauties of a fellow servant to her lover, for the description of the big bum, white thighs, and hairy belly bottom, the jog, jog of the elbow, and all the other particulars, sank deep into my mind.

We fucked more than ever, recklessly — it is a wonder we were not found out, for one evening, it being dark, I fucked her in the forecourt, outside our street-door; but troubles were coming.

Her father wrote to know why she had not been home at her holidays, she got an extra holiday to go and pacify him; then we had a fright because her courses stopped, but they came on all right again. One of my sisters came home and diminished our opportunities; still we managed to fuck somehow, most of the time they were uprighters. The next holiday she went home by coach (the only way), I met her on the return, and we fucked up against the garden wall of our house. A month slipped away, again we spent her holiday at the pew-opener's; no man and woman could have liked each other more, or more enjoyed each other's bodies, without thinking of the rest of the world. I disguised nothing from her, she told me all she knew of herself, the liking she took for me, her pleasure yet fear and shame when first I felt her cunt, the shock of delight and confusion when, on my twiddling it, she had spent; how she made up her mind to run out of the house when the milkman came, the hysterical faint when I first laid my prick between her slit and spent, the sensation of relief when I had not done, as instinct told her I should, in spending outside, the sort of feeling of "poor fellow, he wants me, he may do as he likes," which she had; I told my sensations. All these we told each other, over and over again, and never tired of the conversation; we were an innocent, reckless, randy couple.

We had satisfied our lusts in simple variety, but I never put my tongue in her mouth, nor do I know that I had heard of that form of lovemaking — but more of that hereafter. I did her on her belly, and something incited me to do it to her dog fashion, but it was never repeated; we examined as said each other's appendages, but once satisfied, having seen mine get from flaccid to stiff, the piddle issue, the spunk squirt, she never wanted to see it again, and could not understand my insatiable curiosity about hers. She knew, I think, less than most girls of her age about the males, having never, I recollect, nursed male children, and I don't think she had brothers.

How is it that scarcely any woman will let you willingly look at her cunt after fucking, till it is washed? Most say it is beastly, gay or quiet; it is the same. Is it more beastly to have it spurted up, to turn and go to sleep with the spunk oozing on to a thigh, or an hour afterwards to let a man paddle in what has not dried? They don't mind that, but won't let you look at it after your operations, willingly — why?

A modest girl lays quietly after fucking, and does not wash till you are away. A young girl who has let you see her cunt and take her virginity, won't wash it at all until you point out the necessity. A gay woman often tries to shove back her bum just as you spend, gets the discharge near the outlet, uncunts you quickly, and at once washes and pisses at the same time. A quiet young girl wipes her cunt on the outside only. A working man's wife does the same. I have fucked several, and not one washed before me. I incline to the opinion that poor women rarely wash their cunts inside, their piddle does all the washing. "What's the good of washing it?" said a poor but not a gay girl to me, "it's always clean and feels just the same an hour afterwards, whether washed or not." Is the unwashed cunt less healthy than one often soaped and syringed? I doubt it. An old roué said to me he would not give a damn to fuck a cunt at night which has been washed since the morning.

About sexual matters each of us knew about as much as the other, and we had much to learn. A girl, however, in the sphere of life of Charlotte, usually knows more about a man's sex than a youth of the same age does of a woman's; they have nursed children and know what a cock is; a girl is never thought too young to nurse a male child, no one would trust a boy after ten years of age to nurse a female child; but she had never nursed. From Charlotte I had my first knowledge of menstruation and of other mysteries of her sex. Ah! that menstruation was a wonder to me, it was marvellous, but all was really a wonder to me then.

After Christmas, my sister went back to school, our chances seemed improving, we spent another holiday at the pew-opener's. I had got money, and we were indiscreet enough to go to see some wax-works. Next day her father came to see her; he ordered her to tell where she had been. She refused, he got angry, and made such a noise that mother rang to know what it was. He asked to see her, apologized, and said his daughter had been out several holidays without his knowing where she had been. My mother said it was very improper, and that he ought. A friend was with us in the room, and I sat there reading and trembling. My mother remarked to the lady, "I hope that girl is not going wrong, she is very good looking." Mother asked me to go out of the room, then had Charlotte up, and lectured her; afterwards Charlotte told me, for the first time, that her father was annoyed because she would not marry a young man.

A young man had called at our house several times to see her; she saw him once and evaded doing so afterwards. He was the son of a well-to-do baker a few miles from Charlotte's home, and wished to marry her; his father was not expected to live, and the young man said he would marry her directly the father died. Her mother was mad at her refusing such a chance. Charlotte showed me his letters, which then came, and we arranged together the replies.

She went home, and came back with eyes swollen with crying; some one had written anonymously to say she had been seen at the wax-works with a young man, evidently of position above her, and had been seen walking with a young man. The mother threatened to have a doctor examine her to see if she had been doing anything wrong; no one seemed to have suspected me; her father would have her home, her mother had had suspicion of her for some time, "The sooner you marry young Brown the better, he will have a good business and keeps a horse and chaise, you will never have such a chance again, and it will prevent you going wrong, even if you have not already gone wrong," said her mother.

It was a rainy night, I had met her on her return, and we both stood an hour under an umbrella, talking and crying, she saying, "I knew I should be ruined; if I marry he will find me out, if I don't they will lead me such a life; oh! what shall I do!" We fucked twice in the rain against a wall, putting down the umbrella to do it. Afterwards we met at the dressmaker's, talked over our misery, and cried, and fucked, and cried again. Then it was nothing but worry, she crying at her future, I wondering if I should be found out; still, with all our misery, we never failed to fuck if there was a clear five minutes before us. Then her mother wrote to say that old Brown was dead, and her father meant to take her away directly; she refused, the father came, saw my mother, and settled the affair by taking back Charlotte's box of clothes. I had not a farthing; at her age a father had absolute control, and nothing short of running away would have been of use. We talked of drowning ourselves, or of her taking work in the fields. I projected things equally absurd for myself. I tended in her agreeing to go home, — she could not help that, — but refusing to marry.

Charlotte wrote me almost directly after her return. My mother had reserved the right of opening my letters, although she had ceased to do so. That morning seeing she had one addressed to me, in fear I snatched it out of her hand. She insisted on having it back, I refused, and we had a row. "How dare you, sir, give it me." "I won't, you shan't open my letter." "I will, a boy like you!" "I am not a boy, I am a man, if you ever open a letter of mine, I will go for a common soldier, instead of being an officer." "I will tell your guardian." "I mean to tell him how shamefully short of money I am; Uncle °°° says it's a shame, so does aunt." My mother sank down in tears; it was my first rebellion; she spoke to my guardian, never touched my letters again, and gave me five times the money

I used to have; but, to make sure, I had letters enclosed to a friend, and fetched them.

Charlotte was not allowed to go out alone and was harassed in every way; for all that, I managed to meet her at a local school, one Saturday afternoon when it was empty; some friendly teacher let her in, and she let me in. We fucked on a hard form, in a nearly dark room, about the most difficult poke I ever had, it was a ridiculous posture. But our meeting was full of tears, despondency, and dread of being with child. She told me I had ruined her, even fucking did not cheer her. A week or so afterwards, having no money, I walked all the way to try to see her, and failed. Afterwards, in her letters, she begged me never to tell anyone about what had passed between us. Her father sent her away to his brother's, where she was to help as a servant; for somehow he had got wind that she had met some one at the school-house. There she fell ill and was sent home again. Then she wrote that she should marry, or have no peace, wished I was older, and then she could marry me; she did not write much common sense, although it did not strike me so then. She was coming to London to buy things, would say she would call on my mother on the road, but would meet me instead. How she humbugged the young woman who came to town with her, I don't know, but we met at the baudy house, cried nearly the whole time, but fucked for all that till my cock would stand no longer; then, vowing to see each other after she was married, we parted.

She married soon, my mother told me of it; she lived twelve miles from us, and did not write to me. I went there one day, but, although I lingered long near their shop, I never saw her. I did that a second time, she saw me looking in, and staggered into a back room. I dared not go in for fear of injuring her. Afterwards came a letter not signed, breathing love, but praying me not to injure her, as might be if I was seen near her house. Money, distance, time was all against me; I felt all was over, took to frigging, which, added to my vexation, made me ill. What the doctor thought I don't know; he said I was suffering from nervous exhaustion, asked my mother if I was steady and kept good hours. My mother said I was the quietest and best of sons, as innocent as a child, and that I was suffering from severe study — she had long thought I should; the fact being that for four months I had scarcely looked at a book, excepting when she was near me, and had, when not thinking of Charlotte, spent my time in writing baudy words and sketching cunts and pricks with pen and ink.

Thus I lost my virginity, and took one; thus ended my first love or lust; which will you call it? I call it love, for I was fond of the girl, and she of me. Some might call it a seduction, but thinking of it after this lapse of years, I do not. It was only the natural result of two people being thrown together, both young, full of hot blood, and eager to gratify their sexual curiosity; there was no blame to either, we were made to do it, and did but illustrate the truth of the old song, "Cock and cunt will come together, check them as you may," and point to the wisdom of never leaving a young male and female alone together, if they were not wanted to copulate.

In all respects we were as much like man and wife as circumstances would let us be. We poked and poked, whenever we got a chance; we divided our money, if I had none, she spent her wages; when I had it, I paid for her boots and clothes — a present in the usual sense of the term I never gave her; our sexual pleasures were of the simplest, the old fashioned way was what we followed, and altogether it was a natural, virtuous, wholesome, connexion, but the world will not agree with me on that point.

One thing strikes me as remarkable now: the audacity with which I went to a baudy house; all the rest seems to have begun and followed as naturally as possible. What a lovely recollection it is! nothing in my career since is so lovely as our life then was; scarce a trace of what may be called lasciviousness was in it; had the priest blest it by the bands of matrimony, it would have been called the chaste pleasure of love and affection — as the priest had nothing to do with it, it will be called, I suppose, beastly immorality. I have often wondered if her husband found out that she was not a virgin, and, if not, whether it was owing to some skill of hers, or to his ignorance? I heard afterwards that they lived happily.

At the Manor house. — Fred's amours. — Sarah and Mary. — What drink and money does. — My second virgin. — My first whore. — Double fucking. — Gamahuching. — Minette. — A Belly up and down.

One aunt as said lived in H°°°shire, a widow; her son, my cousin Fred, was preparing for the Army. I wanted a change and went by advice to stay there. Fred was a year older than me, wild and baudy to the day of his death, he talked from boyhood incessantly about women. I had not seen him for some time, and he told me of his amours, asking me about mine. I let him know all, without disclosing names; he told me in nearly the words that it was "a lie," for he had heard my mother say that I was the steadiest young fellow possible, and she could trust me anywhere. This, coupled with my quiet look and the care I took not to divulge names, made him disbelieve me; but I disclosed so many facts about women's nature that he was somewhat astonished. He told me what he had done, about having had the clap, and what to do if I got it; then he had seduced a cottager's daughter on the estate; but his description of the taking did not accord with my limited experience. One day he pointed the girl out to me at the cottage door, and said he now had her whenever he wanted.

She was a great coarse wench, whom he had seen in my aunt's fields. He had caught her piddling on one side of a hedge; she saw him looking at the operation from a ditch, and abused him roundly for it; it ended in an acquaintance, and his taking her virginity one evening on a hay-cock, — that was his account of it.

Her father was a labourer on my aunt's estate, the girl lived with him and a younger sister, her name was Sarah; he expatiated

140

on her charms from backside to bubbies, but it was soon evident to me that with this woman it was no money, no cunt; for he borrowed money of me to give her. I had squeezed money out of my aunt, my guardian, and mother, and had about ten pounds, — a very large sum for me then, — so I lent him a few shillings.

He had his shove, as he called it, and triumphantly gave me again such account of his operations and the charms of the lady that I, who had been some time without poking, wondered if the girl would let me; arguing to myself, he gives her money — my girl never wanted money, — why should his? He had been dinning into my ears that all women would let men for money, or presents, or else from lust. "Kiss and grope, and if they don't cry out, show them your prick and go at them." These maxims much impressed me.

"Fred," said my aunt at breakfast, "ride over to Brown about his rent, you will be sure to find him at the corn market," and she gave him other commissions at the market town. I promised to ride with him, but had been tortured with randiness about this great wench of his; so made some excuse and, as soon as he was well off, sauntered towards the cottage, which was about half a mile from the Hall.

It was one of a pair in a lane. Scarcely anyone passed them, excepting people on my aunt's lands. One was empty. The girl was sweeping in front of the cottage, the door was wide open. I gave her a nod, she dropped a respectful curtsey. Looking round and seeing no one, I said, "May I come in and rest, for it is hot and I am tired?" "Yes, sir," said she, and in I went, she giving me a chair; then she finished her sweeping. Meanwhile I had determined to try it on. "Father at home?" "No, sir, he be working in the seven-acre field." "Where is your sister?" "At mill, sir," — meaning a paper mill. I thought of Fred. It was my first offer, and I scarcely knew how to make it, but, chucking her under the chin, said, "I wish you would let me — " "What, sir?" "Do it to you," said I boldly, "and I will give you five shillings," producing the money; I knew it was what Fred gave her usually.

She looked at me and the five shillings, which was then more than her wages for a week's work in the fields, burst into laughter and said, "Why, who would ha' thought a gentleman from the Hall would say that to a poor girl like me." "Let me do it," said I hurried-

ly, "if you won't I must go — I will give you seven and six pence."
"You won't tell the young squire?" said she— meaning Fred. "Of
course not." She went to the door, looked both ways, then at the
clock, shut the door, and bolted it without another word.

The house consisted of a kitchen, a bed-room leading out of it,
and a wash-house. She opened the bed-room door, there were two
beds which almost filled the room; at the foot of one was a window,
by its side a wash-stand. She got on to the largest bed saying,
"Make haste." I pulled up her clothes to her navel and looked. "Oh!
make haste," said she. But I could not, it was the third cunt I had
seen, and I paused to contemplate her. Before me lay a pair of
thick, round thighs, a large belly, and a cunt covered with thick
brown hair, a dirty chemise round her waist, coarse woollen blue
stockings darned with black, and, tied below the knees with list,
thick hob-nailed boots. The bed beneath was white and clean, which
made her things look dirtier; it was different to what I had been
accustomed to. I looked too long, "Better make haste, for father will
be home to dinner," said she.

I put my hand to her cunt, she opened her thighs, and I saw
the cleft, with a pair of lips on each side like sausages, a dark ver-
million strong clitoris sloped down and hid itself between the lips,
in the recesses of the cock-trap; the strong light from the window
enabled me to see it as plainly as if under a microscope. I pushed
my finger up, then my cock knocked against my belly, asking to
take the place of my finger, and so up I let it go. No sooner was I
lodged in her, than arse, cunt, thighs and belly, all worked energeti-
cally, and in a minute I spent. Just as I pulled out, her cunt closed
round my prick with a strong muscular action, as if it did not wish
the warm pipe withdrawn, a movement of the muscles of the cunt
alone, and it drew the last drop of lingering sperm out of me.

I got on my knees, contemplating the sausage lips half open,
from which my sperm was oozing, and then got off sorry it had
been so quick a business. She laid without moving and looking kind-
ly at me said, "Ye may ha me agin an yer loike." "But your father
will be home?" "In half an hour," said she. "I don't think I can,"
said I. Such coolness in a woman was new to me, I scarcely knew
what to make of it. She got hold of my tool, I had not had a woman
for some time, soon felt lust entering my rod again, and sought her
cunt with my hands. She opened her legs wider in a most conde-

scending manner, and I began feeling it. I was soon fit, which she
very well knew, for immediately with a broad grin on her face she
pulled me on to her and put my prick in her cunt herself, lodging
it with a clever jerk of her bum, a squeeze, and a wriggle.

I fucked quietly, but it was now her turn; she heaved and
wriggled so that once she threw my prick out of her, but soon had
it in again. "Shove, shove," said she suddenly, and I shoved with
all my might, she clipped my arse so tightly that she must have left
the marks of her fingers on it, then, with a close wriggle and a deep
sigh, she lay still, her face as red as fire, and left me to finish by my
own exertions.

I felt the same squeeze of the cunt as I withdrew, one of those
delicious contractions which women of strong muscular power in
their privates can give; not all can do it. Those who cannot never
can understand it. Those who can will make a finger sensible of its
clip, if put up their cunts.

She got up and tucked her chemise between her legs to dry her
split, she did not wash it. "I am always alone," said she, "between
eight and twelve just now," and as any woman just then answered
my wants, I made opportunities, and I had her again two or three
times, till a rare bit of luck occurred to me.

We were in the bed-room one hot day; to make it cooler I took
off trowsers and drawers, laid them on a chair, carefully rolled my
shirt up round my waist, so as to prevent spunk falling upon it, and
thus naked from my boots to waist, laid myself on the top of my
rollicking, belly-heaving, rump-wriggling country lass.

I always gave her five shillings before I began; she had taken
a letch for me, or else, being hot cunted and not getting it done to
her often, dearly liked my poking her; and, seeming to want it that
day unusually, began her heaving and wriggling energetically. We
were well on towards our spend, when with a loud cry of "Oh! my
God!" she pushed me off and wriggled to the bed-side. I got off and
saw a sturdy country girl of about fifteen or sixteen years standing in
the bed-room door, looking at us with a broad grin, mixed with
astonishment, upon her face.

For an instant nobody spoke. Then the girl said with a mali-
cious grin, "Pretty goings on Sarah, if fearther knowed un——"
"How dare you stand looking at me?" said Sarah. "It's my room as
well as yourn," said Martha, for that was her name; and nothing

further was said then. But Martha's eyes fixed on me as I sat naked up to my waist with my prick wet, rigid, red, throbbing, and all but involuntarily jerking out its sperm. I was in that state of lust, that I could have fucked anything in the shape of a cunt, and scarcely knew, in the confusion of the moment, where I was, and what it was all about. Sarah saw my state, and began pulling down my shirt. "Go out of the room," said she to her sister. "Damn it I will finish, I will fuck you," said I making a snatch at her cunt again. "Oh! for God's sake, don't, sir," said she. With a grin out went young sister Martha into the kitchen, and then Sarah began to blubber, "If she tells fearther, he will turn me out into the streets."

"Don't be a fool," said I, "why should she tell?" "Because we are bad friends." "Has she not done it?" "No, she is not sixteen." "How do you know she has not?" "Why we sleep together, and I know." "Who sleeps in the other bed?" "Fearther." "In the same room?" "Yes." "Don't you know anything against her?" "No, last haymaking I seed a young man trying to put his hands up her clothes, that's all; she has only been a woman a few months." If she tells of her, she will tell of me, I thought. It might come to my aunt's ears, Fred would know, and I should get into a scrape.

"It is a pity she has not done it," said I, "for then she would not tell." "I wish she had," she replied. One thing suggested another. "She knows all about what we were doing?" Sarah nodded. "Get her to promise not to tell, and get her to let me do it to her, and I will give you two pounds," said I, taking the money out of my purse.

It was more money than she had ever had in her life at one time, her eyes glistened; she was silent a minute as if reflecting, then said, "She has always been unkind to me, and she shan't get me turned out if I can help it." Then, after further talk, some hesitation, and asking me if I was sure I would give her the money, she said, "I'll try, let's have a jolly good drink, then I'll leave you together," and we went into the kitchen. I saw her dodge.

Martha was leaning, looking out of the window, her bum sticking out, her short petticoats showing a sturdy pair of legs; she turned round to us, it was about eleven o'clock in the day, the old man was at work far off and had taken his dinner with him that day, Sarah had told me.

"You won't tell fearther," said Sarah in a smooth tone. No reply but a grin. "If you do, I will tell him I saw young Smith's hand up your clothes." "It's a lie." "Yes, he did, and you know you have seen all he has got to show." "You are a liar," said Martha. Sarah turned to me and said, "Yes, she did, we both saw him leaking, and a dozen more chaps." "She saw their cocks?" said I. "Yes." "You took me to see them, you bitch," said Martha, bursting out in a rage. "You did not want much taking; what did you say, and what did you do in bed that night, when we talked about it?" "You are a wicked wretch, to talk like that before a strange young man," said Martha and bounced out of the cottage.

In a short time she came in again; the eldest told me scandals she knew about her sister and made her so wild that they nearly fought. I stopped them, they made it up, and I sent off the eldest to fetch shrub, gin and peppermint; it was a good mile to the tavern in the village.

When she had gone, I told Martha I hoped she would do no mischief. She was nothing loath to let me kiss her, so there was soon acquaintance between us. She had seen me half naked, how long she had been watching I knew not, but it was certain she had seen me shoving as hard as I could between the naked thighs of her sister, and that was well calculated to make her randy and ready for the advances of a man. "Here is five shillings, don't say anything, my dear." "I won't say nothing," said she, taking the money. Then I kissed her again, and we talked on.

"How did you like him feeling you?" I asked, "was he stiff?" No reply. "Was it not nice when he got his hand on your thigh?" Still no reply. "You thought it nice when in bed, Sarah says." "Sarah tells a wicked story," she burst out. "What does she tell?" "I don't know." "I will tell you my dear; you talked about Smith's doodle and the other men's you saw pissing." "You are the gentleman from London stopping at the Hall," she replied, "so you had better go back and leave us poor girls alone," and she looked out of the window again.

"I am at the Hall," said I, putting my hand round her waist, "and like pretty girls," and I kissed her until she seemed mollified and said, "What can you want in troubling poor girls like us?" "You are as handsome as a duchess, and I want you to do the same as they do." "What is that?" said she innocently. "Fuck," said I boldly. She turned away looking very confused. "You saw me on your sister, between her thighs, that was fucking; and you saw this," at the same time pulling out my prick, "and now I am going to feel your cunt."

I put my hand up her clothes and tried to feel, but she turned round, and after a struggle half squatted on the floor to prevent me. The position was favorable, I pushed her sharply half on to her back on the floor, got my fingers on to her slit, and in a moment we were struggling on the floor, she screaming loudly as we rolled about.

She was nimble, got up, and escaped me, but by the time her sister came back I had felt her bum, pulled her clothes up, and talked enough baudiness; she had hollowed, cried, laughed, abused, and forgiven me, for I had promised her a new bonnet, and had given her more silver.

Sarah brought back the liquors; there was but one tumbler and a mug, we did with those; the weather was hot, the liquor nice, the girls drank freely. In a short time they were both frisky, it got slightly into my head; then the girls began quarrelling again and let out all about each other, the elder's object being to upset the younger one's virtue and make her lewed. I began to get awfully randy, and told Sarah I had felt her sister's cunt whilst she had been out. She laughed and said, "All right, she will have it well felt some day, she's a fool if she don't." We joked about my disappointment in the morning, I asked Sarah to give me my pleasure then. "Aye," said she, "and it is pleasure; when Martha has once tasted it, she will like it again." Martha, very much fuddled, laughed aloud, saying, "How you two do go on." Then I put my hands up Sarah's clothes. "Lord how stiff my prick is, look," and I pulled it out, Martha saying, "I won't stand this," rushed from the room. I thought she had gone, and wanted to have Sarah; but she thought of the two pounds, and, shutting Martha's mouth, "Try her," said she, "she must have it some day, she'll come in soon." When the girl did, we went on drinking. What with mixing gin, peppermint, and rum shrub, both got groggy, and Martha the worst. Then out went Sarah saying she must go to the village to buy something, and she winked at me.

She had whilst the girl was outside told me to bolt the front door, and if by any chance her father came home, which was not likely, to get out of the bedroom window, and through a hedge, which would put me out of sight in a minute. Directly she was gone I bolted the door and commenced the assault. Martha was so fuddled, that she could not much resist my feeling her bum and thighs, yet I could not get her to go and lie down; she finished the liquor, staggered, and then I felt her clitoris.

I was not too steady, but sober enough to try craft where force failed. I wanted to piss, and did, holding the pot so that she could see my cock at the door, but she would not come into the bed-room. Then I dropped a sovereign, and pretending I could not find it, asked her to help me; she staggered into the bed-room laughing a drunken laugh. The bed was near, I embraced her, said I would give her two sovereigns if she would get on the bed with me. "Two shiners?" said she. "There they are," said I laying them down. "No — no," but she kept looking at them. I put them into her hand, she clutched them saying, "No — no," and biting one of her fingers, whilst I began again titillating her clitoris, she letting me. From that moment I knew what money would do with a woman. Then I lifted her up on to the bed and lay down besides her. All her resistance was over, she was drunk.

I pulled up her clothes; she lay with eyes shut, breathing heavily, holding the gold in her hand. I pulled open her legs, with scarcely resistance, and saw a mere trifle of a hair on the cunt; the novelty so pleased me that I kissed it; then for the first time in my life I licked a cunt, the spittle from my mouth ran on to it, I pulled open the lips, it looked different from the cunts I had seen, the hole was smaller. "Surely," thought I, "she is a virgin." She seemed fast asleep, and let me do all I wanted.

In after life, I should have revelled in the enjoyment of anticipation before I had destroyed the hymen; but youth, want, liquor, drove me on, and I don't remember thinking much about the virginity, only that the cunt looked different from the others I had known. The next instant I laid my belly on hers. "Oh! you are heavy, you smother me," said she rousing herself, "you're going to hurt me, — don't, sir, it hurts," all in a groggy tone and in one breath. I inserted a finger between the lips of her quim and tried gently to put it up, but felt an impediment. She had never been opened by man. I then put my prick carefully in the nick, and gave the gentlest possible movement (as far as I can recollect) to it.

Her cunt was wet with spittle, I well wetted my prick, grasped her round her bum, whilst I finally settled the knob of my tool against it, then, putting my other hand round her bum, grasped her as if in a vise, nestled my belly to hers, and trembling with lust, gave a lunge, — another, — and another. I was entering. In another minute it would be all over with me, my sperm was moving. She gave a sharp "oh!" A few more merciless shoves, a loud cry from her, my prick was up her, and her cunt was for the first time wetted with a man's sperm; with short, quiet thrusts I fell into the dreamy pleasure, laying on the top of her.

Soon I rolled over to her side; to my astonishment she lay quite still with mouth open, snoring and holding the two sovereigns in her hand. I gently moved to look at her; her legs were wide open, her gown and chemise (all the clothing she had on) up to her navel, her cunt showed a red streak, my spunk was slowly oozing out, streaked with blood, a little was on her chemise; but I looked in vain for that sanguinary effusion which I saw on Charlotte's chemise and on my shirt when I first had her; and, from later experience, think that young girls do not bleed as much as full grown women, when they lose their virginity.

Her cunt, as I found from ample inspection afterwards, was lipped like her sister's; the hair, about half an inch long, scarcely covered the mons, and only slightly came down the outer lips, her thighs were plump and round, her calves big for her age; she was clean in her flesh, but alas! hick blue stockings with holes and darns, bit boots with holes at the sides, a dirty ragged chemise, dark garters below the knees, made an ugly spectacle compared with the clean whiteness of Charlotte's linen.

But the sight took effect, my prick had her blood on it, quietly I slid my finger up her cunt, it made her restless, she moved her legs together, shutting my hand in them; she turned on her side, and showed a plump white bum, over one side of which a long streak of bloody sperm had run. I pulled her on to her back and got on to her, then she awakened struggling and called out loudly, but I was heavy on her, my prick at her cunt's mouth, and I pushed it up until it could no further, whilst she kept calling out, I was hurting her.

"Be quiet, I can't hurt you, my prick is right up you," said I, beginning the exercise. She made no reply, her cunt seemed deliciously small, whenever I pushed deep, she winced as if in pain, I tried to thrust my tongue into her mouth, but she resisted it. Sud-

denly she said, "Oh! go away, Sarah will be home and find us." I
had my second emission, and went to sleep with my prick up her, —
I was groggy. She slept also.

I awakened, got up tired with heat, excitement, drink and
fucking. She got up, and sat on the side of the bed, half sobered
but stupid, dropped a sovereign, and did not attempt to pick it up.
I did, and put it back into her hands; she took it without saying a
word. When buttoned up, I asked her what she was going to do,
but all the reply I could get was, "You go now." I went into the
kitchen, banged the door, but held the latch, the door remained
ajar, and I peeped through.

She sat perfectly still so long, that I thought she was never
going to move; then sat down on the chair and laid her head against
the bed, looking at the sovereigns at intervals; then put them down,
put her hand up her petticoats carefully feeling her cunt, looked at
her fingers, burst into tears, sat crying for a minute or two, then
put a basin with water on to the floor, and, unsteady, partially up-
set it, but managed to wash, and got back on to the chair, leaving
the basin where it was. Then she pulled up the front of her che-
mise and looked at it, again put her fingers to her cunt, looked at
them, again began crying, and leaned her head against the bed, all
in a drowsy, tipsy manner. Whilst so engaged, her sister knocked
and I let her in; she looked at me in a funny way; I nodded; she
went into the bed-room and closed the door, but I heard most of
what was said.

"What are you sitting there for?" No reply. "What's that basin
there for?" No reply. "You have been washing your grummit?" No
reply. "What have you been washing it for?" "I was hot." "Why,
you have been on the bed!" "No, I ain't." "You have, with he." "No,
I ain't." "I know he have, and been atop a you, just as he were atop
on me this morning." "No, he ain't." Then was a long crying fit.
Sarah said, "What's the good of crying, you fool, no one ain't going
to tell, I shan't, and the old man won't know." Then their voices
dropped, they stood together, but I guessed she was asking what
I had given her.

Then I went in. "You have done it to my sister," said Sarah.
"No," said I. "Yes you have," and to Martha crying, "Never mind,
it's better to be done by a gent than by one of them mill-hands, I
can't abear 'em; leave off, don't be a fool." I went out of the room,

Sarah followed me, and I gave her the two sovereigns. "You know," she said, "some one would ha done it to her; one of them mill-hands, or Smith would, he's allus after her, and I knows he got his hands upon her."

Fred went up to London next day, and I was at the cottage soon after; the girls were there, the elder grinned, the younger looked queer, and would not go to the bed-room. "Don't be a fool," said the elder, and soon we were alone together there. Half force, half entreaty got her on to the bed, I pulled up her clothes, forced open her legs, and lay for a minute with my belly to hers in all the pleasure of anticipation, then rose on my knees for a close look. My yesterday's letch seized me, I put my mouth to her cunt and licked it, than put my prick up the tight little slit and finished my enjoyment.

Afterwards when I had her she was neat and clean underneath, although with her every day's clothes on. She was frightened to put on her Sunday clothes. She was a nice plump round girl, with a large bum for her size, with pretty young breasts and a fat-lipped little slit; the lining of it, instead of being a full red like Charlotte's and Sarah's cunts, was of a delicate pink. I suppose it was that which attracted me. Certain it is that I had never licked a cunt before, never had heard of such a thing, though "lick my arse" was a frequent and insulting invitation for boys to each other.

I saw her nearly every day for a week, and her modesty was soon broken. Sleeping in the same room with her father, accustomed to be in the fields or at a mill, such girls soon lose it; but she seemed indifferent to my embraces, and all the enjoyment was on my side. "I've not much pleasure in that," said she, "But more when you put your tongue there." I could not believe that was so in a young and healthy lass, but being always in a hurry to get my poking done lest her father came home, used to lick, put up her, spend quickly, and leave; but she soon got to rights. I licked so hard and long the next time I had her, at the side of the bed, that all at once I felt her cunt moving, her thighs closed, then relaxed, and she did not answer me. I looked up, she was laying with eyes closed and said, that what I had done was nicer than anything. I had gamahuched her till she spent.

After that she spent like other women, when I had her. I tell this exactly as I recollect it, and can't attempt to explain. She worked at a paper mill; slack work was the reason of her being at home, now she was going back to work; I feared a mill hand would get her and offered to pay her what she earned; but if she did not go to the mill her father would make her work in the fields, and she dare not let him see she had money.

Indeed the two sisters did not dare to buy the finery they wanted, because they could not say how they got the money. So back to the mill she went, it being arranged that she should stay away now and then, for me to have her. "Oh! won't she," said Sarah, "she takes to ruddling natoral, I can tell you." Sarah said she told her everything I had done to her, including the licking, and I felt quite ashamed of Sarah knowing that I was so green, as I shall tell presently.

Fred returned, and I had difficulty in getting her often. My cousins walked out in the cool of the evening, I with them; often we passed the cottage, and I made signs if I saw the girls. I sometimes then had her upright in a small shed or by a hay-stack in the dark, where the hay pricked my knuckles.

Fred was soon to join his regiment, was always borrowing money of me "for a shove," and never repaid me; but he was a liberal, good-hearted fellow; and when in after life I was without money and he kept a woman, he said, "You get a shove out of °°°," meaning his woman, "she likes you, and I shan't mind, but don't tell me." I actually did fuck her, nor did he ever ask me, — but that tale will be told hereafter. Nothing till his death pleased him more than referring to our having looked at the backside of his mother and at his sisters' quims, he would roar with laughter at it. He was an extraordinary man.

One day we rode to the market-town, and, putting up our horses, strolled about. Fred said, "Let's both go and have a shove." "Where are the girls?" said I. "Oh! I know, lend me some money." "I only have ten shillings." "That is more than we shall want." We went down a lane past the Town-Hall, by white-washed little cottages, at which girls were sitting or standing at the doors making a sort of lace. "Do you see a girl you like?" said he. "Why, they are lacemakers." "Yes, but some of them fuck for all that; there is the one I had with the last half-a-crown you lent me." Two girls were standing, together; they nodded. "Let's try them," said Fred. We went into the cottage; it was a new experience to me. He took one girl, leaving me the other; I felt so nervous; she laughed as Fred (who had never in his life a spark of modesty) put his hands up her companion's clothes. That girl asked what he was going to give her, and it was settled at half-a-crown each. Fred then went into the back-room with his woman.

I never had had a gay woman. A fear of disease came over me. She made no advances, and at length, feeling my quietness was ridiculous, I got my hands up her clothes, pulling them up and looking at her legs. "Lord! I am quite clean, sir," said she in a huff, lifting her clothes well up. That gave me courage, I got her on to an old couch and looked at her cunt, but my prick refused to stand; her being gay upset me. She laid hold of my prick, but it was of no use. "What is the matter with you?" said she, "don't you like me?" "Yes, I do." "Have you ever had a girl?" I said I had. Fred who had finished, bawled out, "Can't we come in?" This upset me still more, and I gave it up. In Fred and his girl came, and he said, "There is water in the other room." I went in and feigned to wash myself, and hearing them all laughing, felt ashamed to come out, thinking they were laughing about me; though such was not the case, it was because Fred was beginning to pull about my woman.

I had more money than I had told Fred, and when he said he was thirsty, offered to send for drink, thinking my liberality would make amends for my impotence. Gin and ale was got; then I began to feel as if I could do it. "She's got a coal-black cunt," said Fred, and I seemed to fancy his woman; then he said to mine, "What colour is yours?" and began to lift her clothes; "let's change and have them together," and we went at once into the back room, whither the two girls had gone. One was piddling, Fred pulled her up from the pot, shoved her against the side of the bed, bawling out, "You get the other," and pulled out his prick stiff and ready. An electric thrill seemed to go through me at this sight, I pulled the other into the same position by the side of Fred's; then the girls objected, but Fred hoisted up his girl and plunged his prick into her. Mine got on to the bed, leaving me to pull up her clothes. The same fear came over me, and I hesitated; Fred looked and laughed, I pulled up her clothes, saw her cunt; fear vanished, the next moment I was into her, and Fred and I, side by side, were fucking.

All four were fucking away like a mill, then we paused and looked at our pricks, as they alternately were hidden and came into sight from the cunts. Fred put out his hand to my prick, I felt his, but I was coming; my girl said, "Don't hurry." It was too late, I spent, laid my head upon her bosom, and opening my eyes, saw Fred in the short shoves. The next instant he lay his head down.

I believe now that really all four felt ashamed, for directly after we were all so quiet, one of the girls remarked, "Blest if I ever heard of such a thing afore, you Lunnon chaps are a bad lot." A long time afterwards, I again had the girl for two and sixpence; Fred was then in Canada; she recollected me well, and asked me whether gals and chaps usually did such things together in London.

Fred and I used to examine our pricks for a few days after, to see if there were any pimples on them. Fred soon forgot his fear and shame and offered to bet me the fee of the gals that he would finish first, if we went and repeated the affair, but we did not.

Martha became very curious about me and my doings with Sarah. New to fucking as she was, she got jealous at the idea of anyone sharing my cock with her. She was curious too to know about her sister's pleasures; the elder had, I think, got all she wanted to know from the younger, and had made but little return for it in information.

Then my amatory knowledge was increased by an event unlooked for, unthought of, unpremeditated; I am quite sure I had neither heard nor read of such a thing before, and should, at that period of my life, have scouted the idea as beastly and abominable, though I had done it. How I came to lick Martha's cunt even then astonished me, I thought that it was the small size, the slight hair, and youthfulness of the article; but I used to lick it very daintily, wiping my mouth, spitting frequently, and never venturing beyond the clitoris. It occurred to me one day instead of kneeling, to lay down and lick; so I laid on the bed, my head between her thighs, my cock not far from her mouth, and indulging her in the luxury; for it was much the idea of pleasing her which made me do it. She played with my cock and wriggled as my tongue played over her clitoris, then grasped my prick hard, which gave me a premonitory throb of pleasure. "Do to me what I am doing to you," said I, "put it in your mouth," scarcely knowing what I said and without any ulterior intention. She with her pleasure getting intense, impelled by curiosity, or by the fascination of the cock, or by impulse, the result of my tongue on her cunt, took it in her mouth instantly. How far my prick went in, whether she sucked, licked, or simply let it enter, I know not, and I expect she did not either; but as she spent I felt a sensation resembling the soft friction of a cunt, and instantly shot my sperm into her mouth and over her face. Up she got, calling me a beast. I was surprised and ashamed of this unlooked for termination, and said so to her.

I had as said arranged signs, as I passed the cottage, about our meetings, yet had difficulty now in getting at her without being found out, and never should, excepting for the elder sister, to whom I gave every now and then money. She took care of the house, rarely went out, but worked at a coarse sort of lace and earned money that way. She used to sit outside the cottage door if fine, working, and curtseying when we, who were called the Hall folks, passed. My aunt said one day, "What a strapping wench that is, don't you think so, Walt? you always look at her as you pass." I might have replied, "Yes, she is, and her arse is remarkably like yours," but I did not and was after that more on my guard. Fred had not had the girl for a long time, that freed me a little. Then Martha shammed ill two days to stay from the mill and let me have her, and I spent a good many hours with her. As I turned my head quickly one day, I thought I saw the bed-room door close, and it occurred to me, that the elder had been watching; she looked lecherously at me as I came out.

I went one day soon after and found Sarah alone. She made some excuse about her sister being obliged to go to work. I was going away angry, when she asked me to look at her new boots and stockings. Amused at her vanity I looked, and she put them on. "Them fits fine," said she, showing her legs amply. I was not excited about it, and was going. "Ain't you never going to ha me agin?" said she. "I've no money." "We are old friends, never mind money, if I hadn't got you Martha we moight ha been good friends still, — ar wish a had'nt." "You did it to save us," said I. "Ah, but yer shouldn't leave old friends, and I ha watched and made yer both comfortable." Well, thought I, this is an invitation to fucking, — she had a wonderful clip in her cunt, and I began to rise. "You have lots of friends," said I. "I take my oath, that no friend has seen me since the day you got my sister; ain't I been allus on watch for yer? did yer ever pass without seeing me?"

A woman who wants fucking is not easy to resist, even if she is ugly and middle-aged. There she sat, the picture of health, her petticoats nearly up to her knees; I had never before seen them excepting in coarse blue woollen stockings. I rolled her clothes up, saw the big thighs, the next instant had my fingers in the slit; up knocked my doodle. She shut the shutter, locked the door, and with a pleased look got on to the bed. Her cunt struck me as quite a novelty, and I got ready for insertion.

"You like her better than me," said she. It was a poser, but a man always likes the woman he is going to poke better than any other, and so I denied it. "Why don't you do to me what you do to she then?" "What is that?" "You knows." "No." "Yes you do." "I feel it like this." "More than that." "What?" "You know." "I don't, tell me." There was a pause. It came into my head that she knew I had licked Martha's quim, and it had such an effect on me, that down went my doodle, and I was almost ashamed to look at her; for, as said, until I licked Martha I had never done such an act, and did it with a sort of belief that I was a great beast, and should have said so of any man who did anything of the sort. Indeed after spending in her mouth, I had felt so very much disgusted with myself that I left off the licking altogether and had made the girl promise she would never tell her sister, nor refer to the matter again. So I was silent, standing with one hand on her belly just above her split, and in an uncomfortable state of mind.

She broke the silence. "Do it as you do it to she." "I don't know what you mean," I again stammered. "Yes yer do now." "What has Martha told you?" "Nothing, but I knows." And finding I was about to get on the bed, "Naw, naw, kiss it." So I put my mouth down on to the hair and gave a loud kiss. "Naw," said she, "do it as you do it to she, I am a finer woman than she by long chalks; what is't yer sees to take to her so? you knows you tickles hers with yer tongue." The murder was out. I wanted to mount her, she baulked me, and kept repeating in a jocular, playful manner her request. So I got her to the side of the bed, her large thighs wide open, and legs hanging down in a favorable position, intending to please her; she gave her cunt a dry rub with her chemise.

I began with dislike, but there was something in the novelty which warmed me. What a difference between her and her sister. I could lick the younger one's all but hairless orifice with comfort, and she always laid quiet; but I had to pull open this one's sausage lips and hold back the dark thick fringe, which got into my eyes and tickled my nose. No sooner had my tongue touched her clitoris, than the lips closed round my mouth, and, as my saliva worked up on to the cunt-hair by her movement, it wetted my nose and face, she heaved and bounced her arse so much. Then her thighs closed round my head tightly enough to squeeze it off, she buried her hands in the hair of my head, and up went cunt again, bringing my nose into the hole, then with a jerk she got her cunt away from me. I was not at all sorry to desist.

"Oh! do it natural, — do it natural," said she, and her thighs opened and hung down, showing a slobbered cunt. I went into her, just as she lay at the side of the bed, and in a minute her cunt was wetter than ever.

I have no doubt that the wench spent almost directly I licked, but I did not know it. When I asked her if she liked it, she said, "The old fashioned way be the best, but I have done the same as she." I questioned her, but never knew whether her sister had told her or not, or whether she had peeped and seen us together at it.

I made her promise she would never tell her sister what I had done. She hoped I would see her again, but having promised Martha that I would not have Sarah again, told her so. She said she was tired of watching for us. The sisters were often quarrelling, and I believe out of jealousy about me, yet I fucked her again.

I may mention the risks I ran, that I was once with Martha on the bed when I heard my cousin's voice asking Sarah, who was at the door, if she had seen me pass.

I could not get the younger readily enough, had been long from home, and was about returning. I had spent all my money, and told Sarah one day after I had poked her that I was going away. Her sister was then at the mill. Said she, "What will Martha do?" I supposed she would get another sweetheart. She shook her head, "Martha be poisoned." "What?" "Don't be afraid," said she, "she be in the family way, we call it poisoned in these parts, when a girl ben't married." It was true. The girl had only menstruated once or twice before I first had her, and now her courses had stopped. There was no attempt at making a market of me, all needed was to get her right again. The elder took Martha to a fortune-teller, and she got better of her difficulty. I borrowed money of my aunt and, giving Martha all I could, went back to London. She left the neighbourhood.

I saw Martha two years afterwards, when visiting again my aunt; she was in household service, and was out for the day. I waylaid her, hoping to have her again; we kissed and fondled, and with difficulty I felt her quim but could not accomplish my wishes; she was going to be married, and soon after I heard that she was.

Sarah also was going to be married to a farm labourer, and when I joked her about his finding her out, she laughed and said, "Lord, he war my first sweetheart," from which I inferred that cousin Fred was mistaken about taking her virginity.

My first cunt-licking, and cock-sucking took place with Martha; I had never before played such amatory pranks, and all came about by instinct. For a long time I was ashamed of myself and never breathed a word on such subjects to anyone; I don't think I should have done so even to Fred, but he was then away. Gradually I was learning by instinct the whole art of love. What made me offer money to get Martha I can't say, I don't think that I had ever heard of tempting women's virtue by money, but I never forgot the lesson, and much improved on it as time went on.

I now had had four women. The difficulties in the way of getting at them were very useful in preventing excesses, and kept me in health. It seems surprising to me now how little I seemed to have thought of baudy attitudes, and lascivious varieties; for belly-to-belly poking on the bed was nearly all I did. I had still the modest, demure demeanour which deceived my mother (coupled with her ignorance of life generally) and relations, and, though very proud of my achievements, kept them much to myself, never disclosing the names of my women, and only telling one or two intimate friends of what I had done; who reciprocated by telling me their achievements. Fucking had eased my prepuce. I made a practice of pulling it backward and forward several times a day; in fact, whenever I piddled. My prick had grown bigger in the two years, which pleased me much, but about the size of it I had a curious doubt, which will be told of further on.

I was, though demure, quite a man in manner and look, and with women behaved in a way which one or two of my relatives remarked. I used to think to myself when talking to them, "Ah! I know what sort of opening you have at the bottom of your belly." The cousins, whose cunts I had had a partial glimpse of, I used to like to dance with, wondering how much the hair had grown on them. I used also to think about my sister's cunt that I had seen when in the cradle, but just then she died. My experiences indeed much increased the charm of female society to me.

Chance had given me two virgins out of four women; that was a luxury unthought of, uncared for, and in no way appreciated; the virgins were no more liked by me than the others.

Cousin Fred will appear at less frequent intervals; he was away sometimes for months, then for years, but he is named whenever he played an important part in my adventures, — he was participator in others which will never be written about here.

Charwoman and daughter. — At a key-hole. — Cutting corns. — A shower and a barn. — A fat rumped Devonian. — Suggestive pictures. — A bum-hole offered. — Erotic madness. — Remorse.

We could not get servants for some time. A middle-aged charwoman came to assist, and one of her daughters came from time to time, stopping generally the night. Their cottage was not far off, I had seen the girl from an infant, she was then about eighteen years old. I had often smiled when I met her, of course I smiled now. She was quite a slim little girl, there was nothing of her, but I was at an age when anything having a cunt attracted me.

Profiting by experience, I now used key-holes; fortune favoured me, for, for some reason, instead of one large bed, two small ones were put into the servants' room; between them a wash-stand and a chair on each side of it were nearly opposite the key-hole. How I chuckled at this, for unless the key-hole was covered, I could see nearly all one bed and both chairs and wash-stand. I saw the old woman wash and use the pot, put on her stockings and other things; the other bed was a little out of range. I could not so often see the girl, but did at times.

One evening the girl only stopped. So soon as I heard mother's door closed, out I went in my night-shirt, and through the key-hole saw the girl naked. She put the light on the floor, one leg on the chair, and with a small handglass looked at her quim, her bum was towards me. Not satisfied she turned round, sat down facing me, putting the candle on the floor and with legs as wide open as she could went on with her investigation. I had a reasonably good look at her, and her cunt. As said, she was nothing to look at, but I got in a fearfully excited state and made some noise at the door which alarmed her, for up she got and stood still listening. I went to my room, looking through the half-closed door, hers opened and out came her head. I nodded and back she went.

The next day she was going home, and as I now (although having rows with mother about it) went out when I liked, just before she left I went out and walked. It was dark. In two or three minutes out she came. After walking by her side for a time I asked her point blank how she liked the look of it last night. "What do you mean?" I told her all I had done. "Oh!" she said with intense surprise, "what a mean thing to do." I told her how one of our former servants used to look at me naked. After a minute she did not appear to be at all disconcerted at having been seen naked; from my description she could have had no doubt whatever that I had seen all. "What did you look at your quim for?" asked I. "Ah! that's my business; what did you look at me for?" "To see your cunt." Being at a dark part of the road I began kissing her, and got my fingers on to her belly. She made no row, but crossed her legs; and small and seemingly weak as she was, succeeded in preventing me feeling. I was out with her an hour, kissing, coaxing, attempting; I got my fingers and hand over her bum and belly, but not on to her slit. At each failure she laughed and said, "Done again." I swore I would some day. "No you won't, you're not the first that has tried," said she, and I went home without having felt her quim properly.

I attempted it the next day and at every opportunity in the house and out of it, till new servants came. She felt my prick, would look at it, squeeze the balls, talk about fucking and baudiness to any extent, tell me what she had seen and what she had heard about such matters. She at length scarcely resisted my feeling her bum, belly, and legs, yet I never got my finger on to her slit, so as to feel the moisture; for she closed her little legs and wriggled, or got away from me somehow. Once or twice when I got a little rough, she set up a squeal, and I desisted. I offered her money. She replied, "No thank you, I am not going to spoil my chance that way." Our conversation used to begin by my saying, "How is your duff?" "Oh! nicely, thank you; how is your jock?" "All right, and stiff, waiting for your duff." "Then it will wait a long time," and so on. It always ending in my trying to feel her, and getting no further. At length they left, new servants coming.

I frequently saw her afterwards, and always began the same

game. My mother was told I had been seen talking to her, so after that I only spoke to her at dusk. Some time afterwards she married a gardener, and I occasionally saw her, but recognition came to a knowing nod and smile, which she always returned. Meanwhile I had got my fortune, as I shall tell, had no end of women, and had forgotten her when, walking across a field not far from our house, I overtook a short woman with a little child, and it was she. A shower came on, and we went into a barn, no one was in it. She told me I was said to be a "dreadful chap after the gals." "You know all about that now," said I. "Yes," she replied with a grin, and gradually talking baudier, we went on, until in a few minutes I had laid her down and fucked her on the hay. "I told you I would do it," said I. "But you didn't when you said you would, — now it won't matter." That was her notion. The rain continuing, she said she must go, whether wet or dry. Neither of us had an umbrella. She pulled her gown over her head, and saying, "You won't tell anyone, will you?" took the child by the hand and was going, when my appetite came again. I pulled her back, and with little persuasion, again went up her. She enjoyed the fuck greatly. As I lay on the top of her we heard a bang, and the barn grew dark; a man was shutting the door. "Ulloh!" said he, "I didn't know any one was there; I hope I ain't disturbed you." We made no reply, but out we went. "You will have a boy out of this," said I. "I hope I shall," said she. That was the end of my adventure, for I never had her again, and she soon left the neighborhood. It was her own little child that was with her.

Though I have (as I shall in other cases) told all I had to do with her consecutively, yet between the time when she was in our house and the time of meeting her at the barn, three or four years must have elapsed; and didn't we talk baudy in the barn before I got into her. That may have warmed her up, yet I believe she wanted me, as soon as she found herself alone with me. Her little child witnessed the business.

Just at this time or a little later, an adventure of a serious kind occurred to me.

The streets leading out of the Waterloo Road were then occupied much by gay women. Some were absolutely full of them; they were mostly of a class to be had for a few shillings if they could not get more, but many a swell I have noticed lingering about there. My mother now took nearly all my money for my board, but with the little re-maining I had a knock off occasionally. It was one of my pleasures to walk up these streets when dark and talk with the women at the windows, which were always open whatever the weather, un-less some one was within engaged with the ladies.

Each woman had generally but one room, but two or three used to sit together in the front room in their chemises. There was the bed, wash-stand, chamber-pot and all complete. Perhaps one lolled out of the window, showing her breasts, and if you gave such a one a shilling, she would stoop so that you could see right down past her belly to her knees, and have a glimpse of her cunt-fringe. Sometimes one would pull up her garter, or another sit down and piddle, or pretend to do so, or have recourse to other exciting de-vices when men peeped in.

I used to look in and long. Sometimes had a shilling peep and then bashfully asked for a feel of the cunt for it. I so often suc-ceeded that, ever since when I wanted that amusement, have of-fered a shilling for a feel and met with but few refusals in any part of London. Sometimes it ended in a fuck. Once or twice to my as-tonishment they took mere trifles, and, as I think of it, there is wonderfully little difference between the woman you have for five shillings, and the one you pay five pounds, excepting in the silk, linen, and manners.

One night I saw a woman with very fat breasts looking out of the window (I was then fond of stout women); and, after talking a minute, asked her if she would let me feel her cunt for a shilling. "Yes," said she. In I went, down she shut the window, and in an-other minute I was groping her. She did not let me feel her long. I had not felt such a bum since Mary's (already told of), and it so wetted my appetite that I struck a bargain for a fuck. She was soon stripped, and all I now recollect about her is that her cunt was large and covered with hair of a brownish colour; that her eyes were dark; and that she seemed full twenty-five years of age. I fucked her on a sofa.

When I had buttoned up, she produced a book full of baudy pictures, of which I then had seen but few; and I went a second time, to see the book rather than her. Looking over it, she pointed out to me, with a laugh, several pictures of men putting their pricks into women's arse-holes, and into the rumps of other men. Having never before seen such pictures, and having no idea of the operation, I felt modest and turned to others; but she so regularly, as we turned over the leaves, pointed out this class that my sense of shame gave way to curiosity; and, not believing, asked if it was possible to do it so. "Lord yes," said she. "Does it not hurt?" said I. "Not if properly done," she replied, and went on to say it was delicious, some men thought; and she talked altogether in a very knowing way about it; told me how it was best to grease the hole first, then the prick, and to shove gently, and went on so that I said on a sudden, "Why, you have done it, I think." "Yes, but only with a particular friend of mine who is very fond of it, — and so am I; it is better than the other."

I felt shocked, bewildered, and excited. The subject dropped, but she sat feeling me, slipping her finger under my balls, and pressing my arse-hole with her finger. I prepared to fuck. She suggested she should kneel with her buttocks towards me, so that she could feel my balls when my prick was up her. I assented, and her bum-cheeks were presented to me. Excited by her conversation and her hints, I looked curiously at her large slit, and then at her bum-hole; I touched the latter, and she drove her bum back upon my finger with a laugh. I did not take her hint, but drove my prick into her quim and pushed in the regular fashion. Thinking of the pictures excited me, and without knowing what I said, I suddenly pulled it out, saying, "Let me put it into the other." "Not tonight," said she, "put your thumb a little way in, your nail is quite short (she had noticed that I used to bite my thumb-nails short)." I instantly did, the next moment spent, and dropped over her back, waiting for the last drop of sperm to run off into her.

Her hints, her pictures, of which she had actually scores, stirred my curiosity; her manner disgusted me, yet my brain seemed affected. Is it possible, thought I, that a man's prick can go in there? — Impossible. And yet she says she has had it done to her, and my thumb went in easily enough. The more I thought and the more I reflected how a hard turd hurt me sometimes in passing it, the more I was puzzled about the intense pleasure which she said the operation gave! To solve my doubts (although I had determined not), I went to her again, and saw the pictures. She again talked about them, until, scarcely knowing what I was doing, "Will you let me?" I asked. "Yes, if you do what I tell you." I consented. "Don't talk loud," said she, "it will never do to let any one know what we are at." Our voices dropped to a whisper, whilst by her advice I pulled off trousers and drawers, and she stripped stark naked.

Then she carefully greased my prick with pomatum, and put some on her arse-hole; it was the work of a minute, not a word was said. She then, start naked, sat by the side of me on the sofa, began fondling and kissing me, took my hands in hers and rubbed my fingers on her clitoris, half frigged herself with my fingers, I let her do what she liked. Then she turned round. "Put it in," she said when her rump was towards me, "then give me your hand, and don't push till I tell you." Her arse-hole was at the level of my prick as I stood by the side of the sofa, my machine was like a rod of iron, my brains seemed on fire, I felt I was going to do something wrong, dreaded it, yet determined to do it. "Put it in, slowly," said she in a whisper. The hole opened, felt tight, but to my astonishment almost directly my whole prick was hidden in it without pain to me or any difficulty. "Give me your hand." I did. Again she began frigging herself with my fingers. "Rub, rub, push gently," she said, and I tried, but was getting past myself. "Now," said she with a spasmodic sort of half cry, half grunt. I felt my prick squeezed as in a vise, I shoved or rather scarcely began to do so when I discharged a week's reserve up her rectum. My brain whirled with excitement, whilst she, leaning over the pillows on the sofa, kept breathing hard and half snorting like a pig, still frigging herself with my fingers.

As my senses returned, I could scarcely believe where my prick was; excitement still kept it stiff, but desire had left me. I pulled it out with an indescribable horror of myself.

"Wasn't it delicious?" said she. "I like it, don't you? you may always do it so." What I replied I know not; I washed, dressed and got out of the house as soon as I could. When in the street, I was sick. I ran off, fearing some one would see me, got into a Hackney-coach and drove in the wrong direction; then got out and went a round-about way home, fearing some one was following to upbraid or expose me. I scarcely slept that night for horror of myself, never went up the street again for years, and never passed its end without shuddering, have no recollection of having had pleasure, or of any sensation whatever; all was dread to me. And so ended that debauch; one I was deliberately led into by that woman, having never thought of such doings before as possible, or at all, as far as I can recollect.

Preliminary. — My taste for beauty of form. — Sarah Mavis. — Midday in the Quadrant. — No. 13 J°°°s Street. — A bargain in the hall. — A woman with a will. — Fears about my size. — Muck. — Cold-blooded. — Tyranny. — My temper. — Submission. — A revolt. — A half-gay lady. — Sarah watches me. — A quarrel. — Reconciliation.

[I had early a taste for beauty of female form. Face had for me of course the usual attraction, for beauty of expression always speaks to the soul of a man first. A woman's eyes speak to him before she opens her mouth, and instinctively (for actual knowledge only comes to him in his maturer years) he reads in them liking, dislike, indifference, voluptuousness, desire, sensuous abandonment, or fierce reckless lust.

[All these feelings can be seen in a woman's eyes alone, for they express and move with every feeling, every passion, pure or sensual. They can beget in the male pure love as it is called, which is believed to be so till experience teaches that however pure it may be, it cannot exist without the occasional help of a burning, throbbing, stiff prick, up a hot, wide-stretched cunt, and a simultaneous discharge of spermatic juices from both organs. The rest of a woman's body, the breasts and limbs, can move lust unaccompanied by love, and if once admiration of them begins, lust follows instantly. A small

166

foot, a round, plump leg and thigh, and a fat backside speak to the
prick straight. Form is in fact to most more enticing, and creates a
more enduring attachment in men of mature years, than the sweetest
face. A plain woman with fine limbs and bum, and firm, full breasts
will (unless her cunt be an ugly gash) draw a man to her where
the prettiest-faced miss will fail. Few men, unless their bellies be
very big, or they be very old, will keep long to a bony lady whose
skinny buttocks can be held in one hand. I early had a taste for
female form, it was born with me. Even when a boy I selected
partners for dancing because they were what I called crummy, and
admired even at one time a fat-arsed middle-aged woman who sold
us bull's eyes, because I had caught her exhibiting her large legs
when squatting down to piss.

[For years I had had at the period named, two friends, one of
whom was a sculptor, who alas! drank himself to death; and one a
painter still living as I write this. I had been in their studios, seen
their naked models, heard their opinions on both male and female
beauty, and had the various points of female perfection shown me
on the lady-sitters. I had them explained in two instances by the
ladies themselves, in private sittings, and with them I had sexual
pleasures which they said the artists had neither got out of them
nor given them. I had myself sketched from the nude, and was
thought a not bad hand at it, and had therefore by training, instinct,
and a most voluptuous temperament become a good judge of the
beauty of female form.

[I did not write the above paragraphs, when I wrote what fol-
lows about Sarah Mavis. They are added now many years after-
wards, when I am wondering at what I did in those early days,
marvelling at my judgment in selection, and seeking the reasons
which guided me then in getting for my sexual embraces as many
models of female beauty of form as perhaps any one Englishman
ever had, — short of a prince.]

One summer's morning about midday, I was in the Quadrant.
It had been raining, and the streets were dirty. In front of me I
saw a well-grown woman walking with that steady, solid, well-
balanced step which I even then knew indicated fleshy limbs and
a fat backside. She was holding her petticoats well up out of the
dirt, the common habit of even respectable women then. With gay
ladies the habit was to hold them up just a little higher. I saw a

pair of feet in lovely boots which seemed perfection, and calves which were exquisite. I fired directly. Just by Beak Street she stopped, and looked into a shop. "Is she gay?" I thought. "No." I followed on, passed her, then turned round, and met her eye. She looked at me, but the look was so steady, indifferent, and with so little of the gay woman in her expression, that I could not make up my mind as to whether she was accessible or not.

She turned back and went on without looking round. Crossing Tichborne Street she raised her petticoats higher, it was very muddy there. I then saw more of both legs, my prick stood at the sight of her limbs, and settled me. I followed quickly, saying as I came close, "Will you come with me?" She made no reply, and I fell behind. Soon she stopped again at a shop, and looked in, and again I said, "Máy I go with you?" "Yes, — where to?" "Where you like, — I will follow you." Without replying a word, and without looking at me, without hurrying, she walked steadily on till she entered the house No. 13 J°°°s Street, which I entered that day for the first time, but many hundreds of times since. Her composure, and the way she stopped from time to time to look at the shops as she went along astonished me: she seemed in no hurry, nor indeed conscious that I was close at her heels, though she knew it.

Inside the house she stopped at the foot of the staircase, and turning round, said in a low tone, "What are you going to give me?" "Ten shillings." "I won't go upstairs then, so tell you at once." "What do you want?" "I won't let any one come with me unless they give me a sovereign at least." "I will give you that." Then she mounted, nothing more being said. Asking me the question at the foot of the stairs astonished me, I had been asked it in a room often before, and in the street; but at the foot of a staircase, — never.

We entered a handsome bed-room. Turning round after paying for it, and locking the door, I saw her standing with her back to the light (the curtains were down, but the room was nevertheless light), one arm resting on the mantel-piece. She looked at me fixedly, and I did at her. Then I recollect noticing that her mouth was slightly open, and that she looked seemingly vacantly at me (it always was so), that she had a black silk dress on, and a dark-colored bonnet. Then desire impelled; I went close to her, and began to lift her clothes. She pushed them down in a commanding way saying, "Now none of that."

"Oh! here is your money," said I putting down a sovereign on the mantel-piece. She broke into a quiet laugh. "I did not mean that," she remarked. "Let me feel you." "Get away," said she impatiently, and turning she took off her bonnet. I then saw she had thick and nearly if not quite black hair, and recollect that I noticed these points just in the order I have narrated them. Then she leaned her arm on the mantel-piece again, and looked at me quietly, her mouth slightly open, and I stood looking at her without speaking, my sperm fermenting in my balls; but I was slightly bothered, almost intimidated by her cool manner, — a manner so unlike what I usually met with in strumpets.

"You have beautiful legs." "So they say." "Let me see them." She laid down on the sofa, her back to the light, without uttering a word. I threw off coat and waistcoat, and sitting at the foot of the soft threw up her dress to her knees; higher I tried, but she resisted. Then my fingers felt her cunt, and the delight at the feel and sight of her beautiful limbs overwhelmed me. "Take off your things, — let me see you undressed, — you must be exquisite." My hands roved all about her bum, belly and thighs, and just seeing the flesh above her garters, I fell to kissing it, and kissed upwards till the aroma of her cunt met my nostrils, and its thicket met my lips and mingled with my moustache, which I then wore, though so few men then did. I fell on my knees by the side of her, kissing, feeling, and smelling; but she kept her thighs close together, and pushed her petticoats over my head whilst I kissed, so that I saw but little of her beauties. Then excited almost to madness by my amusement I rose up. "Oh! come to the bed, — come." She lay quite still.

"No, — do it here, —leave me alone, — I won't have my clothes pulled up, — I won't be pulled about, — if you want it have me, and have done." "Well get on to the bed." "I shan't." "I can't do it on the sofa." "Well I'm going then." "You shan't till I have had you, — only let me see your thighs." "There then," — and up went her clothes half-way. "Higher." "I shan't." Now my prick was out. "Get on the bed, — I won't do it here, — take your things off." "I shan't." "You shall." All was said by her in a determined way, but without signs of temper.

She rose without saying another word. I think I see now as I write her exquisite legs in beautiful silk stockings as they showed when getting off the sofa, and getting on to the bed. "But I want your clothes off." "I won't take them off, I'm in a hurry, — I never do." "Oh! you must." "I won't, — now come and do what you want to do, — I'm in a hurry." She lifted her clothes just high enough to show the fringe of her cunt, and opened her thighs a little. I thrilled with lewed delight as I saw them, and mounted her, laid between them, and inserted my prick. Ah! at my first shove almost I was spending in her.

"Oh! lay quiet dear, I've only been up you a second." "No, — get off, and let me wash." I resisted, but she uncunted me, and got off the bed quickly. "Now don't come near while I wash, — I can't bear a man looking at me washing myself." I insisted, for I was longing to see the form I had scarcely yet had a glimpse of. Putting down the basin, she pulled the bed-curtains round her to hide her whilst she slopped her quim. I would not be rude, and saw nothing. Then on went her bonnet. "Are you going first, or I?" said she. "I shall wait as long as you will." "Then I will go first," — and she was going away when I stopped her.

"When will you again meet me?" "Oh! when out at all, I am up to one o'clock in Regent Street." "Where do you live?" "I shan't say, — good bye." "No, — wait, — come to me this afternoon." "I can't." "This evening." She hesitated. "I can't stay long if I do." "Well, an hour and a half." "Perhaps." "Will you take off your clothes then?" "No, — good bye, I am in a hurry." "Meet me at seven o'clock to-night, — do." "No." "At eight then." "Well I will be here expecting you, — but I shan't stop long." "Will you let me see your form up to your waist?" "Oh! I hate being looked at," — and off she went, leaving me in the room.

I dined at my Club, and was in a fever of lust all day. "Will she come?" for she had only half promised. Half-an-hour before the time I was at the house, and had the same room again. It was handsome throughout, had a big four-post bed with handsome hangings (this was thirty years ago mind) on one side of the room, on another side by a partition was a wash-hand stand of marble, against the wall on the opposite side a large glass just at the level of the bed; at the foot of the bed a large sofa opposite to the fire; over the chimney-piece a big glass sloping forwards, so that those sitting or lying on the sofa could see themselves reflected in it; in the angle of the room by the windows a big cheval-glass which could be turned in any direction, two easy-chairs and a bidet, the hangings were of red damask, two large gas-burners were over the chimney-piece angles. It was the most compact, comfortable baudy house bed-room I have perhaps ever been in, although by no means a large room. They charged seven and six for its use, and twenty shillings for the night. Scores of times I have paid both fees.

I noticed all this, and that a couple could see their amatory amusements on the bed, on the sofa, or anyhow in fact, by aid of the cheval and other glasses. I was delighted with the room, but in a fever of anxiety lest the lady should not come. I walked about with my prick out, seeing how I looked in the glasses, laid on the bed, and noticed how it looked in the side-glass, squatted on the sofa, glorying in the sight of my balls and stiff-stander. Then I had a sudden fear that she would think my prick small; what put it into my head I never could exactly say, I used when at school to fancy mine was smaller than that of other boys, and some remark of a gay woman about its size made me most sensitive on the topic. I was constantly asking the women if my prick was not smaller than other men's. When they said it was a very good size, — as big as most, — I did not believe them, and I used when I pulled it out to say in an apologetic tone, "Let's put it up, there's not much of it." "Oh! it's quite big enough," one would say. "I've seen plenty smaller," would say another. But still the idea clung to me that it was not a prick to be in any way proud of, — which was a great error. But I have told of this weakness more than once before, I think.

I recollect well that night fearing she would think my prick contemptible, and it pained me much for I was hooked, although I did not know it. I brushed my hair, and made myself inviting with a desire to please her, without thinking that I was taking the trouble to do so for a woman who was going to be fucked for twenty shillings, and whom I now know did not then care how I looked, or who I was, long as she got her money as soon as she could, and got rid of me to make way for another man, or to go and spend what she had earned.

She did not keep her time. I kept listening, and peeping out as I heard footsteps and saw couples bent on sexual pleasure going up the stairs, and heard them overhead walking about. This and the excitement at the recollection of my instantaneous spend be-

tween her magnificent thighs, my pulling about my prick and con-
templating it in the glass, the moving about of the various couples,
made me in such a state of randiness that I could scarcely keep
from frigging. A servant who had noticed my peeping, came in and
begged I would not look out, for customers did not like it. Did
they know where my lady lived? and would they send for her?
They did not. Then the servant came to say I had been an hour in
the room, — did I mean to wait any longer? I knew what that
meant, and was about to say I would pay for the room twice, when
I heard a heavy, slow tread, and the lady's face appeared.

I grumbled at her delay, she took my complaints quietly, she
could not come earlier, was all she said. She pulled off her bonnet,
put it on the chair, turned round, leaned her arm on the mantel-
piece, and stared at me again in a half-vacant way with her mouth
slightly open, just as in the morning. I gave her very little time to
stare, for I had my hand on her cunt in no time, and nearly spent
in my trowsers as I touched it. She tried the same game, — she
would not be pulled about, — she would not let her cunt be looked
at, — if I meant to do it, do it, and have done with it. My blood
rose. I'd be damned if I would, — nor pay, nor anything else, unless
she took her gown off. So she took it off laughing, and laid down
on the sofa. No, on the bed. No she would not. Then damned if
I would do it (though I was nearly bursting). Again she laughed,
and then got on to the bed. I saw breasts of spotless purity and
exquisite shape bursting out over the corset, threw up the petti-
coats, saw the dark hair at the bottom of the belly, and the next
instant a thrust, a moment's heaving, — quietness, — another thrust,
— a sigh, — a gush of sperm, — and again I had finished with but
a minute's complete sexual enjoyment only.

"Get up." "I won't." "Let me wash the muck out." "No," — and
I pinned her down, squeezed to her belly, grasped her haunches.
"I've not done spending." "Yes, you have." A wriggle and a jerk,
and I was uncunted and swearing. She sat down on the basin, I
stooped down, tore aside the curtains, and put my hand on to her
gaping cunt. She tried to rise, and pushed me, — I pushed her. She
tilted on one side, her bum caught the edge of the basin, and
upset the water.

"Damn you," said she, — then she laughed and got up. I pushed her against the side of the bed, and again got my fingers on the cunt, — slippery enough it was. "You're one of those beasts, are you?" said she.

"I've never felt your cunt properly, and I will." "Well let me wash it, and you shall." She did so, I felt it, and then begged for another fuck.

"You are not in a hurry." "Yes I am." "You said you would give me an hour and a half." "Yes, but you have done me, and what is the good of keeping me?" "I mean to do it again." "Double journey, double pay." "Nonsense, — you so excited me, that I've never had a proper poke yet." "Well that is no fault of mine." She laughed, and turned questioner. "Do you often have the women from Regent Street?" "Yes." "Do you know many?" "Yes, I vary so." "Ah! you are fond of change, — I thought so," — and she got talkative after that. I had thought her almost a dummy.

Meanwhile I was gloating over her charms, her beautiful arms, the lovely breasts I now played with, the lovely limbs I saw, for she had sat down in the most enticing position with the ankle of one foot resting on the knee of the other leg. I wanted to pull the clothes higher up the thighs, she resisted, but I saw the beautiful ankles, the tiny boots and feet, the creamy flesh of the thigh just above the garter, thighs thickening, folding over, squeezing together, and hiding her cunt from view when I tried to look up.

I had hid my prick, the fear had come over me of her thinking it small, and that prevented it standing again. An hour ran away. "I'm going," said she rising. My prick stood at the instant. "Let me." "Make haste then." As she stood up I put my hand up her petticoats. She put her hand down, and gave my prick a hard squeeze. I hollowed, — she laughed.

"I've a good mind not to let you, — you've been so long, — but you may do it." She got on to the bedside. "Oh! for God's sake don't move, — that attitude is exquisite." One leg was well on the bed, the petticoats were squeezed up, and the leg on the ground from the boot-heel to about four inches above her garter was visible. She was half turning round, her lovely breasts, or rather one of them, showed half-front, and with her head looking round at me as she was moving, it altogether made a ravishingly luscious picture. I put my hands up from behind between her thighs. That broke the spell, she moved on to the bed directly, — I on to her.

"Oh! God you are heavenly, lovely, — oh! God my darling, — ah!" I was spending and kissing her too quickly again; lust almost deprived me of my pleasure. In a dozen shoves I was empty. It was all over.

"How quietly you stood in that attitude," said I. "I can stand in an attitude nearly five minutes without moving, almost without showing that I am breathing, without winking an eye." I thought nothing of this at the time, excepting that it was brag.

"Give me five shillings, for I have been a long time with you, — I've a reason, — I won't ask you again." I gave it her. "Shall you be in Regent Street to-morrow morning?" "Yes."

I was in Regent Street, met her, and had her you may be sure, and repeated these meetings for a week daily, and sometimes twice a day; but got no more than the shortest time with her, the quickest fuck, a rapid uncunting. She did not spend with me, and showed no signs of pleasure, scarcely took the trouble to move her bum, would not undress, would not let me look at her cunt. I submitted to it, for I was caught, but did not know that then, — she did. That is, she knew that I was damnably lewed upon her, and used that knowledge to suit her convenience. I had no right to grumble at it, I need not have had her, had I not liked, upon those terms. But I did. At length I grumbled, and at last almost had a quarrel. "I won't see you again," said I. "No one asks you," said she.

As my means were not large, and my purse grew rather empty, I was glad to keep away a few days. Then again I saw her in Regent Street; and after giving her the wink, followed her. She walked on, but instead of going to the house, passed the end of the street. On she went, I went close to her, it was the second time I had spoken to her in the street. "Oh! I did not understand you," she said, "besides I'm in a hurry." "Oh! do come." "Well, I can't stop five minutes." "Nonsense." "Well then I can't, — and she went on walking. My prick got the better of my temper. "Well, come back." She turned round and bent her way to J°°°s Street, saying, "Don't let us go in together."

When in the house, she got on to the bed without a moment's delay. I had her, and she was out of the house again in less than ten minutes, leaving me in a very angry state of mind; but she promised to meet me the following night if she could, and to stay longer with me.

She came an hour late, and found me fretting and fuming in the bed-room. They did not hurry me now at that house, I being already known there, and gave me whenever they could the same chamber. "I'm in a great hurry," were the first words Sarah said. "Why, you told me you would stop longer." "Yes, — I am sorry, but I can't." "You never can, — but take off your gown." "I really can't, — have me at the side of the bed, — you wanted it so the other day." "No I won't." "Then I'll get on the bed," — and on she got. I tried to open her legs, to turn her round to see her bum (I had never seen it yet properly). No, she would not undress, she would do nothing, — I might have it her way, or leave it alone and go. How green it was to submit to all this.

I lost my temper, for my delight I see was in her lovely form, in her physical beauty; whilst she seemed to think that the only joy I could have was to spend in her cunt as fast as I could. "I won't have you at all," said I getting resolute at last. "All right," said she getting off the bed, "I'm really in a hurry, — another night I will." "Another night be damned, — you are nearly a bilk, — there," — and I threw the sovereign on a table, and put on my hat. "Are you going?" "Yes, I'm going to get some woman who is not ashamed of her cunt." "Go along then." Off I went. When half-way down the stairs I heard her calling to me to come back, but savage, I went off.

I walked up Regent Street savage with her, and with myself too, for not having had my fuck, even if she had gone away a minute afterwards. Randy as the devil, I saw a woman at the corner of the Circus, and accosted her, she turned away, I accosted her again. "Will you come with me?" "Yes, if you like." "Do you know a house about here?" "No, I'm a stranger." Then I took her to J°°°s Street, had her two or three times and toyed with her a long time, stopping till she would stop no longer, saying she should be locked out if she was not off. She was only half-gay I think, and wanted a fuck. I had just offered myself in time. She was a biggish woman of about thirty years of age. After I had fucked her the first time, we laid on the bed together; she played with my prick till it was stiff again, and then turning on to her back said, "Come on, — let's have it again."

I thought much of my fine-limbed Sarah Mavis, but it was with anger. A fuck for ten shillings was all very well when randy, but even when in a hurry I never was satisfied till I had pulled the cunt open, and given it a general inspection, although it was generally but a rapid one in those days. If I had the same woman again another day, it was because I liked her and liked to talk to her, for I always found them more complaisant the longer I knew them. But here had I been having a woman daily, and sometimes twice a day, mainly because she was so exquisite in form (for I had some idea even then that her cunt was not a good fit to my prick); yet I had never seen her cunt, nor her backside, nor her bubbies, nor her arm-pits, nor her navel, nor anything properly, and so I determined not to have her again, and to dismiss her from my mind. But I was hooked.

To economize I again went with cheap women, and seemed to get just as nice women for ten shillings as I did for twenty; but I had taken a liking for the house in J°°°s Street, which was an expensive one, and liked the best room, and took my cheap women to my dear room. One woman said, "Well you might give me a little more, and have a cheaper room, — the room gets nearly as much as you give me." And I saw a woman there one night pocket the comb, and a piece of soap, — she stole them. I heard in pleasant conversation afterwards, that soap and combs were often stolen by the women, — especially the soap.

About a fortnight afterwards I saw my Venus again, and again was closeted with her. I could resist my desire for her no longer, having never ceased thinking of her even when fucking other women. She was just as calm, but there was a little, quiet spite about her. When she had taken off her bonnet, and looked at me for a minute with her mouth open as usual, she said, "I suppose you have been having other women." I can't tell why it was, but I lied, and said, "No." "What did you go upstairs with one for?" said she, "the night after you left me, — I was in the parlour, and peeping through the door saw you and the woman who stumbled at the foot of the stairs" (which was the fact). "Well I did," I replied, "and saw her cunt, — and that's more than I ever saw of yours." "You've seen as much as you will." Putting on my hat in a rage, "Then I may as well go, — here is your money," — and I turned towards the door. "Don't be a fool," said she, "What do you want? — what do all you men want? — you are all beasts alike, — you're never satisfied." She was angry. "Don't be in a hurry, and let's see your precious cunt." I recollect saying that very distinctly, being angry, — and that up to that time I had been chaste in my remarks. I was at that time of my life not at all lewed or strong in word with women when we first met, but was somewhat less so so soon as I warmed, and only when randy to the highest degree or by fits and starts, spiced my conversation highly with lewed expressions.

She laughed. "Well I will, — but don't make me undress, — I'm in a hurry." "Of course, — you always are." She laid on the sofa, and pulled up her clothes, — she was yielding. "No, — come here." She came, and laid on the side of the bed. At length I saw those glorious thighs open wider, the dark-shaded crack with the swelling lips showed itself more freely than I had ever seen it before. I dropped on my knees, and propping up one of her feet with my hand, lifted the leg so that the thighs distended, and a large bit of crimson nymphæ began to show, the faint but delicious odour of her cunt stole up my nostrils, my lips closed on her gap, and kissed it lecherously, my brain whirled as my nose rubbed in the thicket of dark hair, and my lip touched her clitoris. I know nothing more excepting that I was up her as she laid there, and spending as quickly as ever, before I had in fact well plugged her. "Are you satisfied?" said she as she looked up from washing her cunt by the side of me. "No, it's so quick, — you fetch me so quickly." "That is no fault of mine." She had said so often before. I recollect all these apparently trivial, these various feelings and circumstances as well as if it were yesterday, for she had made her mark on me.

I had partly conquered, and saw my victory. "I like seeing you so," said I, "but won't see you, or any other woman who won't let me see her charms, and who is always in such a hurry, — it would

178

be all very well if I saw you for the first time — ("Why you have a new black silk dress on." "Yes, I bought it with your money," said she), — but for a regular friend as I am, it is unsupportable." I conquered more, and subsequently told her that I might be in Regent Street one day, but I did not go there (I had made no promise). She said she went out against her will to see me, — could I write to say when she was to meet me? No, — but I could write to the baudy house, and they would send on the letter. I called there one morning, and left a letter. The Mistress was a shortish sandy-haired woman about thirty years old, with a white face who looked very fixedly at me, and smiled. She would send on the letter to Miss Sarah Mavis which I found was the name she went by; but Sarah never came to my letter, and I paid for the room for nothing. Then I sent for the Mistress; had a bottle of champagne with her, and she opened her heart a little, she was soon a little screwed, and this was what she told me. Her name was Hannah.

She had not known Miss Mavis long, — only a month or so before she had come in with me, — did not often see her now excepting with me. Mavis had been asking if I had been seen in the house with any other woman, "and of course I did not tell her," said Sandyhead. She thought her a nice woman, and had struck up acquaintance with her. Now she often came into the parlour to chat with her when I had left, or before she came upstairs to me, when I was at the house before my appointed time.

Things went on thus for a little time longer, Sarah doing much as she liked, but certainly becoming more complaisant. She stopped longer, we began to talk; I was of course curious about her, she about me. I dare say she got much out of me, I but little out of her. What I mainly learned was that she only came on the streets occasionally, and from about eleven to one o'clock in the day, — never afterwards; and when she had sufficient money to "go on with," as she said, she came not out at all. "I hate it," said she, "hate you men, — you are all beasts, — you're never satisfied unless you are pulling a woman about in all manner of ways." "It pleases us," said I, "we admire you so." "Well it does not please me, — I want them to do what they have to do, and let me go." "Why don't you go out in the afternoon or evening?" "No, I get my money in the morning, and have other things to do the rest of the day."

She had not been gay long, — not more than a month before

I had met her, — was taken to the house in J°°°s Street by the first man who met her in the streets, and had been there often since. No, she never had been gay before she would swear, and often wished she were dead rather than have to come out and let men pull her about, and put their nasty muck into her, — "nasty muck" was always the pleasant way in which she spoke of a man's sperm.

"One would think you never cared about a poke, — I wonder how often you spend." "Oh! it's all the same to me whether I have it, or whether I don't, — if I do it once a fortnight it's as much as I care about, — you beasts of men seem to think of nothing else, and you leave us poor women all the trouble that comes from putting your muck into us." "What the devil do you care about?" said I, after a chat with her one day in which she had just said what I have narrated. "Oh! I don't care about anything much."

Another day she said, "I like a nice dinner, and then a read in an arm-chair till I go to sleep, or a nice bit of supper, and to get into bed, — I'm so tired of a night, I like to get to bed early if I can." We went on talking about eating and drinking; she told me what she liked and what she disliked with much gusto and earnestness. "I'll give you a good dinner," said I, "and we will come here afterwards." "Will you?" "Yes, — but I won't unless I have you three hours here." "Impossible, — I dare not be out after half-past ten." "Come early." "I can't come very early, for I must be home in the afternoon." There were all sorts of obstacles, — so many that I gave it up, not going to be humbugged. But *she* would not give it up, and it was arranged that if she might name the evening, she would be with me at six o'clock, and stay with me till ten, — an immense concession, — it was the dinner that did it. I saw she was fond of her stomach, and that made me offer the dinner as a bait.

She would not come in after me to the restaurant, I was to meet her at the corner of St. Martin's Lane in a cab, and go with her, — and so it came off. We went to the Café de P°°v°°°e in Leicester Square, I had already ordered a private room, and a nice dinner. My God how she enjoyed it! "It's a long time since I've had such a good dinner," said she, "but never mind, better times are coming again for me, I feel sure." She ate largely, she drank well, and to my astonishment when I got up to kiss her, she kissed me in return, and gave my piercer the slightest possible pinch outside my trowsers. "Let's feel you," said I. Equally astonished was I when

she said, "Bolt the door, the waiter may be in," — and then I had
a grope, and she felt my prick. "Let's go, — let's go, — I am dying
for you." Off we went arm in arm. Directly we were well away from
the Café she let go my arm. "You go first, and I will follow." I
thought she was going to cheat me. "I dare not be seen walking arm
in arm with a man, — but I will follow." In five minutes we were in
the room together. Sarah Mavis was just in the slightest degree
elevated, and perhaps more than slightly lewed.

To pull off my things, to help her off with hers partially, was
the work of a minute. "I must piddle first, — champagne always
makes me want to piddle so." "Does it make you randy?" "Oh! Lord
it does sometimes; but it's such a time since I tasted it before to-
night, I almost· forget." "Are you so now?" "Oh! I don't know, —
come on the bed," said she. She opened her thighs wide, she let me
grope and smell, and kiss, and see. "Come on, — do." Instinct told
me she wanted it, I embraced her, and was enjoying her, when
she clasped me firmly, sought my mouth. "Oh! my darling, I'm
co — com — h — hing," said she, spending as she cried out, and
fetched me at the same instant. It was the first time she had ever
spent with me.

We laid in heavenly quietness, prick and cunt in holy junction,
distilling, slobbering, and bedewing each other's mouths and pri-
vates, whilst the soft voluptuous pleasure was creeping through our
limbs, bodies, and senses. She was in no hurry to wash out the
muck. "Oh! I'm choking," said she after a time, "get off." "I won't."
"Oh! do, — my stays choke me when I lie down after food, — I'm
almost suffocated." I held fast. "If I get off, you won't let me do it
again." "Yes, — yes I will." She jerked my prick out of her cunt,
I got to the side of the bed, she sat up, and was about to get off,
when I stopped her, and together we undid her stays, and took
them off. "Let me wash now." "No, you shan't, — I've never yet
fucked with my first sperm in you, — let me now, there is a darling."
She laughed, and fell back; then for a few minutes we kissed and
toyed. Her magnificent breasts were now free, I buried my face
between them, and kissed them rapturously; her moistened quim
I felt, and it drove me wild with desire; so gluing my mouth to hers
I mounted her, and we were soon in Elysium again, Sarah enjoying
her fuck in a way I thought from her cold-blooded manner previ-

ously she was quite incapable of, — and there we laid, nestling cock and cunt together, till a slight sleep or doze overtook both of us.

In a minute or two Sarah sprang up, and rushed to the basin. I lay still, contemplating her, and saying I would not wash my prick for a week, so that I might retain in the roots and its moistened fringe our mixed juices, the remnants of our first spend together. When she had washed, she laid down by the side of me. "Let's have a nap," said she. The wine seemed to be getting into her head more and more, though she was but in the slightest degree fuddled.

I could not sleep. The sight of her breasts relieved from her stays, the free manner in which she let her petticoats lay half up her thighs, the delight at finding her take pleasure in my embraces exulted me beyond measure. I joked and tickled her. "Let's see you naked." "You shan't." "Well, stand up, and let me see your limbs naked, — take off your petticoats, even if you keep your chemise on." She was yielding, took petticoats off, but would do no more. I had seen more than any other man, and she would do no more, she said. The wine had evaporated, and she was herself again, quiet, composed.

Maddened with desire, "I'll give you a sovereign," I said, "to take the chemise off." "Will you?" "Yes." "No, I won't." "I'll give you two." "What can you want to see more for?" "Hang it, take the money, and let me, or I'll rip it off without paying." I closed with her, and struggled, pulled the chemise up above her haunches, pulled it down below her breasts, tore it. "Now don't, — I won't have it," said she, getting angry, "it won't please you if I do, — you will not like to see me half as well afterwards, I tell you." "Yes I shall, — here is the money, — now let me see you naked, — I'll give you three sovereigns."

She pushed me away, and sat down. "Where is the money?" said she. I gave it her. "I've got an ugly scar, — I don't like it seen." "Never mind, — show it." Slowly she dropped the chemise, and stood in all her naked beauty, and pointing to a scar just below her breasts, and about four inches above her navel, "There," said she, "is it not ugly? — does it not spoil me! — how I hate it!"

I told her no, — that she was so beautiful that it mattered not. Yet ugly it was. A seam looking like a piece of parchment which had been held close to a fire and crinkled, and then glazed, star-shaped, white, and as big as a large egg lay between her breasts and her navel. It was the only defect on one of the most perfect and beautiful forms that God ever had created.

"There," said she, covering it up, "you won't want me naked again, — now I dare say you don't like me as much." Yes I did. "Do you?" "Yes." She came and kissed me. I often had her as naked as she was born afterwards.

"What is the time?" "Ten o'clock." "I must go." "Another poke." "Make haste then." We had it. "Oh! now don't keep me, — if I'm not home by half-past ten I shall be half murdered." She had let expressions like that drop more than once; but I got no explanation excepting that she lived with her father and mother, — and at that time I believed it.

At the next meeting she had her old quiet manner, her old "keep your distance" was attempted; but it was impossible. A woman must always give again what she has once given, she cannot help it. Then came more dinners, but she was more cautious now in what she eat and drank, less reckless in her embraces of me; but we were closer acquaintances than we had been; she let me pull her about more freely and as a matter of course, washed her quim without hiding herself for that operation, and so on, — yet still she held me at a great distance, and was reserved. She conquered me, in a degree.

In fact she did pretty well what she liked with me; saw me when she liked, stopped with me as long as she thought proper, let me fuck her just as often as she liked and no more (and it was rarely she let me do that more than once a day), see to her knees, or to her cunt, or pull her about just in the degree she for the time thought fit to permit. I grumbled, said I would see more complaisant women. Well I might if I liked, — but I did not. Her indifference to sexual pleasure chilled and annoyed me and for a reason I never could understand, her cunt never seemed quite to fit me, nor fetch me with the voluptuousness that scores of other women have done. Yet I saw her almost exclusively for three years, and when she gave herself up to pleasure with me, my delight was unbounded; when she let me have her with her cunt unwashed after our first copulation, I thought of it for days afterwards. Altogether she had her way with me in a manner I did not see, and have only comprehended since.

This went on for some months. Whether she had other male friends or not I don't know, but I never found her in Regent Street or other places where I had once been able to find her, after I began to see her regularly, and have reason to think that she ceased casuals after she had me, and perchance another, that is all. Hannah said often at a future day that I was her only friend.

I have not yet described her. She was of perfect height for a woman, say five feet seven, her form from her chin to her toe-nails was faultless, if anything inclining to too much flesh, and to too great a backside; but then I liked flesh, and a woman's bum could not be too big for me. I used to rub my lips and cheeks over her bum for a quarter of an hour at a time, when she condescended to turn it upwards for so long a time for that worship. Handsome her face certainly was, but it was of a somewhat heavy character: her eyes were dark, soft, and vague in expression which together with the habit of leaving her lips slightly open, gave her a thoughtful, and at times half-vacant look. Her nose was charming and *retroussé*, her mouth small, with full lips, and a delicious set of very small white teeth, her hair was nearly black, long, thick, and coarsish dark hair in large quantity was in her armpits, and showed slightly when her arms were down, her arms and breasts were superb. Her cunt was thick-lipped, and with largish inner lips which showed well on nearly the whole length of the split; her mons was very plump, and covered well, but not widely, with crisp black hair. She looked twenty-six, yet was not more than twenty-two, and she looked most handsome when lying asleep.

If I were asked the most perfect thing about her, I should say her feet and legs up to her notch — they were simply perfect; I have seen them as handsome in smaller women, never in one of her height. I must add that her cunt was large both outside and inside, and that she was not a voluptuous poke to me, but why I can only guess at now; I did not know it whilst I was acquainted with her.

"A little of that satisfies me," she would say of poking, "once a week, — once a fortnight, excepting at times, — you men are beasts, all of you." She at first refused my mouth, never moved her bum, and laid like a log. "Here I am, — do what you like, — do it, and get it over, — or leave it," was her common mode of meeting my grumbling. Her first sexual pleasure with me was, I believe, the night she dined with me; afterwards she took pleasure with me more frequently, but uncunting me and rushing out of bed to wash the instant I had spent, before I had indeed done spending; until a sudden change in her took place which I shall tell of, and then she was kinder, more lustful, or perhaps I might say more loving, and more reckless; letting me enjoy her after my own fashion, and abandoning herself to enjoyment as much as it was perhaps in her nature to do so.

I found that she often now was with the keeper of the house, or rather she who represented her, — Hannah. So I got acquainted more closely with Hannah, would go into her parlour, and talk with her before Sarah came. This began one day when I was awaiting Sarah by her asking me if I would cast up a column of figures, nearly the whole of which was in five shillings and seven and sixes. I did it once, then I did it a second time. Going in one day just afterwards, she stepped out from her parlour and thanked me. I stepped into the parlour, and got into the custom of doing so, — if ladies were not in there, — but there was a good introduction business done, as will be seen, and often-times ladies were waiting there till their swains arrived.

One day she cooked a luncheon for me, once a breakfast, the latter was during the time I had quarrelled with Sarah, and took another woman to sleep with me there. I complimented her on her cooking, she was half groggy (as she often was), and was very talkative. "Lord," said she, "you have tasted my dinners many a times." "Nonsense." "Yes you have." "Where?" "Do you recollect a ball at °°°°, where all the servants were allowed to look at the table before supper, and your coming down with Mr. °°°, and we all scuffling back?" "Perfectly." "Well, I cooked that supper." Then it turned out that she had been cook at a house where I was a constant visitor, she had recognized me at once, but did not recollect my name, or so she said, — indeed it was not probable that she knew it. She had been caught with a soldier in the house, and had been kicked out.

Now by chance of fortune she was keeper of a baudy house, and her soldier visited her there when in London, — he was a Guardsman, — and she supplied him with money, and lots he had, for she robbed her Mistress wholesale of the baudy house profits.

Hannah had two sisters, one a married woman with a bad husband, and several children. She often came and assisted at J°°°'s

Street, sometimes acting a chambermaid, — and about two years after this period of my history a second one appeared who had been a housemaid, and who had I suppose also lost her character. A pretty blue-eyed girl about twenty years old with a cast in her eye, and a lovely leg up to within a few inches of her cunt. I never saw higher, and shall have more to say about her hereafter. Her name was Susan — a sailor was said to be in love with her.

Sarah at the end of some months asked me to give her five pounds, and soon afterwards ten pounds. She was going to make up a sum of money to buy a business for her father. She had been dressing very shabbily I noticed, and said she knew I did not mind that, and it was all because she was trying to save money, — to quit that life she hoped, — and I believed it. I could not get her for several days, yet could have sworn I had heard her voice one day in loud altercation with a man in the parlour when I was waiting for her upstairs. I rang and asked for her; the servant came, and asserted that Miss Mavis was not there, and I never saw her that night. Next day I made an appointment (through Hannah) for eleven a.m., and waited a long time before she came up. She looked ill. "You've been crying." "I have not." "Yes you have, — your eyes are red, — aye, and wet now." She asserted she had not, and then burst out sobbing saying she was unwell. I was distressed, and sent for wine. Hannah came up and comforted her (I saw Hannah knew all about it). Then we were left to ourselves. "I've never been a bed all night," said Sarah. "Come to bed now." To my extreme astonishment *into* bed she came, after looking at me in a very earnest manner.

I had often asked her before, and she never would; saying she never had been in bed but with one man, and never meant. I was enraptured, stripped to my skin, and was soon pressing every part of her body to mine. She gave herself up to me entirely, her tongue met mine as we spent. "Don't throw me out now dear." "Very well." Oh! miracle, I thought, and there we lay, prick and cunt soaking together, till we had another fuck, then she dozed off in my arms, and I soon afterwards. We slept more than two hours, then my fingers sought her cunt directly and awakened her. I told her the time, she sighed saying, "It's no matter, — it serves them right." It was a day of miracles, Hannah sent up food, we eat it in bed, we fucked again and again. I was delighted with the spunk we left on the sheets; then we dined at the Café, and went back to the baudy house, — more fucking, no cunt-washing, all was free, baudy abandonment.

Hannah came up to us about the time Sarah usually left me, and told her it was time to go. Sarah said she did not care a damn, Hannah begged her to go, — she would go home with her. She agreed to go, kissed me, and said I was a kind fellow. I waited outside, and tried to dodge her home; but was unsuccessful; the two discovered me, stopped, and upbraided me, and came back to the baudy house. Then she made me promise not to follow her, and went out to piddle as she said. Hannah followed, I waited five minutes for them, and then called to the servant. She came in with a demure face, and said, "Lor sir they have both gone out five minutes ago."

For weeks after that Sarah was changed, and with the exception of not stripping entirely, did as freely as I wished, she did everything I wanted but sleep with me all night; she kept out later, but away at night she went; she embraced me, enjoyed her fucking, and in fact treated me like a husband. Then she said one day, "I'm some months gone in the family way." "Who's the dad?" "You perhaps." "No I'm not, — it's some man you are fond of, not me." "I am fond of no man," said she. Then she was ill, and away for three weeks, she had had a miscarriage. I was in despair, and sent her money all the time of her illness, but could learn nothing from Hannah, excepting that Sarah was a dear good woman, and too good for him. That was said before the sister, who cried out, "You shut up, Hannah." So I came to the conclusion there was some other man in the way.

Another day I pumped Hannah, but she was an old bird, and not easily caught. "She is fond of a man," I said. "She is not a fond sort, — if she is fond of any man at all it's you, — but she has got her duty to do." "What's that?" "Ask her, — I don't know her business. Now you get out, there are some ladies coming here directly, and Miss Mavis won't like your being here with them." "I'm not her property." "Pretty nearly you are, — at all events go, there is a good gentleman." Whilst Sarah was away I did get acquainted with three or four ladies, and two of them I had. Sarah had then either gone abroad, or I had had a desperate quarrel with her.

When Sarah met me again she was still miserably ill, and

thanked me for my kindness warmly. We resumed our meetings, and again she was cautious, but no longer bounced me. She spent with me, enjoyed me, but entreated me, "Oh! let me wash out the muck, — now do pull it out, — I am so frightened of being ill again." So I let her have her way. She refused to say anything about her illness, excepting that it was I who had caused it; but I did not believe her. She usually now gave way to pleasure with me; at the end of the month I gave her twenty pounds to make up a sum, then she got still more exacting about money. "Oh! I do stop a long time with you, — give me more money, — do, — I want to make up a sum," &c., &c., — and then of course came a lie. At length she said (one bright sunny morning it was, I had poked her, and was laying on the sofa afterwards, she sitting on the easy-chair, her lovely breasts out, one beautiful leg over the other showing slightly the flesh of her thighs), "You won't see much more of me, — we are going abroad."

I started as if I had been shot at. "You? — nonsense, — never." "I am indeed, — I'm sick of this life, and will go anywhere, do anything to get out of it."

I sank back on the sofa sobbing, it came home to me all at once that I was madly in love with her. I was dazed with my own discovery, — I in love with a gay woman! one whose cunt might have had a thousand pricks up it! who might have sprung from any dung-hill! — impossible! I felt mad with myself, — degraded! — impossible, — it could not be, — and for a time I conquered myself. I tried then to draw her out about herself. It was useless. Her quiet way of asserting that she *was* going at length brought home the conviction that she spoke the truth. Then I laid and sobbed on the sofa for half-an-hour. "Oh! you will soon get another friend," said she. "No, no, — I can get a woman, but not one I shall like, — Sarah my darling, Sarah I love you, — I dote on you, — oh! for God's sake don't leave, — come with me, — you shan't lead this life, — we will go abroad together."

"That is impossible, — if I did you would leave me, and then what should I do? — come back to this life, — no." "You are going with somebody else, — who?" "I can't say, — I'll tell you when I am gone." "When are you going?" "Perhaps in a fortnight, perhaps a little later on."

I calmed for a time, a fortnight might give me a chance of

persuading her, and I began it at once; but it was all, "No, — no, — no, — it's all for the best for both of us," — and again I fell into deep despair, my heart felt breaking, I had been so happy with this woman for months, she had so filled my thoughts, so occupied my spare time, that I had half forgotten my home life. Now I felt alone again, I had told her some of my troubles, — not all, — now I poured them all out, and offered everything, — all I had, — to go that next day abroad, and never return; that I would make her love me though she did not now, I promised all man could promise, — and meant it.

"No, — no, — impossible," — and again I fell back on the sofa sobbing like an infant. I have almost the deadly heart-ache now as I write this. She sat looking at me for some time, then she arose, stooped over me, and kissed me. I turned round, and — how strange that in my despair I noticed it, and now recollect noticing it! — as she stooped her chemise opened, and as I put my arm round her, her breasts touched my face, and as I moved to kiss them I saw her whole lovely form down to her feet, the dark hair of her motte, the bright white scar; and all in the soft subdued light which is on a woman's body when enveloped in a thin chemise, — and my prick stood whilst kissing her and sobbing, and she was soothing me.

"It's of no use your loving me," she said, "and it's of no use my loving you, — don't take on so, — perhaps when I am gone you will be happier at home, — I can't love you, although I like you very much, for you have been a good, kind man to me, — I nearly do love you I think, — if I were with you I'm sure I should, — but it's of no use, for I am a married woman, and have two children, and am going with them and my husband."

I was amazed, and doubted it. "I'll bring you my children to see," said she, "it was to get them their dinners and tea that I always left you at times as I have." "And at night?"

"I always go home before he comes home." "You always go home to your husband?" "Yes."

How I loathed that man! — my loathing rose to my lips, "That miserable contemptible cur lives by your body, — a dirty vagabond." "No he's not, — poor fellow, he would earn our living if he could, but he can't." "I don't believe it, — a man who lives by a woman is barely a man, — I would empty cesspools to keep a woman I loved, rather than another man should stroke her, — no good can come of it, — he'll leave you for some other woman some day." Sarah turned nasty, said she was sorry she had told me so much, that all I said against him only made her like him the more; and so leaving me in sorrow she went away.

Now that I felt sure she was going away, I could not see too much of her; morning, noon, and night I had her. She brought her two children to me, and very proud she was of them. How it was I never noticed the marks of childbirth on her before I know not, but I never had. I spoke of that now. "I took good care you should not," she said smiling, and I recollected that when I had her by the side of the bed, when I looked at her on the sofa, it was nearly always with her back to the light; when laying on the bed, and I tried to gratify my passion by opening her thighs and gazing on her hidden charms, she nearly always half-turned towards the window, and her belly was in shadow. "I don't like to be pulled about, — I won't have it, — if you want me have me, and have done with it, — get another woman if you like who will do it, or allow it, — I won't." These and similar answers always settled me, and I submitted, for I was under her domination, and in my folly I had actually feared that if I persisted, she would not come to see me.

She brought her children in the morning to me at J°°°s Street, and I had her that afternoon. Now she was free enough, pointed herself to the marks of childbirth (very slight they were), and voluptuously held her cunt lips open, — she had never done so before. From that day and afterwards she allowed me to see her in every way or manner, if not to let me do what I wished. The mystery was over, I knew most if not all, — certainly all about her person.

Poses plastiques. — Sarah departs. — My despair. — Hannah's comfort. — Foolscap and masturbation. — Cheap cunt. — A mulatto. — The baudy house accounts. — Concerning Sarah. — The parlour. — The gay ladies there. — My virtue. — Louisa Fisher. — A show of legs. — The consequence on me. — Effect on Mrs. Z°°i.

I dined with Sarah repeatedly until her departure. She was now often in low spirits, and drank very freely of champagne; then would fuck with a passion and energy which did not seem natural to her, for by look and general manner one would have sworn she was even tempered, and without much passion, — had I not found that out by experience? One night soon after she had brought her children to me, she seemed wild with lust. What was the matter with me I don't know, but I had no desire for her, and could scarcely stiffen for the embrace; yet she was in ecstasies with me as I fucked her. "Do it again," said she. "I can't." "You must do it, — I've not washed." "I can't." "Yes, — yes, — I'm mad for you," said she, — and we kept on fucking till early the next morning. "I am in the family way again I think," said she as she left, "and if so will jump over Westminster Bridge." But she was not, and after that night she persuaded me not to spend in her, but to withdraw just as my emission took place. "It will spoil all my plans if I am in the family way," said she, "all I have done will be of no use if I cannot act." "Act?" "Yes, I am an actress." "Does not your husband spend in you?" "No one has spent in me but you since my miscarriage, — I won't let him, and he doesn't want me in the family way."

"You an actress!" "Yes, — have you never see me?" "No." "Are you sure?" "Yes." "Did you ever see the *Poses plastiques* and Madame W°°°t°n?" "Yes, two or three years ago." "Well I was one of her

191

troupe." "Good God! — and what do you do now?" "Nothing, — but we have a troupe going on the Continent, — I am the principal, — I am Madame W°°°t°n now."

Then she told me she had in her youth been a model for artists, had sat to Etty and Frost, hers was the form which had been painted in many of their pictures, — and then she would say no more.

I grew sadder and sadder as the time came for her departure; so did she. She said I worried and unsettled her; she wondered sometimes if she were doing the best thing for herself and children, or not. She was so frightened lest she should get in the family way that as already said she made me withdraw before the critical moment, spending my sperm on her thighs or on the crisp hair of her motte. I got an idea into my head (a stupid one enough), that if she were to get in the family way by me she would stay in London; and one night after we had dined, and she had had pleasure in my groping, and as usual had said, "Now don't do it in me," I plunged my prick up, and spent a full stream in her cunt. "I hope to God that sperm's all up your womb," said I. Her own pleasure had so overcome her that she could not move for a minute; then jumping up she washed herself with a sponge, — she recently had used one. I never had a spend in her again for months afterwards.

Then for hours I used to look her over and over from head to foot, as if I wished to recollect every part of her person for ever afterwards: the roots of her hair, her ears, the way the hair grew on the nape of her neck; the way it grew on her cunt, and in her armpits, and every other part I used to look over as if searching for something; the only part of her which escaped my investigations was the bum-furrow, which was to me an uncomfortable part in all women, and in my wildest sexual ecstasies and aberrations I neither felt it nor saw it, and don't know whether the hole was round or square, red or brown.

After she had told me she had sat as a model, she brought me a small oil-painting of herself made by an artist of some rank. She was proud of it, and so was her husband. I offered such a price for it that placed as she was she could not resist, and I bought it. She gave me one day a photograph of herself; both had the characteristic opening of the lips well shown. It is only recently that I have destroyed these mementos of a dead affection.

When I saw that nothing would keep her in England, I did my best to help her enterprise, gave her money freely, paid for dresses, boots, travelling cloaks, children's dresses, and in brief, for everything. During the nine months I had known her she in fact ran me dry, and in debt. I spent upon her more than I could have lived on for four years at the rate I lived at just before I met her. But I was now in better circumstances than I had been for years, and the money was my own.

As the time approached, I could neither sleep nor eat, and used to be at J°°°s Street hours before I knew she could come; would wait any time for her, treating Hannah and the ladies, and doing nothing but talk about Sarah. Sometimes I used to think about following her abroad. When she came to the house, I used to spend my time in crying, and she after telling me not to be foolish, would cry too. Then, "Oh! let me see you naked." "There then." Then came kisses all over her body. "Oh! now for God's sake don't spend in me." Then came a delicious fuck; then crying and moaning recommenced. She left a week at least before she had said she should, and did so to prevent me the pain of parting with her, — I must give her that credit. Hannah told me so.

I had arranged to meet her one morning, and was as usual there before my time. Hannah stepped out from the parlour. "Has Sarah come?" She beckoned me into the parlour. "Why, they all sailed this morning, — my sister went to see them off, — did you not know?" I staggered to the sofa dizzy, speechless, then senseless. When I came to myself, Hannah was standing beside me with brandy and water and a spoon with which she was putting it into my mouth.

"Don't take on so," said she, "don't think any more about Sarah, — she is a fine woman, but there are lots as good, — I know a dozen, and any one would be glad to know a man like you, — have some brandy and water," — and she took a great gulp herself. "There now," said she, bending over me, "would you like to see Mrs. °°°°; — she who met you the other night in here with Sarah, — she has taken quite a fancy to you, — don't cry. Sarah will come back, and if she don't you'll get another woman whom you will like as well. There is Mrs. °°°°, a splendid shaped woman who only sees one gentleman here, — she took quite a fancy to you, though she only saw you once." But I was desperate, and rushed out of the house. Where I went to, I don't even recollect, but went home at last very drunk, — an extraordinary occurrence for me.

For some days I was prostrate in mind, and almost in body, but at length recovered sufficiently to attend a little to my affairs which had gone altogether to the bad for a month, and had been going bad for many months. I resolutely set myself against going to J°°°s Street, and would not have women; indeed scarcely knew where to lay my hand on a shilling, so necessity had perhaps as much to do with my virtue as anything else; but I was generally in a weak, low state of health, and really believe, though it seems to me almost incredible now, that it was well nigh three weeks before I touched or saw a cunt after Sarah left.

Then one Sunday I had erections all day long. After dinner lust drove me nearly mad, so I went to my room, took a clean sheet of white paper, and frigged myself over it. My prick only slightly subsided, I frigged again, and then as the paper lay before me covered with sperm-pools I cried because it was not up my dear Sarah's vagina, laid my head on the table where the paper lay, and sobbed with despair, jealousy, and regrets, for I thought some one would fuck her if I did not, that it would be her hateful husband whom she had helped to keep with my money.

I may say here that on several occasions of my life I have frigged myself over a clean sheet of foolscap paper; it was mostly done for curiosity, to see what my sperm was like, whether it was as thin, or as thick, or as large in quantity as at the last time I previously had masturbated.

I could not after that Sunday keep away from J°°°s Street, and went there the next day. "I don't expect she'll write to you," said Hannah, "even if she said she would, — what will be the use? — it will only make you miserable." But I felt sure she would; and kept away from women still for some time after that, — I was stumped for money among other reasons. Then I began to spend involuntarily in the night, which to me was more hateful than frigging myself; so one night I went out for a bit of cheap quim.

I went first into the streets near a large well-known tavern at a spot where several big thoroughfares meet, and where there is a large traffic, and picked up my cheap women there. But the women, their chemises and petticoats, and their rooms shocked me more than they used, and kept me chaster than I otherwise might have been.

One night I went home with a tall straight woman who would not take my fee. "No," said she, "I've got two nice little rooms of my own." If you get a woman for five shillings you have to pay for the room besides, and ten shillings is only a small sum; so I went with her for ten shillings, and saw her at intervals for a few months.

She was about five feet nine high, was not stout, was as straight as a lath, yet not thin, had very firm but quite small breasts, and a biggish bum. She had mulatto blood in her veins she told me, and was brown-skinned, had a large mouth and *very* thick lips, the Negro blood showed there plainly; her hair was dark, and so were her eyes; her cunt was a pouter: it was small, but the lips pouted out more thickly I think than those of any woman I ever yet saw, yet they were not flabby, but protruded largely like two halves of a sausage; the hair was black, short, and intensely crisp and curly; it felt like curled horse-hair. I used to think her a plain woman, one of the plainest, but she was a glorious fuckster; her cunt was tight inside, and yet so elastic as not to hurt or pinch (and I was at that time when just at spunking point as often said before tender-pricked). The hair of her head was coarse yet straight, her large mouth was filled with teeth of a splendid whiteness, and when she smiled she showed the whole set. It was seeing her large white teeth that first attracted me before I could distinguish any other feature of the face; you could see them at night right across a road, they were dazzling, and almost made one forget the great thick-lipped orifice which opened to expose them. I have before told of women who attracted me by their teeth, and particularly of a creole.

This *mulatto* as I called her, amused me with her lecherous postures; she was as lithe as a willow branch, and was willing to please. I was fond of making her kneel on the bed with bum towards me, and her legs nearly close together, and then the backward pout of her cunt was charming to me, so much so that I took to poking her dog-fashion.

One night when I was full of sperm I made her remain in the exact posture until all my spunk had run out of her cunt, and sat holding a candle towards her rump till I was satisfied with the sight; and more than once I kept her in that position, looking at the gruelly lips until I fucked her a second time.

She had such a very remarkable steady walk that she scarcely seemed to move, she glided, her feet were so nicely carried forward, and her body so evenly balanced from her hips. In this respect she resembled a talk dark woman named Fletcher, whom I knew quite recently. There must have been something in the arrangement of their thighs and hips which caused this. Women who are accustomed to carry heavy loads on their heads always walk straight, and never roll from side to side as most people more or less do; but I don't know that either of the women named had carried baskets on their heads, — I knew the walk of that class of women, having been born in the neighbourhood where they worked.

She, I imagine, had a liking for my doing it naked with her, for she was always suggesting that we should strip, but she could not bear my fucking her dog-fashion. When I stripped and got into her on her belly, she would twist her legs right into mine in quite a snaky fashion, and sometimes lift her legs up till her heels were almost up to my blade-bones. She also, like a few others I have poked, seemed to have the power of holding my prick in her cunt quite tightly after I had spent, — perhaps because she had not spent herself, for about her pleasures in the copulation I am not sure, though she always impressed me as being a hot-cunted one.

After I had once been to J°°°'s Street again I went more and more frequently. Hannah was always nearly screwed, — champagne or brandy pleased her best. When she was so, she would at times gradually let out much that she knew, — and this is what she let out one day.

"Bah! her husband indeed! — she is not married, — he's got a wife besides, and Sarah knows it, — he's blackened his wife's eyes more than once when she has been annoying them; but that don't pay, for she is his lawful wife, so he allows her something, and it keeps her quiet, and she won't last long, for she is drunk from daybreak till night. Sarah's a real good one to keep the lazy beggar, — she keeps them all, poor thing, ever since he could not get any engagement; there's she, and their children, and her sister, who lives with them, and then there is her old mother who she keeps, and his wife as well, — she has enough to do, poor thing." This came out one day after Hannah had dined; I had brought her a bottle of specially fine brandy, and we were sitting in the parlour drinking it together, mixed with water.

I had long been getting into Hannah's good graces. I stood wine and brandy, was always respectful to her and the gay ladies I met in her parlour, and never used coarse, rude language to them, nor in speaking of them or of ladies of their class. Hannah told me I was a great favorite with several of them, as indeed I found to be the case. I may say that all my life I never spoke disrespectfully to or of gay ladies, so long as they behaved themselves; they have been mostly throughout my life, kind and true to me after their fashion, they gave me pleasure, and I treated them as if I was grateful for it.

But I was moreover serviceable to Hannah. Once or twice as told she had brought me some figures to cast up, and when Sarah had left, she brought me others on various little scraps of paper. She asked me never to mention my having done so to her sister, and I did not. I became curious at finding the items were all in five shillings, seven and sixpence, ten and twenty shillings; at last it struck me what it was, and taxing her with it found it was the takings of the baudy house. She told me so with a laugh. She could not write herself.

The takings were put on slips of paper by the servants, and by some process of her own which she could not explain, she got a rough sort of check on the servants to prevent them robbing her. She had to account to the real owner of the house, — and how she did it she alone knows. This is certain (she once admitted it), that from the takings she put a pound a day into her own pocket. Whether she robbed the owner to that extent, or whether it was her admitted share I never knew. She was well dressed, had excellent food, allowed her Guardsman money, her sister's husband money, and others too I rather think. But after she had taken her three or four hundred pounds a year, there was a splendid income handed over to some one. This house had but eight rooms and two mere closets, to let out for fucking; they often took twenty pounds a day, and sometimes much more.

I did this arithmetic pretty regularly, and she became my fast friend. She told me all about Sarah that she knew (what Sarah at a future day told me agreed with it), and much about the habits of other loose ladies which will be partially narrated in due time, and a good deal about baudy house management.

And now more about Sarah's antecedents. A new species of entertainment had sprung into existence a few years before this time, called *Poses plastiques*, in which men and women covered with silk fitting tightly to their naked limbs and made quite white, placed themselves on stages in classical groups to the sound of music. Women and men of great physical beauty formed these groups, they were in fact actors of that class. Madame W°°°t°n, known as a splendid model, first got them up; her husband was a splendid man, Sarah was her niece, and also had the beautiful form which ran in the family; she was poor, and Madame W°°°t°n took her to live with them, and at seventeen years of age she appeared as Venus.

At nineteen she had a child by Madame W°°°t°n's husband, at twenty a second. Madame found out the father, and kicked Sarah out. Mr. W°°°t°n then kicked Madame out, and went to live with Sarah, rows ensued, other companies of *Poses plastiques* came into competition, the thing got overdone, he could not get his living; he knew a trade, but was I expect too lazy to work at it; so Sarah took to letting herself out as model, and that being poor pay, to letting out her cunt to get their bread; she had just begun it when I first met her. They seem during a year or more to have parted with all their goods, before she took to showing her belly-parting for money.

So beautiful a form of course succeeded, and for a time I became the principal milk-cow. Then a proposition was made to form a troupe to go to the Continent; there seemed to be a grand opening, and with Sarah's money (most of it got from me), the apparatus, costumes, properties, and troupe were got together. Off they had gone. She and her husband were the exhibition-managers, speculators, and chief actors.

Hannah made a mouth when I asked what sort of a man Mavis was. She did not think much of him, — why did he not work? — he had a trade? — No, because he was no longer able to get on as an actor, he preferred to let Sarah get the living for the whole of them. "Ah! you'll see her back, mark my words, — they won't succeed, — and then what will take place? — you'll see, — is she, poor thing, to work and do everything, that he may lay a bed, dress as a gentleman, and do nothing but take her out for a walk on a Sunday; she is as proud of his taking her out for a walk on a Sunday as if he kept her a carriage." After much reflexion I came to the conclusion that Sarah had only just turned harlot about the time I had first met her, that she did it to keep her man and her family, and he got accustomed to his woman getting his living for him.

I kept on calling at J°°°s Street, always expecting to hear of Sarah. Hannah was glad to see me, for now I cast up her accounts weekly. I got acquainted with two or three ladies there who came at intervals to meet their friends. They were very nice women, none were ever to be seen in the streets, they had either their own acquaintances whom they met at J°°°s Street, or Hannah had introduced them to gentlemen there. They were not a bit like whores in dress, appearance or manners, and my acquaintance with them opened my mind to the fact that there is a large amount of occult fucking going on with needy, middle-class women, whose mode of living and dressing is a mystery to their friends, and who mingle with their own class of society without its being suspected that their cunts are ever wetted by sperm which lawfully may not be put there.

I began to stand wine when I met them, and was introduced as a friend of Miss Mavis who had gone abroad. I was, I found, well known by name and character for kindness, and I expect also for being a fool. All the women were shy at first, Hannah's sister (the servant), I overheard telling Hannah that the ladies did not like my being in the parlour. Hannah at times would ask me to leave, as a lady wanted to come into the parlour and wait there, and so on. But gradually Hannah would say, "Who is it? — oh! she knows him," — or "Oh! she won't mind, — let her come in." So by degrees I became intimate with these privately gay ladies, and several of them on more than one occasion joined their sweet bodies to mine in the game of under and over.

I had never had a woman in the house since Sarah had gone; firstly because I did then not pay more for the girls than I did for the room alone at J°°°s Street, and because I feared if Sarah came back Hannah would tell her, — as if it would have mattered to Sarah in any way excepting that another woman would get the

money she might have had. Still I had that stupid idea about the
matter, and although I had longed for one or two of the other ladies,
and although they had looked languishingly at me, I never had
then proposed a private interview upstairs.

One day Hannah said she had heard from Sarah who had
asked after me. "They are (Sarah and the troupe) getting on well,"
said Hannah. "If she says so I suppose they are, — but we shall
see." Suddenly, "Have you had another woman since she left?" The
question startled me. "No." "Oh! I don't believe it, — if you haven't
you're a nasty man." Then I confessed, and told her what I had
done. "Why don't you have Mrs. Fisher?" said she. "I'm poor, and
can't, — I'm not going to do what I did with Sarah." "Lord she
won't mind, — she'd like you, I know, — but don't say I said so, —
she's got a lovely leg, — she's a fine woman, — nearly as fine made
as Sarah Mavis, and she is taller, — she never gets it done at home."
Hannah was unusually muddled with liquor that day, and let out, —
her sister was not there to check her with "Now then Hannah
you'd better shut up," — and Hannah described Mrs. Fisher's hid-
den charms till my cock stood.

I would pass hours sketching from recollection Sarah Mavis'
limbs and form, her bum and cunt being the most favorite subjects;
then so randy that I did not know what to do with myself, I would
rush out into the streets to prevent my frigging myself, — and erotic
night-dreams were frequent.

"Why don't you see Mrs. Z°°i," said Hannah to me, "she likes
you, and would come up any day if I wrote to her (I had supped
two or three times with that lady), — I would not fret about
Sarah, although she is a fine woman, — you let her see you have
another woman, and she will come round if she comes back." But
I did not for a time.

One afternoon, however, being in the parlour, Mrs. Z°°i was
there, a splendid woman about twenty-six years old. Also was there
a young woman who had two children by a man with whom she
was about to go abroad, and she was a lovely woman. The two
ladies had just had a two o'clock dinner with Hannah, I had just
come from my Club after luncheon, and sent for champagne. All
our talk got frisky, — all knew Sarah, my love. If I could get any
one to talk with me about her, I was delighted, and began at it.
Said the Mistress, "Well, she is a splendid-formed woman certainly,

— splendid, but there are lots of others, — I've a good leg to my knee, so has Mrs. Z°°i, and Mrs. °°° (meaning the other whose name I forget). "Show us your leg," said one. "There," said Hannah, pulling up her clothes, "now show yours." They all showed their limbs, one after another. "You might fancy you had Sarah's legs round your thighs, if you had Mrs. Z°°i's there," said Hannah. I was nigh bursting for a fuck. Mrs. Z°°i pulled her clothes up higher, and stood up to show the leg better; the other ladies did the same. I felt my pleasure coming, and objecting to wet my shirt, began to unbutton. "Oh! I can't bear it," I cried, "oh! my God I'm coming," — and the instant my prick was free from my trowsers I spent copiously, the three women their petticoats still up nearly to their cunts, looking and laughing. I had not frigged, it was fullness, and the voluptuous delight at seeing the limbs of the three fine women which fetched me. "There is lots of stuff in him," said one. Ashamed of myself, I begged their pardons, and sent for more wine. "He had better have given one of you ladies that good spunk," said the Mistress. I overcame my bashfulness, they laughed about what Sarah Mavis had missed, one professed to feel annoyed at my behaviour. "Oh! you are damned modest," said Hannah.

Mrs. Z°°i soon afterwards went upstairs into the bed-room to a gentleman she had come to meet, the Mistress said she should lay down, — she always did after her dinner, and slept for two hours, — she was fuddled, and indeed always was. The mother of the two children and I were alone; from the instant I had spent she had never taken her eyes off me, — never. I recollect the look of her dark eyes and their expression quite well. Hannah snored almost directly. "Let us have a kiss," said the lady to me, "I know you are fond of a well-formed woman," — and she pulled up her clothes a little. She was sitting on the sofa, my prick rose, I bolted the door, and we fucked whilst the Mistress kept snoring.

Mrs. Z°°i came down. "What, you here still? — What have you been doing?" The mother replied, "He has been smoking, and talking about his dear Sarah." The woman was actually sitting at that very moment with a flood of my sperm up her cunt, for she had neither wiped, nor washed, nor pissed since I had fucked her. Then they talked about Z°°i's friend who was a clergyman. Z°°i was the wife of a man who lived with her, but never had her (so she said); she hated him, he had clapped her once.

The mother went out of the room, and came back, Hannah awoke, we had tea, I paid, it was my rule then to pay for everything for the ladies whenever I was in the baudy house parlour. I rose to go, shaking hands with the two ladies. The one whom I had embraced put a bit of paper privately into my hand. Outside the house I read it. "Wait outside," it said. I had been delighted with her pleasure, and did so. She came out, we walked quickly off. "You go to the top of the next street," said she, "and I'll meet you," — and she went another way, and met me at the top. "I did that in case Z°°i came out," said she, "let us go and have dinner together." "I have not enough money," said I. "Never mind, I have." We went to the Café de P°°v°°°e, and dined; I fucked her again and again on a sofa. She was a charming woman. As we sat on a little sofa dallying after dinner, she said she had not had it for a month, her friend had gone to Germany where they were going to live, to make arrangements, he would return in a few days; then he, she, and the children were going to Germany with him. "I liked you," said she, "but when I saw what you did before us this afternoon, I could scarcely stop myself, I wanted it so badly, — I dare say I'm in the family way, — oh! don't look, — it's full, — it's dirty, — you shan't." The next instant I was up her again; afterwards she washed, and I saw her cunt. I paid for the dinner partly, she the rest, — I had not a sixpence left. "I'm sorry," I said to her, "that I have no more money." "I did not come here for money," said she. "Let me leave you half a dozen pair of gloves at No. 11." "No, I've lots of gloves." "Then give me a kiss." She stood putting her tongue in my mouth for a minute, then giving me a hearty kiss off she went. I never saw her, nor had her again. Hannah told me she was in Germany, and very happy there.

I knew an elderly couple who were childless and lived in a nice little house in the suburbs with a long garden in front, and one at the back as well; they were in comfortable but moderate circumstances, and kept two servants only. Every year they went to the seaside, taking one servant with them, and leaving the other at home to look after the house; and usually some one to take charge of it with her. This year they asked if I would, when I passed the house (as I frequently did), call in and see if all was going properly, for the housemaid left in charge was young, and her sister, a married woman, usually only stopped the night with her, leaving early each morning for work in which she was daily engaged. She was an upholstress.

I knew the servant whose name was Jane. She had been with the family some months. I often dined at the house; and once or twice when she had opened the garden-gate (always locked at nightfall) to let me out, I had kissed her, and tipped her shillings. She was a shortish, fat-bummed wench. Not long before this time I gave her bum such a hard pinch one night, that she cried out. A day or two afterwards I said, "Was it not black and blue?" "I don't know." "Let me see." "It's like your imperance," she replied.

After that I used to ask her when I got the chance, to let me see if the finger-marks were there, at which she would blush a little, and turn away her head, but nothing further had come of the liberty.

When I called at the house I had no intention about the girl,

as far as I can recollect. She opened the door, and heard my errand
and questions. Yes all was right. Did her sister come and sleep
there? Yes. Was she there now? No, she would not be there till
nearly dark. I stepped inside, for then I thought of larking with
her. "I am tired, and will rest a little," and stepped into the parlour,
sat down on a sofa, began questioning her about a lot of trifles, and
in doing so thought of the pinch I had given her bum, and my cock
began to tingle. Then I thought she was alone in the house. Oh!
if she would let me fuck her! — has she been broached? — she is
nice and plump. Curiosity increased my lust, and unpremeditat-
ingly I began the approaches for the attack, though I only meant a
little amatory chaffing.

"Is it black and blue yet, Jenny?" She did not for the instant
seem to recollect, for she asked me innocently enough, "What sir?"
"Your bum where I pinched it." She laughed, checked herself,
coloured up, and said, "Oh! don't begin that nonsense sir." I went
on chaffing. "How I should like to have pinched it under your
clothes, — but no I would sooner kiss it than pinch it." "Oh! if
you're agoing on like that I'll go to the kitchen." I stood before
the door, and stopped her going out. "Now give me a kiss." I caught
and kissed her, then gave a lot, and got a return from her. "I won't,
— Lor there then, — what a one you are," — and so on. "Well,
Jane one kiss, and you may afterwards kiss whenever you want, you
know." And so she seemed to think, for I got her to sit down on
the sofa, and we gossiped and kissed at intervals, till my cock got
unruly. "What a fat bum you have," said I. Then she attempted
to rise, I pulled her back, we went on gossiping, and kissing at in-
tervals. She got quite interested in my talk as I sat with one arm
round her waist, and another on her thigh, outside her clothes of
course.

So for a while; but I was approaching another stage, was get-
ting randy, and reckless. "Lord how I'd like to be in bed with you,
to feel that fat bum of yours, to feel your c — u — n — t," spelling
it, "to f — u — c — k it I'd give a five-pound note," said I all in a
burst, and stooping, got my hand up her clothes on to her thigh.
She gave a howl. "Oh! I say now, — what a shame! — oh! you
beast." I shoved her back on the sofa upsetting her, got my lips on
her thighs, and kissed them. Then she escaped me, and breathing
hard, stood up looking at me after her struggle. "Oh! I wouldn't

have believed it," said she panting with the exertion. What a lot of women I have heard say they would not have believed it, when I first made a snatch at their privates. I suppose they say what they mean.

Begging her pardon, "I could not help it," I said, "you are so pretty and nice, — I'd give ten pounds to be in bed with you an hour." "Well I'm sure." "Think what it is not to have a woman you like." "Well I'm sure sir, you are a married man, — you've got a partner, and ought to know better, — missus would not have asked you to call if she'd a know'd you, — she thinks there's no gent like you, — what would she say if I tell her?" "But you won't my dear." "She thinks you a perfect gentleman, and most unlucky," the girl went on to say, "and she is sorry for you too."

"Oh! she does not know all, but you've heard, have you Jenny?" I tried to make her sit on the sofa again, and promising that I would not forget myself any more, she did so. We kissed and made it up, and talking I soon relapsed into baudiness.

The quarrelsome life I led with the oldish woman at home was, I knew, well understood by the old couple. "I lead a miserable life," said I. "Oh! yes I know all about it," said the girl, "master and missus often talk about you, — but you're very gay, ain't you?" Then I told this girl a lot. "Think my dear what it is not even to sleep with a woman for two months, — for two months we have never slept together, — I've never seen her undressed, — never touched her flesh, — you know what people marry for, — I want a woman, — you know what I mean don't you, — every night what am I to do? — I love laying belly to belly naked with a nice woman, and taking my pleasure with her, — so of course I can't keep from having other women at times, — you don't know what an awful thing it is to have a stiff prick, and not a nice woman to relieve it." She gave me a push, got up, and made for the door at the word prick. Again I stopped her. She had sat staring at me with her mouth wide open, without saying a word, all the time I had been telling the baudy narrative of domestic trouble, as if she were quite stupefied by my plain language, until she suddenly jumped up, and made for the door without saying a word.

I was as quick as she, caught her, put my back against the door, and would not let her go, but could not get her to look me in the face, I had so upset her. There we stood, I begging her to sit down, and promising not to talk so again, she saying, "Now let me go, — let me out." "No, — sit down." "No." But in about a quarter of an hour she did, and then again I told her of my trouble, avoided all straightforward allusion to my wanting other women, but hinted at it enough. She got interested, and asked me no end of questions. "Lord, why don't you separate? — if I quarrel with my husband so, I'm sure I will, — I tell my young man so." "Oh! you have a sweetheart." Yes she had, — a grocer's shopman, — he lived at Brighton, came up third class to see her every fortnight, starting early, and going back late. She was flattered by my enquiries, told me all about him and herself, their intention to get married in a year; and I sat and listened with one hand outside her clothes on her thigh, and thinking how I could best manage to get into her.

"He goes with women," said I, to make her jealous. "He don't I'm sure, — if he did, and I found it out, I'd tear his eyes out, and break off with him, though he says Brighton is a dreadful place for them hussies." She got quite excited at the idea. "When he comes up, you and he enjoy yourselves, — his hands have been where mine have to-night." "No he hasn't, — if he dared I'd — now I don't like this talk, — you said you wouldn't, — leave me alone, — you keep breaking your word." Another little scuffle, a kiss, and a promise. "Why should you not enjoy yourselves? — who would know anything about it but yourselves, — it's so delicious to feel yourselves naked in each other's arms, your bellies close together." "Get away now," — and she tried to get up. I got my hand up her clothes, pulled her on to the sofa, and holding her down with one hand, pressed myself sideways on her, and kissed her, pulling out my prick with the other.

Then she cried out so loudly that I was alarmed, for the window at the back was open. "Hush, — be quiet, — there, — I've touched your cunt." I pulled one of her hands on to my prick. "Oh! for shame Jane you touched my prick." Again she got up, and made for the door; so did I, and stood there with my back to it, and my poker out in front of me. "Come and open the door my dear, and you will run against this." She turned her head away, and would not look. "Why don't you come on? — if you run up against it, it won't hurt you, — it's soft though it's stiff." "I'll write to my mistress tonight," said she, and turned away. "Do my pet, — tell her how stiff it was, and the old lady will want to see it when she comes back." "It's disgraceful." "No, my dear, it's to be proud of, — why you're looking at it, I can see."

Then she turned quite away. "That's right dear, — now I can see where I pinched your bum, — it was not far from your little quim, — oh! if that could talk, it would ask to be introduced to this, — it's hot, isn't it Jenny?" I said, this and a lot more. She had walked to the back window, and stood looking into the garden whilst I rattled on. "You're laughing Jenny." "It's a story," said she, "I'm insulted," — and turned round with a stern face. I shook my tooley-wagger. "How ill-tempered you look, — come and feel this, and you'll be sweet-tempered at once." She turned round to the window again.

"I *will* write my missus, — that I *will*." "Do dear." "My sister will be here directly." "You said she comes at dusk, — it won't be dark for three hours." "I wish you would go, — what will people say if they know you're here?" "Don't be uneasy, — they will know no more than they know of your doings with your young man." "There is nothing to know about, but what is quite proper."

So we stood. She looking out of the window, and turning round from time to time. I standing by the door with my prick out; then I approached her quietly. "Feel it Jenny, — take pity on it." "Oh! for God's sake, sir, what are you doing?" She turned, and pushed me back, then retreated herself, keeping her face to the window as she stepped backwards. "Oh! there is Miss and Mrs. Brown walking in the next garden." Sure enough there were two ladies there; they could have seen everything close to the window over the low wall which separated the gardens; and had they been looking, must have seen Jane, me, and my prick. "Oh! if they have seen, they will tell my missus, and she'll tell my young man, and I shall be ruined, — oh! — oh! — oh!" said she sinking back into an arm-chair with a flood of tears, — half funk and shock, and perhaps randiness, causing it.

I was alarmed. "Oh!" she sobbed, "if they saw you, — hoh! — hol — and it was no fault of mine, — you're a bad man, — oho! oho!" She sat with her hands to her face, her elbows on her knees. I dropped on my knees imploring her to be quiet, was sure no one had seen me, and tried to kiss her. The position was inviting. I slid my hands up her clothes between her thighs, she took no notice, was evidently in distress, not even conscious of the invasion. A bold push, and my fingers touched her cunt. I forgot all in the intensity of my enjoyment, at feeling my fingers on the edge of the soft, warm nick. No repulse! I looked up, she sank back in the chair, seemingly unconscious and deadly white.

I withdrew my hand, then came a mental struggle; my first impulse was to get cold water, the next to look at her cunt. I went towards the door, turned round to look at her. Her calves were visible, I ran back, and lifted her clothes, so that I could just see her cunt-hair, gave her thighs a kiss, and then rushed downstairs, got water, and as I entered the room she was recovering. She knew nothing, or next to nothing of what had occurred, nor that my fingers had touched her clitoris, though she had not actually fainted.

"I wish I had some brandy," she said, "I feel so weak." "Is there any in the sideboard?" "No." "I'll go and get a little." A few hundred feet from the house down a side-street, was a public-house. As I was going, "You will let me in again?" I said. "If you promise not to touch me." She looked so pale that I fetched brandy, but put the street-door key in my pocket as I went. "If she don't let me in," I thought, "she shan't have the key, — and what will she tell her sister about that?" It was a key almost as big as a shovel; she never noticed that I had taken it away. She thought by her dodge that she had got rid of me, and told me so afterwards.

I brought back the brandy and knocked. "Let me in." "I won't." "Then you shan't have the street-door key." This was spoken to each other through the closed door. A pause, then the door opened. "You are coming Jenny." We went downstairs into the kitchen, she had brandy and water, and so had I. It was a hot day, the pump-water was deliciously cool, I made hers as strong as she would take it, — it was an instinct of mine. She got her colour back, and became talkative, we talked about her fainting, but she tried to avoid talking about it, and did not want me to refer to what had led to it. I did, and was delighted to think that it was owing to what is called "exposing my person."

"I don't think the ladies saw it, so you need not have been so frightened Jenny, — but you saw it, did you not?" No reply. "I saw you looking at it." "It's a story." "Why did you faint?" "I always feel faint if I am startled." "What startled you?" "Nothing." "You saw it, and you put your hand over it to hide it, and you touched it." "It's a story, — I wish you'd go." "You ungrateful little devil, when I've just fetched you brandy." "It's through you that I felt ill." "Why?" No reply. "Don't be foolish, — it was for fear that the ladies should have seen my prick so near you, — now look at it," — and I pulled it out, it was not stiff. "It was twice the size when you saw it, — feel it, and it will soon be bigger."

The girl rose saying she would go and remain in the forecourt till her sister came, if I did not leave, but I prevented her going out of the kitchen. She began to cry again, and had a little more brandy and water. My talk took its old channel.

"Do you know how long you were fainting?" "I didn't faint, but only a minute or so." "Do you know what I did?" She was sitting down, then got upright, looked at me full in the face, her eyes almost starting out of her head. "What did you do! — what? — what? — what?" She spoke hurriedly, anxiously, in an agitated manner. "I threw up your clothes, kissed your cunt, and felt it."

"It's a lie, — it's a lie." "It's true, — and the hair is short, and darker than the hair of your head, — and your thighs are so white, — and your garters are made of blue cloth, — and I felt it, the dear little split, — how I wish my belly had been up against it! — what a lovely smell it has!" (putting my fingers to my nose).

"Oho! — oho! — oho!" said she bursting into tears, "what a shame to take liberties with a poor girl when she can't help herself, — oho! — oho! — you must be a bad man, — missus had no business to send you to look after me, as if she could not trust me, — she don't know what sort of man you are, — and a gentleman too, — oho! — and married too, — it's a shame, — oho! — oho! I don't believe you though, — oho — o — o." And when I told her again the colour and the make of her garters, she nearly howled. "You mean man, to do such a thing when I was ill."

I kissed her, she let me, but went on blubbering. "I've a good mind to tell my young man." "That will be foolish, because you and I mean to have more pleasure than we have had, — and he'll never be any the wiser but if you tell him, he'll think it's your fault."

This had occupied some hours, it was getting dark, but it seemed only as if I had been there some minutes, so deliciously exciting are lascivious acts and words. The charm of talking baudily to a woman for the first time is such, that hours fly away just like minutes.

I got her on to my lap and kissed her. She was so feeble that I put my hands up her clothes nearly to her knees before she repulsed them. Then I feared her sister coming home; she promised to hide the brandy, and we parted. She kissed me, and let me feel to her knees, to induce me to go. "Oh! for God's sake sir, do go before my sister comes." My last words were, "Mind you've felt my cock, and I've felt your cunt." "Pray go," — and I departed, leaving her tearful, excited, and in a state of exhaustion which seemed to me unaccountable.

Probably had I persisted a little longer I should have had her, such was the lassitude into which she had fallen; but I felt that I had made progress, and went home rejoicing, and forming plans for the future. When I had had some food, and thought over the matter, I came to the conclusion that I had been a fool in leaving her, and that had I pushed matters more determinately at the last moment, I should have certainly fucked her before I had left. I was mad with myself when I reflected on that, and the opportunity lost, which might not occur again.

Jenny had not fainted quite, but though unable to speak, resist, or indeed move, she must have been partially conscious. I think this from what I knew of her nature afterwards.

*When are women most lewed. — Garters, money, and promises. —
About my servant. — The neckerchief. — Armpits felt. — Warm
hints. — Lewed suggestions. — Baudy language. — Tickling. —
"Fanny Hill." — Garters tried. — Red fingers. — Struggle, and es-
cape. — Locked out. — I leave. — Baudy predictions, and verifica-
tion.*

I have a confused recollection of thinking myself the next day
an ass, for having missed a good opportunity of spermatizing a fresh
cunt; yet for some reason or another it must have been three days
before I went to try my luck again.

I had about this time of my life begun to frame intentions, and
calculate my actions towards women, although still mostly ruled
by impulse and opportunity in love matters. My philosophy was
owing to experience, and also in a degree to my friend the Major,
to whom some years before I had confided my having commissioned
a French woman to get me a virgin. He was older, poorer, and more
dissolute than ever. "He is the baudiest old rascal that ever I heard
tell a story," was the remark of a man at our club one night. Ask
him to dinner in a quiet way by himself, give him unlimited wine,
and he would in an hour or two begin his confidential advice in
the amatory line, and in a wonderful manner tell of his own ad-
ventures, and give reasons why he did this or that, why he suc-
ceeded with this woman, or missed that girl, in a way as amusing
and instructive to a young listener as could be imagined.

"If you want to get over a girl," he would say, "never flurry
her till her belly's full of meat and wine; let the grub work. As long
as she is worth fucking, it's sure to make a woman randy at some
time. If she is not twenty-five she'll be randy directly her belly is

211

filled, — then go at her. If she's thirty, give her half-an-hour. If she's thirty-five let her digest an hour, she won't feel the warmth of the dinner in her cunt till then. Then she'll want to piss, and directly after that she'll be ready for you without her knowing it. But don't flurry your young un, — talk a little quiet smut whilst feeding, just to make her laugh and think of baudy things; then when she has left table, go at her. But it's well," the old Major would say, "to leave a woman alone in a room for a few minutes after she has dined, perhaps then she will let slip a fart or two, perhaps she'll piss, — she'll be all the better for the wind and water being out. A woman's cunt doesn't get piss-proud like a man's prick you know, they're differently made from us my boy, — but show any one of them your prick as soon as you can, it's a great persuader. Once they have seen it they can't forget it, it will keep in their minds. And a baudy book, they won't ever look at till you've fucked them? — oh! won't they! — they would at church if you left them alone with it." And so the Major instructed us.

About three days afterwards, taking a pair of garters, two small showy neckerchiefs, and *Fanny Hill* with me, I knocked at the door. "Oh! you!," said she colouring up. "Yes, — is everything right?" "Yes! all right, what should be the matter sir?" She stood at the street-door holding it open, though I had entered the hall. I turned, closed the door, and caught hold of her.

"Now none of that pray sir, you insulted me enough last time." "I could not help it, you're so lovely, it's your fault, — forgive me, and I won't do so any more, — here is a sovereign, take it, kiss me, and make it up." "I don't want your money," said she sulkily. "Take it, I give it with real pleasure, — what I had the other day was worth double."

"I won't be paid for your rudeness, if that's what you mean." "Lord, my dear, I've no occasion to pay for that, I took it without pay, — I wish I could get what I told you yesterday, — I'd give ten times the sum." "You are going on again." "Don't be foolish, — take it, buy a pair of silk stockings." "I don't want silk stockings." "Your plump legs would look so nice in them," — and I forced her to put the money into her pocket.

Then I got her to the parlour, to sit down, to allow me to kiss her, and then to talk about me and my "missus," as she called her, a subject which seemed to excite her, for she began asking me question after question, and listened to all I said with breathless attention about my daily habits, rows, and fast doings. Once I stopped at some question. "I won't tell you that." "Oh! do, — do." "No it's curious." "Do, — do." It was about a pretty servant-girl whom I had noticed in my house. "It will offend you if I do." "No it won't." "Well give me a kiss then."

She kissed me. She had stood up a moment, now she sat down again by me on the sofa. I went on with my story, every now and then I stopped till she kissed me, it came to a kiss every minute, as I sat with my arm round her waist, talking.

Said I, "It was a servant whom my wife turned out at a day's notice, — a pretty girl, — I had taken to kissing her, and then I nudged her somewhere you know. One night when she opened the door, I saw by the light that my wife was in our bed-room. 'Is your mistress upstairs?' 'Yes sir.' 'And the cook?' 'Yes.' Then I closed with her. 'Don't sir, missus will hear.' I hugged her closer, shoved her up against the wall, got my hand on to her cunt, felt her, and gave her half a sovereign. How delicious it was to get the fingers on to the wet nick of that pretty girl, and say, 'How I should like to fuck that, Mary.'" I told it in words like that to Jenny, as she sat listening. At the word "fuck" up she got.

"You are a going on rude again." "You asked me." "Not for that." "But that's what I had to tell, what you kissed me to tell." "I didn't think you would say rude things." "Sit down, and I'll tell you without rude words." And so I did, telling all over again with additions, but instead of saying "cunt," "fuck," and so on, said, "I got my hand you know where," — "and then she let me you know what," — "she was frightened to let me do, you guess what I wanted."

"Luckily, though she foolishly told her fellow-servant, she did not say who had been feeling her. That sneak told my wife, who told me about it, or she knew, and said she could not keep such an improper girl in the house as that. 'But the other servant may have told a lie to spite her.' 'Perhaps, but I'll turn her out too,' — and so she did, both left."

Thus I talked to Jenny till I expect her quim was hot enough; then said I, "Here is a pretty neckerchief, — put it on." "Oh! how pretty." "I won't give it you unless you put it on." She went to the glass and unbuttoned the top of her dress, which was made to button on the front. I saw her white fat bosom, she threw the kerchief round the neck, and tried to push it down the back. "Let me put it down, — it's difficult." She let me. "You are not unbuttoned enough, — it's too tight." She undid another button, I pushed down the kerchief, and releasing my hand as I stood at the back of her, put it over her shoulder, and down in front, pushing it well under her left breast. "Oh! what a lovely breast you have, — let me kiss it."

A shriek, a scuffle. In the scuffle I burst off a button or two, which exposed her breast, and getting my hand on to one of the globes began feeling and kissing it. Then I slid my hand further down, and under her armpit. "Oh! what a shame, — don't, — I don't like it." "How lovely, — kiss, kiss, — oh! Jenny what a lot of hair I can feel under here." "Oh!" — screech, — screech, — "oh! don't tickle me, — oh! — oh!," — and she screeched as women do who can't bear tickling. I saw my advantage. "Are you ticklish?" "Yes, — oh! — (screech, — screech). — Oh! leave off."

Instead of leaving off I tickled harder than ever. She got my hand out, but I closed on her, tickling her under her arm, pinching her sides, and got her into such a state of excitement, that directly I touched her she screeched with wild laughter; the very idea of being touched made her shiver. We were on the sofa, she yelling, struggling, whilst I pinched her, she trying to get away from me, but fruitlessly; I buried my face in her breasts which were now largely exposed, and she fell back I with my face on her, holding her tight. Then I put one hand down, feeling outside for her notch; that stopped her screeching, and she pushed me off as she got up.

I soothed her, begged pardon, spoke of the hair in her armpits, wondered if it was the same colour that it was lower down. Now she shammed anger, boxed my ears, and we made it up. I produced the garters. "Oh! what a lovely pair." "They're yours if you let me put them on." "I won't." "Let me put one half-way up." "No." "Just above the ankle." "No, my stockings are dirty." "Never mind." "No." Then she made an excuse, said she must see to something, and left the room. I thought she was going to piddle.

She came back. I found afterwards she had been out to lace up her boots, they were untidy. It was coquettishness, female instinct, for she wanted the garters, and meant to let me try them on, though refusing. "Where do you garter, above knee?" "I shan't tell you." "I've seen, — let me put them on below the knees." "No,"

"Then I'll give them to another woman who will let me." "I don't care." I threw the garters on to the table after some fruitless attempts. I was getting awfully lewed with our conversation.

"Do you like reading?" "Yes." "Pictures?" "Yes." "I've a curious book here." "What is it?" I took the book out, *The Adventures of Fanny Hill.* "Who was she?" "A gay lady, — it tells how she was seduced, how she had lots of lovers, was caught in bed with men, — would you like to read it?" "I should." "We will read it together, — but look at the pictures," — this the fourth or fifth time in my life I have tried this manœuvre with women.

I opened the book at a picture of a plump, leering, lecherous-looking woman squatting, and pissing on the floor, and holding a dark-red, black-haired, thick-lipped cunt open with her fingers. All sorts of little baudy sketches were round the margin of the picture. The early editions of *Fanny Hill* had that frontispiece.

She was flabbergasted, silent. Then she burst out laughing, stopped and said, "What a nasty book, — such books ought to be burnt." "I like them, they're so funny." I turned over a page. "Look, here she is with a boy who sold her watercresses, is not his prick a big one?" She looked on silently, I heard her breathing hard. I turned over picture after picture. Suddenly she knocked the book out of my hand to the other side of the room. "I won't see such things," said she. "Won't you look at it by yourself?" "If you leave it here I'll burn it." "No you won't, you'll take it to bed with you." There I left the book lying, it was open and the frontispiece showing. "Look at her legs," said I, for we could see the picture as we sat on the sofa; and I began to kiss and tickle her again.

She shrieked, laughed, got away, and rushed to the door. I brought her back, desisted from tickling and lewed talking, though I was getting randier than ever. "Now have the garters, — let me put one round the leg, just to see how it looks, — just half-way up the calf." After much persuasion, after pulling up my trowsers, and showing how a garter looked round my calf, she partly consented. "Promise me you won't tickle me." I promised everything.

I dropped on one knee, she sat on the sofa. "Put one foot on my leg." She put one foot there, and carefully raised her clothes an inch or two about the boot-top. "A little higher." She raised it holding her petticoats tight round the leg, and I slipped the garter round it. "It's too loose, raise a little more." "I won't any higher, — I can see how it looks." "Won't they look nice when they are above the kneel and won't your young man be pleased when he sees them there." "My young man won't see them any more than you will." "Let me slip on the other." The same process, the same care on her part. She bestowed all her care on the limb I was gartering, lest I should slip the garter higher up. The remainder of her clothes were loose round her other leg. Then I pushed my hand up her clothes and herself back on the sofa, relinquishing the leg I was gartering.

Rapidly my hand felt thighs, hair, cunt. How wet! What is this which catches my fingers? — what is it they are gliding between? With a yell she pushed me away, and got up as I withdrew my fingers. She had a napkin on, my fingers were stained red. "Oh you beast," said she bursting into tears. I caught hold of her, and began to tickle her; she pushed me violently away, and escaping, rushed downstairs, slammed the kitchen-door in my face, and locked herself in. I have been accustomed to this behaviour on similar occasions.

I stood outside begging pardon, talking baudiness, I tried to burst open the door, and could not. I was not fond of poorliness in women, had a keen nose, and oftentimes could smell a woman if poorly, even with her clothes down; how it was I did not smell *her*, considering how near my nose had been to her split and her breasts, I can't say, but suppose randiness overcame my other senses. I played with my prick which was in an inflammatory state, feeling it made me much randier, I called through the door how I wanted to fuck her, how my prick was bursting, how I would frig myself if she did not let me. "What a hard-hearted girl, — I'll give you ten pounds to let me, — who will know it, but you and me?" and a lot more; but it was of no use, and at length I went upstairs, determining to wait, and thinking that in time she might follow me.

On the sofa I sat thinking of what I had done. There lay one garter, I took it up, and rolled it round my pego, I rubbed the tip with it, thinking it might be a spell. I took up *Fanny Hill*, got more excited by reading the book, looking at its salacious pictures, and feeling my prick at the same time. Then the sense of pleasure got beyond control, and laying down the book on the floor just beneath me, where I could see a baudy picture, I turned on my side on the sofa, and frigged till a shower of spunk shot out.

Then down I went. The door was still locked, my senses were calmed, but I talked baudy, and offered her money without a reply; growing tired I bawled out, "I'm going, — you will let me in a day or two, and get the ten pounds towards the new shop, — you won't be so unkind when I come again." "I'll take good care never to let you in," said she. They were the only words I could get out of her. I went upstairs, took a slip of paper, and wrote on it, "I have wrapped the garter round my prick, it is a charm. Directly you put it on I shall know, for my prick will stiffen, — you will put it on I am sure; and directly my prick stiffens, your cunt will long to have it up it, even if I am miles away. You will put the garter on, for you can't help doing so, — I'm sure to fuck you, neither you nor I could avoid it if we would. Why should we deny ourselves the pleasure, — no one will know it, and you will be ten pounds the richer." I wrote that or something nearly like it, and charmed with my own wit, rubbed the garter over the top of my prick till I left the smell on it, then laid it on the table over the paper I had written, and went away, taking *Fanny Hill* with me.

It is a positive fact, that about two hours afterwards I had a violent randy throbbing in my prick, and found out later on that just at that very time she had put that garter on.

[And now for the complete understanding of what follows, it it must be stated that the house was in plan nearly like that which I inhabited when I had my beautiful servant Mary. Kitchens in the basement, two parlours with folding doors between them, nearly always open; and rooms back and front over the parlours; and that my absent friend did with those rooms whilst absent at the seaside, what was not unusual with people of their class in those days, lock most of them up, leaving only sufficient for the servant, or caretaker, to inhabit.]

I waited a few days to ensure her poorliness being over. I had not left her *Fanny Hill*, but why I cannot tell, for I knew how baudy books excited a woman. The night before my next attack I wrapped up the book, directed it to her, gave a boy sixpence to deliver it, hid myself by a lilac which was in the front-garden close to the road, and saw the boy give it to her, and go off quickly as I had told him. It was just dusk, and too dark inside the passage of the house to see; for Jenny stepped outside the house so as to get light, and stripped off the envelope. I saw also that she opened the book, closed it, looked rapidly on both sides, then stepped inside, and closed the door. I expect that her cunt got hot enough that night. I saw her sister who slept with her nightly, going through the front-garden soon afterwards, and Jenny open the door for her. I had then moved off to a safe distance, the other side of the road.

Jenny was fond of finery, and I had heard the old lady of the house declaiming about it. Her pleasure at the showy neckerchief and garters was great, so I bought a pretty brooch, and filling my purse with sovereigns determined to have her at any cost, for my letch for her had got violent. The next day I had a good luncheon, went to the house just after her dinner-time, and took with me a bottle of sherry. I recollect the morning well. It was a sultry day, reeking with moisture; it had been thundering, the clouds were

218

dark and threatening, the air charged with electricity. Such a day makes all creation randy, and you may see every monkey at the Zoological Gardens frigging or fucking. I was resolute with lustful heat, the girl was, I expected, under the same influence, and taking her as I did after a lazy meal, everything was propitious to me. How shall I get it? — if I knock she may not open; and if she sees me go up the front-garden she won't open. But I had to try, so walked up to the door, and gave one single loud tradesman's knock.

There was a little porch and a shelter over the street-door. Standing flat up against the door, so that I might be hidden from her sight if peeping, I heard an upper window open. She looked out, but where I was she could not see me. There was delay, so again I knocked, and soon the door began to open, I pushed it and stepped in. The front-shutters on the ground-floor to my wonder were closed.

"Hoh! sir, — you," said Jenny amazed, "what do you want?" I pushed the door to, and caught hold of her. "I've come to have a chat and a kiss." She struggled, but I got her tight, and kissed as a randy man then kisses a woman, it is a magnetizing thing. "Oh! there it is again," she cried as a loud thunder-clap was heard, "oh! let me go, — oh! it do frighten me so." "Where are you going?" "Oh! into the parlour, — I've closed the shutters." The girl was in a panic, and did not know what she said. The parlour-door was open, the room nearly dark, which suited me. She went just in, and then turned round to go out, but I pulled her to the sofa. A flash of lightning showed even in the darkened room, the girl cowered and hid her face with her hands. I took her round the waist. "Shut your eyes, and lean your head against me." Mechanically she did, she was utterly unnerved. I felt down with my right hand the form of her thighs and haunches through her clothes. My prick began to stand. Pulling it out, and taking her near hand I put it round my prick just as the thunder roared. She kept her hand unconsciously on it for a time, then with a start took it away and jumped up. "Oh! it's wicked," said she, "when God Almighty is so angry," — and just as she got to the door a terrific flash made her turn round again. I caught her, and sitting down on a chair pulled her on to my knee; she hid at once her face on my shoulder in terror.

Coaxing and soothing, and exciting her, in her fear she listened, at times twitching and oh-ing. I was sorry I had touched her cunt the other day I said. "Oh! now don't." "Feel my prick again, — do dear." "Let me go, — you've no business here." Another flash came, I put my hand up her clothes, the tip of my fingers just touched her quim. She struggled and got away, and in doing so upset the chair which fell down and broke. "Oh! now what will my missus say!" said she. Then a screech, and she got to the other side of the table.

This went on a little longer, a gleam of sunshine came through the shutters. Then she opened one shutter, and said if I did not go she would open the window and call out. The light showed my pego, stiff, red-tipped and ready. "Look what your feeling has done for this Jenny," said I shaking my tooleywag at her.

But her resoluteness daunted me, so I promised not to do so again. "Here is some sherry that I was taking home to taste, — let's have a glass, — it will do both of us good after this thunder, — you look white, and as if you wanted a glass." I had got out of her on a previous day that she liked sherry. "I'll go and get you a glass," said she. "No you shan't, — you will lock the door," said I, — I knew that was in her mind. No she would not. "We will go together then."

We did, and returning to the parlour under my most solemn promise of good behaviour, down she sat, and we began drinking sherry. One glass, — two, then another she swallowed. "No I dare not, it will get into my head, — no more." "Nonsense, — after your fright it will do you good." "Well half a glass." "Isn't it nice Jenny?" "It is." "Does not your sweetheart give it you?" "At Christmas, but only one glass." The sherry began to work. "Only another half-glass," — and I poured it out nearly full. Soon after I got up after filling my own, and standing before her again filled up hers which she had sipped without her seeing me. "Finish your glass dear." "No I can't, — it's making me so hot." "Just another half-glass." "I won't." But she began to chatter and told me again all about her young man, of their intending to open a grocer's shop when they had two hundred pounds; that he had saved a certain sum, and when he had a little more his father was to put fifty pounds to it. She also had put money in the savings bank. I got closer to her, and asked for a kiss. "Well I'll kiss you if you promise not to be rude again." A kiss and a promise. She was one of the simplest and most open girls I have ever met with, and once a half-feeling of remorse came over me about my intentions, whilst she was talking on quite innocently about her future; but my randy prick soon stopped that.

"What nonsense dear, your young man won't know that I have

felt your thighs, and you my thing, nor any one else what we do, —
I have thought of nothing else since I touched you, — kiss; — now
let me do it again, — just feel it, — only where my hand's been
before, — I swear I won't put my hand up higher, just above your
garters, — have you got those garters on?" "No." "Oh! you have."
"Well I have." "Let me just see." "I shan't." "I'll give you a sovereign
to let me." "Shan't." I pulled out the sovereign, put it on the table,
and spite of her resistance pulled up her clothes just high enough to
see one garter; then clutching her round the waist I pushed my
hands up, and touched a well-developed clitoris. She struggled, but
I kept my hand there, kissed her rapturously, and frigged her; her
cap fell off in her struggle. "Oh! I — can't — bear — it — now —
sir; — I — don't — oh! — like it, — oh!" Then with a violent effort
she got my hand away, but I held her fast to me.

"What a lovely smell your cunt has," said I putting the fingers
just withdrawn from her thighs up to my nose. I have always
noticed that nothing helps to make a woman more randy than that
action; it seems to overwhelm them with modest confusion; I have
always done that instinctively to a woman whom I was trying. "Oh!
what a man, oh! let me pick up my cáp." Just then I noticed her
hair was short, and remarked it. She was annoyed, her vanity hurt,
it turned her thoughts entirely. "Yes," she said, "I had a fever two
years ago, — but it's growing again." "Well it has grown enough
on your cunt dear, — did it fall off there?" "Oh! what a man! — oh!
now what a shame!" My hand was on her thighs again, and I
managed another's minute frig, and kept her close to me.

The heat had become excessive. What with struggling, and the
excitement, sweat was on both our faces. Her thighs by her crack
were as wet as if she had pissed them, her backside began to
wriggle with pleasure, which I knew I was giving her; but again
with a violent effort she freed herself from me, and as I put my
hand to my nose she violently pulled it away. The sherry was up-
setting her wisdom.

"There is the sovereign," said I as she stood looking at me,
"that will help you." "Don't want it." Seeing where her pocket-hole
was I pushed it into it. "Oh! what a lucky sovereign, to lay so close
to your cunt Jenny," — and pushing my hand into her pocket I
touched the bottom of her belly through the linen. Again a struggle,
a repulse, then she put her hand into her pocket. "You're feeling

your cunt Jenny," said I. "O — oh!" said she taking it out quickly, "I was feeling for the money, — I won't have it."

Then I kissed her till the sweat ran off my face on to hers. "Oh! my goodness," said she as it grew darker, "it's going to thunder again." "Have another glass." "No it's gone into my head already." But she took a gulp of mine. "Let's fuck you Jenny dear." "What?" "Fuck." "Shan't." "Oh! you know what I mean." "No I don't, but it's sómething bad if it's from you." I pulled out my prick, and tried to push her on the sofa. She got away, and then with my prick out I chased her round the table. "Leave off," said she, "a joke's a joke, but this is going too far." She was getting lewed, and was staring at my prick which showed above the table as I chased her. Quick as me she managed to keep just on the side of it opposite to me.

"I'll swear I won't touch you again if you will sit down." "I won't trust you, — you've been swearing all the afternoon." "So help me God I will," said I, and meant it. "Well then not when you are like that." I pushed my prick inside my trowsers, and then she sat down. What a long time this takes to tell, what repetition! but there are not many incidents I recollect more clearly.

Then I took out ten sovereigns, all bright, new ones, laid them on the table, and then the brooch. "Do you like that Jenny?" "Yes." "It is for you if you will let me, and those ten sovereigns also." "You are a bad man," said the girl, "and would make me forget myself and be ruined, and without caring a bit," — and she began rocking her head about, and rolling her body as she sat beside me, and looking at the money. "Who will know? — you won't tell your young man, — I shan't tell my wife, — let me." "I shan't, — never, — never, — never, — never, if it was fifty pounds," said she almost furiously. "He won't find it out." "Yes he would." "Nonsense, — half the servants do it, yet marry," — and then I told her of some I had had who had married. "No, — no, — no," she kept repeating, almost bawling it out, as I told her Mary So-and-So who married a butler, and Sarah So-and-So who married my greengrocer, though I'd fucked them over and over again. "No, — no," looking at the money; then suddenly she took up the brooch, and laid it down again.

Before running round the table after her, I had thrown off my coat and waistcoat. "It's so hot, I've a good mind to take off my trowsers," I had said; but I had another motive. She seemed weaker, and was so, for gradually she had got inflamed and lewed by heat, the electrical condition of the atmosphere, the titillation of my finger on her seat of pleasure, and the sight of my stiff penis. She had I expect got to that weak, yielding, voluptuous condition of mind and body, when a woman knows she is wrong, yet cannot make up her mind to resist. Just then it came into my mind to tickle her; and then followed a scene which is one of the most amusing in my reminiscences.

She shrieked, and wriggled down on to the floor. I tried to mount her there. She kicked, fought, so that though once my prick touched her cunt-wig, I could not keep on the saddle. She forgot all propriety in her fuddled excitement, and whilst screeching from my tickling, repeated incoherently baudy words as I uttered them. "Let me fuck you." "You shan't fuck me." "Let's put it just to your cunt." "You shan't, — you're a blackguard, — oh! don't, — leave me alone, — well I will feel it, if you'll let me get up, — oh! — he! hi! hi! — for God's sake don't tickle, — hi! — I shall go mad, — you shan't, — oh! don't, — oh! if you don't leave off." "I shall, — I must." "Oh! pray, — you shall if you leave off tickling then, — oh! don't pray, — oh! I shall piddle myself, — he! he!" She was rolling on the floor, her thighs exposed, sometimes backside, sometimes belly upwards with all its trimmings visible. "Oh! it's your fault," and as she spoke actually piddle began to issue. I had my hand on her thigh, and felt and saw it.

Randy as I was I burst out laughing; and she managed to get up, began to push in her neckerchief which I had torn out of the front of her dress, and arranged her hair.

"Oh! look at me, — if any one came, what a state I am in," said she looking in the glass, and there she stood her breast heaving, her eyes swollen, her mouth open, and breathing as if she had just run a mile, but attempting nothing, saying nothing further, awaiting my attack. What randy, pleasurable excitement she must have been in, though unconscious of it, whilst only thinking of how to prevent my fucking her against her will.

"You began piddling." "Didn't." "I felt the piddle on my hand." She made no reply, but passed on, and wiped her face. When I said more she merely tossed her head. "Don't be a fool Jenny, — let us, — you want it as bad as me." Then I rattled out my whole baudy vocabulary, "prick," "cunt," "fuck," "spunk," "pleasure," "belly to belly," "my balls over your arse," "let my stiff prick stretch your cunt," — everything which could excite a woman; to all of which she merely said, "Oho! — oh!" and tossed her head, and never took her staring eyes off me, nor ceased swabbing up her perspiring face, and at the same time looking at my throbbing, rigid cunt-stretcher.

Finding she took to yelling, and even hitting me, I desisted a moment. "Where is the book I sent you last night?" I had till then forgotten it. That opened her mouth. "Have not had a book." "I saw the boy give it you, and you open it." "He didn't." "He did." "I burnt it, — a nasty thing, — I would not let my sister see it." An angry feeling came over me for the moment, for I thought it probable, and should have had difficulty in replacing it. Then came an inspiration to help me, — a man always gets somehow on the right track to get into a woman if he has opportunity. Nature wills it. The woman was made to be fucked, and the sooner for them, the better for them.

"You have not burnt it, — I'll bet it's in your bed-room, — in your box." "It isn't." "I'll swear it's there, — you have been reading it all night, — I'll go up and see." She started as if electrified into life as I made for the door. She got there before me, and stood before me. "You shan't go, — you've no business up there, — I've burnt it, — it's not there." "It's in the kitchen then." "No, I've burnt it," she went on rapidly and confusedly. "I'll go and see," said I pulling her from the door, she screeching out, "No you shan't go up, — that you shan't, — you've no business there." Then I pulled up her clothes to her belly, she got them down, but still she kept her back to the door. I kept pulling her till her cap was off again, and felt sure she was getting weaker and weaker.

Then she turned round suddenly, opened the door, and ran up the stairs rapidly like a lapwing, I after her. Once she turned round, "You shan't come up," said she, and tried to push me back; and then again on she went, I following. I stumbled, that gave her a few steps ahead; I sprang up three stairs at a time, recovered the lost distance, and just as she got into the bed-room, and slammed the door to, I put my foot in it, — it hurt me much. "Damn it, how you hurt my foot, — I will come in," — and pushing the door my strength prevailed; the door flew open, I saw her running round the bed, and there on the very pillow of the unmade bed lay *Fanny Hill*, open at one of the pictures. I threw myself across the bed, and clutched the book. She then stood motionless, panting and staring at me, she had clutched at it, and failed just as I caught it. She would have got it, but for having to go round the bed.

I laughed. "Have you not had a treat Jenny dear!" Her face was a picture of confusion. I was stretched half across the bed, and now went right across. Then to escape me she ran away, and had nearly reached the door when throwing myself over the bed again I grasped her petticoats under her arse, and managed to pull her back. "Damned if I don't fuck you," said I, "by God I'll shove my prick up your cunt if I'm hanged for it," — and pushing a hand up behind I clasped her naked buttocks. She turned round, I pulled her petticoats clean up, she yelling, struggling, panting, imploring. I dropped on my knees, kissed her belly, and buried my nose between her thighs. The petticoats dropped over my head, her belly kept bumping up against my nose and lips, which were covered with her cunt-moisture.

I rose up, pushed and rolled her against the bed, my hand still up her clothes. "Oh! don't, don't now, — you are a great gentleman they say, and ought to think of a poor girl's ruin, — oh! if it was found out I should be ruined." "It won't darling," I had got my fingers well over the whole slit. "Pray don't, — well I'll kiss you, — there." "Feel it." "Will you let me get up if I do?" "Yes." "There then," and she felt me. "Oh! I must fuck you." "Oh! pray don't, — oh! let me go now, and I'll let you another day, — I will indeed sir, — oh! you hurt, — don't push your fingers like that." "Kiss me my darling." "You shan't." "Then there." Another struggle. "Oh! I can't — be — bear it." Her arse began to twist again, her head sank on my shoulder, her thighs opened; then with a start, "Oh! my God it's lightning (it began to thunder and lightning badly), — oh! I'm so frightened, — oh! don't, — another day, — it's wicked when it's lightning so, — oh! God almighty will strike us dead if you are so wicked, — oh! let me go into the dark, — oh! don't, — I can't be — bear it." Her arse was shaking with my groping and frigging.

"Now don't be a fool, — damned if I don't murder you if you are not quiet!" "Oh! oh!" I had got her somehow on to the bed, she was helpless; with fear, liquor, and cunt-heat. I threw myself on to her. A feel between thighs reeking with sweat, with her cunt in a lather, with the sweat dropping in great drops from my face, with sweat running down my belly on to my prick and my balls; I shoved. One loud "aha!" and my prick-tip was up against her womb-door. A mighty straight thrust; and the virginity was gone at that one effort.

Right up there with but a shove or two as far as I recollect, and without trouble, my sperm spouted directly my tool rubbed through the wet, warm cunt-muscles. Then I came to my senses; where was I? had she let me, or had i forced her violently?

She laid quietly under me with closed eyes and open mouth, panting; I was upon her, up her, pressing heavily upon her rather than holding her; then thrusting my hands under her fat bum I recommenced thrusting and fucking. She lay still, in the enjoyment of a lubricated cunt, distended by a stiff, hot prick. Soon she was sensitive to my moments, her cunt constricted, a visible pleasure overtook her, her frame began to quiver, and the soft murmurs of spermatic effusion came from her lips. She spent. On I went driving as if I meant to send my prick into her womb, fell into a half dreaminess, and became conscious of a great wetness on my ballocks; it was her discharge more than mine, the most copious I recollect, excepting from one woman. Then I dropped off on her side. She lay still as death, the thunder rolled over us unheeded by her in the delirious excitement and delight of her first fuck.

She turned on her side slightly, her thighs and backside were naked, she hid her face, and shuddered at the thunder unheeding her nakedness, then buried her face in a pillow, and so we both dozed for a minute or two. Her backside was still naked, when I looked at her in all ways as she lay, and saw traces of sperm on her thighs and chemise. A little lay on the bed, but no trace of red, no signs of a bloody rupture of a virgin cunt. My shirt and drawers were spermed, but had not a trace of blood. The light fell full on her backside, I could see lightish brown hair in the crack of the parting of her buttocks; a smear of shit on her chemise. Her flesh was beautifully white. She had on nice white stockings, and the flashy garters; she had a tolerable quantity of hair on her quim on the belly side. I sat at the side of the bed, got off boots, trowsers, and drawers; then laying down gently inserted my longest finger and delicately began rubbing her clitoris which I could see protruding of a fine crimson color. Then she moved; she was not asleep, but dazed by the fuck, fear of the lightning, the excitement, the heat, and the fumes of the wine combined.

She stared at me, pulled down her clothes, and tears began

to run down her cheeks. What a lot of women I have had cry at
such times! "Don't cry my darling." She turned on to her face, and
hid it. For a quarter of an hour, I talked, but she did not answer.
I told her she had spent, that I knew she had had pleasure. Then
I pushed my fingers up her cunt; still she did not speak, but let me
do just what I liked, keeping her eyes shut. So soon as my rammer
was up to the mark, up her it went fucking, and again I felt its
stem well wetted. She was a regular streaming spunker.

After that, "I am going downstairs," said she. "I'll come." "No
don't." "You only want to piddle." "Yes," said she faintly. "Piddle
here, — what will it matter?" "I can't." "I'll go out if you won't bolt
the door." "It's no good bolting the door, — you have ruined me."
I went outside, closed the door, and heard the rattle in the pot.
When I re-entered she was sitting at the side of the bed crying
quietly; she did nothing but look at me, but without speaking.
"Arrange yourself in case any one comes to the door." "No one will
come." "The milkman?" "He will put it down inside the porch."
She sat down the picture of despair. Never had I felt more lewed,
I was mad that day with lewedness. "Let's feel your cunt," said I,
"I have spent in it three times." "I don't care what you do, you
may do what you like, — it's of no consequence." I felt up her cunt,
she hung her head over my shoulders whilst I paddled my fingers
in the wet. "Don't hurt me," said she. "I have not hurt you." "Yes
you have." "Let's look." That roused her. "Oh! no, — no, — no, —
you shan't." "Wash your cunt." I fetched the sherry, but she had
not washed her cunt. "You should wash it out." "Oh? — oh!" said
she. "If I should be with child I shall never be married."

She drank more sherry, and promised to wash. Then I went
downstairs, fetched up the brooch and the ten sovereigns, and gave
them to her. "How shall I say I got it?" "Does he know how much
you have saved?" "Yes." "Is it a year's wages?" "Yes," — and she
began to cry again. "What shall I say about the brooch?" "That you
bought it, — let's lay down and talk." She yielded instantly, I threw
up her clothes, she pushed them down. Then I lay feeling her quim,
and got out her bubbies, she submitted, laying with her eyes closed,
till my rubbing on her clitoris made her sigh. Then up her, I felt
her wetting my prick-stem, and shot my sperm into her at that in-
timation of her pleasure.

It was about seven o'clock, I had been nearly five hours at

my amusements, and was tired; but had that day an irrepressible prick. It began to stiffen almost directly it left her cunt. I went down with her to tea, there I pulled her on to my lap, and we began to look at *Fanny Hill.* I could not get a word out of her, but she looked intently at the pictures. I explained their salacity. "Hold the book dear, and turn over as I tell you." Then I put my fingers on her cunt again. How sensitive she was. "Let's come upstairs." "No," said she reluctantly, but up we went, and fucked again. Then she groaned. "Oh! pray leave off, — I'm almost dead, — I shall have one of my fainting fits." "Lay still darling, I shall come soon," — but it was twenty minutes hard grinding before my sperm rose.

Then she laid motionless and white through nervous exhaustion, excitement, and loss of her spermatic liquor, which I kept fetching and fetching in my long grinding. She told me afterwards that she could not tell how often she spent. I had never been randier or stronger, nor enjoyed the first of a woman more.

She was a most extraordinary girl. After the first fuck she was like a well-broken horse; she obeyed me in everything, blushed, was modest, humbled, indifferent, conquered, submissive; but I could get no conversation out of her excepting what I have narrated. She cried every ten minutes, and looked at me. After each fuck she laid with her eyes closed, and mouth open, and turned on her side directly, putting her hand over her quim, and pulling her clothes just over her buttocks. Then after I had recovered and began to talk, a tear would roll down her cheek.

About nine o'clock she said, "Do go, my sister will be here, — and the bed wants making." At the door I put her against the wall and rubbed as well as I could my flabby cock between her cunt-lips. She made no resistance. "We'll fuck again to-morrow Jane." "I'll never let you again," said she, "for you shan't come in," — and she shut the door on me with a slam.

My soiled shirt. — Jenny's account of herself. — Fucking and funk-ing. — Poor John! — Of her pudenda. — Its sensitiveness. — Erotic chat. — Startled by a caller. — Her married sister's unsatisfied cunt. — How she prevented having children. — Doubts her husband's fidelity. — Jenny taught the use of a French letter. — Hikery-pikery, and catamenial irregularities.

When I got home I looked at my linen; never had it been in such a mess after female embraces. I had taken no care about it, it was be-spunked in an unusual degree, and lots of thinnish stains were on the tail which made me think that one or both of us must have spent copiously. Then I recollected that Jenny's cunt seemed very wet to me when I felt it after I had spermatized her. There were no signs of blood, and taking stock of the sensations I had experienced, "Jenny has had it before," I said to myself. Then came a fear that her discharge was from a clap, but I dismissed that from my mind. I had only once had the clap from a woman not gay.

So I washed the tail of my shirt, laid it under my arse to dry, gave it a natural stain of piss, and went to bed reflecting and wondering who had first penetrated Jenny's privates.

A day or two afterwards I went to see her, and shammed a knock. She opened the door. "Oh!," she exclaimed as I entered, "now you shan't, — you shan't again." "I shan't what my dear?" "I know why you come here, — but you shan't." "I want a chat, — don't be foolish, — come here, — I won't do anything, — I don't want anything, — but come here."

I got her into the parlour, and on to the sofa, then talked, then got baudy. "Do just let me feel your thighs, — what harm can it do when I have been between them." "No." "Just a feel, — there

229

I won't put my finger further, — oh! Jenny you like my finger, — be quiet dear, — just let me feel it." Half an hour after she had said, "Now you shan't," my prick was in her. No woman can refuse the cock which has once stretched her cunt, she is at its mercy. We spent another afternoon in talking and fucking, and she partly in crying and bemoaning her evil deeds.

I had not only opened her cunt, but opened her heart and mouth at the same time. She was the funniest, frankest little woman I ever knew. She told me all her past life, her future expectations, asked my advice, deplored her wickedness to her young man, and all in an hour. She spoke the same incessantly afterwards. In a fortnight I knew everything about her from her birth, and about all her family; it was as if for the first time in her life she had had a confidant.

"What shall I do with your money?" "Put it with the rest." "But he knows what I've got, — we always tell each other." "Keep it to get you a good stock of clothes before you are married." "But he knows all about my clothes." "Put it in a little at a time, or don't tell him till you are married; then say you kept him in ignorance for a pleasant surprize, or tell him nothing at all about it, — you will have more than that." "I don't want your money, I fear it will bring me harm." "Well give it back to me Jenny." But Jenny did not seem to see the advantage of that; so she kept it, and had more besides in time.

"What will become of me and poor John? — he'd die if he knew how ill I behave to him, — now don't, — you do upset a body so a talking, and putting your fingers there, — oh! leave me alone, — no no more." "Once more dear, — how hot your little cunt is, — it's longing for a prick." "Oh! take care of my cap, you will tear it, — I'll take it off." "What a fat backside you've got Jenny, — how wet your cunt is, — shove, shove, fuck, — where is my prick Jenny now?" But Jenny became speechless always after three cock-shoves, and began moistening the intruder with all her cunt-power.

After fucking she was tranquil for a time; sperm seemed to soothe her, but then she had funks. "Oh! dear what have you made me do? oh! if I am in the family way! — oh! if he finds it out, he won't marry me! and he is such a good young man, and so fond of me, — o — o — ho — ho! — I've behaved very bad to him, — and I didn't mean, — oho! — it's all your fault, oho! — I didn't know what I was about, — I never do when it lightnings, — oho! Do you think he will find it out when we are married?" she would ask in her calmer moments, after she had cried herself out. This scene occurred every day I fucked her for a time, then less frequently.

I tried to comfort her, told facts, and many inventions of my own, of how I had had women, who afterwards married and whose husbands had never known that they had been broached.

"Is it true really! — oh! do tell me the truth, — if he finds it out I will drown myself, — I'm sure he will, — it's all your fault, — you must be a bad man to take advantage of a poor girl in the house alone." "But if you're not in the family way, he can't find out until you are married, and then it will be too late. You won't tell him, and your cunt can't speak." "Oh! sir you do say such funny things."

This went on for weeks. "Oh! it's my time, and it's not come on." Then with joy, "Oh! I'm all right, but you can't do anything to-day, — oh! if my mistress should find out, or if my sister should come home and catch you here, — oh! if the next-door neighbours should see you come here so often, and tell my mistress." One or other of these fears was always upon her, but did not prevent our fucking. At that time Sarah was away, and Louisa Fisher still ill, so Jenny had all my essence; and later on as much as Louisa and Sarah spared me. As to my home, I had pretty well done with fucking there.

Jenny's cunt was well-haired, and had rather large inner lips; not so large as I have seen in many women, but larger than I liked. Her tube was easy. What a fight I had when first I saw it. "I won't be pulled about like that, — no it's shameful." "I dare say your John has seen it." That always sent her off howling, and when she had subsided she let me do as I liked. "It's a nasty thing to pull me about like that." But it came soon to the old world-wide habit: a feel and a look before the entry. The same woman who won't let you see the bottom of her belly at first, will hold her cunt open for your inspection in a month. It is breaking in a woman to baudiness which is the happiness of the honeymoon, not the hard burst through a bit of gristle.

It had weighed on my mind ever since I had had her, and about three weeks afterwards I told her my doubts of her then being a virgin. She swore that no man had even put his hands on it till

I did. "Am I different from other women?" She was indignant at the doubt, and honestly and truly I believe. A schoolfellow used to look at her quim, she at her schoolfellow's, she always thought hers was the most open of the two, she always could put her finger up easily. "But you did hurt me through, though I did not bleed. My sister says she did bleed a little when she first had her husband," —and Jenny now described her sister's first night, and her sister's form, and rather wetted my lust for her sister.

I came to the conclusion that she was born loose at her inlet, or had broken through the cover when quite young, and that no prick had rubbed her but mine; but her organ was a peculiar one in its habit of distilling its liquids.

I have told how my shirt was stained at first, and soon found that Jenny was one of those women who spend rapidly, frequently, and copiously. I have met I think two like her in my career, to the time I correct this.

On the second day's poking I noticed this and became fully aware of it afterwards. When I put my prick up her, and began my movements, a shiver and a sigh escaped her almost directly, her bum gave a heave, a discharge came from her, and if I pulled my prick out then, it was perfectly wet. It used in fact to run out a little, and if pushing one hand well under her arse (which was not so easy, for she had a fine backside), I felt the root of my prick or rather the end of the stem, I could feel her moisture running down one of her bum-cheeks, or between them. That over, by the time I spent we usually discharged simultaneously. Her voluptuousness was greater when we spent together, than on her preliminary discharge. She said she could not account for it, but that a delicious sensation crept over her the moment the prick entered; that her cunt tightened and seemed to wet itself copiously; that her spend at the climax was longer, more thrilling, voluptuous, satisfying, and exhausting; that when our spunks had mingled her whole body was satisfied; but that the first spend seemed only to confine its pleasure to her cunt. It is difficult to describe these sensations.

I frigged her several times, and got a copious discharge from her, thin, milky, and barely sticky, yet it left a strong stain on linen. She was astonished when I told her of her peculiarity. Perhaps she wondered what her poor John would think of it. I can't say I altogether admired her wetness; I took a dislike to a tall thin girl who was much of the same sort as Jenny, but that girl was quite sloppy-cunted, though not with the whites. This was since.

[Another woman who had this sensitive and sensuous (for it was both) organization, was the sister of an intimate friend, and whom I have fucked since the above was written. I don't know that I shall say anything more about that lady, so tell of her cuntal peculiarity here. She was plump, fair-haired, had a fine complexion, and in face strongly resembled the queen. She was to be married.]

When her young man came to town, and Jenny went out with him, the girl upbraided herself. When I next saw her after his visit she felt herself a deceiving wretch, and cried. Now would I please desist, and not make her sin any more. But the persuasion was too great, the recollection of her pleasure too strong, and never did I go away without having plugged her.

Did she love her young man? Yes she supposed she did; he was kind, attentive, and would make a good husband. She wanted to get married, to have a home of her own; besides he was not a workman, but a tradesman, and when married they would have a shop, and be in a higher position. She always spoke more of the house and shop, and her liberty, than of her young man.

She was of a highly nervous organization, and through me she was to be shocked severely. She half fainted the first day I took liberties with her, thunder and lightning gave her an inclination that way, twice afterwards she nearly fainted, any sudden thing annoyed her and turned her white. One occasion I'll tell of now, the other in due course.

We fucked on the sofa after the first day; but though large, it was not like a bed, so afterwards we used to go to her bed-room. I used to leave my hat and stick downstairs, so that in case of surprize I might stand in the hall, and say I had called to enquire. It was a stupid thing to do as I found out, and then I used to take it into the bed-room. I had fucked her one afternoon, when a double knock came at the street-door, I knew it. "It's my wife," I said. Down I rushed for my hat, and returned to the bed-room; and then Jenny opened the door. She had called to make some enquiry, and went away. I heard the door close, but no further noise or movement, then crept downstairs. There sat Jenny on a chair, just recovering from a half faint. "Oh!" said she, "I nearly dropped down." "Ah! she would have knocked you down my dear, if your cunt could

have spoken and said what was inside it." But Jenny never could
joke. It was always dreadful, and she was to be punished in some
way for her evil deeds with me. A few tears, and then a little baudy
chaffing brought smiles again on her face.

I delighted in talking baudy to her, told her smutty stories
about the women I had had, described their charms, and any special
lasciviousness connected with them. Her astonishment was great, her
curiosity intense; she in return told me all she knew about every
other woman, and all her own little baudy doings. Never was
woman so frank about such matters. When I left her I doubt
whether her dear John could have told her half what she could
have told him about fucking, and the two articles that copulation
is done with.

Her talk was all about her sisters, and principally of the married
one who came to sleep with her; a woman about twenty-eight years
of age, who had been married some years, and had two children,
the last one four years old. She, or rather he, did not mean to have
any more, they could not afford to keep them. "How did they stop
it?" I asked Jenny. She did not know. But one night the sister
wanted particularly to sleep at home, and had asked Jenny if for
once she would sleep in the house alone. She consented though
frightened. I proposed sleeping with her, and we passed a very de-
licious night together: a man and woman fresh to each other always
do in bed. What a night of feeling, frigging, sniffing, inspecting,
and fucking it was!

At all times, no matter what we began talking about, cunt and
cock were sure to become the subject. That night I learned that her
sister had slept away, expecting to catch her husband out in some
infidelities. Since he had determined to have no more children, he
made her frig him instead of fucking; so the sister went short of
cock and had to frig herself. That annoyed her. Then when he
fucked her he did not do it properly, he cheated her sister, Jenny
said. I was a long time in getting out of Jenny what the man did,
at length she said, that just as the stuff was coming, he pulled it
out, and it went all over her sister's thighs or her belly, and often
before she had had her own pleasure. Her sister thought it was
just as well not to be married, as to go on like that.

That was not all. He used at first to do it every night, and
now not once a week, said he could do without it, that he did not

care about it, and so on. She believed that he had other women, and that was more aggravating because she wanted it herself more than ever. She was not so well, she told Jenny for want of fucking, she liked it, and would willingly have more children though she was so poor. I asked cautiously if she had heard of the skins which people put over their pricks, and into which they spent their seed? Jenny had not. I explained what they were. She said she would ask her sister about it. I cautioned her about showing that she knew too much. A few days afterwards Jenny told me her sister had tried them, but they did not like them, besides they could not afford them. What Jenny's sister paid for French letters I don't know, I used to pay nine pence each. I fucked Jenny with one on, just to instruct her.

These two women talked often about such matters; and each day Jenny told me what her sister had said. Soon I knew all about her sister's doings, from the night she lost her virginity to the birth of her last child. The little fucking that the sister had, and her longing for more affected me considerably; I quite longed to see this hot-bummed, cunt-neglected wife.

Jenny and I settled down quite matrimonially, I saw her certainly four days a week, or else every day excepting Sundays. At times I spent the whole day there, took wine, and meat, and newspapers. She cooked, and very badly. We eat and drank together, and fucked, she cried about John and her wickedness, and her fears of being found out. Then I read to her the news, and also every baudy book I could get hold of, and explained to her every use that could be made of our tools, both male and female, from flat-cocking to buggery, so far as I knew, — but I did not know so much as I do now.

To prevent its being known I was there, we got quite cunning. I was not to come at eleven o'clock, because then the butcher came; nor at twelve, because the girls were always at the window next door; between one and two o'clock I was safe, because the family was always at dinner at that time; at three the milkman came, and I avoided him. So with a little trouble I pretty well escaped observation, during the eight or ten weeks which I did husband duty, and perhaps as much as some two husbands would have done.

Once she was awfully uneasy, for her courses had not come on, and shed floods of tears. She would lose her John, poor fellow!

When in that way she was always pitying him, but she was always irregular in her menstruation, which rendered it difficult to judge of her condition. Oh! she was sure she was now in the family way, she had symptoms; she had asked her sister how she had felt when she had conceived, and her own symptoms were the same. "My God what shall I do! — I'll drown myself, I will, — I shall never be able to face him, — poor fellow!" "Go and get something, go and see some one." She went, took a dose of what she called "hikery-pikery," and the ugly red stream came on. I don't believe she was in the family way. Years after I heard she had never had a child, though long married.

A sailor, a whore, and a garden-wall. — The newly-made road. — Windy and rainy. — Bargaining overheard. — Offer to pay. — Against a garden-wall. — A feel from behind. — A wet handful. — Blind lust. — Into the sperm. — The policeman. — A lost umbrella. — A new sort of washing-basin. — Fears of ailment.

Amidst all this saturnalia of cunt, I don't believe I ever did anything with one, excepting to feel and fuck it, though in attitudes varied. Recherché erotic pleasures were not in my custom, and not even in my thoughts. Amusements with a man would have shocked me, had they been suggested. His spunk would have upset my stomach to look at. To put into a cunt which another man had just quitted, would have revolted me; yet I was doomed to do all this, unpremeditatedly, on the spur of the moment and opportunity.

I lived then on the western outskirts of London where they were building on what had been and were still largely pleasant fields. About five minutes' walk from my house was a street made not five years before, and leading out from it a new road, a sixth of a mile long, connecting two main roads, and made to enable the fields on either side to be built upon. There were gas-lights at long intervals, just enough to encourage people to use it at night. The carriage and footways were of coarse gravel, and quite newly made.

Under wheel and foot these roads crunched as people went across them. At one end of the road was a new row of houses, the garden back-walls of which abutted on the open fields, and the side-walls of two formed the entrance to the road, — both houses just then were empty.

It was about eleven o'clock at night, windy and rainy at intervals, and there was a small moon hidden by thick clouds scudding across it. Sometimes there was a gleam of light, at other times all was dark. It was very windy as I came through the road for a short cut, after thinking whether it was safe or not, and just then I met a policeman at the further end, and bid him good night. The crunching of my footsteps on the newly-laid gravel annoyed me, both by its fatigue and noise, so I stepped on to the meadow-land which lay alongside it, and walked quite quietly. As I neared the street into which it led, I could distinguish what looked like a man and woman standing on the footpath close up against the garden side-wall of the empty house, and well away from lamps. Thought I, "They are fucking or finger-stinking," so walked further from the footpath to prevent noise, and more slowly to see the fun. It excited me lewedly, for I wanted a woman.

As I got near them I was under cover of the back garden-walls. The idea of catching a couple fucking made me more randy. "I won't, unless you give me the money first," said a female voice. I stopped, but heard no male reply. "I shan't then, — what have you got?" the shrill voice said. No audible reply, but I saw a struggle as if a man was trying to lift a woman's clothes, and heard a laugh. Then I stepped on to the path, and walked on. "I shan't then, — if you have no money what did you come here for?" came clearly on my ear, though said in a somewhat lower tone. Just as I came to the angle of the wall I saw plainly a fair-sized woman with her back against the wall and a shortish man in front of her, pulling her about as if he was trying to feel her, or lift her clothes. The amatory scuffling prevented them noticing my approach. The woman said as I neared them, "I won't without the money," — and then was a hush as I walked on.

What then occurred exactly I can't recollect, but I said as I was close to them, "Let him have you, and I'll give you five shillings." "All right, — give it here then," said the woman. I stopped, and saw by the small light of the distant lamps that the man had the cap and open collar of a sailor. A desire sprung up quicker than I write this, and what I meant for a baudy joke became the reality of action, — I followed my impulse without thought of consequences.

"I'll give you five shillings if you let me see you do it." "All right," said she — and to him, "Will *you?*" "I'm right for a bloody spree," said a male voice almost inarticulate either from drink or cold. "Give me the money first." "Certainly, if you let him do it." "Come round the back of the gardens," said the woman, walking off with the man to the rear, and well out of the line of road, I following. We stopped. "Give me the money." "Won't the policeman catch us?" "He won't be back for half an hour," said the woman, "he has just passed." I knew he had, having met him. We were now away from the lamps, it was dark. "Let's feel your cunt," said I getting into reckless baudiness. The man close to us kept chuckling to himself, and I thought staggering, but was not sure. He closed on the girl as I did. "Let me feel your cunt," said I.

The girl lifted her petticoats, her back against a wall; I put my hand between her thighs, and met the man's hand on the same errand, — we were both trying at the same spot. "Bloody spree," said a hoarse drunken voice. We both groped together. "One at a time," said she. I withdrew my hand, and it knocked against his prick, I laid hold of it, and believe to this day that the sailor thought it was the girl who was feeling it. I clutched it, and a strange delight crept through me as I drew my hand softly up and down his stiff stander which seemed longer than mine. "Hold hard you bugger," said he.

Excited beyond all thought, I still clutched and glided it through my hand. "Where is your prick?" said the girl. I felt her hand touching my hand. Letting his prick go, "No sham," said I. "There is no sham," said she, "where is your money?" I put my hand in my pocket feeling for the money, took it out, and gave it her. "Come on," said she to the man. Instantly they were close together. "Bloody spree," I heard mumbled again. "Lift up yer clothes, I can't feel yer arse." I felt that her clothes *were* up. I put my umbrella against the wall, grasped a thigh with my left hand, and my right went towards her quim, but was stopped by contact with the man's prick which was against her belly. "I'll put it in," said she. The next instant the to-and-fro movement had begun, I felt the wriggle of her arse-cheeks which I held with my left hand, his hands were now round her arse above mine, and under her clothes. "It's out," said she, "stop, I'll put it in again" — and all was still. His prick had slipped out through his energy. The woman guided it up again, and the backside jogging recommenced. I know what she

said, I guessed much what she did from what she said. The buttock
movement there was no mistaking.

It was too dark to see. I heard him breathing hard, and felt
her thighs quivering and wriggling. Changing sides and stooping,
I pushed one arm and hand right round her buttocks, between her
thighs from behind, and under her cunt till my fingers passed her
arse-hole, felt his prick, and grasped his balls. I doubt whether he
knew it, for his pleasure was making him blow like a man who had
run himself out of breath. I felt his prick-stem as he drew back,
and that it was wet with the moisture of her cunt. Then with hoarse
muttering, of "blood-prick spunk, bloody cunt," I felt him shove
and wriggle hard, and then both were stationary and silent. I kept
my hand still groping under her cunt, and feeling his prick-stem
from beneath, with my thumb and forefinger.

He did not hurry himself to withdraw. "You've done, — get
away." "Let's fuck agin," said he. "You shan't." As she spoke, his
prick flopped out right on to my hand, wetting it. She moved away,
the man swore. Mad now with lust, "Let's feel your cunt," said I
lifting her clothes. She let me. "My God what spunk, — how soft
your cunt feels, — let him fuck you again, — I'll give you more
money, — feel me, — frig me."

I don't recollect the girl speaking, but she seized my prick
whilst I groped up her cunt with fingers saturated with sperm. No
disgust now. For the moment I loved it. She stopped frigging. "Put
it in me, it's nicer." "No." "Oh! it's all right, — it's nice, — put it
in." "No." "Do, — I want a fuck." "You've just been done." "You do
it." I yielded, and putting my prick into her reeking cunt fucked her.
"Oh! I'm coming." "So am I." "Oh! — ah? — ah!" I spent, and think
she did, am not sure; but she shagged hard, and squeezed me up
to her. The sailor had taken my place, and was looking on I suppose,
standing with his back against the wall, mumbling something.

As my pleasure subsided I could just see the man by the side
of us working away, I suppose at his prick, with his fist like a steam
engine, I felt the sperm oozing on to my apparatus, all round. "Let's
fuck yer agin," said the hoarse man's voice. "I'll give you money to
let him," said I. Out came my prick. "All right," said she, "let me
piddle first." "Where is your prick?" I said, "does it stand?" "Bloody
fine." I put my hand on it, and grasped it. A new desire and

curiosity about a male organ came over me. The woman had pissed, and was standing up, she caught hold of my prick which was hanging out, whilst I had hold of his prick. Then I took out money, and gave all the silver I had, — I don't know how much.

"Put it into her," I said, frigging it; it was not stiff, and I was impatient to feel him fucking again. He turned to her front. "Let go my prick," said he. The girl took it. "It's not stiff." "Bloody something," I heard him say. Again I heard the rustle of the frig and of her clothes lifted. "Your cunt's bloody sloppy," said the husky voice, and he chuckled. "Make haste," said the woman.

"Oh! the policeman!" Half-way down the road I saw the bull's-eye of the policeman's lantern. I was now standing feeling my own prick with excitement; but at the same instant a glimpse of moonlight came from between the heavy clouds, and showed me the man pressing his belly up against the woman, and her petticoats bunched up high. The policeman's bull's-eye far off was throwing light across the fields. "The police!" I said. "Come further along," said the woman dropping her clothes, and moving off still further into darkness, I moving off in the direction of the road. My lust went off, — what if the policeman saw and knew me! I got to the road, turned to the left along the crunching gravelled path, walking very quickly, and so soon as I turned the corner took to my heels, and ran hard home, ran as if I had committed a burglary.

Letting myself in with my latch-key I found I had left my umbrella behind me. Then a dread came over me. I had fucked a common street nymph, and in the sperm of a common sailor, both might have the pox, — what more probable? I could feel the sperm wet and sticky round my prick, and on my balls. I had then taken to sleeping in my dressing-room. My wife I thought must have been, according to habit, an hour abed. On entering my room there sat she reading, which was a very unusual thing. I sat down wishing she would leave the room, for I wanted to wash and wondered what she would say if she saw me washing my prick at that time of night, or heard me splashing. But she didn't stir, so taking out the soap unobserved, "I've bad diarrhœa," I said, and down I went to the water-closet. Sitting there I washed my prick well in the pan, and went upstairs again. (How many times in my life has a sham ailment helped me? — how many times yet is it to do so?).

Fear of the pox kept me awake some time. Then the scene I had passed through excited me so violently, that my prick stood like steel. I could not dismiss it from my mind. I was violently in rut. I thought of frigging, but an irrepressible desire for cunt, cunt, and nothing but it, made me forget my fear, my dislike of my wife, our quarrel, and everything else, — and jumping out of bed I went into her room.

"I shan't let you, — what do you wake me for, and come to me in such a hurry after you have not been near me for a couple of months, — I shan't, — you shan't, — I dare say you know where to go."

But I jumped into bed, and forcing her on to her back, drove my prick up her. It must have been stiff, and I violent, for she cried out that I hurt her. "Don't do it so hard, — what are you about!" But I felt that I could murder her with my prick, and drove, and drove, and spent up her cursing. While I fucked her I hated her — she was but my spunk-emptier. "Get off, you've done it, — and your language is most revolting." Off I went into my bed-room for the night. What I said whilst furiously fucking her, thinking of the sailor's prick and the spermy quim of the nymph, and almost mad with excitement, I never knew. I dare say it was hot.

For a fortnight I was in a state of anxiety, and twice went to a doctor to examine my prick, but I never took any ailment. I went early next day to see if my umbrella was in the fields, but it was gone, — I wonder who had it. I never saw the woman again that I know of, but had I seen her five minutes after the event I should not have known her, nor the sailor. He seemed to me a young man of about twenty, groggy and hoarse with cold, his prick seemed about the size of my own. She was a full-sized woman with a big arse, but flabby.

Though I could not find my umbrella I saw the spot on which it had stuck into the wet turf; and the place where we had played, for a yard or two square was trodden into mud, whilst all around was green.

After I had got over my fears I had a very peculiar feeling about the evening's amusement. There was a certain amount of disgust, yet a baudy titillation came shooting up my ballocks when I thought of his prick. I should have liked to have felt it longer, to have seen him fuck, to have frigged him till he spent. Then I felt annoyed with myself, and wondered at my thinking of that when I could not bear to be close to a man anywhere, I who was drunk with the physical beauty of women. The affair gradually faded from my mind, but a few years after it revived. My imagination in such matters was then becoming more powerful, and giving me desire for variety in pleasures with the sex, and in a degree, with the sexes.

A big maid-servant. — A peep up from below. — Home late, dusty and stupid. — Chastity suspected. — Consequences. — Dismissed. — My sympathy. — The soldier lover. — Going to supper. — At the Café de l'E°r°°e. — In the cab returning. — Wet feet. — On the seat. — Mutual grasping and gropings.

I have forgotten to say that I had been again much better off, but by extravagance had to draw in, and now lived in a larger house, but kept only three servants. During the latter part of the time of my liaison with Mrs. Y°°°s°°°e we had for a month or so but one servant. A charwoman came to do rough work; but why this temporary arrangement took place need not be told.

She was a big country woman quite five feet ten high, and speaking with a strong provincial accent. When she was alone in the house I used to cross the streets to see her kneel, and clean the door-steps. She had such a big arm, and her bum looked so huge that I wondered how much was flesh, and how much petticoats. She cleaned the windows on the ground-floor, which in the house I then inhabited were got at by an iron balcony with open bars beneath. Seeing her cleaning them one day I went stealthily to the kitchen, and then into the area, and peeping cautiously up her petticoats, saw her legs to her knees. They were big and suited to her buttocks; but though the sight pleased me much, I never thought of having her, for I avoided women in my own house and neighbourhood. She was plain-faced, sleepy, and stupid-looking; the only thing about her nice, was bright rosy flesh. She looked solid all over. Her hair was a darkish chestnut colour, her eyes darkish, and one day she lifted a table as heavy as herself. There was not the slightest amorousness in her face or manner, and she dressed like a well-to-do country woman. Give her lots of nice, good, white underclothing; it was better than a sham outside, I heard she had said. She was about twenty-two years old, but she looked older.

About two months after she came (and just then when without other servants), on arriving home one Sunday night at about ten o'clock, I found she had been allowed to go out as usual, but had not returned. Another hour crept on. Savage, I thought of locking her out. About half-past eleven she returned. I let her in, and asked why she was so late. She looked dazed, muddled, had a very red face, muttered she was sorry, she had fallen down and hurt herself, and without waiting to answer me properly went downstairs. My wife went after her, and when she came up, told me she thought she was in drink, and that her dress and bonnet were covered with dust. "She had been up to some tricks with a man," said she.

Next day I heard she had told as an excuse, that as she was walking along a lane up which she turned to piddle, a man laid hold of her, and had taken liberties with her; that in the scuffle she had fallen down, had screamed, tried to catch him, had failed, and a lot more to similar effect. One or two days later I was told the woman had been dismissed. That I quite expected, for it was the mistress' custom to coax out the facts from poor devils in a kind way, and then to kick them out mercilessly; any suspicion of unchastity was enough for that. Middle-aged married women are always hard upon the young in matters of copulation.

"What is she going for? — a few days ago she was so beautifully clean, strong, and serviceable that none were like her!" "Oh! she has got a sweetheart, and is up to no good with him I'm sure." "How do you know?" "She told me so." "It's hard to dismiss on suspicion only, a poor girl who came up to us from the country." "You always take the part of those creatures." "I know nothing for or against her, nor you." "She is no better than she ought to be. — I have noticed a soldier idling about here for some time past." "As you like, — it's your business — but she came to us with an excellent character."

I pitied the woman, but more than that from the time I heard that a man had assaulted her, a slightly lecherous feeling had come over me towards her. I wondered what he had done, — had he felt her? — had he fucked her? — had she ever been fucked before, even if the man had recently done it to her? I began looking closely at her, getting in the way on some pretext or another, and always

246   MY SECRET LIFE

wondering if this and that had been done. I looked at the broad
backside, so broad that a prick must look a trifle by the side of it.
"Have the male balls banged up against it?" I thought. When I
heard of her being turned adrift I thought I would just like to have
her once or so, and that her leaving us gave me a chance. Curiosity
was I believe at the bottom of my desire for her, — it was her huge
fleshy form, and that spanking arse. Oh! to look at it naked, and
feel it, if I did nothing more.

Finding the charwoman was not coming one day, and that the
big servant would be a short time alone in the house, home I went;
and on some pretext went down to the kitchen.

"So you are going to leave us." "Yes sir." "Why?" "I'm sure I
don't know, — Missus says I don't suit, — yet only a few days ago
she said I suited well." Here she broke into tears. I spoke kindly to
her, said she would get another place soon, — she must take care
not to go up dark lanes again with a man, nor go home late and
dirty. She could not help it, — it was no fault of hers. What liberties
did he take with her? I asked. The woman coloured up, and turning
her head away, said he did what was very improper. "Did he put his
hands up your petticoats?" "What was very improper," she repeated.
"But how did you get so dirty?" They struggled, and she slipped.
"I wish I'd been him, — I'm sure when he felt, he got his hand close
up, — I'd give a sovereign to have mine there." That remark threw
her into a distressing state of confusion.

I talked on decently, alluding to what I thought had taken
place, and wishing I had been the man; but got nothing from her
excepting that the man had taken liberties with her, — yes most
improper liberties.

I told her I was sorry she was going, and thought she was
hardly used, but I could not help it, — how was she off for money?

Very badly off, — she had come straight from the country to
better herself, and had bought nice, good, underlinen, knowing she
was coming to a gentleman's house, and now before she could turn
herself round she was sent off. She had had to pay for her coach to
London, and when she had her wages, and paid for a cab to lodg-
ings, she would not have twenty shillings left. What was she to do
if she could not get another place? Here the big woman blubbered,
left off cleaning, sat down on a chair, and hid her face.

"Don't cry, you're used badly, — I'll give you a little money until you get a place, — it won't be long." "You're a good kind master," said she, "everyone says so, — but Missus is a beast, she ain't no good to any one, — I don't wonder you are out so much, and don't sleep with her." I gave a kiss and a cuddle. "What lovely limbs you have, — how firm your flesh is, — you are delicious, — I should like to sleep with *you*, — come into the lane with *me*, and tell me when you are going to piddle again, and let *me* take a liberty."

"Who told you I went up the lane?" "Your mistress," — and then I left, telling her on no account to let it be known that I had been home.

After this I heard that she had said it was a soldier. Now I knew that a soldier who took liberties with a woman, took no little ones, and generally got all he tried for; so made up my mind that she had been fucked on the night she came home late.

A day or two after I was surprised with the following. "I've got another servant, — she will come the day after to-morrow, so I mean to send Sarah away at once, — of course she will be paid her month's wages, but I shall get rid of her, for I am sure she is an unchaste woman."

"Poor devil! — it's enough to make her unchaste, — but it's your business." "Are you going out to-night?" "Why?" "Because if you are I'm going round to my sister's." "I am," — and off I went after dinner; but waited in a cab not far from the end of the street, watching to see if she really did go out. She did, and directly I spied her I drew myself back, and told cabby to follow her to the sister's house. Then I drove back part of the way, and went home.

"So you are going?" said I to the servant. "Yes, I'm turned out, sir." "A soldier and you went up a dark lane, — what a fool to tell your mistress." "Ah! she has told *you*, — what a bad un, she sneaked it out of me, — but I'm not to blame, he is my sweetheart, and is going to marry me." "Have you got lodgings?" "Yes sir, I'm going out to-morrow to see them, and I've written telling my sister (a servant also), and she has taken them." "Wait for me when you go, and on no account say I've been home, — I mean to help you, — you are badly used, — what can I do for you?" "If you would help me to go to the Tower, — my young man's name is ***, he is a Grenadier, — I've written him, but he has not replied, and I want to know if he is there." "I will wait for you to-morrow night outside, when you go to see the lodgings." A kiss, a hug, and out of my

house I went again, after having ascertained where she was going
to, and the time she was to go out.

Next evening I waited outside her lodgings, she came in a cab
with her box, and told me that her mistress had bundled her out.
She had had nothing to eat since mid-day, and was sick and weary.
"Make haste then, — arrange your things, and we will go and have
something to eat, and you shall see your soldier to-morrow." "God
bless you, I do feel grateful sir," said she.

In half an hour she came out. I did not know where better to
go to, and knew that it was just the time when the place would be
empty, so took her to the Café de l'Europe in the Haymarket. It was
a long drive, but I wanted to be with her in the dark cab. She was
wonderfully struck with the place, but I was ashamed of being
seen with her. She was anxious to go home early, because she lodged
with poor people who went to bed early. She had never tasted
champagne, so I gave her some. Oh! her delight as she quaffed it,
and oh! mine as I saw her drink it, — it was just what I wanted. "A
cock has been into her I am sure," I thought, "so another can't do
her much harm, — if she'll fuddle she'll feel and be felt, or fuck, or
frig, they always go together," my old instructor in the ways of
women used to say.

I arranged to take her the next day to the Tower; our talk
naturally was about the affair. "He did it to you," I said. She
wouldn't or didn't see my meaning. "I could not help it if he did,
or what he did, — he took unproper liberties." "He took them more
than once, I'll bet!" She did not like such joking, she remarked. All
this was when we were going out to supper.

Going home in the cab I began to say a baudy word to her.
"He felt your cunt," said I, "did you feel his prick?" She bounced
up and hit her bonnet against the top of the cab. "Oh! my! sir," —
but she kept on in her excitement, letting out bits of the history,
saying at intervals, it was not her fault, — she was fuddled, —
fuddled with beer and gin, — a little fuddled her. I saw that pretty
clearly from the effect of the champagne; and unbuttoned so as to
have my prick handy. It was a wet night, the bottom of the cab was
wet straw. "My feet are quite wet," said she. "Put them on the seat,
my dear." She did so; I felt them as if solicitous for her comfort,
putting my hand higher than above her ankle, just to see if her
ankles were wet also.

"Why your ankles are wet." "Yes they are." With a sudden push up went my hand between her thighs, — a yell and a struggle, but I had felt the split before she dislodged my fingers. She was stronger than me, but my hands roved about her great limbs, searching under her petticoats round her huge backside. "Oh! don't, — you're a beast." "Oh! what a backside! — what thighs! — what a lovely cunt I'm sure you have! — let me keep my hand just on your knee, and I swear I won't put my hand higher." To ensure my keeping my hand there, she held my wrist as well as a vice would have done. She had by sheer force got it down to there.

I pattered out all my lust, my desire to have her, incitements, and baudy compliments on her form. "Let me fuck you." "You shan't." "You know what it means." "I know what you mean." "What harm could I do? — who would know?" And then the old, old trick. Taking her great fist in mine, I put my stiff prick into it. What a persuader! Though she kept up a show of struggling she did not get it away from that article instantly.

I suppose unless utterly distasteful to each other, that a man and woman cannot feel each other's privates, without experiencing reciprocal baudy emotions. They get tender to each other. The woman always does, after she has got over the first shock to her modesty, and her temporary anger. If after a man has felt her, a thermometer could be applied to her split, I believe it would be found to have risen considerably in temperature. After struggling and kissing, trying to feel her quim, trying to keep my hand on her thighs, it ended in our having our mouths together and my hand being pinched between her two great thighs, whilst the knuckles of one of her hands, with sham reluctance touched my doodle, just as the cab reached her dwelling, and there we parted. All the rest of our conversation was about her soldier, her being dismissed, and is not worth writing.

The next day. — At the Tower. — In tears. — "The wretch is married." — At T***f***d Street. — After dinner. — On the chamberpot. — My wishes refused. — An attack. — Against the bed. — A stout resistance. — I threaten to leave her. — Tears and supplications. — On the sofa. — Reluctant consent. — A half-virgin.

Next day she met me early, and we drove to the Tower. On the road I instructed her what to do when there (it was full six miles off). I tried my best to get her passions up in a delicate way, but amatory fingerings I avoided whilst the poor woman was in search of her lover. The feeling of each other's privates on the previous night, had opened her heart to me. She let out a little more of the history of her escapade with the soldier, and asked my advice how to act in certain eventualities, which could only be applicable to a woman who had been rogered. She was painfully anxious as she approached the Tower. I stopped in the cab just in sight of the entrance, and after instructing her carefully again who to ask for, and what to do, in she went.

In half an hour she came back with wet swollen eyes, got into the cab, and began to bellow loudly. The cabman had opened the door for her, and stood waiting for orders. For a few seconds I could get nothing out of her, then told the cabman to drive to a public house near. There I gave her gin, but still could learn nothing. All she said was, "Oh! such a vagabond!" Into the cab again. I told the man where to drive to, for I had laid my plans. "Tell me, — it's not fair after all the trouble I've taken not to tell me," — sob — sob. Soon after it all came in a gush. "Yes he was there, that is, he was two days ago," but the regiment had gone to Dublin, and would not be back for eighteen months, — a letter would be sent

250

him of course, but his wife would be there in a day, for, — "Oh! —
hoh! — hoh! — the wretch is a married man, and he's deceived me."
"You should not have let him do it." "I didn't mean to." "You let
him do it more than once I'll swear." "He did it twice to me, when
in the house, — he swore he'd marry me three days after, if I let
him, — and so I d — did, — ho! — her — ho!"

Thus I heard in snatches the whole history, which she told me
more plainly afterwards. She had been fucked twice on the eventful
night, once on the ground in a lane, and once in a bed-room.

I drove to T°°°f°°°d Street where I used to meet Mrs. Y°°°s-
°°°e. It was not much more than mid-day. I got a comfortable little
sitting-room, out of which was a large bed-room. A dinner was sent
in by an Italian restaurant close by. After her first grief had sub-
sided, the wine cheered her, and she made a good dinner, talking
all the time of her "misfortun." When we had finished for a while
I sat caressing her. Then I said, "I want to piddle," — and pulling
my prick out before her went into the bed-room and pissed.

"Don't you want to?" "No." "Nonsense, — do you suppose I
don't know? — now go." She went into the bed-room. I quietly
opened the door ajar directly she had closed it. There was she
sitting on the pot, one leg naked, adjusting her garter, and pissing
hard.

Then raising her clothes that side she scratched her backside
in a dreamy fashion, looking up at the walls. The rattle of her
piddle went on. She had been out all the morning, had had gin and
champagne, and her bladder must have been full. The side she
scratched was towards me. She finished piddling, but still she sat
scratching her rump. Then rising she turned round, looked in the
pot, put it under the bed, pushed her clothes between her thighs,
and looking round saw me at the half-opened door. She gave a
start, I rushed up to her.

"What lovely thighs, — what a splendid bum" (though I hadn't
seen it). "What a shame, — you've been looking at me." "Yes my
darling, — what a lot you have pissed, — what a bum, — I saw
you scratch it, — let's feel it, — I did last night, and you know what
you felt." I got my hands on to her naked thighs, pushing her bum
up against the bedside.

"What a shame to think you have been looking, — leave me
alone, — pray do, — now you shan't, — no — you sh — han't."

I closed with her. I had pulled my stiff-stander out. I shook it at her. "Look at this my darling, — let me put it in you, — up your cunt." "No, — leave off, — I won't, — I have had enough of you men, — you shan't."

For a long time the game went on, I begging her to let me have her, she refusing. We struggled and almost fought. Twenty times I got her clothes up to her belly, my hand between her thighs. I groped all round her firm buttocks, and pinched them, grasped her cunt-wig, and pulled it till she cried out. All the devices I had used with others, all I could think of, I tried in vain. Then I ceased pulling up her clothes; but hugging her to me besought her, kissing and coaxing, keeping one of her hands down against my prick, which she would not feel, — but it was useless. Then stooping and again pulling up her petticoats, letting loose every baudy word that came into my mind, — and I dare say the choicest words, — I threw myself on my knees, and butting my head like a goat up her petticoats, got my mouth on to her cunt, and felt her clitoris on my lips; but I could not move her. She was far stronger than me. Then rising I tried to lift and shove her on to the bed. I might as well have tried to lift the bed itself. I tried to drag her towards a large sofa, big enough for two big people to lay side by side, and made for easy fucking. All was useless. Her weight and her strength were such that I could not move her. There she stood with her backside against the edge of the bed, her hair getting loose, one of her stockings pulled by me down to her ankle, and the upper part of her dress torn open, but no, she would not let me. She was frightened, — she would not, — I was as bad as the soldier. In the excitement she no longer cared about her legs showing to her knees, but her cunt she fought for, and get my prick against it I could not.

So we struggled I don't know how long, and then breathless, fatigued, I got into a violent rage, — a natural rage, not an artificial one, — and it told as brutality often tells with a woman.

We stood looking at each other. She kept one hand on her clothes just outside her quim, as if to defend it. I with my prick out, felt defeated and mortified. I had been so successful with women, that I could not understand not getting my way now. "You damned fool," I said, "I dare say fifty have fucked you, and you make a sham about your damned cunt, and your fears, — what did you come here for?" She opened her eyes with astonishment at my temper.

"I didn't know I was coming here, — I didn't know you meant me to do that, — you said you'd be kind to me, and give me something to eat, sir, — I'd not eaten since last night, — you said you would be kind to me, sir." It was said in the deferential tone of a servant.

"So I will, but if I'm kind, you must be kind to me, — why should it be all on one side?" "I'm sure I don't know," she whimpered. "You know he fucked you, and I dare say a dozen others have." "No one's ever done it but he, and he only did it twice," said she blubbering. "Let me." "No I won't, — I'm frightened to." "Go and be damned." I put in my prick which had drooped, went into the adjoining room, put on my hat and coat, took up my stick, and returning to the bed-room, there was she still with her arse against the bed, crying. She started up when she saw me dressed to go out.

"Oh! don't leave me here alone sir, — you won't, will you?" "Yes I shall, — you can find your way out." "Oh! let me go with you sir." "I shan't, nor see you again, — why should I? — you won't let me have you, not even feel you!"

"I would let you, but I'm frightened, — I've got my living to get, and I've been ill-treated enough by that vagabond, — I didn't think you brought me here for that." "What did you think then?" "I didn't think about it at all, — I was all along thinking of him." "You didn't think of him when I felt your cunt in the cab last night, — good-bye."

"Oh! stay only a minute, — do stay sir, — don't leave me here." She still stood against the bed. "Will you let me? — what a fool you are." "Oh! don't call me names, — I would, but I'm frightened, — I've got my living to get." "Haven't you been fucked?" "Y — hes, — y —hes," she sobbed out, "but it wasn't no fault of mine, — I was — aho! — fud – dled," — and she blubbered as loud as a bull roaring.

A sentiment of compassion came over me, for I never could bear to see a woman cry. I threw off my hat and coat, and going up to her as she stood, kissed her. "There then, — let me feel your cunt, — that can't hurt you."

She did not struggle any more. I lifted her clothes, and placed my fingers on her quim. I frigged hard at the right spot, but could get my fingers no further towards the sacred hole. Her massive thighs shut me off from the prick-tube as closely as if it had been a closed door — I could not get my hand between them.

But my fingers were between the cunt-lips, twiddling and rubbing. "Don't cry, — you'll let me I know, — who will know but we?" I fetched a tumbler of champagne from the sitting-room, and she took it like a draught of water. Up went my hand again, and with fingers rubbing her clitoris we talked and kissed side by side. Then turning myself more towards her, up went my other hand round her big bum, which felt as hard, and smooth, and cold as marble.

This went on a long time. She began gradually to yield when she felt the effects of titillation. She then grasped my fiery doodle. Then frigging her harder, her head dropped over my shoulder, and I got my fingers under the clitoris, and there to the hole. "Oh! (a start) you are scratching me, — you're hurting me there."

Taking away my hand. "Come here, — don't be foolish," said I, "let us do it, — you will enjoy it, — come," — and I pulled her. Her big form left the bed, and slowly she came with me to the sofa. "Sit down, — there, dear, — kiss me, — put up your legs, there's a darling." Slowly, but with much pushing and begging there at last she lay, and the instant she was down I threw her petticoats up, and myself on to her.

I saw the great limbs white as snow. A dark hairy mass up in her thigh-tops. "Oh! don't hurt." "Nonsense I don't." "You do indeed, — oh!" My hands are roving, my arse oscillating, I'm up a cunt, — all is over, — she is fucked.

"Did you have pleasure (I always asked that if I had doubt), — answer me, — did you? — do say, — what nonsense to hold your tongue, — tell me." "Yes I did, after you had done hurting me." "Did I really hurt you?" "Yes." "Impossible." "You did." What a sham, I thought to myself, a woman always is, — a Grenadier has fucked her twice, yet she says my prick hurts her.

I turned off on my side, the sofa being large enough. We had done the trick, and the recklessness of the woman who has tasted the pleasure, and feels the man's spunk in her quim, had come over her. The champagne added its softening influence. She pulled her dress half-down, we laid and talked. I felt her quim. "Don't." "What is it?" "I'm sore." "Why, you are bleeding." "You've hurt me." Out stood my prick, then rose upright again in a moment. Her blood on my finger and her pain gave me a voluptuous shiver. My trowsers were in my way. I tore them off, and stood by her side. "Let me see your cunt." She resisted, but I saw her big thighs closed, and the dark-haired ornamentation. Then getting between her thighs kneeling, I pulled open the lips from which blood-stained sperm was oozing; then I dropped on to her, and again drove my prick up her. A glorious fuck it seemed as I clutched her huge, firm buttocks, and felt her grasping me round my arse. All women, and even girls without any instruction put their arms round the men who are tailing them, the first time they feel the pleasure, but not before. Then we dozed in each other's arms. Then we got up, she confused, I joyous and filled with curious baudiness. "Wash, — won't you?" "You go then." I did, but back I went soon. She had just sluiced it. "You are not bleeding." "I am a little." "You are poorly." "I am not."

I brought her back into the sitting-room. We drank more wine, she got fuddled, not drunk, or frisky, or noisy, but dull, stupid, and obedient. We fucked again and again, and stayed at the baudy house, drinking and amusing ourselves till nine at night. How that big woman enjoyed the prick up her! And the opening of her cunt opened her heart and mouth to me as well.

The big servant's history. — The soldier at the railway station. — Courting. — In the village lane. — On the grass. — At the pot-house. — Broached partially. — Inspection of her privates refused. — Lewed abandonment. — Her first spend. — A night with her. — Her form. — Sudden effects of a looking-glass. — The baud solicits her. — Sexual force and enjoyment. — She gets a situation. — We cease meeting. — The butcher's wife. — An accidental meeting. — She was Sarah by name.

This was her history. As she came up from the country to us, her box was missing at the station. A big soldier seeing she was a stranger made some enquiries for her, saw her into a cab, invited her to have a glass of gin, which she took, and told him the place she was coming to. The next night he showed himself there, he made love to her, wrote to her, met her on Sunday nights, and at other times when allowed to go out. He offered to marry her, and she had written to her sister to tell her about it all.

On the notable Sunday night, he took her to a tavern, and they had gin and beer till she was fuddled. She knew partially what she was doing, and thought it unwise to go up the lane in the dark with him; yet spite of herself she did. He would marry her that day month, then they would sleep together. He cuddled and kissed her, then began to take liberties. She resisted. Then if she would not let him, she might go home by herself, — why not let him? when soon they would be one in holy matrimony, — and so on. She felt as if she could not struggle. He tried to get into her upright against some railings. Then asking her to lay down on the grass, and she refusing, he pulled her down, and got on to her. She struggled and cried, but felt so frightened, that he seems to have had his way.

For all that, he did not, she thought, broach her; he pushed and
hurt her, and must have spent outside, she could not be at all
certain about that. Steps were heard, they got up, she was crying.
Her clothes were, she knew, dirty (though it was dry and fine), her
bonnet was bent. She was frightened to go home; he said she
must get brushed up, and took her to some low tavern to do so.
Terrified at what had been done, and about losing her place and
character, she scarcely knew what she did. She had more gin, went
into a bed-room with him to wash and brush, and then he persuaded
her that now he had done it once, he might as well do it twice.
Then he fucked her on the bed. Now the man had turned out to be
(there was no possible mistake about his identity) a married man
— a sergeant — with two or three children.

"Are you sure he got right into you?" "Quite when on the bed,
but I scarcely know what he did or said in the lane, — a little
fuddles me, — yes I did bleed, for it was on my smock when I got
home, and he did hurt me very much."

I wanted to see her cunt, for her blood-stains made me wonder,
and the rather hard pushing I had had, though only for a second or
two, set me thinking. I felt her cunt, she winced, — it hurt her. An
almost imperceptible stain was on my finger. "You *are* poorly." "I'm
not really, — I was so last week." "Let me see your cunt." I coaxed,
caressed, tried to pull her thighs open. It was useless. She was much
stronger than me, and when she laid hold of my wrist to free herself
from my rovings, she removed it easily. Force could do nothing, —
she was what had been said of her, as strong as a horse.

So again I got savage. I had conquered by my anger two hours
before, and now took to damning and cursing her mock modesty.
Then she began again to whimper. "Oh! you do frighten me, — you
do 'bust' out so, — I'm quite afeared, — it's not nice to have your
thing looked at." "You damned fool, I've fucked it, — I dare say
your soldier looked at it." "He didn't, — he didn't, — not that I
know of." By abusing I got her consent. Pulling open her thighs I
saw her quim. Had she been gay, she would have taken care to turn
her bum from the light; but she laid with her arm across her eyes,
as if to hide from herself, the sight of a man investigating her
love-trap.

There was the ragged jugged-edged slit of a recent virginity,
and near the clitoris the jagging seemed fresh, raw, and signs of

blood just showing on it. I touched it, she winced, and nipped my
hand with her great thighs, which set me damning again. Again
they opened, I probed deep with my fingers up her cunt. There was
no stain from the profundity, and the blood came from the front.
I looked till my cock stood, and then fucked her again.

I could never make this out, and we never met without talking
about it. She was perfectly sure the soldier had been up her, and
spent in her when in the bed-room. As to his prick, whether it was
short or long, thick or thin, she knew not, for she had never seen it,
though he had put her hand to it in the lane. His prick must have
been a very small one, and only split up enough for its entry, and
I had finished her virginity, that is my conclusion.

What is more remarkable, is that her cunt was one of the
tightest I ever met with in a full-grown woman. It felt more like
the cunt of a girl of fourteen, excepting in its depth. It was a full
size outside, and handsome to look at between huge white thighs
and huge globular bum-cheeks. It was fledged like a young woman's.
I expected to find it hairy up to her navel, but it was only slightly
haired, which helped to satisfy me that she was what she said, only
turned twenty-one years of age.

She was great in bulk, but poor in symmetry. Her bum was
vast, but she was thick up to her waist, and had large breasts as
firm as a rock. Her thighs were lovely, but her knees so big, that
no garter would remain above them, and she was clumsy in ankle
and foot. She had a lovely skin, and smelt as sweet as new milk,
sweet to her very cunt. I recollect noticing that in her, because
some time before I had been offended with the smell of Fisher's,
a woman I fucked, as already told.

I spent the rest of the day with Big Sarah, told her I would
keep her as long as she was in her lodgings, and advised her to live
well, and to enjoy herself. But she did not need idleness and feeding
to make her randy, she was a strong fucker, now that her passions
had been once gratified.

I made her twice or thrice stop out all night. She told at her
lodgings that she was going to stay with an aunt. I took her to J°°°s
Street, which I liked better than T°°°f°°°d Street, for that though
the quietest, and only frequented by swells of middle-age, was
old-fashioned, dingy, and dull; whereas J°°°s Street had looking-
glasses, gildings, red satin hangings, and gas-lights. We had a supper

at the Café de l'Europe, and at nine p.m., we were in the room in which I had poked many a woman. I was delighted to see her white flesh under a bright light. "Now drop your chemise — look at me," — and I stripped to the skin. I exposed her bum, belly, and breasts in turn, whilst she laughing tried to prevent me. Flattery of her beautiful form did it. "Am I so beautifully made?" "A model my darling," — and she stood naked excepting stockings and boots. I had shifted the cheval-glass, and we laid on the sofa. "Look at your thighs and cunt my darling in the glass, — see how my prick looks in it." "Law! to think there be houses with all this, — are there many such?" she asked.

I placed her on the sofa, kneeling, her head against the bed, her backside towards me, and introduced my penis dog-fashion. How randy I had made her! — how randy I was as I felt my belling pressing against those two stupendous globes. "Turn your head there, and look in the glass." "Oh!" said she wriggling her backside, "what a shame for us to be looking like that." The sight made her breathless, and wriggle her cunt closer on to the peg, — how soon a woman learns to do that.

There was a large glass against the wall, so placed that those on the bed could see every movement, — I drew the curtain aside. We fucked enjoying the sight of our thrustings, heavings and backside wrigglings, and passed the night in every baudiness which then I practised. "Do you like looking?" "Yes I like it, — but it makes me do it all of a sudden." It was true, for I found that when fucking her, if I said, "Look at us, — look at me shoving," directly she looked it fetched her; her big arse quivered, and her cunt squeezed my prick like a vice. It was the same always on future days, or when if not in the same room I placed the cheval-glass at the side of the bed. The sudden squeeze and jerk of her arse as she looked amused me, and I always arranged for the spectacle with her. I did not usually do this with women.

It was a delicious night. We were both start naked. Her lower limbs looked so much better when quite naked, than when she had stockings and boots on. The room got hot, we threw all the clothes off. She was a juicy one, and the sheets in the morning were a caution, — I wondered whether it could have all come out of one cunt and one cock. "What will they think?" said she.

I showed her in the evening where she would find the closet, and advised her strongly if spoken to, not to reply to any one. We had breakfast in bed, then fucked. Her need to evacuate came on, and half dressing herself she went down. When she came back, out I went on similar errand. She had washed, and I found her on my return anxiously looking at the seminal stains on the bed-linen. We got on to the bed again. Questioning her, she told me that the woman of the house had said to her, "What a splendid woman you are, — I wish you would tell me your address. — I could make your fortune." She had made no reply. I had her as already said several times after, at J°°°s Street, but took care never to let her out of my sight.

She went after a situation. Such a strong, big, fresh-looking woman was sure to get one, I knew. The next time I saw her afterwards she was in low spirits. "I've boiled myself a pretty kettle of fish," she said, "I could have married well in the country, but thought I should do better in Lunnun, — and now what am I?" "My dear, your cunt can't speak, and if you hold your tongue, no one will know anything about our little amusements, and you will marry well."

I soon tired of her. She was a good-natured, foolish, stupid, trusting creature, and my wonder is that she had lived twenty-one years in the country, without having had a prick up her. As a lovely-cunted fuckstress she left nothing to be desired. She had her fears about consequences, for her courses stopped, but she somehow managed to set that to rights, and at last went to her situation. Once afterwards I fucked her, — my God how she enjoyed it! She was in service not far from me. A butcher's man very soon after married her. They opened a shop, and did very well, then they moved some distance away, and I lost sight of her for years. Then I met her walking with two or three children, I suppose her own. We passed, only looking at each other.

But I almost spoke, for she came upon me so unexpectedly, and my first impulse was to speak. She stopped short, threw her head back, and her lower jaw dropped, so that her mouth opened wide, and it would have been ludicrous, had it not been for the expression of fear and pain which came over her face. I recovered myself, passed on, and never saw her more.

I paid her expenses at her lodgings, and gave her a ten-pound note as a present. It was very economical, — but I never knew a woman so delighted with my liberality. "I had two pounds, and now I've twelve," said she, "I shall send a pound to my mother." When I gave her the ten pounds she asked what it was, never having seen a bank-note in her life before. One or two country-women of the same class whom I have had, were just as ignorant of a bank-note.

A gap in the narrative. — A mistress. — A lucky legacy. — Secret preparations. — A sudden flight. — At Paris. — A dog and a woman. — At a lake-city. — A South American lady. — Mrs. O°b°°°e. — Glimpses from a bed-room window. — Hairy armpits. — Stimulating effects. — Acquaintance made. — The children. — "Play with Mamma like Papa." — A water excursion. — Lewed effects. — Contiguous bed-rooms. — Double doors. — Nights of nakedness. — Her form. — Her sex. — Carnal confessions. — Periodicity of lust.

I pass over many incidents of a couple of years or more, during which I was well off, had a mistress whom I had seduced, as it is stupidly called, and had children; but it brought me no happiness, and I fled from the connection. All this was never known to the world. My home life at length became so unbearable, that I at one time thought of realizing all I had, of throwing up all chance of advancement and a promising career which then was before me, and going for ever abroad I knew not where, nor cared. My mother had died, one sister was married, and was not much comfort to me; the other was far off, my brother nowhere. Just then a distant relative left me a largish sum of money, it was scarcely known to any one of my friends, quite unknown at home, and to none until I had spent a good deal of it. I kept the fact to myself till I had put matters in such train that I could get a couple of thousand pounds on account, then quietly fitted myself out with clothes. One day I sent home new portmanteaus, and packed up my clothes the same day. "I am going abroad," I said. "When?" "To-night." "Where to?" "I don't know, — that is my business." "When do you come back?" "Perhaps in a week, — perhaps a year," — nor did I for a long time. I never wrote to England during that time, excepting to my solicitors and bankers who necessarily knew where I had been at times.

I went first to Paris, where I ran a course of baudy house amusements, saw a big dog fuck a woman who turned her rump towards it as if she were a bitch. The dog licked and smelt her cunt first, and then fucked. He was accustomed to the treat. Then I saw a little spaniel lick another French woman's cunt. She put a little powdered sugar on her clitoris first, and when the dog had licked that off, somehow she made it go on licking, until she spent, or shammed a spend, calling out, "Nini, — cher Nini, — go on Nini," — in French of course.

I could make a long story out of both of these incidents if it were worth while, but it is not, and only notice that the Newfoundland, whose tongue hung out quite as long as his prick as he was pushing his penis up the French woman's quim, turned suddenly round when it had spent, seemed astonished to find he was not sticking arse to arse with her, and then licked the remains of the sperm off the tip of his prick. It was not a nice sight at all, nor did I ever want to see it again.

There were few large cities of Central Europe I did not see, and think that the best baudy houses in most large cities saw *me*. It was a journey in which my amatory doings were especially with the priestesses of Venus. Beautiful faces and beautiful limbs were sufficient for me, if coupled with ready submission to my wishes. Although I learnt no doubt a great deal, and had my voluptuous tastes cultivated in a high degree, yet they developed none of those outside tastes which ordinarily come with great knowledge and practice in the matters of cunt. I shall only tell the most remarkable fornicating incidents.

I was at the Hotel B°°° in a Swiss town by a great lake, had arrived late, and was put into the third story, in a room overlooking a quadrangle. It was hot. I threw up my window when I got out of bed in the morning, and in night-gown looked into the quadrangle, and at the walls and windows of the various bed-rooms opening on to it on three sides. Looking down on my right, and one story below me, I caught sight over the window-curtain of a bed room, of a female head of long dark hair, and a naked arm brushing it up from behind vigorously. The arm looked the size of a powerful man's, but it was that of a woman. She moved about heedlessly, and soon I saw that she was naked to below her breasts; but I only caught glimpses of that nakedness, for seconds, as she moved backwards and forwards near the window. Then she held up the hair for a minute, and seemed to be contemplating the effect of the arrangement of it, and showed what looked like a nest of hair beneath one armpit. Her flesh looked sallow or brown, and she seemed big and middle-aged. My window was near the angle of the quadrangle, so was hers, on the adjacent side of it. Perhaps from the window where I was, and that above mine only, could be seen all what I saw.

The armpit excited me, and I got lewed, though the glimpses were so few and short. Now I only saw the nape of the neck, and now her back, according to the postures which a woman takes in arranging her hair, and so far as the looking-glass and blinds and my position above let me. Once or so I saw big breasts of a tawny color. Then she looked at her teeth. Then she disappeared, then came forwards again, and I fancied she was naked to the waist. Then I lost sight of her, and again for an instant saw just the top of her naked bum, as if she were stripped, and in stooping down had bent her back towards the window. When she reappeared she was more dressed. She looked up at the sky, approaching the window to do so, caught sight of me, and quickly drew the blind right down.

I went down to breakfast, met some friends, and sitting down to table with them in the large breakfast-room, saw close to me this very lady. I had seen so little of her face that I did not recognize her at first by that; but the darkness of the eye and hair, the fullness of bust, and the brown-tinted skin left me in no doubt. We were introduced to each other. "Mrs. O°b°°°e, a lady from New Orleans, a great friend of ours, — been travelling with us for some weeks, with her two little children," — and so on.

I found out from my friends as we smoked our cigars in the gardens after breakfast, that she, with another American lady, and themselves, were going for a long tour, and had been touring for some weeks in Europe. She was the wife of a gentleman who owned plantations, and had gone back to America; intending to rejoin his wife at Paris at Christmas. The lady with the very hairy armpits and her husband were intimate friends of my friends.

I found this party were travelling my road, and I agreed to wait at °°°° as long as they did. We met at meals; I joined in their excursions, and took much notice of her children who got quite fond of me. She seemed to avoid me at first, but in two or three days showed some sympathy. I guessed that my history had been made known to her, and found out at a latter day that it had. "A married man travelling without his wife is dangerous," said she to me one day when we were a merry party. "A married woman without her husband is a danger to me," I replied, and our eyes met, and said more than words.

I objected to my room, and in a few days the hotel-keeper showed me some better rooms. I had then ascertained which hers were, and pointed out the room next to them. "That," said he, "won't do — it's large, and has two beds." "Oh! it's so hot, I want a large room, — show it me." He did. "It's double price." "Never mind," — and I took it at once. Luck, thought I. Her own room was next, and adjoining it a room in which her two children slept. A half-governess, half-maid who travelled with her, was on another floor, — why I don't know, — perhaps because the next room to the children's was a sitting-room.

My new room had as usual a door communicating with hers. I listened one or two nights and mornings, and heard the slopping of water and rattle of pots, but with difficulty; and nothing sufficiently to stir my imagination or satisfy my curiosity. There were bolts on both sides of the doors, and double doors. I opened mine, and tried if hers was fastened. It was. But I waited my opportunity, intending to try to have her, thinking that a woman who had not had a man for months, and might not for some months more, would be ready for a game of mother and father if she could do so safely.

She was not very beautiful, but was fine, tallish, handsomely formed, with a large bust, and splendid head of hair. Her complexion had the olive tint of some Southerners. One might almost have supposed there was a taint of Negro blood in her, but her features were rather aquiline and good. The face was coldish and stern, the eyes dark and heavy, the only sensuous feature of her face was a full, large-lipped mouth, which was baudy in its expression when she laughed. I guess she was a devil of a temper.

After a day or two I gave up all hope, for she would not understand double entendres, coldly returned my grasp when I shook hands with her, and gave no signs of pleasure in my company, excepting when I was playing with her children. Yet when she

looked into my face when laughing; there certainly was something
in her eye, which made me think that a pair of balls knocking
about her bum would delight her. I used to think much of what a
friend of mine, a surgeon in a crack regiment in which I had some
friends, used to say, which was this.

"All animals are in rut sometimes, so is a woman, even the
coldest of them. It's of no use trying the cold ones, unless they have
the tingling in their cunts on them; then they are more mad for it
than others, but it doesn't last. If you catch a cold woman just
when she is on heat, try her; but how to find out their time, I
never knew, — they are damned cunning." So said the surgeon.

I must have caught Mrs. O°b°°°e on heat I suppose, and it
came about soon. We went out for some hours on the lake in a
boat. She was timid, and when the boat rocked I held her, squeezed
her arm, and my knees went against hers. Another time my thigh
was close against hers. I put one of her children on to her lap. The
child sat down on my hand, which was between her little bum and
her mother's thighs. I kept my hand there, gradually moving it
away, creeping it up higher and higher, and gripping the thigh as
I moved it towards the belly, but so delicately, as to avoid offence,
and I looked her in the face. "Minnie is heavy, isn't she?" I said.
"She is getting so," she replied, looking with a full eye at mine.

Now I felt sure from her look, that she knew I was feeling her
thigh. I had stirred her voluptuousness. The water got rougher. "I
shall be sick," said she. "What! on such a lake!" "Oh! I'm a bad
sailor." Placing my arm round her for a minute I pulled her close
to me. It became calm, and lovely weather again. The water always
upset her, it seemed to stir her up, she said. "I'd like to see you
stirred up," said I. Then to avoid remark I changed sides with a
lady, and sat opposite to Mrs. O°b°°°e. We faced each other,
looking at each other. I pushed my feet forward, so as to rub my
foot against her ankle. She did not remove her foot, but looked
at me.

Arrived at °°° we dined, and sat afterwards in the garden.
It grew dusk, and we separated into groups. I sat by her side, and
played with her children. One child said, "Play with me like Papa,
— play with Mamma like Papa does." "Shall I play with you like
Papa?" said I to Mrs. O°b°°°e. "I'd rather not," said she. "I'd
break an arm to do so," I replied. "Would you?" said she. "Oh!

put the children to bed Margaret," — and the governess with the children and Mrs. O°b°°°e walked off. I for a minute joined my friends smoking, then cut off by a side-path leading to that through which Mrs. O°b°°°e would pass, She had just bid the children good night. "I shall come up to see you directly," said she to them, — and to me, "I thought you were going into town." "Yes I think I'll make a night of it, — I'm wild. — I want company." "Fine company it will be, I dare say." "Let me keep you company then." No one was near, I kissed her. She took it very quietly. "Don't now, you'll compromise me." It was now quite dusk. I kissed her again. "I'm dying to sleep with you," I whispered. "You mustn't talk like that, — there now, they will see you," — then I left her.

I had noticed her habits, and knew that usually she went up to her children soon after they had gone to bed, so I waited at the foot of the stairs. Soon she came. "What, you here?" "Yes, I'm going to bed like you." It was a sultry night, everybody was out of doors, the hotel servants lolling at open windows. No one met us as we went upstairs. "Why that's not your room, — it's next to mine." "Yes it is, — I've been listening to you the last two nights." "Oh! you sly man, — I thought you were sly." "Look what a nice room it is," said I opening the door. There was a dim light in the corridors, none in my room. She looked in, I gave her a gentle squeezing push, and shut the door on us.

"Don't shut the door," said she turning sharply round. I caught and kissed her. "Stop with me, my darling, now you're here, — I'm dying for you, — kiss me, do." "Let me go, — there then, — now let me go, — don't make a noise, — oh! if my governess should hear me, what would she think!" "She is not there." "Sometimes she stays till I go up to the children, — oh! don't now, — you shan't." I had her up against the wall, my arm round her, I was pressing my hand on her belly outside her clothes. She pushed my hand away, I stooped and thrust it up her clothes on to her cunt, and pulling out my prick, pushed her hand on to it. "Let me, — let's do it, — I'm dying for you." "Oh! for God's sake don't, oh! no — now, you'll compromise me, — hish! if she should be listening." For a moment we talked, she quietly struggled, entreating me to desist; but my fingers were well on to her cunt, frigging it. I don't recollect more what she said, but I got her to the side of the bed, pushed her back on it, and thrust my prick up her. "Oh! don't compromise me — don't now." Then she fucked quietly till she gasped out, "Oho — oho," as a torrent of my sperm shot into her cunt.

Excepting from the clear light of the night, which came from the sky through the window in the quadrangle, the room was in darkness. I don't know that my prick ever lingered longer up a woman after fucking and declare that whilst up her, I told how I had seen her brushing her hair, and so on. She said that I should compromise her, — and oh! if she should be with child, — "what will become of me." Feeling the sperm oozing out over my balls, and my prick shrinking, I uncunted. "Oh! what have you made me do, you bad man?" said she sitting upon the side of the bed. "Oh! if they should see me going out of your room, — oh! if she has been listening."

I drew down the blind, and lighted a candle, much against her wish. She sat at the edge of the bed just where she had been fucked, her clothes still partly up. I listened at the door between our two rooms, but heard nothing, then told her again how I had watched her from a top-window, and seen her breasts and armpits. My prick stiffened at my own tale. Sitting down by her side, "Let's do it again my love," I said, and pushed my hand up her clothes. I shall never forget the feel. The whole length of her thighs, as she closed them on my hand felt like a pot of paste. Only a minute's pleasure, and such a mass of sperm! She repulsed me, and stood up.

I stood up too; kissing, coaxing, insisting, she looking at me, I fingering, pulling backwards and forwards the prepuce of my penis. No, she would not. Then I threatened to make a noise, if she would not, and swore I would have her again. She promised to let me if I would let her go to her bed-room first, — she would unlock her side of the two doors, if she could. She was not sure if there was a key, — if not she would open the door on to the corridor, but only at midnight, when the gas was turned out, and few people about. She promised solemnly, and sealed it with a kiss. "Oh! for God's sake be quiet." I opened the door of my bed-room, and saw no one in the lobby. Out she went, and got into her own room unnoticed. Then I opened the door to her room from my side. There were double doors.

She seemed to keep me a long time waiting, though she had

scarcely been in her room five minutes. I stripped myself to my shirt, then knocked at the door gently, then louder. A key turned, the door opened. She had only gone in to be sure that the children were in their bed, and the governess not with them. "Oh! I have been so fearful lest she should have been there," she said.

The children were asleep, she had bolted their door. "And now go to bed, and let me also, — there is a dear man, and don't ask anything more of me." "To bed yes, but with you." She begged me not, all in a whisper. My reply was to strip off my shirt, and stand start naked with prick throbbing, and wagging, and nodding with its size, weight, and randiness. "Only once, one more, and then I will be content." "No."

"Then damned if I won't," said I moving towards her. "Hush! my children will hear, — in your room then," — and she came towards my door. "Oh! nonsense, not with your clothes on, — let us have our full pleasure, — and this hot night too, — take off your things." Little by little she did, and stood in her chemise. I tried all the doors, they were securely fastened, and then I brought her quite into my room. "Leave me alone a minute," she said. But as randy as if I had not left my sperm up her fifteen minutes before, I would not, and pulled her gently toward my bed, tore the clothes off, so as to leave the bottom sheet only on, and got her on to the bed. "Do let me see your cunt." "No, — no, — no." As I pulled up her chemise, down she pushed it. "Oh! no, — I'm sure I shall be with child," said she, "and if I am I'd just best make a hole in the water." Her big breasts were bare, her thighs opened, a grope on the spermy surface, and then fucking began. "Oho!" she sighed out loudly again, as she spent.

Off and on until daybreak we fucked. After the second she gave herself up to pleasure. The randiest slut just out of a three months quodding could not have been hotter or readier for lewed fun with cunt and ballocks. I never had a more randy bed-fellow. She did not even resist the inspection of her cunt, which surprised me a little, considering its condition. Our light burnt out, our games heated us more and more, the room got oppressive, I slipped off her chemise, our naked bodies entwined in all attitudes, and we fucked, and fucked, bathed in sweat, till the sweat and sperm wetted all over the sheet, and we slept. It was broad daylight when we awakened. I was lying sweating with her bum up against my belly, her hair was loose all over her, and the bed. Then we separated and she fled to her room, carrying her chemise with her.

Oh! Lord that sheet! — if ten people had fucked on it, it could not have been more soiled. We consulted how best to hide it from the chamber-maid, and I did exactly the same trick as of former days. Have not all men done it I wonder?

I got a sitz-bath in my room, which was then not a very easy thing to get. I washed in it, wetted all my towels, then took off the sheet, wetted it nearly all over, soiled it, then roughly put it together in a heap, and told the chamber-woman I had used the sheet to dry myself with. She said, "Very well." I don't expect she troubled herself to undo or inspect the wet linen, or thought about the matter.

I went to breakfast at the usual time. "Where is Mrs. O°b-°°°e?" I asked. The governess appeared with the children saying the lady had not slept owing to the heat. She showed up at the table d'hôte dinner. I avoided her, knowing I should see her soon afterwards, and said I should go and play billiards; but instead, went to my bed-room and read; nursing my concupiscent tool, and imagining coming pleasures.

I heard the children, having opened the door on my side and found that the key of her door was luckily so turned as to leave the key-hole clear. The doors connecting all the rooms were as is often the case in foreign hotels, opposite each other, and I could see across into the children's bed-room. They were putting their night-gowns on in their own room. Then the governess came into her mistress' room and I heard her pissing, but could not see her. To my great amusement, for the slightest acts of a woman in her privacy give me pleasure, she then came forward within range of my peep-hole, and was looking into the pot carefully. Then Mrs. O°b°°°e came in and the governess left. Mrs. O°b°°°e went to look at her children and returned, opened our doors, and then we passed another amorous night, taking care to put towels under her bum when grinding. We did not want the sheets to be a witness against us again.

Mrs. O°b°°°e was not up to the mark, and began to talk that sort of bosh that women do, who are funky of consequences. After a time she warmed, and yielded well to my lubricity. I would see her cunt to begin with. It was a pretty cunt, and not what I had expected, large, fat-lipped, and set in a thicket of black hair, from her bum-hole to her navel; but quite a small slit, with a moderate quantity of hair on her motte, but very thick and crisp. I told her again how I had seen her from the window. The recital seemed to render her randier than either feeling my prick, or my titillation of her quim. The hair in her armpits was thicker, I think, than in any woman I ever had. Her head-hair was superb in its quantity. I made her undo it, and spread it over the bed, and throw up her arms, and show her armpits when I fucked her. She was juicy-cunted, and spent copiously; so did I. The heat was fearful. We fucked stark naked, again.

Later on she told me that she cared about poking but once a month only, and about a week before her courses came on. At other times it annoyed her. Going on the water always upset her stomach, and made her lewed, even if in a boat on a river, and however smooth it was, it upset her that way. At sea it was the same. It made her firstly feel sick, then giddy, then sleepy, but that always two or three hours afterwards, randiness overtook her. After a day or two, the lewedness subsided whether she copulated, or frigged, or not. She told me this as a sort of excuse for having permitted me to spermatize her privates, the night of her excursion on the water with us.

She was curious about my history. I told her I had women at every town I came to. She declared that no other man but I and her husband had ever had her.

CHAPTER XV

Frantic coition. — A priapus. — Purging and resting. — Priapus humbled. — Carnal exercises resumed. — The governess. — A peep through a key-hole. — Bathing. — The after-frig. — My politeness. — The silk mantle. — Travelling resumed. — The new hotel. — Felt, and all but. — Unproductive seed. — A thin partition. — Scared by a laugh. — Unsuccessful. — The mantle given. — Still no success. — I leave.

On the third night which I had her, she had undressed to her chemise, and had lifted one leg to pull off her boot. It was a small foot, and a fine fat leg. A letch to have her with her boots and stockings on struck me. She was now complaisant in everything, and I fucked her thus at the side of the bed, and then with her bum towards me I had her again. She was tired, and prayed me to desist. I felt tired, but so heated, and irritated in my privates, and so furiously lewed, that though my sense told me I had done enough, my prick refused to be quiet, and kept standing. It was still fearfully hot. I had been abstinent from women for some time, until I had seen Mrs. O°b°°°e's armpits, and had since been idling, eating, drinking, smoking, and thinking, almost dreaming, of nothing but baudy things and of fucking her.

At last I let her go to her own bed, and laid down outside my own. My prick had come out of her stiffish, and soon got as hard as iron, and kept so till I could bear it no longer, and went into her room. She was asleep, and outside her bed with her boots and stockings on still. She had laid down fatigued, and fell asleep thus. I think I see her now as I pulled up her chemise, and felt her still wet cunt. I made her angry, but she came to my bed. Again my pego pushed up her. Now she had said "Oh! I'm so tired, — pray let me

go." "I will my darling after this." "Oh! I'm spending again," she
almost shrieked, and so did I. Then I let her go. I tell all this with
minuteness, for the circumstances were so exceptional, that they are
impressed on my memory in the minutest detail.

I fell asleep and awakened with prick harder than ever, heard
her snoring, and not liking to disturb her, pissed, thinking that that
might reduce my concupiscent machine to a wagging size. It did
not, and thinking about her bum, armpits, and all her charms, I got
furious. My prick had none of the soft voluptuous sensation in it,
which comes from sperm-charged balls, but ached from its roots
to my arse-hole; yet the tip was sensitive to pleasure. Rubbing my
finger on it made it throb, and my whole body quiver, though I had
none of the incipient pleasure of a spend.

I awakened her. No I should *not* do it any more. But I threw
myself on to her, and fingered her cunt with passion. Her thighs
opened again, and I drove up her with violence and baudy ejacula-
tions, for my brain seemed on fire. "Oh! pray, — oh! if the children
should awake." "Come to my room then." I uncunted, and she came.
Ram, ram, ram. "Oh! I'm doing it," she cried, but it took me a mile
of shoving to spend. She spent twice before I did, and when I un-
cunted my prick was still stiff. I would not let her leave, but lay
fondling her (almost sticking together in our sweat), and making
her feel my iron-bound prick till I mounted her again.

"Oh! what a man, — you're hurting, — why it's stiff still, —
don't push up so hard, — I feel as if my womb was falling, — oh!
I'm spending, — oh! you'll kill me, — don't, — leave off." At day-
light I was still feeling her cunt, kissing, and pushing my prick up
her, almost as soon as I had uncunted. Then she refused angrily
to let me do it any more, — and no wonder, but I held her to me.

Now I could not spend at all, yet had pleasure in the fucking.
She on the contrary spent quicker, and quicker, had got inflamed
and excited both in mind and cunt. She kept begging me to stop
after each of her spends, and saying I should kill her. At the last
spend she gave a scream, and began to sob, uncunted my penis by
a violent jerk, and there was blood on it. I think some of it was
mine. How often I spent that night I never could tell. I was fucking
for about eight hours, off and on almost without stopping. Then I
slept, and when I awoke, had still a prick stiff, but it was aching
fearfully.

She had locked herself in, never answered my whispered calls,
nor my discreet raps, and did not appear that day. She was ill.
I looked a scarecrow, and told a man of our party that I had been
at a baudy house all night. My prick all day kept standing at
intervals. Seeing in the afternoon the governess take out the children
for a walk, I went to my room, saw Mrs. O*b***e, and promised
not to exact anything that night; but at bed-time insisted on
plugging her cunt again. She said I was a brute, that I only cared
about my own pleasure, and refused me positively, entreating me
not to make a noise and compromise her, but I fucked her till she
screamed, and so did I, with mixed pain and pleasure.

My stiffness without much desire, still continued and much
annoyed me. Such a copulative fury had never occurred to me
before. At last I began to think that there was some ailment coming
on. I had heard of such things, of men going mad through it, and
got alarmed.

Then I frigged, hoping to reduce it, and after immense trouble
got a pleasure, but so mixed with pain that I groaned. I could
scarcely see any sperm, felt burning hot all over me, my mouth was
parched, I was trembling, and thought I had better see a doctor.
I carried medicine in my trunk, took a violent dose, in a few hours
nearly shit my guts out, then took more medicine, and laid a bed,
all day, eat nothing, and my prick gradually became tranquil. Mrs.
O*b***e's cunt was mulberry in colour, my prepuce was raw, we
rested from our amatory labours for several days, but we talked
about it a great deal.

Then both with re-invigorated privates, we fucked, and covered
again some towels with sperm. She was sure she was in the family
way. Again I got symptoms of a priapus, and wore her out by
ramming, and making her spend. At last she spent thrice before
I did, I felt a peculiar wetness on my prick, pulled it out, it was
covered with her courses. "Thank God," said she.

Then I had a weakness which I thought was clap. It was
nothing but the result of over-fucking. She got her courses over,
and refused to let me have her again. My gleet cured itself by
quietness and careful living.

We kept as secret as we could that my room was next to hers.
We always looked into the corridor before leaving or entering
our rooms, and never did so at the same time. She had special fear

of the governess finding her out. I thought that she need have no fear on that head. But one never knows.

One evening she said to the governess, "Give the children their bath just warm." The girls had a bath once or twice a week, before going to bed. Instinct which has always helped me so in these affairs, made me go directly afterwards to my bed-room. Instinct was right. The bath was in front of the key-hole in Mrs. O°b°°°e's room. I saw the girls washed, could just see where their little hairless splits began (it was daylight still), and then oh! luck! The governess, a dark-eyed, short young woman about twenty-four years of age, an American, gave herself a bath, and soaped and rubbed herself from the nape of her neck to her toes. She rubbed her cunt dry in a most irritating, cock-stiffening manner, within two yards of my eye, and then dressed herself again, and sat down on a chair.

Scarcely had she seated herself, than she began to pull up her clothes in all manner of ways, as if hunting for a flea; then got a book, and turning her back to the light began reading, keeping her right hand up her petticoats. Then she went and pulled down the blind. She lighted candles, and sat down reading again, nearly facing me. Her hand after a while went up her petticoats on to her quim, and moved gently. She put the book on a little movable table, one of her legs on the edge of the bath, the other on the floor, and pulled her petticoats a little up to ease her hand, showing her legs a little above her knees (she had not put stockings on after the bath). Then her legs opened wide, her hand moved, she frigged hard and quick, I saw the shake of it, her legs quiver, stretch open then close, her bum wriggle, her legs open, her head fall on one side and her eyes close. Her hand then appeared from under her clothes and hung lifelessly over her petticoats, which fell down, and so she sat for a minute as if asleep. Then she put her hand under her petticoats, withdrew it, looked at it, washed it in the bath, and moved away. Then I heard her pissing. Then the chamber-maid appeared, and took away the bath. When doing so Mrs. O°b°°°e came in and asked why the bath was still there, and if the children were asleep. I closed my door, and slipped downstairs, not desirous of having it known that I had been in my bed-room.

It was a delightful sight. Nothing gives me more pleasure than seeing a woman dress and undress, wash, piddle, and do all she wants, not thinking any one is looking at her. I'm not sure that it is not as exciting as the baudiest sights a woman can give a man. Three women, — chaste women, — have I seen frigging themselves, when they could not have thought they were observed, and the sights will never fade from my memory. I have seen and heard full twenty chaste women dress, undress, wash, brush, piddle, without their knowing I did so.

Later that night I had Mrs. O°b°°°e and fucked her thinking of the governess. How strange it seems that when my genitals have been in a woman, and the sperm rising to moisten her cunt, I have at times thought of some other woman, and copulation with them.

Mrs. O°b°°°e and I did not allude to our married condition. One evening laying face to face, kissing, I fingering her clitoris, she holding my prick, I put a question. She said no, her husband's prick was not quite as large as mine, very nearly she thought, and then, "Oh! don't let us talk about such things," — and we never as far as I can recollect referred again to similar subject.

Her first night with me seemed the highest development of randiness and sensuous enjoyment I ever witnessed in a woman, who was what may be called chaste. Her long abstinence from a doodle, the effect on her physical organization of the rocking of the boat, and my stimulating words acting upon her mind caused it. She seemed almost mad with pleasure. When fucking, her sighs were continuous, though she was quiet in tongue, until the crisis came on. The copious discharges she made were like a flood, but it was that night alone, afterwards she was different. Towards the end of our acquaintance, she said she was worn out, and did not care about it. She was a strong-scented woman. When she got hot, a sort of baudy, cunty, sweaty exhalation evolved from her. I shall always think it was that among other things, which got me such an attack of stiff-standing, and that the aroma of her body excited me, though it somewhat offended me.

I had been at the Lake hotel some weeks, and the party were about to move off. I was going in the same direction, but expected a friend to meet me, and they left a day before I did. The last night I begged her to let me have her and she consented under a solemn promise not to spend in her. I always loved to spend hard home, but kept my word, and spent outside her cunt, pulling out my prick just when the ejaculation of sperm began, and letting it fall on to her buttocks. Then we parted. She said if ever we met again we must try to forget what we had been to each other, and that I was to blame more than she was. We saw each other two days afterwards, but I never had her again, and she did not go to Paris at Christmas. I did, and heard she had gone back to America.

From the night I saw the governess frig herself, I lusted for her. Talking about her to one of the party, he told me he thought she knew the feel of six inches of stiff up her; but I got no more out of him. I met her walking in the town, and looking at a mantle in a shop-window, and asked her if she were going to buy it. "Oh! no I can't afford it, though it would just suit me." "I'll give it you if you will let me —" "Let you what?" Her eyes met mine. "Let me bring it to you some evening when they are all a bed." She shook her head, and walked away. I bought the mantle, and took it to the hotel.

I took it with me three days afterwards to the town of °°°. There we were all again together at the same hotel. She was not far off from Mrs. O°b°°°e's room this time. I got a bed-room as near to hers as I could, but was bothered because my friend with whom I was going to travel had a bed-room very near to mine.

I told her I had bought her the mantle. No she would not take it, nor let me take it to her, Mrs. O°b°°°e would ask her where she bought it, would wonder how she could afford it. Spite of all her objections I knocked at her door one evening just before she could have undressed, and after Mrs. O°b°°°e had gone to bed, "only to show it to you." I saw her, and got into the room. There was as occasionally happens, no door between hers and the adjoining rooms, but the partitions were so thin that you could hear through them easily any one cough, snore, or fart. I begged and besought her to feel me, to let me feel her. I threatened to make a noise and compromise her. She did not want the mantle, if she was to be ruined and insulted for it, — she had not asked me for it, which was true enough. But little by little we kissed, I pulled up her clothes, saw her thighs, and got the smell of her cunt on my finger; but she would not let me do it, though she felt my prick. "Oh! do leave me, — I'll do anything but let you do that, — I mustn't, — if Mrs. O°b°°°e found anything out, I should be ruined and turned off in a strange land." And in the midst of this I spent whilst her hand was round my prick, one of mine on her thighs, and I was vainly trying to push her on to the bed. Then I desisted.

With her hand covered with sperm she stood looking at it, and at me, and saying, "Do go," I tried for another hour I suppose, and was about to conquer, had got her on to the bed, and was just getting on myself, when we heard a loud burst of laughter in the adjoining room. That disconcerted us both, for it seemed as if they were laughing at us, and she jumped up in terror.

She recovered herself, when we heard the talking and laughing continuing, but it had spoiled my chance, though I tried for hours afterwards. Then angrily leaving her, I left her the mantle; but the next morning I asked her for it, which was mean. She sent it into my room. I felt a little ashamed of myself for taking it. I never got into her room again, so I amused myself by talking the hottest and lewedest I could to her, for the three or four days I remained there; principally asking whether she would like any of my sperm on to her cunt and if she had frigged when I had left the room. She took it very quietly, but used to colour up and look randy. Then I was obliged to leave, so I sent the mantle to her with a note saying it was hers, and departed without having fucked her, nor do I know whether a penis had ever probed her or not, but I think that had I remained longer, I should have found that out. A woman who has had a man's sperm on her fingers must feel yielding afterwards.

Camille the second. — Stripping. — The divan. — Cock-washing. — Camille's antecedents. — Face, form, and cunt. — Mode of copulating. — Avaricious. — Free fucking offered. — Gabrielle. — Cunt, form, and face. — Minette. — My daily dose of doxies. — At M°°g°°e. — Lodgings at the greengrocer's. — Louisa the red-haired. — The lodging-house servant. — The shop-boy. — My friend's daughter. — Piddling, and presents. — Loo's bum pinched. — The servant kissed. — A stroke on the sands. — With Loo on the beach. — Chaff, and cunt-tickling. — A declaration of love. — The virtuous servant.

I do not recollect having gone with a French woman excepting when abroad, my tastes ran on my own countrywomen. Now in the year 18°°, a year of national importance, and one in which strangers came from all parts of the world to London, I was to have a French woman again.

Was it for the sake of change only, or because they were more willing, salacious, enterprising, and artistic in Paphian exercises? — was it my recollection of having that when I did not want it? — I cannot say.

At quite the beginning of the month of June, about four o'clock in the afternoon, I saw a woman walking slowly along Pall-Mall dressed in the nicest and neatest way. I could scarcely make up my mind whether she was gay or not, but at length saw the quiet invitation in her eye, and slightly nodding in reply, followed her to a house in B°°y Street, St. James. She was a French woman named Camille.

I named my fee, it was accepted, and in a quiet, even ladylike way she began undressing. With a neatness unusual in gay women, one by one each garment was folded up, and placed on a chair, pins stuck in a pin-cushion, &c., with the greatest composure, and almost without speaking. I liked her even for that, and felt she would suit my taste. As each part of her flesh came into view, I saw that her form was lovely. When in her chemise, I began undressing, she sitting looking at me. When in my shirt, I began those exquisite preliminaries with this well-made, pretty woman, feeling her all over, and kissing her; but my pego was impatient, and I could not go on at this long. Smiling she laid hold of my prick. "Shall we make love?" this was in the bed-room. "Yes." "Here, or in the salon?" "I don't like a sofa." "Mais ici," said she pushing the door open wide, and pointing to a piece of furniture which I had not noticed, though noticeable enough.

In the room was a sort of settee or divan, as long, and nearly as wide as a good-sized bed; so wide that two people could lie on it side by side. It had neither head nor feet, but presented one level surface, covered with a red silky material, and a valance hanging down the sides. At one end were two pillows, also red, and made flat like two bed-pillows. "There, on that," said I at once.

I never saw any divan or piece of furniture like it in my life since, neither in brothel, nor in private house, here or on the Continent, excepting once when quite in the extreme East of Europe.

It was a blazing hot day. "Shall I take off my chemise?" "Yes." Off she took it, folded it up, and took it into the bed-room. "Take off your shirt." Off I drew it, and we both stood naked. She laid hold of my stiff prick, gave it a gentle shake, laughed, fetched two towels, spread one on the divan for her bum, laid the other on a pillow for me, went back to the bed-room, poured out water in the basin, then laid herself down naked on the divan with her bum on the towel. I kissed her belly and thighs, and she opened them wide for me to see her notch, without my having asked her to do so. To pull it open, have a moment's glance at the red, kiss and feel her rapidly over, mount her, fuck and spend, was only an affair of two or three minutes, so strongly had she stirred my lust for her.

I laid long up her, raising myself on my elbow to talk with her whilst my prick was still in her sheath. At length it slipped out.

Gently she put her hand down, and caught it, taking off the excess of moisture. Delicately she raised the towel, and put her hand on her cunt, and saying with a smile, "Mon Dieu, il y en a assez," went to the bed-room, I following her.

She wiped her cunt with the towel, half squatting to do so, then rose up quickly saying, "Shall I wash you?" I had begun, but the offer pleased me. I have no recollection as I write this, of any gay woman having made such an offer. "Yes wash it." "Hold the basin then," — and taking it up she placed it under me, so that my testicles hung into it whilst I held it. She washed me. "Soap?" "Yes." "Inglis sop" (laughing), — the first English words I heard her speak. My prick washed, she performed a similar operation on herself. All was done so nicely, cleanly, and delicately that I have never seen it excelled by any woman.

"Causons-nous?" said she leading the way to the divan. Then both laying down naked we gossiped. She was from Arles, in France, eighteen years of age, had been in London a fortnight, had been tailed six months and lived with her father most of that time. A month ago had been persuaded to go to Lyons by an old woman who there sold her pleasures, and kept her money. Another old one snapped her up there, and brought her to London, to a house in B°°n°°s Street, where a young French woman more experienced than Camille induced her to work on her own account. They two got away, Camille set up in B°°y Street, her friend elsewhere. That was told me laying naked with her on the divan.

[She was alone in London, and still exercising her occupation the other day, thirty-one years after I first had her. I have known her, and had her occasionally during all that time, though sometimes two or three years have elapsed between my visits to her. She has been in poor circumstances for years past, and oftentimes I have gone out of my way purposely to meet her, and give her a bit of gold, out of regard for her.]

We lay during her narration (which was soon told) naked. Hot as it was I felt a slight coolness, and drawing myself closer up to her, "It's cool," I said. Without reply, she put one hand over me to help my embrace of her, with the other handled gently my prick, the next instant kissed me, and I felt her tongue peeping out of her pretty lips, seeking my tongue. My fingers naturally had been

playing gently about her cunt all the time of our talk, and her
hand rubbing gently over my naked flesh. So for a minute in
silence our tongues played with each other, and then without a
word and with one consent, and like one body we moved together
gently, she on to her back, I on to her belly, my prick went up her,
and with slow probing thrusts, with now and then a nestle and a
pause, till the rapid clip-clip of her cunt drove me into more rapid
action, to the rapid in and out and the final short thrusts and
wriggle against her womb, till my prick with strong pulsations sent
my sperm up her again. "Ah! chéri, — mon Dieu, — a — h — a!"
she sighed as she had spent with me. "You fuck divinely," said she,
but in chaste words, afterwards.

A wash as before, and then with chemise and shirt on, we
talked about France, London, beer, wine, and other topics. "Let
me look at your cunt." I had scarcely looked at it. Without reply
she fell back, opened her thighs, and then I saw all, all, — and so
for two hours we went on, till it was time for me to dine, and with
a parting fuck which we both enjoyed, we parted. I added another
piece of gold to what I had already put on the mantel piece before
she began to undress. A custom of mine then, and always followed
since, is putting down my fee, — it prevents mistakes, and quarrels.
When paid, if a woman will not let me have her, be it so, — she
has some reason, — perhaps a good one for me. If she be a cheat,
and only uses the money to extort more, be it so. — I know my
woman, and have done with her henceforth.

Camille was a woman of perfect height, about five foot seven,
and beautifully formed, had full, hard, exquisite breasts, and lovely
legs and haunches, though not too fat or heavy. The hair on her
cunt, soft and of a very dark chestnut colour, was not then large
in quantity, but corresponded with her years. Her cunt was small,
with small inner lips, and a pretty nubbly clitoris like a little button.
The split of her cunt lay between the thighs with scarcely any
swell of outer-lips, but had a good mons, and was altogether one
of the prettiest cunts I have ever seen. I am now beginning, after
having seen many hundreds of them, to appreciate beauty in cunts,
to be conscious that there is a special, a superior beauty in the cunts
of some women as compared with others, just as there is in other
parts of their body. She had pretty hands and feet.

Her skin had the slightly brown gipsy tint found in many women in the South of Europe. I never saw a woman in whom the colour was so uniform as in her. From her face to her ankles it was the same unvarying tint without a mottle, even in any cranny. It had also the most exquisite smoothness, but it neither felt like ivory, satin, nor velvet, it seemed a compound of them all. I have scarcely felt the same in any other woman yet. That smoothness attracted me at first I expect, but it was only after I had had her several times, that I began to appreciate it, and to compare it with the skin of other women. She had with that, a great delicacy of touch with her hands.

Her face was scarcely equal to her form. The nose was more than *retroussé*, it bordered on the snub. She had small, dark, softly twinkling eyes, and dark hair; the mouth was ordinary, but with a set of very small, and beautifully white, regular, teeth. The general effect of her face was piquante rather than beautiful, but it pleased me. Her voice was small and soft, — an excellent thing in a woman.

[Such was the woman I have known for thirty-one years, but of whom there is scarcely anything to be told. No intrigue, nothing exciting is connected with her and myself. I cannot tell all the incidents of our acquaintance right off as I do those of many of my women, who appeared, pleased me, and disappeared; but she will be noticed from time to time as I had her, or sought her help in different erotic whims and fancies, which took hold of me at various periods. I write this now finding that her name appears in my manuscript a long way further on. She was moreover a most intelligent creature, clean, sober, and economical, and saving with a good purpose and object, to end alas! for her in failure.]

I never had a more voluptuous woman. Naked on that divan, or on the béd when the weather was warm, I had her constantly during that summer. I know nothing more exciting, than the tranquil, slow, measured way in which she laid down, exposing her charms; every attitude being natural yet exciting by its beauty and delicate salacity. She always seemed to me to be what I had heard of Orientals in copulation. She had the slowest yet most stifling embrace. There was no violent energy, no heaving up of rump, as if a pin had just run into her, nor violent sighs, nor loud exclamations; but she clung to you, and sucked your mouth in a way I scarcely

ever have found in English women, or in French ones; but the
Austrians and Hungarians in the use of tongue with tongue, and
lips with lips are unrivalled in voluptuousness.

Beyond a voluptuous grace natural to her, she had not at first
the facile ways of a French courtesan, they came later on. I saw
the change, and from that and other indications feel sure she had
not been in gay life long before I had her. I could tell more of her
history, but this is a narrative of my life, not of hers.

[I have destroyed some pages of manuscript solely relating
to her.]

She soon got a good clientele, picked up English rapidly,
dressed richly, but never showily, and began to save money. She
made affectionate advances to me which I did not accept. After a
time she used to pout at what I gave her, and got greedy. So one
day saying, "Ma chère, here is more, but adieu, — I don't like you
to be dissatisfied, but cannot afford to come to see you," — she
slapped the gold heavily down on the table. "Ah! mon Dieu, don't
say so, — come, — come, — I am sorry, — you shall never pay me,
— come when you like, — I did not want you to pay me, but you
would, — come, — do come, — that lovely prick, — do me again be-
fore you go, — don't go, — my maid shall say I have not come
home" (she expected some man), — and she never pouted about
my compliment, till many years afterwards.

I suppose that having had this charming fresh French woman,
made me wish for another; for spite of my satisfaction and liking
for her, I made acquaintance with another French woman, as un-
like Camille as possible. Her name was Gabrielle, a bold-looking
woman with big eyes and a handsome face, very tall and well-made,
but with not too much flesh on her bones, with a large, full-lipped,
loud-looking cunt in a bush of hair as black as charcoal. I never told
Camille about her, and think it was the great contrast between the
two which made me have her. That woman also seemed later on
to have taken some sort of fancy to me.

She had all the ready lechery of a well-practised French harlot,
I saw it from the way she opened her thighs, and laid down to
receive my embraces. About the third visit she brought water; and
made me wash my prick, on which the exudation of healthy lust
was showing whitish, before she let me poke her. I liked her
cleanliness, but to my astonishment no sooner were we on the bed,

than she reversed herself laying side by side with me, and began
sucking my prick. I had no taste for that pleasure, nor since a
woman in the rooms of Camille the first did it to me, had my penis
been so treated that I recollect, though I had made ladies take it
into their mouths for a second. I objected. "Mais si, — mais si," —
and she went on. My head was near her knee, one leg she lifted up,
showing her thighs, which opened and showed her big-lipped cunt
in its thicket of black hair. She played with my prick thus till ex-
perience told her she could do it no longer with safety, then ceasing
her suction, and changing her position, I fucked her in the old-
fashioned way.

The amusement seemed not to have shocked me as much as
I thought it should have done, and it was repeated as a pre-
liminary on other days, without my ever suggesting it. After I had
had my first poke, the delicate titillation of the mouth seemed
vastly pleasant, my prick then being temporarily fatigued by ex-
ercise in its natural channel; but I felt annoyed with myself for
relishing it at all.

I had not overcome prejudices then, though evidently my
philosophy was gradually undermining them. Why, if it gives
pleasure to the man to have his prick sucked by a woman, who
likes operating that way on the male, should they be abused for
enjoying themselves in such manner? A woman may rub it up to
stiffen it, the man always does so if needful, — that is quite natural
and proper. What wrong then in a woman using her mouth for the
same purpose, and giving still higher, more delicate and refined
pleasure? All animals lick each other's privates, why not we? In
copulation and its consequences, we are mainly animals, but with
our intelligence, we should seek all possible forms of pleasure in
copulation, and everything else.

With these two women I was satisfied till towards the end of
August, both of them trying to make me see them much. Gabrielle
for some fancy of her own took to calling me Monsieur Gabrielle.
I did not see her nearly so often as Camille, but one or other I saw
almost daily, Camille generally between luncheon and dinner, Ga-
brielle after dinner. I have seen both on the same day, and then
both were fucked; but I usually copulated but once daily. I was in
good health, and one daily emission of semen kept me so, and
seemed as needful to me as sleep. I had much lewed pleasure in

comparing mentally their two cunts, their being a most striking difference in the look of the two.

I was so amused with them that year, that I would not leave till near September. Then, "You've stopped all the long days, and the hottest weather, when I wanted to be by the seaside, — and now I won't go at all." I was glad of it, and without waiting for change of intention in that quarter, had my things packed up, and without delay, took myself off to the healthy, but vulgarish town of M°°g°°e. It was a place where I expected a little fun, a few kisses from healthy lips, and a little intrigue perhaps, and the chance of getting some young healthy, unfucked cunt. I know pretty well now that with town-women out for a brief holiday like most of those who go to M°°g°°e; that idleness, better air, more and better food than they are accustomed to, heats the cunts, and makes many a modest one long for a male, and discontented with her middle-finger.

I had not been at my hotel a day, before I met an intimate friend with his wife and eldest daughter, — a girl of fourteen. He had taken the upper part of a house over a shop, being a man of but moderate means, and intended to have brought two other children, and a maid, but something prevented that. I liked both him and his wife, and at his suggestion went to occupy one of his rooms, and live with them (paying my share). I found the rooms were over a greengrocers, which I didn't like, and think I should have cried off, had I not seen that the servant was a healthy, full-fleshed bitch, and I thought there might be a chance of prodding her, like Sally on a previous autumn.

The house newly built, and evidently for lodgings, was bigger, more comfortable than most of its class, and had a side or private entrance-door, opening on to a passage separated from the shop but with a door into it at the end where also was a kitchen with a bed-room over it, and a water-closet, all looking into a little garden with one or two trees in it. The sitting and bed-rooms over the shop were occupied by my friend and wife, and of two rooms above, one was mine, and one his daughter's; the attics the landlady and the servant I thought occupied. There was also leading out from the staircase, the bed-room over the kitchen which my friend had also hired, to avoid having strangers in the house with them. This was entered from the staircase-landing, as was the lodgers' water-closet, a convenience which few such houses had then.

The shop seemed flourishing. Any one going in at the private door could not fail to see the whole of the shop, down to a small parlour having a window on to the garden. The first thing I noticed was a strong, healthy, red-cheeked, saucy-looking girl about sixteen years of age, with a curly but dishevelled head of deep-red-coloured hair, — a very unusual and peculiar deep-red, and but rarely seen. The girl standing at the shop-front stared hard at me when I arrived, and nudged a big boy about fifteen years old who was half-sitting close by the girl, upon a sack of potatoes. The girl called the woman of the house "Aunt." She attended to the shop I found when the aunt was away (cooking chiefly when so). The boy took home the goods purchased, and left nightly after closing the shutters. Red-Head slept in the attics over me, and took off her boots at times as she went upstairs, so as not to make a noise over the lodgers' heads, — the aunt slept there also. They two eat in the kitchen or the shop-parlour.

I was at once cheery with the servant, but it did not promise much. The red-haired one (another Louisa, and called Loo), pleased me, though I did not like her hair. She spoke so loud, laughed so heartily with customers, took chaffing, lifted such heavy weights, and then flung her short petticoats about so much in moving her haunches, that I longed to pinch her. She looked so hard at me (and also my friend), when we passed the shop, for she was generally at the door, and often outside it, goods being placed there, — that I made up my mind she had just come into the first lusts of womanhood, and was pretty strongly in want of a man.

In a day or two I was buying fruit two or three times daily. "Keep the change Loo (I hear that's your name), — it will buy you some ribbon." "Oh! thankee sir," — and she put it quickly into her pocket without hesitation. Emboldened I gave her half a crown. "Keep the change, and you shall give me a kiss for it." Into her pocket it went. She looked quickly towards the back of the shop, — there was the boy. She slightly shook her head. "I can't," said she in a low voice, taking the change out of her pocket and tendering it to me. I winked, pushed out my lips as if kissing, and left the shop, leaving her the change. The boy was out of sight somewhere when I was buying the fruit.

Between eleven and one o'clock she was mostly alone, her aunt in the kitchen, the boy out, and the same for an hour or two in the afternoon. Unfortunately those were the bathing and prome-

nading hours, so there was difficulty in getting at the girl un-
observed, but nothing stood in my way when cunt-hunting, and
never had. From always thinking how, and where, I all my life
have got my opportunities with women. I also found that of an
evening, her aunt just at dusk went out at times to get, I heard her
say, a mouthful of fresh air. Then the girl was alone with the boy
till he left.

About the fourth night, the boy had left, Loo was alone in
the shop-parlour, my friends upstairs. I went out (as I said), to
have a cigar, and a stroll, but when just at the bottom of the stairs
the shop-door in the partition opened, and Loo appeared. "Hist, —
hist," said I. She stopped, I caught hold of her, and kissed her.
"Oh! don't, — Mary [the servant] is in the kitchen." I kissed
again. "Oh! don't." "You owe me a kiss." "Oh! not here, — go to
the front-door," said she. I did. She came there, just outside the
door, but up against it, she kissed me, and went rapidly back. "I'll
wait for you as you go to bed," I said, and did so with slippers off.

About half-past ten she passed my bed-room. I heard Miss
°°°° moving about in the room opposite to me, but on the landing
I pinched Loo's bum hard, — very hard as she passed. She winced,
and passed on very quickly, shaking her head and smiling, candle
in hand. I put my head down shamming to look up her clothes.
We were intimate already, I had begun double entendres which
she took, and I began to think that the fresh-looking, saucy one,
young as she was, knew a prick from a cucumber. Then I found
that the servant went home each night to sleep.

I hadn't been at M°°g°°e a week before I wanted female
assistance, and picking up a casual, and thinking of my intention,
gave her five shillings to show me a baudy house or two, which
she did. One, a very quiet one, was in the old part of the town, over
a china-shop.

Parting with the woman I strolled on to the beach, and met
her there again, and felt her cunt, I sitting on a seat, she standing
by the side of me. My cock stood, and I gave her money for a
poke. It was not a dark night. "There is sand low down," said she,
"no one will notice us when we are lying down." But a fear came
over me, — I told her so. "Well I've got your money, and if there
was anything the matter with me, I'd hardly ask you to have me,
— I'm here every night, and live up at °°° with my mother." Then

near to the waves, she laid on her back on the soft dry sands, and I fucked her, and enjoyed her very much. "How do you wash your cunt?" "I piddle now, and wipe it with my handkerchief, down there (nodding her head) — there are rocks and pools of water, — I'm going to wash it there, — I always do after gents," — and she went off to do it.

Next day buying something, "Come Loo, and kiss me in the passage." "I can't — he'll be going out at half-past eleven." Excusing myself from accompanying my friends, I was at the lodgings at that hour. The servant above had then all the beds to make, and the aunt was cooking. It was risky, yet I had a brief talk with Loo in whispers in the passage, and kissed, and hugged her, and told her I had fallen deeply in love with her. I had not begun smut, but her bold manner made me wonder why I had not. That afternoon I overheard a quarrel between her and her aunt, and saw Loo wiping her eyes. Loo said to me when I told her what I had heard, that she wished she'd never come, and would sooner go to service.

I noticed also, for I was dodging in and out all day, and listening in the passage where I could hear much said in shop and parlour, what seemed to me a very familiar manner between the girl and the boy. One day he took her round the waist. She, seeing me enter the shop, pushed his hand away and boxed his ears. He stooped, pulled her petticoats a little way up, and then suddenly appeared very busy. Evidently she had given him a hint. It annoyed me, and I wondered if the boy had felt her.

I did not quite give up hopes of the maid, who looked five-and-twenty. I kissed her, and gave her a little present for cleaning my boots nicely. She took that fairly well. Then I felt for her notch outside her clothes. She repulsed me violently, and with a look which I didn't like. So for a time I desisted, but recommenced, and at length kissed her every time I got her alone. My friend's daughter caught me at it, and her father spoke to me. *He* didn't mind, but his *wife* did, — I must take care, — it wouldn't do to let a young girl see that game going on. Nothing more was said, but I noticed that he and his wife looked after me. One night when we were walking out alone, he said, "You want that woman, — and a damned nice woman she looks, — if my wife wasn't here I'd try to get her myself, — but for God's sake don't let either of the ladies catch you, — it won't do."

The young lady's room was opposite to mine, and such was my insatiable desire to see females in déshabillé or nude, that it passed through my mind to bore a hole (which I had done at foreign hotels) through her door, to spy her. I could have done so, but I did not, though I could not restrain myself from listening to hear when she piddled and a few times succeeded. Then I thought of her piddle and little hairless cunt, which gave me such pleasure, that I quite felt a liking for the girl, but not sexually, and brought her presents which pleased both her and her parents.

In a fortnight I had often kissed Loo, and pinched her bum till she said it was blue. I told her I should like to sleep with her, for I loved her, — this was on the first night she got for a walk at dusk. I had heard her aunt say she'd keep a tight hand on her, and I found Loo was fast almost to a gallop. We walked and sat down on a beach-seat. "How can you love me? — you're married, — Mary heard Mrs. L°°g saying so." "I never said I wasn't, but I hate *her*, and do nothing to her, and love *you*." "Oh! gammon," she replied. I had now a little changed my opinion about the girl. She wanted to know the meaning of my "doing nothing," was free in manner, and any delicate smut which I began using she answered frankly to. "Oh! I knows what you means well enough, but don't you go on like that." I concluded she had been brought up with coarse people who spoke of all their wants, and acts openly, so that the girl saw no harm in such things. She had only been with her aunt that summer. She told me of her relatives, and where they lived in Northumberland, — there was a large family, — but that was all I could get out of her. "Yer don't want to call on em," said she laughing.

All was soon finished with the servant. One morning I waited indoors in hopes of getting at Loo, and spied the servant as she brought a slop-pail to the closet which as said was close to the bed-room over the kitchen. When she came out I asked her into that room which I had never entered before. "Come here, I've something particular to tell you, — come." Reluctantly she came in, then I kissed, and gradually getting to the unchaste, got my hand on to her cunt. "Be quiet, — you shan't, — oh! don't, — Mrs. Jones will be up to see if all's right." "No she's out — oh! what lovely thighs, — what hair on your cunt — don't make that noise." She resisted hard, and pushed down her clothes, at first spoke in suppressed tones, then louder. "You shan't, — oh! you wretch, — I don't want a dress, — you shan't, — oh! oh! leave off, — I'll tell Mrs. Jones, — I will."

I desisted for the moment, but only to pull out my prick. She had taken up the slop-pail looking very angry. With prick out I rushed at her, she banged the pail down, I pushed her against the bedside, and got my fingers on to her cunt again. "Let me have you." "Oh! — you — shan't, — I'll call." "I'll say that you asked me in here." "You liar, you beast, — I won't, — oh! hi!," and she cried out so loudly that I desisted.

"I won't stop here any longer, and I'll tell Mrs. Jones." She went out of the room crying and nodding her head furiously at me. There will be a row, thought I. Later on I offered her two sovereigns. "Don't say anything, — you'll only lose your character if you do, — I've done you no harm." Indeed I rather funked the affair. She took the money without a word, and pushed me off when I tried to kiss her, and I never got at her again. Two days afterwards she left, — she was only a weekly servant. I don't think she ever told about me, — she said she didn't like the place.

Loo on the beach. — The shop-boy's attempt. — Caught at the water-closet. — A knowing one. — The gay sister. — Success despaired of. — Over the china-shop. — Virginity slaughtered. — Alone in the lodgings. — The bed-room on the stairs. — Poking like blazes. — A gamahuche. — Aunt at market. — Clever dodges. — Naked in bed. — Homage to Priapus. — Belly to belly. — Belly to bum. — She on he. — The hand-glass. — Am I with child? — I leave M**g**e. — Sequel.

I had no one now but Loo. She had gone out one evening without leave, and met me. Her aunt scolded. I got very warm in my hints and words. She laughed at them, but still I hesitated, she was such an odd, unusual girl. I did not know what to make of her, and my failure with the servant made me cautious.

It was slow I found being always with my friends, the lady didn't like my taking her husband out of a night without her, so though dining with them I went out by myself, but usually came back just when the shop was being shut up, to catch Loo, — even if I went out afterwards.

The night after the new servant came, I left my friends at a concert, and went home. Entering I heard voices wrangling, and stealthily crept as near the partition-door as I could. Loo and the boy were scuffling. One second I couldn't hear a word, the next minute everything. "Don't, — leave off, — I won't let you," — then a chair or something made a noise. "Oho," cried she, — "shan't." "I've felt it, — aint it hairy?" chuckled the boy quite loud. Another scuffle. "I'll tell aunt, — don't, — oh! — the lodgers will hear." Again a scuffle. "Oh! — now — you — shan't." "Cunt," — "Oh" — "Prick," — a slap. One of them banged right up against the partition, some-

292

thing dropped, and all for a moment was silent. I mounted the stairs out of sight, and listened. The door opened, the two came out at the same moment, and the servant, who had not gone, came out of the kitchen. "I dropped the candle, and couldn't see, and jumped agin the door," said the boy. "You're a stupid clumsy," said Loo. The boy went out of the house like a shot, the servant and Loo into the kitchen. He's been feeling her cunt, — perhaps she him, — the little bitch has been fucked, thought I.

A day or two before I made a hasty offer to take her to London for a week, — would she go? — "Oh! won't I just, — I'm longing to see London." Then, "How can I get away? — aunt would tell father." No she could not. "Take a walk with me when the shop is shut up." But the aunt rarely let her go out in the evening, nor in the day, except on Sundays. Put up to it by me she told her aunt she would. "We'll go out together," said aunt, — but it rained a little, aunt said it would spoil her clothes, and would not go.

Next night the aunt was out, the girl had the shop shut directly it was dark, and spite of aunt came out to meet me on the beach. I told her what I had heard. She admitted the boy had tried to feel her, but had not succeeded. "But I heard him say it was hairy." "He's a liar." "I don't believe you've got any hair there," said I. "Oh! ain't I though," said she laughing. "Let me feel." Then in the dark, little by little, I managed to feel a fat pair of thighs, and the tip of a cunt. She sat quiet, at last kissing me, and I her. One of her legs was over the other, so that my finger could only just rest on her clitoris. Then she felt my prick. It was a lovely hour I passed on that seat by the shingle. I whispered in conversation, "prick," — "cunt," — "fuck," — that magical triad. "Oh! I knows what yer means." "Open your thighs now," "there then, — oh! you hurt," — and she got up. "You wicked little devil, let me." I thought her cunt seemed open enough. There was a row when she got home, but she cheeked her aunt boldly.

Next morning I went to the closet, some one was there, and wanting to bog badly I went down to the closet in the yard, pulled open the door sharply (it was not bolted), and there stood Loo with petticoats up, showing both legs nearly to her backside. She was just turning to seat herself. "Oh!" she shouted dropping her clothes. "Oh!" said I banging the door to, startled as much as she was. I went off, but an hour afterwards bought some fruit, — no one was in the shop. "I saw your bum." "You didn't," said she without a blush. "I did." "It was no fault of mine if you did." "Show it me now, — there is no one here." "Shan't." She really blushed, and sat down, but could not contain herself from laughing. I showed her my prick, and was nearly caught doing so, by some one entering the shop.

She got out another night to walk with a female friend whom the aunt thought Loo could be trusted with. Directly clear of the house, that girl went off with her lover, — five minutes later I was with Loo on the beach. It was moonlight. How I cursed the moon, then luckily heavy clouds hid it. Now I talked about copulation openly. She knew all about it she said, and at last admitted laughing that she had felt the shop-boy's prick. "No," no other man's excepting quite small boys, — she had felt those. "Let me do it to you, — fuck you, — it's such pleasure, — you know all about it, — why not?" "I would, but I am frightened, — suppose I had a child." I told her how I would prevent her having one. No, she was frightened. We felt each other well. How I restrained myself from frigging God only knows; but we were only about an hour gone.

Next day I felt her quim in the shop and again as she went up to bed, and showed her my prick. What risks I ran, and how I escaped! Had my friend opened his door, or the girl opposite opened hers, I must have been caught.

I found she did not like being in the shop, did not like her aunt, and soon after said she would go away with me to London, if I liked (I'd now offered to keep her). That bothered me, I had only just got rid of a woman, and did not want another. "But in London you'd come to grief, — perhaps go on the town, and be miserable." Well she didn't care, she wouldn't stop with her aunt, didn't want to go home — had had enough of *them*. She had a sister who was gay at ° ° ° °, who told her she was very jolly. The murder was out, her cheek and frank acceptance of baudy suggestions, her knowledge of fucking, were due to her gay sister. At once I said, "What's the good of sitting here by the sea where we may be known? — let's go and have a chat and a glass of wine in a house." "No." "Why you know you've been fucked, Loo," said I angry, not mincing words now, and believing she was shamming for a purpose. "I'll take my solemn oath on any Bible, I ain't had it done to me," said she earnestly, — but I didn't believe her.

There were constant quarrels now between her and her aunt, —
we heard them upstairs. Mrs. L°°g, my friend, complained of the
noise. Then I found that Loo had been sent there by her father,
to keep her away from her gay sister. All this time my friends had
never noticed my goings on with the girl, all having been done by
us two with such stealth.

After that night I talked open smut to her, and felt her, and
she felt my prick on every opportunity. We discussed fucking, and
getting with child, as if we were married. She a girl of sixteen would
look me in the face, and laugh about it without the sign of a blush.
It was the most extraordinary state of things I ever have experi-
enced; but matters stopped there. A month nearly had passed, I
had shagged the woman (already named) on the sands two or
three times, to keep myself from fist-fucking, and liking the novelty
of the place; but I was very lewed on Loo. She liked the spooning,
and liked my feeling her cunt, but, "No, I'm frightened, — I won't
go anywhere with you, — I won't let you do it." "I fucked a girl
on the sands, as you would not let me," said I in just those words.
"Lor you didn't." "I did." She became quite silent.

My friends were now leaving. "I'm going away with them Loo,
as you won't meet me." I said that on two successive days. She
made no reply. Sunday came. "Come out this evening." "I'm going
to church with aunt." "Well, meet me instead." She did, and I got
her without any trouble to the china-shop, and five minutes after
that, we were sitting close together, her hand round my prick, I
titillating her clitoris, our mouths glued together, speechless. Oh!
those lovely five minutes. Her thighs and bum gently moved. "Oh!
don't." "Get on the bed Loo, — don't be foolish, — we'll feel each
other better there." She rose. "Take off your gown, you will rumple
it." She took it off in silence, and got on to the bed herself with-
out help. We laid down. "What a lovely fat bum you have. — I
must kiss it." I loosened my trowsers. "There now, let my prick just
touch your belly, — feel me." My fingers slipt along her cunt, and I
tried to put one up it. "Oh! you hurt." Is she virgin? Then without
any resistance I laid on her. She sighed, her thighs opened, I ad-
justed my prick, grasped her buttocks firmly, and thrust. "Oh —
ohoo! — har!" one loud cry only. I had shattered it in three or four
hard thrusts. She was a virgin, and a tough one. My sperm was
filling her cunt the next minute. She had meant fucking some hours

before, I am sure of it, and almost fancy now, that she had made up her mind to have it done to her, long before that Sunday.

Coming to my senses, "Did you like it? — did it give you pleasure?" "No it hurt," said she with perfect tranquillity. I laid still, kissing her, nestling up her my still stiff prick, put my fingers down, and found them red. I had put a towel on the bed, and now pushed it under her buttocks, and uncunted, — I thought soiling her linen might cause her difficulty. For a moment to my delight, I saw the unusual sight of a virgin cunt just fucked, and then pushed the napkin between her thighs. "You never have had it before," I remarked. "I told you so," she replied. She laid still till I suggested her washing. As she washed, "You've made me bleed," and she laughed. The affair did not seem very serious to her. Then we talked, I saw her cunt, and fucked her twice more, — the second poke I stopped in the middle. "Don't you feel pleasure now?" "Oh! yes — oho, ah!" She did not get home till past ten o'clock. I went home first. Her aunt rowed her in the passage. Walking with a friend, — walking with a friend was her only reply. My friends heard the row in the passage, as well as I, and next morning remarked, they were afraid that shop-girl was giving her aunt much trouble, — Mrs. L°°g said she looked an impudent minx.

Then came that delicious time when a couple both on heat scheme how to fuck on the sly. It seems to me the most delicious gratification of sexual passion, when it is done thus successfully. To kiss, and finger your privates, whisper as you pass, give signals to each other, cunt in one's mind, cock in the other's; to think all day when, where, and how the copulation is to come off; to watch this one who is in the way, scheme to get the other out of the way, hatch excuses for getting out of the house, tales about where you have been, and reasons for coming in late is delightful. I love the secret joys of success in deceiving, the passionate fuck here, there, anywhere, just as the opportunity offers; the rapid spend from genitals in which from thinking constantly of it, with lewed desire for hours, the sperm and sexual juices have been accumulating, ready for mingling. I had all this with Loo, have had it with many other women since the age of sixteen, and know nothing in life so soul-absorbing, so delicious.

Next day we felt each other in the shop, on the staircase, and going up to bed. Next day promised to be unsuccessful for us, but

I was so lewed that I was ready for any risk, — she much the same. We could think of no place, till suddenly, "There is the bed-room on the stairs, — it's empty, — no one will think of your being in there." I went in the evening to a bazaar with my friends, left them there; and then slipped into the house, and into the bed-room unobserved. The servant had left, the aunt went out, and Loo slipped into the room.

She had left the boy in the shop. I fucked her quite in darkness on the bed-side, — the boy thought she had gone up to her bedroom. I sat patiently half an hour, then up she came, and we did it again. Nearly another hour, and again she came, and was fucked. "You haven't washed your cunt, have you?" "No, — ought I?" said she. "Isn't fucking nice?" "Oh! ain't it just!" The boy wondered at her keeping the shop open so late. "The bed (a feather one) will show," said I. "As I come down in the morning, or directly Tom's gone, I'll set it to rights," said she.

For the rest of the time of my acquaintance with this red-haired damsel, my dodges and devices to get her were mostly like those with little Sally, already told of. The circumstances were nearly the same. A sea-coast town, a lodging-house, a landlady, a young lady anxious to get her cunt buttered, a man in full health, intent on buttering it for her. Who could under those circumstances prevent copulation?

The next night she went out without asking leave, and I had her in the china-shop. "My darling let's look at your cunt." She opened her thighs quite freely. "Does it look much different to what it did?" She had been trying to look at it in the glass, but couldn't see, — she hadn't a hand-glass. "But it feels quite different," she remarked. We fucked like blazes for a couple of hours. There was a great row, and threats of the aunt about her absence, when she got back.

She was biggish, almost a woman in form, but with girlish expression in face. Excepting for that she looked eighteen. She had large thighs, a fat backside, and nice plump, but little breasts. Her flesh was beautifully white. She had a pretty cunt, a very fully-developed clitoris, and the hair on it was more carroty than that on her head. I had never yet seen a regular carroty cunt, but there was not much hair, — in that respect it looked sixteen. The edge of the split hymen was well jagged, any one could have seen that it

had not been split up long. I looked at it till the exceptional letch
seized me. I tickled the clitoris with my tongue till she gave a sigh,
then the idea of giving her full pleasure enchanted me. I closed
my mouth on it, and licked and licked, and thrust my tongue in
and out, till she writhed. "Leave off, — oh! — it's dirty, — oho!" My
jaws ached, my tongue was weary, I thought it was impossible to
finish her, till with a strong effort, gliding my tongue over her
clitoris, with all the rapidity that fatigue would let me, her thighs
opened, and with a low yawling, half-moan, half-sigh she spent,
clutching my hair spasmodically, and her thighs nipping. I don't
know how long I had been operating on her, and wonder why I
did not fetch her sooner. I never did it to her again, and can't
account for this sudden letch, — I never can give reasons for gama-
huching one woman, and not another.

Next day my friends left, I stayed, and hired their two rooms,
and the odd bed-room, — the old landlady said she could only let
them together. The weather was getting cold, no other lodgers
were expected, the shop-business fell off. The landlady next day
asked if I would mind her waiting on me, as she and her niece could
do all I wanted, unless other lodgers came. Though delighted I said
in a dissatisfied manner that I expected to be properly cooked for,
and waited upon; that I didn't like persons above their positions
about me, and so on. Oh! she'd take care, and her niece should wear
a cap. Soon after she returned. Would I excuse the cap, — her niece
would not wear one; — she added that the girl had given her father
lots of trouble, and now gave her trouble, — and she should send
her home. How I laughed in my sleeve; the servant left, the shop-
boy remained, a charwoman came for an hour daily, and the land-
lady, Loo, and I were alone in the house at night.

I gave lots of trouble, sending the landlady out to buy this and
that. Whenever I wanted her out of the way I sent her to buy
something. I kept her hard at cooking, and did not care what it
cost to get her out of the house, nor did she, for she got profits.
When she was out up came Loo. In a trice I had her on my bed,
and shagged her. The landlady laid the cloth, my beefsteak was
burnt, and I grumbled. She was very sorry. Then she laid the cloth
an hour before my meal, so that she might cook. I wasn't going
to have a table-cloth on in the room all day, — I should dine out.
Oh! she was so sorry. "Get a servant then." Well she would, — but

would I mind her niece without a cap laying it? "No, let her," — and up came Loo. What a lark! the woman was cooking whilst I was pulling up Loo's petticoats, slapping her backside, kissing her motte, she laying the cloth. Then I slipped into my bed-room. Then knock, knock, "Your dinner's on table sir." In I went. "I see the young woman has laid it all right." "Yes sir, I'll see that she does." I rang, and up came Loo. "A bottle of pale ale." The shop-boy fetched it, Loo cleared the table, and had a glass of ale, her aunt had gone out to buy me something, so we fucked. A randier little bitch never had a prick up her. At a late dinner it was the same game, and Loo's cunt had another seminal libation. What a jolly day! Is it my luck, or my clever maneuvering? I think the latter, for I have had much practice in this sort of thing.

For a week, twice a day, and mostly three times I had the girl. She gave me hints when to get her. "Aunt will go out at such a time." "Where will the boy be?" "In the shop, — I'll tell him I must be in the kitchen, — he daren't leave the shop, — if he goes into the parlour even, aunt would send him about his business, — he puts any money he takes down on to the counter, till aunt takes it." Then up skipped Loo directly she thought it safe, got on to my bed, and almost pulled her own petticoats up, so longing was she for the prick. Directly afterwards, and often with her carroty quim unwashed, off she went. I grumbled about her want of attention to her aunt, to keep up the deception. The old woman let out about the girl being a wild one, and giving her trouble, and then for a couple of days the woman attended to me herself, and I had no poke.

"Aunt goes to market herself to-morrow," whispered Loo grinning. During the season a relative went to the market for her. At six o'clock next morning off aunt went, Loo partially dressed, let her out. The boy was to have been there to open the shop. He entered by the private door to do so, and Loo had cunningly told him to come later. The lock was always bolted back when the door was opened in the morning, so that lodgers could let themselves in and out. The lass omitted this, and there were we in the house alone and secure, I in bed ready.

Upstairs she ran like a hare, "Pull off all your clothes, — yes, naked." "No I won't," — the only objection I ever heard her make. But I stripped her and myself, and in a minute we were both start naked in my bed together. What a delicious cuddle we had on that chilly morning! Then I gratified my eyes, never having seen her naked before. A little reddish hair was just showing in her armpits. A kiss on her pretty little breasts and her red-haired motte, a peep at the ragged, jagged opening to her cunt. I knelt over her, and she kissed my prick, — never before, and she did it with such delight. Then ouf! in tight libidinous naked embrace our genitals coupled. Oh! what a divine fuck it was, — luckily with a towel under her backside, I don't spoil sheets, and give trouble now, — I deluged her cunt. Everything is nice to people in copulation. "Put your hand down darling, and feel my prick in you." "Oh! isn't it wet!" "Do you like fucking naked in bed?" "Oh! yes, it *is* nice, — do married people do it naked?"

Then lying coupled, nestling our bellies, talking of fucking, instructing her (half the delight of having a virgin is in instructing her in libidinous acts, and instilling into her mind ideals of copulation), kissing, tongue-sucking at intervals. We passed a time. "Can you feel that my prick's getting smaller in your cunt?" "Yes it is." "Do you like the feel of the spunk in it?" "Oh! yes I do" (a question I have put to all my virgins before, but ever fresh it comes). "Feel my prick now it's out. Isn't it small!" "Yes, — I shall try to make it stiff." "Do love, — let me look at your cunt." Thighs wide opened I saw the offering my prick had left there. "Would you like to see your cunt now?" "Yes, — but it looks nasty, don't it?" "No dear." I stiffened. "Look love, look at my prick, — let's fuck before your aunt comes in, — get up, — kneel, — there, that's it," — and then with her white, smooth, hard backside against my belly as I knelt at the back of her, I had another glorious fuck in her smooth, sperm-lubricated vulva.

"What am I doing dear?" "Oh! — ah! — a doin it to me — ah!" "Say fucking." "Fuck — hing, — ah! — ah!" We are quiet, I am bending over her, hands quiet on her buttocks, motionless all but in the last throbbing of my prick, and the gentle clipping of her cunt round it, as my ejaculation finished.

My prick kept in its channel, her bum close into my belly. What delicious tranquility, and soft baudy dreaming. "Is it nice this way dear?" (the first time I had done it so). "Oh! yes, — do married people do it this way ever?" A silence. "How long's aunt been gone? — oh! that's the boy ringing." "Don't move Loo, — my prick's stiff

yet." A pause. "Oh! I'd better, — he'll keep on a ringing, — what a
nuisance." "Let him ring." "Oh! take it out, — he might tell aunt,
— and I've got to dress." Out I pulled it, she dressed (a frock over
her chemise). "I shall tell him I fell asleep." Then she let him in,
and again came to me. We kissed, felt each other's genitals. "Don't
wash your cunt, Loo, and we'll do it again at breakfast." Off she
went, dressed properly, and lighted the kitchen-fire.

When she brought my breakfast, "I wish we could sleep to-
gether." "So do I," she replied. "We'd sleep naked." "Yes," said she
grinning, but we never did. We could not manage a poke till after
luncheon, and then did it on the sofa, backside to belly again, be-
cause it took so long to make the feather-bed look square, after we
had rumpled it. How quickly she rumped up to my prick! — how
gloriously she fucked! She was made for fucking, and loved it. I
guess that in a year or two, when full-grown, it will take a strong
man to do all her carnal work. Her exact age was sixteen years and
one month the day I broached her.

We were baulked all the next day, for the aunt attended to me,
but the next morning went to market. The boy's mother was ill, so
Loo told him he might come late, and again in bed naked we
strummed. I put her on the top of me. Libidinous devices, played
with the young lass, pleased me fifty times as much as with an
accomplished courtesan. "Are you coming Loo?" "Y — hes, y — hes,"
— our salivas were mingling. "Do married people do it like that?"
said she as she lay on the top of me after her spend.

I had every meal at home, and had cooking and things fetched
at intervals all day long, to get the aunt out of the way. To my
annoyance she said she must get a servant, for it was too much for
her. "Why don't you make your niece do more?" "She don't like
waiting [all arranged], — the girl's a rare trouble to me, and to her
poor father; but I must send her home." "As you like, but I am
not likely to dine at home so much." No servant was got, — one
would have spoiled all, — so I did not lose my lass. Every other
morning the aunt was away for about two hours, and did not know
the boy came late (he was glad to come late), for the shop was
always open before she returned. We lost no time, my prick was
in Loo's cunt five minutes after her aunt went out, and generally
in it a quarter of an hour before she came back. Between our carnal
exercises, she with only a frock on lighted the kitchen-fire, and let

the boy in, stripping and getting into bed with me like lightning
between those performances. She now kissed and toyed me most
lasciviously directly she got into bed.

One morning I lent her a hand-glass, and helped her to inspect
her cunt. She contemplated it with great satisfaction. I pointed out
to her the edges of the ruptured hymen, — it almost looked like a
cock's-comb on each side, she said.

"I wonder if I'm in the family way," said she one day just
after we had fucked, and whilst she was taking away my breakfast
things. She had had no symptoms, no sensations that she knew of,
but she wondered, — she would know by the following Monday.
On Monday she was all right, the redness showed, and for three
days she was untouched. Then we resumed our fornication, and
for nearly a month more carried on this sweet little game of copu-
lation, and I believe unsuspected excepting by the boy.

It was close to November, all visitors were gone, and I told
her then that I must leave, and then for the first time she showed
anxiety about her future, and shed tears. But from conversation,
though she had now got very close, I firmly believe she had made
up her mind to turn strumpet. Her aunt and she quarrelled daily.
Aunt was always threatening to send her home, she threatening
to run away. I urged her going home, and one morning feeling
uneasy about her, I gave her twenty pounds in sovereigns. That set
her crying violently (she had never asked me for a farthing). As
I could not take her to London (which it was impossible for me to
do), perhaps she'd go home. "If you don't go home, stay here, —
you're handsome, — you'll get a sweetheart, and marry if you're
careful, — he won't find out what you've done." Only common shop-
people spoke to her she remarked with a toss of her head, as if
she thought them not good enough.

Two of her monthly periods had passed since I first had her,
without signs of pregnancy. I felt quite comfortable about that, and
after a heavy day's fucking, and three fucks on the last morning
done with great risk, to my astonishment she suddenly cried bitterly,
and just before her aunt came home, put her bonnet on, went out,
and I never saw her more. The aunt was in a state of anxiety when
I left, and so was I, the girl being so peculiar in character. I feared
she would come to London, but I never saw her, if she did. The
following spring, being about twenty miles from the town, I went

there purposely to enquire. As I saw the aunt in the shop I went in, and bought something.

The aunt knew me, smiled, and asked if I were coming to M**g**e again. "Where is your niece?" said I casually. "Oh! gone home — or somewhere." After a pause, "She gave my poor brother lots of trouble." I asked one or two fishing questions, but learnt nothing further. I am convinced that she turned gay, and would have done so whether I had had her or not. She was made for much fucking, was ready for it, waiting for it. I believe she often had felt the shop-boy's prick though she denied that. She admitted once having done so, but they were always scuffling.

It is funny that I should so soon after I had a lady with a ginger-coloured motte, have fallen upon a red-haired motte. Liking neither of the colours I yet much enjoyed both women, but Loo far better than the other, owing to her youth, freshness, and inexperience. But each woman as she succeeds another, seems fresh to me, and brings her own peculiar charms and enjoyment. The delights of women are inexhaustible.

[I was alone nearly all this time at M**g**e, the season was over; what acquaintances I had had left, and these notes were written partly whilst there, and the rest soon after, for I had just then strongly on me the desire of describing the incidents of my private life, and writing them gave me the greatest pleasure. The account of my doings with Loo the red-haired, are word for word as I then wrote them.]

Camille. — Gabrielle and a female. — Temporary impotence. — After supper. — Minetting. — Gamahuching. — Flat-fucking. — Screwed and lewed. — Libidinous posing. — A triad of debauchees. — Next day recollections. — At Naples. — An agent for pederasts. — Reflexions about sodomy. — At Milan. — At a bagnio. — Cheap women. — In a diligence. — Mother and child. — At G°°n°b°e. — The chambermaid's mistake. — Noisy incitements. — Through a door. — Invitation and surprize. — A warm room. — Warm suggestions. — Warm actions. — A hot pudendum. — A scorching hot penis. — A burning conjunction. — A moist conclusion. — A good night's work. — A hairy bum furrow.

When I came to London, Camille received my attentions but I was not constant to her, for a change of women was necessary to me. Gabrielle I had lost sight of, for she had changed her lodgings, till one afternoon going up an obscure street near Regent Street, I heard called out, "Monsieur, Gabrielle." Looking up I saw it was she. Upstairs I went, and very soon was up her. I saw her several times afterwards, and one evening had a desire to see two women naked together, — it was years since I had done so. Gabrielle got me another woman as tall as herself, and with a cunt of similar hairiness and look. I sent for champagne, we all stripped naked, the two women sat on my knees, then laid on the bed side by side, and then knelt on it with rumps outwards, whilst I investigated their genitals; but my prick would not stand, and though I tried to fuck the stranger who used every blandishment, I could not do it.

I have before, and since, at times been unable to poke one woman when another was present, — why I cannot understand. Neither can I account for passing by dozens of nice women without putting my tongue to their cunts, and then frantically gama-huching one, without perhaps any greater charms, although for the moment she may have appeared to me to have possessed them. I have as already said, poked women in the presence of others, though but rarely.

Gabrielle found out my weakness, went out of the room, and soon after I was in coition with the other French lady. We went on champagning when Gabrielle returned. Having put chemise and shirt on, and made up the fire (for it was cold), in an hour or so Gabrielle said it was her turn to be fucked, and began, unasked, her favorite move of stiffening me by a delicate application of her tongue to the naked tip of my penis, and very shortly my lust was rampant again. Then began one of my unpremeditated orgies.

Our talk had been of the loosest; all three had been smoking, sitting round the fire, the women with chemises above their knees, letting the warmth of the fire reach their cunts. At times I looked up between their thighs and amused myself libidinously with them. Time went on and I did not fuck. Gabrielle asked me to give them supper, and consenting, they sent out for ham and French sausages, which they devoured, — I made them sit quite naked to do so. Again we smoked, had more champagne, and our talk was of the lewedest. I felt Gabrielle's cunt. "Let me feel it too," said the other woman suiting the action to the word, and feeling Gabrielle. Then both women kneeling down, one licked my prick-stem, one my balls, till I nearly spent, but restrained myself.

Voluptuous excitement then filled my mind with libidinous fancies. "Gamahuche, Gabrielle," I said. She scarcely needed a second request; both women laughed, moved on to the bed, and the stranger, kneeling between Gabrielle's legs, gamahuched her, whilst I looked at her fully-developed, thickly-haired cunt from behind, as her big rump was raised up by her kneeling with her head low. Gabrielle had two pleasures, or else shammed them, but I think not, for I can now pretty well tell between the real and the sham in baudy exercises. After that, again we all smoked, and drank champagne sitting round the fire, and then Gabrielle gamahuched the other woman.

My lewed imagination worked still, and made other sugges-tions. I said, "Flat-fuck her, faites la tribade." The two were now pretty screwed, and up to anything, and I now believe amused each other this way when by themselves, though I did not then even fully realize that tribadism was more than a sham.

On the bed got the two tall French women, naked, boots and stockings excepted. Gabrielle mounted the other, who passed her thighs high up over Gabrielle's haunches, and they joined their cunts. I felt the mass of hair made by the two cunts close together. They kissed each other, then they rubbed cunts together, till they moaned with pleasure; and then laid silent. Then as they laid flat and tranquil in each other's arms, I got between Gabrielle's thighs, put a hand round between the two bellies, and it lay embedded in the hair of their cunts. I somehow inserted my prick in her cunt, whether much or little up it I can't say, — and spent my seed up her in a shove or two. Then as my prick came out, Gabrielle, with a cry of pleasure, rubbed her cunt lubricated with my sperm against the cunt of her friend, and they rubbed, and wriggled, and screeched, and spent in voluptuous frenzy.

I was going away after that, but looking out found it still pouring with rain, as it had been all the evening; so I stopped, — it was passed midnight. We had more wine, and my brain was whirling with lust. I made Gabrielle and her friend piss over my hand; I held their cunts open, and the pot under each whilst the other held the candle, whenever either of them wanted to empty her bladder (and the champagne ran through them freely), so that I could see the function performed. Then Gabrielle laid down again, I knelt over her and she sucked my prick, whilst her friend again gamahuched her. My antipathy to minette was overcome, a desire to finish my prickwork in its lodging came over me. "I shall spend, — I'm coming," I cried. Gabrielle sucked my prick harder and I spent in her mouth, and bent over her, until her own pleasure came on as her friend rapidly licked her cunt. She spent almost simultaneously with me. Then we got up, rested, and recommenced. At last having fucked both women again, all on the bed now together. At four o'clock in the morning I found my way home exhausted, and two-thirds drunk.

It was a long time since I had had any debauch. Women, and lots of them, were my delight, but I took them one at a time. With a strong constitution, I could copulate without fatigue once or twice daily, could do so without excitements, without stimulants of any sort, excepting the glorious contemplation and amusements that the beautiful woman for the time could give me. I disliked the idea of minette, yet now I had consummated in the lady's mouth, and, actually enjoyed it; had set women flat-fucking, and enjoyed seeing that. Did they do it properly? — did they enjoy each other? — were they only shamming? I sat reflecting on all this with an aching head the next morning, and wondering how many times I had spent. I certainly fucked each woman twice or more, and spent in Gabrielle's mouth — and that was all I knew.

Next evening I went to Gabrielle's. Both women had got drunk she said, and slept together. "Did they flat-fuck afterwards, — did they really enjoy that?" "Mais certainement oui," it was "une fantaisie," and they did it till they could do it no longer — "Mon Dieu," till her friend fell asleep on the top of her. She was "une femme charmante, et cochonne." They both had headaches, had enjoyed themselves — look at the bottles. The bed was unmade, the room still in disorder. Should she fetch her friend again? — she had only just left her. "Mon Dieu" she did not recollect how often I had spent — seven times she thought. I fucked her, left, and did not see her again for months, but frequented Camille, who with her soft, almost feline ways and delicious manner in copulation, charmed me much.

To get away from home, I went abroad again early in December to Naples with a friend, and had women there of course. One evening coming out of my hotel, an elderly man exceedingly well dressed, accosted me in Italian. He was so gentlemanly in appearance and manners, that I stood and listened to him, at first not being able to make out what he said. It was that he had some charming ladies he could introduce me to — not common women, not whores. I listened, for it was the first time I had been solicited by a man on such matters, though I had made many a valet-de-place pimp, and go to brothels with me. They were charming he said in a quiet voice, and one a delicious young lady only fifteen years old. I told him no.

"Ah! the Signor would perhaps like a fine young man." I did not quite understand him at first, not understanding Italian well, and repeated after him interrogatively the word "young." He misunderstood me. Ah! yes, if I preferred young, he had two lovely boys, quite young, one thirteen, one fourteen years old, without any hair on them — they were most delicate. Finding I had to make him repeat, because I did not understand him and that I answered in French, he addressed me quite fluently in that language, and told it all over again. Yes, only thirteen and fourteen years, — no hair on them, but though so young they both could spend. I declined, he took off his hat with a gloved hand, "Buona sera, Signor," — he was often on the Chaia, if I changed my mind, and I several times saw him there accosting men just at dusk.

This set me thinking very much, and on reflection, though amusing one's self that way seemed to me most objectionable, yet if men liked it, it was their affair alone. A man had as much right to use his anus as he liked, as a man has to use his penis — that was the conclusion I came to. But it set me wondering if many men took their pleasure up other's backsides. Was it more pleasure than fucking women? — did the buggaree have pleasure like the buggerer? — and so on, till I thought I should like to try, but I never did. For a little time afterwards I thought over all I had seen, heard, and done with my own sex from boyhood to the present time. My curiosity on the matter was aroused, and the curiosity has become stronger since.

I was extremely unhappy whilst away from England, felt as if banished, yet hated to go back, and was so depressed that I never had fewer women. I seemed to care nothing about them or indeed anything else, till parting with my friend, I went to Milan. There I found that at the very best house where they kept women, the price was only something less than four shillings for a woman, and fresh handsome women they were. A sexual rousing took place in me, but it was not the result of the cheapness of cunt, it was the niceness of the women, and out of eight women in the house I fucked seven. Then to Turin I went, and sledged over Mount Cenis, and afterwards by diligence much of the way, and the rest by rail, reached Paris with a few adventures, and the first, strange to say, again with (I believe) a married woman.

I travelled in the coupé of a diligence with a tall, dark-eyed, handsome lady, looking thirty, and a boy about five years old, her child. She was well, even expensively dressed, but most quietly (quite the style then when ladies dressed for travel, with its roughness, and not as tho for show). Eight hours were we together. It was very cold, and I longed to get near her for the warmth which a nice woman gives a man; but the child sat in the middle. Of course we talked during the whole journey. She was going to the same town as I was, but I found not to the same hotel. She had been there before, and pronounced the F°°c°n Hotel excellent, so I altered my mind, and went to it at the town of G°°n°b°e.

It was a big old-fashioned hotel (the railway had then not quite reached the town), and none of the hotel-servants could speak anything but French and Italian (commonly the case in those days). We went up speedily with others to get bed-rooms (no telegraph then), a chambermaid showed them to us together, evidently thinking us married. I selected one. The lady looked at the one next. "The little boy will sleep with me," said she, "I must have a large bed, — this bed won't do." "Lucky boy," said I. She fixed her eyes on me, and coloured. "Boys recollect what they see when very young, I know that, I do," I went on to say, and laughed. "Do they?" — and she laughed too. "This room then?" said the maid. It had a large bed, but I had selected that. "There is a little room leading out of this (the smaller room) which will do for the little boy," said the maid, showing it. The lady took the two rooms, the chambermaid then unlocked the door between my room and the lady's. "Shall I bring your supper here, or will you go downstairs?" said she to us. The lady laughed, and (in French of course), "No, no, — the gentleman is not with me." "Mais pardon, Madame," said the chambermaid much confused, and shooting a bolt on Madame's side of the door, she went into my room and locked the door on my side, leaving there the key. I was standing in the corridor. Then my prick began suddenly to swell with a voluptuous sensation, the idea of being alone in the bed-room with the lady caused it.

The lady was a well-informed woman, and spoke French and Italian well. We had crossed the frontier in the diligence, and I heard her speak both languages; but though with her for hours, not a word, not a sign of voluptuousness had passed between us, and I had never thought of love till that moment.

Now lust seized me. "She means us to visit each other presently," said I. The lady laughed, "A pretty visit for me, that would be." "A bachelor on the visit to a widow." "But I'm not a widow." "You've been a long time without a husband you told me." "And truly enough," said she with a sigh.

We went into our rooms, washed, and soon after she went downstairs. Seeing no one, I went into her room, unbolted the door, and went then downstairs. The table d'hote was over, we each

ordered dinner, and at the waiter's suggestion agreed to dine to-
gether, she paying her share. "Do you like champagne?" I asked.
"Yes, but I can't afford it, so don't order any for me," said she
quite anxiously. "We are in old France again, and champagne I
must have," and I ordered some, begged she would favor me by
taking a glass, and we soon got through one bottle, and began an-
other. The little boy who had a small quantity, fell asleep, the
mother said she must put him to bed. "Good night, sir," said she.
"I'll say good night to you upstairs, for I shall go to bed too." She
looked hard at me.

It was a very cold night, the corridors of the hotel were silent.
Almost directly after she left I went up to my room. We could hear
every movement in each other's room; it was always so in old-
fashioned hotels in those days. I listened, — a door closed. "You're
nice and warm, — good night dear, — go to sleep, — I'm close to
you." The next instant the rattle of a long strong piddle reached my
ear. I laughed loudly and intentionally, and said through the door,
"Good night." "Good night," she replied in such a tone, that I felt
sure she was trying to stifle her laughter.

In conversation, I had discovered that she had travelled much
in Europe, and tried to draw her out about herself, but found it
useless, — she was close as an oyster. She tried the same with me I
noticed, with what success I cannot say. Who is she? — what is she?
— her husband has been long away she says, — she looks quiet but
invitingly, — she advised this hotel, — she laughed in a lady-like
manner at little boys recollecting things, — does she want poking?
— shall I try it on? — so ran my thoughts rapidly.

With lewed intent, but nervous about my intentions, I still lis-
tened and heard movements as of a woman undressing. Then I
half-undressed myself, brought the pot nearest to the door, and
pissed, making it rattle as much as I could to excite her. Anything
which brings man and woman to think of the genitals of the opposite
sex has a stirring lewed effect! Then I knocked gently, and called,
using the name (Mrs. M°°°l°°d) she had entered in the hotel-
book. "What do you want?" said she coming to the door. "To talk
to you, — I feel so dull." "And I'm so cold, — good night." "Haven't
you a fire?" "There is no stove." "There is one in my room, — and
it's quite warm, — come in and chat, — you are not going away to-
morrow?" A long pause. "No thank you."

Rustling movements again, and a cough. I hesitated, for she

had given me no encouragement. My prick got voluptuous, it had not entered a woman for a week or more. I put wood on the fire, summoned courage, and knocked again. "Come and have a chat." "No thank you, I've my gown off." How rapid is human thought. I saw in my mind's eye her half-naked breasts and arms, and my prick rose stiff. Has she bolted the door, or found out that it is unbolted? I turned the key, then the handle, and the door opened! "Oh! who's that?" said she running to the door. "Oh! you really must not — the maid ought to have locked it." Her voice had dropped, and we stood looking at each other, when she found it was I who had entered.

"Don't be frightened, — it's too early to go to bed, — come and chat, — your room is like an ice-well, mine like an oven. Leave the door open, it will warm your room." "I don't mind the cold." "You complained of it." "I shall be warm in bed." "You'll be warmer in mine, there is room for two." "Oh! don't talk such nonsense." "It's not nonsense, — we are alone, — come." "No." "Come and have a glass of champagne (the bottle scarcely commenced was in my room), — you'll sleep better." No she'd had more than enough; but she hesitated, and stood still looking at me. "Fetch me a glass." "Come in, — it's warm, and your boy won't hear us talk." "Poor little fellow, he is so tired," said she standing still, "and it's really freezing here," (throwing a shawl over her shoulders). "Come, it's warm in my room." A little more persuasion and she came, sat with me before the fire, and had champagne. The door was left open, so that the heat might penetrate her chamber. No one was in the bedroom next to mine, — I had ascertained that.

We talked cosily, then warmly. Gradually I felt her arms. How plump she was, — she did not look so plump in her gown. Really, — didn't she? Then with coquetry and pleased vanity, she showed her arm nearly to her shoulder. I kissed it. "What sweet, smooth flesh you have." "Now don't, — you must not." I had lifted the shawl, and she tightened it. "Oh! do let me see your bust again, — it's beautiful, — I saw it when I opened the door." With a twitch I pulled off the shawl, clutched her, and kissed her shoulder, but little of her breasts were visible. She would go if I went on so, and put the shawl back. I made her pull off her stockings, — her feet would get so warm. She turned her back to me, and did, — and nice white little feet she showed.

But one of my nervous timid fits was on me, and I could not make the attack boldly that I wanted to make. She was a lady, evidently married, and I didn't then see that whether conscious of it or not, or whether she intended it or not, that she really was ready for fucking, — she really was ready for fucking, — she could not help being so. I hesitated, and went on talking quietly and respectfully. When did she see her husband last? "Oh! some time ago." When expect to see him? She didn't know, — she expected a letter there from him. I had heard all this in the diligence; and got bolder. "You're longing for him to be in bed with you, aren't you?" "No, — but it's quite natural if I did," — and she laughed, and looked at me. In half fear I kissed her. "You mustn't really," but now I had struck the lewed gamut, and ran rapidly up it after my usual fashion. "Let us sleep together." "Oh! no, — I ought not to have come in here." "Do." "I dare not." She half rose to go, but I kept her down on the chair. "Don't go, — it's quite early, — your room will get warm soon," and I threw more logs on the fire.

"What pretty white feet — you've a lovely leg I am sure. — Do let me." And gently I put my hand high up on her calf, I did it so respectfully, but she stopped me. "Oh, let us sleep together," I burst out. "It's impossible." I coaxed and carnied: "Do, — look what a state you've put me in," and in rutting excitement, out I pulled my prick in its randy rigidity. She looked. "Don't do that now or I'll go, you don't know what risk I should run." Again I prevented her rising. Our seats were close together. "Well let me feel your leg. Let me feel your flesh — only to your thigh — there, just there." — Her resistance was that of an infant, and my fingers reached her cunt. —"Feel me love, feel my prick, — let us — kiss me." I could not place her hand on my prick, for with one of mine I was holding her waist, the other was on her cunt. "Feel me — do, — let us. — Let us fuck. — Kiss me." "Oh — aha — I dare not." We ceased talking, but our lips kept on kissing. — She laid hold of my prick — I alternately groped up her cunt, or frigged the clitoris; and so in silence for a minute or so I suppose. But how count time in such delicious enjoyment — tho certainly she had been in my room an hour and a half before we reached this stage. She got restless under my fingering. — "Let us," "Oho — no — oh — I daren't," but she kept on kissing. Her fatigue, the companionship in the strange hotel, the warmth of the fire, the champagne, our kisses, my lewed talk, and the feeling of her cunt had stirred her lust and subdued her. She grasped my prick quite hard and sighed, "Aha." Then as if conquering herself relinquished it. "I must go," said she, rising. But I rose, the bed was at the back of us, and holding her to me I pulled her against it. Then desire conquered her. Without a word, without resistance, she laid on the bed, I mounted her, saw for an instant dark hair between her thighs, and we were one; cock and cunt in conjunction, cock ejaculating its sperm, cunt distilling its moisture, sighs and gasps of pleasure, soft kisses, and no other sound but the bursting and quiet cracking and hissing of the logs on the red hot embers. — What a delicious treat after a week's abstinence. It was Paradise Elysium to us both, certainly to her, as much as to me.

We lay copulated, kissing and tonguing long after the ecstatic pleasures were over, but at last disjoined. "Let us sleep together." She stood quite still for a minute, and then, "I'll take off my things in my own room," was her only reply. She locked her boy's door, and got into the bed with me. She had risked it — and was ready for further risk. My sperm had only made her more voluptuous. She knew too well the soft pleasure of a second fuck in the lubricated cunt to diminish it by washing, and as I had left it five minutes before, so I found it. No sooner had my fingers touched the lips, and felt the smooth sperm covered surface, than my prick rose, and the next minute was engulfed and drowned in the bath of our joint making. How exquisite is the smoothness that a man's sperm gives to the vulva. I tried to prolong our pleasure, but our reservoirs were too full. Again we spent, and then overcome with pleasure and fatigue, fell asleep in each other's arms.

She awakened me in two or three hours. The fire was out. She was next the wall, and was getting over me. "I want to pee," said she. So did I. We both pissed in the dark, got into bed again and cuddled. Her modesty was gone, she handled my prick, I felt her cunt, and we kissed and kissed, feeling and handling. — "Let me see your charms, I'll strike a light." "No, don't" — but I did, and throwing up her chemise, saw a dark-brown motte, and handsome haunches, and belly. My prick stood again, I knelt for an instant between her thighs, shaking my stiff machine at her in baudy waggery. Then putting out the light we covered up, and talked lust, lewedness, and love, till again we consummated, and went to sleep, her bum against my ballocks, her back against my belly, my hand over her haunches touching her motte. The loveliest of all ways of sleeping with a woman in cold weather. We slept for hours. When I awakened it was six o'clock, and quite dark. Her rump was towards me and she was fast asleep. I was lying on my back, with as grand a prick as ever opened cunt lips. I never could have too much of a woman. Even when fucked out I still like to see, feel, and kiss her. I soon turned round, and felt my lady pretty freely over her body, but without awaking her. Then I slid my fingers between her buttocks and thighs, in what seemed much crisp hair, till the soft elastic covers of her quim met them. I wriggled quite slowly my middle finger up it, how warm, soft, and smooth, it felt, and I revelled in it for a minute. I believe it to be impossible to keep a finger up a woman's cunt long without awaking her. Mrs. M°°°l°°d's bum began to move quite gently, and her cunt to clip when my finger had been in her a little time, then she half turned round, and my finger came out. "What is it, what are you doing, what is it? Oh, it's you," she said, suddenly becoming conscious that she was in bed with me. Lust was raised in her. I pulled our night clothes well up, and belly to belly, with hands on each other's arses we kissed. "Let's do it again." — She turned on to her back, I on to her belly, and we had that fuck with pleasure peculiar to the morning, and fell asleep again.

But she awakened me soon. — "I must get out." "To piddle?" "Yes." I groped for the pot and handed it to her, she pissed, and went to the boy's door. "Arthur," she called. "He's fast asleep," said she, and came to bed again. — We cuddled, but fucking was over. At the first glimpse of daylight, "I must get into my bed before my boy comes in," said she. She bolted the door between our rooms, I went to bed, and it was late when I went to breakfast. She had breakfasted and left the room long before. — We had agreed not to notice each other much. The towel I had taken to bed with us was handsomely stained. — I am too old a hand now, and have had too much trouble with stained sheets to forget a towel on such occasions as this.

False names. — Mrs. M°°°l°°d. — Baudy tales. — Naked by a trick. — My smooth flesh. — The child's mother. — The hairy bum furrow. — I leave G°°n°b°e. — Who was she. — At the town of N°v°°s. — Spy holes. — Marital frolics under the bed clothes. — Husband and chambermaid. — Chambermaid and self. — The brooch. — Conflicting emotions, desire, and disgust. — Suzanne's complaisance. — I leave N°v°°s. — At Paris. — The Bal Masque. — Gabrielle and Violette. — Baudy exercises and groupings. — An orgy to exhaustion. — To London.

After her luncheon she left her child down stairs, and came into my room. "When should I leave G°°n°b°e?" she asked. "Just before you do." "Which road are you going?" "Towards Paris — and your road?" "Not to Paris." "Your name is not M°°°l°°d, but you have entered it so in the hotel-book." She laughed and coloured up. "No, and yours isn't — °°°°." "True, we don't want to know each other's name, but they were entered from our passports at the frontier, what if the police find we have changed them?" (Passport regulations were very severe then.) "Directly you have got your letter I will leave, I won't cause a suspicion of you, and if we ever meet elsewhere we will be utter strangers to each other." This seemed to satisfy an anxiety she shewed in a conversation much longer than this.

I had begun kissing and hugging, she was cool to me, and without reply resisted my lifting her petticoats, but she mollified as we talked. Standing up at first, we were soon sitting on the edge of my bed, my finger on her cunt, and arm round her waist. It was a clear, brilliant, January day, but cold and frosty. "Let us do it." "No, I've run a dreadful risk." "Risk it again." "I'm frightened." "Feel me," and out my prick came. She laid hold of it. "Let us." "My little boy is alone." "Never mind, let us — I must see your lovely thighs." "A-h-a, leave off, take your hand away." "Get on the bed then, love." She got on. I threw up her clothes, and kissed her belly and motte. Had she come to be fucked, I wonder. — I can't say. Women are so cunning; but her cunt had just been washed, the hair was moist and not with piddle. Pulling aside the lips, I fingered it and lightly tickled her clitoris, I was standing by the bed side, she laying along it, so that was all I could do with my tongue. Her thighs and belly looked lovely on a beautiful white chemise with work round the bottom. The winter sun shot a brilliant ray right on to her cunt as she lay — it was that which seduced me into the lingual incitement. — Then I laid my head on her thighs, contemplated her charms, and smoothing her belly said, "How many children have you had? You have no marks of child-birth." "Oh! pull down that blind, I don't like being exposed so." "My darling you can stand any amount of exposure, your thighs and belly are lovely." But she pushed down her clothes, I pushed them up again, she down. — Then rapidly for fear of refusal, I got on to her and fucked right off. Curiosity seized me whilst lying on her, and I repeated the question. She laughed, and the laugh jerked my prick out of her. — She got up and washed her cunt. — I repeated my question. "You don't know where to look," said she laughing. "Let's sleep together to-night." She shook her head, locked the door between our rooms, and went down stairs.

She walked about the town with her boy; I met her, bowed, and passed on. I barely noticed her at the table d'hôte. I ordered a fire in my room, more lights, wine, and cakes, and went there about 8 o'clock (it was dark at about five) and waited till I heard her and the boy's door closed. Then I knocked — no response — louder and louder I knocked. "Don't," said she, speaking thro the door. "Come." "No." I gave a violent bang, and the door opened. "Don't make that noise, the boy will hear. I'll come when he's asleep," — and she came.

We sat by the fire drinking champagne, put inquisitive questions to each other and fenced replies. — "You won't find out anything more," said she laughing. "Well it's stupid, I'd better not, nor you of me." Then I began kissing, talked baudily, told story after story. "Good gracious, I never hear such things," she kept remarking.

"Hasn't your husband told you such things?" "Never, he never uses such words." "Not cunt?" "No, never." "Not fuck?" "Never." "You've heard them." "Of course I have." Then on I went in my lewedest strain, charmed with such a listener.

She would not let me take voluptuous liberties, whilst this conversation went on. No she would leave if I did. So leaving off, I began quietly love making, kissing, and cunt feeling. "Come to bed love, we can talk just as well there, let me look at your thighs as you sit, let me undress you." — She objected but yielded. I helped her and took off garters and stockings, charmed with the disclosures of her flesh. She carried her clothes into her room; I went with her. "Bring your night-gown into my room. It's so cold here." "No, you go and I'll put it on here." But I carried it into my room, she following me. "Let me put it on you." "No I won't." She took it from me, pulled her arms out of her chemise, which she held up for the second with her teeth; opened the night-dress, raised it over her head, and as she did so, let the chemise drop to her feet; just then I snatched the night-gown out of her hands, and she stood as naked as she was born. "Oh, what a shame," said she very sharply, and put her hand over her cunt as if to hide it, "give it me now." — I dropped on my knees, buried my lips in the hair of her cunt, kissing it, and clasping her round her smooth buttocks.

Her struggles were slight. "Now let me put it on, I'm cold." I rose and holding her close to me, looked at her beauties as well as I could in that position. Then she insisted so strongly, that I let her put on her night-gown. She pardoned me, I undressed, we both sat before the fire and again recommenced billing and cooing. She let me expose her thighs. "Let me see your lovely bum." "No." "Do." — "No." But coaxed, she at last consented, and stood up modestly with her bum to the fire, whilst I looked at it, felt, and kissed it. — "Look," said I, with a sudden impulse of lust, which made me desire to show myself; and stripping off my night-shirt, I stood naked with prick stiff in front of her. . "Feel me dear, do feel me," and I placed her hand on my thigh. — In a modest way she felt my flesh all down my thigh, and then up one side. Said she, "What lovely flesh, — you're just like a woman." "Many other women have said so."

Into bed we got — and without more dalliance — my burning prick went in her hot, soft, cunt. We fucked, we spent, and lay coupled together long. "Feel my flesh and talk now, love." She ran both hands over me. "It is just like a woman's — I thought — men were always hairy." I uncunted, turned on my back, and she felt my belly and breasts. "It's like a woman's, it's lovely," again she said. I wondered who and what she was, that she should lay lasciviously enfolded in my arms. "Am I smoother than other men?" "I've only felt my husband and you — and gracious Heaven — what risk I am running." "When were you fucked last?" "Oh, months ago." She had seen a few men partly naked, working — and some fishermen and labourers, they were all hairy, she said.

In an hour we talked ourselves into lewedness again, and she let me see her form and beauties, but did not then open her thighs. Again we fucked and slept, she awakened, went and listened at her boy's door, pissed in her room, and got into bed with me — I had a night lamp — and we passed a voluptuous but restless night, which left us weak when the morning came; and in one of our burning, lewed caresses, she said she had never had a child, that the boy was her step-child, and had never known his real mother. That is the utmost about herself I learnt at any time.

For two days she would not let me have her in the day time, but an hour after the table d'hôte she was in her room, put her child, whom she had tired out by walking, to bed, then got into bed with me, and we fucked all night. I was in first-rate condition, and it was a sort of honeymoon to us both, but specially to her. My smooth flesh seemed to excite her wonderfully, and on the last night she kissed me all over. The last time I had her it took me half an hour to get an emission, stopping from time to time at the work, but never taking my prick out. She who had her pleasure quickly, with short sighs and clasping me very tightly to her, and had been fetched oftener by my unremitting ramming, groaned, "Oh, do leave off." "I'm coming in a minute love," — and I went on violently at the rate of two shoves a second, finishing the fuck almost with pain, and with a sore prick. At daylight we were a hollow eyed, fucked out couple.

The child on the third night cried "Mamma, mamma." — She must have slept but lightly, for she was out of bed in a minute, awakening me as she got out; he soon went to sleep again, and she came back, shivering, to my bed. She was exceedingly kind to the boy.

She was not a short woman, and had ample flesh, her calves

were thin, the thighs swelled out rapidly to fine haunches, her cunt was full lipped. By the last night I had eradicated all modesty in her, she let me look and feel as I liked, and I verified that she had short, crisp hair, like horse hair, along the bum furrow, from her cunt to her back-bone. The hair of her cunt was thick, very curly, and lay close on her flesh. She was dark eyed, dark haired, had unusually large thick eye brows, and was a boldish looking, handsome woman.

She had been twice daily to the *poste restante*, and every day made me promise to leave when she asked me. One morning "Now you must leave to-night if you can." I left that night and have never set eyes on her since. From a slight accent, I think she was Irish.

After luncheon that day she refused me. Fatigued sexually as I was, yet the idea of losing her excited me — no she would not, but she let me into her room. Then letting down my trowsers (what strange incitements come into my mind), I held my shirt up all round me. "Well feel my flesh for the last time," the invitation succeeded, her hand smoothed and felt up to my breasts in silence. As I hoped, it stirred her lust. "Let me feel you, dear, for the last time." "Well that's all." — I felt her cunt. — My prick stiffened, she felt it, and a few minutes after I was groaning in the delight of having her, rather than the need of ejaculating my sperm. "I'll get you with child," said I, as vague baudy thoughts floated thro my brain with my increasing pleasure. — "I've never been-with-child — oho-har," she sobbed out as her spending began. — She told me the same as she washed her cunt afterwards. "I didn't mean to say it, and I'm running a great risk."

I had been wondering daily who and what she was, I was surprised at my easy success. Did she want money, or was she only satisfying her lust — she had no servant — said she couldn't afford champagne — yet drank excellent Claret, had the best rooms — was well clothed — had very fine linen, and lots of baggage. Risking it I said delicately, "If you want money I can lend you some." — "No thank you I have enough, and have only to write to get what I want."

We kissed. "I shall often think of you." She made no reply. "I hope we shall meet again." "Gracious heaven, I hope not." She kissed me. "You're very handsome," — she said, then shut the door, and I never have met her since. C C M was marked on her linen.

After the first day we never took but the slightest notice of each other when we met in the town, nor did I dine near her, nor do much more than bow slightly when in the hotel. No one could have guessed our secret amusements unless it were the chamber-maid, nor she unless she listened, which was not likely; but fearing that, I slipped into the adjoining bedroom unobserved. The room was empty, and a wardrobe placed against the door, so that hearing there was not easy, and we spoke always in a low tone.

On my road to Paris I stopped at the (then little visited) town of N°v°°s. At the hotel was a big Frenchman and his young wife. I thought he must be commercial. His wife was a young, buxom wom-an, and I fancied they had not been married long. My bed-room was next to theirs, and I noticed that spy holes had been bored in the door between our rooms, but carefully plugged up, which gave me a desire to have a peep at the lady. It is a delicious sight to see a pretty young woman at her toilet. So with scissors, I pushed open some holes and could see clearly through some of them, a bed, and pot cupboard by the side of it. This so excited me, that instead of going to see the cathedral, and other things I had come to see, I did nothing but watch this lady; and whenever I thought she was going to her bed-room, I went to mine. I have ever been indefatiga-ble in watching for opportunities with women, nothing ever turned me off the scent, no amusements ever drew me aside, when a lewed intention, or hope, had laid hold of me.

After breakfast up stairs she went, I also, and mounted a chair (the holes were high) to peep, but saw nothing worth seeing. She put on her bonnet and went out with her husband. I went out but returned before her. About half an hour before luncheon, she came back, and I had the pleasure of seeing her sit down and piddle by the side of the bed, from which I guessed that it was her bed. Simple as this operation was, hundreds of times as I have seen women, both dressed and naked, piddle, the sight of this pretty woman doing so gave me such wonderful pleasure, that I set to work to open a hole lower down — in the direction of a washstand — guided in so doing by hearing the china rattle. I feared that the hole being so low it would be obscured, but risked it, and got a fair view through it.

She had luncheon at the hotel. Soon after, up she went, up I went, and quickly saw her pee-wee, and then, — oh, joy! her husband came in. Then she put herself on the bed side, he turned up her clothes, contemplated her dark haired cunt for a minute (and so did I), and after she had sat up and felt his prick for a minute, he shagged her. There was not much ceremony between the two, they both wanted it, were very quick about it, and enjoyed it. I watched her face whilst she was spending. Then they both went out, and she never washed. I should have heard the basin if she had. Whether she gave her cunt a dry rub or not, I can't say.

I only intended stopping a day at N°v°°s but now resolved to stay longer. I thought all the remainder of the day of what I had seen. It was delicious to look at her (a bright eyed brunette), at the table d'hôte, and think of her cunt, and her thighs hanging over her husband's arms, and sexual pleasure in her pretty face as she spent. I had been a long time wishing again to see a couple fucking, and now my desire was gratified fully, and I might perhaps see more; so sooner than lose a chance, I went to my room directly after dinner, waiting and waiting until about 11 o'clock, when in they came, seemingly very happy, for they talked loudly and laughed. I watched, but her bed was all I could see from one peep hole, and I could not be constantly shifting, so some times I saw her, some times not, and him the same. After a time she appeared in chemise, sat on the edge of the bed, pulled her stockings off, piddled, pulled off her chemise, showed her back-side quite naked for a second or two, put on her night dress and got into bed. He came into view in his shirt, and pulled down the bed-clothes, and she pulled up her nightgown to let him look at her cunt for a minute. She evidently quite understood his wants. Then he mounted her, but it was cold; he uncunted, they covered themselves up with the bed-clothes and fucked under them. I had only the pleasure of seeing the bed-clothes heaving. He had put the candle, which had been by her bedside, on to the wash-stand, and I could not so well see her face as I had in the day time. He then got off of her and went to his bed, taking the candle with him and extinguishing it. She had turned on her side, and seemed to sleep directly he had left her, with the soothing effects of her pleasure and a cunt full.

I watched all this with intense pleasure, standing on a chair, with my prick out stiff, and feeling it, and longing for a pleasure.

I resisted frigging myself, determining to get a woman next day. To my annoyance, I awakened in the night with a baudy dream, and spending copiously on my night shirt.

I passed most of my time when waiting thus, in writing my doings at Naples and G°°n°b°e with Mrs. M°°°l°d. Next morning I did not see them copulating, tho I got up at day break and watched till breakfast. Then I heard the lady say, "I may as well go there at once; and you come to dinner." Then I watched her go out of the hotel, and fancying there would be no fun for me till night, I thought of going out myself, and in half an hour or so, went up to my room for my great coat. When there, I heard male and female voices talking quietly in the adjoining room. Oh, thought I, she has come back, so got at once to my peep hole.

But the husband was there alone, and I was about to get down, when in came a chambermaid, who closed the door, bolted it quickly, and in a minute was on the bed side with her thighs wide open, and he was tailing her, just where he had done it to his wife the day before. I watched them fucking. The instant it was over, she shook down her petticoats and left the room, in another minute he was out of it, neither washed. I was staggered, and soon after I left my room and saw the chambermaid talking to some travellers at the end of the corridor. Oh, how I longed to have her.

I went out, could not find a whore, came back, had luncheon, and went to my room thinking of the chambermaid, and wondering at her tricks, and her impudence, in doing it in a room with a married man, and where I supposed she must have known there were peep holes. The man and she seemed acquaintances. Then I wondered if she would let me. Impelled by my throbbing prick, which kept urging me to please it, I went up and down stairs to my room, trying for an opportunity, till I saw her in the corridor. She was a good looking, dark eyed woman, seemingly about twenty years old, and was dressed better than an ordinary chambermaid. I rang for hot water, she brought it, I began a conversation. — It was very cold. — "Yes, will you have a fire, sir?" I knew she would send a man to light it so declined. "You warm me." "I don't know how," said she with such a sly lewed look, that I felt sure she was game. "I'll show you," and I kissed her. She resisted after the manner of women, but so feebly, that I easily held her close, and repeated my kiss. "Now leave off, they will wonder where I am." "I'm warmer already, ma chere, I'll give you a lovely cameo brooch if you make me warmer still, and no one but you and I will know it." "What do you mean?" "Why this," — and I put my hand up her clothes. She scuffled. "Oh, no, certainly not," but she would not have dislodged a child's fingers from her cunt, which I got well hold of. "I won't." "Don't make a noise, ma chere, or they will hear us in the next rooms." "I'm frightened," said she, "I can't, I won't," — and I thought my chance was gone.

Talking one evening with the friend who had recommended me the house in L°°°f°°°d St. (where I had been with Mrs. Y°°°s°°°e) on the subject of women, he said that he did not offer servants and that class of women money, that a bit of jewellery caught them much more readily than gold, and that it was very much cheaper. "They may refuse a sovereign or two, they may be offended, but jewellery they can't refuse." I had found boots, and bonnets, backed with gold, do very well, but certainly had failed in two or three instances signally, and had missed opportunities in other cases, where a mere offer of love could not be made, with chance of success.

Struck with some pretty cameo brooches at Naples, I bought half a dozen for presents (they were not nearly so costly thirty years ago as now). "I've got such a pretty brooch which I'll give you. Do you like brooches? Look at this." "Yes," said she taking it. I caught hold of her again, pulled my prick out, and got my hands on to her cunt. "Now don't, I don't like it," — was all she said, and she stood leaning her bum against the bed, looking at the brooch with her thighs closed, and my fingers fumbling about her cunt lips.

Sure now of having her, I let her go, then rapidly bolted the door, and in a minute had her on the bed with her petticoats up. She meant fucking. I was on her, and my prick had touched her cunt when, my fingers feeling its moisture, the idea of her not having washed the Frenchman's sperm out of her seized me, and my prick began to dwindle. Tho the fucking took place hours before, tho my knowledge of copulation generally should have taught me that I should find none of his leavings, even if she had not washed, yet all occurred just as described, and then followed in succession, an absurd variety of contradictory emotions, and actions, which must have astonished her.

I rose on to my knees between her thighs hurriedly, and holding my prick looked at her. Shall I ask her if she has washed, I thought. "What's the matter?" said she hurriedly. Mentally then I saw the husband fucking her at the side of the bed, and my prick stiffened, again the idea of his sperm lying in her haunted me, I felt I could not fuck her, and thrust my fingers up her cunt to feel if his sperm was there — as if it was a more delicate thing to feel it with my fingers, than with my prick. "Oh, you hurt!" she cried out loudly. Then down I fell on her forgetting the sperm, thinking only of the two as I had seen them fucking. My prick was like a horn, my lust got furious, and with fierce thrusts I spent in her. "Oh, you hurt — oho," she sobbed and she spent with me.

This conflict of desire and disgust, a prick stiff one minute, the next dwindling to flaccidity, stiffening again as a different thought flashed through my brain, and furiously emptying its semen in a violent paroxysm of pleasure into the cunt which a minute before it had refused to enter, strikes me as one of the singular events of my amatory life.

She interrupted my tranquillity by uncunting me. "Let me get up." — I got off of her, my mind again recurring to her not having washed, but she washed now, turning her back to me, when a bell rang. "It's the call bell," said she, rising quickly from the basin, "look and see if any one's in the corridor." I did. "Yes." "Peep, and tell me when no one's there," in a whisper standing at my back. The bell rang again. "There is no one." Out she went, leaving the brooch on the pisspot stand.

Temporarily satisfied, I soon wanted her again, kept peeping out of my door, and at an opportunity beckoned her. "Presently," said she in a whisper, as she passed the door, "there are travellers about just now." In an hour the corridor was again quiet and she came in. "I cannot stop long," said she, getting on to the bed without hesitation at my request. I got by the side of her, had a pleasant grope, kiss, a partial look, a few minutes baudy talk, and then I was up her again, and we had the nice second fuck of two people who wanted it. As our privates unjoined, the call bell rang again, "Sacré," said she, "what does she want now?" — and off she went quickly with her cunt unwashed this time. She had not asked for the brooch which I had put by, tho I saw her for a moment looking round the room, as if seeking something. She promised to see me after the table d'hôte.

It was quite dark when I went to my room — no travellers were in the rooms on my corridor excepting the couple in the adjoining room. — I lit my candle and kept my door ajar. Suzanne kept her word and came. "Have you washed your cunt," said I, "since we made love?" "Of course." "Where?" "In my room." "Let's look at you." "No, I don't like that." But I would. We got on to the bed "We must not make a noise," said I, "for there is a married couple next to us. Who are they, do you know?" "Yes." It was a manufacturer. He used to live in the town, and had not been long married to a lady whose relatives lived there. "I heard them fucking last night." said I. "That's what they married for," she supposed, laughing as she said it. "I dare say he has fucked you before he was married, as you know him." "Mon Dieu, non." How I longed to tell her what I had seen, but did not, and then we enjoyed each other. I gave her the brooch, which pleased her immensely. No, she could not sleep with me for fear of being found out — but her room was by itself, two flights up thro a door, which she indicated. She would leave the door ajar. Following her at distance, she showed me the way by going straight to, and entering the room.

The married couple came home. I saw him fuck his wife. At the hour appointed, all was silent. I slipped up to the maid's room and had pleasure with her, went back to my own room, passed a tranquil night, awaking just in time to see my neighbours fucking on the bed. After their breakfast they left the hotel.

Then I slipped into their room, and found that apparently after the peep holes had been bored, their room had been painted and traces of the holes obliterated. Those freshly opened by me now alone shewed.

I passed the entire of two days there, keeping much to my room. Suzanne slipped in to me at my request, and I gave her pleasure several times daily. In the intervals writing the narrative of my liaison with Mrs. M***l***d at G**n*b*e. Then having fucked myself out of my rutting fit, with a kiss I left her, and left the town for Paris, stopping at several towns on the way, and using spyholes whenever there were any, but saw nothing worthy of recording.

In a week or two I was at Paris, and went to a *bal masque* at the opera house, Rue Lepelletier. A tall woman, masked, dressed as a man entirely in white, but not as a Pierrot, tho with a Pierrot's

hat on, and with breeches which terminated at her knees, was
dancing a furious cancan with others. Her legs were flung about
high and low, her gestures were lewed and suggested fucking. I,
with a group, stood much amused at the dancing. At a pause of the
dance she accosted me. — "Je vous connais, Monsieur." "Mais non
ma belle." "Mais oui, souvent je vous ai vu à Londres." "Qui êtes
vous donc." "Donnez moi un petit souper et vous verrez." — She
spoke in a high pitched tone to prevent recognition. Dancing re-
commenced; I thought nothing more of it so moved off among the
crowd. A dozen women in masks had said they knew me. I was
soon afterwards talking to a beautiful creature with exquisite legs,
and dressed as a ballet dancer, and was thinking of seeing her legs
with her silks, when the man-woman in white appeared. — "Ah,
you run away from me then!" "No." "I know you." "You don't."
"Bet." "No." "Will you give me a supper with my friend here if
you do?" "Perhaps." She lifted her mask and I saw Gabrielle. The
ballet dancer moved off, muttering. Gabrielle, her friend, and I
were soon supping at a cafe, and an hour after were in Gabrielle's
room. "Not your friend," said I. "Mais oui. You will find Violette
charming. Si cochonne, elle fera tout ce que vous voudrez. Do you
remember that night with two at °°° Street? We will so you
amuse to-night." And the two women and I went together to Ga-
brielle's bed room.

Indecent familiarities began, obscene if you like; the more
libidinous, the better they seemed to please me. I felt Violette's
blonde cunt as she straddled across me. Whilst sitting, Gabrielle
knelt and had commenced her favourite minette with my prick. It
was her fancy not mine, but lasciviousness is contagious, and I
yielded. Violette was partially undressed, Gabrielle still in man's
attire. She explained to me the way the trowsers were put on, and
how opened when she wanted to piddle. "No, don't take them off,
Gabrielle. I'll fuck you with them on at the bedside." "Ah, si," and
laughing, "then you can fancy you are buggering a man." — We
stripped the other lady who was a blonde, laid her across the bed,
put pillows under her arse to elevate it, and Gabrielle stooping,
licked her cunt, whilst I putting my prick into Gabrielle's cunt from
behind; we all took pleasure together. We two fucking, soon spent,
the other lady was longer. Gabrielle, who seemed as if she could not
take her mouth away from the cunt, persisted till she had finished

Violette twice. Most of the time I looked on from behind; my prick, still more or less stiff, up Gabrielle's cunt.

Alas, — these delicious, enervating, sexual amusements will end. The stiffest prick will leave the loveliest cunt. The randiest cunt feels full and satisfied. The strongest and most agile tongue fatigues with minette. — The gamahuchee even needs a little repose. So our groupings terminated, our bodies separated, and with moistened genitals we sat talking and looking at each other. All were still lewed, lascivious, libidinous, tho every letch we could think of had been gratified. The women had sucked each other. Both had resuscitated my prick with their mouths when other means failed, tho I did not ejaculate under that suction. — I fucked both of them more than once, and at day break was fast asleep lying close to Gabrielle, whilst her friend lay snoring on a sofa. At midday we got up and breakfasted. — I fucked them both and left.

After a week's amusement mainly with Gabrielle and Violette, but with one at a time only, I returned to London. There were signs of spring.

The little episode at N*v**s set me trying at every hotel I went to afterwards to see if there were any spy holes, and I often found them. I had seen them at hotels before, and had looked through them, but had no very satisfactory sights when I did. I really cannot understand why I had not been more on the look out for them. I think they were more numerous in France then than in other countries, and that the plan and arrangement of the rooms then favored them. — At all events I have since looked most cunningly after them. Just about this time also I had begun to shave in a new and careful fashion, and had bought a gimlet to enable me to fix a hand glass to the windows for that purpose, and now began to use it at times for making holes, or opening those which had been made and stopped up.

When I found that in my room there was no opportunity of peeping, I changed it as soon as I could. When arriving at an hotel, I waited to see which room was selected by young women, or by a young married couple if there were any, and if possible got the room next to theirs. If there was no door communicating with it, I found some objection and refused it. Thus I got many opportunities, and had some very pleasant, and at times, chastely voluptuous sights.

With Gabrielle and Violette, my libidinous tricks were much the same as I had with Gabrielle at London. The orgy at Paris was but a reproduction. I have had Gabrielle with another woman together since, and see that she loves licking another's cunt, as well as prick sucking.

Explanations. — Reflexions, and observations about myself. — My private establishment. — Easy circumstances. — My new house. — James the footman. — Lucy the parlour maid. — Love exercises in the dining room. — Two dismissals. — The cook and James. — Kitchen and housemaid. — A general turn-out. — Lucy's despair. — My kind intentions. — At her lodgings. — A dinner with her. — On the sofa. — On the notch. — Her confession. — At J°°°s St. — Her form and features. — Gamahuching interludes. — Frig precedent. — Fuck sequential. — Paradisiacal copulation. — Instructions in oral obscenity. — An exquisite cunt. — My gamahuching letch.

[I have not looked through and corrected the foregoing manuscript. — The abbreviations may damage the narrative but there is no help for it, if it is to be printed; yet but few incidents having any novelty have been erased, and the conversations with my women are just as I wrote them originally — the excisions excepted. — How delightfully the episodes come back to my memory as I read the manuscript. Incidents fading into forgetfulness come out quite freshly to me, and I almost seem to be living my youthful life over again. Would that I were going to do so, for it was a lovely time with women; and was only cursed by that one lasting, deep, irremediable error.

[I am not sure about ages in one or two instances, nor the exact order of two or three of the more fugitive amours. I could perhaps set these quite right by reference to books now hidden and dusty, but it is not worth the trouble to do so. — None are of any real importance. I write for my pleasure alone, and if I print, shall print for my pleasure alone, so let the manuscript stand as it is paged.

[I notice now in reading it, that some of my raciest adventures, those which being unsought, those which fell to my lot as it were by accident, and which tho brief were among the most voluptuous, occurred whilst I had other and more enduring liaisons on hand. Such was my weakness and fondness for the sex, that I never could keep faithfully to any one woman absolutely, however much I loved her. I have wished and intended to do so, have tried hard, so hard, to avoid infidelity, but surrendered at last to the temptation. The idea of seeing another woman naked, of piercing a fresh cunt, seemed to foreshadow to me voluptuous pleasures never tasted before with any other woman. As my prick entered the cunt it had never touched before, the sensation always seemed to me more exquisite than that I had ever had with others. Yet many a time after such pleasures I have been disgusted with myself for my weakness, and tried to atone for it, without the object ever having been aware of the reason for my ultra kindness.

[The quantity of manuscript still left for revision, alas, is long. Amongst it is an essay on copulation, written I think somewhat earlier than some I have revised, and written with such knowledge of the subject as I then had, as well as with some ignorance which I now see. It has that freedom of expression which I at once adopted in my narrative, and leaves no doubt in my own mind about what I meant then, and at all times. — It pleased me much when I wrote it, yet it must be sacrificed to time, money, and expediency — for it is not an incident, and forms no part of the history of my private life, tho it illustrates well my frame of mind and knowledge of things sexual, at the period of my life when I wrote it.

[This perusal brings prominently before me all my acts, deeds, and thoughts for full twenty years, and I perceive clearly, that altho I had done most things which were sexually possible once, and almost out of curiosity, or else on sudden impulse (up to about this period), yet that my habits with women in my lust were for the most part simple, commonplace, and unintellectual; and that I had not sought for out of the way lascivious postures and varied complex delights in copulation or its preliminaries, which a fervid, voluptuous, poetical imagination has since gradually devised for my gratification. This desire for variety seems to have commenced some time after I became acquainted with Camille.

[But by that time I was evidently no longer displeased with that which, in years previously, would have shocked me. My prejudices have now pretty well vanished with the approach of middle age. I have conquered antipathies and reaped the reward, in seeing before me a great variety of frolics, suitable to my maturity, but which I am glad I did not have prematurely in my youth when I did not need them, and should not have appreciated them as I do now. — It is amusing now to notice the gradual change from simply belly to belly exercise, which contented me, to the infinitely varied amusements since indulged in.

[No doubt in this I tread but in the ordinary footsteps and ways of male-kind. What I have done, thousands of others are doing. It is only when lustful impetuosity is weakened that reflexion and experience begin to devise new pleasures to aid it. As we get older we invent them as a stimulus, and women thus become more and more charming, needful, and important to us; and just at a time when our responsibilities towards them become greatest. So by aiding and administering to us in our salacious devices, they reward us. In the end they are more and more needful to us, and we repay them by our generosity, our care of them, and our sacrifices for them. Nor are they behind us in desire to participate in these frolics, for they have lust as well as we. In a quiet, hidden way, they like lasciviousness if taught it gradually. But lust is mainly in we men — women are the ministers to it, it is the law of nature. — No blame attaches to woman for liking or for submitting to such frolics, abnormal whims, and fancies, which fools call obscene, but which are natural and proper, and perhaps universally practised, and which concern only those who practise and profit by them. In my experience many women delight equally in them, when their imaginations are once evoked. Nothing can perhaps be justly called unnatural which nature prompts us to do. If others don't like them, they are not natural to *them*, and no one should force them to act them.

[The foregoing and similar paragraphs, written long after the manuscript, are to be enclosed in brackets thus [   ] so that I may identify them when I see them (if I do) at a future day in print, and this writing is destroyed.

[The headings of the chapters are now written for the first

time. — They will be needful if this be printed. Now I resume my narrative.]

Whilst away I arranged it, and directly on my return to England gave up a snug, quiet, illicit establishment elsewhere, and to the satisfaction of both parties. Both agreed to it, and thought it was for the best. We had no quarrel. It cost much money down, and an annuity paid still, but no one was injured, no one wronged. All interested were provided for. I wonder if this will ever meet her eyes, or if so if she will know that it refers to her. It is not probable, for neither names, places, nor initials are given, and no clue afforded; yet nothing is impossible.

I had not returned to England a fortnight before a domestic turn-out took place, which caused me much annoyance but led me to unlooked for pleasure.

It has, I think, been said before that I had been for some time in better circumstances, had a larger house, more servants and so on. Among the servants whom I found on my return, was a parlour maid, a lovely girl with a superb pink and white complexion, and a skin which looked like ivory. She had darkish chestnut hair, soft hazel eyes, and a lovely set of teeth, was well grown, plump, and altogether a most desirable creature, and who looked a lady. Her name was Lucy. It passed through my mind that she would be an exquisite sweetheart, but I resisted incipient desire, avoiding by prudence and custom all intrigues with my own household.

Suddenly this girl was dismissed, and I was requested to dismiss my man, who had lived with us before I had left England, indeed had been in my service nearly two years. He was the best man I ever had, and was moreover a fine, handsome fellow, five feet ten high, and pleasant to look upon. He had been caught in loving familiarities with Lucy, who it was said also was with child by him; the poor girl had let this out to the cook or some one else, and the cook split upon her. James was impudent and denied it all, but I think the case was proved. It would not have done to have passed over open fornication. Had I done so, the habit would have spread throughout the household; so I reluctantly gave him notice. The poor girl went off very quietly in tears. I never felt so sorry for a woman, especially as whilst denying that she had let him have her, she said that he had promised her marriage, which James, when I told him, said was a lie. But this statement of hers confirmed me in the belief that he had tailed her. Lucy was however promised a character, and that nothing should be said about her *faux pas*, unless a question leading to it were asked. It was an unusual piece of charity of my old woman.

So nice a looking girl was of course sought after, and in two or three days ladies applied for her character, but none would take her. James had not gone because I could not get suited with another man. I spoke to him again, and accused him of cruelty and wickedness in promising marriage, but he still denied it altogether. "But the cook asserts she has seen you on the sofa in the dining room more than once." "She's a liar," said James, "but I've several times had *her*, and on that sofa too, and because I'd have no more of her, she's got up this tale." — James got then insolent.

Now in my dining-room was a sofa, tho not an usual piece of furniture in a dining-room; but I liked to lay there by myself and read after dinner at times, so as to avoid the drawing-room and all that was usually in it. The footman and parlour maid laid the dinner things, waited at table, and cleared away, and as no other servant had any right in that room usually at those times, they had a nice chance and had availed themselves of it, I quite believed.

I wished the cook at the Devil for causing me to lose two nice servants, and immediately told my wife what I had heard about her.

She turned up into a high state of moral indignation, and had the cook up, and told her what James had said, I was asked to be present. Cook was fattish but had a pleasant face, was under forty — and I have fucked many a less tempting bit of flesh. — Never did a woman turn so red as she did. She was almost speechless, then almost choked, denied it, and dared the villain to say so to her face. I called him up. My wife said she could not have such investigations before her — yet she stayed. James repeated that he had been "very familiar" with her. — Cook howled, shed tears, and said he lied. He retorted that the kitchen maid knew it. The kitchen maid was called up and questioned in a most delicate way. — She first denied knowing anything about it, but catechised by James, said that the cook and he had certainly been to the top of the house to-

gether at times when missus was out. She didn't know why, it
wasn't her business to spy her fellow servants, and so on. And then
said that the housemaid who slept with Lucy knew more than she
did about Lucy and James. A regular shindy ensued among the
servants, and it ended in the whole lot being discharged, except-
ing the lady's maid. Altho by no means sure that the footman had
not accused the cook out of spite, I felt sure that he had got into
Lucy under promise of marriage.

At the end of a week the poor girl came crying to us, and im-
ploring that nothing should be said to prevent her getting a place.
Then I found out her lodgings and went really and truly to comfort
her. It was about ten o'clock in the morning. "Three pair front,"
said the landlady, not looking very pleasantly at me, and directly I
had gone, as I heard afterwards, said "I ain't a going to have any
of them games here. You take yourself off if swells like him visit
yer." — So as I really was much interested in the girl, and had de-
termined to help her, I arranged for her to meet me at Charing
Cross that afternoon. I declare I had no intention of trying to have
her, tho I had felt a desire for her. But I meant to try to get her
married to my man. That was my vague notion.

She was a little late, and as I could not well talk with her in
the street, I took her to the Cafe de P°°v°°e and ordered a little
dinner in a private room. — She had had very bad food since she
had left my house, and this nice dinner delighted her. Like all wom-
en of her class she refused it at first, was nervous, said she could
not eat before gentlefolks, and was most uncomfortable, but it grad-
ually wore off as the food warmed and the wine cheered her. Her
lovely eyes began to sparkle and her tears dried up. Then cheered
myself, a sudden throb of desire went through me. She has had it
up her cunt, has been spent in, has clasped a man in her arms, has
felt his prick. — I wonder if she has a pretty cunt, much hair on it,
and a group of cognate thoughts came on and my prick was stand-
ing, and was within a couple of yards of that cunt. Did my lust
communicate itself to her by subtle magnetic influence? how can
that be known? But I became silent for the moment, and so did she,
staring intently and, as I thought afterwards, voluptuously at me.

The dinner was not long about. Whilst eating I told her that I
meant to help her out of her difficulties. "How?" she asked. Well I
must feel my way, try if I could get James to marry her, or send her

home, or get her a place, or a doctor if she wanted one. But I must know more than I did, must feel sure I was on the right path, she must tell me the truth, or I could do nothing. — This was varied by talk about myself and household, and I heard much that had taken place, and what had been said, during my absence; for this girl had become our servant just after I went abroad. The talk however always got back to the subject of her *faux pas* with James, and there was an undercurrent of lewdness, for it all referred to cock and cunt; tho not a word of smut had I used, as we sat eating so close together, with my legs touching hers under the table.

The dinner was removed, but wine left, it was only sherry. Unnoticed I bolted the door, and down I made her sit with me on the sofa. "Now, Lucy," said I, "let us talk quite seriously about you and your belly; before I can do you any service, you must tell me the truth. Has James done it to you or not?" — After long hesitation she said slowly, "No." "And you're not with child?" "No." She did not look me in the face and became quite cast down. "He has never put it up you?" said I, revelling in the idea of evoking voluptuous recollections in the girl. "No sir," "Then if that be so, I don't see what use I can be to you, I was going, had you been fucked, and had you been with child, to have helped you to get rid of it, or to have sent you to your parents, till you were confined, or to some where else, and to pay for it all, for I much pity you. But now all you have to do is to get another place, which you are sure to do in time, so give me a kiss for my good intentions. I watched her closely as I said fucked, and saw her blush and wince, with a sense of modesty, and I felt a delicious lust creep through me when uttering the lewed words, and calling to her mind sexual pleasure.

For a minute she sat looking down speechless, and I repeated all I had said. She seemed to be struggling with herself, and at length raised her face to mine and kissed me. Then I kissed her passionately, and hugged her to me and kissed every part of her face, her ears, and eyes, and neck. — Her eyes filled with tears, she broke from me, buried her face in her hands, began crying violently, and saying that I was very kind. I tried to comfort her, putting my arm round her, kissing her, asking what it was all about, repeating, "Has he fucked you, has he? tell me, now tell me," but getting no reply for some minutes. Then her tears subsided and she sobbed out, "I told you a story, I'm past two months with child by James."

And having made the confession she came to herself, kissed me whenever I asked her, and told me the history of her seduction (for that it was), whilst I cuddled her to me affectionately, making her sip sherry at times to comfort her, and keep her spirits up.

James had promised to marry her. One night he took her to the theatre, and then to have some drink in a house, and there he induced her to let him have her. Since then he had her repeatedly, and nearly always on the sofa in our dining room. For half an hour I questioned her and she told me all the detail, as if I were her confessor.

Then I repeated my promise. She was to consider what would be the best for her to do, but perhaps James would marry her. No he would not for she had written him, and he had not answered her letter. — I told her on no account was she ever to mention me to him, that she might be easy about money, for I would pay for all she needed, till she was out of her trouble. She said she didn't want money, having by her two or three pounds. I gave her more saying, "That will prevent your fretting." She was deeply grateful, and cried and kissed me again and again.

I can do her no harm thought I, for she is with child, and my prick swelled proudly. Voluptuous thrills passed through me as I thought of her cunt being within reach of my fingers, and I resolved to try for it. We finished the wine, she was heated, I again began talking about her love affair, and now in burning words of lust. My embraces, kisses, and lewed words excited her. Did he hurt her, when his prick first went up her cunt? Wasn't it pleasure to her, doing it. "Kiss me, Lucy." She kissed but did not answer. "How exquisite the sensations are just when the prick stiffens to its utmost when up the cunt, aren't they?" "Oh don't, sir, talk so," she burst out. "Why not, love? You know." Then my hand began roving about. "Have you much hair there, Lucy?" "I won't tell you, now leave off." "You garter above knee, don't you?" "Yes, sir." I pulled her further on the sofa, and still closer to me. "Let me feel." "Oh, sir, you mustn't now." But pressing her closely to me, kissing her, telling her of my desire for her, in a few minutes my hand was on her thighs and roving up and down, then round her haunches as far as I could reach, it went over her smooth, sweet flesh; and then the fingers nestled between her notch, and when half hidden by the plump lips and the thick, silky hair which curled over my knuckles — there they rested — "I'm feeling your cunt, Lucy, I don't hurt you, do I now?" She replied not, but our kisses met, and we laid in silent enjoyment. I· am feeling her, she is being felt. The fingers of a man, even if motionless, on a woman's cunt, inflame her.

Now I got burning with fierce desire, as my fingers played delicately with a well-developed clitoris. "Fucking is lovely, isn't it dear Lucy, feel my prick, love." Removing my hand from her cunt, I got out my prick, and placed her hand on it. Back went my hand between her thighs and recommenced its delicate fingering. "Open your thighs dear, and let me feel lower down." "Oho," she gasped, as they widened apart, and softly with a burrowing motion, two fingers buried themselves in her vagina.

"How wet your cunt is, love — you want a fuck." Not a word she said, her breath seemed short, her eyes closed, she kissed me when ever I asked her, she was swooning with voluptuous feelings. "Let me do it, I want it so badly. You are so lovely and it can't hurt you now, let me," and I kissed her rapturously. "No," she whispered but almost inaudibly, holding my prick still in her hand. I took no denial, gently pushed her back, lifted her legs up, without resistance mounted her, and the next instant my pego was sheathed in a most heavenly cunt. With deep drawn·sighs, Lucy clasped me to her and we fucked. "It's lovely, isn't it, dear?" "A-ho, o-ho," she whispered, and the next instant we were both spending in ecstasy.

What voluptuous, triumphant joy I had as, raising my self up partly, I looked at that lovely face. — My prick still buried up her. Then in tranquil enjoyment I lay kissing her, till my prick slipped out. How uncomfortable the sofa suddenly seemed to be. I have had scores of women on sofas, but how few sofas gave full comfort in copulating. That which we were on now was a miserably small one. I got up, so did she. "Wasn't it lovely, Lucy?" "Did you bring me here to make me do that?" said she sorrowfully.

I swore that I had not, — that it was only the result of her beauty, — an accident — that I suddenly had lusted for her. She shook her head as if she doubted me.

"I wish I could wash," said she. — I rang the bell, the chambermaid showed her a room. When she came back we had more wine. "I'm fuddled," said she, but she wasn't. "Never mind, I'll see you home, but come with me, we have some hours before us, and we will go where we can be more comfortable, finish your wine." In ten minutes I was in the room which I first entered with Sarah Mavis.

"It's a bad house," said she. "So they call it, my love, but it's good to us, so why is it bad? Take off some of your things, and we will talk about your troubles lying down." She was docile. Soon we were on the bed half undressed. — "Now don't be foolish dear. Let me look at it. I've fucked it, what can be the harm in looking at it?" In half an hour I had seen all, and we fucked as often as we could, till it was time to go. I took her to within sight of her lodgings in a cab.

The next day we dined together. I was wild to have her again, and as quickly as we could, we adjourned to J°°°s. St. I passed a delicious four hours with her. We both stripped to shirt and chemise. She was exquisitely formed, plump to perfection, without an ounce too much fat, and had the loveliest little cunt I ever saw, with a little nutty shaped clitoris, with a mere line of inner lip, and delicately puffed lips covered with bright, chestnut colored, silky, yet crisp hair, which only just covered her mount, and stopped half way down towards the bum hole. Her flesh enervated me with its sweet smell, she was one of those delicious-smelling women. The smell of her cunt was also exquisite, and I opened the lips again and again to smell it. My prick rose as its odour permeated me, I could not wait to enjoy my eyesight, but mounted her and fucked her madly.

When we had reposed a little, and her dear little cunt had absorbed some of my libation as we lay talking, I made her wash it clear of the remnant of the pearly sperm, and brought her with modest reluctance to the side of the bed, where I could get the best light. Then I looked well at her exquisite rosy aperture, and smelt, and sniffed its fragrance with rapture. At once my prick stiffened as the aroma penetrated me, but I refused to be hurried by it into blissful exhaustion so rapidly. Restraining myself, I gloated speechless on its beauty, and revelled in my inhalation. — What voluptuous thoughts rushed thro my brain as I knelt with the wide spread thighs before me. Then gently I put my tongue on her clitoris, and licked lightly, then it played over the whole surface of her cunt, now it protruded up her vagina as far as it could reach, then went again to the clitoris, then broadly over the whole lovely pink surface, covering it as it were, with a plaister. Suddenly in her lust, "Oh, what are you — doing?" she cried, writhing, "Oho-a-ha." "Isn't it. pleasure love?" "Oh, yes, oh — but don't — aha." On I went licking, sucking, tongue probing, now covering her cunt with my saliva, now sucking it up, mixed with her salt effusion. "Oh — don't — leave off — shall do it else," — she cried, with a bum jerk. "Spend, love, spend in my mouth," I cried, and licked still faster. — My hands were under her lovely white buttocks which wriggled gently side ways, then gently but quickly, up and down, rubbing her cunt against my tongue; her thighs opened wide and shivered, I took the whole surface of her cunt in my mouth, sucking, inhaling it, until — clutching the hair of my head with both hands, with a prolonged moan of pleasure — "Oh — o-ha," and a quiver of her belly, and short sobs, her muscles relaxed, her thighs and belly were quiet, a salt discharge came over my tongue, and all was silent all quiet, but my rigid, restless, prick, which was throbbing and knocking up towards my navel.

In full tide of lust and love for my delicious partner, I sucked her cunt dry, scarcely knowing that I did so. Then I arose. She lay motionless, with eyes closed, thighs distended, and hanging down, as I had dropped them. Every hair on her cunt was saturated, and the juices were running to waste down toward her bum-furrow. It hung round my mouth, and wet moustaches. I felt it there with delight. Holding up her thighs, I pushed my prick up her, and gave it a delicious lodging for a minute or two, till it got too impatient and threatened to finish without me. Then I withdrew it, and wiping her cunt dry outside with my hand, and drying my moustache, I laid by the side of her on the bed, and we talked of the tongue pleasure, which she had never tasted nor even heard of before. What delight I felt in having given that girl a new pleasure. She had fucked and frigged, but had never been gamahuched, until by me.

I feared to fuck her, tho burning to do so, lest my over excited machine should too hastily finish its enjoyment without giving her her share. "Feel my prick, there love, isn't it stiff? If I put it in you now, I shall spend directly, and you won't. Frig yourself a bit first." "Oh, I can't." "Nonsense, no stupid modesty, love — you've often done it to yourself. You've just told me so — haven't you?" "Yes but by myself." "Frig now." "Oh, no, no." "Let me then frig you, turn on your back." The lovely creature did so at once. I turned on my side against her, covered one leg with mine partly, and her mouth with mine, kissed her with wet lips and tongue, and excited her. Then I put two fingers as far as I could up her cunt. "Now love, do frig yourself." I stretched her cunt and felt its corrugated, wrinkled surfaces. "Frig, love, now whilst my fingers are up you, till you feel pleasure coming on."

Persuaded at length she did so without reply, gently as if ashamed. Then my prick now less rigid, I pressed up against her thigh as she lay, I whispered lustful words, a restless movement of her body came on soon, as her fingers moved nimbly over her clitoris. "Do you feel the pleasure, love?" "Yes," she whispered. Then gliding over her, I pushed my prick between the delicate lips and silken fringe, and it glided slowly and deliciously up her lubricious tube, till it touched her womb door.

Then gently backwards and forwards I moved it. We fucked. That glorious word expresses it all. Slowly, till urged by spermatic wants, that inner sovereignty or force within my balls, hurrying to ejaculate itself; quicker and quicker went my thrusts, her buttocks responded, her cunt gripped, till with short, sharp, thrusts and wriggles, my prick hit against her womb, her cunt constricted and ground, and sucked round my prick from tip to root, moistening both itself and occupant, and my sperm shot out, and filled it. "Ah — oho — my — love — darling — a — har — fuck — a har," and we were silent, well pleased in each other's arms, our tongues together. Can paradise give any bliss like that which a man and woman enjoy, when loving each other and their prick and cunt perfectly fitting each other they join their bodies in copulation, till they pour out and mix together the unctuous salt juices, which reproduce their kind.

Again I gamahuched her, again I fucked, and again gamahuched. Her heavenly, voluptuous look as she spent I shall never forget. — I was frantic with lust for her. — Indeed had a love for her rapidly springing up; for not only did she seem to me, and indeed was the very perfection of sexual enjoyment, but she was lady like in look, in voice, and in manner, and so utterly unlike a servant, that any gentleman, had he married her, might soon have made her a lady; yet here was this poor girl with child by a footman. As laid by her side that day, I vowed to myself to do all I could to prevent her going to ruin, for I noticed that her very docility would enable any rogue, male or female, to lead her easily. I have had more pleasure in writing this narrative about her than had when writing about other women, whose doings I have told about.

The girl was also chaste in words and in manner, which pleased me much in itself, and also because it gave me the opportunity of teaching her to use lewed words. It is to me one of the great charms of liaisons with women who are not gay, to make them speak in the coarsest language of their organs, wants and sensations, whilst I look them in the face. Two or three days afterwards in the middle of a fuck, I raised myself up and leaning with both hands on the bed, whilst my belly pressed hers, and my prober was to its full length up her cunt: "Where is my prick now?" said I. No answer; her cunt tightened and moved my prick in it, but she replied not. "Where is my prick? say dear, say in my cunt," and I gave a thrust. "Say in my cunt," another thrust. Her eyes closed, she was coming spite of my prick being motionless. The grip of her cunt was on me, "Say in my cunt, or I'll pull it out. Say cunt, love." I moved spite of myself. "Say cunt." "Oh — a — har," — she sobbed. — "Cunt, dear." "In my cunt a — ha," — burst from her. "Oh," and dropping on to her and thrusting my tongue into her sweet mouth, in a transport of all-pervading voluptuousness we lay speechless in each other's arms, whilst the juices of our mouth mingled, and the thick hot sperm filled her cunt to over flowing. Then in the soft fondlings of satisfied lust, I made her repeat the four words, which express at once the simple loving function. I love to make a modest woman say them.

Daily she went after situations uselessly, and for nine or ten days I had this exquisite creature, and had I not just repented and got rid of a similar folly, really believe I should have offered to keep her, so nice was she in every particular. As a fuckstress she was perfection. Rarely have I found such an exquisite fitting cunt as Lucy had. Its delicate tightness and elasticity, its lubricity and smoothness, its depth, its nutcracking grip when the spending spasm was over — for she had involuntarily that gift — I have never found coupled in greater perfection in any women yet, tho I have had some as nice, and one always has a tendency to praise the charms of the woman in possession for a time.

My desire for gamahuching her increased instead of diminishing. I was never tired of looking at her cunt. — So every time I fucked her, I made her wash, then bringing her to the side of the bed, I put pillows under her head so that I could see her, and sitting down on a chair, took her thighs over my arms, and looked at her exquisite pink orifice, till I dropped on my knees and put my mouth to it and sucked, till I gave her pleasure. Each day we parted both of us exhausted. But I must not any longer dwell on the charms of this lovely creature.

She could not get a situation, for her uncharitable brute of a mistress, always after giving her a good character, some how let out about this *faux pas*, so Lucy and I both agreed that she should get an abortion. — I told her to spare no money, and put her in the way of getting the thing done. She took other lodgings and got relieved (at her third month), and then went home to her parents. I gave her twenty pounds the day she left, and told her to write at any time to me at a club if she wanted any more; but never to mention me, or any thing about our connection, or her miscarriage, to any living soul as long as she lived, even if she married, or was dying. I never told her about the general turn out of servants in my house, or what James said he had done to the cook, thinking the less I said about those things the better.

I had got a new set of servants, for even the lady's maid it was thought desirable to send off, but James remained for I could not get suited. I took a dislike to him for his brutality in not answering the girl's letter; and taking no notice of her when out of place. So one morning, "James," said I, "what has become of that poor Lucy, has she got a place? She has ceased coming here about her character." He replied that he didn't know. "Well, it's no business of mine, but I have an impression that you have wronged her. Poor creature, and such a nice young woman. If it be really true that you seduced her by a promise of marriage, you will some day regret it, it will be on your conscience heavily. She would make a good wife to a man of your class, and a man even far above you. I never felt more for a poor creaure, than I did when I saw her going away crying." "How am I to keep a wife?" said he. "Set up a shop for her, or let her take in washing, and you can work as either indoor or outdoor servant, you are both strong and healthy." "Where does she live?" "I don't know, I can find out; but I know where her parents live in the country, and dare say she's gone home." I noticed all this time that James had ceased to deny having had her. Then impulsively I said, "Poor thing. I'd give fifty pounds to help her, and prevent her become a street walker, for that will be the end, if it be not already." Then turning away I said sharply, "That will do, you will leave on Wednesday." — "Are you suited, sir?" "No, but I won't have you about me any longer." The man retired — crest fallen — he had been, I know, flattering himself that I would after all still keep him on as my servant. He liked me I must add. On Wednesday he left.

A fortnight elapsed before I heard anything of him, and was surprized he had not applied for his character. Then he came to me. He was trying for a place in the country, would I give a written character as footman or valet. It was a place where he was to live out. Yes, if I was certain all was square. — Where was it? At °°°° near the village where Lucy lived. Then he volunteered that she was with her parents, and that he had been down to see her. I was startled, and began to think about my own little games in Lucy's receptacle, but said, "What did you go there for? Is she with child really, or not?" "Well its quite true she was so and it was my fault, but she's had a miscarriage and is all right, and we've made it up." "More fool she," said I, "you will serve the poor girl the same dirty trick again." No he wouldn't, he was a thinking of marrying her. "That's like a man," said I. "I'll give you fifty pounds to help you if you do." "Will you sir?" said he. I reflected. "Well, I really think I would." "By gosh I'll marry her in three weeks," said he, "for it would just set us up, and I've saved a little money, and can go home of nights." "Well I must think it over. Come to me tomorrow morning, and if the gentleman writes to me for your character, I will see what I can do for you."

I was really very glad, but did not quite see why I should give fifty pounds. I had done the girl no harm, had given her lots of money, and enabled her quietly to get over her trouble which I had not brought on her. But I had deep sympathy for her, almost an affection seemed springing up in my vacant heart. So thought I, it may do good to her. She is a sweet creature and deserves it; and next morning I told him I would give him fifty pounds, so soon as he was married to her. Not knowing how I might be compromised by this act, I instructed my solicitors in the matter, told them all the circumstances (excepting that I had tailed the girl), and arranged for them to pay the fifty pounds, so soon as they were satisfied that they were married.

He got the place he wanted; soon my solicitors got a letter from her saying the marriage was to take place on a certain day, and subsequently a copy of the marriage certificate. They then paid him the money. He went to service near the village, and so did she for a time, they heard. Two or three months afterwards I received a letter with these words in it: "Sir, God bless you for your kindness, please burn this, I felt that I must thank you. Lucy." — and I never heard of the couple afterwards. It was one of the shortest, but one of the most delicious of my amours, and I look back to it with intense satisfaction.

From first to last I had about three weeks enjoyment of her, for she was only a day past her monthly period, when the accusation came, by which she lost her situation, and I had her up to a day or two before her courses were forced on by the doctor.

I can't explain to myself why I had such a letch for gamahuching her, excepting the extreme beauty of her cunt, and its sweet, inciting smell. I have been always fitful in this taste. To most of the women — including some splendid women — young, beautiful, lascivious, whom I have much liked, I have never done it. I have done it with a half dislike, to several lovely creatures who insisted on my doing it to them, and I licked, spitting frequently, and wiping my mouth on the sly afterwards to avoid offence; but occasionally I have liked it much, tho as I write and look back years, I don't recollect one woman to whom I gave such cunnilingual attention as I did to Lucy. The idea of giving pleasure to a woman seems to actuate me more in what I now do, than it used. Once I seem mainly to have thought of my own pleasure. There is a strange feeling of enjoyment comes over me now, when my tongue touches the clitoris of a sweet young woman, if I like her.

Although Lucy willingly kissed my prick and balls, I never even suggested her taking it into her mouth, — do not indeed recollect the idea having ever occurred to me. I was of course curious about James' amatory tricks, but there was little to tell, and what there was, she told me quite freely when I had had her a few days. Excepting at the house, where he shattered her virginity, he had only once had her in another house, the rest of the doings were in my house. When they had brought the dinner or luncheon things up stairs to lay the cloth, he shagged her quickly on my sofa and sometimes on the table. Directly we had left the dining-room, he did the same whilst they removed the things. So very frequently, sweet Lucy waited at table with his sperm both in and out of her cunt, and it is to be hoped that before the dinner bread was cut they washed their fingers, tho I greatly fear they did not. His prick seemed to her about the size of mine, but she had scarcely seen it, and she got with child at the second or third fucking, so she had not had much fun for her trouble. She never had the pleasure with him that I gave her, and that is all she said.

I have had a dozen women with their backs on a dining room or other table, and have found them a most convenient couch. For impromptu coition, tables are just the height for me. I can see, feel, and fuck easily on them, and can save the lady's clothes from inconvenient rumpling. One night in the smoking room of my club, the conversation turning as usual upon women, I alluded to tables, and wondered if every man present had used them. Ten men were present, and each said he had often times done so. One man, since dead, said he had shagged every servant he had on them. He was in the F°r***n office, not well off, and kept but two servants. "It's the safest place in the house," said he, "just before the cloth is laid. Your wife is most likely dressing, the cook cooking, and neither can interrupt you. I expect every man has put a woman's arse on that piece of mahogany."

Then again I sought Camille's society, and for a long time thought her the most charming of courtezans. — She had plumped up still more, took a warm bath every day, and her skin, always good, had the most delicious, velvety smoothness. I use that word advisedly, because having an exquisite sense of touch, I notice that some women's flesh feels like ivory, some like satin, and some like velvet, and some (which is the perfection of all) which seems a compound of all them, and I call that perfect flesh.

Moreover she had a slow, lazy, voluptuous manner of fucking, by which she seemed to prolong my pleasure, and this with her, I think, was art grafted on natural aptitude. She was never in a hurry for me to go, never said she was engaged, or that some one was coming at ** o'clock, or would I excuse her for a few minutes, or similar devices of strumpets with which I am now fully acquainted. Nor did she borrow, nor be dissatisfied with my gifts, nor say she was short of money, that her rent was due to morrow, and so on. She had plenty of friends I know, for her splendid tho quiet dresses, silk stockings, boots, and fine chemises told me that. Indeed she admitted it, showed me various men's cards, saying that she supposed if they left her their cards, they did not object to their being seen, or why leave them. And so I used to sit for hours with her, poking her at intervals, and talking upon sexual matters, as well as all sorts of subjects, and drinking Claret and smoking.

Indeed she was a most enticing creature, for she had among other qualities, a small, soft, exquisitely feminine voice, and a silvery quiet laugh. In cold weather clad in a lovely loose sort of silk wrapper, she sat half fronting the fire, with perhaps one leg just over the arm of the chair, or in some attitude by which I could see half way up her thighs. As it got warmer she would loll about with a chemise so fine, that you could see the hair of her cunt through it, and her rich darkish toned flesh looked exquisite against the white by contrast.

[I had until within a year or two of the period of time now entered on, read but little erotic literature, and that in English. Now I had read much of that written by the French. How coarse and commonplace the average English baudy book is, compared with the French; and the same may be said of the pictures. With certain facilities recently possessed, I must I think (if they exist) have come across English engravings in which the workings of love (called lust), that potent factor of human action implanted in him by nature for his pleasure and the woman's, and for the perpetuation of the human race, are artistically portrayed; yet I have scarcely seen any which, as engravings, are not coarse; designed by those evidently unaccustomed to draw the human figure at all, and quite unable to portray the male and female either in the varied incitements to, or the varied attitudes, in which they copulate. Whilst in the French are to be found copious engravings, true to life in every one of these particulars.]

This literature amused me much, as did the pictures of fantastic combinations of male and female in lascivious play and in coition. Their impossibilities even amused me, and brought frequently to my mind what I had heard of in my now wide experience with Paphian ladies. There is no end of variety in such amusements, and no limits to eccentricities in lewedness, and no harm in gratifying them, either alone with one woman or man, or in society, to whom it is congenial. A field of lascivious enjoyment new to me, seemed opening, and I thought about the out of the way erotic tricks portrayed, and of those I also might play, and that I should like to try them. I began to see that such things are harmless, tho the world may say they are naughty, and saw through the absurdity of conventional views and prejudices as to the ways a cock and cunt may be pleasurably employed.

Why, for instance, is it permissible for a man and woman to enjoy themselves lasciviously, but improper for two men and two women to do the same things all together in the same room? — Why is it abominable for any one to look at man and woman fucking, when every man, woman, and child would do so if they had the opportunity? Is copulation an improper thing to do, if not, why is it disgraceful to look at its being done? — Why may a man, and woman handle each other's privates, and yet it be wrong for a man to feel another's prick, or a woman to feel another's cunt? Every one in each sex has at one period of their lives done so, and why should not any society of association of people indulge in these innocent, tho sensual, amusements if they like in private. What is there in their doing so that is disgraceful? It is the prejudice of education alone which teaches that it is.

Such reflexions for some years had crossed my mind; they tended to sweep away prejudices. And tho I still have prejudice, yet for the most part I can see no harm in gratifying my lust in the ways which the world would say is highly improper, but which appear to me that men and women are intended by instinct as well as by re-flexion to gratify. This frame of mind seems to me to have been gradually developing for some time past — and accounts for much that follows.

In these opinions I was strengthened by repeated conversations with Camille. She was one of the most philosophic whores I ever knew, was fairly educated, and had a wonderfully cool common sense way of looking at things. When I had doubts of the propriety of doing this or that, she would solve them with answers which ap-peared to me irrefutable, at length. We seem to have been on the subject of unusual pleasures whenever we met. — In fact we were constantly talking about varieties in lustful enjoyments. She would sit down smoking a cigarette, and I a cigar, and consider whether there was wrong in frigging, gamahuching, minetting, tribadism, or sodomy. — In men frigging each other, or women doing the same, and other things. Our conclusion was that there was no harm in any of them. With that clear conscience, and aided by my imagination and by the French books and prints, erotic whims began to suggest themselves to me gradually.

I then fell ill for a short time, and during that, arranged some more of these memoirs. Soon after, disappointments, troubles of various sorts, and other considerations made me nearly burn them. Getting well I drowned my sorrows in female society, and had many of the fair mercenary ones, whom I had known before I left England. To their class I owe a debt of gratitude, and say again what I think I have said else where: that they have been my refuge in sorrow, an unfailing relief in all my miseries, have saved me from drinking, gambling, and perhaps worse. I shall never throw stones at them, nor speak harshly to them, nor of them.

They are much what society has made them, and society uses them, enjoys them, even loves them; yet denies them, spurns, damns, and crushes them even whilst frequenting them and enjoying them. In short, it shamefully ill treats them in most Christian countries, and more so in protestant England than in any others that I know.

Then came the weariness of spirit, the vacuous dissatisfaction of an affectionate man, without a woman to attach himself to. Hat-ing still my home, again with less money (my own fault), I went on a round of visits to my relations of whom I had many. Among them, I went to my aunt in H°°°f°°dshire; I had not been there for four or five years. She was now an old woman, and all her children were married excepting one still at home. Fred was dead, little Joey, whose nursemaid years before I had shagged, and caught with Page Robert, lived with my aunt. His mother, whose cunt I once saw when young, was poor and had a large family. The old butler was dead, and with the exception of one old gardener and the old farm yard keeper, not one was on the estate who was there in the jolly days, when I had Pender, Whiteteeth, and Molly. My mother I should say was also dead, and the house in which I was born was inhabited by one of my married sisters, whom I did not like, nor she me.

I found life at the manor house slow. Walking and riding out with my cousin, even tho she was the handsomest of the lot, did not satisfy me. Why she had not married was always a wonder. So after I had paid visits to some neighbouring friends I thought of leaving, when something detained me. It was a woman again. God bless cunt! copulation for ever! God bless it for all the sweet associations and affections it produces. This act described as filthy, and not to be alluded to, is the greatest pleasure of life. All people are constantly thinking of it. After the blessed sun, sure the cunt ought to be worshipped as the source of all human happiness. It takes and gives and is twice blessed.

Joey had grown a big hobledehoy before his time, and was turned fourteen years old. — Forgetting what I had been at his age, — my desires to know what a cunt really was, — my languishing inclinations towards females, I now treated him as a child, and only thought of him as the little piddling imp, who formerly gave me the excuse for getting acquainted with his nursemaid, a dozen years before.

He came home at about a quarter past one and went back at three, to a school about a mile from the Hall. To suit him (tho indeed it had nearly always been my aunt's principal meal), we had dinner at half-past one. After dinner, I used to smoke and read till three or four, then go out, — and often with my aunt or cousin. The simple meal rarely occupied three-quarters of an hour, then my aunt took a nap in her room, — Emily sitting with her. — Joe always disappeared immediately, and either went back to play at school, or look at some rabbits he had in the stables. Nobody heeded where he went.

There was no man servant just then in the house, one was expected soon. A parlor maid waited at table. A fine, strapping, but some what bold looking woman, apparently nearly thirty years old. She was no great beauty, but the picture of health, blue eyed and light-brown haired, fleshy and strongly built. My aunt had a favorite dog ill at the farm, cut off meat for it at our meals, and used to send this woman with it to the farmyard directly she had done waiting. When I began to want a woman, I wondered if this woman would assuage me. Her name was Tomlin.

Smoking and strolling out of the library, directly after the midday meal one day, in the direction of the farm, I thought to my surprize that I saw a man kissing a woman in the laurel shrubbery, not far from the memorable privy in which I once had Pender. As I approached I heard male footsteps going off. — Going on then to the farm, and thinking of the fuckings I had had in cow house, dairy, and barn, — after about a quarter of an hour I saw the parlor maid come quickly across the rick yard, and pass into the laurel walk towards the house. Not thinking of that, and walking leisurely back, I saw Joe in the distance on the extreme edge of the lawn, on the other side of the grounds, making for the stables very quickly. Then it struck me of a sudden that he had been in the summer house called the grotto, — perhaps thinking of my own tricks in that grotto put the idea into my head, that the servant had been there as well.

At our supper I watched Joe, but saw no signs of intelligence between him and the woman. — At the next midday meal I fancied that he eyed her in a peculiar way, so when she went off with the dog's food, I went off to the stables, and thence to a point from which I could see the walk leading to the grotto. The grotto was hidden from view, and so it was from the house. Master Joe after a time came away from it in a hurry. I hid in a stable, and saw him pass out towards the road, then going back near to the laurel walk, I saw the parlor maid going very quickly towards the kitchen entrance of the house, and looking demure enough. There is a game up for certain, thought I, between that woman and that boy.

The grotto has already been partly described: it was a big building, an expensive toy. The back and sides were built of rock, burs, and lumps of stone; ferns and ivy grew on it, the boughs of big trees overhanging it. The roof partly was rockwork, the remainder, formed of trunks of trees rustically put together and boarded, was falling into decay. My aunt would not incur the expense of restoring it. — I suspected that the boy and full grown woman had been there. How could I manage to watch them. I spent an hour in the grotto before I could devise the means.

It was almost surrounded and covered by big trees and shrubs, and by climbing up the rock work at the back (easily enough done), I reached the arch, and leaning over that reached the wooden part of the roof, which was so decayed that in many places the ivy had worked itself thru the boards, and hung down inside. — At a convenient spot, I thrust a walking stick thru it, and made a hole big enough to see half the place below. It was so big that indeed any one looking up carefully, might have seen an eye placed there, or certainly have seen the hole.

Next day saying I should not be at midday meal, and putting on an overcoat — really to lay down upon and prevent my hurting myself on the stones, I posted myself on the roof. Soon after, in came Joey and — bless him — sat down on the side nearest the peep hole, pulled out his cock, looked at it and put it back. Almost simultaneously in came the woman. He kissed her, in an instant his hands were up her clothes, they scarcely had time for talk, there was no wind, and I heard them fairly well.

Opening her legs she let him feel her. "Don't you wish your uncle (so they called me) was gone?" said she. "I just do," said Joey. "Oh, let me see it," pulling up her clothes. She pushed them down. "No, you saw it the other day, it's just the same; where is your thing?" Joe pulled it out stiff enough, she took hold of it, and quietly felt it. Joe continued his groping, and begging for a look. "Not to day. I can't wait." "Oh, its coming," said Joe all on a sudden. The woman let go his cock and sat down. He sat on her knee. She caught hold of his cock again, and after a few frigs Joey cried out again, "Oh, it's a coming," and out spouted his sperm. "What did you do that for?" said he. "You won't tell any one ever, will you now?" said she. "If your father knew he'd send you to Van Diemens' land. He said he would if you troubled him, you know. Here, look." She lifted her petticoats right up in front of Joey, who was sitting on the seat, feeling his cock and sulking, but instantly dropped them, almost before he could have seen anything, and laughing, went out. They were not together five minutes. Joe put by his machine and, looking out first carefully, went off.

I felt now sure the boy had had her, and next day I did not dine with my aunt, but again got to the top of the grotto. Joe came in first, she after. "Your uncle is looking sharp after you," said she directly she entered. "Does he guess?" said he. "Don't know, but don't you look at me when I'm in the dining-room." While saying this they felt each other, both standing up. He had thrown his left arm over her shoulder, his right was up her petticoats. "Make haste," said she, and placing her bum against the edge of the heavy rustic table, she pulled up her petticoats, caught hold of his prick, guided it to her cunt, straddling her legs apart to get to the proper level, and, so both standing, they fucked with heads over each other's shoulder. They were quiet for a minute after the spend, then she kissed him loudly, gave him a push, down dropped her clothes, and she went off instantly saying, "Tomorrow, if it don't rain." — They had only been a few minutes together. — She alone was in a hurry, Joe leisurely looked at his cock and then went out. Something must have disturbed him, for he came back and stood by the side of the grotto, not far from the front of the slope by which I got up to the roof. — Then he ran off. — I was frightened he would see me, for I was getting down from the roof when he returned, and I caught sight of him thru the foliage. They said a few more words to each other than I have written here, but I only heard them partially.

A convalescent amusement. — *On copulation, and the copulative organs.*

During my illness° I was as chaste as men usually are, when they cannot be unchaste; but I thought much about women, and the complicated organs of the sexes, by the agency of which the species is continued. I reflected on the secrecy with which human beings envelop their amours — of the shame which they so ridiculously attach to any mention or reference to copulation in plain language, or indeed at all — altho it is the prime mover of humanity, and finds expression in every day life in some shape or another, by word, or deed; and is a subject which passes thro the mind, almost daily, of men and of women who are in a healthy state of body, and have once fucked, and perhaps before that.

It was a wonder to me that when both sexes feel so much pleasure in looking at each other's genitals — that they should take such extreme pains to hide them, should think it disgraceful, to show them without mutual consent, and penal to do so separately or together in public. — I came to the conclusion that in the women it is the result of training, with the cunning intention of selling the view of their privates at the highest price — and inducing the man to give them that huge price for it — the marriage ring. Women are all bought in the market — from the whore to the princess. The price alone is different, and the highest price in money or rank obtains the woman. Then I wrote what follows, because I never had found it written in plain language elsewhere.

This description of the genitals, and their mode of meeting, has probably in it many errors and omissions, for I am not a doctor, but it was all I knew about it when I wrote it. No attempt is made

° ED. NOTE: At this point the author had contracted venereal disease.

at anatomical definition or exactitude. — It is what may be termed essentially a popular description, suitable to the smallest capacities, and fit for both sexes — or if you please — instructive reading for the young. It is, to the young, essential knowledge — yet the great aim of adults seems to be to prevent youths from knowing anything about it.

Providence has made the continuation of the species depend on a process of a coupling the sexes, called fucking. It is performed by two organs. That of the male is familiarly and vulgarly called a *Prick*, that of the female a *Cunt*. Politely one is called a penis the other a pudenda. — The prick, broadly speaking, is a long, fleshy, gristly pipe. — The cunt a fleshy, warm, wet hole, or tube. — The prick is at times and in a peculiar manner, thrust up the cunt, and discharges a thick fluid into it, and that is the operation called fucking. — It is not a graceful operation — in fact it is not more elegant than pissing, or shitting, and is more ridiculous; but it is one giving the intensest pleasure to the parties operating together, and most people try to do as much of it as they can.

The prick is placed at the bottom of the belly, and hangs just between the thighs of the man. It consists of a circular, pendulous pipe, or tube of skin and gristle, with a hole through it, by which piss and sperm is sent out. — It has a knob or tip at its end, like a blunt pointed heart, and is covered with a most delicate thin skin, which has the most exquisite sensitiveness to touch. Over this knob or tip is a thickish skin of the same character as that which covers the stem of the prick, and is formed in such manner that it can be easily pulled from off of the tip. It shields the tip from injury, and keeps it moist and sensitive. It is called the foreskin, or prepuce. The prick is usually flabby and hanging down, is about three inches long, and soft to the feel. — The outer skin feels loose all over it as does the foreskin or prepuce, which covers the tip. — But when the man is lewed, that is to say, wants to fuck, it lengthens, thickens, stands up quite stiff, and the foreskin comes a little off the knob, which is then of a fine carmine colour. If the skin does not then move off readily — it is easily pulled back a little. When put to the cunt, it goes back at once, and the knob in its exquisite sensitiveness goes up the cunt uncovered, followed by the rest of the prick, until the whole is up it, to the *Balls.* The balls, or stone bag, is a wrinkled, skinny bag, hanging at the root of the prick and a few inches on its under side from the bum hole. — It contains two stones called also testicles, which feel from the outside about the size of bantams' eggs, and some people call them their eggs. Sometimes this bag feels firmer than at other times — and is always a good handful. If it feels firm and full, and is covered with well defined close wrinkles, it is generally a sign that the man is in fucking order. — This bag is sometimes called a ballocks, but oftentimes when a man speaks of his ballocks, he means his prick and balls all together.

The stem of the prick is smooth, and usually free from hair until towards the point at which it connects with the belly and balls, where it is covered with hair which curls round it. It seems to come out of a hairy thicket, which grows up the stomach towards the navel but stops short of it. There is usually but little hair on the balls, but it grows round beneath them, and sometimes down the inner side of the thighs a slight way, and under the balls' bag to the arse hole, and sometimes even there is short hair round that hole. If there be much it is called hairy-arsed, and is not convenient, for it interferes with the comfortable cleaning and wiping of the bum, after voiding.

The prick is naturally dry excepting the tip, which is usually covered by the foreskin, and which has at all times a tendency to be moist. If a man is randy for a long time and cannot ease himself by fucking, or frigging, or by getting his sperm out somehow, this tip sweats a white pomatum looking stuff, which covers the tip, and collects under the knob, where it joins the stem. This randy exudation called sebaceous, emits strongly a peculiar male smell. A fuck clears it all off. — Inside the body of the male are organs for secreting and forming a stuff called sperm, or spunk, which is whitish, partly thickish, and resembles paste which is thin and badly made, — or thin lumpy gruel. This is spit up the woman's cunt, through the tip of the prick when fucking. — This emission in popular language is called spending, or spunking, and is the period of the highest pleasure of the fuck, and the ending of it. — This stuff, is the male seed, and impregnates the woman, or as it is called in simple language, — gets her in the family way.

The cunt is the woman's organ, and is placed at the bottom of her belly between the thighs. It consists, firstly and outwardly, of a slit about five inches long, looking like a gap or cut, with lips. It begins near the bum hole, and curves upwards towards the lower part of the belly in the direction of the navel, and finishes in a hillock, or pad of flesh, a little above the thighs. This pad gradually dies off into the general surface of the belly, and is called a mons, or pincushion. In some women the slit, or cunt gap, is less than in others but in all they begin near the bumhole, and the lips gradually thicken, and then die out again into the mons. In some women these lips are in part of their length, twice as thick as those of a man's mouth. — In others they are thin, and some scarcely have the form of lips at all, but look like swollen flesh. The cunt looks like a mere cut, in such women.

There is hair all over the pincushion, or as it is called the motte, and round the outer lips of the cunt, down to its bum hole end. The hair getting usually less thick, and shorter, as it gets there; but at times as in the man, the hair grows a little round the bum hole itself, and up the bum furrow. The pad, or pincushion, or mons, is placed there to cover certan bones which go over that part of the cunt, and prevent the man hurting his belly, when thrusting up the cunt in fucking. This in his excitement, he might at certain moments do by shoving violently. — The mons, or motte, is more thickly covered with hair than the rest of the cunt, particularly at the spot where the slit begins, or opens.

If the outer lips be pulled open, their inside will be seen to be smooth, fleshy, almost pulpy, and like the inside of a mouth and of pink or carmine colour according to the age of the female and the usage of her cunt. — A little way below the beginning of the slit at the belly end of it, is a little lump or button of flesh called the *clitoris*. This is red, and smooth like the rest, and in some women, is much larger than in others. — When the woman is not sexually excited, or wanting a fuck, or is not randy that is to say, — this is softish, but when randy it gets a little firm or solid, or as they say stiff, but not in all. — It is the chief seat of pleasure in a woman, for tho the prick rubs against it but little in fucking, the woman often gives herself pleasure by rubbing it with her finger, or frigging herself there, till she spends.

This is a description of what may be termed the mouth of the cunt, or its externals, and its inner parts must now be described. Just under the clitoris, almost in continuation of it in fact, but just at the beginning of what I call the prick tube, it being specially made to take the prick, is a little projection in which is a hole. — This is the woman's piss duct. — Both clitoris and piss duct are for the most part covered by the outer hairy lips, the hair curling round in front, and partly overshadowing the gap, hides all of it more or less in most grown women; but when women want to piddle, nature induces them to squat down, so that their bums are within a few inches of the ground. In that position the cunt gapes and opens, the clitoris and piss-vent come to the front, and the piss comes out with force. The hair of the cunt is shortish, opens with the lips but nevertheless it is frequently wetted by the stream. If there is longish hair, you may see drops of piddle, like drops of dew, clinging to it when she stands up after pissing. — Some of the piddle also runs down to the mouth of the vagina, or fucking prick hole, yet to be described, and that part being not unfrequently a little sticky, the piss cleanses it. Thus the outer hair, and the inside of the cunt mouth and lips, are wetted generally by the woman's piddle, — and when she gets up, she usually tucks her clothes for an instant between her thighs to dry it. — This is vulgarly called "mopping her cunt."

Beneath the piddling orifice, the soft red surface slopes down, and inwards, to a hole very near to the bum hole, so near in fact that you may readily put one finger up the cunt and a thumb up the bum hole, and pinch the partition which separates them. This is the vagina, or prick receiver — the hole which goes up into the woman's belly, and in which the operation of fucking is done, by the man's prick.

The opening is in some a little tight, but inside is more capacious. — In all cunts, it easily distends, and will take any thing from a little finger to a rolling pin, — and will gently close on, clasp, or embrace it, with an evenly tightening grip all round, whatever its size may be. — This fucking hole is deep enough usually to take a stiff prick six inches long, without pain to the woman. If it hurts, they have a knack of dropping their buttocks, so as to prevent the prick going too far up. — This vagina, as it also is called, at the top or end, rounds off and contracts, and the tube of the womb enters it. In the neck is a small orifice usually closed but at the proper time during fucking it opens. It is against this opening that the man's prick knocks; and the sperm is shot out in fucking.

From the clitoris, and inside the outer lips of the cunt slit or gap already described, are little thinnish red flaps or cartilage, which descend on each side, and terminate by the prick hole. They are in fact a sort of inner cunt lips, and are called Nymphæ, or vulgarly often called lapels, or lappets. They are of the same pink or carmine tint as the inside of the whole of the cunt mouth. — In most women these lips are so small that when a woman's legs are closed, or only just slightly opened, the outer and hair cunt lips hide and cover them, or they only just show the thinnest red line between them. — In other women they are large, and hang out even like large red flaps. These lapels are always moist inside, and when large, and a woman opens her legs so that the outer lips separate, the lapels stick together, the clitoris peeping above them. — The prick of course opens and passes between them, and they rub on each side of it in fucking.

In virgins — just inside the tube, prick-receiver, or vagina, and behind the piss-vent, is a little red film or membrane covering the hole, all but a little perforation through which the monthlies, or courses, or bloodies, as they are called, and other cunt juices of the woman escape. This is the hymen, or virginity, which is broken by the prick the first time the women is fucked, leaving the membrane with a ragged edge like a cockscomb, but which raggedness disappears in a year or two after fucking.

The hole or tube which receives the prick, is also pink, soft, and smooth inside, and feels like the kernels on the inside of the mouth. The sides will give ready way to the push of the finger, and being elastic it directly recovers itself when the finger is withdrawn, and therefore closes gently on the prick whether a large or a small one. — This quality makes it a very pretty plaything for the man. — Nothing pleases some so much as putting their fingers up it, or playing as it is called at stink-finger, whilst the woman plays with his cock and balls. — This mutual handling and titillation of each other's privates, makes them both lewed or ready to fuck. — I forgot to say that when the man's prick is randy and the woman squeezes it, that the hole at the tip opens slightly, and a strong smell comes out of it. — Some women when randy like that smell.

The cunt is always wet inside. If anything be put up to dry it, it is wet a minute afterwards. — If a woman wants fucking it gets wetter, and in some women if they have their clitoris titillated, their cunts get very wet indeed. — This moisture is very smooth and slimy, and is salt to the taste, which condition is intended so to lubricate it, and to make it smoother and nicer for the man's prick, the red, fine skinned tip of which is very thin and highly sensitive. It is the seat of pleasure in fact. The cunt has always a peculiar smell, slightly fishy or cheesey it has been called, tho I never detected that sort of smell. This is the case even with the cleanest women, and it is stronger if a women has been very randy for some time, and has not washed her cunt, — or in one who rarely washes it, but depends on her piddle and her cunt mopping afterwards to keep it sweet and wholesome. This cuntal smell from a healthy, clean, woman, is pleasant and stimulating to most men.

Fucking consists in putting the two organs just described, together. That is, in the man making his prick stiff and pushing it up the cunt as far as it will go, and quite plugging it up. Then pushing it backwards and forwards in it, and gradually quicker and quicker, his prick getting stiffer and stiffer, and her cunt getting wetter, and tighter and tighter, until at last the pleasure which both feel from the instant their privates meet, and which increases gradually as the fuck goes on, gets maddening almost in its intensity, and terminates by the balls shooting out through his prick into her cunt, a quantity of sperm, and the whole surface of her cunt at the same time clipping his prick, and exuding a thinnish milky liquor described before. This done, with intense pleasure to both, they are both quiet, satisfied, and almost insensible for an instant from excess of pleasure. Then the cunt gets lax, the prick shrinks out of it, and the fuck is over.

But before this occurs both of them *should* feel, and the man actually *must* be randy or want to fuck, for without that his prick will not be stiff, and the symptoms of lust or randiness must be understood in the first place.

Randiness in a man shews itself by his prick feeling uneasy, yet with a voluptuous sensation, by its swelling, lengthening, and stiffening. His thoughts go to women who look beautiful in his eyes then, even if they did not before. He longs for them, gets fidgety, and, if sitting, has a desire to wriggle his backside backwards and forwards. — He can scarcely keep his fingers from his prick, but wants to feel it and fondle it. His prick burns, his balls, if he has not recently done too much fucking, are firm and covered with well corrugated, close wrinkles. — If he touches his prick much, it begins to throb, and knocks up toward his belly. His bumhole tightens and squeezes, as the prick knocks, and, when in that state, he is ready to fuck anything, from his sister to his grandmother, from a ten-year-old, to a woman of sixty, for a standing prick has no conscience. — Woe be to the female whom he gets a chance at, if she does not want *him*, for he will have *her* if he can.

Randiness in a woman shows itself in some respects in the same way, but it gives much less outward sign. — She feels restless, has an inclination to press her legs close together, then to open them wide, then close them again. To squeeze her cunt tight by the muscles at the orifice of the prick hole, — the same action closing tightly her arse hole, which thus acts sympathetically with the cunt. — To move her bum about uneasily on the chair, to sigh with a sensation of pleasure, and throw herself about. To put her fingers on her cunt and play with it — and to rub her clitoris. Her cunt feels hot — burning — some times it gets wet — very wet — with a languishing swooning sensation — and yet she does not exude or spend as when being fucked — she is sensitive with men. — If one touches her hand or squeezes it, it gives her pleasure. — Any attention from a man fills her with vague desires of she knows not what. — Her eyes seek his, then drop — and if she has seen or known much of men's nature, — she eyes askant his trowsers, just where his prick lies, and blushes at what she is doing, as if he knew what she was thinking about. If she is of a very sensitive, or warm nature, or what is called "hot arsed" or hot cunted, or "randy arsed" — and this lewedness has continued for a long time without the relief given by fucking, she is subject to hysterics. In young women a good fucking sets them to rights, but this is by the way. — Some girls when randy, giggle and laugh a great deal, and laugh at all a man says to them. — Their eyes brighten and languish, they involuntarily return the pressure of the man's hands. All this is just what incites men to desire to fuck them.

When both the man and woman are randy, they are in the best condition for fucking, but when not so, and nature is impelling them both toward copulation, they make each other lewed if they get an opportunity.

Let us suppose a couple together — he having had women before — she having had it once or twice on the sly, but has been a long time without it, and determines not to risk it again. He knows nothing about this but begins to long for her. — They are quite alone, and there is no chance of being disturbed.

He looks at her, chats pleasantly, draws nearer and nearer, till they sit quite close. — He wonders what her secret charms are, if her thighs are round and plump, her bum big. — Then his mind goes to her cunt. He thinks of its hair, its color, and then his prick stiffens and he longs to fuck her, and wondering if she wants it, or will let him, is impelled to try.

Then under the impulse of intention, his desire to discharge his sperm up her becomes stronger. Reckless, he begins kissing, which is resisted at first by her, but at length permitted once and with protest. — Then his arm goes round her waist — he draws her closer, and so they sit whilst for a time he murmurs love.

Then one hand goes on her knees outside her clothes — and more kisses follow. If not randy before, — the pressure of his arm, and hand now drawn still nearer to her belly, or pressing on her thighs but still outside her clothes, makes her randy now. — He kisses her more passionately and in doing so, his hand pushes against her belly. — She guesses he had done it purposely but says nothing. — Her cunt and bum hole tighten and a voluptuous shiver runs through her. — She fears herself, and threatens to cry out but does not. — Gradually she returns his kisses, but begs him to go and leave her.

Meanwhile he has stooped a little, has felt her ankles, has thrust his hand up her petticoats and it is on her thigh just above her knee. — She resists violently, but lewedness now pervades her system. — She is in a sweet confusion, and overwhelmed with lustful sensations, one moment makes a half cry — then laughs, — then says "hush" as baudy wishes now find utterance from him. — She perhaps kisses him to leave off, but does not wish him, likes what he is doing, knows it is wrong, but makes up her mind that he shan't do the trick to her.

This lasts for a time. She is getting sick with lewed desire. A cry — a struggle — and he has forced his finger between her cunt lips — it is rubbing her clitoris, whilst she with closed thighs is pushing him away with one hand, and trying to pull down her clothes with the other. She shifts her bum back, tightens her thighs together, but he keeps his finger there still. — Then he pulls out his prick, a stiff, ivory, red-tipped rod, with its pendulous, firm balls. — Its look fascinates her. — He tells her to look at it. — She turns her head and eyes away, — but can't help turning them again.

He struggles now to get her clothes up — she to prevent him. — Now he pushes the prick against her hand and a thrill goes through her as she feels the hot rod. — Again and again it knocks against her hand — he snatches her hand and makes her clasp his prick. With a cry, she snatches it away. — In doing this he has for the instant withdrawn his hand from her cunt, and with a slight feeling of relief she thinks for the moment he is going to cease.

Vain hope, if she hopes it, which is often doubtful, for the feel of her hand on his doodle has made him curious. — Seizing her, he pulls up her clothes, — sees her thighs, and the dark hairy shadow above the split, and ere she can prevent it, his finger is pushed further towards the prick hole. — She cries out that he hurts, but he pushes on his fingers. — She entreats, resists, but voluptuous sensations are coursing thro her veins. — The stiff prick dances before her eyes, — and altho she would resist if she could, feels her power to do so going, for lewedness has possession of her body, and desire to let him have his way is taking possession of her soul; and so both panting, they for a minute cease — he keeping his fingers where he had forced them.

Nature has placed the woman's clitoris so that it cannot escape man's fingers. — If a woman closes her thighs tightly, a man cannot from the front get his finger to the cunt hole; and from the back, the arse cheeks close, so that without violence he cannot do it, even when she be standing up, altho as easily then, as from the front. But without hurting her, and do what she may to prevent him, the clitoris can be reached by this middle finger. By pushing it through the closed thighs, — it reaches the upper part of the cunt where the clitoris lies, and was so placed to enable the man to incite and incline the woman to submit to his will in copulation.

In a minute he recommences. — In vain she tightens her thighs —his finger rubs heavier and heavier against it, he holds her close to him with one arm, kissing and beseeching; whilst just under her eyes is the throbbing prick ready to plug her. Her thighs are exposed, she is now too excited to pull her clothes down, and her cunt feels wet. — "Ah! — Ah! — What is this?" A shiver of pleasure runs through her, which makes her, spite of herself, open for a second her thighs — her cunt feels wetter, her face inclines towards his —

her resistance is gone, her eyes close, she is nearly spending, she only murmurs, "No — no — oh don't — leave off — I won't," to his earnest entreaties, and the next instant falls back under his pressure, or is partly dragged, partly lifted, lustfully conscious, to the nearest bed or couch, all resistance is gone, she is saturated with lust and is quiet. — Then their bellies meet, his hand insinuates itself under her round warm haunches, something stiff and hard, yet smooth and soft, pokes between her thighs and glides quickly down over her clitoris. She feels it at her cunt entrance, — it thrusts, it enters, — it is up her, — she feels it in her vitals and the balls knocking against her buttocks, and then for a minute both are quiet.

Then up to her womb, then down nearly to her cunt lips, backwards and forwards goes the prick. Long shoves — short shoves — quick, quicker, — a sigh from him, a wriggle from her, and then again a slight rest. — A shove again, and then perhaps (tho but rarely) he, curious, withdraws one hand from her smooth bum, and feels the stem of his tool gently closed round by her cunt lips, gently yet firmly, and the hairs of their organs mingling. — His finger gently touches the clitoris against the lower end of which his prick had rubbed. — A shiver of delight goes through her as she feels him, and juices begin to exude from her cunt. — On go the thrusts — quick — quick — quicker and harder, his rigid prick knocks at the portals of her womb. — Now a sigh from her, — her eyes close — her mouth gently opens. — Shorter and quicker are now the thrusts, and his arse wriggles, he thrusts up her cunt as if he would engulf his whole body in her, his balls covering her arsehole, wag and rub, and knock against her bum cheeks, her belly heaves — her thighs open wide — her knees move up gently, her legs stretch out, then close on his again and squeeze his thighs, his prick stiffens more, and begins to throb violently in her, — her cunt juices have wetted it from tip to root — it is running out and wetting the hairs round his prick stem.

Now a more delicious and almost maddening sensation pervades their whole bodies. — Gradually more and more powerful, it usurps their senses in a voluptuous delirium. — If her father were now to come into the room, she would cling to the man. — If he knew his mother was being murdered in the next room, he would not, to save her, withdraw his prick from the cunt.

Now their kisses are moist, their tongues meet, their salivas mingle, — he sucks all he can from her mouth, his hands tighten

round her backside, he clasps her to him as if to squeeze the breath
out of her; her hands tighten round his waist, or rub convulsively
over his buttocks, or up his back. Up go her thighs gently again, and
press tightly against his haunches, he grasps her bum like a vice and
with a long drawn breath — with a sigh from him — and perhaps
a convulsive cry of "cunt," — out shoots his spunk against the por-
tals of her womb which open to receive it, — her cunt at the same
moment tightening round his prick and grinding it, and distilling
over it on all sides its thin, salt, milky, juices. What sperm her
womb does not suck up and absorb, unites with her juices, making a
bath in which his prick lies weltering. — Some squeezes out, making
still wetter the hair of both their genitals, and then with gentle and
gradually diminishing wriggles, and backside movements of both,
with gentle murmurs, sighs, and kisses, they lay quiet in each other's
arms in luscious Elysium, with limbs stretched out, and every
muscle tranquil, — what senses they have left, absorbed in dreamy
thoughts of prick, cunt, sperm, and fucking, and in loving delight
in each other.

So they lay for a few minutes until he moves again, when the
friction of his prick, even in her lubricated cunt, causes it sympa-
thetically to tighten, tho but slightly only, for sated with pleasure
that channel to her womb has lost its muscular power for a while.
Yet the gentle grip it gives sends a thrill of pleasure through him,
and his shrinking prick; this sends forth one drop more of lingering
sperm now in its thinnest liquidity. It is the last. — Then his weight
oppresses her, she moves, and his shrunken, wet, cock, comes out
dripping over her anus, and with a kiss he rises. — In doing so a
drop falls on to her thigh, or on the thicket of cunt hair — it is the
parting dew. She also rises, pulling down her petticoats and for a
minute they are both silent and look at each other. — On his face is
a smile of satisfaction. — She blushes and looks abashed at her do-
ings, and is in the dreamy pleasure of a sperm saturated cunt.

If the happy couple have fucked before, and are in bed tran-
quilly together, the game is slightly varied. Their spend is over; but
naked, limb to limb, he lingers on her belly, nestling his balls up to
her and trying to keep his prick in its soft, smooth, wet, warm lodg-
ing. — He lingers on her long, the hair on both their privates stick-
ing and drying together, so close and intermingled have they got.
— His weight, which she did not feel whilst thrusting and moving
up her and their postures varied each moment, now oppresses her;

and she moves, or has a cough or feigns one, which shakes her belly and his shrinking prick uncunts.

Still he will not get off, and the red wet tip, is still dribbling out a little sperm which drops on her bum hole — or against her bum cheeks. Then following his withdrawal, — some of their mixed essences which her womb has not sucked into it, rolls out like a great thick tear towards her arsehole. He turns off of her. She turns on her side towards him and the spunk tear changes its course, and lodges on her thigh near to the arsehole end of the cunt. She need not put down her fingers to feel that her cunt fringe is wet, she feels unmistakably that her cunt lips are slabbered, wet, and spermy; and it gives her pleasure to feel it there for it came from out of his body into hers. — She loves him for putting it there. — He also turns towards her, — his prick still shrinking, flabby, and sloppy, falls on his thigh and wets it, and he loves that wetness for it came from her cunt. Then belly to belly — or belly to bum — naked and touching, with soft baudy words of love, and baudy images floating dreamily across their minds. — She thinking of balls, prick, fucking and of the spunk lying in her cunt. He of cunt, spunk, and tongue sucking, they fall asleep — and that is fucking.

But often times something comes of this cunt basting — not quite unknown, but mostly unthought of during the hot fit of lust and pleasure, and certainly unhoped for excepting by married women. Something which, had it been thought of whilst with clasped haunches, wriggling buttocks, prick thrusts, heaving bellies, sighs and murmurs, the couple were insensible to all but pleasure, their souls steeped in Elysium, — would certainly have made the lady at least a little anxious. That second or two's mixed spending, and spunk sucking up of the womb, sometimes causes the lady to be in the family way, and that day nine months, after much fainting, sickness, longing for all that is out of season and out of reason, with a swollen turgid belly — much spewing, five minute pissings, farting, shitting, and the whites: — an infant comes down that cunt, — the result of such fucking, and this is how it comes about.

High up in the belly of the woman and in recesses just outside the womb, are little organs or parts of her body, containing what are called ova — and which common people call eggs — it is a sort of enclosure in which a woman breeds eggs within herself, out of herself, and parcel of her nature. Leading from this egg nest, is a little tube connecting with the womb, and at monthly periods, an egg is squeezed out of it into the womb through this passage, and it only wants to be touched by the man's spunk — when man and woman are both discharging in their spasm of pleasure, and lo! — the thing is done. That which had no life, lives, — the egg is vivified, the woman is impregnated, is with child. Then it will grow bigger and bigger in her, and her belly will swell, until in the nine months, out comes a child through her cunt.

And this is the exact process and time when the egg has life given to it. — As far as is known, the thing takes place at the moment when both man and woman are in the greatest state of voluptuous enjoyment, and at the crisis and termination of the fucking. If the man alone spends in the woman's cunt, it will not do it. — If the woman spends alone, it will not do it. — If they spend some time after each other, it may or may not do it. — But as the fuck goes on, and their mutual pleasure increases — just at the moment that the woman's cunt tightens, just as the man shoves short or merely wriggles his prick as far up the cunt as he can — the egg either being there ready, or being then squeezed out of the bag into the womb — the woman's juices exude from her into her cunt. — The man's spunk squirts, — the womb sucks in the male and female mixture, — the egg is touched, and life begotten. Thus in the delirious ecstasy of the fuck, the job is done.

Such is a prick — such a cunt — such fucking — such the consequence. — The fucking organs excepting to those who have them, would not perhaps be thought handsome. — No one thinks a dog's prick handsome, or a cow's cunt beautiful, — yet they are not unlike those of the human species. — No one who sees a dog fucking a bitch, thinks that their action is elegant, or their faces edifying, yet their movements are much like those of the human species. — The wriggling of the lady's buttocks when a prick is moving up her, and the up and down movements of the man's haunches, and the saucers he makes in his arse cheeks are not elegant, — their slabbered privates when they have finished not nice, — their faces during the operation not expressing intellect. In fact the motion is somewhat monotonous, is inelegant, almost ridiculous, and the end, sloppy and odorous; yet they both think the operation most beautiful.

And if a woman in stature, form, colour, skin, and in beauty of mouth, teeth, nose, and eye, were perfect; if her limbs were perfection, her breasts ivory — her breath sweet as a honey suckle, her voice tender, her temper perfect, and if in brief she comprised all that we call perfection in a woman; — yet were she without that hairy mouthed, slippery, half slimy, salt, and odorous cunt, a man would sooner sleep with his grandmother or lie down with a cow than with her.

And if a man be tall as a guardsman, formed like Apollo, be strong as Hercules, and a grand model of strength, beauty, and all that is attractive in man — if he even be gentle and kind to a woman — and yet had not that bit of distensible gristle, with its pendant balls, or if having it, it would not stiffen and swell at times so as to enter, fill, and plug up the cunt entirely, and shed into the innermost recesses and end of the cunt — that thickish, semi-opaque, gruelly essence of man's blood — she would not care a far for him, and would sooner sleep with a male monkey.

This is a description of the organs employed, and the object, art, and manner of using them, which is called fucking — together with its results. It is written in this simple, homely, yet classical manner; so as to enable the dullest, simplest, and most unsophisticated to understand it. It is specially suitable for ignorant boys and girls from twelve to fifteen years of age, — at which period they begin to think of such matters, and when they may study it with most advantage, because and at that age the world tries its best to obscure the consideration, and to hinder all real knowledge about it getting to them. It may be read usefully after evening family prayers also, by older members of the family, to whom at times, it may serve as an aphrodisiac, and it will spare many young, but full grown people, trouble and loss of time in searching for knowledge which ought to be known to all, but which owing to a false morality, is a subject put aside as improper.

[At the time I wrote this, I had but little of the anatomical knowledge of the sexes which I now possess, and vulva — vagina — clitoris — and other terms or their exact signification were only partially known to me.]

Big-eyed Betsy Johnson. — Early acquaintance. — Brothels closed. — Ten years later. — It's you Betsy! — Her huge nymphæ. — Protuberant eyes. — Witty baudiness. — My erotic requests. — Her help. — With Betsy and a man. — Hesitations. — His offers. — I frig him. — His arsehole offered. — No erection available. — Pestles and bumholes. — Spunk and a toothpick. — I poke Betsy. — His thumb on my bum. — A little virgin wanted. — One found. — At J°°°s St. with her. — Another Molly. — Betsy's baudy antics. — Molly modest, stripped, and liquored up. — Pitching shillings at cunts. — Molly refuses my amatory advances. — Betsy's threats.

[Before I tell about my acquaintance with this woman, — I must recall some facts to explain how that acquaintance was first made.

Some time before the termination of my acquaintance with Sarah Mavis, with whom I was so desperately infatuated, the London public had a fit of virtue to which it is subject periodically. It commenced a crusade against gay women; and principally those frequenting Regent and Coventry Streets, and others in that neighbourhood. Many nice, quiet accommodation houses were closed, and several nice gay women whom I frequented disappeared. Indeed, for a time, the police were set on with all their brutality. Women by dozens were taken before magistrates ruthlessly, and altho mostly cautioned and set at liberty, some were imprisoned; and the effect was, that for a short time the streets named, and a few others, were all but cleared of gay women.

Among the women who disappeared was one named Betsy Johnson, a lovely little creature under twenty, and in the perfection

369

of her youth. Just before she disappeared, she said one night to me in her jocular way — "Fucking is done for here except for love, so I shall take to washing for my living." — She disappeared, and I was now to meet her again some nine or ten years after].

It was in the middle of November. — I was walking along the Strand, one very nasty, muddy, dank, dark night. The whores were lifting up their petticoats, partly to escape the mud, but more I expect to show their legs, as high as they dare, and I was gazing on them with pleasure, my mind wandering from their legs to their backsides. I passed a female nearly, then stopped — as I seemed to recognize an old carnal acquaintance.

"Why, it's you Betsy." — I turned round, and passed into a side street, followed by the female. "I don't recollect you, yet I know the voice," said she. — I made myself known. Several years had passed since I had seen her. It was Betsy Johnson, whom I had fucked just after she had turned gay, and at about the time I was in love with Sarah Mavis, and had quarrelled with her.

Betsy was a middle-sized female, but her plumpness and roundness were delicious. Her form was lovely then. She had a delicious skin, as smooth as ivory, fine chestnut hair, the same color on her cunt hair, of which she hadn't much. She had two defects. Her eyes were excessively prominent, the clitoris was large, and the nymphæ very large. They hung out when first I knew her, and when she was not twenty years old, full half an inch below the outer lips, and for the entire length of the split. — I did not like that, yet I used to have her, for she was so beautiful in form, so smooth in skin, and fucked so divinely and her cunt fitted me heavenly. She was the wittiest woman of her class I ever met — it was good neat wit — and baudy wit as well at times, for she was fond of baudiness — She enjoyed it. She at that time took a fancy to me, but I did not return it — tho I saw her once or so, when I quarrelled with Sarah, as to the best of my recollection I have already narrated.

We went to a house and she stripped. She was as beautifully shaped as ever — but her genital deformity had increased. — The nymphæ hung down outside the cunt lips, I am sure one inch and a half along her whole split. — We had a long conversation about it and I told her of women having them cut off, I had read of that being done. — She was immensely interested in that, and also had heard of its being done. — She must muster up courage to have them cut, she said. — Men, she was sure, didn't like those flaps — tell her, "Did they?" — Since she had been back in London, she could not secure any regular friends, and kept very poor. "These precious nymphæ must be the cause, they do not please I expect."

She was always lascivious. — "Your fucking is delicious, me dear. You still do it well." — On my preparing to leave. "Why sure, and you're not going after doing it once, and all these years since I've seen you? — I recollect you, when I had to tell you you had done enough for your money. — Ah, I'm older, but sugar me if you go yet," — said she, clutching hold of my prick. So we fucked again, and again, for I could not resist her. — "You'll go home straight me dear tonight, won't you, a fresh cunt won't make it stand again, till you've laid on your back a little, and filled yer belly with grub, me dear." — "Won't you see me again?" "Perhaps." — "Ah," said she reflectingly. "You don't like me, I'll go back to S°°°b°°ry. I'm not getting on here — whoring is not my game now." — She was one of those who boldly spoke of whoring for her living — I did not like that. — "Why, it's what it is, isn't it?" she had said when I checked her for her plain speaking.

I did see her again, but her large flapping nymphæ rather turned my lust off. I wanted to go to her rooms. — "You can't, it would horrify you," said the poor woman. — "You see, I've only a gown and chemise on — it's all I've got, but I must show my legs nice." — "My legs are my fortune sir," she said. — She had a lovely leg still, and had silk stockings on, and nice boots, tho almost without under-clothing. "I sleep on the floor on a mattress, there is no bedstead, only a mattress, a table, and a jerry in the room, that's all. I've not even a blind, me darling." — She was not Irish, but affected the brogue.

When we were parting, "Can I do anything for you?" — she asked — what she meant I didn't exactly know, but chaffingly I replied. — "Yes, Betsy. Get me a nice young cunt without a bit of hair on it — and a man to frig." "Och, yer baste, is it a young cunt yer wants, — not for Joseph. But I'll get you a man easy enough if you mean it." — "I do," said I — suddenly thinking I should. — "Well, there are plenty of them." — "But in your room." — "Impossible, you and the sod too, would not stop in it five minutes." When I told her those wants, I didn't mean what I said, but at a subsequent meeting *she* suggested them, and it ended in my arranging to meet her with a man, and we were to go to his rooms together two or three days after, for she had stimulated my curiosity.

I met them in S°°o S°°°°e. — He took off his hat respectfully. — "Go ahead, and I'll follow," said I, and on they both went. — She then fell back — I was nervous and told her so. "If I go with you and him is all square?" — "It's all safe, but mind he shan't touch me, he shan't fuck me if that's what you mean — I can't bear the beasts." — "All right, go on, I only want to see what a man of this sort is like." — On the two went, crossed O°f°°d St:, to a long street, out of which turning up a paved court, he opened with a latch key a door and up we all well went to a first floor over a shop, and into a well furnished sitting-room, and bed-room. As we entered she again fell back, and whispered, — "Mind he don't touch me." — "All right, but no plant Betsy, eh?" — "All square, my pet." — It was a dark night, and I was awfully nervous, but an extraordinary curiosity was on me. I wondered if it was great pleasure to bugger — Betsy had said that men had told her it was.

At last then, the erotic caprice, which I been thinking of at intervals for years, a caprice which had subsided, been forgotten, but from time to time been roused by the sights through key holes, and peep holes, of couples fucking: a caprice which had got strength, by each succeeding prick I had seen, and specially by the big furnished young man, whom I last saw (poking his wife at Paris) was to be gratified — I had overcome all scruples, and satisfied myself that there was no more harm in feeling another's prick, than in feeling my own. — There was the man before me, on whom I might satisfy all my curiosity — and yet I began to tremble. — Once indeed on the road I stopped Betsy, and said I should not go home with them — but on her laughing at me, I persevered.

Indeed my heart had palpitated so violently as I followed them, and I felt so afraid of what I was doing, that once I thought of running away — (I have, since that time, had a similar fear) — Pride, bravado, and the curiosity of handling another man's prick, of seeing his emotions in spending, kept me going. — It was nothing but curiosity, for I never liked a man even about me. — But to frig one! — Ah! So many years had elapsed since I had done that, that I seemed to have forgotten all about it.

We went into the bed-room together. She stayed in the sitting-room. — "She is better there," said he. — "Let's see your prick," I said as soon as I had a little overcome my tremor. — He pulled it out, it looked small. I touched it with a sort of dislike. — "Are you fond of a bit of brown?" — he asked. — I did not understand and he explained. — "We always say a bit of brown among ourselves, and a cunt's a bit of red." — I had a feeling of nausea, but went on. — "Let's frig you." — He took off all but his shirt, and seating him on my knee I began to frig him. He questioned me whilst doing so — had I been up a man? — "No." — Then there was no pleasure like it. — I frigged violently but his prick would not stand, I talked baudy and about women. He said "A bit of brown is worth a hundred cunts." I felt quite disconcerted, for his cock remained small and flabby. I had thought that talking about cunts would stiffen it.

The conversation, then led by him, took an arsehole turn. — He asked me to let him feel my bumhole. — I consented. — In for a penny, in for a pound, I began to think. Taking down my trowsers, he looked at my bum, and his prick stood at the sight. "Is it virgin?" said he, and felt it. — Then, standing by my side, my left arm round his waist to steady me, I frigged him, and the little bugger spent, but a very little. I rushed to wash my hand.

When he had composed himself, he washed his tool, and became very curious about me, and most energetically felt *my* prick. — "Put it up me," — said he. — "I can't, my prick won't stand." — "Shall I suck it?" — "You?" — "Yes." — "Do you do so?" — "Lord yes, I have had it so thick in my mouth, that I've had to pit it out of my teeth with a toothpick." — I turned sick, but after a time I turned his arse towards me, and got my prick stiff by hard frigging, determined to try what buggery was like. But the moment I put it against his arsehole down it drooped — He was kneeling at the side of the bed. — "Wet it well with your spittle," said he, wetting his own hole. — It was useless, and I desisted. — "You will presently," he remarked. — But tho I tried again and again, determined to know everything, and to do everything once in my life, it was useless.

Then he went to a drawer, and produced a small marble pestle such as chemists use, and asked me to let him put it up my bum, extolling the pleasure I should have. — "It must hurt," I said. — "Oh dear no, look." — Going to the side of the bed, he laid down, and cocking up his legs, shoved it up his own arsehole a little way. — That only made me feel more sick, I was so unsophisticated in such matters. I expect he saw that, for he took it out. But then he produced two more of different sizes, one quite a large one, and told me there was a friend he visited every week, who met him in his stables, and he put the larger one up his fundament. — That man said it was not large enough to give him pleasure. "I put it up him to there" said the sodomite marking with his thumb the spot on the pestle. But the description made me feel more modest. — "You should have the small one up first, I will do it for you, and I know such a sweet young man who would suck your prick at the same time if you would like." — "Oh, no." — "Do let me sod you," — said he all at once and quite affectionally, "I should so like to do it to you and take your virginity," and he shook his prick, and frigged it a little. — It was not stiff, and was very sharp pointed, but not at all a large one.

I was now quite flabbergasted. His coolness and his tale of picking his teeth free of semen, made me actually shudder. — Then the pestles. — Fancy two men together in a stable, one shoving a pestle up the other's bum. — How curious I thought, yet how abominable — it's incredible. Yet still I felt curious. — "Does it make him spend?" I asked — "His prick stands after I have worked it up and down in the brown for a while, then I go on gently, and suck his prick, till he spends," — he replied coolly.

Again I frigged him, curious to see his emotions, and watched his face when with difficulty he spent slightly. — But my cock would not stand. — So I went into the room to Betsy, determined to try her cunt. — She had been, she told me afterwards, looking thro, and listening at the door all the time. "Don't come near me," said she to .to the sod. — After much ado she made my cock stand, I mounted her, and fucked, feeling his prick whilst I did so — that either suggested itself to me, or he suggested it — and it seemed to increase my pleasure.

Then as I rammed up Betsy's cunt, I became conscious he was feeling me behind, and that his thumb or finger was intruding into my bum hole. — "Feel her brown," said he. — I was in the height of my pleasure. "You beast," said Betsy. — Whether I obeyed his advice or not, I can't say. I spent, and fetched her, and then we quickly parted. — I gave him a sovereign, no more, and her two, before each other. — They made no remark. — I promised to see him again, but had no intention of doing so, and never did.

I met her soon afterwards, and she was curious. "Did his arsehole seem large?" I was unable to tell her, disliked even to refer to it, yet my curiosity seemed unsatisfied and I had a sort of desire to learn more, yet a dislike to myself for desiring it. — When she asked me if she should get him again, I refused point blank, yet all the time longing to try, and dissatisfied at not having put my prick up him, to see if it gave some unknown pleasure or not.

But I spoke to Betsy again about an unfledged virgin cunt. — She shook her head — did not know where to get one — the boys had all the girls when quite young. — Didn't she know what games boys and girls were up to when quite young. — She had lived at ***** — and there was not there a girl over fourteen who had not had it done to her — and by the boys — boys not men — and in the fields, tho sometimes at home. I had heard similar accounts from women years before, and believed her. — "I'll get you half a dozen little ones without hair, but they all know as much as I do about fucking." — That offer I declined, for I knew there were plenty like that about the streets, whom I could get without her assistance. — "A virgin, a virgin, and with no hair on her cunt, or nothing." — Well, she would if she could, but she shook her head. — Her last words were, "Just a little hair on it you wouldn't mind, would you?" — "Perhaps if only just shewing, but mind, I'll have a good look at her cunt, with thighs open, before I have her. No virgin, no pay. I won't be gammoned." — "All right, me dear, but you'll have to wait pretty long."

I met Betsy a little time afterwards by mere chance, and was going to pass her, but somehow she recognized me and touched me on the elbow, saying hastily, — "Come here, come here, I've been looking for you for a week." — We turned up a side street. — "Oh, if you mean it, I think I've got such a nice girl for you, but I shall run a risk." — We had a long conversation, I gave her money to make presents to the girl, and some for herself, but not much. — "I think she will, but if I can't get her, I can't, and then you'll think I've chiselled you." — "No I shan't," and we parted.

I looked for Betsy and a few days after saw her. — "She's a virgin," — said she, "but I don't see my way to it yet." — "Ah, the old game." — "Thought you'd say so, you old fox." — Betsy tried hard to make me go to a house with her, but I would not, tho I made her again a little present, and agreed also the price for her services if they were of use. — "I fear I can't manage it," said she, "tho she is a randy little bitch, and is longing to know what fucking is like, the boys have felt her cunt and she their pricks — she's told me so — ah! she is a regular hot-arsed one, and *you* may as well have her whilst she's got it to give, and you'll give me the money on the night you have her first?" — "Yes, if she be a virgin, not otherwise, and I'll see her cunt well before I do her." — "All right, you old fox, she was a virgin last night, I'll take my oath."

More than a week passed. Then I looked out for and saw Betsy. — I passed her, touched her lightly, said "hish" — and passed on, turning up the next convenient by street. — Betsy followed me and began breathless. — "Oh! It's such a chance, — I've walked up and down here for three nights, and never left the street till midnight, nor left with a man, for fear of missing you."

"She *is* a virgin." — Then she told me that the lass had only the signs of hair on her cunt. — Yes, she had seen her cunt, and had looked at it well. — "Yes — wide — wide open — and you can scarcely get your little finger up the hole, me dear — it's just large enough to let her monthlies through — and she's only had her monthlies twice, — you've got a rare chance — and such a plump, fine, little divel, I'd like to do her myself. But give me a sovereign to rig her out, you'd like to see her look nice. Honor bright — did I ever deceive you? Oh no, not next week, meet us tomorrow night, don't lose a night, or you may miss your chance, she has been sleeping with me three nights, and I don't let her out of my sight. She is such a hot-cunted little devil, that God knows what she'll be up to. — I'll give her boots and stockings, and say you sent the money for them — and you tell her you'll give her a silk dress — and a crinoline — don't forget the crinoline, she is mad for one (they were just in fashion), you'll be pleased, she is as well shaped as I am. — I'm only frightened they won't let her in the house, but they know you well there in J°°°s St., and that's a good deal. — If they do object you must come to my garret, tho I fear they'd hear us there." — Thus she talked on energetically, without stopping, and saw her ten pounds almost in her pocket.

Next night was dark and cold, and they met me in L°°c°°t°r S°°°°e. — The girl looked young and a little object. — Betsy told me to say the girl had been in with me before if they objected. — We entered. The door sounded the warning click. I went in first, feeling a little nervous, and had gone up a few stairs, when the door-woman said, — "She can't go in Miss, I can't let her — she is very young." — "Oh, she's not young at it — she has been half a dozen times before with me and my friend — hasn't she sir? — For she is sixteen, tho she looks so young," said Betsy in a low tone.

"She looks very young," said the woman hesitating and standing at the door. I turned round. "It's all right, she's been in here with me before, why object now?" — "She looks very young," the woman said again — just then another couple pushed open the street door. — "Go on, go on," — said the woman — "first floor front," and up Betsy and the young one came with me. — The door-keeper was anxious to get us out of sight of the couple just entering, they helped to settle the question.

The woman soon followed us into the room, and staring hard at the young one, — "If it's all right, I've nothing to say," said she. I put a sovereign into her hand. "We shall stop all night." "Two ladies, sir." I gave her another, shut the door in her face, and bolted it. — Betsy winked at me. "I knew she would if you spoke, and you've stumped up handsome." I had indeed, and had never been charged for two ladies before in that house.

Betsy had made up the girl in the oddest way with a big bonnet, and she looked almost a bundle of clothes too big for her. — It was an error in the disguise I saw at a glance. — But there we were, all three snugly in the best room in the house. Betsy pulled off her bonnet and shawl as quickly as possible. Then she pulled a great shawl off the little one, and a bonnet big enough for a grenadier, and I saw a lovely girl of about fifteen, looking up earnestly from rather deep-set eyes. — "This is the friend who sent you the boots and stockings, and he'll give you a lovely crinoline," said Betsy. — "Won't you, sir?" — "Yes," — said I.

I stood staring with delight, whilst Betsy undressed both of them in an agitated manner. First she pulled off her own gown — then the girl's. — Then she stripped herself to her chemise, then the girl. — When the girl was in her chemise, Betsy pulled her slap down on the sofa, and putting her hands under charming plump, little breasts — "Ain't they a pretty pair," said she — "and, oh! she has such a fat bum, and pretty little cunt." — She lifted the chemise, and the girl pushed it down. — She had never taken her eyes off me, nor I off her. "Don't, Betsy." — "Don't you be a little fool, look here," — and Betsy throwing up her own chemise, rolled back on the sofa, threw up her legs, opened her thighs well, and pulled her cunt lips

wide open. — "There, look at that, me dear — there's a sight for a
stiff prick." —"Oh! — Oh! Betsy, don't," — said the girl. — "Didn't
we do so last night my dear." — "Oh, not before a man," — said the
girl, colouring up and trying to pull Betsy's chemise down. — "Don't
— for shame." — "Shan't — Pough — all my eye, Molly — show him
yours." — "Shan't — you're dirty." — "Didn't we look at each other's
last night, Molly?" — "Not before a man — don't now, Betsy. — Oh,
don't before him." — It was said quite naturally.

But Betsy pulled right off her own chemise, turned to the girl,
and in a jiffy had pulled hers off also. — There they were, both
naked except their boots and stockings. Then with a laugh, she
threw herself back on the sofa, and pulled her cunt lips open again
— calling on Molly to do the same. The girl stood timidly looking
at me, putting one hand modestly in front of her cunt to hide it, and
trying to regain the chemise, which Betsy Johnson had put under
her own backside.

I sat down, pulled the little one to me, felt her pretty breasts,
her plump round little bum and thighs. She all the time kept her
hand in front of her sacred split. I pulled her then on to the sofa,
and got my hand between her thighs, talking baudy, and kissing her.
— Betsy had got up, and stood naked with her arse to the fire look-
ing at us, letting out baudiness, and inciting the young one to com-
ply with my wishes. — Then I pulled off my clothes to my shirt,
and showed her my pego, stiff as a poker and like a burning coal.

"Oh! There's a glory," said Betsy. — "Oh, don't hide it Molly, I
wish it were going up my cunt instead of yours," — and stooping,
she kissed it and pulled me towards her by it. — "Kiss it, Molly," —
said she — "kiss it before it goes up you. — Oh! Wow — wow —
wow" — and she put my prick in her mouth till it was nearly out
of sight. The little one stared. "Oh, ain't you dirty?" — "Dirty, you
little fool — a prick's nice wherever you put it, nice anyhow, and
anywhere. — You'll think so before a week — you'll be ready to eat
one a week after it's been up your cunt, Molly." — "Oh — oh," and
she went on putting it in and out of her mouth, and kissing it down
to my testicles.

I sat down again, got the little one on my naked thigh, and put
her little fist round my prick. — Betsy keeping up her baudy patter
all the time. Then I pulled the little one to me, her legs apart, mine
between them, and my pego rubbed between her plump thighs. I

grasped her plump little bum, and kissed her, whilst she kept strug-
gling — mildly tho — "Oh, don't now — oh, Betsy — don't let him
— it's dirty — don't" — and so on. Then I got out wine and liqueur
which I had brought with me. — There was only a water tumbler
in the room, and we all three drank out of it. I would not ring for
glasses lest the servant should come in, and see the youth of the lass.
The liquor was nice to her for she drank freely, became talkative,
and laughed. — Up to that time she had, tho tolerably passive under
my handlings, looked scared and fixedly at me, only uttering, "Oh
Betsy, don't do so — Oh, I'm — astonished." — Now she was more
at home. —

I delighted in talking to her — anticipating the delight to fol-
low. — "You've never had any man's hand between your thighs,
have you dear?" — "No sir." "And never put your finger up your
cunt?" — "Lord," said Betsy, "you could not get your finger up it.
I tried the other night, didn't I Molly?" — "No." — "Oh, you little
liar. — I did and I showed her the difference, and told her she
couldn't have any pleasure till her hole was as large as mine, and
she put her fingers up mine to feel." — "Oh — o-oh — o-oh Betsy, I
didn't." — "You did, you little fool, you got your hand nearly up it."
"Oh, you beast, you said you hoped you might be struck dead if you
told of me," — said the young one, looking quite aghast. — Betsy
laughed. — "I said any other girl but not a man, it don't matter to
him. — He's a man and going to make your cunt like mine. — Oh,
won't your little hot arse shake, where his balls are close up to it. —
You'll bless me tomorrow, when you get your new dress and crino-
line — and you'll be asking him to put his prick into you again and
again."

"Let's look at your cunt Molly," said I, trying. I threw her on
her back on the sofa and knelt down in front. She resisted vigorously.
Betsy caught hold of her arms and pulled her back, whilst I pushed
her legs wide open — the little pink gash widened, but I could not
in the struggle and excitement satisfy my curiosity, so desisted for
a while. We then drank and talked more, till my lust made me furi-
ous to begin.

What strange whims and caprices I have had with women,
and usually quite impromptu. I wonder if other men have suddenly
thought of such amusements and tricks. — I now had one. I took
some shillings out of my pocket, and sitting down on the floor with

my back to the fire, — "Open your legs wide Betsy," said I, "as you
sit on the sofa, and I'll throw shillings at your cunt. Every time I hit
between its lips, the shilling is yours — if I miss, I'm to have three
throws more with it and then it's yours." — Betsy screamed with
laughter, brought up both heels to the level of her buttocks on the
sofa, and spread out her thighs, shewing a wide split, that a half
crown could have gone into. I pitched the shillings at her cunt —
one on two hit it, and she made Molly pick them up. — The girl
stood looking at me — then at Betsy, and repeating, "Well, you *are*
dirty," astonishment in her eyes, manner, and voice, but she picked
up the shillings fast enough — and gave them either to me or Betsy
as she was told. — At length she laughed, and hid her face with her
hand. — "Oh, ain't he one," said she.

"Let's throw at yours, my darling," said I. — "Let him," said
Betsy, "or I shall have all the shillings." — The girl hollowed, refused,
resisted, till Betsy lost her temper, so we had more wine. At length,
"Now I'm going to look at your cunt." The wench was now well
warmed by wine, baudy conversation, and tricks, yet still there was
delay, and she refused. — Betsy said she was not going to be fooled
— what she had come to do, she would have to do. — She might go
away if she would not. — Go and get a lodging where she could. —
"Lay on the steps all night if you like, you shan't come home with
me — and *you know*," she said in a significant tone to the girl, which
I did not then understand. — With a little more persuasion, the
naked lass laid on her back on the edge of the bed, her legs hanging
down. — It was at the side of the bed away from the gas, Betsy had
pushed her on that side of the bed.

For half a minute I gazed at her with delight as she lay with
wonderfully large thighs, and legs, and would never have believed
her youth, had it not been for the hairless cunt, and youthful face.
She was country born, she had said, and early used to work in the
fields, such work soon develops the form, and hence her beauty; but
I soon began my investigation into her virginity.

Molly's virginity verified. — All three on the bed. — Molly refuses me. — Betsy's rage. — My prick up Betsy temporarily. — Molly convinced. — I mount her. — A wriggler and screecher. — The bed pillow employed. — Stroke number one. — The bloody sequel. — Stroke number two. — Betsy screwed. — Stroke number three. — Molly spends. — A night's cock-work. — Three in a bed. — Three weeks with Molly. — My erotic whims. — Difficult postures. — Betsy's assistance. — Molly on Betsy. — I fuck Betsy. — Molly jealous. — Betsy frigging herself. — Sudden disappearance of the two. — Reasons months after. — The washerwoman in quod. — The Priest's interference. — With Betsy in a Bath. — Fucking under water. — The Brothel in J°°°s St. closed.

I had doubted Betsy, and thought she was going to sell me about the virginity, spite of her protestations, and spite of my telling her that if not satisfied, I would only give her the price of a fuck of herself, and a little present to the girl: and knowing the room and the way the furniture was placed, and where the gas was, this now occurred to me again. I had to prevent my being cheated, and to get a good look, brought a candle with me which I now lighted, and stood by the side of the bed, — Betsy close to me. — I took one of the girl's legs, Betsy the other. — "Open your thighs and let him look, you said you would — you promised me you would — there's a darling," said she.

The girl's legs opened wide — I gave Betsy the candle, and with the vacant hand pulled open wide the lips of the little cunt, which was of a delicate pink, with the slightest signs of dark hair just on the mons. — Excited as I was, and with a prick throbbing as if it would burst, or spend without a touch, I saw that the cunt had never had anything larger than a finger up it. With an impulse I have always had with hairless cunts, I put my mouth to it, and gave it a little lick. — Such a mouthful of saliva came, and ran out of my mouth at once. — The girl struggled as she felt my tongue, and closed her thighs on my head. The spittle had covered her cunt — I threw off my shirt, pushed Molly straight on the bed, got on it by the side of her, and Betsy got on the other side.

But she would not let me mount her. In vain Betsy coaxed and bullied by turns. — "No — no," — she had altered her mind. — She was frightened — it would hurt, that great thing would hurt her, — it would make her bleed. — Then she burst into tears and cried. I desisted, Betsy quieted her, for fear of the people of the house, and when she had done she spoke to her in a subdued voice as nearly as possible thus.

"You bloody little fool. I had pricks up me twice as big as that, and longer than his, before I was your age — don't I get a living by fucking? — Don't I get silk stockings and dresses by fucking? — How are you going to live? — Who's going to keep you, I want to know? — What did you come here for? — Didn't you promise me? — Didn't you say you'd let him? — Didn't you say you'd like to be fucked if it was nicer than frigging yourself?"

The girl made no reply, and was confused and shaking. "All right, you may go, and you may get home as you can," — saying that, she jumped off the bed and rolled up in a bundle the girl's chemise and petticoat, which were quite new. — "You shan't have the things I've given you, damned if you shall." Then she came to the bed, violently pulled off from the girl both boots and stockings, and rolled up the stockings with the petticoat. — "Now you may go — put on your dress and your boots, and go, you're not wanted here, my friend and I will stop all night."

The girl looked scared out of her senses. "Don't Betsy, where am I to go to?" — "Go to Hell and buggery, go and shit yourself, I don't care a bloody fart where you go to." — The girl blubbered and sobbed out, — "I will then, I will let him." — "Hold your snivelling, and don't make that noise. — Someone's at the door perhaps, — let him do it to you, — if you don't — go — and you know. — You know what," — and Betsy, tho slanging in the foulest way (and I have not told a quarter what she said), — did it all in a suppressed voice.

I got on to the bed again. So did Betsy, who helped the girl to her old place. Again the girl said she should be hurt and refused. — "You do it Betsy, with him — you let him do it." — "Lord," said Betsy, who had recovered her temper, "he may fuck me till his spunk come up into my mouth if he likes — show her how to do it — let's have a fuck, my dear," — and she winked at me — "show her how it's done, and then she will let you, won't you Molly" — Molly made no reply.

I knelt between Betsy's legs naked, with prick stiff, dropped on to her, and put my prick up her — "There, feel, Molly." — She took hold of the girl's hand and guided it between our bellies — "Feel, his prick's right up — turn a little on the side," said she to me. — We did, keeping copulated. When her arse was a little turned towards Molly, she threw one thigh high up over my hips so that the girl could see the prick as it lay squeezed into Betsy's cunt — "Look under, look Molly — look there, nothing but his balls to see, is there." — The girl put her head down, and curious, touched my balls. — "Oh fuck, fuck, isn't it lovely my darling," said Betsy.

We turned flat again and Betsy began fucking and heaving in earnest. She thought she was going to have the treat for she wanted it. — But I slipped my prick out of her cunt, tho I kept on ramming and driving, as if I was going to fuck her backside up to her blade bones. — "Sham," — I whispered. — Betsy, tho disappointed, took the hint, and we heaved and pushed together, my prick now outside her, and at length screaming out, "Fuck — cunt. — Oh, lovely — ah my spunk's — coming — oh, push hard — dear — fuck — fuck." — We both shammed ecstatic pleasure and sunk quietly down, whilst the lass sitting up naked on the bed by our side looked at us all the while intently.

"Let him now do it to you," — said Betsy, again coaxing and threatening Molly. — My prick had drooped, just as the girl at last allowed me to get between her thighs — but it sprung up stiff directly I dropped on to her. I worked cunningly, rubbing the tip just outside till I had lodged it. She trembled. I pressed her, and gave a tremendous thrust, and was on the right road. — "Oho — hah — ar," — she screamed — "You hurt — get off —I won't let you — har." — She screeched loudly, and struggled violently. "Hish, you damned howling little bitch," said Betsy, pushing a pillow right over the girl's head. I pressed my head on the pillow, the girl's head was hidden from me, but I could hear her cry. — I had not got up her, was funky about the noise we were making, but in the excitement thought only of my work. — "Hish, they will hear," were the last words I heard Betsy say. — Then I felt my sperm was coming, and with a violent effort, and grasping the fat little buttocks like a vice — my prick went up her, leaving my sperm all the way up as I entered. I felt the tightening of her hymen round my prick, as it went through it with a cunt-splitting thrust.

It was all over in a minute. Then, "Oh, don't," — I heard in muffled tones. — "Have you done her?" — said Betsy. — "Y — hes — y — hes." — She pulled away the pillow, and there I lay with the little naked one palpitating, but quiet in my arms, my prick up to its roots in her. I kept it there, tho it was shrinking, but I kept on gently thrusting, just enough to keep it half stiff. Then I partially withdrew it, the girl winced and murmured. — "Oh, take it out, you do hurt," that stiffened me quite. — "I am fucking again. — I shall spend again," — I said to Betsy, who turned on her side to see better, and in a few minutes of exquisitely prolonged pleasures — I spermatized again the little virgin quim.

[It is the last time but one or two that I recollect doing so without uncunting, for I am approaching a time of life, which makes a pause between fucks usual with me.]

I rose on my knees, and looked at the girl, who lay quite quiet with her thighs wide open, and her hand over her face. — A bloodier mass of spunk I never saw on a cunt. — Her blood had run down on to the counterpane, and lay in a red rim all round my prick near to its root. I was delighted beyond measure. She bled more than any virginity of her age which I ever yet have had, I think.

Betsy chuckled. — "Well, Moll — you've been fucked and no mistake, ain't you? — How do you like it? — It didn't hurt you, did it?" — The girl made no reply, but lay with her nice round thighs wide open, her eyes covered with the back of one hand. — Betsy got off the bed and put a towel under Molly's buttocks and thighs. "You've spent enough and you have spoiled the counterpane." — The girl closed her legs on the towel, turned on one side, and began to cry. Betsy pulled her up and gave me the towel. I wiped my prick, and we all three got up — the girl ceased crying, and then sat on the sofa naked, in front of the fire; and we began drinking again.

Our talk was all about fucking, and we chaffed the former virgin, who sat without answering in a meditative way, seemingly wondering and upset by what had taken place. — At length, looking at Betsy. — "What will mother do if she finds it out?" she said. — "Find it out, how is she to find it out? — You won't tell her, and she does not look at your cunt, does she?" — "She might find it out." — "You little fool, she can't — and if she asks you, tell her to ax your pooper — and come to me, I will get you on to earn your living." — "She might find it out, tho," said the girl, giving her head a hard shake, and looking at the fire and as if speaking to herself. — "Say it's one of the boys in the court who did it, but I'll tell you what to say tomorrow," said Bet.

Betsy had had so much liquor that she was very jolly. The girl was on the sofa between us, when Bet put her hand across and began frigging my cock. "Is the next for her?" said she. — "Look Molly, that's what did it — isn't it nice? — Tell us how does it feel when it's up you? — It didn't hurt you, did it?" — "It hurts me now," said Molly sullenly. — "Wash it, Molly." — I would not hear of that, — I wanted her as she was, I liked to see the bloody smears on her belly and thighs, and know her cunt was full of my semen. "Don't you want to piddle?" — "Yes," said the girl in a whisper. — "Do it then." — "I shan't" — "Why you little fool, you must, we'll all go to bed directly, and you must before you go to sleep. I'm not going to bed with you, unless you do, you'll be pissing over us in the night." — The girl piddled, singing out — "ooooho" in a whisper, as the piddle I suppose touched the torn edges of her virginity.

Time had passed on in this amusing and exhilarating conversation till again I wanted the lass. She would not consent, she would not be hurt again, but we persuaded her, got her on to the bed, and again I sent my pego up her. At first she gave little subdued cries, and then took the thrusts very quietly. — "Isn't it nice now?" "No." — "Don't it give you pleasure?" — "No — no — no," — was all I got out of her. But I raised myself upon my elbow to look at her, whilst I went on fucking. She laid so quiet and closed her eyes in such a manner, that I am sure it did give her pleasure, tho she might not have spent.

We got hungry, and did not like the woman to fetch anything, for fear she would ask questions, but at length did so. "Let her get more wine," said Bet. She brought it and something to eat. We took it in thro the door ajar. We finished the liquor, and Molly got drowsy. We asked her how her cunt was. — "It aches and oh, it's so

hot, it feels as if it was afire," said she. — We laughed at her candour.
— I felt up it, so did Bet. We looked at it well and then into bed we
all got and I fucked the little lass again. She moaned as I put my
prick up. — Bet, whose baudiness was most amusing, pulled the
clothes down and slapped my arse whilst I was fucking. — "Isn't it
nice, Moll — isn't it?" The girl quietly gasped out — "Yhes — yhes,"
and at that fuck, the torn, heated, irritated little cunt, brought up by
long friction, stretching, and the pushing of my prick to its proper
crisis, gave out its juices, spent, and she had her first pleasure in
fucking on the first night that the male sperm had bedewed it.

Then all fell asleep. When I awakened, the lights were out,
for they had turned off the gas. I was outside, my face towards
Molly who was snoring. I felt her sticky cunt, and pushing her on
her back got into her. — She gave a loud cry not knowing where she
was. — Again I fucked her and she liked it, and told me so in broken
words, as I stretched her cunt.

When I awakened again it was daylight. We were all tired and
thirsty, drank water, pissed, got into bed again, and twice I fucked
the little one. — We had breakfast in the room, taking it in thro the
door. — Betsy was anxious to get out before me, for fear of the
baudy house-keeper, so I saw her out first with the young one, and
then followed. I had given her the ten pounds, and the little one
some money, or rather gave it Betsy for her. I was fucked out. How
many times I did it I don't know, but had rarely been baudier and
stronger. I so enjoyed the girl, that my cock stood the moment I laid
my hands on her thighs, and I parted with her longing to meet her
again.

The next night but one I again had them both, and passed a
delicious evening. — The baud no longer objected. The girl came
naturally dressed and looked older than she did in her makeup,
which was a failure. — This night was, if less exciting, more enjoy-
able in its lasciviousness. The lass raised no objections, and for some
hours my eyes were feasted and my fingers or my prick were investi-
gating her cunt. What a delicious satisfaction to push into the little
tight tube, and compare it mentally wih full grown capacious cunts,
to compare the jagged, pink slit, with the open port of Betsy, who
told us about the pricks she had seen and had up her, and of such
baudy pranks, that the lass declared she did not believe them. I did.
What pleasure I had when again the girl spent, and admitted that

it was better than frigging — even if Betsy did it to her. — "You seem comfortabler after it," said she, "than when you do it yourself, don't you Betsy." — It was an evening of mental and physical enjoyment to Molly and myself, and even to Betsy, who kept frigging herself.

Night after night, almost without intermission, did I then have Molly. — One night, Betsy said it was a shame that I did not give her a turn, and Molly consenting, I fucked her whilst Molly looked on. — But Molly seemed to think she had a right to all that would come out of my doodle.

I now get more whimsical in my lusts and more versatile in my enjoyments. Different poses suggest themselves to me continually. I have bent most women to obedience in these, of late years, those who would not obey I ceased to visit. But if a woman likes fucking, she takes as much pleasure in lasciviousness as a man does. — Betsy with her witty lewedness was fond of lascivious postures, but altho she did lewed things, she always seemed to do them with a certain witty gentility that was peculiar to her. The great pleasure she had in placing Molly, and shewing her how to move, and perform with me, was evident. — It was a baudy play, or a rehearsal.

I wanted to fuck Molly dog fashion. — When she leant over the bed she was too low, when she knealt on the bed too high. Bet, who always watched our fuckings, was ready with a suggestion. — She threw herself on her back at the edge of the bed with her legs dangling. — "If she lays on me, her cunt will just be at the right height," — "Nonsense." — But I put Molly, laughing, on the top of Betsy, and they were naked, belly to belly, face to face. — Bet clutched her, threw her heels up on to Molly's buttocks and jogged up and down for a minute, as if fucking. "Now you can see two cunts with one eye shut, said Bet, if you look." — Pulling open the little one's legs, I saw two cunts, nearly meeting. Have I ever seen that before? — I forget.

I did not think of flat-cocking (tho I have often thought of it since), — but easing Molly down towards me a little, I got her cunt just at the right level, and drove my prick pretty well home, then holding her legs with difficulty on each side of my hips, began fucking. — Betsy threw her legs up high, when Molly's were so placed. I placed one of my hands between their two bellies, and could just feel with my knuckles the hairy surrounding of Betsy's split, whilst with my fingers I felt Moll's clitoris. Then with my hand thus, I fucked and spent. Then I shoved Moll up higher on to Betsy, stooped, and saw her cunt dripping out its sperm onto Betsy's cunt.

Betsy, thoroughly worked up, having felt every jog and my balls almost knocking against her, as I poked Molly, as she now felt the spunk drop on to her cunt, pushed Molly off of her, and shutting her eyes began frigging herself. — "You're not going to have all the pleasure, my darlings," she said. — Molly and I looked on whilst she frigged. "Let's feel your prick," said she suddenly, I moved close to her — she seized it. — "It's sticky. The spunk's all over it." She gasped out, squeezing it hard, — "Oh, ahar, my God." Her imagination, as she felt my cock, helped her, and she spent. It is wonderful, what ungainly attitudes, and what difficult uncomfortable poses, men and women will put themselves in, to get variety of attitudes in fucking.

"Do you often frig yourself?" I asked her. — "Yes she do," said Molly, "she likes it." — "Shut up you," said Bet, "I frig when I can't get fucked, and I haven't had much chance lately, I've been with *you* every night — the other night I gave a Peeler a treat." — "Where did he have you?" — "Against a shop door," said Betsy, nothing abashed.— "I don't believe you." But Molly told me that she saw Betsy and the Policeman at it. So the girl was training up very nicely in the way she should go.

I tried to ascertain where the little one lived but never could get at it from either of the girls. I wanted Molly alone, and to save the expense as well, for I had to pay double for the room, and to pay both Betsy and Molly. That the girl went home with Bet, and that she had a mother, I learnt from scraps of conversation, especially when the flap-cunted one had had her full share of wine, yet the home was kept secret and Bet, when questioned at length said, "you'd better not bother yourself — or you'll get perhaps into more trouble than you'll like." — So I ceased enquiring.

Nearly a month had passed away, when Bet said the girl was going back to her mother. "She must stop at home three days, and then I'll get her out again, but she must go home early." That I agreed to. At the house on a night arranged, the mistress told me that Betsy had called to say she should see me soon, but not that night, nor did she meet me afterwards, and some months rolled by, before I met Betsy again. She was then looking very poor and unwell. — We turned into an accommodation house, and then she told me all that had occurred.

The girl was the daughter of a laundress, a friend of Betsy's, and she was allowed to be much with her, tho the mother knew how Betsy got her living. The girl was growing, had had her courses, and wanted fucking. — "Fucked by someone I knew she would be soon. — Some ragged-arsed coster perhaps. She'd been felt by youths, and had felt them, and as you wanted a fresh one, I thought I might as well have a few pounds for the virginity, as let it go for nothing" — So she led the girl up to it. It was easy enough, the little one nothing loath, was longing to have a prick up her, and get a silk dress, but Betty scarcely knew how to get her away. Just then the mother got drunk, assaulted a Policeman, was abusive, and was quickly sent to quod for a month. — Betsy said the girl should stay with her, till she was out of prison, and so she did, and she was then brought to taste my prick.

After the last time I had Molly, the mother came home, and soon told Bet her daughter had been ruined, and that Bet was at the bottom of the business. She denied it — and Molly denied it, but it ended in a row. The mother got again drunk and assaulted Betsy. The whole neighbourhood got to know and was up in arms. Betsy was obliged to leave her lodgings and at last to leave the neighbourhood. — She was afraid even to take to her old Strand walk, because of the mother. Since then, Molly and her mother had gone she knew not where.

Betty's belief was that it was owing to a Priest, for Molly had sworn she had never told her mother. When a doctor to whom she took the girl, had examined her cunt, he said that if a man had not been up her, she had put something up as big as a man. Molly still resolutely denied knowing anything about the matter, or that her cunt was any larger than it always had been, and said that she *had* put things up it. They were Roman Catholics. The mother took Molly to confess. The girl would not tell Betsy anything she had told the Priest, saying that she should go to hell if she did tell — and declared in ambiguous terms that the Priest had never asked her *that* — but only what he had asked her other times before — and she had taken care not to say too much. For all that, Betsy declared that from what the mother had let out that the Priest must have cautioned her, against letting her having anything more to say or do with Betsy. It seems that whilst Molly had been living with Bet, the two had talked a great deal about Priests, and what women told those holy men when confessing — and Betsy declared that tho the Priest might not have said the actual thing, he had said enough to the mother, to put her on the scent and make her do what she did.

I fucked Betsy that night but never afterwards, and gave her what I could to compensate her for her trouble and loss, for it seemed a probable story. I soon afterwards lost sight of her, and Molly I have never seen since.

The episode lasted about four weeks, and I had plenty of amusement during the time. — I was delighted with the little one. I could gaze for half an hour at a time at the little delicate pink slit, its jagged rupture, its little fleshy hairless lips: and then look at Betsy's well-haired cunt, as she laid by the side of her. When the little one's cunt was fresh washed I would tickle the little clitoris with my tongue till she closed her thighs on me — or pushed my head away, but I never made her spend that way, nor thought of doing so, nor desired it — It was simply instinctive, lascivious play which pleased us both — and delighted Betsy to witness.

In arranging these later portions of manuscript, I came upon a narrative of copulation in a bath, which I had with this big-eyed Betsy — I knew that I had written it, and at one time looked for it fruitlessly, then forgot it, and only thought about it again, when in arranging the loose leaves telling of my secret life at about this date, it suddenly turned up. It must therefore be kept in place here, altho what occurred took place certainly ten years earlier. — It was the only time I ever fucked a woman under water.

I have since tried to stroke a woman in a bath in the southwest of Europe, and failed, but fucked her directly we left the bath (in which I let as much water playfully up her cunt as I could) on a sofa in the dressing room. — It was at about 10 o'clock a.m. She was a lovely-formed, dark-eyed, dark-haired creature, a ballet girl, and an Italian about twenty years old, and (for now my amusements were far wider in range, obscenity, and eccentricity) I made her piss over me from the edge of the bath, and I pissed against her cunt, before our ablution. This was to her great amusement — and during all breakfast time afterwards, she did nothing but talk about it, for it was her first essay in such class of erotic diversion. — After breakfast, we adjourned again to the bath, under pretence of taking one, and I fucked her twice in the dressing room and then I went back by myself to P°°°h.

One night, Betty and I talked about the bath which we took together years previously, for it was she who told me of the bathing place. It is strange to me that I have never written full narrative before, for I made the notes at the time, as I well recollect. And now to the narrative.

One day when I had her on my first acquaintance with her, the subject turned on baths, and she asked if I had ever had a woman in a bath. "It takes a good man to fuck under water," said she. Then she told me where I could try, and I met her there soon after.

In J°°°s St., not far from my favourite baudy house, was a small building on the outside window of which in largish letters was written *"Baths."* There were there indeed baths for gentlemen, yet I expect the paying business was the double bath to which the initiated only had access. — Betsy told me not to go in with her, for men and women never went in together, but to wait a few minutes, as she had to see if a bath was ready, and let the keeper know who to expect. I did as told, and was soon in a comfortable little room where Betsy was awaiting me.

Against the wall was a bath like any other bath, but large enough for two. Hot and cold water could be turned on at pleasure. There were several different sized, but large flat cushions covered with soft leather, or something smooth, intended to be placed at will in the bath, for bum, back, knees, or head. We soon stripped, and filled the bath to a height just enough to cover our bodies, and then got into it together. Having heard from Betsy of the difficulty, I had kept myself from fucking for a few days, and now had a rigid prick, and plenty of sperm in my testicles.

Laying by her side I began to feel her cunt. She told me the more I let the water up, the greater difficulty I might have in fucking her. I soon began the work, and to my annoyance could not get my prick up her comfortably. Her cunt felt sloppy, yet dry to my tip, and my prick did not seem so stiff as it had been a minute or two before. She laughed. Then I arranged the cushions differently, so that her cunt might be higher up, for me to get at it more readily.

Then I had to let water out, and then in, because it either covered
her too much, or me too little. Then her head was too low and so
on. But at length all being carefully adjusted after much time and
trouble, again I mounted her under the water, and got my prick
into her cunt. Then the motion of my arse and belly, and her wrig-
gling up to me, sent the water up in waves, slopping all over her
face, and directly afterwards, one of the pillows slipped away from
under us, her head sank down clean under the water, my face went
under the water filling my nose, out slipped my prick, and we both
got up dripping, she annoyed because she didn't want her hair
wetted, I annoyed because I hadn't finished my fuck. Indeed I had
scarcely began it, yet now found my prick quite limp.

Again we went in. We had been a longish time now in and
out, and were getting saturated, and my prick wouldn't stand.—
In vain she frigged it under the water, so I rose up on my knees,
and frigged it stiff, sank down, entered her orifice, but I couldn't
do it. I got up angry and swearing, she rose laughing. Then I turned
her arse towards me kneeling, and knelt myself, trying it from be-
hind, but both cunt and ballocks were above the water then, but I
pierced her and shoved for a minute or so up her, and got it well
stiff again.

But having come to fuck *under* the water and not out of it, I
began readjusting the water level, so as to cover her arse and my
prick. Then it was too cold, then too hot, and it took time to get it
right, but at length it was. With difficulty I then got my prick up
her when just under the water, when the cushion on which her
hands were placed as she knelt, slipped away. A little only, but
anyone floats so easily, that directly she had lost her pose, down
she went on her belly, her head clean under water again, down I
sank on the top of her, out slipped my prick of course, and out of
the bath both got again.

"I told you it took a good man to do it in the water," said she.
—So I found, but was determined to do it, for I knew the spunk
was in my balls ready for issue. Again I tried various positions. Her
cunt had lost all its lubricity, the water had acted on my cock
prejudicially, and tho wanting it, I had to frig it up each time to
stiffen it, and at length I could not get it into her when under the
water at all.

She began to feel chilly, so did I. We stirred the fire, and made the water hotter. I got furious. She wanted to frig me under the water, I would not let her. Had she ever frigged herself under it? — No, but she would try, and she began, the water surging all about, as her hand moved. "I can," said she. But I pulled her hand away, and suspended the operation for I wanted her to spend with me.

At length determined to do it somehow, we put the water very shallow, I turned her arse again towards me, and we fucked kneeling, until our mutual pleasure was just increasing. Then, uncunting, I turned her on her back, and myself on to her belly, and my throbbing prick went up her as she lay with the water just touching her arsehole. Then we shagged on, till I felt that nothing could take the stiffness out of my prick, but a spermatic discharge, and she seconding me with intelligence (for *she* wanted to fuck *under* water, as well as me), she lifted her arse and me up with her slightly, I withdrew the pillow, her arse then sank under the water, which just covered her cunt and my balls, and in a few pushes my spunk filled her cunt, and restored its smoothness. — We lay with our organs in the water, her breasts and my back out of it, and so we lay till my prick slunk out of her cunt, which it soon did.

There was a bed in the room, and a warmer in it. Rapidly drying ourselves, we jumped into the bed. The woman brought us some warm brandy and water, and we laid in bed talking over our adventure, and the difficulties of aquatic copulation, till we wanted each other. Then letcherously we fucked between the warm sheets, and fell asleep.

Before we left the bath, I had felt up her cunt. The water followed my fingers, which in retiring brought with it my sperm, which we saw laying on a cushion, when we looked in the bath afterwards.

Betsy spent with me in the bath. "I was as lewed as you. — Lord God! . . . One fuck in a bed is worth fifty in a bath, me dear, but you did fuck and finish in it. — You're the fourth man who has been in the water with me, but the only one who spent under the water, the others fucked just outside it. — You've something to be proud of. I'll tell Mary S°°m°°rs."

Mary S°°m°°s was a big woman whom I also had at the time

I knew Mavis. She was about twenty-four years old, and weighed fourteen stone I think. She was big all over, but had no undue stomach, no over fat arse, but the flesh was evenly distributed about her. She had the loveliest eyes I ever saw, of the lightest hazel, and a large easy cunt. I recollect that cunt well. She was very handsome, and was always in the Quadrant in daylight, I don't recollect seeing her of an evening. She tried to attach me, and used to say I was the loveliest poke she ever had, but there was something about her which I didn't like, and could not at first comprehend. I thought she was lazy and dirty, from an oppressive odour about her. At last I discovered that her feet had a strong smell, and avoided her. But when she saw me she would follow me. — Women spoke much more importunely in those days to men. "Come along with me dear, I haven't seen you such a time." "I can't, I'm in a hurry and am poor today." — "Never mind the money, I want to see you so."

Betsy told me that Mary Si°m°°rs had sweaty feet, was married, that her husband had run away from her at the time I knew her, and she had just then turned out. She had, since I had lost sight of her, taken up with a thief, and they had both been put in prison.

Betsy and I laid long in the bed. We talked more about the bath, and our sensations when fucking in it, than about anything else. She had tried to frig herself under the water, when with one of the men, just to see how she liked it. It wasn't so nice as frigging in bed. We fucked again, and at about half past ten, left. They charged two sovereigns for the bath, and half a sovereign for the bed. The chamber-woman expected five shillings. — I expect I was cheated but had never asked about prices beforehand.

I never entered the house again. A few years after the baths disappeared. — I have since been in a bath with a lady, and laid naked on her, and we washed each other's genitals in it but never attempted fucking. That we did on a splendid sofa in an ante-room, when still wet from the bath. It was about midday on a scorching day in July.

Very soon after this the house in J°°°s St. was closed, and I lost one of the best kept, best furnished, snuggest accommodation houses I ever was in. — In it I think I must have had seventy or eighty women — for unless very far off, I always brought my chance, or stray women there. The celebrated house at the corner of O°e°d°n Street was closed soon after. Then I found a nice house close to the Thames embankment, and not far from P°°l°°o, and one close to Oxford St., and then half a dozen others, so what good was done by shutting up the others? Such houses are a necessity.

My social conditions. — Dainty whoremongering. — Difficulties in selection of women. — Eccentric fucking attitudes. — Writing my narrative. — The uniformity of fucking. — A peep over folding doors. — Amorous Americans. — The swain's lecture. — An obstructive table. — The lady's legs. — The swain's prick. — An inquisitive look. — I hear but see not. — Sobs and tears. — Momentary nudity. — Next day's repetition. — Conjectures. — A semi-eastern harem. — Beautiful courtezans. — A beauty selected. — "I've no hair there." — Other beautifuls. — A noisy neighbour. — Male inspection of male erection. — England again. — Many expensive mercenaries.

Under changed social conditions I now travelled, I was free from care, had plenty of money (tho getting rid of it fast), and altogether it was a happy time. I raced about Europe for two or three months, and had constant change of scene. When I got to a town, I sought the best brothels, and with my physique in first rate condition, revelled in female charms. After perhaps a week abstinence, that time spent in comfortable travel, how instantaneous my selection of the woman, with what burning lust I clutched my woman when I got her, how rapid my thrusts, how maddening in its ecstacy, as my prick throbbed, and the hot thick sperm gushed up her cunt copiously as ever. Indeed, sometimes I think more copiously than it ever did, but that is improbable.

Yet I gratified my sense of beauty largely. Sometimes when I had fucked a woman, chosen in hot haste, I could scarcely tell why, I again had the women of the house exhibited to me, and selected another for the second libation of my prick. More frequently tho, the first one had my second emission. Then cooled, I left; and waited till the next day, before I had further sexual enjoyment.

Then I had at times woman after woman to look at, dressed, half-dressed, or naked to my eyes, so that I might judge fully of their charms before selecting one for my sexual homage. Then I began to have two at a time, and sometimes three even, in the chamber with me. There, at my leisure, and without observation but that of my Paphian divinities, I could place them in every attitude, and see every perfection, before I chose the one to fuck. I had modes of payment of my own, would give half fees to those whose cunts I had only looked at or felt, and full fee to her whom I spermatized, and so on. At some places they would not agree to this, at some they would.

This contemplation of female charms makes me think I am like Paris, when selecting a Goddess for the golden apple, and I wonder if *he* made a mistake. I often do, and get so bewildered in my choice, that I do not know which to take. This one has such a lovely backside, but has hanging breasts. That one has too much hair on her cunt, and her nymphae hang out too much, but she is otherwise beautiful. That one has a lovely face, but too light a hair on her cunt, and her legs are thin. So I inspected and thought, till my prick would wait no longer, and urged me to let it taste its pleasure. Then when it left their cunts, how different some ladies looked to me, to what they had before. Surely a prick stiff and throbbing, and a prick flabby, wet, and flopping, affect the powers of imagination very differently.

But it was very charming always. At times I paid the full fees for a trio, and placed them as I have seen in engravings, and I invented myself combinations quite as beautiful and exciting. — I discover now, that I have as fertile a fancy as erotic artists, and moreover begin to delight in fucking, in different and oftentimes difficult postures. Postures which give not the voluptuous ease when the prick is in the woman, which the old fashioned way of belly to belly, or belly to backside give, but which nevertheless fire me with a sensation of intense lust, and fill my imagination with ideals of voluptuousness.

During this time I travelled alone, and had no one to interrupt me, or to make demands upon my time for companionship, and so I could arrange my erotic intentions beforehand and surely carry them out. In the intervals of my enjoyment of female society, I amused myself by making notes, or writing the narratives fully. [This

I find now by rough perusal of manuscript not yet touched, has a
• • freshness which is not in some of that revised, and which I think I
have already said elsewhere, was written out from memoranda
(memoranda very copious it is true) many years after and I had
at the end of two years a very large mass of manuscript, mostly
relating to my frolics with professed Paphians. This I largely ab-
breviated soon after, and shall do so, still more now. This following
paragraph I leave exactly as I then wrote it.]

On perusal I find I think much repetition, much which must
have been written elsewhere, tho where, and when, I cannot recol-
lect. Even with my good memory, I cannot at once bring to my mind
what I have written in a narrative of the amours of nearly twenty-
five years. But I shorten it. The roads to copulation are like the act,
very much the same everywhere. Prince and beggar do it the same
way. A policeman thrusts and wriggles his prick like a Duke. A
milkmaid heaves her buttocks and tightens her cunt like a Duchess.
It will be wearisome to tell how I tailed Mary one night, if I have
told that I did it the same way to Fanny the night before. Yet when
I had women I mostly wrote about my doings with them at great
length, described in detail as well as I could our voluptuous move-
ments, and the sensuous ideas which rushed through my brain as I
fucked then. That writing indeed completed my enjoyment then.
Now my pen may run through the greater part of it.

What is a little odd, is that I got few chances of seeing thro key
and spyholes, much worth recording. Perhaps that may be in a de-
gree attributable to spending so much of my time with harlots, and
when at my hotel, being usually very tired, and recruiting by repose
for my next orgie. Yet I saw one or two pretty sights.

At °°°°°, after a mid-day meal, I heard a male and female
voice in the chamber adjoining, which was connected with mine by
folding doors. I had only arrived there that morning. I looked for a
peep hole but saw none. A big chest of drawers was placed across
the door, obscuring the key hole. It was empty, yet with much diffi-
culty I moved it aside, and then found that a piece of furniture was
placed in a similar way on the other side. Balked, I looked for my
gimlet and couldn't find it. Then I noticed that the doors, very badly
made as they usually are abroad, did not shut into a recess, but
folded on my side against the architrave or top framework (I expect
there were also folding doors on the other side, but if so they were •

open), and did not at the top appear to fold close owing to their having warped. I mounted the drawers, but was then not tall enough, so putting one of my trunks on them I mounted that, and then thro a long chink at the top, saw half over the room, which was like mine, an unusually large one; for the hôtel was not of modern build. [This took place quite twenty-five years ago.]

There opposite to me on a large sofa, sat a man and woman. He with his arm round her waist, and his head on her shoulder. She was sitting and quite pensively looking down, and listening attentively to all he was telling her. She looked about twenty, he about twenty-five years of age, and they were Americans. Everything was quite quiet, and I heard word by word nearly everything he said to her. — She scarcely uttered a word in return, and was absorbed in listening.

. He was telling her the whole process of conception as he understood it, how the female got impregnated, and how an unwelcome fœtus could be got rid of. What he said indeed was in some respects new even to me — altho it is a subject on which I don't think I am quite ignorant. Every now and then, she turned her head round towards his, and said something which I could not catch, it was said in so low a tone, and then resumed her pensive look on the floor. — When she made a remark — he said "Yes," or "no — poor dear," — and kissed her. — I had seen neither of them before, and did not know what relation they bore to each other. I first thought when I peeped, that they were a newly married couple. Then from some remarks, that they had been illicitly fucking, or as I suppose it would be said, that he had seduced her.

He must have talked on this subject I think something like half an hour, and in a tone as monotonous as that of a lecturer on science — he never raised his voice a bit, was in no respect excited, but went on speaking with the American nasal accent. Then somehow I fancied he had got her in the family way, for his remarks, were interlarded with "you." Then he took to kissing her, and then gently he put his hands up under her clothes, and I heard him say "cunt."

But in front of the sofa was a table, which partly hid his middle, and hid hers entirely. So tho I knew that he had put his hand up there, for the lift up of her clothes, and his position shewed *that*, I could not see more than to her knees, the table in front of her, tho a foot or so away from her, hid her middle. — But I saw that she

put her legs apart to help, and soon after leaning more back on the
sofa, pushed her bum forward, to facilitate his feeling whatever it
might have been that he felt; and certainly it must either have been
her bum or her cunt.

In doing this he leant forward, stooping for his feel up her, and
tho he went on speaking, I then entirely lost all hearing, excepting
of mere sound, for his face now was turned upwards towards hers,
and the back of his head was towards me. Probably he may have
dropped his voice, for we all I think do so when lust comes on us. A
soft murmuring voice is the voice of love. A man doesn't bawl out
that he wants a woman to let him fuck her. Then I could see that she
lifted her clothes entirely up, and his head bending lower went out
of sight, all being hidden by the table, but the bunch of her clothes,
which shewed above the table. He unmistakably was looking at her
cunt, or kissing it. Lick it, he scarcely could in that attitude, and
they remained like that for a minute or two.

Then he resumed his seat, putting one arm round her, but keep-
ing his right hand out of sight, and unmistakably (the table hid it)
under her petticoats, and he went on explaining and lecturing. Then
smiling, and relinquishing her waist, he opened his trowsers and
pulled out his prick. That I could see as he sat. Then he said some-
thing which I could not catch, she turned to him, I saw her right
hand lay hold of his prick, and she began frigging it clumsily. He
pulled it then more out of his trowsers, and laughing said quite
loudly, "No — so," and gave it himself a gentle frig or two. She took
it in a pretty little hand again, and soon got it by a little frigging
up to a fine erection. — Then they turned half towards each other,
and they kissed, but the table now hid her hand and his machine, tho
I knew she had it in her hand, and that his hand was on her cunt.
I could see a little more of her legs sideways, but could hear nothing
for a minute or two. They were in silent enjoyment of feeling each
other's privates. Then they put arms round each other's necks, and
cuddled. Oh how I envied him, and my prick stood stiff, but I re-
sisted my desire to masturbate.

Then both got up. He stood with prick out stiff, and a fine one
it was. She for a moment looking at it. Then both went out of sight
alas, to a bed which I could not see, and there they fucked, for I
could hear his murmurs of pleasure as he spent. But I could see
nothing of their action, nor of her, or his subsequent ablution, tho

I heard the splashing of water. — Both came into sight, and again sat on the sofa, and he felt her, and they talked long about consequences. — "Have no fear, my love, at a proper time I know what to do," said he. — "Oh, I'm so frightened — so miserable that I can't sleep," said she. — "Who's in that next room?" said he, all of a sudden. — "No one, I think, there was no one last night." — I kept as quiet as the grave. — "I'll look," — I heard her say, tho when she said it, I could see neither of them. I think she looked out of her bedroom door, for soon after she came into sight, and I knew she was in the room by herself from her manner. She sat down at the table, and buried her face in her hands long. Then she cried, and began writing a letter.

I was very tired and sleepy, for I had been traveling nearly all the night before, but the affair fascinated me. I could not keep my eyes off of her. I felt intense delight in knowing that the fair creature had been fucked, and that that pretty hand had before my eyes frigged a great cock up to a stiff stand. — My prick stood asking for a spend, but I resisted frigging. At last I grew so tired that I got down, and laying on my bed slept long. I got ready for the evening table d'hôte. There I saw the lady sitting at table, with her swain not far off. He and her party were all travelling together, there was a lot of them, and all Americans. She had two brothers I think, both mere boys, friendly with the man who had fucked their sister, and they I knew were ignorant of their sister's amorous games. Had I been her brother, I think it would have been different. But what vigilance can keep a willing cunt from an aggressive prick? All history, all experience, tells me that they WILL come together. — Vigilance grows weary of watching, and lulled into security, whilst lust is ever vigilant and ready to seize the slightest opportunity, is cunning in making them, and five minutes suffice for a randy prick to fill a cunt with sperm.

Expecting a nocturnal visit of the man, I kept awake — but nothing was to be seen. I saw the lady undress, and stand for a minute naked by the table, rubbing her breasts and body with her hands, before putting on her night-gown. I saw that she had not much hair on her motte, and that she was very thin, but she was very handsome faced. Next day at the same time, the man was with her. They evidently knew that I, or some one was in my room, for they spoke in so low a tone that I could scarcely hear a word they said. They played with each others genitals, more than the day before, but the table still hid their hands and their middles from me, till he pulled her on to his knee, and then I saw his prick out, and more of her legs, tho' but for a minute or two only. They went soon out of my sight, I heard them fucking, and did not see him again.

After she had washed, she undressed and came in chemise only, straight to my door, and I imagine there was a glass there for she was evidently looking at herself in one. — Such furniture arrangements in foreign hotels are common. Then she laid down on the sofa, leaning her head on one hand, whilst with the other she felt her cunt. The confounded table let me see her thighs as she lay, but just hid the hand which was on her cunt from me — she didn't frig herself. After a little time she laid quiet on her back and began to cry hard. I could hear her sobbing. Tired of looking, I got down. In a quarter of an hour afterwards, I saw her sitting up, still in her chemise and writing a letter seemingly, and so I left her and went out to see the town.

I saw the party at the dinner table, but was not near them. I never took my eyes off the couple, for to look at a woman whom I have secretly seen naked, or fucking, gives me the intensest pleasure; and still more so if I can speak with her. I feel almost a friendship for her and would do anything to please her. — After dinner, I tried to get into conversation with some of the party, so as to get to speak with her, but they were unsociable and I failed. At night, beyond seeing her again put on her night-gown, and her rump as her chemise dropped down, I had no treat, and next morning early, the party left the hotel. I came to the conclusion that the girl was in the family way.

Then I found my way without the aid of a guide to a brothel, where in all my life, I never saw such a selection of beautiful, healthy women. They were not like so many of the flabby breasted, highly got up, yet fucked-out looking women one sees at the houses of certain of the capitals of Europe; but resembled healthy lasses who had just come from the country. — But it was in a country where the women are very beautiful, and I was at a town where the poor women of easy virtue are not used and then abused, kicked, and hooted, and almost branded, but where they often marry and marry well. — A well known traveller is said to have got his wife from one of the houses at this town, and a charming wife and woman she has ever since been, I am told. After a midday meal, walking along in a by, but quite a good street, I heard the merry laugh of women just by my ear, for I was close to the wall in the shade, it being a hot day. Stopping, I could just distinguish female forms thro the close outer blinds, and looking up saw that all the blinds of the house were shut. Fancying it was a harem, I pushed the door, which opened, and I found myself in a fine hall, and mounted a staircase to a very handsome large saloon.

The Abbess of this open-thighed nunnery spoke bad French, but enough for me. Soon trooped in a dozen of the most beautiful women I think I ever saw together in a bagnio, or in any society. I have often been bewildered in my choice at a baudy house, and more so I think when the ladies were naked than when clothed. Here they were clothed, but it was of loose or open make. All were more or less décolleté, their breasts were seen nearly to their nipples, in some the nipples shewed, in some I could see the enticing darkness of the hairy armpits. The majority had the most lovely, tho not flashy or stagey boots on, and the display of calves was fine. They did not all stand up, but most sat down, as if they had taken their places on chairs for the evening. One or two addressed me in a language I did not understand. I spoke then in a language which was replied to by one or two, and I talked compliments and nothings for delay, for I was confused by their loveliness, and a desire to fuck half a dozen of them at the same time.

At length, almost at hazard, and spite of my looking round till my eye balls seemed to ache, I patted a not very tall girl on her lovely shoulders, and left the room with her. She was an exquisite creature, with cheeks like a rose, tho her skin had a darker hue than our English women. She had eyes like a gazelle, and dazzling teeth. In our bed-room, in a second she sat on my knees, and I glued my lips to hers. On a gesture which she understood, she threw off all clothing but boots and stockings, and stood naked, a sight of glorious beauty. She was but eighteen years old. Tho my prick was stiff before I had got up stairs with her, I sufficiently restrained my self to look over, and feel her exquisite form. From neck to breasts, breasts to armpits, armpits to cunt, my fingers ranged, and my lips followed, feeling and kissing, kissing and feeling till I longed to lick her. Then after, opening her lovely cunt-lips, I went on to looking at her bum furrow — for all parts of the pretty creature it seemed, must be pretty to me. To my astonishment she moved herself from off the bed, and turning round with her bum towards me, and pulling the ivory cheeks asunder, so that I could see her anus, "I no hairs there," she said in broken Italian, which with German I found we could best communicate with each other in, tho she belonged to neither nation.

What her object was in informing me of the condition of that part — whether it was an invitation to it — whether its beauty caused it to be often investigated by friends, it never occurred to me to think about, until I began to write this narrative of my visit to the nunnery house, which I did next day. — But the instant she had spoken, so exquisite did her cunt with its crisp dark hair, and pouting lips, look between her buttocks furrow, and lovely thighs, that I inserted my prick, and almost instantly spent the semen in her, which had been boiling in my ballocks, since the time I saw the couple in the bed-room at the hotel: for I did not frig myself there, restraining myself with much difficulty from doing so.

The nymph stood quite still, with my prick in her, satisfied to let it rest there and soak. It showed no signs of shrinking, whilst I stood feeling her marbly buttocks, putting my hand round to feel her clitoris, feeling her breasts and armpits — revelling in her beauty. — Then her cunt clipped it. It was an invitation to go on fucking. But I now wanted her sweet face, her lovely lips towards me. Pulling my prick out of her lubricated cunt, "Get on the bed and lie down, cara mia," I said.

Without reply, and putting her fingers on her cunt, to prevent spilling my spunk out of it, on she got, and smiling, asked for a towel. I gave it her, and she dried her fingers with it. For an instantly only, I saw between her wide apart thighs, the red slash, covered with the pearly essence of my testicles, and then plunged my wet prick up it again. She met me with ardour in a fuck worth two of the first in duration, baudy thoughts, and voluptuous enjoyment of her spunk filled genital. It ended in her spending when I did, and our mouths overflowing into each other, as the juices of both cunt and prick mingled in her.

Then all is told, excepting that I stopped hours with her, conversing in polyglot, but mainly kissing and feeling her, in delicious, thoughtful, baudy half silence, during the hot afternoon.

The next day I had her again, and thought I should never care about another woman. The day after that, I could not go to the house, but the following evening did. She was engaged I found for the night by a gentleman. Disappointed, I yet saw some of the other ladies. Tho some were then fucking in their chambers, I got one taller, but in every other respect, as beautiful and perfect, as the one I had had. The charm was now broken. I had her again once, but my love of change, the desire to see and know what other women were like, was too much for me. I stayed a fortnight at the town, and had fucked half a dozen of the women before I left.

I kept to my bed-room, hoping to see some other sights there, but to my annoyance, two officers took possession of it, and walked about as it seemed to me both night and day, with boots and spurs on. There were military doings in the town. They smoked also incessantly, and had a party one night, on which occasion I don't think they went to bed. Being much annoyed by their noise, I asked for another room, tho for many reasons I liked the one I was in. — The manager told me the officers would leave the next day: which they did.

But the same night, two other men connected with the army, tho apparently not soldiers, were put there. They were quiet, and at night hearing them preparing to go to bed, I had the curiosity to get up and peep. To my astonishment one was naked, and the other, in his shirt, was looking attentively at the naked one's stiff prick, and feeling it. What he was doing it for I can't say, for he soon relinquished it, their light was put out, and both almost immediately snored. Who were they — was one a Doctor, but why a stiff prick? All was so solemn and business like, so unlike erotic amusement, that to this day I can't make the affair out.

The day after, I left ***** and went on traveling, but returned to England soon. I had no intrigue on hand, tho I had thought when free that I should soon have one. I had not a servant even to meet. Those nice, little, randy-arsed, well-fed devils, who can only get fucked now and then on the sly, and of whom I have enjoyed dozens in my time, and hope to enjoy as many again. As it was, the mercenary frail ones, of the highest and most expensive class, absorbed my manhood, and my pocket. Cunt, silk stocking, diaphanous chemises, laced night-gown, and jewels, are costly. Then I found one I liked much, and tho I did not keep to her, for I never can to one woman alone, I frequented her for a couple years. Other adventures occurred between my visits to her, but I have collected all about her into a consecutive narrative, and also all relating to an intrigue with a French lady of a very curious kind, which began at Paris at about the same date.

At Cremorne one night late in the summer, I saw a tall, fine woman, whom I mistook for a German. Her hair was of a darkish, half flaxen hue, tho not flaxen. It was a color I did not admire, but it seemed in her very handsome, and to suit her face, which was round, with a thickish, but prettily retroussé nose, sweet, languishing, half sleepy, blue eyes, and pouting lips, such as I love; in a small mouth full of fine teeth. She had a lovely, transparent, white complexion, tho too white and colorless perhaps. She had a quite unusual, graceful, undulating motion in her haunches, indeed of her whole body as she walked. Not a vulgar swing of her rump, which some women affect, but quite an easy movement. It was as if the bum was too heavy for her legs. But the graceful undulations seemed to go over all her body. I went home with her to the extreme west of London.

I have blotted out her surname on my notes, and altho I visited her at intervals quite two years cannot now recollect it. Her Christian name was Amelia, and I call her Amelia German, on account of her German, or perhaps Hollandish look.

She stripped, and in doing that, her movements were graceful, and I found her as I expected, beautiful in form, with thighs which were a perfect model, and a large, tho not overpowering backside. Her cunt was not very hairy. It was small, delicate looking, and retained somewhat the pink or coral tint of youth, and this made it very pretty, coupled with the light colored fringe. The color however was much darker than that of the hair of her head. Clitoris and nymphæ were small, and delicate, and barely shewed thro the full lipped slit. Altogether, it was sweetly pretty, and scarcely looked like the cunt of a full grown woman of two and twenty.

I slept with her, and found her a most charming bed-fellow. She had much of the manner of fucking that Camille has. — A slowish, reciprocating movement of her haunches to my thrusts, and when spending, no violent action (which I hate in a woman), but a sort of squeezing, prick engulphing, wriggle of her cunt, and heave up of her backside, which was most exquisite. When found in other women I expect I have always told of it. We both slept start naked, for her body was of exquisite plumpness, yet without fat. Her mouth and teeth had first attracted me and I fastened on it. I could scarcely keep my tongue from her mouth, nor she her tongue from mine, for she liked that sensuous junction of the mouth as much as I do, when I get the mouth I like. At my wish she did not wash after copulation, she did not care to if she liked the man, she said. I fucked her to my utmost and passed a most delicious night. We both slept profoundly till about eleven o'clock next day. Kissing her in the morning, I said to her, "You spent with me always." — "I don't know who wouldn't spend with you, your way of doing it would make any woman spend if she liked men at all," she replied. She was one of those who didn't use language either baudy or blasphemous. Yet she was lustful, full of juice, and as greedy of sperm, as well nigh any woman I ever yet have had. A strong, healthy woman, in the very prime of life, and quietly fond of all voluptuousness.

I had her a night or two after, and then satisfied by a more careful look, that which I had fancied by fingering and fucking her before, that the opening of her vagina, or mouth of the prick tube, was very small, and that immediately the mouth was passed, it grew if anything larger than it usually is in women. As I fucked, I found that

sensation of undue capacity even round my prick. At a future day,
I noticed this particularly at the second poke, if she had not washed
my sperm out. It was the smallness, and the shape of this opening of
the vagina, which helped to make her cunt look so pretty. She told
me it had been noticed by most of her friends, and she seemed very
proud of it, for when I looked at her cunt as I always did before
entering it, "Isn't it small?" she used frequently to say in a gratified
tone. I once before had a woman who was proud of her smallness
there. I never told Amelia that her cunt inside was extra sized. I
never do anything which may vex or wound a woman I like, or cause
her to think I am not quite satisfied with her charms. I have known
many women much offended by remarks of mine about their person,
remarks made quite innocently by me. Many gay women are as
proud of their cunts as they are of their faces.

She was a voluptuous creature, and enjoyed my embraces much.
I had ample signs of that and am not deceiving myself. She was not
a talkative person either, and had a soft voice which I like. We used
to pass much time when together, in billing and cooing, as it may
be termed: for once on her bed, our mouths joined and our tongues
set to work, and we did nothing else for a long while. We licked
each others teeth, wetted copiously our lips with saliva, and rubbed
them together till they dried, every now and then just protruding
the tips of our tongues and all as silently as possible. — "You've a
lovely mouth, Mealy." — "And so have you, and the sweetest
breath." This was repeated often enough, just as if both were spoon-
ing. I don't usually take the wet mouth of women of her class, or of
any woman, unless I like the look of their mouths; tho wet kissing
of that sort, I love intensely now, and it is most exciting to me, and
makes my cock stand without handling it.

She was skilled also in prolonging our sexual enjoyments. "Lay
quiet in me, dear" — this was often said when my prick was up her,
and quiet I used to lay as long as my prick let me, but it was an
imperious organ. "Oh, don't move it," she would murmur thro our
wet lips and tongues, when voluptuously slabbering each other. Then
when she spent, the pupils of her eyes disappeared, the white only
could be seen, her mouth opened quite wide, and she breathed
short, and hard, for a second or two. But before the spend had quite
finished, her liquid lips were joined to mine again, giving subtle
enjoyment, till the luscious enervation came on. In fact she was

gifted by nature with the art of love, and loved the art, tho she never seemed baudy, nor talked it. Then I began to take to her, then resisted myself — no more affection for me if I can help it.

She had a nice ten-roomed house, well furnished. I found after a week, that she inhabited it all herself, and there was no lodger in it. Then I found that her rent was paid by Captain ••••• of the ••• Infantry, the son of a Baronet and his heir. He was very fond of her, and came up to see her as often as he could. At the time I speak of, he was at Aldershot. This information was given me one day, when I said I was going to call on her. She begged me not as she would be engaged for a week. On other occasions that also occurred and then she told me further why. I saw, after I was better acquainted with her, his photograph, and also of that of his father's house. At a later date she shewed me photos of his sisters. All were taken by the same man in the country. [Photography then was not in its present state of perfection.] He promised he would marry her, she told me. I have a faculty in getting the confidences of gay women, and without soliciting it. — How many have asked my advice in their troubles, and in the belief that they have no true friend in their own sex.

She had at that time living with her, a woman whom she called her house-keeper and companion. A fine, well grown woman, about twenty-eight or thirty years old seemingly, and in tone and manner, quite superior to what is usually found in the house of a gay woman. In fact a gentle-woman. This very much astonished me. In bed with Amelia one night, after a champagne supper, and we had fucked once, talking about the house-keeper, she told me that she had been a governess, but had lost her position, and had had a child. Her manners indeed were quite those of a lady. When I called she placed a chair for me, and left the room in quite a different manner from a servant.

I did not always tell Amelia when I should be with her, but took my chance, calling sometimes even in the morning, but mostly in the afternoon or evening. Sometimes I waited an hour or two for her, if she happened to be out, or engaged. I don't recollect her being with a man at home when I called, more than once, and think that two or three men mainly supported her. She told me one night that a married man was very good to her.

I had known her somewhere about two months, when one evening now quite late in the autumn I called. She was out and would not be in for an hour or two, would I call again. I preferred waiting. The companion who had opened the door to me saying that both servants were out (as was at times the case), was leaving the room. It was cold and there was a fire in the parlor, and thinking of her comfort only, I said, "You can stay, unless you have a fire in the drawing-room." — No, there was no fire, but she could go to the kitchen. At my request she stayed in the parlor. We began talking, and I thought she looked very nice. She was a dark eyed, dark haired woman, tallish like her mistress, and was dressed nicely in a quiet colored silk. I began whilst conversing, to think over what had been told me about her having had a child. I wondered whether she was fucked by any one now, and arrived at the conclusion, that a fine woman like her in the prime of life, would not go without conjunction with the male, whatever might be said about her chastity to the contrary. No cunt can refuse a prick when once it has had it. Amelia had said, she was sure she was quite steady, having had enough of men, and being disgusted with him whose cock had produced her child, brought her to grief, and neglected her afterwards. How could a gay woman believe that?

I got lewed. "Sit nearer the fire, it's cold out there." She drew near it, and so did I. Something in her movement brought the easy swing of the haunches of her mistress to my mind. I had been longing to talk about love matters, but didn't know how to begin, had one of those stupid ignorant ideas about its not being fair, that her mistress would be told and mischief made, and so on, as if I had not as much right to poke the maid, as the mistress. But I was fondish of Amelia. The movement of her companion's haunches destroyed all such thoughts, and I burst out, — "Your bum moves just like your mistress'" (tho it was not a bit like it). "Does it?" said she, laughing. — "Yes, and I expect it's the same size." — "There's not much difference when we are both naked." "Really? I should like to see." — She never replied, but shook her head, laughing quietly all the while to herself.

I drew close to the tender and put my feet on it — "Put your feet up, Mrs. A°t°n (She was spoken of always as Mrs.). — She did. — "Lift your clothes and give it a warm." — "I'm warm enough." — "I'm too hot," said I, adjusting my prick in my trowsers, for it was

stiffening, and could not rise up owing to my drawers, and I pulled
it about outside my trowsers, in such manner that she must have
known the reason, for she laughed, then stopped herself and looked
demure. But I'd made her want to open her thighs I was sure, lust
is so contagious, words raise ideas, ideas heat cock and cunt quickly.

"Did any man sleep with Mrs. German last night?" I asked. I
had been several times in the room with the house-keeper before,
but had never asked any question, knowing that I should only get
a lie in reply. — "No." — "Someone did, now." — "Yes, some one
did." "You told me just now no one did." — "Oh no I didn't, you
said a man — I slept with Mrs. German"; — She told me that when
her mistress was alone, she slept with her, and that was most fre-
quently, for that she only let one or two men sleep all night with
her.

Then I rattled on, forgetting quite that I was waiting for Mrs.
German — did they sleep naked together as I did with her? Had
she as little hair down there as her mistress? I knew it was dark
whilst Amelia's was light. Did she cuddle her? — Mrs. A°n answered
those, and a lot of other questions, quite discreetly and evasively,
said she slept with her because she was timid. She did her hair —
dried her after taking a bath, did all sorts of things for her to make
her comfortable, for she had been very kind to her. I hesitated to
say it, but at length, — "You've seen her cunt I expect." — "Of
course." — "You've frigged her." — "Don't be a beast and ask me
such questions," said Mrs. °°°°, all on a sudden turning half indig-
nant. "Well, don't tell Amelia what I've been saying." — "It's not
likely that I shall."

That somehow encouraged me. I got up and kissed her. "Don't
tell her that," and I tried a feel. — "Don't be foolish sir," — "Let me,
my prick's bursting, and I can't wait for Mrs. German — look." —
Out I pulled my pego on a state of high inflammation, — "Don't you
now be foolish — I won't feel it. — She'll be in directly, or the serv-
ants will, — Don't — I'll tell her — now don't you." — I was stand-
ing up now. She still sitting with feet on the fender. I stooped
quickly, ran my left hand up her petticoats, and touched her cunt
in a trice, holding her back in the chair with my right hand whilst
I felt with the other. She did not resist much, did not even close
her thighs, and my hand easily covered the whole slit from clitoris

to vagina. I kissed on and fumbled about, and thrust a finger up her cunt for a minute, she half laughing. Then she closed her thighs. — "No, leave off, that's enough, you did not come here for that."

Relinquishing her quim, "Let's do it," I said. — "No, that I won't." — "You shall." — "Mrs. German may come in at any minute." — "Well she can't get in without ringing." — "Yes she can, she has the latch key." — "I'll bolt the street door." — She didn't say no. — I bolted it, and returned. She now was standing by the table, I pulled her on to the sofa and felt her cunt again. — "You'll never tell Amelia." — "Never, how can you think I should be such an ass." — "I don't know about that." — Not another word she spoke, but laid hold of my prick which had been out all the time, we kissed, she laid in a hurry almost her length on the sofa, I threw up her clothes, saw that it was a dark, fully haired cunt, as I guessed it must be, and the next minute my prick was at work up it, we were fucking energetically, and finished our pleasures at the same moment. — Said she as she rose. — "If Amelia knew about this, she'd turn me out the next minute — so don't you do me that harm, God knows I've had enough misery."

I felt immediately as if I had been treacherous to Amelia. — Of course that was very foolish, but I did. — Mrs. A°t°n went to the kitchen and washed her cunt, came up, sat down on the sofa, and said that if her mistress was not home soon, probably she wouldn't be home till late, as she had gone to dine with a friend, and might go from there to the Argyle rooms, but I had better leave. — I wouldn't go. — If she came in she could say I hadn't been there long. "We'll do it again." — Mrs. A. was of opinion evidently, that in for a penny in for a pound was a good motto, and tho she had told me to go, was awaiting another cunt basting. She wouldn't undress, but all that could be seen by lifting her petticoats above her waist I saw. All I could see and feel by loosening her dress above, I did. I investigated her cunt, held a candle to look at it, and a good, bold looking cock trap it was. She helped me quite willingly in my inspection, for she had nothing to hide, till I took a candle. Then she resisted. Directly I had satisfied my eye-sight, — "You'd better make haste," she said, and laid down with thighs wide open. She was either hot cunted, or fearful of her mistress returning, and I think both, but certainly hot cunted — and as I feared being interrupted by Amelia's return, I shagged her again at once.

"You like fucking jolly well," — I remarked. — "Who doesn't, but it's brought me to grief, I'd vowed never to let a man again." — "Gammon, my dear." — Her remark might have been a pumper — and I had promised Amelia never to tell her companion what she had told me about her, and never did. Then Mrs. A°°° begged me to go. The servants would certainly be in soon, if I went off at once she should never say I had even called, that would be best, and I was never to tell Mrs. Amelia about my having done so. Off I went, called at the Argyle, saw Amelia there, told her I had merely looked in to see her, and went home.

Soon after, in conversation with Amelia, she told me that she felt timid, and frightened of being robbed or worse, if she slept by herself, and that Mrs. A°t°n usually slept with her. "Does she gama-huche you?" — Amelia gave me a slap. — "Oh you beast, no. — I don't like women — I like poking too well." — Certainly she did that, there was no mistake about her voluptuous delight in coition, nor in her spending freely with me, but then might she not have liked the other variety of lustful enjoyment as well?

I told Amelia that I saw no objection to women amusing each other sexually if they liked, but she affected dislike — or really felt it. Did she? These thoughts only occur to me as I think over matters, and write this narrative, and [still more as I revise them after many years], Amelia was a quietly voluptuous woman, Venus in all ways pleased her I am sure, and it is more than probable that she had Sapphic tastes, as well as lechery for men, tho the double taste I believe is unusual, but there are such singular sexual idiosyncracies. — If she liked a woman for lustful games, it did not prevent her get-ting in the family way by a man.

Other females, however, had my caresses. I did not keep to Amelia, nor disguise that from her. Then I went abroad (I put this part of my narrative separately) and when I returned, Amelia was in the family way by her captain. In vain I told her before it was too late that she had better get rid of the fœtus. No, she was de-lighted. — It was his, he knew it was his — he had stopped with her an entire month — she had had no other man all that time, and he wished for a child by her, said he would keep it, and so on. It was to me almost incredible, that a woman with such experience as she must have had, young as she was, should have believed all that. — But she did. Now he was supplying her with plenty of money, and

did not wish her to see any other man. His regiment was ordered to
●●●● and he could not see her for many months. I guessed how all ● ● ●
that would end, but attempted no more to destroy the happy illusion
she was under. — She was fond of the captain, poor thing. But what-
ever the captain might have been, or whatever her promises, it did
not prevent Amelia from fucking heartily with me. Her enjoyment
of my prick indeed got intense. She certainly ceased going to the
Argyle almost entirely.

I like to see all of a nice woman when I have once had her, and
altho I did not really care about her, got Mrs.A°t°n to a baudy
house, and passed about four hours with her there. Having made
several calls hoping to find Amelia out, and to have Mrs. A°t°n, I
failed in doing so. Difficulty in some cases increases desire, and it
was so with me now. I thought that I longed exceedingly to have
the woman, so wrote her, and slipped it into her hands when I
called, and told her where to write to me. She named a day, and
eleven o'clock in the morning. It is funny that the woman never
appeared to leave the house, I never found her out of it, or heard
of her going out, and she frequently was in the house alone. She
said one day that she never wanted to go out, which I believe to
have been a lie. I fancied she was hiding there, and feared to go
out, tho my reasons for that belief are not very strong.

Soon after eleven o'clock, there we were in a house (not my
favorite one) and ten minutes after that, she in chemise, I in shirt
were on the bed together. I inspected her charms which she seemed
a little modest about, she inspected mine, which pleased me much.
Now I looked out for the signs of childbirth. — She was absorbed
intensely in handling and contemplating my prick, when I began
the search. I was standing by the bed-side. Suddenly she relin-
quished my prick, and pushed down her chemise. By my investiga-
tions she was evidently taken unawares. "Don't. I don't like to be
pulled about so, don't," — said she very angrily. "You've had a child,
my dear." — "I haven't." — "Yes, I have just seen the marks." — "I
haven't, but what if I have?" — "Nothing, my dear." — "But I
haven't, I've had a miscarriage." — "How did that happen?" — "I
shan't tell you. — I'm sorry I've met you." — "Nonsense. It doesn't
matter to me if you have, or not." A fuck restored her temper.

I tried to get out of her when she'd been fucked first, but learnt

I expect nothing true. She'd been seduced, had been ruined by a
scoundrel who had promised to marry her, her career was gone.
She'd since had no other man but me. — How curious I was, did I
ask all the ladies I had such questions. She didn't want men for she
hated them. — Well! She did frig herself, if I wanted to know —
why shouldn't she, she must do something, naturally. — "Frig
Amelia?" — "Certainly not — she has quite enough of it without
doing that." — "Enough of what?" — She hesitated. "Well fucking,
there! — I knew you wanted me to say that word, and I've said it,
and do you feel any the better for it?" She was nasty, snappish, and
disliked being questioned. So I desisted, having come out for pleas-
ure, and not to annoy.

"I won't look at your belly," said I, after she had washed her
cunt, for that she insisted on doing quickly after I had spent in her,
and I wanted again to see her charms, for unless I am in bed for
the night, I nearly always look at a woman's cunt before each fuck.
I am indeed never tired of looking at a woman's hidden charms.
"Now, don't be nonsensical, you may pull your chemise down below
your navel, but I've seen all I want there," — and I pulled it down
myself. — "Now open your thighs wider — you did it on the sofa the
other night." — Open they went, for it makes some women lewed
to have it looked at. I had a good look at a cunt of the usual class,
a cunt of thirty, well haired and full lipped, nothing in it to call
either pretty or the reverse. But she was tawny skinned, there was
a slightly bilious, brown tint in her skin, just as there was in her
face. She was what may be called a dark skinned woman, which I
don't much admire, but fleshy and well proportioned. When I had
seen all this, and done my utmost in tailing her that morning, I was
satisfied, and never desired her again.

In the four hours, she kept me closely up to my work. She
wanted fucking more than I did, but I did it four times. She was
curious about my prick, and looked at it repeatedly. When I said
after my second poke, — "Let me look at you, open your thighs." —
"Let me look at *you* then," she said, and laughed. — Of course I let
her. I couldn't help thinking that really it was a long time since she'd
had a man, or she wouldn't have handled and looked at my prick
so much. She was like a young girl with it, and her hurry to let me
up her was undisguised. Yet as I had made up my mind from her

evasive replies to my questions that she was lying, I didn't care to think much about her, or whether she had been much or little fucked, or by one man or more.

She had come out that morning to buy a dress, she said, which I think was true. I tipped her, which I half fancied she didn't expect, and we parted as if we were acquaintances, and nothing more. — Nor did she make any signs of recognition or pleasure when I saw her again at Mrs. German. (This all took place, before Mrs. German told me she was in the family way.)

Some months elapsed during which I was much abroad, and I went a long voyage across the sea, which I omit telling here for the sake of continuing about Amelia. It was on my return that she told me she was in the family way and the particulars just given. Then I resumed sleeping with her, and did so at times for one or two months, till her belly began to get large. — After a while she got fretful and tearful, for her captain tho he sent her money and kind letters, said it would be long before he could see her again, that he had been found out, and had had an awful row with his governor about her. She began asking me if I thought he would do what he had said. How could I tell I replied when I only knew what she had told me. Then she said she was sure she could trust me, and showed me a bundle of his letters which I read, and saw he was cooling down. I did not like to add to her trouble by telling her that, but said if he didn't, she might perhaps sue him for a breach of promise, tho I didn't think she could — but that even comforted her.

I did not care about poking her with her big stomach, and left off calling much. She then went to the Argyle, as she said, only to divert herself. Whether she got friends there or not I didn't know, but she so managed to dress that there were no signs of the size of her belly. At the Argyle she came up to me one night directly she saw me (I had always told her never to notice me unless I made her a sign, it was my custom with all women). "I *must* speak with you," said she. "What do you think, I went home last night, and found my house-keeper had delivered herself of a seven month child, and it was dead, and was lying on the table wrapped up in a napkin, she was lying on the sofa fainting — what shall I do — the dead baby's there still." — I suggested calling in a doctor. She said she was frightened to do that. — "Perhaps she's killed it," I remarked. — She

was sure she didn't know, she hoped not — but Mrs. A°t°n wouldn't
reply, would tell nothing, wouldn't open her mouth. — There she
lay now in bed ill, only saying that she wouldn't have a doctor and
wished she was dead.

I could not assist her, but still advised a doctor. — She asked
me to go home with her and see Mrs. A°t°n. — I declined doing so
as long as the dead child was there. I could do no good, but would
be at the Argyle a few nights after.

A week after, Amelia told me the child was buried, and that it
was stillborn. That A°t°n was ill, and that she meant to send her off
directly she was better. A week after that she was gone, and I slept
with Amelia. She was mysterious about her companion, and said
she would never have believed that she would get into such a scrape
again. I asked no further questions, not wishing to know anything
more about the matter, but had my suspicions that the child was
born alive. — I never heard of A°t°n afterwards. — But I wonder
much at Amelia thinking that a woman who had once had fucking,
would go the rest of her life without it. — There were fresh servants
in the house soon after. If I had anything to do with begetting that
child, it could not have been more than five months old, but sup-
pose I had not.

But there is one thing I ought to have named before. I was very
salacious one night, and delighted much in the beauty and white-
ness of Amelia's form. She was, I think, in much the same condition
of lust. How exquisite is the pleasure, when a man and woman are
both lewed, and play erotic tricks together. Her belly had then
scarcely began to swell. I postponed consummating, and indulged in
many lewed preliminaries. I was fanciful in the highest degree, and
full of erotic inventions. — "Kneel over me dear, and let me see your
pretty cunt," and I moved into the middle of bed. She was naked
as she was born, for she had had her night-gown on ready to get
into bed with me, and I made her take it off. Laughing she placed
herself on her knees, straddling across me, her coral split slightly
opened by the position. I gazed with sensuous delight and stiff prick,
on the pretty light haired division, and fingered it, using at times
both hands at once. When doing so she put one of her hands behind
her bum and felt my cock. — "Oh — hah — isn't it stiff. — Oh, do
me." — "Not yet love, feel my prick again." — Kiss it, kiss, I'm so

lewed,"—said she, wriggling her thighs and buttocks, as well as a kneeling position permitted. "Come nearer then."—She moved on her knees more forward, they widened out as she came near my shoulders, and her cunt met my mouth. Rapturously I kissed it, then involuntarily put my hands round her smooth white buttocks, and pulled her closer to me. "Get lower down dear."—Her cunt covered my mouth, I put out my tongue and tickled her clitoris with it, then licked, then closed my lips on it, then licked it again. "Oh—oh, if you do that I shall spend. Oh—ohoooo,"—she said, and her cunt moved backwards and forwards, covering my mouth and my nose. For a moment I desisted, saying "Shall I gamahuche you, Mealy?"—"Oh, do—go on, do, I'm nearly spending," and her belly and backside shook with her lust.

I clasped her buttocks with both hands and put my tongue to her clitoris again. "Keep your cunt quiet when you spend" for in her pleasure just before, she had moved her cunt about so, that I lost the clitoris, my tongue went on to her vagina, and her clitoris rubbed my nose. I don't like my nose and my lips to be covered by a cunt. Then I licked and gently bit, and nibbled at her clitoris, till I felt her backside vibrating with pleasure, her whole cunt, spite of her, seemed to drop all over and cover my mouth, and with a sharp cry of pleasure the dear creature spent. "You never did that before to me," said she, when she laid by the side of me a minute or two afterwards.—"Do you like being gamahuched?"—"Yes, very much at times, but I want it done properly to me afterwards"—and properly it was done by me then in a few minutes.

Two or three times after that, the letch seized me for gamahuching her, and I always did it in that fashion. It was only done when she was hot cunted, when we had been talking libidinously, and when I had gone home with her after a good dinner. (For I had taken to give her dinners at °°°°, then not long opened.) I was not ashamed of her, for she dressed well and quietly, and tho there was an unmistakably voluptuous air about her, she scarcely looked like a gay woman, when away from a harlots' gathering. The gamahuching also was due to *her* incitement, more than my own suggestion. Her captain always did it to her, she told me when I questioned her. —"Yes—yes, once another has." And so on, till talking begat the want. Then she washed her cunt, and mounted to my mouth again.

And this is what I wrote then. It is better left as it is, than put into narrative form like the rest. "Licked Amelia's cunt last night, did I want to do it, or did she want me to do to her? I have done it to her several times, now don't like doing it, yet I do it. She seems to like it so. — Her frame as far as I can judge, lying under her cunt as I do, and seeing nothing, and only able to clasp her bum or her thighs, seems to thrill with a higher enjoyment than when she is fucked, and I like giving her pleasure for she deserves it, and she is so beautiful. But I want to wash my mouth and moustache directly after; whilst she says after a moment's repose only, "Go on, dear." But I don't like the taste, and eject my saliva both whilst doing it, and after it, till it runs down over my chin and I long to wash my mouth. Yet last night I gamahuched her long, without ejecting. But I do it as it seems to me through her talking about it. It is she who always begins talking about it first. I wonder whether Mrs. A°t°n did it to her. I half suspect it. I'll ask again. But why shouldn't she if they both like that fun?"

Again I was away from England. When I came back, she was very big and miserable. Her time was approaching for her confinement. The captain sent her money, but I saw from his letters (she insisted against my will on making a confidant of me) that he was cooling, and just before her accouchement, wrote to say he deeply regretted it, but there was no help for it, if he didn't, his Father would leave him nothing, he should be ruined, so he was going to be married. I saw her a few days after she received this letter, and in a sad state of distress she was. At one time she cried and said she loved him, the next moment cursed him. She had lost her good friends thro him, they would not visit her with her big belly, and now she should have a wretched child to keep, and much more. She raved about it, and her energy (in one habitually so placid) surprized me.

She had the child and luckily it died. But it nearly killed her in coming into the world, and I wonder if it was owing to that small opening. I shall write no more about it for this is not a history of Amelia German. She quite altered in appearance afterwards. I had other women, was much away, and only had her once or twice after she recovered from her confinement. Some months afterwards going to the Argyle, I met her and went home with her. She was then in lodgings, had lost her nice quiet manners, and was a flaunting vulgar whore. I was sorry for it. Suddenly she disappeared, no women whom I asked could tell about her, they hadn't seen her anywhere for a long time, was all I got from the sisterhood.

[For the reason that by naming either the season of the year, or the exact spots visited, clue may be given to identity, so both are omitted. For similar reasons, the narrative of some adventures, tho carefully written, will be destroyed. Unfortunately, soon after they occurred, I made them the subject of conversation at my clubs, and told some of the incidents to friends and relatives. To repeat them here would be to declare myself, and others still alive. So to the flames they go — how many, many pages of manuscript have been so destroyed.]

Sarah's jealousy. — Her ballet posturings. — My postures. — An escape of wind. — Wheelbarrow fashion. — A young lass suggested. — Harriet, sweet sixteen. — Financial arrangements. — Doctor H°°m°°d again. — Tooth brush and tooth powder. — Virginity doubtful. — Harriet screwed, unscrewed, and opened. — A tight vagina. — Sarah's strange behaviour. — Three in a bed. — Harriet jealous. — Runs away. — The baudy-house with spyhole closed. — On the size of my prick and others. — On the capacity, elasticity, and receptivity of cunts.

When I went back to Sarah, she was surprized at the length of my absence, and thought she had lost me. She was spiteful, as gay ladies are when they have missed their man and their money. I expect she had begun to regard me as a regular source of income.

We went to the peep hole and for one or two evenings had various amatory frolics, and then I made a discovery about Sarah.

She had surprised me by the ease with which she posed in difficult, lewed, and odd attitudes that I put her in. — This evening we had been sitting drinking, and she was larkish. I remarked the ease with which she attitudinized. — She laughed and got up. "Look here then." — She threw off her chemise, put up one leg nearly to the level of her shoulder, and placing the tip of the toe against the wall so as to rest it, inclined her body downwards towards the floor with her hand touching it. — It *was* a sight. Her cunt was gaping, showing the broadest red face which a cunt can show with-

422

out being pulled open by fingers, the dark thick hair shewing all around it, until lost at her bumhole. The thicket in one armpit was quite visible, and all this was seen at a glance. — I went on my knees to look at her split, and put my finger on it in baudy ecstasy.

She stood upright and I begged her to do it again. — "Look, I don't think I can do it now but will try." Throwing up her leg, she caught hold of the toe with her hand, then pulling it higher and higher, she turned round and round on her left foot. It was a quite fresh view of the cuntal territory. The dark fringed lips were now not open, but were slightly squeezed together, yet made prominent. The red stripe was scarcely perceptible but the lips shewed the crimson beginning, and a peep of the arse valley was got. The sight was entrancing, and in a minute hurrying her to the bed, I plugged her cunt. She was in rare lewed mood and soon spent. I had that night pissed against her cunt, and we now both spent together lusciously.

"I am as randy as be damned," said she. "I always am just before my month — fuck me again."

We sat down after our exercise. Said I, "You must have been a dancer." She laughed. — "Did you never see me before you met me in the street?" "Never." "Are you sure?" "I think so." "Did you ever see the play of °°° at Covent Garden!" "Yes." "Ah. Then you saw *me*. — I used to dance in it." Then I drew from her that she had been a figurante — but never learnt why she left the theatre. She did not mean to go on again — altho she could if she wished. — "There are reasons, I'm not going to tell if you ask me all night."

In the attitudes then she placed herself again, then danced naked, and postured as the ballet dancers do. — "Come and hold me so, and so — take off your shirt." — I did. — Then she placed me so as to hold her in various attitudes, as men hold female dancers in ballets. — There were we naked before a large glass. — She in attitudes exposing her backside and cunt, — I now with stiff prick holding her. — Sometimes she held by my prick. — Soon after posing in a few attitudes she again got my pego into her cunt, and again afterwards till I was fucked out. — She was hot that night. This was at the baudy house with the glasses.

I went away delighted. — Thought I, some fellows would give no end of money to see her. How often since I have wished as I saw the ballet dancers cocking up this leg, or throwing out that,

that their drawers were away and I could see their quims. — Now it must be wide stretched, now what a sight it would be. — I fucked a ballet girl some years ago as I think I have told, but perhaps that is one of the narratives omitted in order to shorten this history, but that was for the pleasure of fucking thro a cut I made in her tights. I think I have told this but am not sure. She for a minute or two had pirouetted, but I only had with her a momentary amusement. — But now I have a fine limbed woman who can do it all, and will do it when I like — so I thought on.

A night after when I wanted her to posture naked she refused. — We had words, I paid her, and to her astonishment went away without fucking her. Again I met her and asked her. Again she would not, and again away I went. — The third time she said she would posture a little, and so to the A°°a we went.

When indoors she refused, was sorry she had ever "shown off so," wondered how she came to be such a fool as to let out about herself. "Champagne and lewedness did it, Sarah." — As she still refused, I put down the money and was going away, when, "Don't go without poking me, I'll do it." — Twenty minutes afterwards, altho sulkily, there she was, one toe against a metal shelf, I naked with cock upright — now looking at her gaping quim, now peeping under her buttocks, now looking at the reflection of our naked bodies in the glasses. I made her throw up her leg and catch the toe, and as with an effort she did so, out slipped a little fart. — "There," said she, "I swear I will never do it again," and she wouldn't that night. — I fucked her and left her in the sulks.

I would not go with her again until she promised, and soon her posturing was part of my evening's amusement. We used to attitudinize before the looking glass, laugh at our postures, and say what money men would give to see us two naked together. — I dare say rich men have induced ballet girls to do as much, but more they could not; and I was fortunate to have had such voluptuous entertainments so cheaply.

Then I fucked her wheelbarrow fashion. I have tried that, I think, with other women but am not sure. It seemed now a novelty. With Sarah's long limbs I could accomplish it well. She put pillows on the floor for her head and arms to rest on. I sat myself at the side of the bed naked. She was naked also, put her legs gradually up on to the bed, one on each side of my haunches, then I held her legs at the proper level. It was a beautiful sight to see her bum gradually coming up. The buttocks' furrow only shewing a little at first, and then the dark hair, thick and curly on the sides of her cunt, coming into sight, and between it the red gap. Then I leaned back for a few seconds in admiration, pulling open the bum cheeks, and burying my finger in the red lane. — Then pressing down my prick, which resisted elastically, being moved out of its perpendicular, I inserted it in her cunt and drove it home, passing my hands under her thighs, shoving and exciting her to the crisis. My senses recovered, I sat down on the bed again, keeping my doodle as close into her cunt as I could, and passing one hand round to her belly felt her clitoris, till my prick came out of its pool, and the lascivious junction was over.

This was very exciting, but as a fuck the position is inferior in pleasure to many attitudes. The man's prick is bent down, the clitoris end of the cunt loses its friction. The woman's posture with both her hands and head down low is fatiguing. If they both spend there is no repose after the emission, and the tranquil, languid pleasure which follows the active ramming, ballocks wagging, bum wriggling, twisting, and after squeezing, is lost.

I had not thought anything more about little unfledged cunts, was satisfied for the time, I suppose, with my past amusement with deaf little Emma. I went then once or twice to Sarah's lodgings. She let me in herself for she didn't always keep a little servant, but had often only a charwoman. — There I made her do a little fantastic fucking, as well as posturing, when the following occurred.

I suppose that having got money by supplying me with a youthful virgin, she wanted another bonus, and became the temptress. She said one night when I met her out and stopped only to have a chat that she'd just got such a nice young maid, would I have her? — My letch for youthful quims was, I suppose, smouldering, and it at once blew up into flame. I asked the price and agreed to pay as before, *if the girl was virgin.* But there was difficulty about the virginity, for the girl was quite sixteen, had had her courses for some time, and had been in service. Sarah thought she was virgin, but knew she couldn't deceive *me* — would I go and see her? She gave an inciting account of her nice looks, and as she was at a charming age, an age at which I had had of late years few, my women having been either younger or much older, I arranged to go and have a look at the girl.

I was to be Doctor H°°m°°d again, Sarah indeed always now called me Doctor — I went and saw a tall, thin, bright looking, dark eyed, dark haired girl, who looked quite sixteen. Her eyes flashed as she spoke, and I said that I fancied she knew a prick from a rolling pin. — Said Sarah, "I never knew a girl who was sixteen who didn't, girls who have nursed their brothers have seen a prick stiff, even if they haven't stiffened them — but she is worth a poke whether she's had one before or not, tho I believe if she had been poked, that she wouldn't come to me." She had done her best. — "She may never have been poked, even altho she may not give you trouble to get up her." — I made up my mind at once that the girl was not virgin.

Sarah was for my getting it over soon if it was to be done. *She* was not going to hide her being gay from the girl, as she had from the deaf girl at first, had already told her how she got her living, and that a good easy living it was. This girl's name was Harriet. If I wanted to be sure that she was intact, making her drunk and looking was the way. Sarah would help me, but the sooner the better. It was of no use keeping her if I did not want her. — She did not want a good looking girl there. "Afraid of Mr. F°°z°r?" Perhaps she was, but that did not matter to me, Sarah said snappishly.

The girl was told I was the doctor to Sarah and I once used to *"Do her over"* (her usual term) — but now tho I came to see her as doctor, I never fucked her, but I talked freely, baudily, and never charged for my medical services, I was an odd but good man.

The girl I found answered perfectly to Sarah's description of her. Her flashing dark eyes had an unusually soft expression in them. A sweet expression of lewedness and voluptuousness, which some girls have just after their first menstruations have settled down to the exact monthly period, leaving them fresh tinted, soft skinned, and ready to receive the love of man. — This struck me to be the case with Harriet, who I think came from one of the outer suburbs of London, but somehow I was never as curious to verify this impression, or to learn anything about her, as I have been about some women.

In a day or two I was again at Sarah's lodgings. — "Do you mind Harriet sitting in this room? There is no fire in the bedroom." "No." I did not. The girl then sat down at needlework, I sent her for brandy and wine, giving her the change. We all drank, and the girl quickly enough. Sarah went into the bedroom. Whilst absent, after joking the girl I pinched her bum. She cried out. Sarah came in. — "What's the matter." "The gentleman's pulling me about." "Lord, I thought he was kicking your arse you make such a noise." The girl opened her mouth wide, stared, and sat down confused. — We laughed. I said I should like to kiss Harriet's and not kick it, I was sure it was as pretty as her face.

Presently I went behind her, putting my hand under her chin, kissed her and noticed then that she had good teeth, but not too clean. "You have a nice set of teeth, but you don't clean them." "My brush is worn out, Sir."

"Let me see your teeth better." She resisted. "Don't be a fool," said Sarah, "let the Doctor see your teeth." When I had done so, "Here," said I. "Go to the chemist, buy a toothbrush and a box of tooth powder as quickly as you can." Off she went — I never could bear any woman with dirty teeth.

I had given her five shillings. She was back in five minutes, and pleased enough — especially when I told her to keep the change. — She opened the box to look inside at its contents standing close by the lamp. I was standing with my rump to the fire smoking. "When that is gone I will give you more — clean your teeth every morning and night, and in a week your mouth will be as sweet as your cunt, just after you have washed it."

The girl dropped the box, spilling the contents over the table —stared at me for a second — turned her back, burst out laughing, checked it, and rushed into the bedroom. Sarah cried out, "Damn you, you careless little beast, you've spoilt my table cloth," and fetched her back. "It's no use minding the Doctor." The girl got up the tooth powder, I threw half a crown to Sarah, saying, "It was my fault, black-cunt, and that will help to clean the cloth."

It's too long to tell all, but I kept up that style of talk, and got the girl to sit by the fire with us, her mistress saying, "Come if he wishes it, he always has his way here." And I talked baudy enough to have turned a clergyman's hair grey. The girl's eyes from shunning at length looked at me, Sarah kept telling her not to mind me — not to be a fool — that she must hear men talk so some day. Perhaps she had already, I thought.

I asked her questions which a medical man might. When she did not reply, Sarah rebuked her. "What can it matter to *him* — you might be ill some day, and want him."

As I got heated by wine and the look of the girl, I promised her money for boots and stockings provided she would let me put them on. "Take the money — don't be such a fool — take it," said Sarah.

I took my leave, saying, "Dark hair, and dark eyes just like Sarah — I wager your cunt hair is dark like Sarah's." The girl blushed and did not reply. "It is black," said Sarah laughing. "I have seen it."

The girl became so quiet that I began to think she had heard such talk before — but her manner afterwards convinced me she was not accustomed to it.

I saw Sarah next night in the street. "We'll make her drunk and look at her cunt tomorrow night," said she. — But we were baulked, for the girl's menstruation came on, and we deferred the job. But I asked the girl all about her courses, as a doctor might. She gave me plain but modest answers. By the time her monthlies were over, she had ceased to evade my questions even when baudy. When Sarah laughed, the girl did so altho uneasily — four or five nights' smutty talk were breaking down her modesty.

Then Sarah told me she had shown her my baudy book and advised me to bring another, and we arranged that when she was tight, Sarah should go out and I should examine her cunt and do what I pleased.

I had taken quite a different liking to this girl from that which I had for the deaf one, who was like a child, and whom I desired because she was so. But Harriet, more than a year older, had made me feel lewed in a different sense. — It was the charm of getting into a very young woman, whose passions were getting roused by nature and quickened by me. — She was not so young as I had wished, but young enough to be a pleasurable novelty. Tho I don't know really what can be called very novel to me in the way of women and the manner of playing with them.

One evening behold me at the house. Wine and brandy and water was had. It was a cold night and we sat facing the fire. —

Baudiness was on, altho we had not planned what to say, but it
was to be enough to stimulate the girl's lust to the highest, and
after having made her either screwed enough to permit me to do
anything with her, I was to look at her virginity, or for it, and fuck
it out of her if she had got it as best I might. I did not like this
business, tho I consented to it, as I have before in my career.

"Come and sit here," said I to the girl. "It's cold there." —
She did, and we were all three in front of the fire, I in the middle.
I gave her two glasses of wine without much effect. Sarah winked
at me, half filled a tumbler with boiling water and lots of sugar and
brandy. It was as strong as the devil but the sweetness disguised it.
—"Here Harriet, take a good drop." She gulped it, Sarah and I took
a little, then again the girl took large gulps. Soon her eyes bright-
ened, and she giggled in the way girls are often affected, at the
beginning of a lush, and before the stupid stage comes on.

Then Sarah raised her own petticoats to her knees, to let the
warmth of the fire reach her bum, as the most modest woman will
do if by herself, or with her female friends, or husband, present.
"Let me see your new stockings and boots," said I, for I had given
the money for them. She hesitated. "Shew them to the Doctor."
The girl let me raise her petticoats to her knees, showing a thinnish
but neat pair of legs.

I praised and stroked them. "Keep the petticoats up like your
mistress, you see she likes the fire to get to her cunt." "Oho," said
the girl, dropping the clothes. Sarah laughed — "I like to warm my
cunt. What do you drop your clothes for, you little fool." I pulled
up her clothes again, she let me, and we had more brandy and
water. Then I felt Sarah's thighs, then gradually felt the girl's thighs.
— "I don't care — *there*," said Sarah in answer to me, and she pulled
up her clothes quite to her navel, put one leg up against the chim-
ney-piece and, half turning round in her chair, shewed her cunt.
"I like my cunt looked at — like it fucked — you've seen and fucked
it many a time, haven't you, Doctor?"

Harriet stared, said "Oho!" and giggled, but resisted me, who
was now trying hard to feel her. She was gradually getting screwed,
and her resistance grew less as I insisted.

Then Sarah pulled out my prick, I felt Sarah's cunt, got Harriet
on to my knees, and felt all about her limbs, and then was a con-

fusion of baudy deeds and baudy talk. Sarah rose, winked at me, said she must go out, and in a minute had gone — I locked the door.

Harriet seated herself in Sarah's arm chair, I dropped on my knees, throwing up her petticoats, and saw that she had slight blackish hair at the bottom of her belly. I pushed between her legs and pulled them round me, and that brought her bum to the edge of the chair, and my prick which I had pulled out just touched her cunt. With a cry she got back, but she being in a sitting position, easily I pulled her to me again, my stiff prick now touching her thighs. She was now laughing a drunken laugh. "Feel my prick," said I, putting down her hand. — "Oh! oh!" said she trying to do so as if delighted. "It's my prick," said I. "Yes," she answered.

"Let me fuck you — come to the bed." "Oh, no! I can't." — "Have you ever been fucked — wouldn't you like it." She giggled, and had just sense enough left not to answer. I had now my hand between her thighs, was fumbling at her cunt, and she did not resist.

Then I got up, sat on a chair, pulled her on to my lap, held her back, and putting my prick in her hand felt her cunt, and kissing her said, "Let me fuck you." I got no answer, but she kissed me, grasping my cock. — Her eyes closed. — Saying "oh — don't sir, — oh don't" — in a thick stammering manner. "Did not you hear what Mrs. F°°z°r said." "Oh, yes," and she held my cock so tight that she hurt me. Sarah had not left ten minutes.

I led her to the bedroom and without resistance got her on to the bed. There was a candle left alight. — Partly by gentle force and partly by entreaty, I got up her clothes and separating her legs tried to look at her cunt. She tried to rise and I pushed her back. Her head fell on the pillow. I lugged her to the side — "Don't — don't" — forced apart her legs and pulled open her cunt lips. — Drunk as she was, she resisted enough to make my look uncertain, but I saw that it was an opened split. Passion then vanquished me, I forgot my object in looking, her flesh looked so nice, the slight hair on the pretty little pouters made me beside myself — putting her straight on the bed again, I covered her without resistance, unconsciously she wanted fucking. The next instant my prick was lodged at the entrance.

"Oh you hurt — oh you mustn't — oh pray," was all she said.

I felt I had broken thro nothing, no obstacle had met me, yet I seemed to make but very little way. Thrust after thrust, further I entered yet but slowly. At length I was up it to its top and spending. A tight fit and no mistake if it was not a virginity. — Beyond "Oh! oh! don't" — not very loud, she had given no utterance of pain, and by the time my prick could go no further, and my balls were banging against her buttocks, she was quiet.

I had spent too excitedly, was she or was she not virgin? The thought was working. With prick up her still, I rose on my elbow to look at her and put my hand down to feel her cunt. By the light of the solitary candle, I could see no blood on my fingers. Just then she opened her eyes. "Oh I am so ill — I shall be sick, get away, sir, let me get up," said she in incoherent tones, and began to retch. I pulled out my prick, and with my shirt tail wiped the whole face of her cunt. Then I raised her up and got her a basin, into which she vomited. — "Oh my head, I am so ill." She kept moaning, I got her warm water and made her drink it, which brought up the remainder of the liquor. Then she fell back and fell asleep.

I looked at my shirt tail on which were spots of sperm, but no blood — I doubted if she were a virgin and resolved not to pay Sarah. Looking at her made me lewed again — I lifted her clothes and looked at her cunt, pulling wide apart her thighs, then put my finger up it — never had I felt anything so tight, even as the sperm rolled out round my finger. The little deaf one's cunt was loose by comparison. — Soon I mounted her, then she awakened but let me do what I liked. Again my prick went up inch by inch through her slimy tube, so tight was it, and enjoying it I consummated slowly. Stupid as she was, my prick roused her passions and she spent. She awakened to it, and gasped like a fish out of water.

Indeed I never saw a girl more agitated but in a peculiar way when spending. The majority of young ones are so quiet about it. But this girl's mouth opened, her eyes turned up till nothing but the white was visible, her lips quivered, and the next instant she seemed asleep. She had spent, but scarcely seemed to know it. Sarah just then came in and I told that she was not a virgin and should not be paid virginity price.

"I believe she is virgin, for all that — did you ever have a girl of that age with such a little quim?" "How do you know that," said

I. "I have seen it." "When?" Then came an account of doings which I have heard similarly before, and I believe it is much the way in which the elder female usually proceeds, when she wishes to seduce the younger.

Talking the night before with the girl about fucking, she had excited her by all the means in her power. — The girl, curious and finding her mistress so communicative, asked if it hurt at first, and was told sometimes, but so little as to be a mere imagination. That many women it didn't hurt in slightest degree, and that she could tell by looking at her cunt if it would hurt *her* or not. — That and the offer to show Harriet her own cunt settled the matter. She had shown the girl hers, and had looked at the girl's. Sarah admitted that she had not seen what is usually a virginity, but was nevertheless sure if the girl had been fucked with a prick of the ordinary size her cuntal opening could not be as small as it was. "If you fuck her much, I'll bet her cunt gets much easier."

"You must like looking at cunts." Sarah said she did, at the cunts of girls who had never had it, but — "I did at Harriet's for your sake as well as my own, for I want the money."

But I wouldn't pay but half, with which she was not at all contented. I was in fact angry and under the impression that she had tried to sell me. I liked my girl — there was a genuine freshness about her, yet at times I thought the girl was shamming. Why did Sarah hide her being gay from the first young lass, and ostentatiously proclaim it to this one? I afterwards thought. The game for this one was clearly not the same as for the other. But why when she knew that the hymen was not there, did she not tell me? Because she thought I shouldn't find it out. — "You are a downy card," said Sarah. "For all that I believe that the girl never has had a man put into her, don't let's quarrel, I'll send her away."

I did not want that and said I should have her again. — This conversation took place whilst Harriet was snoring on the bed with two spermatic libations up her. Sarah spiteful about the half fee said she'd wake the girl — was I not going? No, I would hear. Sarah did not seem to wish that. — To the bedroom we went. "To think of that little devil having been fucked," said Sarah, as she looked at her. Shaking Harriet, the girl sat up bewildered — the fume of the liquor still strong in her. "What are you doing on my bed?" said Sarah. Rubbing her eyes — "I don't know — Oh my head — Oh, I'm so ill." "Why, you have made a mess on my bed." "Oh I couldn't help it, I am so ill." "You have been on the bed with the Doctor — he has fucked you, you little bitch." No reply. "Hasn't he fucked you?" No reply. Another shaking, and the girl began to sob. "Hasn't he fucked you?" "I don't know." "You do, your clothes were up. — Hasn't he?" "I think so, but I don't know." "He has, and I will turn you out."

"Oh — Oh — Oh don't — you told me to let him do what he liked — Oh my head." "Yes, but I did not think you'd let him fuck you, at your age you little beast — how often did he do it?" "I don't know," said she blubbering. Then suddenly, "Oh don't hit me, I am going to be sick again" — and she went to the basin and retched.

It seemed cruel work — the tears and pain the poor girl was in. "It's my fault," said I. "Oh here he is," said the girl. "Tell mistress it arn't my fault." Sarah laughed. — "How often has he done it to you?" "I don't know. I was asleep. Oh don't let her turn me away sir, I am so comfortable here." — "I should think you are," said Sarah, "and to let him fuck you." "You told me to let him do any-thing." "I meant if he wanted to kiss you, and put his hand up your petticoats, and feel you — but who'd have thought of your letting him fuck you, at your age, you little beast." "I could not help it — Oh!" — and she tumbled back on to the bed.

We went into the sitting room, and saying that I meant to have the girl again I departed. The next night I was at Sarah's and, making no bones about the matter, said I wanted Harriet in the bedroom. Said Sarah, "It's funny, you come to see *me*, and yet want my servant, Doctor. — Well if you will, I suppose you must." The girl wouldn't come, so I pulled her gently into the bedroom.

I was thoroughly lewed, she sullen, had taken medicine, and what with that, the night before, and only having slept a drunken sleep, she gave so much trouble when I wished to look at her cunt, that I called in Sarah. — "You little fool," said she — "when a man has fucked you, you may let him do anything — let him see your cunt or anything else," and away she went.

The girl yielded. At the side of the bed, thighs distended, I opened her cunt whilst I held a candle to it.

Her love seat was that of a girl of full sixteen, an age at which I have seen but few. It looked long and delicate but with unusually pouting lips for her age. A strongish clitoris shewed and nymphæ full and thicker than usual. — Clitoris and nymphæ in fact, were much more developed than is usual in girls. (I wonder if that be a sign of a warm temperament.) The channel of coition was unusually small at the mouth, and I fancied looked as if it had been just torn or stretched at its upper part. — Was it that her hymen had only been partially destroyed, or stretched and opened, and had I completed the stretching? — Altho the membrane with a *small* hole was not visible when I first saw it, was there a membrane with a *large* hole? In the excitement of my first look and hurried fuck, I now could not be sure. She had a very full mons or mount with short thick hair but small in quantity on it, close to the top of the nick, and but a little way only down the lips. Altogether tho unusual in appearance, it was a pretty and libidinous looking, exciting cunt. There is a physiognomy in cunts, some are prettier than others, some more exciting to look at than others, tho it is difficult to say what it is in the appearance which excites in one more than in the other.

Tho I couldn't discern signs of hymenal rupture, on my putting two fingers up it she called out. Then lust stirred me to action, and pushing her on to the bed I entered her. Its feel was the same as on the previous night, and she said I hurt her. For about three hours I pulled her cunt about, for in her way she was a novelty. The deaf girl was a full grown child who would talk and fuck but not always spend. This girl was bursting with randiness, her young lusts were on with all their force. She soon took delight in everything I said or did, all was new to her, her lustful sensations were even new to her.

The look of a prick, the feel of its smooth skinned rigidity, its friction and lubricating overflow were all new to her, I believe absolutely new, spite of the absence of a hymen. So she took to all the preliminaries and exercises of love with delight and with the eagerness and ardour of a hot cunted one. I had not been deceived in my first impression about her. She was dying for the juice of the male, restless with lewed sensations, in the springtide of her lust, and under the urging of sexual curiosity — I had just caught her in time, and she with me revelled for weeks in unrestrained lasciviousness. If I had not had her, some one would. The first man who had kissed and fondled her might have felt her cunt, she couldn't have helped letting him; and once felt she would have let him do anything. Her warm nature was commanding her to surrender her person to the male. She was dying for a prick.

I took a fancy with her· (I always have some special fancy with each woman) to lay in bed both of us start naked. Thin as she was I somehow liked this — tho why I am unable to say. How give reasons for any letch? There in clean sheets which I made Sarah provide (and indeed bought one new pair) we used to indulge in lewedness. Her slim young form pleased me much, and naked I used to cover her, or put her on the top of myself — fuck her belly to belly, or to bum, till I was satiated. These varied postures test whether the female is a hack or a greenhorn. If accustomed to salacity they fall into them readily, and in a way which cannot hide their knowledge whatever innocence they may allege, whilst the neophytes show an astonishment and quiet delight not easy to imitate and deceive. — "You can't do it so, Doctor." "Yes, we can try — see — there" — was said more than once during my varied performances with Harriet.

I had her frequently for more than two months, and it is certain that the mouth of the vagina, the site of the hymen, got bigger. Whether it stretched or split I can't say — but easier for my prick to enter, it certainly got. Inside it remained a tight sheath to my penis, tho quite elastic, and perhaps large enough for the greatest male cunt stretcher. I incline to think she never had a true hymen, or had broken it early in life, leaving a larger orifice than is usually found before male penetration. — I used to fancy that the mouth of the prick hole had opened gradually more at the top than elsewhere, but cannot pretend to assert that it was so. She told me that when about nine years old, she and another girl, a schoolfellow, used to push their fingers up each other's cunt. At all events I came to the conclusion that a prick had never been up her till she had mine.

Sarah, after I had once or so had Harriet, used to go out leaving us together, first asking me if I wished her to stay. She felt sure of her double pay and wished to make a little more out of doors — I often let her go. If she returned before I had left, she would tell me before Harriet if she had had a man — or two — or none, as the case might be; but she didn't any longer use baudy language before the girl, altho she had done so freely until I had fucked her.

— Then she grew impatient about keeping her. Hadn't I done with her. — "Take her away and keep her, I can't have her here much longer. She won't work, and it won't do to have a charwoman in whilst she is here."

It is one of the charms of life that the pleasures of women never tire. When weary of one, I change and all old pleasures come fresh again. — One woman you may best like to fuck on her belly — another with her bum to your belly, another to grope, then one to frig, then one to gamahuche. It is rarely that the entire round is equally pleasurable with one. — When I change, almost forgotten pleasures revive. So it certainly is with me. — With fresh cunt not only comes fresh courage, but fresh amusements. The variety depends on the difference in the sexual make and tastes of the woman, for all women cannot fuck so well in the same fashions. They also like men, have when their passions are fully evoked their own lascivities and letches. — The man who is well versed in amorous games, is sure to hit on that fashion of fucking which is best suited to both. This is most true of modest women, but in larger degree of gay women. — "Men are fond of variety, I like to see what a new man wants to do with me," said Sarah one night when we were talking.

One night Sarah was in the sitting room, I in bed with Harriet with my finger up the tight little cunt, when I thought I should like to feel Sarah's cunt. — I jumped out of bed and to the astonishment of Harriet brought in Sarah and made her get naked into bed. I laid between them and quickly had a middle finger up each cunt. Then I put my prick into one after the other and probed alternately, comparing size and feel, and discoursing on the effects of age, growth, and fucking combined, in enlarging and stretching a pudenda. However large a cunt it may be, it mostly sufficiently compresses the prick to make it spend. — Few exceptionally large cunted ones I have however known in this particular.

Harriet, who used to nestle up to me and feel my balls incessantly, asking many questions about fucking, and so on, was now quiet altho I did not then notice it. — Soon I thought I would fuck Sarah, and got on to her, she nothing loath. "I think it's time I had a turn," she said, after I had put my prick in her. I wanted to compare, so out I pulled it and got on to the little one, who had turned her bum towards us. When I had a few thrusts up her, then again

I put into Sarah, who was in a mood for pleasure, and we had a very voluptuous fuck. The girl had again turned her rump towards me.

I tried to pull her round — but she resisted, got out of bed, and ran into the other room start naked as she was. — "What's the little devil up to?" — said Sarah, who, also quite naked, followed her. — I went after them and there were we all start naked in the parlour. The girl wouldn't come back and made no reply. Sarah boxed her ears. — I swore. "You've done it to her," said Harriet. "You little bitch what of that," said Sarah. "He has a right, he would do it to me often if he had not seen you, blast you. You'll go out of my house, you shan't keep here." The young one was jealous, which was funny, and it both annoyed and amused me.

Sarah was slightly screwed, let out finely, and it took an hour to get things to rights again. Then in bed I began in Sarah and finished up Harriet, which terminated the night's amusement. I have had before a young girl, who grew ridiculously jealous of her mistress when I fucked her. — It was now late spring and light at nights, which interfered with my going to Sarah's lodgings. Then I went out of town and when I returned the girl was gone — Sarah said she had run away, that she would not work, was always frigging herself, and thought herself as good as her mistress. They had had words and the girl had bolted one night, taking her things with her. — I offered Sarah money to get her back. She said she tried, tho I don't believe she did. I never saw the girl again. — "I'm glad she's gone, for she is in the family way," said Sarah. "I don't believe it." "She is, she'd her courses on just before you had her, and hasn't since." "It's some other man." "None other has had her I'll swear." Had I done the trick again?

Some where about this time I went to the peep hole one day and found it closed. Perhaps as the baud once said to me it had been "blown upon." She may have caused that herself, may have slain the goose with the golden egg. It paid well, we began to find difficulty in getting the room, it was so often engaged. Too many knew of it evidently, and it no doubt was "blown upon."

Its rooms were arranged cleverly in every way, for the purpose of spying the temporary occupants of the back room; who whatever they did, and nearly wherever they placed themselves, could not escape observation, nor the glare of the gas which seemed to concentrate upon them. The partition at the peephole could not have been three quarters of an inch thick, so wide was the range of vision through it over the room. It was, I think, thicker in other parts, but we could hear well usually thro it. The way the hole was bored thro a dark spot in the pattern of the wall paper, the cork which filled the hole was colored to match, the way the pictures on each side could be raised and lowered, were all most cleverly managed. The house in a bye street which had but little traffic of any sort had only noise outside about every five minutes, and excepting then, we heard fairly the talk in the back room. It was not a swell bagnio, tho, and had but five available rooms. [I have since seen an equally well arranged house at Paris, where every word said by the performers could be heard, and everything seen.]

What I saw through the peephole had one special consequence. It satisfied me that my prick was a full sized one, and well beyond the average rather than less. — Out of a hundred which I saw, there were not as far as I could judge twenty larger than mine, and Sarah said there were not ten. I saw one or two Brobdingnagians, perfect battering rams, but the largest of all was the titanic shaft of the man who whacked Sarah's buttocks with it and knocked it hard on the table as well, tho its big plum shaped, swollen head was bare of foreskin, and was carmine with lust. Sarah said his was the largest she had ever seen, and that talking with others of her class who had also seen it, they were all of the same opinion.

But tho for some reason Sarah would not take that titanic, potential machine into her body, and tho I saw some Paphians' handle other Brobdingnagian tools hesitatingly and affect to think them too big, say they would hurt, and so on; they one and all *did* insert them in their cunts, and as it seemed to me with pleasure. I believe there never was a prick so big in any way that a cunt could not take it without pain, and even pleasurably. Its tip might perhaps knock at the portals of the womb too hard for some, but that is all. I have heard women say that the harder those knocks were the more pleasure it gave them. All the talk I have heard of pricks being so large that women could not, or would not, take them up them is sheer nonsense. Several women have told me so. Some said that they loved to see and handle big ones. None said that such stretchers gave them more physical pleasure than those of moderate size. The elasticity and receptivity of a cunt is in fact as wonderful as its constrictive power. The small prick of a boy of thirteen it will tighten round and exhaust, as well as one as big as the spoke of a cartwheel, and it will give pleasure to both equally.

Recherché eroticisms. — An outcome of the brothel spyhole. — An abnormal letch. — A man for a month. — Alone with him. — Mutual nervousness. — The ice broken. — Pricks produced. — An exiguous tool. — Unavailing masturbation. — Sarah's participation. — Cuntal incitation. — Prompt rigidity. — Onanistic operation. — Spermatic ejaculation. — Instantaneous copulation. — One on and one off. — A gorged cunt. — Masculine minetting. — A gristly mouthful. — Sucking cum fucking. — After supper. — Sarah's oration. — The end of the orgy.

Then took place the crowning act of my eroticism, the most daring fact of my secret life. An abnormal lust of which I have been ashamed and sorry, and the narrative of which I have nearly destroyed, tho according to my philosophy, there was and is no harm in my acts, for in lust all things are natural and proper to those who like them. There can be no more harm in a man feeling another's prick, nor in a woman feeling another's cunt, than there is in their shaking hands. — At one time or other all have had these sexual handlings of others, yet a dislike to myself about this sexual whim still lingers. Such is the result of early teaching and prejudices.

Twenty-four years had elapsed since my frolics with the first Camille. — Then I had frigged a Frenchman. Then I did the same with the man that big eyed Betsy got me. Then I'd felt the Captain in the dark at Lizzie M°°°d°n's. Since that I had not touched a male. What I witnessed through the baudy house partition put new inclinations into my head. The handsome pricks which I had seen women play with, the ease with which their doodles were handled, the ready way a girl brought a rebellious prick to stand and spend by coaxing it up in her mouth, etc., raised again desire to feel and

440

play with a prick myself. Other men's seemed different to *me*, and at times I said this to Sarah in some such terms as these. — "I should like for once to feel a man's prick, to see closely his prick standing, see his spunk come out much or little." And so on.

The baudy house sights always terminated in fucking Sarah, and then for a time the desires which arose during my peeping ended abruptly. I talked about them at times when lewed nevertheless with Sarah, who said, "One man's prick stands and spends much like another, play with your own, but if you want, I can get one easily enough, and I'll let him come here for you, if Mr. F°°z°r is out of town."

But I thought she meant a fellow who let out his rump and prick, and of that class I had an insufferable dislike and fear. They were I had heard thieves, their pricks used up, and I wanted nothing to do with an anus [at that time, not having found out the pleasure you both take and give by pressing the bumhole of a woman when fucking her] so for some months, altho she described some men as eligible, I would not see them.

At length in the winter she said, "My old woman (a crone who did her charring, and was in fact her servant altho she did not sleep in her rooms) can get a young man about twenty who's not a sod — he is a working man who has been without employment for two months and will be glad of a sovereign." I thought I was going to be sold, but as I had only promised her a sovereign for getting me a man, I came to the conviction that I had really a chance, so arranged that he was to go to her rooms.

But unpleasant notions came. A poor man! he will be dirty and smelling of sweat — be rough — his linen ragged. — To get over that Sarah said, "Give me a sovereign, he shall have a new shirt, and socks, and drawers, I will buy them" — so I gave that money.

The evening came. I felt so nervous and even shocked at myself that I wished I had never undertaken the affair. — It was in vain that I argued with myself, and spite of my conviction that there was no harm in my doing it, when I came to her door I nearly turned back. I had been trying to strengthen my intention by thinking over my former wishes and curiosities, of the various amusements I should have with him, and how much I should learn of the ways of a man, to add to the lot I knew about women. All was useless, I almost trembled at my intention. I entered, saw Sarah. "He

is in the bed room — such a nice young man, and quite good look-
ing, I never saw him till I went to buy the things." I said I felt
nervous. "That is stupid, but you are not more nervous than he is,
he's just said you were evidently not coming and he was glad of it,
and would go." Again she assured me that he was all the char-
woman had told, a young man out of work, wanting bread, and not
a sodomite.

I followed her into the bedroom. Saying, "This is the gentle-
man," she shut the door and left me with him. He stood up respect-
fully and looked at me timidly.

He was a fine young man about five feet seven inches high,
rather thin looking as if for want of nourishment, with a nice head
of curly brown hair, slight short whiskers, no moustache, bright eyes,
and good teeth. He was not much like a working man and looked
exceedingly clean. "You are the young man?" "Yes sir." "Sit down."
Down he sat and I did the same.

Then I could not utter a word more, but felt inclined to say,
"There is a sovereign, good night," and to leave him. All the desires,
all the intentions, all expectations of amusement with his prick, all
the curiosity I had hoped to satisfy for months left me. My only
wish was to escape without seeming a fool.

With the exception of the sodomite whom Betsy Johnson had
got me, it was the first time I had been by myself in the room with
a male for the clear intention of doing everything with his tool that
I had a mind to. My brain now had been long excited by anticipa-
tion, and wrought up to the highest when this opportunity came,
and every occurrence of that evening is as clear in it now as if it
were printed there. Altho the exact order of the various tricks I
played may not be kept, yet everything I *did* on this first night, all
that took place, I narrate in succession, without filling in anything
from fancy or imagination. I could even recall the whole of our
conversation, but it would fill quires (and I did fill two or three). —
I only now give half of it, and that abbreviated.

I sat looking at him for some minutes — I can frig him, thought
I — but I don't want to now. — What an ass he will think me. —
Why does he not unbutton? — I wonder if he is a bugger — or a
thief. — What's *he* thinking about. Is he clean? — How shall I begin
— I wish I had not come — I hope he won't know me if he meets
me in the street. — Is his prick large? — These thoughts one after

another chased rapidly thro my brain, whilst I sat silent, yet at the same time wishing to escape, and he sat looking at the floor.

Then an idea came. "Would you like something to drink?" "If you like, sir." "What?" "Whatever you like, sir." — It was an immense relief to me when I called in Sarah, and told her to get whiskey, hot water, and sugar. — Whilst it was being fetched I went into the sitting room, glad of getting away.

Sarah, in the sitting room, asked, "How do you find him?" — I told her I did not know and was frightened to go on, — "Oh! I would now, as you have had him got for you, then you'll be satisfied." — Again she assured me he was not on the town, and I need not be afraid. The whiskey was got, and behold me again alone with him. I made whiskey and water for myself and him and took some into Sarah. I began to ask him about himself. He was a house decorator in fine work, such work was at its worst just then, being a young hand he had not full employment, had been out of work nearly two months, he had pawned everything excepting what he had on. This all seemed consistent. He told me where he lodged, where he was apprenticed, the master he worked for last, the houses he worked at. "If you are a decorator your hands will be hard, and if you kneel your knees will." "Yes but I have had scarcely anything to do for two months, and but one day's work last week. Look at my nails." — They were stained with something he had used. Then he had had one day's chopping wood which had blistered both his hands, for it was not work he was accustomed to. Blisters I saw. There was evident truth in what he said.

This relieved me, together with the influence of whiskey and water. I got more courage and he seemed more comfortable, but not a word had transpired about our business, and an hour had gone. Then my mind reverted to my object, and I said, "You know what you came for." "Yes sir." He changed white, then red, and began to bite his nails.

My voice quivered as I said, "Unbutton your trowsers then." He hesitated. "Let me see your cock." One of his hands went down slowly, he unbuttoned his trowsers, which gaping, shewed a white shirt. Then never looking at me, he began biting his nails again.

The clean shirt, coupled with his timidity, gave me courage. "Take off your coat and waistcoat." He slowly did so. — I did the same, gulped down a glass of whiskey and water, sat him down by

me, and lifting his shirt laid hold of his prick. A thrill of pleasure
passed thro me, I slipped my hands under his balls, back again to
his prick, pulled the foreskin backwards and forwards, my breath
shortening with excitement. He sat still. Suddenly I withdrew my
hand with a sense of fear and shame again on me.

"May I make water, sir, I want so badly," said he in a humble
way, just like a schoolboy. "Certainly, take off your trowsers first."
He looked hard at me, slowly took them and his drawers off, and
stood with his shirt on. I took up the pot and put it on the chair
(my baudy brain began now to work). "Do it here, and I'll look
at your cock."

He came slowly there and stood. "I can't water now — I think
it is your standing by me." "You will directly, don't mind me." The
whiskey and excitement having made *me* leaky, I pulled out my tool
and pissed in the pot before him.

He laughed uneasily, it was the first sign of amusement he had
given. Directly I had finished, I laid hold of his prick and began
playing with it, I pulled back the skin and blew on the tip, a sudden
whim that made him laugh, and his shyness going off, I holding his
prick, he pissed the pot half full — I was delighted and wished he
could have kept on pissing for a quarter of an hour.

The ice was now broken, I took off *my* trowsers, and then both
with but shirts and socks on, I sat him at the side of the bed and
began my investigation of his copulating apparatus.

"I want to frig you," said I. "Yes sir." "Has any man ever
frigged you." — No living man had touched his prick since he was
a boy, he declared. — Then I began to handle his cock with the
ordinary first fucking motion.

I had scarcely frigged a minute before I wanted to feel his balls.
Then I turned him with his rump to me, to see how his balls and
prick looked hanging down from the back. — Then on to his side,
to see how the prick dangled along his thigh. Then I took him to the
wash stand and washed his prick, which before that was as clean
as a new shilling, but the idea of washing it pleased me. Then laying
him down on his back, I recommenced the fascinating amusement
of pulling the foreskin backwards and forwards, looking in his face
to see how he liked it. — He was as quiet as a lamb, but looked
sheepish and uncomfortable.

His prick at first was small, but under my manipulation grew larger, tho never stiff. Several times it got rather so for an instant, and then with the desire to see the spunk come, I began frigging harder; when instead of getting stiffer it got smaller. I tried this with him laying down, sitting up, and standing, but always with the same result — I spoke about it. — He said he could not make it out.

His prick was slightly longer than mine, was beautifully white, and with a pointed tip. I made it the stiffest by gently squeezing it — I had had no desire in my own doodle, but as I made his stiff once when he was lying down, my own prick came to a stand, and following a sudden inspiration I laid myself on to his belly, as if he had been a woman, and our two pricks were between our stomachs close together. I poked mine under his balls, and forced his under my stones, then changing, I turned his bum towards me, and thrusting my cock between his thighs and under his balls to the front, bent his prick down to touch the tip of mine, which was just showing thro his thighs. But his prick got limper and limper, and as I remarked that, it shrivelled up. We had been an hour at this game, and there seemed no chance of his spending. No sign of permanent stiffness or randiness or pleasure. He seemed in fact miserably uncomfortable.

Then he wanted to piss again from nervousness — I held his prick, squeezing it, sometimes stopping the stream, then letting it go on, and satisfying my curiosity. That done, I made a final effort to get a spend out of him, by squeezing, frigging slow, frigging fast. Then I rubbed my hand with soap, and making with spittle an imitation of cunt mucous on it, titillated the tip. "I think I can do it now," said he — but all was useless. "It's no good, I'm very sorry, sir, but I can't, that is a fact. — I don't know how it is."

The last hour had been one of much novelty and delight to me, tho he couldn't spend; but the announcement disappointed me. It came back to my mind that he might be, after all that Sarah had said, but an overfrigged bugger, who could no longer come. For I had heard that men who let themselves out for that work at last got so used up that it was difficult for them to do anything with their own pricks, and that all they could do was to permit men to feel their cocks, whilst they plugged their arse-holes. So I repeated my questions, and he again swore by all that was holy that no man had ever felt him but me; and he added that he was sorry he had come, but the money was a temptation.

I laid him then again on the bed and felt his prick. We finished the whiskey, and I sent for more; and in a whisper told Sarah that there was no spunk in him. She brought in the whiskey herself, and laughed at seeing us two nearly naked on the bed together.

Then I asked him when he had a woman last, if he liked them, how he got them, and so forth. He told me that he liked women very much — sometimes he got them for nothing, and they were servant girls mostly. When at houses if servants were left in them, or even if the family were only for a short time out — young fellows like him often got a put in; or else made love to them, and got them to come out at nights. He warmed up as he told me this, and his prick began to rise, but on my recommencing to masturbate him, it fell down again. He declared that the woman he last had was ten days previously, when he gave her a shilling out of the trifle he had gained, and that he had never spent since. Then he began biting his nails, adding that he hoped I should give him the money, for he could not help not spending, and was desperately badly off — "I have had some bread and cheese, and beer, but I have not tasted meat for six days."

Three hours with him had passed, the frigging seemed useless, but talking about women had brought *my* steam well up, so I began to think of letting him go, and plugging Sarah to finish. "Sarah is a fine woman isn't she? Did you ever have her, or see her naked," I said suddenly, thinking to catch him. — She *was* fine, but he had never seen her in his life, until the day but one previously. — "Would you like to see her naked." Oh! would he not. I knew Sarah would do anything almost, so called her in, told her his cock would not stand, and that we wanted to see her naked. "All right," said she, and began to undress.

He kept his eyes ardently fixed on her as she took off her things — I remarked to him on her charms as she disclosed them. He said "Yes — yes" — in an excited way. Then he ceased answering, but stared at her intently. When her limbs and breasts shewed from her chemise, a voluptuous sigh escaped him, and he put his hand to his prick outside his shirt. Feeling him, I found his prick swelling. "Don't pull off yet Sarah." She ceased taking off her chemise. "Pull off your shirt." Helping him he stood naked with his prick rising. — "Now show us your cunt." Down Sarah lay (after stripping off her chemise) on her back, one arm raised and shewing her dark haired arm pit, her legs apart, and one raised with the heel just under her bum, the black hair of her cunt curling down till shut in by her arse cheeks, the red lined cunt lips slightly gaping. — It was a sight which would have made a dead man's prick stiffen, and mine was stiff at the sight altho I had seen it scores of times. I forgot him then, till turning my head I saw his splendid cockstand. — His eyes were fixed full of desire on her, and he was a model of manly, randy beauty. — "Is not she fine?" said I. "Oh! lovely, beautiful, let me do it," addressing her. "No," said I, "another time perhaps," and I seized his tool with lewed joy.

For an instant he resisted. Sarah said, "Let my friend do it, you came for that." I frigged away, he felt its effects and sighed — I frigged on and felt the big, firm, wrinkled ball bag. A voluptuous shiver ran thro him soon. "Oh! let me feel her — do." "Feel her then." Over he stooped. "Kneel on the bed." Quickly he got there and plunged his finger into her carmine split. Again I grasped his tool and frigged. He cried out, "Oh! I'm coming. — I'm spend — ing" — and a shower of sperm shot out, covering her belly from cunt to navel. I frigged on until every drop had fallen. Then letting go his prick, he sat down on his heels, his eyes shut, his body still palpitating with pleasure and now fingering his still swollen doodle.

The effect on me was violent. Sarah's attitude on her back at all times gave me a cockstand — it had stood whilst frigging him. — There she lay now, a large drop of his spunk on her motte seemed ready to drop down on to her clitoris, higher up on her belly little pools lay. Tearing off my shirt, scarcely knowing what I did, crying out, "Move up higher on the bed" — which he did, I flung myself on her and put my prick up her cunt. — My prick rubbed the spunk drop on her thatch, my belly squeezed the opal pools between us, the idea delighted me — I fucked away, stretched out my hand, grasped his wet prick, for he was now conveniently near me, and fucked quickly to an ecstatic termination.

. The greater the preliminary excitement, the more delicious seems the repose after a fuck — the more it is needed, and I had had excitement enough that night. At length I roused myself. My cock did not seem inclined to come out of its lodging. I felt that

I could butter her again without uncunting. So keeping it in, I raised myself and looked at him sitting at the head of the bed, naked and still feeling his prick, which was again as stiff as a ramrod.

"He can spend after all," said I, my prick still up Sarah. — "I told you he was a nice young man." "Should you like to fuck her?" "Just give me the chance." The tale of the soldiers putting into each other's leavings came into my head. "Do it at once." "Lord," said Sarah, "you don't mean that." But I did. "Do it now." — I rose on my knees. — As I took my belly off of Sarah's, they were sticking together with his spunk. It made a loud smacking noise as our bellies separated. — My prick drew out sperm which dropped between her thighs. — As I got off, he got on, and as quickly put up her. The next minute their backsides were in rapid motion.

The second fuck is longer than the first, and I had time to watch their movements. — A man and woman both naked and close to me, were copulating — I could see and feel every movement of their bodies — hear their murmurs and sighs — see their faces. — There stood I with my own prick now stiff again watching them. — My hands roved all over them — I slipped my hand between their bellies — I felt his balls. — Then slipping it under her rump it felt the wet spunk I had left in her cunt, now working out on to the stem of his prick as it went in and out — I got on the bed and rubbed my prick against his buttocks. I shouted out — "Fuck her, — spend in her — spend in my spunk," — and other obscenities I know not what. — I encouraged his pleasure by baudy suggestions. A sigh, a murmuring, told me he was coming. My fingers were on his balls, and I let them go to see his face. He thrust his tongue into Sarah's mouth. — "You are spending, Sarah." — No reply. — Her mouth was open to his tongue, her eyes were closed, her buttocks moving with energy, and the next second but for a few twitchings of his arse, and their heavy breathings, they were like lumps of lifeless flesh. Both had spent. The fancy to do her *after him* came over me — my spunk — his spunk — her spunk — all in her cunt together. I will spend in her again. — The idea of my prick being drowned in these mixed exudations overwhelmed me libidinously. — "I'll do it to you again. — Get off of her." — "Let me wash," said Sarah. — "No." — "I will." — "You shan't. — He was getting off, she attempting to rise, when I pushed her down. — "It's wiser" — I didn't know what she said

scarcely. — "No — no — no — I want to put into his spunk." —
Her thighs were apart, her cunt hole was blinded, hidden by
spunk which lay all over it and filled its orifice. I threw myself on
her, my prick slipped up with a squashing noise — I know no
other way of describing it. I think I hear it now.

I felt a sense of heavenly satisfaction. Her cunt was so filled
that it seemed quite loose, the sperm squeezed out of her and up,
until the hair of both our genitals were saturated — I pushed my
hand down, and making her lift up one leg, found the sperm lay
thick down to her arse hole — I called out, "Your spunk's all over
my ballocks," and told all the baudy images which came across
my mind. I told him to lay down by the side of us, and made
Sarah feel his prick at the same time I did — I felt my pleasure
would even now be too short and stopped myself. Sarah with a sigh
cried, "Oh — my God — go on," her cunt tightened, she let go his
prick and clasped my buttocks to her — I still held his prick, and
tried to lengthen my pleasure but could not, her cunt so clipped
me. Abandoning myself to her the next instant almost with a
scream of pleasure, I was quiet in her arms and fell asleep — and
so did she, and so did he — all three on the bed close together.

Awakening, I had rolled off close to Sarah on to my side, my
prick laying against her thigh. — She lay on her back asleep, he
nearly on his back. All three were nearly naked, myself excepted
who had on an under shirt next my skin. — She had silk stockings
and black merino boots on. My foreskin had risen up and covered the
tip of my prick. In the saucer at the top was spunk which had
issued from me after I uncunted. — The lamp was alight. Two
candles (they had been short pieces) had burnt out, and the fire
had all but expired. The room had been hot all the evening, for
there were three of us in it, three lights burning, and the fire. Now
it had got cold, and a sensation of chillness was over me.

I got up and looked at the pair. — She a splendid woman, firm
and smooth skinned, and of a creamy pink tint — with the dark
hair of her cunt in splendid contrast. He a fine young man with
white flesh, and with much dark brown hair clustering and curling
round his white prick, and throwing his balls into shadow. His prick
still large was hanging over his thigh, the slightly red tip half
covered by the foreskin pointing towards Sarah, and as if looking

at it. Then sexual instinct made me pay attention to her. — She lay there with two libations from me, and one from him in her cunt. I desired to see how it looked and felt it, but was so distracted by my various erotic impulses that I cannot recollect everything accurately. — All I know is that I laid hold of her leg nearest to me, and watching, pulled it slowly so as to leave her legs slightly open. I put my finger down from the beginning of the cleft. It felt thick and sticky, yet but little spunk was to be seen — looking down towards the bum cheeks, I saw the bed patched in half a dozen places with what had run out from her — I thrust my finger up her cunt and she awakened.

She sat up, looked round, rubbed her eyes, said, "it's cold." Then she looked at him. "Why — he's asleep too, have *you* been asleep?" — Then she put her fingers to her cunt too, got off the bed, and on to the pot — looking at me smiling. — "You *are* a baudy devil and no mistake — I don't recollect such a spree since I have been out." "Your cunt's in a jolly state of batter." "It will be all right when it's washed" — and she proceeded to wash, but I stopped her.

He was snoring and had turned on to his back — his prick which seemed large lolled over his thigh. "He's a fine young man and his prick's bigger than yours, and what a bag," said she gently lifting up his prick and shewing his balls. I saw it was very large, as it had seemed to me when I squeezed and felt it before, but then I had been far too excited to notice anything carefully. Now I began to frig him as he lay. "I thought you had done me, for for two hours I could not make his cock stand." "Ah! it was nervousness. — He has never been felt by a man before, some would give ten pounds for such a chance and you are to give him a sovereign." "Do you think he can spend again?" "Yes, see what a lot he spent over me; if he was well fed, that young chap would be good for half a dozen pokes, he's been half starved for two months."

I gently laid hold of his prick, and pulled the skin down. One feel more and it rose to fullish size, and lay half way up his belly. "I thought it would directly you touched it from its look," said she. Said I, "I will frig him," and commenced in the slowest and gentlest manner, scarcely touching it. The stiffening began and the foreskin retired, the tip got rubicund and tumid, an uneasy movement of his thigh and belly began, and muttering in his sleep his hand went to his prick. — I removed mine. Soon his hand dropped by his side again, and he snored and muttered something.

Sarah, who had put on her chemise, then laid hold of his prick and frigged it. — "He can't spend, he's done too much already," said I. "I think he will tho." Then I, jealous of her handling, and lewedly fascinated, resumed the work. — Had he not drunk and eaten heartily, and been very fatigued, he must have awakened, but he didn't. Not spending, I spat on my finger and thumb, and making a moist ring with them, rubbed his prick tip through them. That did it. He muttered, his belly heaved, and out rolled his sperm, as he awakened, saying, "I've had a beastly spending dream, and thought I was fucking *you*." Seeing us laughing he seemed astonished, and was angry when told of our game. We all washed, we men put on shirts, and he got good humoured again.

I had scarcely eaten that day, felt empty and said so — Sarah said *she* was hungry, he that he could eat a donkey, for he'd not had food since the morning — I had never eaten in Sarah's lodgings, for the style didn't suit me, but felt that I must eat now. "Shall I fetch something at once? It's near midnight, and all the shops will be closed." — We had been five hours at our voluptuous gambols, but it did not seem half that time.

I gave Sarah money. She fetched cut beef and ham, bread, cheese, and bottled stout, and also whiskey. — Whilst she was away, he recovered his temper and felt his cock. He said he hated "beastly cheating dreams." "Are you fond of feeling men?" "It's much nicer to fuck a woman," I replied and told him that for many years I had never put finger on a prick but my own.

Spite of dirty knives and a dingy table cloth, we all fell to at the food. — He ate ravenously and told me that the last time he had meat, a mate gave him some of his dinner. I gave him a cigar, we had more whiskey and water, the room was hot again, we sat round the fire with our shirts only on — Sarah was dressed. — He told me again about himself, and soon the conversation drifted into the fucking line. He had lost his modesty and with it much of his respect for me. Instead of only answering and saying "sir" he began to ask me questions. Just as a woman's manner alters towards a man, directly he has once fucked her, so did his alter now that I had frigged him.

I asked if he liked being frigged. — No he did not like — "spending in the air" — did I? "No" — but I did such things at times Then Sarah alluded to his big balls, we both felt them, and such a large bag I have never seen before. He said the boys at school joked him about it. Boys know the sizes of each other's pricks.

I wanted to go on. The novelty was so great that I could not see and feel him enough; circumstances which I did not expect had brought Sarah into the fun, which increased the amusement. I am in the prime of life, and altho never attempting such wonders as some men brag of, can easily do my four fucks in an evening with a fresh woman, and sometimes more, altho then used up a little next day. I had now only spent twice and my prick seemed on fire. Wine, beer, and a full stomach soon heat a young man who has not spent for ten days. I pulled his prick about as we sat round the fire, and it readily swelled. He prayed me to desist, he'd had enough that night, but I had not. So I made Sarah take off her clothes to her chemise, and sit opposite. I sat next him smoking and looking at his prick, and feeling it at intervals.

Often in my youth, my prick has stood before my dinner was finished. A dozen times have I got up and fucked in the middle and finished dinner afterwards. — This meal began to tell on all. Sarah raised her chemise to let the warmth of the fire reach her legs, and showed her silk stockings and red garters. — "What a fine pair you have," said he — and down went his hand to his shirt. I saw a projection, and pulling up his shirt, there was his prick as stiff as ever.

"I'll frig you, and you look at Sarah's legs." He objected, had had enough of *that*, he would sooner fuck Sarah. — I had not brought him to fuck my woman — my letch was for frigging him. — Whilst this talk was going on I held his prick. Sarah showed us one of her thighs and told him to let me do what I liked — I had a stiff one and was dying to let out my sperm. I would frig him, and he should fuck her afterwards. A young man with a standing prick always thinks that there is enough sperm in it for any amount of fucking. — How often I have thought whilst my cock was standing and burning to be in a cunt what wonders I would do, and directly after one coition did nothing more.

I put Sarah on the bed, myself by her, him by the side of us on his back, and upside down; his belly so placed that his prick was near my shoulders, and I could conveniently feel it. His prick was throbbing with lust — I laid on Sarah with prick outside her and began frigging him. He sighed and cried out, "Oh! let me do it to her — do — oho — do." I meant to play with him long, but Sarah was lewed, placed her hand between our bellies and put my prick up her. — Then all went its own way. — If a woman means you to go on fucking when up her you can't help yourself. Without moving their bums, they can grip with their cunt muscles and grind a man's tool so that he *must* ram and rub. I was soon stroking as hard as I could, but holding my head on my right hand resting from the elbow, so as to see his prick which I went on frigging. It was a longer job than before, with all our lewedness and good will, for both of us. At length out came his sperm. At the sight of it out shot mine into Sarah, who responded with her moisture, and all was quiet.

We reposed long, then I got off. "Now you may have her." — Sarah washed. He laid on the bed, and after wiping up his now thin spunk from his belly, began frigging himself up. Sarah laid down by his side and let him feel her clean cunt, but it was useless; and after some violent fisting of his tool, he rose saying, "I'm done up" — and again we all sat down before the fire, smoking and drinking, and talking about fucking, the causes and the consequences thereof.

This talk went on for an hour or so. Sarah said jeeringly to him, "Why don't you have me." — Every ten minutes he frigged his cock uselessly. Then he ate more food. — Sarah went to the watercloset, which was in a yard, and dressed partly to go there, for it was cold. — His prick looked beautiful but lifeless. — My baudiness was getting over and I was tired, but thought then came into my head — a reminiscence of my frolics with French women. But tho I had done everything but one with Sarah, I did not suggest what was in my mind before her — I had a stupid lingering modesty in me. — We were both fuddled and reckless, and Sarah now down stairs. I locked the door, saying, "If you'll promise not to tell her, I will make you stiff enough to have her." He promised. — I laid him on the bed and putting his prick in my mouth began to suck it, first with the skin on, and then gently with the skin off. The smoothness delighted me. I no longer wondered at a French woman, who told me a prick was the nicest thing she ever had in her mouth. I did exactly as it had been done to me as nearly as I recollected; spit out after the first taste, and then went on mouthing, licking, and sucking. It took effect directly. — "Oh! it's as good as a cunt," said he. It was stiffened by the time Sarah came back. I went to the door and unlocked it, he had resumed his seat, then Sarah washed her backside and went back to her seat by the fire. He'd never had his cock sucked before.

We finished the whiskey — it was getting towards one o'clock — Sarah said, "It's time we got to bed — why don't you both stop all night? — it will be cold, for I have no more coals." The lamp was going out, and she went to the next room to fetch candles. When she came back, "If he is going to fuck you, he should begin," said I. "Yes, and I am going to bed whether he does or not." She stripped to her chemise and got into bed. "If you don't have her now, she is not to let you when I am gone, get outside the bed." — Sarah did. — With cock stiff he got on to her in a minute. I saw by a cross twist of his buttocks and a sigh that he was up her — Sarah gave that smooth, easy, wriggling jerk and upwards motion with her buttocks and thighs, which a woman does to complete the engulf-ment of a doodle — I put my hand under his balls. His prick up to the roots was up her cunt.

Then not a word was spoken. A long stroke ensued, and grad-ually after hard quick ramming, their last pleasure shewed itself. My randiness increased by watching him, I made him leave her cunt before he had well finished spending and again plunged my prick into her reeking, slippery, slimy vagina. I gloried in feeling their sperm upon me. I was not in the habit of giving Sarah wet kisses, but as I thought, I longed to meet her mouth with mine, and with our tongues joined, and hard thrusts, a pain in my pego, and slight pain in my arse hole, I spent, and Sarah spent. "My God I'm fucked out," said she.

It was three o'clock a.m. — eight or nine hours had I been in one round of excitement — I had frigged him three times and he'd fucked thrice — I had fucked six times — I had fucked in his spunk, and had sucked his prick — Sarah had been fucked quite eight times. How many times I had spent I did not then know, being bewildered with excitement and drink. — As Sarah got up she seemed dazed, sat in a chair, and said, "Damned if ever I had such a night, I'm clean fucked out." Then paying them I left. It was at our next meeting that Sarah said I had fucked her six times. In my abbreviation of the manuscript, I have omitted some of our lascivious exercises, which were in fact but a repetition of what I had done before.

I was thoroughly done up the next day, not only with spending but with excitement. My delight in handling his white prick in repose, half stiff and in complete rigidity, was almost maddening. The delight of watching his prick glide in and out of her cunt was intense. The desire and curiosity of twenty years was being satisfied. My knowledge of copulation and of the penis getting perfected. — Yet I went home in an uncomfortable frame of mind about what I had done with him. There was no one in my home just then to wonder at my being so late, to notice my excitement, or to question me, which was fortunate.

*Unavailing repentance. — Gemini frolics. — Pricks between bellies.
— I on him. — He on me — tip to tip. — Boots and stockings. — A
lascivious triad. — Gamahuching all round. — A looking-glass got.
— Genital manipulations. — Simultaneous fuckings and friggings. —
I fuck, she sucks. — Variations on the same tune. — She on my prick
sits. — He her clitoris licks. — Three on our sides together. —
Amatory exercises with ropes. — Sarah's pudendal capacity. — An
assault of two pegos. — Finger and penis co-operating. — Miscel-
laneous lascivities. — A scare in the street. — A scare at Sarah's. —
A suggestive question. — Desires excited. — Heavy pay for an anus.
— Sodomy cum onanism. — Fear, disgust, and hasty retreat.*

I went home used up, but excited beyond measure. I could not
sleep for thinking of having frigged a man. The smoothness of skin,
the loose easy movement of the outer skin over the inner rod, and
its whiteness — the gradual change in color of its plum shaped
tip from pink to a deep carmine, the shooting out of his sperm, the
voluptuous shuddering whilst he fucked Sarah, the saucers which
came and went in his arse cheeks when he fucked, all danced before
my eyes as I lay in bed, and I saw them as plainly as if the fucking
was actually then going on. — Again her distended cunt lips, with
the thick spunk oozing, my prick pushing between them with a
squash, squeezing the spermatic mixture out on to my balls, and
up to her motte, and gumming our hair together, my grip of his
stiffened cock as I fucked her the second time; all filled me with an
incredibly furious, baudy excitement, making my prick stiffen and
throb, spite of my fatigue and preventing my rest.

Then came reflexion. — Had I really frigged a man — still
worse — got my own prick wetted with the sperm of another man.

Above all sucked his prick! — An act I had certainly heard of being done by men to each other, yet all but disbelieved, and looked on as a very foul action — yet I had done it, had enjoyed it all. Much as I had done and seen before, I was not quite easy in my mind, spite of my philosophy that any sexual enjoyment is permissible — that our organs of generation are for our own use and pleasure, and that what men and women choose to do together they have a right to do, it concerning no one else. Such are the results of prejudices and false education. It ended in reflecting that I never had intended to do those things, that opportunity had let me unwittingly to do them, and resolving that I would never do it again, I fell asleep.

Next morning at breakfast I thought, "That debauch will never be renewed." After luncheon, "What was the harm after all." Then I began to think I should like to feel him once more, to watch the phenomenon of the spend more coolly and philosophically. — Once more to make him spend, and to watch his prick from its stiffening to its shrinking. To watch his face and see how pleasure affected it. Why should I not bring him and Sarah naked together as I had done and see his prick rise, let him fuck her, and watch as I did last night — surely there is no harm — or not more than in looking at such doings through a spyhole. — The man is clearly not a sodomite, or he would not be so ready to fuck her. He is out of work, and probably is what he says he is. It is a chance which never may come again to me.

I thought of the double fuck without the washing, of the prick in my mouth, and then felt ashamed. — "I must have been screwed and so excited that I did not know what I was about, I shall never do *that* again, and hope he won't tell Sarah." I then took a gallop, determining again to get him. I had slept so badly on the previous night that on my return I laid down. My mind wandered to his prick and what Sarah called his purse. I wondered if his prick was really bigger than mine and wished I had measured it — I wondered if he spent more or less than me, and many other things; and at last came to the conclusion that I ought to be ashamed of myself, and being empty in stomach and fatigued, said, "I have done with that business." — Then I went to my club, had dinner, desire to see him again then came back, and soon I was with Sarah arranging for another meeting.

Said she, "You'd a pretty good night, I declare that if I were to tell some women what we did, they'd only believe part of it. — He wanted to sleep with me." She dare say he would come again willingly, she would go and see — I gave her money to buy him trowsers, cravat, and collars, said that he was to take a bath, and also gave her money to feed him well — Sarah met me out an hour afterwards. He would be there the following night.

She had done all I wished, and the fellow looked as spruce as possible — I was again nervous, and so was he, but a few minutes' conversation put us at ease. — We stripped, and behold us close together, I holding that handsome tool of his. He asked if Sarah was coming, but I did not want her then, and sat with his balls in my hand, for a time thinking of the size and fullness of the scrotum.

Of the sovereign — he told me that he first paid fifteen shillings for rent, and the rest where he owed money — that Sarah had got him good food, — that he had not spent since that last night. "When I thought of it all, I got to want it," said he.

Then I washed his genitals and made a complete and curious examination of his penis and scrotum, and had more complete quiet pleasure crowding in that than on the previous occasion. Before when feeling his prick it did not make me randy — tonight it did. My examination began to tell on him, and when I had pulled the foreskin once or twice up and down, his rod was stiff. Then up stiffened mine. — I began frigging him. — "Now I will look at your sperm as it comes." Suddenly he laid hold of my prick. — "Hullo, don't do that."

He relinquished it begging pardon, saying he did not know what made him do it. — My pulling *his* about seemed quite a proper thing for *me*, for I paid him for it; but directly *he* touched *my* prick, I felt disgusted. — The mind is an odd thing — if a gentleman had felt me, should I have been equally shocked?

This preliminary was soon over, he was on the point of discharge when I stopped, and making him sit down, watched his stiff prick gradually droop, and then I went at him again and so on. If a copious discharge is to be got out of a man, that is the way to do it. — At length after playing so for long, he said he must and would come — so I frigged as fine a spermatic ejaculation as I had had on the first night. It spurted out a yard, quite.

I had intended not to let Sarah appear that night, but feeling his cock had made my cock stand. "I'll frig myself," I said. But I hated spending in that fashion. — After trying to restrain myself till I could do so no longer, I called Sarah. She was dressed. Throwing her on the side of the bed, up went her clothes, and I put up her, he looking on. Up came his prick again at the sight. — He asked to have her, but I wouldn't let him, and handled his tool whilst I fucked her.

I carried out my intentions, frigged him four times, and had no end of amusement with him. — I had a taste that night for rolling over him as if he were a woman, when his cock was stiff, and making mine stiff, and laying the two pricks together. I tried all sorts of ways of making his stand. Sometimes by pulling the skin up and down, sometimes by shaking the top — now by giving it a rude pinch — now by squeezing his balls. I tried every way which I could recollect women had used on me, or I had heard or thought of. There was now no difficulty about it, for his cock kept standing after very small handling; and he had still sperm, tho getting at each discharge less in quantity and thinner. At his fourth discharge all was over, but there were still things which I wished to do with him. One was to put his prick in my mouth. Again I rubbed my lips on its smooth white stem, and kissed it, and all but put it in. — But I never will do that again, thought I to myself.

The amusement however seemed incomplete without Sarah. Again I fucked her, and then let *him* do it to her. That was a very long job and finished the evening, and him.

Afterwards. Each meeting I thought would be the last, yet I had him again. Sarah participated in the amusements regularly. The evening did not seem complete without the two. I was infatuated. — Of course four discharges a night could not be kept up, but I did not see him every night. — But as much spunk as could be got out of him I got, pumping him pretty dry with my fist, and myself as well, but into Sarah's cunt. I now tell only some of my amusements, and as near as may be in the succession in which they took place. They could not all be done on one evening.

My baudy imagination being set to work, all sorts of possibilities came into my head. We soaped well our pricks, and under our balls and arse furrows. Then lying on the top of him, we thrust our pricks under each other's balls, and working in the soapy furrows, both spent on each other's backside. — It was not convenient, our pricks rebelled at being so bent and thrust, but the novelty made up for the inconvenience. — Novelty stimulates desire. — I got much amusement from lying on the top of him, when our pricks were not stiff, and feeling the testicles and two cocks in a bunch together. Sarah, then quite delighted, felt our intermingled genitals. Then I put him on the top and myself beneath, Sarah held a looking glass and candle, so that I could see when on my back two ballocks in a heap together. Sarah was delighted with all my lasciviousness and said she never knew such a baudy man as I was.

One day standing up I soaped both our prick tips and we frigged ourselves. We put the two tips so close that they rubbed together, and we spent against each other's glands.

These lascivious vagaries and delicacies did not suggest themselves all at once. Firstly my delight was to watch his face as he spent, then to see the prick stiff, the sperm shoot, the tremulous shaking of his backside, and to hear his quiet murmurs of pleasure. After I had had enough of that, I betook myself to more fanciful amusements.

Spite of myself, my mind recurred to the feel of his prick when in my mouth, and altho I vowed to myself never to let it go into it again. — Yet why? thought I at length. Have you not licked a cunt? Have you not had the fresh warm piddle squirt against your face from Sarah's cunt? — Have you not savoured the salt liquor which distils from and keeps moist a woman's cunt? Nay. Have you not when moistened till almost running out, by its sweating (so to speak) under the action of your tongue on her clitoris, shoved your tongue up her cunt, and brought it back into your mouth with delight and ecstasy at giving her pleasure? Is the putting into your mouth a prick, dry, clean, and smooth as ivory, worse? — But it's a man's. In her mouth a prick is quite proper. He may lick, tickle, and suck her hole, that's quite natural. But a man's! — No I won't.

For all that, one night whilst feeling it, when he had washed after I'd first frigged him, I again washed it carefully, and laid him on the bed. There hung his prick and his testicles, the tip just covered by the prepuce. As I pulled back the foreskin, I put out my tongue and tickled the top. "Your tongue is on it," said he laughing. — Then I took it in my lips. It was like ivory. I longed to minette with it, and passed the limp, soft, flexible tool entirely into my mouth: not a bit was outside. — It went back towards my gullet and there I held it, till it began to swell. I passed it up and down in my mouth, licked and sucked it, put it out and let it stay till it drooped, then remouthed it, and continued this for a long time. At length his sperm had been so accumulated by the dalliance that he said he could bear it no longer and would frig himself if I did not. I then brought it up to the spending throb, pulled it from my mouth, and finishing with my hand, his spunk shot up. There is nothing like coaxing a prick a long time, for accumulating the spunk in the reservoirs of concupiscence. I'm sure more comes then, than from a hasty frig.

Then I fucked her before him, then sent her out, and again sucked his prick which was in powerful order — I laid him on the bedside in the attitude most convenient to lick a cunt, and so that I might see his face whilst I operated. It is easy in a man's face to see when his ballocks are about to send forth their juices. — A red Indian, they say, can preserve his features when being tortured. I doubt if he could when spending. — A man's face then is rather stupid, nor is that of a woman's, as she is holding tightly to her fucker's backside for the full engulfment of his throbbing cock in her cunt, highly intellectual; but it's much more lovely than that of a man's face.

I offered him money to suck my prick. He would not, and that night's amusement ended. Then much to his delight I began to let him fuck Sarah. Whilst they were doing that trick, I handled his balls, put my hand between their bellies, made them turn over on to their sides and lift their legs in all sorts of ways, so that I might see the movement of the prick and the swell of the lips of her orifice. — I made him fuck her standing up, then on the side of the bed, whilst with a candle I moved round them, satisfying my curiosity. Then I fucked her and made him similarly satisfy himself. He was delighted to grasp my balls whilst my prick was pistoning her. — Modesty and timidity had now left all of us. — Unrestrained libidinous enjoyment was everything to us, each doing the best to stimulate each other's lust. Sarah had become more active, suggestive, and libidinous than we two. She delighted in it.

My libidinosity increased by indulging it. I longed to see ourselves in the various attitudes. — Sarah's table glass was small, and having placed it so as to get a glimpse of ourselves, and finding it unsatisfactory, I bought at a broker's shop, a long, large old-fashioned looking glass in a mahogany frame. We together nailed it up against the wall at the level of the top of the mattress, and so that we could see ourselves from head to foot as we lay. Then our sensual delight was doubled, for as we fucked, or frigged, or sucked, we could look in the glass, and talk about our attitudes.

One night all three highly strung — I was near her, he by her side on the bed. "Oh look at his prick." "Ah! it's not stiff — he'll spend." "Frig it, frig him Sarah." She did. "Are you coming, Jack." "Aha." "Yes — my spunk's coming." "Oh fuck me, fuck me," cried Sarah, or "I'll frig myself." "Stop, Sarah, I'll fuck you," and I put my prick up her. — She grasped my rump with one hand, with the other grasped his prick, and so did I. Both Sarah's and my hand were on it. Sometimes she had the stem, I the scrotum. Just before *we* spent out spurted *his* spunk. Then as we felt it, we poured out our sexual tributes, a spasm of libidinous sympathy fetched us both together.

I began then to pay for his baths, his food, and fine linen so that he came perfect from head to toe. He had no hair on his body, excepting on his prick and armpits, and but little on his face. — What with idleness, good living, and baths, he became as smooth as ivory and as nice to feel as the nicest woman. He got in a fortnight plumper, altho I took so much semen out of him; but he was young and strong. — What pleasure for him! — The only annoyance to me was that his prick, when he got randy and it stood, had a strong smell. — The smell of most cunts I like.

After I had sucked him that night, I never repeated it but once. — Altho we had lost all modesty, I did not like Sarah to see all, until late in the evening when whiskey and baudiness told on me. Whatever we did together, I never lost sight of my principal object, which was to frig him, and see either his tool or his face when he was spending. — When Sarah came in, at first we used to sit round the fire drinking and smoking, all as naked as the weather permitted. Sometimes he told his adventures with servants in the houses where he had worked, she about what men had done. The conversation always was erotic. — Until the spirit moved me to action, I usually sat by him in an easy chair, with his tool in my hand. Sometimes he laid hold of mine. "Look at you two feeling each other's pricks," Sarah would say, with a toss of her head. — "Shew me your split, and see if it will give his cock a rise." — She would show it gaping, and his cock would rise. Perhaps he'd kneel

in front of her, fingering her cunt, or licking it, whilst she cocked
her leg up to facilitate his work. At times both *his* and *my* fingers
were up her cunt at the same time, and fifty other baudy tricks we
did.

I had now made Sarah suck my prick, but I disliked still to tell
here that I had had *his* prick in my mouth; yet one evening did so.
Behold us soon all three on the bed, *she* with *his* prick in *her* mouth,
and *he* with *my* prick in *his* mouth. I feeling about *her* cunt and
his balls, as well as the difficult attitude permitted. Another night
we followed it up, by his laying on the bed and she kneeling over
him with his prick in her mouth, her backside over his feet, and I
at her backside fucking her — I alone could plainly see this in the
looking glass, and a most delicious sight it was.

My most satisfactory amusement, I think, was frigging him
whilst I fucked her. I used to lay him down so that his prick was
well within reach of my hand and in view whilst I did so. At times
Sarah laid her head on his chest or his belly, as a pillow, he laying
across the bed, and then his prick was just by my shoulder. Then
putting my hand up I frigged him. At other times, laying partially
on his side with his legs up against the wall at the bed head or near
her head, his prick was equally close to me.

Once his tool looked so beautiful that it seduced me entirely —
I had again vowed to myself that having had his prick in my mouth
and felt it swell within it from flabbiness to a poker, under my
lingual pressures, I would never do it again. — But now lying with
my prick up Sarah, my left hand under her smooth backside, my
right round his prick; my pleasure coming on I could not resist it,
and engulfed his stiff cunt-rammer in my mouth. My backside was
then oscillating, his hand could just reach my arse and he was
feeling my balls. I felt he was near his crisis, withdrew his prick,
and at that instant out shot his sperm, just between Sarah's naked
breast and mine.

Instantly, for such was the lascivious effect, Sarah and I mingled
our mucilages in her cunt. I never had his prick in my mouth after-
wards.

He got fond of Sarah and constantly besought me to let him
have her. Then after I had frigged him, we would all three sit
round the fire. "Shew us your cunt, Sarah?" — She'd open her legs
so that the article was visible. I watched his prick, which perhaps

hanging down lazily between his thighs immediately at the sight of her gaping cunt would gradually thicken until it looked like a short roll of ivory. Then it rolled on one side as if to get away from the big balls. Then with a throb straightened somewhat, its top still pointing downwards, and the little red tipped orifice beginning to show more out of the foreskin. Then it gave a throbbing knock or jump against his thigh and proudly lifted his head, and with other throbs in succession stood grandly stiff against his belly, and the prepuce gently slid off, leaving uncovered two thirds of a deep crimson knob. Then I would gently pull up and down the skin with a slow motion, pleased at the involuntary action of his prick, caused by the mere look of a dark haired cunt. "Let me fuck her — don't frig me this time, you have frigged me enough. — Oh! do let me put into her." Then I let him feel her cunt, and his lust goaded to the utmost, he would sigh and groan almost and lick her cunt. Then I let him have her, or had her myself and frigged him whilst up her. "And so we passed the pleasant time, as well we could, you know, in the days when we were randy arsed a long time ago."

One night, I sat her on my prick whilst I sat on a chair, her bum against my belly, her cunt outwards. — In a looking glass, my ballocks then almost seemed to hang from the arsehole end of the cunt. He knelt down and licked her clitoris whilst I fucked her. Sarah enjoyed the double action, and spent murmuring her lewed sensations; clutching his head, whilst I held her round her haunches tightly, my fingers on the hairy motte. In that position I could only ram gently up her. When she'd spent, he fell back on the floor and frigged himself looking up at her cunt, my prick still up her, and the sperm running out on to my balls, as my cunt plugger slowly left her.

I was slim and supple as an eel. I would on the bed put into Sarah, and then we would both turn on to our sides belly to belly, keeping our privates coupled. Sarah would throw over me her uppermost leg, so as to open her bum furrow, and he laid on his side with his belly close to her rump, thrusting his prick forwards. — The tip would just touch the end of her slit, which was nearest to her bum hole; rub in the furrow, and touch the bottom of my prick as it lay engulfed in her. Then we all began fucking together. I ramming up her, he rubbing his prick up against our coupled genitals, which he had bedewed with saliva. We never hid our pleasures —

I would cry out when coming — Sarah would murmur her pleasure, and he the same. The three voices blended whatever baudy, stimulating words fell from us. "Oh! fuck — cunt — spunk — oh — I am coming — I'm spending — spunk — ballocks — aha — ahre" — I spent up her, he against her furrow and the stem of my prick, or over my balls, or against her arsehole or thigh. If the rubbing against our flesh didn't fetch his sperm, he brought himself to a crisis with his hand, and at the last moment put his prick against her flesh and spent somewhere.

One night as he was tailing Sarah, I felt his hard, wrinkled, full, large scrotum, and slipping my fingers further up, let his stiff lubricated shaft slip through my fingers as it worked up and down her cunt. Then reversing my hand so that his prick rubbed against the back of it, I slowly glided the middle finger up her cunt. "What are you doing," said she. — "Feeling up." — She said no more, the lasciviousness of the act pleased her and him, the whole length of my finger was up her side by side with his prick, whilst he was fucking. His prick glided over my wet finger as they spent together. I had already fucked her, was cool and collected, and noticed the tightening of her cunt as she spent, in a way I never had in any woman; for clear observation of the muscular action of a woman's cunt, at the supreme moment of spending, is impossible; tho my prick is conscious of its constriction.

I did that more than once. Sarah's, altho one of the most delightfully compressive cunts, was undoubtedly largish. — Once she allowed us to try to get both pricks up her together, but we could not manage it.

[It is difficult, even with two very rigid tools to do *that*, for I and another man have tried it since with a woman. But such is the distensibility of a cunt that I'm sure it *will* take two pricks at once.]

Then we reversed our position, and I pushed from behind and spent against *his* balls, whilst he fucked *her*. I liked to vary my pleasures, and when away thought of what I had done, and arranged variations of the fun for our next meeting.

[What whims and caprices lust generates! I have often thought how absurd the following part of my narrative seems, but the deed didn't seem at all absurd to me then.]

Bringing both pricks into use at the same time pleased me much, the difficulty was that our legs got in the way. After thinking how to obviate this, I put a big hook in the ceiling, and a rope hanging from it with loops at the bottom. Into a loop Sarah put her upper foot, and that slung her leg out of the way. Sometimes he put his foot so. Such ingenious devices voluptuous pleasures led me to. They have seemed ridiculous since, but delighted us all immensely at the time.

Afterwards I put up a second hook and rope, at such distance apart that Sarah could easily put through them her legs up to her knees, and she laid for ten minutes at a time with her legs in the air so distended that her cunt gaped wide. We saw her cunt and anus peeping out from under it. — When in that position I fucked her. Before that we men stood and admired her exposure, feeling each other's pricks, and in the looking glass admiring ourselves in the baudy postures.

I made *him* another time fuck her whilst her legs were slung up, and as soon as his prick was out I investigated her cunt and saw his sperm in it. I find now nothing objectionable in semen — that essence of love.

Whilst I fucked her in that position, I once made him kneel over her with his backside towards me and his prick in her mouth. Then I recollect for the first time that I noticed his anus.

Soon after I had him, I took a fancy to see him in silk stockings. He put on a pair of Sarah's, which so pleased me that I bought him a pair, and a pair of kid boots. I never had him afterwards without them. When on the top of Sarah, with legs together in silks and boots alike, altho the male leg is different from the female, I could scarcely tell which was which, from heels to rumps. But the split and the spindle shewed the difference in the sexes.

Once I made Sarah lay on the top of me and do the fucking, whilst he squatted on her back. So placed I frigged him. Some of his sperm came on to Sarah's hair and made her angry. Sarah didn't mind being spent over anywhere excepting her head. Some of his spunk fell on my face, and I did not like it.

During one period of this erotic frenzy, being as it happened by myself in town alone, I was there nearly every night. My curiosity was insatiable. I would sit on a footstool with my head between his legs, and ear resting against his ballocks — I made the two stand up belly to belly touching, whilst I laid down between their legs and looked up at their genitals, sat with my face against his balls, and his prick up against my nose, whilst Sarah delicately tickled *my* prick with her mouth. I pissed against the tip of his prick, and in brief did every fantastic, erotic, frigging, feeling, tickling, skinning, coaxing, sucking tricks to his rod and balls that I thought of, and always with delight. At last always seeing the tip get redder, the rod stiffen, and the gruelly sperm jet out of it.

Sarah said, — "You've ruined that chap. He can now get work and won't." — I had then seen all I wanted, and also felt offended with his familiarity; told her I would not see him again, and then he would go to work. "He won't, I am sure." — But I kept away, and whilst doing so recuperated, for I'd knocked myself up a little with this lascivious excitement. I saw one day somebody like him in the streets, which frightened me, although I had never allowed him to see me with my hat on. When I wrote to Sarah and she met me at a house, she said he was sad at not seeing me, and she had told him I was out of town. — "Have you ever buggered him?" she asked suddenly. The question revolted me, such intention had never once entered my head, had never even occurred to me.

Two or three days after I was again alone in town, and awakened with such lewedness that had my grandmother been in bed with me, I believe I should have gruelled the old lady's quim. Tossing about, and resisting frigging myself, the baudy amusements had with him and Sarah kept running through my mind; and altho I had vowed to myself never to see him again, the desire to do so became overwhelming, and I wrote to Sarah to get him.

The evening came, and how strange! I felt part of my old nervousness. — He put on his silks and boots, which Sarah kept. — At the sight of his white flesh, and roly poly pendant, mine stood upright. We stripped. I pressed his belly against mine, grasping him round his buttocks (he was smooth as a woman), and his prick rose proudly at once.

I handled his prick, pleased with the soft feel of the loose skin. — "Fetch me, or I'll frig myself, I shall spend a pail full" — I wetted both our pricks and bellies with soap and water, then putting him on his back on the bed, mounted him. Our pegos were pressed between our bellies, and grasping each other's rumps, and shoving our pricks about as well as we could, the heat and friction drew both our spunks, and we lay quiet till our tools shrunk down over our balls, forming a heap of testicles and pricks.

Then came a dislike to him and disgust with myself that I often had felt recently. But it vanished directly, I felt lewed again and when I felt his cock. It was stiff soon. As he finished washing it he turned round, and I saw it thick and swollen. Just then Sarah rushed in and prayed me to go. "Do, oh do pray, or there will be a great row — for God's sake go." She was much agitated, I had never seen her so before. "You must — you shall go, — or I shall be half ruined.". Yielding, I went as quickly as I could, and he did after me, I heard.

Next night I saw her out, and could get no explanation about her agitation; but she told me I could not go to the house for a week or ten days.

What gave me about that time such hot fits of lust it is not easy to say, but I was in full rut. At times a fellow's prick stands much more than at others, sometimes it is idleness, sometimes stimulating food, sometimes strength. For some days before I saw him again my prick stood constantly, I was again alone in town, and why I did not ease it by fucking don't recollect — Sarah I could not see any where, and I did nothing but think how I would frig him, and tail her, when we met.

When at length we met, he told me he had not spent since I'd made him. Laughing, Sarah said, "The beggar wanted to have me, but I wouldn't let him." Perhaps a lie — I touched his cock which sprang up stiffly at once. He stripped, and his red tipped, white stemmed sperm spouter would have fascinated any woman — I undressed, my cock stiff as his, and libidinous frolics began.

"Have you buggered him" — Sarah's question came suddenly into my mind as I handled his throbbing prick, his rigid piercer. "Fetch me, frig me, then *you* fuck Sarah and let *me* fuck her after — go on — I'll frig myself — I must spend" — said he, and began frigging.

I stopped him. I put him in various attitudes and looked at his naked rigidity — feeling it, kissing it, glorying in my power — with my own prick upright. Both were wanting the pleasure sorely, yet I dallied and my brain whirled with strange desire, fear, dislike, yet with intention. Then I placed him bending over the bed — his bum towards me, his head towards the looking glass — I stood back to look. There were his white buttocks and large womanly white thighs, his legs in silk, his feet in feminine boots. — No one could have imagined him a man, so round, smooth, white, and womanly was his entire backside and form. It was only looking further off that I missed the pouting hairy lips, and saw a big round stone bag which shewed the male. His prick was invisible, stiff against his belly.

I closed on him, put my hand round and gave his prick a frig — his bum was against my belly. — "Fetch me — oho — make haste, I'm bursting" — looking down I saw his bumhole and the desire whirled thro my brain like lightning. Without pausing or thinking, I felt his prick from under his balls, and whilst he almost shivered with desire — "Oh! make haste, fetch me" — I put both hands round him, feeling his balls with one, his prick with the other; and my own stiff prick I pressed under his ballocks, saying, "Let me put my prick up your bum."

"That I won't," said he disengaging himself and turning round, "that I won't."

Furiously I said, "Let me — I'll give you ten pounds." "Oh no." "I will give you all I have" — and going to my trowsers I took out my purse, and turned into my hands all the gold I had — it was, I think, more than ten pounds.

"Oh no, I can't, it will hurt," said he, eying the money. "It won't." "It will. When I was apprenticed, a boy told me a man did it to him, and it hurt him awful."

I don't know what I replied — but believe I repeated that it would not hurt, that it was well known that people did it, and as I talked I handled his prick with one hand, with the other holding the gold.

"It *will* hurt — I'm frightened, but will you give me ten pounds really?"

I swore it, talked about that of which I knew nothing — that I had heard it was pleasure to the man whose arsehole was plugged — that once done they liked nothing so much afterwards. His prick, which had dwindled under fear, again stiffened as I frigged, he ceased talking and breathed hard, saying, "I'm coming." — I stopped at once.

"Let me." "I don't think you can, it seems impossible — if you hurt me will you pull it out?" "Yes yes, I will."

He turned to the bed again and kneeled, but he was too high — I pulled him off — then it was too low. Again on the bed and I pulled his bum to the level of my prick, I locked the door, I trembled, we whispered. I slabbered my prick and his hole with spittle. His prick was still stiff. There was the small round hole — the balls beneath — the white thighs. — I closed on him half mad, holding him round one thigh. I pointed my prick — my brain whirled — I wished not to do what I was doing, but some ungovernable impulse drove me on. Sarah's words rang in my ears. I heard them as if then spoken. My rod with one or two lunges buried itself up him, and passing both hands round his belly I held him to me, grasping both his prick and balls tightly. He gave a loud moan. "Ohoo I shall faint," he cried. "Ho, pull it out."

It's in — don't move or I won't pay you, or something of that sort — I said, holding myself tight up to him. "Ohooo, leave go, you're hurting my balls so" — I suppose I *was* handling them roughly — but his bum kept close to my belly.

I recollect nothing more distinctly. A fierce, bloody minded baudiness possessed me, a determination to do it — to ascertain if it was a pleasure — I would have wrung his prick off sooner than have withdrawn for him, and yet felt a disgust at myself. Drawing once slightly back, I saw my prick half out of his tube, then forcing it back, it spent up him. I shouted out loudly and baudily (Sarah told me), but I was unconscious of that. She was in her sitting room.

I came to myself — how long afterwards I cannot say. — All seemed a dream, but I was bending over him — pulling his backside still towards me. — My prick still stiff and up him. "Does it hurt now." "Not so much."

His prick was quite large but not quite stiff. A strong grip with my hand stiffened it, I frigged hard, the spunk was ready and boiling, for he had been up to spending point half a dozen times. My prick, still encased, was beginning to stiffen more. — He cried — "I am coming, I am coming" — his bum jogged and trembled — his arsehole tightened — my prick slipped out — and he sank on the bed spending over the counterpane — I stood frigging him still.

He spent a perfect pool of sperm on the bed. The maddening thought of what I had done made me wish to do it again. I forgot all my sensations — I have no idea of them now — I knew I had spent, that's all. "Let me do it again." "That I won't for any money," said he turning round.

Then I frigged myself and frigged him at the same time furiously. Fast as hands could move did mine glide up and down the pricks. Pushing him down with his arse on the sperm on the counterpane, I finished him as he lay, and I spent over his prick. balls, and belly. In ten minutes our double spend was over.

Immediately I had an ineffable disgust at him and myself — a terrible fear — a loathing — I could scarcely be in the room with him — could have kicked him. He said, "You've made me bleed." At that I nearly vomited — "I must make haste," said I looking at my watch, "I forgot it was so late. — I must go." All my desire was to get away as quickly as possible. I left after paying him, and making him swear, and swearing myself, that no living person should know of the act.

Yet a few days after I wrote the narrative of this blind, mad, erotic act; an act utterly unpremeditated, and the perpetration of which as I now think of it seems most extraordinary. One in which I had no pleasure — have no recollection of physical pleasure — and which only dwells in my mind with disgust; tho it is against my philosophy even to think I had done wrong.

A lark in a park. — Alice T°°°°h°°l of Middleborough. — Loving couples in the open. — "Let's feel it." — Alice's narrative. — A frig. — Gamahuche. — Her supper. — Reflexions on fucking. — Idealities. — Two little sisters. — At a German bath. — An exquisite Austrian Paphian. — Delicious fuckstress. — A forgotten appointment. — Enter male. — Mein schwester's bedroom. — A treat at a peephole. — Up a lubricious cunt. — Mein schwester washing herself. — Fraulein gamahuched. — Groping and fucking. — On my gamahuching tendencies. — A family of harlots. — Two sister dress makers. — Anne and Maria. — Feeling cunts. — Forms, features, and cuntal resemblances. — A fart in a fire place. — On harlots farting. — Cunt farts. — H°l°n M°°°w°°d. — Our first meeting. — Her physical perfections. — Money differences. — My promise kept. — A year's interval. — Friendship established. — Mutual meretriciousness. — Unrestrained sexual amusements. — Erotic tastes gratified. — Arcades ambo.

I find that I have misplaced some manuscript, and that the four following little adventures took place in the summer and in the autumn.

The narratives of these little incidents are but little abbreviated, some paragraphs not at all — but the past is put for the present, in which latter tense most of the narratives of my amours were written.

———————

Late one night in Oxford Street looking at the battalion of harlots walking about, a well grown woman faced and pleased me — I was fit, yet had no intention of having a woman, was simply looking at them, pleased and yet sorry as they often made me feel, when in unphilosophic mood. "Good night," said she. "Good night, my dear." — "Won't you say something more?" — "No, good night" — and I turned to cross the road to B°°d Sᵗ. — "Come home with me." — "No." — "Oh-do-I wish so you would."

There was something plaintive in her voice, and her manner was unlike her class. — She had for some time walked by my side looking into my face without speaking. — There was gentility in her manner which pleased me. — "Do you live far off?" — "No only up there." — "I can only give you °°°°." — "That will do." — "Go on then and I'll follow" — and so on we went but on and on so far, that I stopped. — "Where is it?" She named the street. — "Oh! that's a long way let's take a cab dear." We did and drove to G°°°e R°°d. — A respectable looking young man opened the door of a very well and seemingly newly furnished house, and we went into a nice bedroom.

She kissed me several times when in the cab which I don't think I returned, and she felt gently at my ballocks. I had not felt much desire until she did that. Then my cock rose and the delicious lewdness coursed thro my body. — "Oho!" said she with a sigh. "It's a nice one I'm sure" — and she kissed me lovingly. — In the room she sat down with her bonnet on, then rose and kissed me several times. — "Would you believe that the man who opened the door was my father's servant?" — "No," I replied bluntly. "I thought you wouldn't but he was, he's just married and opened this house for lodgers, but he knows I'm gay." — I didn't believe her, thought it brag, tho I did not say so. — "Take off your things." — She left off feeling my prick which she had got out and was fondling, and began undressing.

She took off petticoat after petticoat — warm weather it was, — whilst I sat looking at her. Her arms were very thin, and I saw that she had the smallest breasts. — "Go on," said I for she had stopped. — "What, all? — I'm rather thin, do you like thin women?" — "I have no objection to them if they are nice." It was not true but I said that not to wound her. — She took off more clothing, pausing from time to time for me to say enough. But I made her strip to her chemise. — "I'm very thin," said she, "but I am as good on a bed as another woman," and she sat down on the sofa besides me.

I pulled up her chemise, felt about her, and I have never seen such a thin gay woman. She had scarcely breast or backside. He⸗

thighs were half what they should have been, and below her knees
were broom sticks. —My cock dwindled, and all desire left me, so
after feeling her and talking for a time I said, "That will do dear,
now I am going," and I put the money on the mantel piece.

"Oh don't go without doing me, you'll find me very nice.— do
me, I want it so badly, you've not looked at it" and laying down
on the sofa she exposed her cunt, a youthful dark haired article. —
I went to her and looked at it, not having even wished to see it
before. — It was a neat looking cunt, but my prick gave no such
signs of vitality as a fresh cunt ought to have caused. "Let's talk,"
said she, and I sat down by her. She clutched my prick and my
fingers went on to her clitoris; she was a nice clean woman, but no
sensation came to me for a time, and we talked on, she telling her
history, and kissing me at intervals, and always feeling my doodle.

I was quite cold to her — "I can't do it," I said — "and often
go home with women only to see, feel, and chat with them," saying
this to avoid wounding her. — "You don't like me, because I'm so
thin." — "Not so." — "I don't like doing it," said she, "but I do
want it so — I haven't had it for a week," and kneeling down at
once, she took my cock in her mouth; I had not hinted at such a
thing. — The friction of her lips and tongue took effect, it stiffened,
desire came, she rose up triumphantly smiling. "I'm so glad," said
she. Then we went to the bed, and her cunt received it. In copula-
tion it seemed as nice as that of other women's, but I almost won-
dered what I held in my hands as I recovered from my pleasure,
and moved them over her skinny backside. She spent almost di-
rectly my prick went up her. "Oh, it's lovely," said she "keep it in,"
and twining her spidery limbs round mine she held me to her,
clipped my cock well with her cunt, and then easing off from me
slightly begging me to keep my cock in her which I did pretty well,
she got her right hand between our bellies and frigged herself
whilst I was still in her. Her eyes closed. — "Lovely prick, lovely
prick," she kept ejaculating to herself as if to excite herself till she
spent again, and then her legs stretched out, and she laid tranquil.
— My cock was actually stiffening in her, thro. her cunt clipping
as she spent, but I drew it out intending to leave her, her thinness
displeased me so.

But she held me. "Don't go yet — wait and do it again." —
"I can't it's late." — "Not very, you could do it now if you like —

I haven't enjoyed a poke like it in I don't know how long — what a lot you have spent — shall I wash it?" — It was irresistible. — My penis had been getting more sensitive for some time, and a fresh washed cunt even hurt me sometimes, and if washed out with anything but water I could tell it directly. — I like them just as nature has made them when left untouched for some hours, moist, smooth, lubricious; to feel my prick gliding as if over oiled ivory. — "No don't wash." — We talked for a time. She was from the country, of well to do parents, had been seduced, had a child now dead, was turned out by her parents, and turned gay. — The landlord knew all about her, and would tell me if I asked him, but not her real name, nor where her home was. She volunteered all this, and then to her seeming joy I fucked her again, after she had made me piddle, and wash it, and she had sucked it up to stiffness.

"I dare say you won't see me again will you?" — "I rarely see any strange ladies, there is a lady I see constantly who has all I can do." — "Tell me what she is like." — I did and lied eloquently. — "You don't like thin women — men don't, I get on badly, nearly every farthing I get goes to pay my lodging and washing. I can scarcely get enough to eat — I will drown myself — I often think of doing so in the night." — "Nonsense, go home." — "Never — I wouldn't show my face there again, it would kill the old people. — If I don't get on better soon I'll drown myself — I go and look at the canal sometimes as I go home." — I doubled her fee, pitying her, and left her sitting on the sofa crying bitterly. She had not been drinking — it was true despair I feel sure.

Passing a park entrance one misty and warmish night at about ten o'clock, I thought I should like to feel a cunt. I had felt many in earlier days there. I entered and saw couples sitting on the seats close to each other, and further from the walk, couples indistinctly in more compromising attitudes. Moving on to the grass nearer so as to see better, — looking at couples fucking always delights me — there was a man on a seat bending a little forward and a woman standing up in front of him — stink fingering of course. — A little further on was a woman sitting, and a man standing up in front of her. Her arm dropped down as I approached. The man turned round from me, turning again the other way as I passed him, tho

it was too dark to see faces or even a prick if out — I know well
that the girl was frigging him — most likely — I passed on not look-
ing round, for why should I disturb couples in their amorous play,
I should not like it myself. But I should have liked to have seen
him frigged, and an old desire returned as I saw this fun obscurely
in the misty darkness, a desire which I thought satisfied and gone
for ever. — How soft and smooth, tho solid, stiff, yet semi-elastic
is the male love truncheon. How smooth and nice to the hand, and
I thought I should like to feel one once again. — Alas for my virtue.

A square built, shortish female passed me, walking rather
quickly. "Are you going, Mary, to piddle?" — "No, I'm going
home," and she stopped. I laid hold of her arm which was a thick
one, and knew from that and her outline that she had a fattish bum.
— "Come on to the grass, let me feel your cunt and I'll give you a
shilling." In half a minute I had my hand between her thighs. —
"There is spunk in your cunt." — "That there's not, I wish there
was, no such luck. — I've not had it done to night." — "What are
you going home for?" — "I've been crying at not getting a chance,
and going home to bed, for I've not had a mouthful to eat or drink
since breakfast." — "Why?" — "I've no money and have pawned
everything. I'll get something to eat now with this shilling."

"Sit down here and feel my prick." She did, and then my
baudy imagination was stirred. — "Piss over my fingers and I'll give
you another shilling." — "I'll try, but I can't do much, come further
off, for the police may see us here." — She squatted and poured
a little warm stream over my hand. — "Do you like the girls to do
that to you?" — "Sometimes, don't you do it to other men?" — "I
have only done it once before, London men are so funny." She
spoke with a strong provincial accent. — There was a frankness in
manner, a readiness and ring of truth about her.

We adjourned to a seat near a tree after I had dried my hand
on her thigh. It was getting more misty and I felt secure from
observation. — She told me her history, perhaps a lie, perhaps true.
— Alice T****h**l of Middleborough — ran way with another girl
to London to better herself, the other girl was gay and she knew
it but Alice then was not. — "No I was in service at home, and had
put by seven pounds in a saving bank." — They slept at a coffee
house in a street leading out of the E°g°w°°e Road, a servant was
wanted there and she took the place, but found the pay bad, the

work worse than at Middleborough, and the food muck, so her friend advised her to leave and see gentlemen. — She would not at first, but not getting another place went to stay in the lodgings of her friend, and went with her to a music hall. They came home with a gentleman, who fucked her friend before her, they had all been drinking, and her friend then persuaded her to let the gentleman fuck *her*. "She made me let him. — I'd never had a man before. No, I'd never even put my finger up it — of course I likes fucking now, what gal doesn't? but I don't get on. — I've got my seven pounds away from the bank at Middleborough, she told me how to get it, and we have spent it. I wish I were back at Middleborough. — I did get my belly full there — here I often don't get enough to eat. — Liz says I haven't got cheek. — I've only been in London two months altogether."

She had a decent little room but a long way off she said, so gents had her in the park — or in houses close by. Would she let me have her for half a crown? — I wished to know how cheap it could be had. — "Too glad," said she, and she twiddled my prick till I began to feel I wanted to spend badly. — "I'd like it done too," said she. — "We can do it here, but I'm rather short and the grass is too damp to lie down to night, I do it standing generally over there, there are fences over there to lean against." — We went still further off, and found a vacant seat near an out of the way walk. — "Here is your money, half a crown — now don't let me fuck you if you are not well." — "Thank you, sir — I'm all right as far as I know." — I sat down, and turning her back towards me, she pulled up her petticoats and put her buttocks towards my pego — I felt her cunt, but prudence restrained me tho her flesh felt fat, smooth, and clean. — But I had scarcely seen her face. — "Let me frig you. — I'm frightened to fuck you." — "I don't like that done to me sir, but you may if you like." — I turned her round into a convenient position and frigged her. — "Are you coming?" — "Yes, do it a little higher up" — with a little more frigging she spent. — I felt her agitation coming on, felt the quivering and jerking of her loins and buttocks, round which I kept my left hand. — "You haven't spent" — "Oh, I have, feel, I am quite wet — I haven't done it for two days." — Her tight little cunt was wet I felt.

That grope made me salacious beyond control almost, yet I feared to fuck in a channel I had not seen. — "I'll give you half

a crown to suck my prick." — "No, I can't." — A little persuasion
did it. — She sat down on the seat, bent forward, I stood up and
fucked in her mouth. — She was a novice at it — "Don't I do it
right?" — "No — you hurt," — "Oh don't let it go inside." — "I
must." — "It will make me sick." — "No it won't, I shan't spend
much." — "Oh, don't squeeze my bonnet" — I had put my hands
on her head. I then laid my hands on her cheeks, pulling her mouth
to me and spent. She retreated it as the life giving fluid spurted,
but I pulled her head to me tightly, holding her cheeks till my full
pleasure was over.

"I'll have a good blow out before the public's closed, my belly's
regular wobbling thro emptiness," said she. — I paid her twice as
much as I'd promised, feeling pleased with her, and again sat down
feeling her backside. — "You've a fat solid arse, for a London park
woman." — "I was fat when I came to London, but have been
getting thinner ever since," said she, and walked off quickly, thank-
ing me gratefully for the much larger gratuity than I'd promised. —
Said I — "You know you've been lying." — "What have I been ly-
ing about — come to my lodgings and I'll soon make you believe."
— "Good night dear." — "Good night sir, I hope I'll see you again."

Strange it is how I enjoyed this prank in the open. — It made
my cock stand several times since when I've thought of it, and
even when with a lovely woman. But my mind often wanders away
from the woman in whom my prick lies, to the recollection of other
cunts and their pleasures — I have questioned gay ladies, and find
that when being fucked, they also often think of other men and
other baudy deeds. For years my mind when poking women, ran
occasionally on fucking two short girls whom I met in Piccadilly at
day break one summer's morning. Two short girls, — sisters they
said, and I had both of them.

Soon after this in early autumn I was at the baths of ●●●●●●.
At seven o'clock a.m. I was on the promenade near the brunnen,
and saw a woman looking about twenty-five years old, with whom
in form, height, features and complexion, few could compare. She
was one of the most beautiful women I ever saw, and unmistakably
a whore, tho she neither looked right or left or at any man. I fol-
lowed her up and down discreetly til I caught her eye, gave her

a significant look, and followed her to her lodgings. At the foot of the staircase told her that after breakfast I would be with her at half past ten that morning.

There at the time was she expecting me, in a loose peignoir which thrown off, left her but a chemise of finest cambric, and that removed left her nude, all but blue silk stockings and kid boots. She was one of the finest, most beautiful perfect creatures, that God ever created, yet she was but a Paphian, facile to a degree, and without any nonsense about showing it. Soon she was on the bed, and between a pair of thighs and buttocks perfect in form, smoothness and color, opened a smallish, delicate aperture, fringed sufficiently with chestnut hair. It was of the most enticing description, was indeed one of the loveliest cunts I ever saw. — Neither clitoris, nymphæ, vagina or lips, were too large or too small, — ample crisp and fine hair was around it, and shadowed the mons, but not a hair was on her buttocks, nor near a little tight anus looking too small and close to let a straw through it. The oval buttocks with their gradual elongation into the loveliest tapering thighs was exquisite. In fact, buttocks, belly, thighs, fringe, gap, clitoris, nymphæ, color, all were perfectly beautiful.

Tearing my clothes off rapidly in lustful impetuosity, throwing myself upon her greedy of her charms, hurrying to pierce her, to fill that divine gap with my spunk, with a plunge up went my prick into her. It was a bottomless cunt, my tip found no obstacle, all was divinely soft, lubricious, elastic, compressive. In a thrust or two it found its place, no thrusts were needed more, it was in a fleshy paradise, needing no exertion to enjoy it, and where it loved for a minute to remain quiet. But the lovely sheath had its own desires, its own way of acting, of evoking pleasure, of getting out from my testicles the emulsion which was to soothe its heat. — With the gentlest heaves, with imperceptible compressions, it received my equally gentle movements, constricted, pinched my pego more and more, and yet with exquisite delicacy, till at length from out of my reservoirs, spurted my spermatic mucilage, and I died off in her arms faint with pleasure, sleepy almost with sensuous fatigue, clasping her buttocks, sucking her sweet tongue as I lay quietly up her; whilst her thighs gradually sank lower, her belly ceased its heavings, her cunt its grips, and wallowing in my sperm, both prick and cunt lay joined in blessed quietude.

How I wish I'd been younger and at liberty, I think I should have had her night and day till exhausted, but that was physically and for other reasons impossible. But I enjoyed looking at her, and as she appeared in handsome clothing at the various places, sat and looked, or followed and looked at her, and in my mind's eye saw those lovely thighs and belly, that exquisite cunt, as well as if she'd been undressed. Then I began to wonder what other man had enjoyed those charms, and longed to see a man as handsome as she was, giving her pleasure, injecting his semen into her.

Of this divine creature I can say no more than that for some weeks I saw her often. I could have loved her, big woman, sausage eating, beer drinking woman, harlot tho she was. I could have loved her, for she was for sexual pleasures absolute perfection. She loved her profession, yet was not greedy of money. "I can have as many men as I want, I expect a friend at half past eleven," said she, on the first day, "and you must go." — How many scores of women I have had, whose cunts never seemed to give me such complete physical pleasure as this woman's did. — To be happy with any woman the cunt must fit the man's prick. — A subtle refinement of sexuality this, but such is my belief, and then in conjugal life all is happiness.

One afternoon on a blazing hot day, I called without notice, and had not been in her room five minutes, was not undressed nor she, and I had placed her on the bed with her clothes negligently thrown up so that her magnificent backside and cunt were visible. I sat in a chair opposite the bed enjoying the luscious spectacle, when a knock came. "Oh" said she, "I'm so sorry, I'd forgotten. I was to see a man at this time, and he's here, go into the other room for a minute, it's Mein Schwester's room, till I've sent him away." Quick as lightning came the letch. — "No, I'll wait, let him fuck you, let me see him fuck you, then come into your sister's room, with all his sperm in your cunt and let me see it full of it, make him quite naked, you be so too, and I'll pay you well." In polyglot language, in half whispers, all this was said, but I was understood. — "Yah, yah, — but you cannot see — the sparm yes — schnell, — go — he is outside." — More knocks were heard, and in a few seconds I had passed through the door into the sister's room, locked it, peeped, and Oh joy! found I could see the lower half of the bed, and a tall handsome fair haired young man standing there, talking to my woman.

Until that moment I did not know my charmer had a sister —

I had seen her walking about with a shorter and younger woman, and this was Mein Schwester who began her blandishments in a very quiet way and spoke in a quiet voice. — Did I mind her dressing? — certainly not — whereupon she stripped to her waist and began washing a lovely youthful breast. But I wanted to see a fine couple fucking, and could not take my eye from the keyhole. Finding that, — "If you get on a chair you'll see better" — said the Fraulein pointing to the door; and sure enough thro a natural crack high up in an ill made door, I now saw the whole bed.

He was caressing her, feeling her cunt, sitting on the bedside with her. She had got his prick out which looked like a rolling pin, its tip uncovered, red as crimson, and ready for insertion. They spoke in foreign language of which I understood but little, but from occasional words and from her movements, knew that she was urging him to undress. A blazing hot day it was. All at once he began undressing in haste till in his shirt. "All, all," said she, and off that went whilst she threw off her chemise. There they stood naked, a splendid couple, he nearly six feet high with clean white flesh without hair, with a stalwart prick full seven inches long, and thick as well. On the bed quickly she laid, her exquisite thighs apart. I could see her adorable gap which he licked for a minute as he stood, then laid down beside her for a second only, she handling his splendid organ whilst he felt hers. But all was too quick, his prick must have been standing whilst waiting outside her rooms for me to escape, it was rigid when he undressed, and the next second he was on her fucking. Then I could only see his back and a bit of his balls at times, as he thrust and withdrew, which he did with such energy, that in a minute I saw by the movement of his arse and his pressure on her, that the libation was given. Then they lay languid and quiet.

Wild with lust, not willing to lose any of the spectacle, I beckoned the sister to me, and pulled off coat and waistcoat as I stood and gave them to her whilst looking still thro the aperture. — Soon I heard her say something, which I knew was that she'd go into her sister's room and wash. Down I got, pulled off every thing I had on but shirt and socks, and just as I'd finished doing so in she came, holding her finger to her mouth for my silence, holding her cunt to prevent the sperm from dropping, but speaking aloud to her sister. — At once she knowing my letch laid at the bed side and

opened her thighs. Oh accomplished Paphian! and how they like
their trade when they succeed.

There was the lovely cunt, its red surface well nigh hidden by
white thick sperm. The sperm hung to the fringe, it lay thick low
down on the orifice of the avenue into which the libation had been
poured. — My brain whirled with sensuous excitement. I scarcely
knew what I did. — Intending only to have seen the copulation and
the results, now the desire to have her just as she was, to cover
my prick with his sperm, overwhelmed me. Motioning her on to
the bed, I threw off my shirt, mounted her, and plunged my prick
into the soft semenalized vagina, revelling in baudy delight as I
felt the grateful lubricity on my prick, then felt all round the stem
where her cunt lips touched it, and rubbed my balls against her
bum furrow, so that all his spendings might be on and about me.
Then not so young now, or so full as my predecessor, I lingered
quietly up her, thinking with salacious delight of what I'd seen and
where I was. — "Have you spent with him?" "No he was so quick,"
was all that was said. Then at the idea of giving *her* pleasure, of
fetching out *her* juices I began my thrusts, my prick squashing the
sperm as I moved it up and down. My beauty's passions were
roused, I know that this fucking in another's sperm excites women;
murmurs of fuck, prick, cunt, sperm, ejaculated in three languages
were given, and with our tongues exchanging and mingling their
salivas, we spent together, and the essence of two males and her
own spendings mixed together in her cunt.

Before my stiffness had gone she uncunted me, washed, and
went back to him. I with prick still moist mounted again the chair.
There he laid naked on the bed (it was a scorching hot day) feel-
ing his prick. "Have you washed?" said she. — "No, I'll fuck you
again," and pulling her on to the bed he began feeling her cunt.

Tho tired and reeking with perspiration, I wished to see more,
but got down and washed. Silently. Mein Schwester held the wash-
hand basin for me. Then I mounted the chair again and watched
them at their amorous dalliance. Soon after on looking round, I
saw the sister was start naked sponging herself all over. Was it to
wash herself, or to show me her charms?

He did only what I have done hundreds of times, and de-
scribed many times in this narrative of my secret life, but how
fresh, ever fresh and voluptuously exciting are such scenes, such

amatory amusements. To me this was exquisite. There were these superb creatures in the fullness of youth and beauty, feeling each other's genitals, feeling all over their bodies, and kissing almost in silence, for speech is useless almost in such delights. Then his mouth settled on her cunt and he gamahuched her. How I envied him, for I have already sucked and tongue titillated that lovely gap. Soon her lovely backside writhed, her belly heaved, and as he kneeled I could see sideways his prick, stiff and nodding as his lust got stronger with his delicious amusement. Why did they not consummate? I was impatient to see the termination, to see her thighs around his — his buttocks oscillating with the thrusts of his prick up her cunt, I longed to be feeling his buttocks whilst at the exercise. But he was now in no hurry, wisely delaying the lust destroying crisis. — There I stood peeping, start naked, sweating now with excitement, every now and then looking down at the sister leisurely washing herself from head to foot. Soon she had put on chemise and slippers, and looked up smilingly at me. Another peep, they were talking side by side, his prick lolling on his thigh not now quite stiff. The glorious finale would not be yet, and down I got, for my companion began to rivet my attention.

Questioning her, she declared that she was the sister, was twenty-one, her sister twenty-six. Her eyes and face showed family likeness. "Is your cunt like your sister's?" — "I don't know." "Show it to me, take off your chemise." — Without reply she took it off, and laid on the bed. I saw that potential almost omnipotent charm of the woman, that red, central, hairy framed furrow, that scented, red lipped, division of her belly, that orifice which subjugates the male whether emperor or beggar. The gamahuche of her sister was in my mind, she was perhaps being gamahuched at that moment. The letch seized me, and applying my tongue to the Fraulein's cunt, I licked it rapidly, thinking of her sister's gamahuching, wishing we were all in the same room, and gamahuching side by side.

When the Fraulein had enjoyed my lingual treat, when the twitching of her thighs and bum gave warning of her coming crisis, she pushed me off. "Nein, nein, fuck me." — I stood up, prick stiffening, and looked at her rosy flesh. Much younger, neither so tall nor so stout as her sister, but plump and fine in form, with solid bubbies was she. She'd such a pretty mouth, that I cried,

"Suck me." — "Wash it then." — Rapidly I sluiced my injector, heard speaking in the adjoining room, ceased frigging the Fraulein, mounted the chair again, and saw her sister opening wide her thighs for the entry of that grand love staff. — "He's fucking" — I cried, and then with rapid multiplication of desires in my brain, wishing for all things voluptuous, to be fucking both the sisters at once, to be frigging him, cried out, "Suck me, suck me, mein lieben." Without a word or any hesitation, she took my penis in her pretty mouth, and so I stood, her tongue and palate ministering to my pleasure, whilst I saw the other two joined into one body, heaving, thrusting, writhing, as he plunged his pego up and down, till one long cry of pleasure, told that his sperm was shooting into her.

Then getting down furious for similar pleasure I mounted Mein Schwester, fucked hard and quickly, and just as my pleasure was increasing, in came the elder start naked as before. I stopped for a second. "Come to the bed," I cried and moved my beauty and myself close to the wall to make room. The elder laid down, I buried my fingers in her lubricious cunt, put my prick again in the younger, and fucked out my sperm into her in a delirium of baudy desires, and visions of what I had just seen.

The man went away, the two washed their cunts, I spent another hour with them, they and myself naked, for it was a day on which nudity was alone tolerable, and then fucked my favorite after putting my prick first into her sister, then into her. The elder said she didn't know of that natural crack in the door: perhaps not, but perhaps thro that crack some one has seen *me*, fucking *her* — what matters?

I could not for health's sake fuck her as often as I desired, but visited her at times solely to see her naked and to gamahuche her, for now I love gamahuching a pretty cunt whether quite a young one or not — love to give a woman that pleasure which few whether harlot or modest can refuse.

She told me she was born at ●●●●● and had four sisters. — One was kept by an Austrian nobleman. — Another was a gay lady at ●●●●. She and her sister there made the fourth. They were a **harlotting family evidently**, *all* beautiful and open to all the male sex. — Thank beneficent providence for that.

I had returned to England, at the end of the autumn and was going along °°°°° Street at about half past eight one night in early winter, when I saw two, young, shortish women standing at the corner of a cross street. It was away from any main line of thoroughfare where doxies mostly pick up their friends. I looked hard at the one facing me as I crossed the road. — "What do you think of me? You'll know me again," said she. — Gay from that I knew she was, I had not before been quite able to make up my mind whether they were strumpets, or not.

I felt larkish. — "You're pretty, and I should know you again, if I felt you as well as saw you." — "You'd better feel me then." — I passed up the side street and at a few yards from the street lights stopped. She had followed me, and I offered her a present to feel her cunt. It was refused. I increased my offer, and next minute was groping a youngish quim, as I knew by the feel and the quantity of hair on it. "Come home and see me naked, we are only at number fifteen in next street," — and she put her hand down and squeezed my ballocks outside my trowsers, whilst I was busy with her split. I agreed her fee for the amusement at her home. Then, "That's my sister and we live together." — "She's not." — "She is, look at her, we are like two peas." — The other came now quite close. "Let me feel her cunt then and if I like the feel I will." — "What are you going to give me," said sister. "Nothing for the feel unless I should go home with you." — "Look if any one's coming Annie," said she to her sister, and so saying raised her clothes a bit. I felt her cunt and agreed she should come with us. — In three minutes I was in their rooms, which were comfortable enough, in a respectable looking eight roomed house in a quiet street, and with fires both in sitting room and bed room. There was also a small bed in the corner of the sitting room.

They undressed, and whilst doing so we chatted. I'm so fond of seeing women undress. Both had blue eyes, brown hair, and were exactly the same height, they were not good looking. — "You're not sisters," I said, tho I believed from their look that they were. "We are tho," both cried out in chorus. "She's the eldest." — One was nineteen, the other eighteen, they were dress makers, but couldn't get enough to live by work. — "So you both turned out together, who was fucked first?" — The eldest was, neither had been fucked more than a year.

By that time they were naked. The eldest was a little stouter than the other, but both were slim, well made, and in form, colour and feature unmistakably sisters. — "Now let me see your cunts." — At the bed side, and then with their backsides towards me kneeling on the bed, I inspected the divisional slits of their bellies, and really in hairyness and colour, and generally in look of the locality they were wonderfully alike. I have before noticed in sisters a family likeness in cunts. It's a subject I have been curious about. On the contrary I once had two sisters (so calling themselves) who tho alike in features and form, differed much in colour, and between whose cunts there was no likeness whatever. I wonder whether the pricks of the boys of a family resemble each other, if cunts do, why should not pricks?

The elder had slightly more hair on her gap, and I selected her for my exercise. Undressing myself, I laid beside her and titillated her a good deal. She rubbed my already rigid love staff up and down vigorously and more than I liked, for I was in no hurry. "Leave off, I'm in no hurry." — "Don't frig me then so much." — "I'll do it till you're ready to spend, and then you'll spend with me." — "I shall spend with you, I'm nearly spending now, get on me." — But I was going to prolong my pleasure, so leaving off frigging her, whilst she relinquished my tool, I cuddled her close to me, and put my prick up against her belly and squeezed it there with mine, and so we held ourselves close, clasping each other's naked arses.

The younger one all this time was standing naked with her rump to the fire looking at us, and suddenly let a short, sharp, ringing fart. "Maria you *beast*," said her sister relinquishing me, and turning round (for her *rump* as she lay was towards her sister and my *face* was towards her). As she spoke, out from her sister's bottom came another short, sharp, cracking fart. — "You dirty beast, what are you doing?" — "It's better out than in — we all do it sometimes," said the girl laughing. — "Go into the sitting room" — she went — I was disgusted, for I hate to hear a woman or man fart, but turned to my companion, mounted her, my prick began its work, and very soon we both spent with much enjoyment of each other, saucy whore tho she was. — Then I dressed and gave the elder more money than the other. — "Oh! give me the same as my sister." — "I've not fucked *you*, and *it's* all I promised you." — "You may fuck me tho if you like, — do" — and she threw herself on the bed, widening out her thighs and exposing her little crack invitingly. — "You're a dirty little devil to stand there farting." — "So she is," said the elder.

The idea of leaving a cunt untasted which was at hand, and a nice, tight, youthful looking one, upset me. I didn't want another spend, yet longed to put into the cunt. It began to make me waver. — "I can't, my prick won't stand." — "I'll make it." — "You must gamahuche it then." — "I won't gammerouss," said she. But finding I was going she agreed to do it. I undressed again, laid naked with her on the bed, groped the little tight cunt, then had my shrunken pego brought to the stand in Maria's mouth, and fucked her cunt whilst the elder played with my balls, and incited by me (for the idea suddenly came to me as I fucked her sister) pressed my bumhole with her thumb. But it being so soon after my first emission, I took a long time in getting the second, and fucked away in her tight cunt long and heartily. — "Oh I'm coming," said Maria, and I felt from her movements that she was. Then sensual excitement came at once to fever heat in me as I heard her words and sighs, and brought me to a crisis, and we mingled our juices in her cunt at the same instant.

"You're a dirty little devil," said I, laughing afterwards. "I never knew her do such a thing before," said the elder quite seriously. — "Will you come and see us again, there are no other lodgers, we are believed to be dressmakers, and never go out or bring gentlemen home till it's quite dark, ask for Miss ***** if you call" — I never did call.

I've seen a thousand and more females piddle and wash their notches, but don't think I've heard an accidental windy exhalation from half a dozen of them when at those operations. Of one or two of those I'm sure I have told in this history. I have however some dim recollection of a female intentionally farting, and of my disgust, and perhaps it is told of here. But am not at all sure even of the occurrence, and thinking back now more than thirty-five years, don't at this moment recollect the event or the woman.

[But I've heard a woman's cunt fart more than once, a windy exhalation which astonished me at first. I've heard women deny that a cunt could fart, but the woman from whom it escaped whilst I was gamahuching her (one of the sweetest, cleanest and loveliest) asserted it, and the abbess who was present at the interesting controversy, said that such ventuosities were not uncommon.]

———————

One night soon after this, I met at the A°g°°e rooms H°l°n M°°°w°°d and was struck with her instantly. My experienced eye and well trained judgment in women, as well as my instincts, told me what was beneath her petticoats and I was not deceived. I have had many splendid women in my time, but never a more splendid perfect beauty, in all respects.

Of full but not great height, with the loveliest shade of chestnut hair of great growth, she had eyes in which grey, green and hazel were indescribably blended with an expression of supreme voluptuousness in them, yet without baudiness or salacity, and capable of any play of expression. A delicate, slightly retroussé nose, the face a pure oval, a skin and complexion of a most perfect tint and transparency, such was H°l°n M. Nothing was more exquisite than her whole head, tho her teeth were wanting in brilliancy, — but they were fairly good and not discoloured.

She had lovely cambered feet, perfect to their toes; thighs meeting from her cunt to knees and exquisite in their columnar beauty; big, dimpled haunches, a small waist, full firm breasts, small hands, arms of perfect shape in their full roundness. Every where her flesh was of a very delicate creamy tint, and was smooth to perfection. Alabaster or ivory, were not more delicious to the touch, than her flesh was every where from her cheeks to her toes.

Short, thick, crisp yet silky brown hair covered the lower part of her motte, at that time only creeping down by the side of the cunt lips, but leaving the lips free, near to at her bumhole, a lovely little clitoris, a mere button, topped her belly rift, the nymphæ were thin, small, and delicate. The mouth of the vulva was small, the avenue tight yet exquisitely elastic, and as she laid on her back and opened her thighs, it was an exquisite, youthful, pink cunt, a voluptuous sight which would have stiffened the prick of a dying man.

Her deportment was good, her carriage upright but easy, the undulations of her body in movement voluptuous, and fascinating; every thing, every movement was graceful; even when she sat down to piss it was so — and taking her altogether, she was one of the most exquisite creatures God ever created to give enjoyment to man. — With all this grace, and rich, full, yet delicate of frame, she was a strong, powerful woman, and had the sweetest voice — it was music.

I saw much of this in her at a glance, and more completely as she undressed. Then the sweetest smell as if of new milk, or of almonds escaped from her, and the instant she laid down I rushed lasciviously on her cunt, licked and sucked it with a delight that was maddening. I could have eaten it. Never had I experienced such exquisite delight in gamahuching a woman. Scarcely ever have I gamahuched a gay woman on first acquaintance, and generally never gamahuched them at all.

As I went home with her in a cab I had attempted a few liberties, but she repulsed them. — "Wait till we get home, I won't have them in a cab." — Directly we arrived I asked what her compliment was to be. — No she had never less than a fiver. — "Why did you not tell me so, and I would not have brought you away. — What I give is two sovereigns, here is the money, I am sorry I have wasted your time" — and was going. — "Stop," said she — "don't go yet!" — I looked in my purse and gave her what I could — it was a little more than the sum I'd named — and promised to bring her the remainder of a fiver another day. Then I fucked her. — "Don't be in such a hurry," I said, for she moved her cunt as women either do when very randy, or wishing to get rid of a man. That annoyed me, but oh my God my delight as I shed my sperm into that beautiful cunt, and kissed and smelt that divine body, and looked into those voluptuous eyes. I had at once a love as well as lust for her, as my prick throbbed out its essence against her womb. — But *she* had no pleasure with *me*. — She was annoyed and in a hurry, she had another man waiting in another room in the house to have her — as she has told me since.

What was in this woman — what the specific attraction, I cannot say, but she made me desire to open my heart to her, and I told rapidly of my amatory tricks, my most erotic letches, my most blamable (if any be so) lusts; things I had kept to myself, things never yet disclosed to other women, I told *her* rapidly. I felt as if I must, as if it were my destiny to tell her all, all I had done with women and men, all I wished to do with *her*, it was a vomit of lascivious disclosures. I emptied myself body and soul into her. She listened and seemed annoyed. She did not like me.

Nor did she believe me. Two days afterwards, I took her the promised money, she had not expected it, and then deigned to ask if she should see me again. No. She was far too expensive for me — not that she was not worth it all. — Yea more — but blood could not be got out of a stone. — I had not the money and could see her no more. — "All right," she replied very composedly and we parted. As I tore myself away, my heart ached for that beautiful form, again to see, smell, to kiss, and suck, and fuck that delicious cunt, to give *her* pleasure if I could. Tho I saw her afterwards at the A°g°°e rooms — even went to look at her there, I resisted. — What helped me was the belief that I was distasteful to her, why I could not tell, and a year elapsed before I clasped her charms again.

On leaving her that day, I could think of nothing but *her*, went to a woman I knew, and shut my eyes whilst I fucked her, fancying she was H°l°n M. — "You call me H°l°n," said she. "You know a woman of that name I suppose," — I told her it was the name of my sister. Not the only time the same thing has happened to me, and in exactly the same manner with other ladies when fucking *them*, but thinking of *another*.

When I had her again she was in even more complete beauty, had more hair on her motte, and a thick tuft just above the opening of the notch. — Her limbs were larger and finer. I was frank, told her what money I could afford, that I never lied nor broke my word to women. She I think began to believe me, but it's difficult to gauge the depths of a gay woman, and difficult for *any* woman who has been gay long, to believe *any* man. — But things were changing, I began to see her for my pleasures, and her only — if I had an occasional letch, a chance fuck with another, I nearly always told her, but that was after I had known her a year or so. — If she then asked what I did not wish to tell, I said I should tell a lie or be silent. — So our meetings were pleasant, and I revelled in her beauty, and tho no longer young, have many a time fucked her thrice within an hour. — Then she began to spend with and enjoy me, which added to my delight; for in later years, giving pleasure to the woman is almost as great a pleasure to me, as my physical delight in her.

But she would not for long afterwards lend herself to my erotic fancies. She had them in her head, in her mind, in her imagination, and wished for many — I believe most. — She was lewed and voluptuous from her earliest childhood, but hid her desires from *me*, only granting a few of my wishes from time to time as the greatest favour. Yet she longed for them at the very time she refused, and in the night and morning by herself in bed, practised them all mentally, her imagination filled with baudy images, whilst with her pretty fingers she frigged her delicate clitoris, for she was sensuousness itself, and a masturbatrix from her childhood. It was only after I had known her three or four years, and she'd disclosed involuntarily almost in our voluptuous conversations the secret desires of her nature, that she practised with me the frolics she never had done with any other man. — Then we studied lasciviousness in all its varieties, for I had conquered all ridiculous ideas she had had as to the sinful usage of her body — of the wrongfulness, of the shame in certain sexual acts. — She agreed with me that cunt, prick, and arsehole, mouth, armpits, feet and fingers, and all parts of the body, men and women might use to give themselves sexual pleasure, and endear themselves to each other — that nothing they did to each other was wrong, that their doings concerned themselves alone, that all sexual instincts were both proper and natural to gratify.

[This will be seen and the lustful amusements we both enjoyed described — nothing I have done with any other woman which I did not do with *her*. One fancy begot another, and erotic conceptions crept on us gradually.]

She said that she'd never done such things with another man — not even with the man she'd once loved, who had kept her, — nor with those she'd lusted for — for she had strong likings — that men had never suggested strange letches to her. I expect she alone indulged with me in them, because sensuously our temperaments were the same. She matched me in lasciviousness, and moreover knew there was not the slightest chance of my divulging our erotic tricks, to either man or woman.

Many who have not tasted our sexual pleasures will call them beastly. They are not. But what if they are? — What are all the physical functions of man and woman, what are chewing, drinking, spitting, snotting, urinating, farting? — What is copulation? is that beastly? — Certainly it is what beasts do. — They will call that

natural perhaps, but it's a purely animal act, tho not specially
beastly to me. — What is a woman's cunt? — feel it when not re-
cently washed, or when the prick has just left it and the semen
is lying thick inside and out. Is that beastly or not? What is the
joining of two tongues, the mixing of salivas, the gluing of two
mouths together when fucking? — beastly? But there is no harm in
these it will be said, it's natural. — Be it so. — So are other erotic
amusements equally natural and not more beastly. — What more
harm in a man's licking a woman's clitoris to give her pleasure, or
of she sucking his cock for the same purpose, both taking pleasure
in giving each other pleasure. So if a man plugs a woman's bum-
hole with his finger when they are copulating or gamahuching, and
so with other sensual devices and fancies, they are all equally natu-
ral tho many may not enjoy them. — All are permissible if a couple
do them for mutual delight, *and are no more beastly than simple
human copulation*, which is the charm of life, — the whole object
of life, — and indulged in by all as much as their physical powers
permit — yet it's not thought *beastly*.

Imagination plays a most important part in all acts of *love* and
lust, which are nearly if not quite synonymous terms. All human
affections are generated by the act of copulation and its prelimi-
naries. — It is the dull boor, to whom a woman is warm flesh with a
hole for fucking and no more — the man who has no imagination,
— who is incapable of highly wrought sensual delights and fucks
when his seed makes his cock restive, — only thinking of his woman
then, and rumps her directly he has done with her — who is the
*beast — for he only does exactly what the beast, the animal does,
and no more.* — The couples blest with imagination, they who by
various excitements of which a mere animal is not capable, bring
fucking to intellectual height, make it a dream of the senses, make
lust and love in its sensuous elevation ethereal, a poetic delirium,
— *they are not the beasts*. But reduce coition to the mere act, and
the inevitable sequel of the seed laying in the cunt, and the prick
dwindling out wet and flaccid — at once that couple are brought to
the level of *beasts*, and of those stupid asses who in their incap-
ability of doing more than the horse, the hog and the dog, those
who rut and ruddle like every other animal from a louse to an ele-
phant, — such are the *beasts*, and not those who worshipping Eros,

raise fucking by their imagination and sensuous preliminaries almost to a divine level.

H°l°n and I after a time laughed to scorn the crude notions of those animal idiots, who think that all is *beastly* excepting simply putting a cock into a cunt — *which is what beasts usually alone do,* — and amused ourselves erotically as we liked. I wholly for love and lust, she for the same and perhaps also a little for money, — all women are alike in that — but at length she indulged with me in Paphian pleasures for love alone — for our mutual satisfaction.

[Now I follow the course of the events, and have done with sexual essays and opinions as to what is beastly or natural, or what man and woman may do with their genitals.]

A chapter on gamahuching. — The taste cultivated with girls not gay. — A swarthy French woman. — In a Russian bordel. — The red haired French woman. — At the Alhambra. — Miss E°w°°°s met. — Plain face, perfect form. — Our silent supper. — Nudities complete. — Fucking and sweating. — Pale ale in bed. — Gamahuching preliminaries. — Her lovely cunt. — Lewedness. — Double minetting. — I'm deceived. — Her Spanish lover. — Her baudy talk and lascivity. — Friend Eliza. — My narrow escape. — Reciprocating enjoyments. — Frigging herself. — The first floor lodger. — Her opinion of Miss E°w°°°s who disappears. — A Saxon Paphian. — A hirsute cunt. — At the sea coast. — The shell box seller. — A very risky poke. — On the beach at night.

I had early in life and indeed till middle age as told, been indifferent to having my cock sucked or gamahuched, had indeed forbidden French women — who do it as a matter of course, either as a preliminary or finish — to operate on me, altho exceptionally I had permitted it, and of late years even occasionally, sought it. I had gamahuched but little all my life with the exception of my virgins — or very pretty young cunts. — Virgin cunts always attracted me that way, there was scarcely a virginity which I had not licked deliciously before I shattered it, and think I have told in this history, of all those on whom I bestowed that honor. They were nearly all young, but I was not insensible with some women to the endearments of mutual cock and cunt licking, when both I and the lady took a fancy to do it together. — With most gay women I cared not to do it.

———————————

But I liked to persuade quiet girls who had never done it, to tickle my pego with their tongues, and finally put it into their mouths. It was delightful to see their desire to comply under an affectation of dislike, and inexpressibly exciting to gamahuche a nice fresh girl, who had no idea of what a tongue could do on her clitoris, and who after declaring it, "Nasty — oh don't now" — began to quiver and sigh, her pretty bum to twitch and jerk, her belly heave gently up with manifest signs of voluptuous delight. — Then that sudden cry of, "Oh — oh my — aha — leave off — I shall do it else." — The clutch at your head, the catch of the breath, and the sudden escape of salt liquid from her cunt on to my tongue, gave me with such females, the most exquisite voluptuous enjoyment. — But as compared with the large number I have tailed, these were few and far between, for women are not naturally salacious, and there are many who prefer the prick up them to any preliminaries of pleasure — I have I may mention, once or twice deceived *modest* ladies absolutely, by treating their mouths exactly like their cunts when they had no suspicion that I should do so. I found *that* a very amusing novelty, and they really didn't mind that cheating tho they said they did.

I went home about this time one evening with a French woman, a dark swarthy creature with fine eyes. — After undressing enough to show her breasts, she dropped on her knees and began sucking my cock as I sat — I objected, but she said her poorliness was on, so she finished me in that way. — It was done with such art, delicacy of touch, tranquillity and refinement, that when she offered me a second pleasure that way I accepted it, and went away thinking that after all it was a very agreeable variety of sexual pleasure.

Soon afterwards I was abroad, and at a bordel at °°°° in Russia, selected a most delicious, fresh, beautiful creature and quite young. We neither understood each other's language, or but two or three words only. Tho full of sperm, I had one of those nervousnesses come on of which I have told, coupled with a fear of disease, for I was going to travel where I could get no medical help, and fatigue would increase any ailment I might have. — So my cock would not stand.

The house was of its class quite a novelty in that place and had been newly started by a French procuress, and such a collection (at a baudy house) of lovely creatures of different nationalities, I never saw before or since. They were got together for a special occasion which only occurred annually, and different nationalities were needed. But tho I had been two weeks without fucking, I could get no cock stand thro fear or nervousness. The lady laid along the side of the bed, thighs wide open, I stood by her head, could see her all over, and with a little bend could feel her lovely brown haired cunt, and thighs. She was as said lovely in face and form. I made signs for her to gamahuche. "Minette," said I. — She knew the word, and immediately engulfed in her mouth my penis. — After a few movements thro her lovely lips, it stiffened sublimely. — She made signs that her quim was to be its ultimate receptacle, I nodded "Yes." — Then on the angel went, gracefully moving her lovely head, till my prick gave me exquisite sensations, and lascivious intentions came that *I would do*, what I had intimated I *would not*. My pleasure increased. — Shall I fuck her or spend in her mouth? thought I — I stretched out my hand towards her motte, before that I had been feeling her breasts and lovely head of hair. She raised one thigh high up and open, and bent herself so as to help my fingers and I felt the delicate red button which just showed outside the top of her cunt. She looked up at me, I restrained as much as I could my increasing pleasure, and all signs of its advent, seeing that her look reminded me of my promise, till my sperm suddenly jetted out into her mouth.

So quick and strong were the throbs, that the maddening crisis of my pleasure was over before she was aware of my ejaculation. Then she repulsed me, ejecting my libation, hurried off the bed in anger and left the room, — evidently not accustomed to that mode of completion of male pleasure — and came back saying, "Nicht gut! Nicht gut!" But German was not her native tongue. — She sat down, sulked, pouted, wriggled her lovely shoulders, kept repeating "Not good," then asked in bad German, — Was I an Englishman? — I could make that out of what she said, but she said a lot more.

I have rarely deceived women, and now felt ashamed at having lied to her, so gave her four times the present she could have expected. Delighted and with smiles on to her face she thanked me, in a polyglot of Russian, German and other languages, so we made it up. She was Hungarian I heard afterwards. Then I looked at her beauties till I longed for her again. She fetched another woman as she did not quite understand me. I made myself understood at last, the other woman left the room, then and again I pointed to her mouth. She shook her head, and pointed to her cunt. I nodded, and after a little pantomime she took my pego into her mouth. Its resuscitation arrived between her lovely red lips, and when royally stiff and throbbing, I placed it between the fat, soft, lips of her cunt which eagerly opened for its food, and spent in her temple of Venus.

[This was a few years after my adventure with the red-haired French woman, who minetted me, and thumb buggered me at the same time. I now fully realized what a variety of pleasure man and woman could give each other with mouth and tongue.]

Soon after was a lady — nameless — with whom I did something of the sort. She liked to be gamahuched but my taste for lickings had not then set in, and was but an occasional variety of pleasure which I had ceased to think about much; but whether it is, that I am now at an age when I naturally drift towards such pleasures, or whether the instinct of the fair priestesses of Venus divines my wants, I at this time fell in with one who satisfied me with her mouth, whilst mine satisfied her.

Two or three nights after I first made the acquaintance of H°l°n M. I was at the Alhambra, and met a Miss E°w°°°s in the bar room there. I noticed a tall, finely shaped woman talking to some men, her back was towards me, but I saw she was as upright as a dart, and moved with the grace of an Andalusian. The quiet swing of her petticoats told me the sort of haunches beneath, and that no padding or make up was there. — She turned round, and I saw a head of a peculiar character and face decidedly very plain, with lips noticeable for their large size — so large that they reminded me almost of a negress. — There was a clear, sharp, clever look in her grey eyes, and a voluptuous, lewed expression which fetched me. I beckoned her, and she came to my table holding a wine glass in her hand. "Can I go home with you?" — She looked me all over. "I'll tell you in a few minutes" — and she went back to the bar.

I strolled into the corridor, returning in five minutes. — Yes, I could go home with her, but would I wait half an hour, as she wanted to meet some friends — I settled the money arrangements with her, and she went off to speak with the men again. The time expired, I got impatient and went to her. — Would I go to her house and wait for her, she would be sure to be there in time, she asked. — No, if she did not come at once I should get some other woman. — She didn't care she said, and I left the theatre annoyed, but waited outside a few minutes having told her I'd do so. She followed me soon with a short woman who lived in the same house. Would I take her also home? — I agreed, and we all three got into a four wheeler.

On the road I made acquaintance with her thighs. — "Can't you wait till we get home?" But she began to feel my cock. — "Can't *you* wait," said I. — "I'll feel yours," said I to her friend, "to pay me for giving you your cab home." — The woman made no objection, but pushed her cunt forward to meet my fingers. They lingered high up on her thighs, twiddled the hairy thatch, but not quite touched her quim. I kept looking at Miss E°w°°°s face by the gaslamp light, wondering how I could have selected such a plain faced woman, but on feeling her fleshy cunt and thighs, it reconciled me to it. I had soon relinquished feeling the other woman's thighs, and crisp haired motte.

On arriving at the house the other woman went to her room. Miss E°w°°°s sat down, stared at me, and I at her. — "What are you thinking about?" said she. "Where your bed room is." — She opened the folding door remarking, "It's small," — and beginning to undress. — "Oh God! how hot it is." — It was an awfully hot night — I watched her form with delight as she undressed for it was exquisite — I groped between her thighs. — "Wait till I've pissed and washed my cunt, I'm sweating so," said she in exactly those words, and she did. — "I must have supper first, you would not wait or my friend would have given it to me, and Eliza as well." — She was then with chemise on only. — "How long shall you be?" — "A quarter of an hour." — "You've got a man down stairs." — "I haven't, I'll bring supper up and eat it here. — Give me a glass of champagne." — I refused. — "You *are* a queer sort, you like your own way." — "Many have said that before my dear." — "Well, give me some bottled ale." — I consented, she fetched bread and meat and had it with the ale — which she got somewhere — in the room

with me. — We both drank the ale which was good, copiously, and
I undressed to my shirt. — "Let's fuck now," said she. — "You don't
mince your words," said I — "And you don't — just to hear *you* in
the cab, but what's the good of not speaking plain, say fucking if
you mean fucking." — She was a very frank, unusual, amusing
creature, and her manner began to please me, tho I don't like coarse
tongued women.

She ate her supper quite composedly without speaking, but
looking at me all the time. I was lolling on the sofa equally silent,
looking at her lovely arms, shoulders, and breasts, and wondering
at her plain face. At last, "Let's see your legs." Without uttering a
word she rose up, and pulled the chemise well up above her knees.
— With that exception I don't recollect our saying another word,
but we stared hard at each other.

She finished supper and then it was that she said, "Let's fuck
now" — went to the bedroom and put the basin again on the floor.
— "Don't wash again," said I. — "It's so beastly hot I must." — "But
you washed your cunt a quarter of an hour ago." — "You don't like
it dry," said she leaving off and laughing. — Then she got on to the
bed, and without a request from me, pulled up her chemise well
above her navel. — I was delighted, and stood looking at her, feel-
ing, kissing her lovely form, praising its beauty — and its beauty
was supreme. — "Oh! Isn't it hot?" — Rising, she then threw off
her chemise, saying, "There — that's nice." — "You're exquisite,
lovely," said I. — "I'll take off my stockings," said she beginning to
do so — but I stopped that. — Nakedness in bed is delicious — ab-
solute nakedness, — but as long as I use my eyes, I like usually to
have a woman with silk stockings and garters on, and all the rest
naked.

"Lets feel your prick?" — suiting the action to the word. — I
had now stripped to my shirt. — "Take off your shirt and let's fuck
naked." — I did. — "You're a fine man, you've nice flesh, and are
not hairy." — She then felt me all over quickly. — "Come on and
fuck," said she impatiently opening her thighs, then laughing, and
pulling apart her cunt lips with her fingers. I stood gloating over
her delicious red groove, then looked at her, and never saw such
a baudy, randy, lewed expression on any woman's face as was on
hers. — "Come on, let us fuck, you can look at my cunt afterwards,"
she repeated hurriedly, and she wriggled her bottom and loins. I

mounted her, and we fucked in nakedness — a glorious fuck. — There is something odd about my memory: Heaps of things I only recollect generally — others I recollect in every detail. We were both hot, perspiring with heat, ale, and strong lust. My breast stuck to hers with perspiration when we had copulated yet her flesh felt quite cool. I recollect that perfectly.

When we recovered from our pleasure — for she spent rapturously — I lay rubbing my naked breast between her splendid bubbies. — "Fucking naked when it's hot weather is nice." "I *always* like it naked," she replied. Then with cock in cunt, that exquisite connection, we talked. "Get off, your spunk's running out on to my quilt, and it's quite a clean one." "Turn on your side and it will run on to your thigh," I replied — at the same time pushing my prick well up her, and turning and pulling her sideways with me to avoid uncunting. — "You're a baudy devil." — "And so are you." — "You are up to a lot," — said she laughing and kissing me. "I want to piss again," and she uncunted me then, tho I pressed close to her belly. — She pissed and washed, and I expected she would put her chemise on as a hint that all was over, and having had my pleasure, would get rid of me, but she laid down again by the side of me, and asked me to stop all night. "I can only stop an hour or two, and can't give you more than •••••." — "Nobody asked you — here is a towel." — "Are you all right," I asked. — She gave me several hard slaps on my naked rump. "If I wasn't I shouldn't have laid down by you again — look" — and she turned on to her back, opening her thighs wide to shew me her vulva.

I gave my saturated prick and appendages a rub with the towel, then looked her all over, and her cunt inside and out. "Have *you* ever been ill," she asked. — "Yes my dear, many times." — "I hope you have nothing the matter with you *now*" — and she took hold of my prick, examined the glans, gave it a hard squeeze, and relinquishing it said, "You are a rum-un" — and she laughed.

I had ever a keen eye for beauty of female form, and now have seen as much of it as the world can show. — She let me do what I liked with her, lifted up this limb and that, placed herself on her side, her back, her belly as I asked — her complaisance delighted *me,* and *she* seemed pleased as well. — Then she stood up and turned round as if on a pivot. "Put your right arm as high as you can — as if you were pulling a rope," I said. — She did and turned round in that attitude. — "Are you an artist?" — "No." — "Doctor?". — "No." — "I know you are one or the other and you are lying," said she curtly. — Then she told me that artists had said she was faultless, as I had said. We laid down — "Your flesh feels like a woman's, so smooth and nice." She kissed it all over and ran her hand over my breasts, thighs and buttocks, laid hold of my prick, glued her big lips to mine. The next minute I had groped her red love avenue for a second, and we were fucking again start naked still, and I sweating like a blacksmith. It was an awfully hot night.

She put her heels on to my rump to keep me up her when I had done. "Let's have some more ale," said she, and rang the bell at the bed head. — My prick was still in her cunt wh.n in came the lady who'd come home in the cab with us. — "You're enjoying yourselves," said she in no way disconcerted at the spectacle — tho I was. She fetched the bottled ale. E°w°°°s drank a lot — so did I — so did the young lady, looking at us laying naked, and then retired. — We had uncoupled, sat up and now lay down again. I wanted to be off, but she kept hold of my tool saying *I should* do it again, but I got up and put on my shirt, she laying still. — Then I again looked at her lovely form and whilst standing doing so, she caught hold of my prick and played with it, asking when I had fucked last before that night.

What put it into my head then I can't say but think it was the thickness of her lips. I thought of her sucking my cock. — "I should like to do you again but can't." — "You will if you wait." — "Kiss it." — She kissed my prick turning on one side to do so — I felt her lovely haunches, and large firm breasts, yet my cock did not stand. — "You can make it stand, if you put it in your mouth." — "You beast — do you like that?" — "Yes." — "Ever had it done?" — "Yes." — "I won't — I never did such a thing." — "Do it now then — only for a minute — only just a little in — tickle it with your tongue." — "I shan't you beast."

I persisted — "Do." — "No." — "Yes." — "I won't." "Do, and then we'll fuck." — "There then," and she just licked the tip for a second. "Again — longer." — "There then" — a second lick. — "Now put it in further." — "It will choke me." — "Nonsense." — "I never have done so." — "Humbug. I'm sure you know how." — "I don't, show me." — "There — let it go" — and it went half out of sight between her fat lips. — She shut her eyes and palated it, and then spat on the floor. "It's beastly." — "Never mind if we like it." — Then my prick was throbbing, I felt the sperm on her cunt, turned on to her and again we fucked. With me it was a long exercise. — She was passionate now, and kissed me hard when spending.

Then I dressed and left, she came to the street door with me start naked. "When shall I see you again?" — "Tomorrow" — tho I scarcely ever promised to see a woman again. But her splendid form, frank baudy speech, and voluptuous fucking, had caught me.

In the afternoon next day I went, she was having a bath the maid said. In a minute she appeared, chemise and slippers only on, her skin yet moist. — "Did you expect me?" — "Yes, I was sure you would come." In a minute I had her on the bed, *start naked* again, I stripped to my skin, and never left her till it was night and I could fuck no longer. — It was fearfully hot weather still.

She was five feet eight or nine high and dressed her hair high (a fashion just then) which made her look taller. Her form from neck to feet was absolutely perfect; hands, feet, knees were small, the swell of the calves and thighs, the roundness of the thighs as they grew into her large white handsome buttocks, made superb columns. The solid large breasts like half globes of ivory were faultless, and she had the full flesh of a woman of thirty, yet without a pound weight too much. It was lovely to see her walk naked across the room, so beautifully did she put her feet down, so exquisitely did her bottom and thighs move, so stately did her body undulate, so voluptuously yet without any bum-waggle or swagger, did her buttocks move.

Her cunt was fledged with dark auburn hair, in quantity only like a girl's of eighteen and looked lovely as she lay with her thighs open. — A somewhat large clitoris like a button or nut of a beautiful red colour shewing between the lips, she'd not large inner lips. The clitoris invited frigging or sucking. The prick hole was small and not a hair was near her bum hole. — Everything about her was perfectly young and lovely excepting her head. She had beautiful long auburn hair, fine teeth, and clear skin; but the large lips, peculiar nose, and general largeness and long shape of the head spoiled all. I have her photograph now and when looking at it, wonder how any man could take to the owner of it; but the exquisite form, together with the voluptuous power and lewedness of the woman had only to be known. — I liked soon afterwards, her absence of humbug and sham modesty. — Ugly shaped whores often affect that.

"You *are* a randy devil," said she. — "So are you." — "I *am*, and I like fucking with a man who knows how to fuck." That evening she had not eaten for hours, and I had forgotten my dinner. "I must go out and get some one to give me supper, but want no more fucking," were her last words as we parted.

I soon saw her again. My mind had been running much upon cock sucking, my recent experiences in that line had stimulated me, and there was something about *her* mouth which made me specially desire it from her. When a letch laid hold of me it never left till I had satisfied it. She was so frankly baudy in her talk and manner, that I had already lost all modesty with her, and as I lay by her, feeling about her. — "Suck my cock again" — said I. — "No." — "You put it into your mouth the other night." — Still a refusal — I pressed — insisted. "You *gamahuche me then*, and perhaps I will." — Yes, she liked to be gamahuched. — "Gamahuche me first." — "No you minette me first." — Then ceasing our mutual requests, we talked about the pleasure that gamahuching gave a woman.

As I looked at her quim and beautiful thighs, my objection was weakening — "Shall you spend if I gamahuche?" — "Oh shan't I just?" — "Wash your cunt" — quickly she washed and laid down on the edge of the bed. — I knelt on a pillow, the idea of pleasure, of giving *her* pleasure had conquered my dislike, the nubbly, cherry looking clitoris seemed begging to be bitten. I put my hand under her ivory backside, put my mouth to her red split, and gave it a rapid lick, spitting out the salt which met my tongue. — "A little lower — there — just there," — said she putting her middle finger on the spot. Opening the lips I placed my tongue there. — "Ah'r — that's lovely." — Her backside twisted and wriggled a little. — The clitoris felt smooth and nice to my tongue — her voluptuous sighs and thrills randied me more, — my cock stiffened, I lost all dislike to my work, and licked all over and closed my mouth on her cunt. — "Ah-rr — don't — leave off dear, — quicker, aher — quicker, harr — ha — rr. I'm spending — quicker — a — harr" — she sighed and was quiet. — I wiped my mouth and then her cunt with the towel which I had by me. — But I didn't like the work I thought, when I had finished. She wanted me to do it again, she begged, insisted, and on I went gamahuching — she spent again — and again. — "Now gamahuche *me*." — "Not now, presently, let's rest." — My cock would *not rest*, into her mouth I put it meaning to spend there, but the attraction of her form was too much. After her mouth had held it a minute I withdrew it, and putting it into her cunt, fucked my spunk into it. — "It's nicer there," said she, "isn't it now?" I only thought then of fucking, and on the next visit or so it was the same, but the unsatisfied letch haunted me, and one night I went determined to do nothing else to her until I had satisfied it. I oftentimes have made up my mind what I would do to a woman before going to her house, and then forgot it.

After stripping, feeling her all over, inspecting, and the usual amatory preliminaries, "*You* do it to *me*," said I. — "Don't spend then." — "Yes I must." — "If you were not a nice man I wouldn't, and you won't tell Eliza ●●●●● will you?" — Then I thought of a Serbian woman whom I had that way, and laid E°w°°°s on the bed in the same posture, fucked in her mouth and was satisfied; gave her then wine and gamahuched *her*. — I did not care that night to have my pleasure in her mouth again, my letch was over for the time. But I could not escape gamahuching her on other visits. — It was *her* letch with *me*, for she made me do it to her first, and then would do anything after. Soon afterwards I heard her using Spanish words, which a young Spaniard who was spoony on her and whom she thought would marry her had taught her. Her mother kept a small shop at Gravesend, selling there tarts and sandwiches. He had been to see her mother. — She knew the Spanish of every baudy word and I learnt them from her but omit them here.

I called one afternoon, and she had gone away for a few days. — As I was leaving, Miss Eliza ●●●● put her head out of the parlour. I had not seen her for some time, she looked inviting so I walked in to chat. — She told me about the Spaniard. — Didn't believe he would marry Miss E°w°°°s, but E°w°°°s thought he would, she was the baudiest woman she ever knew, all the women said so. — Wasn't it a shame? — She had had her niece up to stay with her, a girl seven years old, and she talked just as baudily before the child — Miss Eliza ●●●● was shocked. — Miss E°w°°°s was idle, loved to be naked, and from the time she got up till she had her bath before dressing to go out, or to see any one, kept on her night dress, or a chemise only, hadn't even shoes and stockings on when the weather was hot. — She let her little niece look at her cunt and play with the hair on it, and once let her remain in the bed room when a man was tailing her. — But she was a nice, kind, generous woman, and had been very kind to her (Eliza). "She is very fond of fucking," said I. — "Awfully fond of it," she replied, and was always talking about it. — "A very lewed voluptuous woman, awfully lewed, most men say so." — "And she's plenty of friends tho she is so plain; she'd fuck all day and night too."

This young demirep had been working all the time she was talking with me about E°w°°°s, and looked nice, pale, and delicate in her light, loose, clean morning gown. The talk had stirred my lust a little. "Show me your leg," said I getting close to her. — She shewed a bit of her calf — I pulled up the petticoat high, was pleased with the sight, then saw more, then felt, then fucked her.

When I said, "Let's poke" — she threw down her work and got on to the bed in such a hurry, wriggled and jigged her bum and kissed me so, that I told her to be quiet, hating a violent fuckstress and sham emotions. — No sooner had we finished, than she cuddled up to me till I did her again, exclaiming, "Oh! I want you so, — Oh I'm so lewed." — Afterwards she asked me not to tell Miss E°w°°°s. — "Why not?" — When she came back I did. "Did you like Eliza?" asked she, giving a peculiar laugh, and looking at my prick curiously as she did so. — Her manner was a little strange, but I did not think about it then much. On the next visit, I heard that the young lady whom I had poked had left the house, and E°w°°°s then told me she had just recovered from a bad clap when I had had her. I had been her first man on her recovering she thought. — No evil effects followed to me from the poke.

I took a liking to Miss E°w°°°s, but for sensuality only, her lovely form delighted me, her freedom of manner, and way in which she let me scrutinize her charms was to my taste. She would lay in any attitude as long as I liked without any impatience, which kept me in a state of tranquil yet voluptuous delight without irritation. She seemed moreover delighted to be scrutinized, drew up the blind to give light to see her charms (close under the window) without being asked when she found my tastes, and almost invited inspection, looking at me all the while with a baudy smile

on her face, which almost asked for copulation, her mouth slightly
open shewing a beautiful set of teeth. She knew her body was
absolutely without a blemish, was proud of being looked at. —
One day she said it made her lewed to let me look, and she liked
feeling lewed. — She was a woman who spent copiously.

But the gamahuching tho at first I avoided it, she often made
me do. — When I had well seen and felt her glorious form, her
baudy smile came on. "Put your head down I've just had my bath,
but I'll wash again there," I took a towel to wipe my lips and
obeyed but did not like it at first. — Again my letch for being
minetted came on. "Suck my cock whilst I do it," said I one day —
"or I won't lick *you*." She turned onto the bed directly. "I may bite
it when I spend, you'd better not." — "If you do I'll bite your
clitoris off." — Then we went at it, and I shall never forget it. We
inverted ourselves on each other, — arsy — versy — mouth to gen-
itals. — I was on the top and spent in her mouth, just as my tongue
on her cunt fetched her. She hurt my prick in her ecstacy.

"I love a double gamahuche," said she. The cat was out of
the bag now, I had had no doubt of it before, for it was she who
incited me to do all this. Now so handsome was her cunt, so beau-
tiful her form, so sweet the smell of her body, that I began to take
to it. She liked the taste of my pego in her mouth, and always put
it there before I commenced licking her clitoris. — "I like it when
it's quite small at first, and to feel it stiffen up in my mouth" —
was her remark one night when I passed a voluptuous evening
with her, for now she avowed all her lusts, and did not care how
openly she told them. She said it as she was laying on the bed with
thighs wide apart, ready for me to cover her reversely, and lick
her clitoris. The next second I was at it, kneeling over her, my
backside well over her head, my prick dropped between her eager
lips, one of her hands clasping my bum, whilst with the other she
held my prick in her mouth, then with my hands under her lovely
thighs, rapidly I passed my tongue over her clitoris. — In a few
short minutes she spent, but my libation shot over her chin and
neck. — "You cheat," — said I. "I couldn't help it, as I began to
spend I let it go" [women in the acme of their pleasure, sometimes
do so when in that position, the stiff stander with difficulty keeps
in their mouths, and in the spasm of their own pleasure, in the

voluptuous after lassitude they frig it for a minute, and let it out, or cease sucking it].

I was annoyed, for part of my enjoyment in this double gama-huching, is in the idea of my sperm deluging my sweet companion's mouth instead of her cunt. — "I won't let *you* spend next time until *my* spend's over." — "You shan't my pet, now let's do it again." — "I'm not stiff." — "I'll make it stiff, let's wash." — Both genitals made sweet and fresh again, and after half an hour's chat lying side by side, feeling each other's fucking tools, we went to work, but in a different position.

I laid on my back, she over me, her knees on each side of my shoulders, and gradually lowering her belly, her glorious white backside came near my face; her bum hole shewed, the crimson cunt opened wide, showing its little inner lips and the clitoris — together looking like a crimson gash in her belly — whilst beyond just a bit of her curly brown haired motte was visible. This for a second, and then it was lost to my delighted gaze, her cunt dropped on to my mouth, and sinking down her belly towards mine she seized my drooping pego and placed it between her big rosy lips. I felt her tongue playing round the plum shaped knob, tickling, and sucking; — a voluptuous feeling shot thro it, it stiffened up and was at once engulfed in her mouth. Then up and down gently moved her head, the friction of her palate and tongue giving me intense pleasure. Out darted my tongue reciprocating her minet-ting, licking the expanded surface of her cunt, now seeking the full clitoris, now shooting it up the avenue to her womb. So for some time went on this luscious play with mutual delight. Then her backside wriggles, her cunt presses closer to my mouth, my prick stiffer and stiffer, involuntarily is jerked upwards by my backside: With gentle fucking motion quicker moves her mouth up and down it, whilst more quickly wriggles her buttocks as I clasp them or rub them and lick her quim rapidly.

With a moan of pleasure from me the sound almost lost in her cunt, out shot with thrills of delight my pearly libation into her mouth. "Aha." A fucking wriggling motion of her backside responds at once, as she feels my warm spunk gush, her cunt settles closer on my mouth, my nose is buried up it, her clitoris is between my lips, rapidly shoots my tongue over it as harder I clasp her ivory buttocks, a salt flux inundates my mouth, her wriggles cease, and heavily she now lies upon me, tranquil in her pleasure. She has spent a flood, my prick and its libation still in her mouth, her cunt still emitting its juices over mine.

"I did it first this time," said I. — "Yes, and it fetched me at once, now give me another gamahuche, I love it tonight, and then we'll fuck my pet." — I did it to her again and again now kneeling at the bedside, watching her face and quivering belly as she spent and spent again, and we fucked for a finish of the evening's amusement. — *Ach Gott!* what exquisite delights the cock and cunt give to those who know how to use them.

Soon after luncheon one day I went to see her and took champagne (I had never done so before) intending a voluptuous afternoon. I found her excited, she had been out of luck and not fucked for four days. Night and day she had been expecting her Spaniard, fearing he had cut her, and that the marriage was off. Now overjoyed she showed me a letter just arrived, written in bad English, filled with baudy words of love. He would be with her that night. She had been drinking with her luncheon, and after my champagne was more screwed tho but slightly so. She quickly unbuttoned my trowsers and got hold of my prick. "Let's fuck pet," said she throwing herself on the bed, stripping herself of chemise and loose gown, — as usual all she had on — and opening her thighs. — It was cooler weather and I would not strip. — "Make haste pet or I shall frig myself." — "Frig then, let's see you." — "No, put your prick up." — Then she began to frig herself.

I wasn't quite undressed, and thought I should like to see her frig. — "Frig away," said I placing myself in kneeling position between her legs and pulling up my shirt. — My cock was stiff. — "Come nearer and let me feel your prick" — said she frigging on — I moved so as to let her, she grasped it, began frigging me, and went on frigging herself. — A fierce lewedness was on her face. — "I haven't spent for quite four days." — "Not fucked, nor frigged yourself?" — "No." — "Oh spend pet, let your spunk fall on me." — "On your face?" — for I was now standing near her. "Any where — I'm coming — spend on me." — With a wrench at my prick which hurt me, she spent and lay quiet — I pulled aside her cunt lips (such a lot of her spending was running out of her like thinnish gruel), threw myself on her, plunged my prick in it and fucked. —

Then our spunk ran over the bed. "Damn the counterpane, let the spunk run on it," said she, holding me tight to her and kissing me.

We had a baudy afternoon, she kept me up her revelling in our spunk, we talked all the voluptuousness which a randy man and woman could, she never let go of my prick for about four hours, fucked me dry, and when she rose to prepare for her Spaniard, what with frigging and fucking, she could have had but little enjoyment left for herself with another man. "I don't care, I like *you*, he doesn't fuck much, he's a little fellow, but he'll marry me I hope."

I followed up that letch of seeing her frig herself for a little time, she was complacent, and after calling me a baudy old beast did what I wanted always — one day, she frigged herself whilst I held her cunt lips open, another day with my two fingers up her cunt. I did these tricks at the beginning of our entertainments, my satisfaction being mainly in seeing what she spent, tho I watched her face and movements during her enjoyment. — She insisted on feeling my prick whilst she operated on her clitoris, and talked baudily all the time, looking lasciviously at me until she spent with eyes closed. One day I knelt over her, and she sucked my prick whilst she frigged herself; she was delighted with my proposal, but I finished up her cunt. — After that my curiosity was satisfied — I knew what her spendings were like.

I think I gave that woman full sensual enjoyment, she seemed to have such pleasure in feeling my flesh. — I have had other women take that pleasure in my smooth skin but none more. She had a letch for me. — As far as her hands would reach she ran them over my flesh when fucking, until the supreme moment when both male and female clutch and press to each other. It is the most ecstatic moment of life when the prick can go no further up, when the cunt lips are squeezed up to the balls, belly to the man's belly, the prick pulsates, the vagina tightens and grasps it, and with convulsive throbs the prick shoots out its sperm against the womb's mouth. I wish I could experience a woman's pleasure at that moment. Does she appreciate or understand a man's pleasure?

Soon afterwards she was away. I called there, she was expected, but never came back. There had been a row between her and her Spaniard and she had gone home, he they thought after her. This was told me by a first floor young lady, who on my calling

a third time, set my cock stiffening as she stood at the foot of the
stairs talking to me. To chat and learn more about E°w°°°s I went
up stairs with her, and there my cock in due time stiffened into
the young lady's cunt. She told me all she knew and perhaps more,
but nothing unfavourable about E°w°°°s, who had said much in
my praise, but that I was the oddest man she ever had. — Miss °°°
thought Miss E°w°°°s very ugly but splendid in shape. All the
women of that and two adjoining houses had seen her naked — all
said she was beautifully made. — But what a baudy woman! I was
a baudy man she knew, had heard her say I was, and I gama-
huchèd Miss E. — Miss E. liked looking at the other women's cunts,
and she liked them to gamahuche *her*, but she didn't flat fuck that
she knew of. I never saw that first floor lady again. — She was thin,
dark haired and cunted, and I believe gamahuched Miss E°w°°°s
herself. I taxed her with it. — Denying it, she laughed, in a peculiar
way.

I never could hear anything about Miss E°w°°°s afterwards,
she never returned to her lodgings. I did not know her four months
nor see her often, yet missed her — lovely in form, enticingly lovely
in her meretriciousness, lovely in fucking, she certainly was. — Had
she remained, I am sure she would have kept me as a friend and
she liked my lewed ways. She may be living now, and many other
of my past ministering angels.

Full thirty years ago I had a woman who in face resembled
her, and whose form and movements of haunches when walking
naked were the same. She however had I think a tinge of the
mulatto in her, and she also had thick large lips. — It was at a
time of my life when straight forward cunt fucking was all I cared
about — I think in these memoirs that I must have mentioned that
woman.

Miss E°w°°°s left me with a more developed taste for gama-
huching a pretty cunt, for whatever my indifference previously, it
was now vanishing. — I often thought of doing it with women
afterwards. Once I did not indulge in it much, young cunts alone
I tongued with pleasure, and did that instinctively. It was the
absence of hair upon them, which I sometimes fancy was the cause
of my taste for their little quims.

After that I went abroad for a very short time, and occasionally visited one or two nurseries of Venus, tho on the whole was true and chaste, which made me enjoy my few furtive amours more, when I had them.

I was at a great Saxon city and went to the swell brothel there, the price per woman was but two thalers, strangers of course paying far above the tariff. — There was music in one of the rooms, and two or three young men smoking and drinking with half a dozen good looking Paphians, who were *décolleté* to their nipples, but otherwise dressed in silks and satins. Not aware that other men were in the salon when I entered it, and not preferring to choose women in male company, I was a little disconcerted, and selected one very quickly but made a very good choice. — I beckoned to her without having spoken to her, pleased with her opulent titties and massive hair, as she was sitting drinking with a man who looked at me angrily, as at once obeying my summons she left him.

She was a tall, stoutish, light auburn haired German, tolerably well formed, but wanting something in grace, as most German women are. Their thighs taper too quickly towards their knees, their hip bones show, they are in fact not voluptuously moulded tho formed to bear big babies in their loins; this one however was fairly well made and with splendid breasts. When on the bed I looked at her hidden beauties, and found such a cunt as I never saw before or since. — About every five years or so I think I have had women whose cunts were very uncommon in some particular.

This Saxon's sexual trough had roly poly lips, with lots of rather uncurled hair on them nearly down to her anus. — A fairly thick bush covered her mount, but not high up. The hair on the lips thinned as usual until their junction with her thighs where it ceased, leaving a well defined, clean flesh line; but on the thighs it began immediately to reappear, and thickened down about three or four inches forming little beards on each side of her cunt, quite handfuls of hair an inch and a half long. It had a mere tendency to curl, and the tufts reminded me of goats' beards. As she stood up with thighs closed, there seemed to be one continuous mass of hair from the top of her motte, to the end of these beards.

I remarked it at once, she thought I admired it (tho it was the reverse), and apparently proud of these hairy appendages, knelt on the bed and invited me to look at them from a rump point of view, without my having asked her to do so. I was in need of a woman, stiffened at once, — novelty always stimulates my salacity — plunged my love lance into her love sheath, and consummated. After ablution, with cooler blood I had again a good look at her curious hirsute growth, intending to write a description of it, and conversed with her about it, as well as I could. She kept twiddling my pego, and what with that and talking and looking at this strange cuntal physiognomy, I thought I should like to spend in it again. — "What are you going to give me?" quoth she when I suggested that.

The financial question being answered satisfactorily, we set to fucking dog fashion, every now and then I drew my prick so far out that the tip alone remained in her cunt, and looked down at the thigh beards which were however only partially visible in that position, but it was my letch. Strange ideas about fucking goats and hairy arsed women, passed through my brain, whilst ever and anon I frigged her clitoris, withdrawing my pego from her cunt altogether. Then resting on my heels I looked at her backside and pouters, and pulled the little beards. I could do it with fair composure, for tho my pego kept its stiffness, my sperm was in no hurry now to issue from my balls. At last I excited her. "Go on fucking, mein Lieben, I want it so, do me on my belly, I like to fuck that way best," — so I turned her on to her back, and after a final look at the thickets, plunged my prick up her quim and satisfied her and myself. — I never saw her again, nor wished. — Next day I wrote this account.

[One or two unusual looking cunts have already been described in my narrative. Seven or eight years after this thigh tufted Paphian, I had a woman whose backside was almost covered with hair. — It will be described in its proper order — perhaps.]

———————

On my return to England late in autumn, I went to the sea side on a well known coast. Girls in the streets and more frequently on the esplanade there offer baskets and boxes for sale, made or covered with shells. Pleased with the appearance of a box, I agreed the price and told the girl who hawked it to bring it to my hotel, giving her my name and address. The girl was very good looking and about fourteen years of age perhaps, but I had really taken no notice of her. I wanted to buy the box as a gift and thought of that alone.

At the time named I was alone in the hotel, which I had not expected to be the case, indeed had named a time when I expected to be far from being alone. "A gal's brought a shell box for you sir," said the waiter. — She came in, I saw the box was sound, paid the girl the money, and as I did so she struck me as being handsome. — Said I, "I'll give you six pence for bringing it if you'll give me a kiss my pretty lass." — "All right, sir," and her face became saucy. She came to me, I sat her on my knees — I was sitting down — kissed her, again kissed, and when doing so desire seized me and I whispered, "And a shilling if you'll let me feel your nice little fat bum, and your little cunny." — "All right," said she, and before the words were out of her mouth, my fingers were between the lips of an almost hairless notch. I felt over belly, navel, and mons well, then thrust my fingers back and one a little way up the prick receiver, which she facilitated tho she said, "Now don't yer do that, sir."

Agitated now with desire for that little cunt, — she now looked beautiful to me, — "Feel my prick," — said I, pulling it partly out, forgetting the awful risk I ran, for my room door might have been opened at any minute. She grabbed it saying, "Give us another sixpence, sir." — "I will my little dear, I'll give you half a crown to fuck you." — "All right, but you can't here, I'll be at °°°° tonight near the beach if you like." — She was a regular little whore I saw at once now.

Delighted and excited with the adhesive feel of her little split, as I kept my finger rubbing along it, and with prick well nigh bursting, I forgot the awful risk I ran for I might have been surprized at any minute, and not only by a waiter but by others, I would have her at once. And how quick I always have found my decision, how subtle under the influence of lust. Out of the sitting room led my bedroom, the bedroom had another door out on to the stairs. I saw my chance and possible escape, looked up and down the street from out of the window, and then on to the lobby, looked and shut the sitting room door again, pushed the girl into the bed room, locked both doors of that, lifted her on to the bed edge, threw up her dirty clothes, saw plump thighs, a little fat, pouting almost hairless notch, and in a second drove my prick up it to my balls. — "Oho" — said she, "don't you do it so hard." — But I fucked with haste and fear, my ears open, yet delighted with the little cunt. Her eyes were fixed on mine, mine on hers, she was quite a fuckstress tho young at it, and I saw that I gave her pleasure. But it was only the beginning of *her* pleasure for my energy and hurry, pumped out my sperm into her tight little cunt too quickly. — No sooner was my spend over than I pulled out my prick still quite stiff, a copious pearly fluid following it. "You didn't spend?" said I. "No I was just agoing to." — The next minute I had paid her half a crown and she went off with cunt reeking.

Two hours later, I went to the place where she had first offered me the shell box. It was the attraction of her little cunt which took me there. She'd got another shell box for sale — I examined it to blind passers by, all the while asking her about herself. — Her father was a fisherman. "Does he know you've been fucked?" — "No, he don't know." — She couldn't be out late, but soon after dark she could, and there were not many people out there, (naming place). At the hour and place that night I fucked her, and made her spend. She was still a little artless, for I frigged her nearly to a second spend before I put into her. — "Oh! I shall do it if you goes on rubbin' me." So then I rubbed her up and down with my prick, and she spent again with me.

I thought I had done with her, when one day she was in front of my hotel offering her baskets, "Buy another on me, I must sell em some how," said she. — I couldn't stand that, I was alone but it occurred to me that the little bitch might have been put up to blackmail me. I told her I'd buy no more, and that if she spoke to me again unless I spoke to her first, I'd put the police on her trail. Saying that I ought to buy something else after what I done to her, she went away and never appeared near my hotel (that I know of) again. At the end of a few days desire for her revived, I stopped, bought some little shell rubbish, and asked her to come to a baudy house with me. She wouldn't hear of it, for her parents might find it out. She knew where the baudy houses were tho.

She said she'd go to the house of a friend when I asked her. I had no gay friend there, but met a full grown harlot, told her my game. (Great risk again.) She met me, I pointed out the little one, who went with her to her lodgings (not late at night this) and there we stripped the lass and washed her, and then I licked her little cunt till she was nearly dead with spending. Then I fucked her and left. She'd never been gamahuched before she declared, never been in a house with a man, she'd had it done to her on the beach, and on the seats, but no where else. Two or three days afterwards I came back to London, and never saw the little damzel afterwards.

H°l°n M°°°w°°d revisited. — Curiosity and plain words. — Confidence begun. — Fucking on trust. — Cuntal essentials to a sensitive penis. — Nelly's assistance. — The cabinet maker naked. — Masks. — Masturbations and copulations. — The naked steel pen hawker. — Nipple and quim. — Sophy's white shoulders and onanism. — Pudenda's piddling. — A fuck for a half crown. — A cuntal purse. — Twin sister harlots, Cissy and Amy. — A fuck for champagne. — My confessions to H°l°n. — On cuntal physiognomies.

. Then the attraction of H°l°n M°°°w°°d took me to her again, and I revelled in her voluptuous and expensive charms. She complimented me by saying, there was plenty of stuff in me and seemed to enjoy my embraces. — On my remarking *that*, she said curtly, — "I didn't say so." — After that I went at times to the A°g°°e to look at her, and she came to me leaving her group of admirers, and actually asked me to go to see her. I refused that — "You're the strangest man I ever had, but I like talking with you. Come and see me, tomorrow, and you can stay as long as you like." I fixed a day a little later, yielding to her fascination spite of myself. On the day, I thought that I wouldn't go. — "It's only a gay woman." But I keep my word even with *them*, and went there.

It was cold weather, large fires were in her rooms, she was but slightly clad as becomes courtezans, whose beauties should be easily seen and felt. — Before the fire I felt her perfumed cleft, whilst the grateful warmth played on her lovely thighs and belly. "It's cold, I wish you'd let me get into bed with you." — "All right." — In three minutes our limbs were interlacing between the sheets — I was silent, thinking of her manifold beauties, feeling the juicy folds, twisting my fingers in the soft curls of her mount, kissing her sweet

516

lips, anticipating the climax. What she was thinking of I know not, but curiously she felt me all over which she'd never done before, and settled on my prick with a handling peculiar to her, which I recognized more fully afterwards. Soon my glowing rod was buried deeply in her warm lubricious cunt, and with frantic thrusts my sperm flushed into her. Soon after that we fucked again, but she annoyed me by getting out to wash after each emulsion which my pego gave her.

When I wanted to inspect closely her pudendal charms, she was capricious, partly refused me, said hastily, "There, that's enough" — closed her thighs and covered herself up. She was not yielding, was inclined to have her own way in everything. — Then said, "I'm going to have a glass of champagne." — "I don't want any." — "Nobody's asked you to" — but I did. — She got curious about me. — "Don't ask me I shall only tell you a lie." — "I don't want to know." — "What did you ask for?" — "Something to say, — you're the oddest man I ever had." — Again we cuddled in the warm bed, in delicious silence I felt all over her lovely body, playing with the ivory hillocks on her breasts, roving over her soft belly and bum, gliding my hand between her smooth thighs till I felt that soft silky fringe, and the lovely aromatic grove it circled round. Then a finger plunged far back in the grove and curved upwards, wetting itself in the warm avenue to her womb, then drew back to the sweetest little clitoris and titillated it. Again, she seized my prick, handling it with her delicate squeeze and motion, and up it sprung to full potentiality. — Without a word she suddenly threw off the bed clothes and looked earnestly at the erection, covering and uncovering its ruby tip. Then hurriedly. "Fuck me," said she. She was a plain speaker in sexual matters. I thought her in a hurry to get me over and away, tho it was but a thrill of lust which made her impatient to satisfy it. She was ever I found impatient to spend directly her lewed sensations began. I did not know her physical forces then, or that spend after spend was easy to her, without fatiguing.

Fuck her I did at once, she joined her tongue to mine, enjoyed my prick with a luscious quiet enjoyment, in a manner which left me pleased with my own performance and with having fetched her. She did not uncunt me after this libation, but kept me longer in her lovely sheath, whilst it drank up my semen, and she squeezed her cunt and moved it gently around it, as if with the intent of prolonging my sexual delight. She had never done so before I fancied, but I had been too excited perhaps to notice these voluptuous details of her copulating. "My love you spent with me this time." — "This time? I've spent with you every time you've fucked me." — "Really?" — "Can't you tell?"

Soon after I got up. — "Are you going?" — "Yes, — I can't poke again." — "I bet I'll make you" — but I could not wait, so bid the voluptuous siren adieu. — "When shall I see you again?" — I would not promise. — "Come in the afternoon the day after to morrow." — "I can't, and if I do, you'll have to trust me." — She thought for a minute, then said, "I'll trust you." — On that day I went, and she would have trusted but I paid her — having the money, and not intending to be in debt. — Two or three months then elapsed before I clasped her charms again.

The delight at the sight of Nelly's overflowing cunt after her married friend had tailed her, some months before this — its exquisite lubricity as my prick glided up it, the soft voluptuous sensation as its tip enveloped itself in fat sperm, the absence of hard friction and irritation on it which I often feel when I begin fucking, and in addition to this the lascivious delights roused in my brain, at the idea of my prick being in the temple which a man had just enjoyed and left, haunted me spite of myself. After a month or two, I asked her if the cabinet maker was still to be had, and two nights after she said he was, tho now at work. I arranged to have him. Then I resolved that we were both to be masked. I was to take his mask off if I wished, but I really neither wished to see his face, nor him to see mine.

On the evening I was anxious, but got over it by drinking champagne. — The masks helped also to steady my nerves. — I don't know the manners of sodomites, but expect they have more confidence than this man had. I had him strip and handled his tool, it was thick and soft, and nice to feel, seemed nicer than the feel of a cunt, but it did not swell till Nelly shewed him her pudenda, when it roused itself. It was an extra sized one, long, thick, and much thicker as it neared the balls — I felt it in silence long, wondering if he had much sperm or not, then put him in various postures to see how his stiff tool looked as he moved about, scarcely speaking a word, and only in a whisper when I did.

Then I laid him on his back on the bed, and turning Nelly's

rump towards him as she knelt, so that he might have the excitement of proximity to her cunt, began frigging him. — "Damn it all, let me fuck her" — cried he with a loud voice, as he felt pleasure coming on. — But that was not my game. Frigging on gently, my own prick sympathetically became rigid, then undressing to my drawers, I watched him and his tool whilst doing so, and he fingered her quim. Seeing my pego standing, he laughed and she chuckled. Then a desire to fuck *her*, came over me — for she is still beautifully formed and good looking, — for an instant I forgot *him*, and cunt resumed its natural sway. But his great stiff prick recalled me, and I frigged on, and my own prick at the same time. — Soon his was throbbing with lewedness. "Oh — a — h — r. I'm coming — I'll spend" — he cried. Then wanting to see his face, and watch his emotions, I pulled off his mask — "Pull yours off" said he. — I didn't, but stood gazing at his face, then at his nodding prick which for the instant I let go. Then my mind reverted to my object, to let him fuck her first — so ceased frigging and saying, "Fuck her." He began to get up.

But again I altered — "No — no — lay — there." — Again I seized his tool, to frig him was now all I wanted, and in a minute whilst he felt her cunt, out spurted on to his belly a copious shower of semen. — An aberration, a lustful delirium came over me, — I had never intended, never thought of it till that instant — I wondered if my sperm was as thick as his — for I hadn't frigged myself to see for sometime — wondered how my sperm would look by the side of his — and the instant that the idea flashed through my brain, I frigged myself rapidly. — Nelly looked on. — "Lay still" — still he lay — my ballocks were full, and I spent over his belly, my sperm falling by, or mingling with his. — In the wild excitement of the crisis, I laid hold of his prick again, whilst with my other hand I finished my own onanistic performance, standing by the bed side with eyes closed, and frigging both pricks at once, till sense slowly returning I found both hands moist with our generative fluids.

He washed, put on his mask again, and we sat down. — I thought of what I'd had him for, was sorry for what I had done — annoyed — and asked if he could fuck Nelly. "Not for an hour," said he. Then I was going to leave and told him he could dress. — He'd no sooner put on his shirt than I altered my mind, said he should wait and fuck her. — "All right, she's a rare good fuck" — said he in a loud tone. "Let me take my mask off." — I wouldn't. I had a dislike to see his face tho a handsome one.

I didn't want to talk, or to feel him. He and Nelly talked and drank, I occasionally said a word. She after her custom played with his prick, and what with her feeling it and his feeling her cunt, before the hour I saw it swelling. — "You can fuck now." — "That I can." — Nelly put herself on the bed side, soon I saw his big tool going to and fro up her cunt, and put my hand under his balls, feeling its movements till his libation was given. I didn't disturb him whilst he bent over her, until from under his balls I felt his prick uncunting.

Nelly lay still with thighs wide apart as his tool left it, her cunt glistening invitingly with clear thin albumen, and beginning to yield up its liquids, for he had spent well. Then plunging my prick up her, it revelled in the grateful lubricity, and my libation mingled with his. — Then rapidly I washed, dressed, and went my way, throwing off my mask only at the door. — He was still masked and naked, sitting on a chair feeling his prick. He fucked her again when I'd left, she told me afterwards.

The excitement during copulation suspends judgment, — almost thought — except baudy thought — reflexion comes afterwards. Next day I felt delight at the mode in which I had made my offering to Venus, in that one of her many temples which lay at the bottom of Nelly's belly, I was sure that the lubricity of her cunt, that softness prepared by the semen of my pioneer, added highly to my pleasure in coition with her, had made it perfect; yet I disliked myself for liking it, and vowed that none but Nell should ever know of my sexual whim [yet now I am narrating it, and have told it to other women — never to men].

Going to Nell's solely to talk about it a few days after, to my surprize she said she'd got another man for me if I'd like one, quite a young respectable fellow who had been a clerk, lost his place, had got down in the world, and now sold steel pens, calling at shops, offices and so on, to sell them. She fired me. "Get him, get him," said I. The idea of copulating after the man in the same female receptacle, again overwhelmed me with lascivious desire.

He was brought, was a short, dark youth, slim and almost boyish. At the first minute almost, he asked me what I was going to give him, and when told, said, "But you'll pay *her*." — Nelly in

vain tried to stop him talking about that. "Pull out your prick," said
I quite boldly finding him to be, or seeming to be a novice. He hesi-
tated as if ashamed, and Nelly pulled it out for him — a little one
— I laid hold of it. — "What are you going to do?" said he. — "What
he likes" — said Nelly answering for me. — "Oh — no — what? —
nothing at the back" — he remarked.

He undressed to his shirt, was clean, had a small prick growing
out of a thick but small bush of jet black crisp hair. — His eyes and
hair were very dark. — Talking with him, he said he'd been a clerk,
but I couldn't get from him why he'd left clerkship. By selling pens,
he made such a poor living, that as soon as he'd got twenty pounds,
he meant to go to America. Miss °°°°° (naming a gay woman) a
friend of Nelly's, told him he could get money if he'd let gents frig
him, and bugger him, but he wouldn't do the latter at any price. —
He was to have Nelly wasn't he? — he hoped so, she was a nice girl,
but he'd never done it to *her*, tho he had to her friend.

My lewed whims, likes and dislikes are so unaccountably curi-
ous. — Somehow I didn't care about his lubricating Nelly's vagina,
the very idea of going where his prick had been gave me offence,
tho he'd been hired for that purpose. — I frigged his little prick
twice, he sitting on my knee whilst I masturbated him. Then I
fucked Nelly and left.

[Then for a time my dislike to another male being even near
me, returned. — Curiosity was I thought at the root of all I had
done, yet the pleasure of a lubricious cunt still dwelt in my mind.

[I nearly burnt these episodes, yet why should I? — education,
prejudice, how powerful are they — what more harm can there be
in feeling a man's prick than his hand, his prick, is the noblest mem-
ber?

[I was certainly wildly erotic after this, and went to Nelly L.
for all my satisfactions. — Whenever I thought of H°l°n M°°°w°°d
my prick stood, but I avoided her, fearing to fall in love — into that
infatuation of lust which leads men to ruin. — How with my volup-
tuous temperament, and my adoration of the beautiful in women I
kept from her astonishes me. Perhaps my erotic whims and Nell's
economical facilities, saved me. My purse was impoverished just
then also.]

I saw flaxen haired Sophy in the streets one night and had again
a letch for her. Nelly got her, and my desire to see light haired and

dark haired cunts together, was again gratified. She had grown stouter, her breasts were very large, but not flaccid, her nipples were very prominent, which perhaps suggested what took place.

Comparing their cunts belly upwards, side by side, then with their bums towards me, we talked about the difference that age had made in them since first I had them; how it had plumped their rumps and bubbies, and thickened the hair on their mottes. — Sophy's motte had swelled up, and was now thickly covered with crisp pale sandy colored hair, indeed was a very fine handful. — She was formed every where for fornication. She had kept a paler tint on her cunt's inner surface than Nelly had. — Dark hair was just shewing round N's bum hole, and we agreed that on *her* motte — where it was wide spread and thick, even when she came out — it had wider spread, had bunched out and was quite horse hairy. — Putting them on the top of each other I wanted them to flat fuck — Nelly refused, tho Sophy was ready for it, half screwed when she came and more so now, for I'd taken a bottle of gin with me. However they laid belly on belly with thighs wide apart, their mottes touching, cunt wigs entwining, but clitoris did not touch clitoris. Whilst fingering, I pulled their lips apart, admired the different crimson tints of their notches, felt their smooth slippery surfaces, saw the fullness of the pouting ridges which closed up the inviting red dells, and the difference in color of the crisp curls. It was a charming sight, a wonderful contrast in two cunts only.

N-y still refusing to rub her cunt against Sophy's, I put them on their backs on the bed, and examined their cunts as they lay that way. — "Lay down with us" — said Sophy. Naked I laid between the two (bed not large enough) and with middle fingers frigged both cunts at once, till their bums wriggled. "Frig faster, I'm coming" — said Sophy, grasping my cock and kissing my naked arm. "Leave off now," said Nelly. Tho lewed to my very arsehole, I got away from them, and pulled away Sophy's hand from her cunt, for she with that reckless lustful abandonment which now characterised her, feeling the want of complete pleasure which I had roused, had when my finger left her clitoris, began frigging herself energetically.

Then noticing her nipples. "Yes, thems growed big thro suckling the brats so long — ain't em?" — said she in her hideous lingo, and voice. — "Put one up Nelly's cunt." — "Oh, you baudy old bugger" — cried she. "What?" said Nelly laughing. — "How is it to be done?" — "I must piddle." — The gin had done its work, both women pissed and began my trick. I didn't know how to manage it at first, but lewed desires soon work themselves out practically with two well trained doxies. Both women now were lewed, excited by drink, and ready for any baudy trick, for a novelty in lust is enjoyed thoroughly by a whore whose cunt is hot, as I have proved many times.

I put Nell on the bedside, and Sophy kneeling in front of her on pillows, to bring her to a convenient height, which wasn't done in a minute. Then standing at Sophy's back, I held Nelly's legs up in the air as wide apart as I could, holding them by the heels, my arms distended, which brought her buttocks to the bedside, her cunt gaping. Then Sophy holding up one breast, pushed the nipple against the cunt, and squeezed her breast flat up against it, hiding all the hair encircled gap but the tip of the clitoris, which just showed itself above her breast. I stood with legs apart straddling over Sophy's fat white back, my balls touching it, and my prick soon erecting, almost buried itself in the hair of Sophy's neck.

"Move it about." — "I can't, it will come out if I do." — "Do you feel the heat on your nipple?" — "Yes, it tickles it." — "Squeeze it backwards and forwards." Sophy obeyed, her breast squeezed up fuller and fuller, then receded, but never quitted the cunt. "Frig yourselves." — Sophy obeyed. — Nell refused, but commanded again angrily did so — her finger rubbed between her clitoris and Sophy's white milk bag. They didn't mind *me*, they were both too lewed and screwed, were both in a minute well off on the frig. Stooping for a moment I put my finger up Sophy's cunt from behind, could feel her finger agitating violently, the whole of her cunt seemed moving with it as my finger buried itself in its folds. Then again straddling across her white fat back, wanting to fuck, to be frigged, be sucked, all at — once — that irresolution as to the act, that desire to have all the sexual pleasures in all ways at once was on me, and intoxicated me with lustful ideas.

Then the loveliness of Sophy's deliciously white skin struck me. Spitting on her back, I rubbed my prick tip up and down on the soft moist surface, frigging the stem with my wet fingers at the same time. I saw Nelly was coming by her looks and manner, that the frigging of Sophy was fetching herself also. She never hid *her* joys, had become a baudy screecher when her pleasure came, and

now sobbed, "Oh — my — dear — fuck me cunt — oh fuck" — I
spurted a shower of sperm on to her white back as she ejaculated
her lustful cries of delight. Nelly who had herself kept up both legs,
when for the minute to frig myself I had relinquished them, was
quiet, had spent, and dropped her legs over Sophy's shoulders, and
there we all remained, Sophy's breast still squeezed gently up
against the other's quim, my prick slowly drooping on to its own
semen, whilst my hand rested on Sophy's shoulder.

The excitement had been very great to us all, tranquillity fol-
lowed, but my erotic imagination never ceased working. Sophy's
nipple was wet from Nelly's cunt. Both stood then in front of me,
both cunts wet, both almost running with their spending. Then we
washed, they drank more gin and talked about our letch — a las-
civious triad — the nipple and cunt work amused us all.

After a time, Nelly put *her* breast on to Sophy's cunt for a
minute, just for the sake of doing it once, and immediately washed
her breast. But the excitement of the novelty was over, I didn't
enjoy the sight as I had the first act, when the caprice had just struck
me. I was most pleased with having spent over Sophy's back. I have
spent over women's breasts, thighs, bums, cunts and faces, but upon
a back never before, and the novelty was delicious.

Afterwards I wanted to fuck Nell, after putting my prick into
both alternately. She positively refused, and wouldn't have my
prick put into her, after the other's cunt, until the prick was washed.
She was snappish with liquor. The fair haired one was ready for
anything, and it ended in both gamahuching me to a certain stage
of pleasure. Then in Sophy gamahuching Nelly at the bedside, and
whilst doing so her bum towards me, I made her stand up, and
pushing between the thighs towards the flaxen hair rift, my prick
entered her deliciously lubricious cunt, that cunt which retains all
its exquisite qualities — fucked by hundreds as it has been, and had
three babies thro it — and spent with my hands on her white but-
tocks, listening to the lapping of her tongue on the other's cunt,
who was spending again.

In another hour Sophy had gamahuched me, taken my liba-
tion in her mouth, and departed muzzy enough. — Nell then told
me that she wouldn't let her cunt touch Sophy's, for she'd heard
she'd had a clap lately. I took no harm. An hour afterwards the
theatres were closed, I had had a lobster supper, was still lewed,

tho not wanting to fuck, and strolled along a street where I knew women pissed freely, and felt the wet cunts of half a dozen. Tired of that and still loitering about, talking baudy to every woman I met, I saw Sophy going along with a young man, followed them to a low brothel, loitered about till she came out, found she was quite drunk, asked if she'd been fucked. "Yes, and the bugger only give me half a crown — no more," said she. She could scarcely speak for drink and scarcely seemed to know me at first. Then all at once, "Oh! Oh! it's you, come and fuck." — "No come here." — At a dark spot I felt her cunt again, it was mucilaginous. — "You haven't washed your cunt," said I. — "Ain't I? — I thought I did when I pissed" she mumbled out. I left her standing there, and soon turning round, saw her going with another man towards the baudy house.

The following incident occurred I find two years ago, but the manuscript got displaced. Altho I did not then see her often, I seem to have relied on Nelly L. to satisfy my erotic whims, and indeed now only went when I had some unusual letch to gratify. She was complaisance itself, I often wondered how it was that with that willingness in pimping, and her personal charms in form and face (she'd shown no signs of fading) she didn't get better rooms, and a better class of men. — Some women have no desire to rise, the lower stage suits them. She was indolent, was not poor, and was content.

Talking with her about a woman who had been taken up for robbing a man, and had kept the stolen trinket in her cunt for two days before it was found there. (This was told in obscure language in the newspapers.) I doubted the possibility. — Nelly averred that it was easy, and it ended in my going out to get the silver, putting forty shillings up her cunt, and seeing her walk up and down the room naked, holding the money in that feminine receptacle. Then she squatted over a pot, and the money dropped out.

I thought much of this, and a few weeks after, resolved to try her pudendal capacity and tenacity. Taking five pounds all in shillings, I talked with her about her cunt which I knew to be very elastic and distensible, altho its muscular action in fucking was so delicious, as before I must have said in this narrative. Telling her the silver I had brought, she entered into a compact at once. Up to forty shillings if held, the money was to be hers, if sixty, fifty hers, if eighty, sixty hers — after eighty all was to be hers, till the silver fell out of her cunt as she walked across the room. She was to walk once up and down if I wished it after each shilling that was inserted. — If she held eighty, I was to fuck her on two other visits without payment. I stipulated that, tho not however intending to act on it, I never like to have a woman without making her a present.

Putting the silver into a basin, she washed and dried it, washed her cunt, dried that well and the insertion began. Shilling after shilling I put up. — After the first twenty — about holding which there was no doubt — until forty were embedded in the elastic gully. Then she walked up and down. "I'm quite sure I can hold twenty more," said she and I put them up by fives, the last five she herself squeezed up in some fashion. — "You've put those up your arsehole," quoth I joking. "Don't make me laugh, that won't be fair." — In a business-like way she now put up shilling after shilling as I handed them to her, till seventy were in her, and triumphantly she walked up and down the room, none falling out of her cunt.

Then I went on slowly, not believing she could hold any more, adding shilling after shilling, and making her walk after each addition to the load, till at the eightieth I put her at the bedside standing, then pushing my finger up a little distance only, felt the mass of coin seemingly but about an inch up from the mouth — I now laid her on the bed for introspection of the infundibular cavern, pulled open the lips for investigation, and could see the silver. Then triumphantly she promenaded the allotted distance, and said, "The money's mine."

Then shilling by shilling others were engulphed in her capacious receptacle, which held them firmly till the eighty-fifth, which tumbled out. Then the game was over, she laughed heartily and more fell out on the floor, her cunt relaxed its grip, I threw her on the bedside, pulled rudely open her cunt, and a dozen rolled out, she laughing almost convulsively, and at each jerk of her belly more silver was ejected. Then over a basin squatting she relieved her cunt of the coin. The last being got out by aid of her fingers, it was then washed and dried, she washed her cunt out with a syringe, we counted the silver, and eighty four shillings were her gain. — "I wish some one would do this every day," said she elated.

The bulk and weight made it seem incredible that any vagina could have held it. But she had done it, and thought that had it been all in half-crowns, she could have held more.

I put then three fingers up her smooth red cul-de-sac, then four up to their knuckles, and believe I could have got my hand nearly up, but she would not allow that, saying it hurt. Then my manipulation having brought the avenue to its natural state of lubriciousness, she feeling randy and my prick being ready, we copulated. The clench of her cunt was delicious, and it seemed impossible that ever it could have dilated, and held eighty five shillings a quarter of an hour before.

[I never tried this trick again with *her,* nor with any other woman but *one* — four or five years afterwards, but told several free mercenary lovers about it. — None had ever heard of such a letch, which was evidently a very original one of mine, and came to me suddenly.]

I did not keep to H°l°n, could not afford to see her often, and one night from the Argyle went home to W°°t°n P°°°e with a sweet faced, dark eyed girl, quite young (wasn't eighteen), a man opened the door, and objecting to his look I nearly left, paid her, and said I had forgotten an appointment. But she pressed me so, — "Come and have me first" — that I went up to her rooms. She'd the prettiest little, chestnut haired cunt between plump thighs, and had a sweet form. We stripped to shirt and chemise — it was very hot — and with great mutual pleasure fucked. — Her manners were nice, modest, yet voluptuous, and I lay with my prick long up her, all the time kissing her — her teeth were beautiful. Our tongues played in silence till our carnal union was dissolved. Then I arose, saying, "You've a lovely cunt." — "You're a lovely poke" — she replied. Just at that moment a knock came. I started, somehow thinking of the sinister looking man who'd opened the door. — "Never mind, lie still, it's only my sister come home" — said she going to the door.

With a ridiculous modesty, I covered my tool with my hand as the sister entered, a girl shorter, but in features closely resembling my woman. — She was very handsomely clad in bright yellow silk (as had been the other), a color then fashionable. Whilst getting something from a drawer, the two began talking. "Yes, he never came, it's the second time he's humbugged me, — So and So wanted to come home with me, but I lost him thro waiting for °°°°, I'll serve him out." She was angry. Then she asked if her sister had supped, *she* hadn't, and was hungry, should Mrs. °°°° get any thing ready? and off she went. I had noticed this girl at the Argyle that very evening, but don't recollect seeing either of them before that night. They'd not been long gay, my woman had told me.

I dressed, and just as I had finished buttoning my trowsers, a voluptuous throb shot through my prick. "You're a sweet girl, I'm longing for you again," said I, kissing her and feeling her breasts. I'd been stimulated by seeing her wash her cunt, always to me a pleasurable sight. She kissed *me*. — "Come on then." — "I can give you no more money." — "All right." — In a minute we were on the bed, she grasping my tool, I twiddling her quim, our tongues meeting. — "Do it, I want it," said she. The next second my prick was buried up to my balls in her tight little cunt, and with prolonged pleasure we spent. How tightly she held my bum I noticed, how she pressed up her cunt to me whilst we spent together. This time we had stripped entirely, and our flesh was in exquisite contact every where. Then we lay and talked till came another knock. "It's only Amy" — saying that she got up and let her in again.

Amy who was eating laughed at our nudities. — "Go and have supper Cis, Mrs. ***** wants to put the things by and go to bed." — "Go, it's a man waiting to have you," said I, jeeringly, and really thought so from the manner of her sister, knowing a bit about the dodges of harlots. "There's no man in the house but Mr. *****. — My rooms are above, and I and sister the only two women in the house." — "You may go up and look," said Amy. — "*Are* you her sister?" — "I should think so" — and she laughed. "You are alike in face, are your quims alike?" — "I don't know, they ought to be for we are twins, would you like to look?" — "I can't afford it to night, shew it me for nothing." — "Oh likely." — Then after a pause, and having heard my woman affirm their being twins — which I had thought a hoax. — "I'll let you look for a minute if you'll give me a bottle of phiz, I've had not a drop of anything to day."

I agreed, saying I'd not pay more than ten shillings a bottle. — She didn't think that the landlord would supply it for *that*, but going to ask, returned with the brute of a man and the champagne. He took the money for it and departed. Then we drank and talked. They had not been long in London I heard, and that was the only house they had lived in. — My woman had been born only three minutes before the other. The champagne, — which was not bad

— was finished. Again my lady washed her cunt. "Now show me *your* quim." — Amy laid on tne bedside, pulled up her petticoats, and I saw a cunt as much like her sister's as possible. — Neither girl had drawers on. — I put my hand to feel her treasure, when she pushed it away and got up laughing, "I didn't say I'd let you feel it."

Just then came another knock and a female voice, — "If you're going to have any supper Miss Cissy, you must come at once." — Asking me to wait only five minutes off she went. "*You* stop," said I to the sister. — She did, and I talked with her till her sister returned, but she wouldn't show me her cunt again. — "How do you like my sister?" she asked — I said I'd fucked her with the intensest pleasure. "*He is* a baudy man," said she to her sister as she entered the room. — "I told you so" — was the reply.

I longed to see Amy's quim again, and said I'd have another bottle if she'd show it, and let me open the lips. She wouldn't agree to that at first, but she'd show it. — I agreed. She then stripped to her chemise, the champagne came and they got frisky with it. — "Shew me your prick," said Amy. — "It's a nice one, and he's a lovely poke," said her sister. I wouldn't shew it, unless she'd let me feel her cunt. She did, and it was a beautiful little split much like her sister's. She caught hold eagerly of my tool, which swelled largely in her hands, but didn't stiffen, quite.

All was most luxuriously inviting. The two sweet girls close to me in their chemises, with bubbies shewing — dark patches every now and then peeping from their armpits — lovely shaped legs in silk stockings and natty boots, formed a delicious sight. Every now and then I felt the elder girl's quim; she lifted my shirt, and gently handled my prick, and our talk got baudier. The champagne was finished, it had got into their bladders, both pissed, and so did I — Amy again felt my prick (not any stiffer) and said, — "I shall go to bed, I wish I'd some one to sleep with, I've not had a poke for two nights." — "I'll give you another bottle of champagne if you'll let me fuck you — if I can — if you can stiffen me." — "Have him," said Cissy. — "All right," said Amy going to the door and hollowing down stairs for the wine. — "He's gone to bed and I can't get it" — said a female.

Up stairs clattering ran the lass, roused the man who came down grumbling (she'd left the door ajar). Soon after the parlor door opened, a champagne bottle was pushed thro, the hand remained. — "The money," said he. I put it into his hand which disappeared. The next few glasses screwed the girls, who had been somewhat chaste in language till then, but now returned my lewed talk. — "Fuck me," said Amy, laying hold of my tool. — "It's not stiff." — "Come on the bed and I'll make it stiff, but it's stiff enough to get into me now." — "Suck it — you must." Both refused, nor would they. — "Mind, I can't give you any money." — "All right, come on." — "Pull off your chemise." — Off it went, off went my shirt. — She laid on the bed thighs wide apart, I investigated her cuntal charms, and my cock then stiffened gloriously; but not feeling pressed by my sperm I still laid by her side. — "Why it's quite stiff, put it in," said she impatiently, and tugging at my prick vigorously.

Who could resist such an eager, loving, invitation? I plunged my pego into her thirsty sheath. She was dying for it, and worked her cunt vigorously, but my tool tho now as rigid as the most exacting cunt could desire, had no libation ready at its roots. Fucking on vigorously to meet her ardor, soon the clip and grind round its tip told me she was coming. The soft, moist relaxation of cuntal friction, her murmurs of pleasure, and tranquillity of thighs, bum and belly, told of her spend. Directly after, "You haven't spent, go on fucking, go on," said she.

On I went fucking with pleasure, grasping her bum, kissing the delicious creature, pleasure in my gland, my mind filled with visions of women, of her sister's cunt, and other exquisite meretricious reminiscences — but without that all pervading voluptuous pleasure, which runs thro every fibre of my body and heralds the advent of spunk, as it prepares to issue from my balls. — She sighed, — she kissed me. — "Aha — you fuck lovely" — I plunged harder and quicker, up and down the lubricious avenue, and sweated copiously with my exercise on that hot night. — Then her cunt gripped and tightened again, then came a voluptuous thrill thro me. — "I shall spend love — it's coming from my balls" — "Aha — so — shall — I — Aher — Aher" — and my spendings mixed with hers in the lovely sheath, and we were tranquil. There sat her sister watching us. — "He's a lovely poke isn't he?" said she. — "Yes." — "How often did he do you?" — "Twice." — "Aha" — said Amy laying with my prick up her, I on her belly, which heaved up.

Then I left. — Many a year was it since I'd fucked a Paphian for a bottle of champagne. It was near daylight when I got home.

A few days after I had the elder in the afternoon. She was fresh as a daisy, looked handsomer than at night. What a long look I had at the little cunt, with what delight I fucked it twice. She then told me she should leave London soon, a gentleman was going to keep her. I gave her champagne as we sat and talked. She said they really were twins, lived not far from London — had been fucked not quite a year, that the same gentleman had the virginities of both of them, and of one not long after the other. They had known him since they were little girls, and their parents as well. He'd helped their parents and had dropped down dead just before they had turned gay. — A curious history if true, yet not improbable; for I know of a case intimately, where a very rich man fucked first two sisters, and left them each small fortunes; some people said he'd fucked their mother as well. She was a remarkably handsome woman. He died suddenly.

Again I called — Amy appeared, said her sister was engaged with a friend. — "I wish I were fucking her instead," said I. — "You might if you'd been ten minutes earlier, but I am glad, for it's the gentleman who's going to keep her." — I examined Amy's charming form, and her little pretty quim was very like her sister's, with but a small quantity of silken hair on it. I fucked her and departed, not liking her as well as her sister, but why can't say. — Calling a few nights after, the sinister looking man opened the door, and said Miss °°°° had gone away. Off I went to the A°g°°e, saw the sister, took her home and had her. Her sister was in a nice house of her own with a great swell she said. I questioned her more. — Yes. One gentleman had had both their virginities, and he was dead, "So much the worse for us."

———————

A day or two after I visited H°l°n. She had now become very curious about my doings with women, and always questioned me. Generally I told her truly what women I had. It pleased me to tell her, especially as I saw it annoyed her when told what the cost of my pleasure had been. She averred that they were *not* sisters, tho they'd given themselves out as such. — She knew them by sight, they had only been seen a few months, and one had recently disappeared. She had enquired about the sisterhood.

They however resembled each other immensely, had voices

alike, and cunts wonderfully alike. Out of a hundred cunts, not one is quite like to another, there is always some difference noticeable in them. — In my belief, there is as much difference in the look of cunts as there is in noses. — But sisters' cunts I think are generally somewhat alike. — One sister often makes another a harlot. All this I've remarked before.

"You say you're fond of *me* but see other women much more frequently." — "Yes but don't give them your compliment." — "But you spend much more money." — "Perhaps, but have three or four women for what I pay you once." — "Well — I won't let any man have me for less than five quid." — But she was annoyed.

Soon after calling on Amy, I found she had also left, both had disappeared from London. They were lovely young harlots, had the sweetest cunts, and each would have let me fuck them as much as I liked — which was less than they wanted.

Sweet as they were I gamahuched neither of them — why?

H°l°n again. — Financial arrangements. — Mutual erotic tastes. — Hers for gamahuche. — Her sexual strength. — Baudy books in bed. — Varied amorosities there. — My smooth skin. — Animalism cum idealism. — Needless repetitions in this narrative. — On a metropolitan railway. — Female costermonger in wrong class. — A stern guard. — My aid and recompense. — At the terminus. — In the half formed road. — Against a wooden fence. — The voice in the dark. — Rapid flight. — Voluptuous sensations in a lusting quim. — White stockings in a fog. — "Ain't you got cheek." — Favours in the mews. — Fucking con amore solamente. — We separate as strangers.

After visiting H°l°n M. a few times, she agreed to accept what I could afford, and I became a regular friend tho I did not see her frequently. — What with presents, and years after assistance when she was in difficulties, the cost of her charms increased rather than diminished, but I was content and saw her whenever the troubles of life made me miserable, and then her intense beauty, and most exquisite sexual intercourse relieved me. By degrees it was that we got to confidences. She left gay life two years after, and gradually each understanding the erotic tastes of the other, our sensuous temperaments being similar, we gave way to all our devices, and she did with me and others, and saw done with me and others, acts which when regularly *gay* — she had never seen or done. — The incidents as written would have disclosed this gradually, but this preface is now necessary, so much manuscript having to be burnt.

As said, — since my lingual amusements on Miss E°w°°°s pudenda — gamahuching had become a greater pleasure to me. — Formerly at the sight of a lovely woman, my first thought was of her cunt, and my first desire to fuck her; now quite as frequently, my first desire is to give her cuntal pleasure with my tongue, — what the special attraction in a woman is, which makes me desire to gamahuche instead of fuck her, I can't say, have often tried to solve that problem without success, but certain it is, that this gamahuching desire is not generated in me by every woman.

This letch was roused in me by H, the first time I had her. On subsequent visits she refused it, and anxious to please her, satisfied by the exquisite pleasure she gave me, I contented myself with fucking her only. But as she learnt a little of my secret life and told me hers, gradually disclosed *her* erotic tastes and letches which all gay ladies have — for lust increases with the knowledge of what lust can do — I found she liked it. Towards the end of this year, one afternoon being in bed together and I ready to mount her, she said looking at me voluptuously, "Put your little head down first." — For the moment I didn't understand, but in a minute my tongue was on her clitoris, she spent under its delicate irritation, and I was delighted.

Subsequently we nearly always commenced our active pleasures with lingual play, and I found out in time her extreme sexual force. She could spend two or three times under the gamahuche, and then enjoy my prick three times, as well as if she'd had no spend before. — Generally she did all this amorous work without a sign of fatigue. I never knew a woman of such sexual strength.

We used at times to lay in bed reading baudy books. Then I would gamahuche her, and she liked the lingual exercise continued almost directly after her spend. A few minutes' repose only and I'd fuck her, then we'd go on reading. Sometimes *she'd* read until suddenly she'd frig herself, laying back, grasping my prick hard with one hand, even hurting it sometimes, with eyes closed, more frequently looking me full in the face eyes wide open, with a wonderful voluptuous expression, till her breath shortened, her lovely thighs and belly quivered, then her eye lids drooped till her body was quite tranquil. — Then with the remark, — "We are beasts," — our reading was resumed. So we went on for hours, fucking, gamahuching, and she frigging herself at intervals — both drinking champagne from time to time — for I always at last took that exhilarating, kidney stimulating liquor to her. H°l°n was made for fucking.

The feminine softness of my skin was always admired by gay women, whose lust often times seemed stimulated by feeling it. Many a one has desired a second poke on account of its nice feel. Now in my maturer years it has the same effect on women, which I should not have expected. The narratives of several incidents shewing this have been destroyed, but enough preserved to prove it.

H°l°n by feeling it, found it increased her liking for me — mere lust that perhaps — but what voluptuousness is added to fucking, when a man and woman like feeling each other's bodies. If only mere animalism this, why speak slightingly about *that*, why not accept it philosophically. Our brains work with our bodies sympathetically in the physical junction of cock and cunt, and for the time the couple love each other, love till the ecstatic crisis is over. Man and woman can both intensify their physical pleasure by thought, can fancy any one or anything, when fucking. — When the carnal exercise is finished, the libation given — all is over.

As I read this later manuscript now, I come upon opinions and scraps of conversation on sexual matters, which altho *apropos* of the event, seem to me to have been said before on many similar occasions, on exactly the same subjects. — If so it is needless repetition, but it's now impossible to refer back — Better perhaps repetition than total omission.

I had been to my stock brokers one day at the beginning of November this year, had luncheon in the City, called at a friend's office, and at about half past five o'clock got into a first class metropolitan railway carriage going to the north west, where I was going to have a friendly dinner with a man. The carriages were full, in ours but one place was vacant, when just as the train started in rushed a woman and took it. She saw at once that she'd made a mistake, and smiled at no one in particular, looking anxiously about, and as if she'd never been in such a carriage before. She then looked at every one of us in turn, with an expression on her face of, — "You know I'm in the wrong carriage and so do I." — They were mostly elderly men, tired perhaps with business, and beyond giving a glance at her, took no further notice and read their newspapers.

I kept my eyes on her for she was coarsely handsome, was opposite to me, and our knees nearly met. Soon I put foot and knee against hers, and a thrill of desire shot through me directly they touched. A desire to see, to feel her cunt, to fuck her, which like lightning goes thro me at times, and almost immediately when I see certain women, I believe that feeling creates a secret sympathy between us, and if the concupiscence in one or other of us be strong, that it is communicated to the other, if he or she be physically in a receptive state which is only if the blood be warm, the organs charged, and cock and cunt be ready for amourous endearments.

She was a well grown, good looking woman about twenty-three years old, of the costermonger class. She looked like one who sold goods from a barrow, or a very small shop. She was commonly but comfortably clad, not warmly enough perhaps for well to do people, but enough so for her class who don't feel cold as we do. She had a vulgar hat — half bonnet — on, yet not a flashy one, and a good, bright, short woolen shawl, over her shoulders. Her face was coarse but good featured, and a little browned (tho winter) by exposure. Her eyes were dark and full, her hair dark brown. She had a full bust, and I knew at a glance had a good fat bum and thighs, from the room she occupied on the seat. — Her hands were discolored with working, a color which would not readily wash off, the color of healthy labor, for she didn't look unclean at all; her nails were quite short and she'd a wedding ring on. I sat looking at her, and she at me at last, till leaning back, purposely I pushed forward both my knees, and touched hers, of which act she took notice, not being accustomed to such refinements. Then my prick began to swell, and she to fix her eyes on me. — Did *she* feel lewed at that moment also? — how I should like to know.

I began to scheme how to have her. How many times I have done so in public vehicles without fixed intention. It seemed absurd, but such seemingly improbable successes with women have fallen to my lot — and thro perseverance mainly I think — that I gave reins to my wishes. — *Nil desperandum.* Pushing myself more forward still, as if better to read a newspaper which I held in my hands, I got her legs well between mine and very gradually closed them on hers, till I could feel the warmth we gave each other. I watched her over the edge of my paper, and fancied I saw that she was conscious that I pressed her limbs purposely. A soft uneasy look came then into her eyes, and she looked round anxiously at the other travellers, twiddling at the same time her third class railway ticket nervously. I felt certain — instinct told me — that she knew I wanted her, and that I was kindling in her desire for a prick, if not for mine; for lust is stirred in a woman, by knowing that a man wants to fuck her. Ostentatiously I put my hand under my great coat on to my ballocks, and moved it there restlessly, looking her full in the face whilst doing so. She turned her eyes away, — she'd not done so before, — and I felt then sure that she was thinking of my prick — I wonder what she thought.

Two or three stations were passed, passengers got out, and at length the carriage was empty all but the woman and myself. As he closed the door, the guard eying her, asked for her ticket, and then, "Wrong class — four pence extra — come out." — She preparing to leave, said she'd got in in a hurry. — "Oh yes — come out — four pence." "I haven't a farthing, I paid all I had for my ticket." — She was quite agitated. — Interposing, I said that she got in as the trained moved off, asked where she was going to, paid the collector the extra fare for her, and off went the train.

We were now alone in the carriage and the next instant I was by her side, she volubly thanking me. — Plunging at once, I said I'd give a hundred times the amount to sleep with her. "Oh I dessay," said she laughing. "But I'll have a kiss." — I took one without resistance. "It's very kind of you." — "What, to kiss you?" — "Oh no, not that" — and she laughed heartily. I took another kiss. — "It's nice to be gentle-folks and ride in such carriages," she remarked.

The kiss inflamed me, no time was to be lost, for in fifteen minutes she would be at her destination — far beyond mine — and other passengers might come in. Placing one hand on her lap, — "I've been rubbing your leg with mine, have been mad for you since you entered the carriage, you are so well formed, so beautiful, get out at the next station and let's have a glass of wine together." — "Oh I dessay — no thankee sir — but you're very kind." — "Let me have another kiss then." — "No — leave off," — but I took a dozen. — "Give me one," and she gave it. — "There now I've paid you, leave off." — "You've a lovely leg and foot (she'd thick ankle jack boots on), let me see a bit more of it, don't mind me, I'm old enough to be your father." — "Oh I dessay." — But she seemed pleased at my praise, looked confused by it, and as I put my hand down didn't resist my lifting her petticoats a wee bit up. I pinched the calf of her leg. "You've a fine thigh I'll swear" — pinching it outside. — "I'm pretty well covered" — laughing. — Certain that she was randy now, — "Let me feel." — "Oh! I dessay, not for Joseph." — Bending I put my hands up her clothes and just touched her flesh, vigorously she pushed her clothes down. — "Now — no nonsense sir — or I'll get out — I'll tell the guard." Just then we reached a station.

But she didn't get out, or tell the guard, and no one got in — so alone together on we went. I now tried to feel her notch, she resisted but laughing always. Several times I touched the hair of her motte, and felt firm fat thighs, yet but for a moment, and never felt the cleft. "Now you're not a going to, I tell yer — now — I'll get out." — "You won't get out — don't be so cruel, I don't know when I've seen a more lovely creature." — "I will tho." "Feel this before you go." — In a state of reckless libidinosity, I threw open my great coat, and exposed my prick in glorious erection. — "I won't you old beast" — I stood up with it in front of her. — "Feel it." — "I won't you beast." — She pushed me away gently, and in doing so touched it. — Again I stood so. — "Oh don't pray. What will they think if they see you?" — Then I hid it demurely, and took my place in front of her, reading my paper, just in time — for at the station some one got in.

We both looked at the intruder who stared at her, wondering I suppose how she came to be in a first class carriage. Soon after I pushed my leg which was nearest the carriage door well forward, and pressed her thigh with it. She didn't move hers away. The other passenger ceased looking, then I put my hand down and clasped my scrotum so that she could see me do it, and a suppressed smile broke over her face. I dropped my glove purposely and picking it up, ran my hand up the calf of her leg. The other passenger was then looking out of the window, tho it was pitch dark. At the next station he got out.

The train next stopped at her station, which was nearly at the end of the line in the western suburbs, a district then only half built over, but with plenty of new roads laid out. I stepped out first not taking any notice of her, waited at the top of the steps till she appeared, followed her till well away from the station, and then went up to her. — It was pitch dark. "Don't follow me now."

—"I must, I will, till you let me — come to this coffee shop and have something to eat." We passed one and I guessed there were· beds there. She wouldn't — I kept on walking by her side, begging her to let me feel her, only feel her, nothing more, extolling her beauty, saying I'd never felt such firm flesh as her thighs. She turned down a dull new half lighted street, newly formed roads without lights and building land enclosed by fences leading out of it, were soon approached. "Give me a kiss you sweet creature, and just let me feel it once only here, and I'll go." She'd been begging me to go, and I was beginning to think I should not succeed. — "I'll kiss you if you'll go." — "Turn down here then and no one will see us." — Not a person was then in sight in the road we were in, we went down the side road about fifty feet, in the dark I kissed her, she me, and next minute my fingers were between the lips of a thickly haired quim. I was enraptured and longed for more. — "I won't let you" — but she stood still — I would go if she'd feel *me*. — In a minute she held my stiff stander. — "I'm frightened — suppose we're seen." — A minute after we were fucking up against the railings, and never had I a more delicious embrace. What a clipper her cunt was, — how she wanted a prick, how she enjoyed it, we even put our tongues together voluptuously as our bellies pressed each other, a lingual embrace which I've not often done when having a woman in the open, or indeed when having uprighters any where, that at this moment I can recollect.

My prick wouldn't leave her, for I was lascivious, she lustful — I'd roused hers and she didn't hurry it out. So we stood conjoined, both my hands round a large solid backside. We talked in a low tone. "If any one passes it will amuse him," said I. — "These side roads don't go through yet, and there's no houses in them," she replied. No one was likely to pass. I was hoping to fuck again without uncunting, and perhaps she was hoping the same, so tranquilly did she stand keeping her belly to mine, but my prick at last came out, her petticoats dropped. With my handkerchief I wiped my dripping doodle, she standing still just where she'd been tailed. "I've done a pretty bit of marketing in the city," said she laughing. — "Have you been to market?" — "Yes, but the price wouldn't do." — "You told the guard you'd no money." — "No more I have excepting what I took to buy with — I must be off — let me go first — don't come further with me, will you now?"

But my passion was not satisfied, I longed to have her again, the adventure so like those of my youth stimulated me. Besides I can still at times fuck twice or trice within the hour. "Let's talk a little longer and we'll do it again," said I, holding her shoulders. — She couldn't, she was late, they'd wonder where she was, yet there she stood in the cold, talking with me in a subdued voice. I asked her where she lived, how she lived, what she'd been to buy. "Oh them's tellings," and I could get no information, nor indeed cared much about it, all I wanted was time for my prick to recuperate and stiffen again, but it didn't. — "I *must* go, I really *must*" — and she walked towards the road, out of which we had turned, I with her, no word about money had passed yet.

It was a dreary half built neighbourhood. Scarcely a person was in the thoroughfare, but she begged me to leave her as she was near her home, and feared being seen. "Now *do* go, you promised. — Oh, impossible to tell you where I live, or meet you again." — "Turn up here then." We passed and now on the other side of the way — what looked like a similar half formed road. I said I could do it again to her. — She now went willingly up the place with me, and soon her back was up against some railings. I found however that I wasn't quite ready for duty, but the feel of her gluey cunt — she'd not piddled since the fuck — and fat firm buttocks, together with her feeling my pego — all of which took place in silence — reanimated it, and before it was thoroughly rigid I put it against her notch. She held up her clothes to aid me, my prick tip touched the spermatized gap, and rose up stiffer, then clasping her bum I gave it a cautious push, and with a throb, to full size it erected, we were off fucking again, and had an exquisite second pleasure — almost greater than the first. — She responded to my thrusts and aided me voluptuously.

My prick had just left her cunt, when a voice not far off, and as it seemed to me on the land behind the fencing, cried out — "I see you. — I'll tell" — and then laughed. — "Oh! God!" — said she, and rising up — for she had just squatted to piddle, — took to her heels and ran off as hard as she could, unheeding my, "Stop, stop, it's only a blackguard." — I lingered to button up my trowsers, saying to the voice, "You go to hell." — The voice made no reply, all was dead silence. — In my flurry I buttoned my trowsers somehow on to my coat, then had to undo it, then buttoned my trowsers to my drawers, then couldn't find the button holes, and so lost time, altho whilst arranging my trowsers I walked slowly towards the main road, thinking she'd wait for me there. But I could see nothing of her, and after walking all about the street and side streets for half an hour, went home, never saw her since, and know no more about her.

What a delicious adventure, beginning and ending in an hour and a half. What led up to it — my lust or hers — or did we both want fucking when we met — or did I communicate the lust to her — or she to me? — I know my evolution of desire, beginning with pleasure in looking at her face and form, then guessing at the sort of cunt she had, then desire, then a voluptuous tingling in my tip, then a stiff prick, then an attempt to possess her, then recklessness. — Did she go thro similar phases of lust? — How I should like to experience a woman's sensations as her cunt heats and moistens, and desire for the man gradually rises till it overwhelms her, and she yields. This woman was not of Paphian class, which made fucking her nicer. Yet how delightful is the facile manner, the frank lewedness, the desire to gratify her lust, which marks the Paphian when in rut. Both in their way are charming, the modest and the immodest, the variety is delightful. This woman was, and will ever be, unknown to me, which makes the episode doubly charming now, when I can rarely avail myself of my chances. It is well that I seize them when I can.

[Once or twice in my life I've been scared when in amorous play — more than once have lost my chance thro scares — I have also scared others, tho I've not told of that here. I should not be so cruel now.]

Legs all my life had almost a greater attraction for me than faces — and distinctly so since I was about twenty five years old. I can now pardon an ugly face even, if the body be beautiful in form. Much as I love a beautiful face, I am sure that my prick has risen more quickly, and lust has thrilled thro me more instantaneously, at the sight of a fine leg and good foot, than it has at the sweetest face. A fine face says to me, — "Am I not beautiful?" — Good legs say to me, — "Fuck me."

One night near Christmas, going along a big, wide, silent street in the suburbs — streets where the houses are detached, with gardens in front and rear — as I passed a gateway, two women — servants evidently — were talking. A tall woman one of them, went off in front of me saying, "Good bye," just as I approached, and I saw that she had thickish ankles in white stockings, and held her petticoats high up. It's strange what simple things will rouse my amatory passions at times. Those white stockings did, and after following her a few hundred feet, I thought I should like to feel her cunt. I'd not seen her face, didn't know whether she was twenty or forty — but she stepped out briskly and I guessed her thirty, and from what I saw at the gate, that she was a servant.

It was a pitch dark night, muddy, and all of a sudden became foggy, and scarcely a person was out. — I'd allowed her to get about thirty feet in front of me, so that I might see the white stockings, and now owing to the thoughts which following her and looking at them had generated, my prick began to throb. If she's game, I can have a kiss or a baudy chaff, which is agreeable; if she's offended, I can but beg pardon, cross the street and leave her. I have done so when I've made such mistakes. Thinking thus, I hastened my steps, and when by her side said, — "You've a splendid pair of legs, I wish you'd hold up the clothes a little higher, and let me see a bit more of them." "They are quite high enough to keep off the mud, and it's like your impudence," said she — laughing heartily tho. — Thought I, she's game, and now *knew* by voice and manner that she was of the servant class. We just then passed a gas lamp, and I saw that she looked thirty years old if not more.

"It's your fault if I'm impudent, for showing your legs so." — "You need not look at them." — "I could not help it and it's set me longing for you." — "Oh indeed." — I got a little suggestive now. — "Do you live about here?" — "No," — I replied, and telling her where I was going. — "It's the other way not this," said she. — "I don't exactly know where it is, you come and show me." — "Oh I can't, I must get back." — "Give me a kiss, you're a fine woman," said I. — She made a sham struggle but I got one, and then another, then I felt sure she liked it. — "You're a rude man." — "You've made me rude, for my cock's been stiff ever since I saw your legs. — Let me feel them." — "You're a *very* rude man." — "Where are *you* going my dear." — "Oh — ain't you cheeky." — "I'll see where you go, and won't leave you till I've felt your lovely legs." — "Oh! ain't you got cheek?" — "Give me another kiss, you've splendid thighs I'll swear" — and again I attempted one. Just then some one approached us. "Leave off, you'll get me into trouble, I live not far from here."

This sort of game went on for a quarter of an hour, she slackened her pace, or else I did, and I went on chaffing. At another gas lamp I thought she looked forty. The houses were now further apart and with larger gardens, the fog got thicker. "I shan't be able to find my way home," said she. — "And I'm sure I shan't find my friend's house." — "Leave me now please sir," — said she seriously. — "I won't till I've felt your legs, come here, this is your way home, let me give you a kiss." — "I shan't." — I laid hold of her arm and led her up what seemed a muddy grassy place, which looked like an entrance to a field by the side of a garden to a large house which we had just passed, or else a mews, the fog prevented my seeing clearly what. She permitted me to pull her but it was really only leading her, and when we were in utter darkness and in perfect silence, I kissed her, and held her close round the waist, my belly against hers, telling her about the excitement her ankles had caused me, she saying, — "Now let me go, I really must go." But instinct told me that she knew I meant fucking. I slipped my hand up her clothes, felt big thighs and a fully haired notch, with scarcely any resistance. — "Now I wouldn't have come if I'd thought you'd be so rude." — Then I put my pego into her hand. "Let's fuck my darling — let me do it."

She at every advance I'd made said, — "Oh! no — ain't you got cheek." — But she was randy and meant to let me. When we were both feeling each other's privates, she asked me to promise not to follow her home, for she was in service. — Two minutes after, my hands were clasping a pair of big buttocks and we were fucking. — She'd had many a fuck in her time I'm sure, and enjoyed it immensely. She'd taken off one glove, and felt my pego before she consented, and I'd introduced it to her quim.

The fucking over, we kissed and parted, and I agreed to meet her the following Sunday. She went out of the dark turning, first. — No money was given or promised. Had I seen her ten minutes after I shouldn't have known the woman. There was something about the business which made me fear a clap, but nothing of the sort occurred. — It took me half an hour to find my way to my friend, —

it was my second visit — tho really it was not ten minutes walk from his house, where I'd fucked this amorous domestic. I fancy that by a little flattery and persuasion, both of which I'd used, any prick would find an easy entry to her. Sure am I that she'd been well fucked long before I had her. I enjoyed the unexpected adventure immensely.

Then again I went abroad for a couple of months, and amused myself with foreign women, the well kept, well drilled whores, of a French lapunar.

These last two episodes are wonderfully similar in character. There is nothing in *that*, but it is singular, that they should have occurred so soon after each other.

H. and I get confidential. — Her voluptuous abandonment. — My sensitive pego avowed. — My seminal ejaculations. — H. likes a big pego. — A big one up her. — I up after the big one. — Mutual delight in a semenalized vagina. — Reflexions thereon.

H°l°n and I now began to understand each other (tho not yet perfectly). She knew I was not easily humbugged, so abandoned largely Paphian devices, treated me as a friend, and her circumstances compelling her to avoid male friends, and not liking females much, and it being a human necessity to tell some one about oneself, I became to some extent her confidant. She then had a charming, well furnished little house, replete with comfort, and her own. I at times dined with her there. She was beautifully clean, you might have eaten off her kitchen boards, and the same throughout the house. She was an excellent cook, cooked generally herself and liked it, was a gourmet. It was delightful to see her sitting at table, dressed all but a gown, with naked arms and breasts showing fully over a laced chemise, with her lovely skin and complexion, eating, and drinking my own wine, she passing down at intervals to the kitchen. We eat and drank with joy and baudy expectation, both of us — for she wanted fucking. — Every now and then I felt her thighs and quim, kissing her, showing my prick, anxious to begin work even during our dinner.

Afterwards adjourning to her bedroom, we passed the evening in voluptuous amusements — we had then but *few* scruples in satisfying our erotic wishes. — Soon after had *none*. — How she used to enjoy my gamahuching, and after a time abandoning herself to her sensations she'd cry out, "Aha — my — God — aha — fuck spunk" — and whatever else came into her mind, quivering her delicious belly and thighs, squeezing my head with them, clutching my hair, as her sweet cunt heaved against my mouth when spending, till I ceased from tongue weariness. Sometimes this with my thumb gently pressing her bum hole, which after a time she liked much. Then what heavenly pleasure as I put my prick up her, and grasping her ivory buttocks, meeting her tongue with mine, mixing our salivas, I deluged her cunt with sperm. — Never have I had more pleasure with any woman, with few so much.

Resting, we talked of *her* baudy doings and *mine* — of the tricks of women. — We imagined baudy possibilities, planned voluptuous attitudes, disclosed letches, suggested combinations of pleasure between men and women, and woman with woman — for Eros claimed us both. In salacity we were fit companions, all pleasures were soon to be to us legitimate, we had no scruples, no prejudices, were philosophers in lust, and gratified it without a dream of modesty.

One day I told her again of the sensitiveness of my pego, that with a dry cunt the friction of fucking sometimes hurt me, that my prick at times looked swollen and very red, unnaturally so. — French harlots — more than others — I found washed their cunts with astringents, which my prick detected in them directly, so when I was expected, I wished H. not to wash *hers* after the morning, her natural moisture then being so much pleasanter to my penis. — No saliva put there, is equal to the natural viscosity, mucosity of the surface of a vagina. — But from her scrupulously cleanly habits, I had great difficulty in getting her to attend to this.

That led one day to her asking, if I had ever had a woman who had not washed her quim after a previous fucking. She then knew my adventure with the sailor, that at Lord A's, and at Sarah F°°z°r's — but not the recent one at N°°l°e L°°l°e's. — I told her that I had not with those exceptions. — "I'll bet you have without knowing." She told me of women where she had lived, merely wiping their cunts after a poke, and having at once another man,

and of its not being discovered; of she herself once having had a
man fuck her, and his friend who came with him, insisting on
poking her instantly afterwards.

We talked soon after about the pleasure of fucking in a well
buttered cunt, and agreed that the second fuck was nicer if the
cunt was unwashed. I racked my memory, and recollected cases
where I had had suspicions of having done so. H°l°n who always
then washed her quim, again said it was beastly. — I said that if
more agreeable to me and the woman, there was nothing beastly
in it; nor cared I if there was, fucking being in its nature a mere
animal function, tho in human beings augmented in pleasure, by the
human brain. "So why wash after, if the two like it otherwise?"

About that time I found I had not quite as much sperm as in
early middle age, testing that by frigging myself over a sheet of
white paper, and wished to see what a young man spent both in
quality and quantity. We chatted about this at times, and one day
she told me she had a man about thirty-five years old, who visited
her on the sly, but very occasionally; a former lover who had spent
a fortune on her (I know since his name, his family, and that what
she told me was true). She let him have her still, for gratitude. He
was very poor but a gentleman, and now he helped her in various
ways. It struck me she liked him also, because he had as she told,
a large prick. I found she had a taste for large pricks, and described
those of her former friends who possessed such, in rapturous terms.
This man spent much, I expressed a desire to see it, and after a
time it was arranged that I should see this cunt prober, him using
it, and her cunt afterwards, but this took some time to bring about.
In many conversations, she admitted that she had not more physical
pleasure from a great prick, than from an average sized one. "But
it's the idea of it you know, the idea of its being big, and it's so
nice to handle it."

I went abroad as said, the incidents there will be given here-
after. On return, I went soon to H. and told her what tricks I had
been up to, and our conversation went to the subject of my sensi-
tive prick and semenalized quims, those I'd seen, and what she had
promised should come to pass.

One afternoon — this was some months later than what I shall
soon tell about — I was in her bedroom as arranged, he was to have
her in the adjoining room. She placed the bed there, so that when
the door was very slightly opened, I could see perfectly thro the

hinge side. We were both undressed, she with delight describing his prick, repeating her cautions to be quiet, and so on. — A knock at the street door was heard. "It's his," said she, and went down stairs. — Some time passed, during which I stood on the stair landing listening, till I heard a cough, — her signal — then going back and closing my door, I waited till they were up stairs and I heard them in the back room. Opening mine ajar again I waited till a second cough. Then in shirt and without shoes, I crept to their door which was slightly open.

They were sitting on the edge of the bed, she in chemise, he in shirt, feeling each other's privates. His back was half towards me, her hand was holding his large tool not yet quite stiff; but soon it grew to noble size under her handling. Then he wanted to gamahuche her, she complied, being fond of that pleasure as a preliminary. He knelt on the bed to do it, tho he'd wished to kneel on the floor. — She insisted on *her* way, to keep his back to me. So engrossed was he with the exercise, that when her pleasure was coming on, I pushed further open the door (hinges oiled) and peeping round and under, saw his balls, and that his prick was big and stiff — I was within a foot of him. — But he noticed nothing, all was silent but the plap of his tongue on her cunt, and her murmurs. When she had spent once, he laid himself by her side, kissing her and feeling her cunt, his stiff, noble pego standing against her thigh, — she pulling the prepuce up and down, and looking at the door crack. After dalliance prolonged for my gratification, he fucked her. She pulled his shirt up to his waist when he was on her, so that I might contemplate their movements. I heard every sigh and murmur, saw every thrust and heave, a delicious sight; but he was hairy arsed, which I did not like.

Then said she, "Pull it out, he'll wonder why I have been away so long; you go down stairs quietly, and I'll come soon." He uncunted, they rose, I went back to my room. He had been told that she was tricking the man then keeping her, and knew that a man was then in the house, and *he* there on the sly was happy to fuck her without pay — for he loved her deeply — and not at all expecting or knowing that his fornicating pleasures, were ministering to the pleasure of another man.

Then on the bedside she displayed her lovely secret charms — a cunt overflowing with his libation. — It delighted me, my pego had been standing long, I seemed to have almost had the pleasure of fucking her as I witnessed him, and now to fuck her, to leave my sperm with his in her, came over me with almost delirious lust. "I'll fuck you, I fuck it," I cried trembling with concupiscent desire. — "You beast — you shan't." — "I will." — "You shan't." But she never moved, and kept her thighs wide apart whilst still saying, — "No, no." — I looked in her face, saw that overpowering voluptuousness, saw that she lusted for it, ashamed to say it. "Did *you* spend?" — "Yes." — "I will fuck." — "You beast." — Up plunged my prick in her. — "Ahaa" — sighed she voluptuously as my balls closed on her bum. I lifted up her thighs which I clasped, and fucked quickly for my letch was strong. "Ain't we beasts," she sighed again. — "I'm in his sperm dear." — "Y — hes, we're beasts." The lubricity was delicious to my prick. "Can you feel his spunk?" — "Yes dear, my prick's in it. — I'll spend in his spunk." — "Y—hes — his spunk. — Aha — beasts." — All I had just seen flashed thro my brain. — His prick, his balls, her lovely thighs, made me delirious with sexual pleasure. — "I'm coming — shall you spend H°l°n?" — "Y — hes — push — hard — ahar." — "Cunt — fuck — spunk," we cried together in baudy duet — her cunt gripped — my prick wriggled, shot out its sperm, and I sank on her breast, still holding her thighs and kissing her.

When we came to, we were both pleased. — "Never mind H°l°n if we are beasts — why say that if you like it?" — "I don't." — "You fib, you do." — After a time she admitted that the lasciviousness of the act, had added to the pleasure of coition greatly — to me the smoothness of her vagina seemed heaven. — I was wild to see all again, but circumstances did not admit of it then, yet in time I did, and one day after he and I had had her, "Go down to him," said I, "Don't wash, and let him have you again on the sofa." — The letch pleased her, he fucked her again, and thought he was going into his own leavings. When she came up, I had her again, I was in force that day. — Her taste for this lubricity then set in, and stirred her lust strongly, — she was in full rut — I gamahuched her after she had washed, thinking where two pricks had been, and half an hour after she frigged herself. Whilst frigging, "Ah! I wish there had been a third man's spunk in it." — "You beast — ah — so — do I." — She rejoined as she spent, looking at me with voluptuous eyes.

We often talked of this afterwards, and agreed that the pleasure of coition was increased by poking after another man, and we did so when we could afterwards with her friend and others. Sometimes it is true she shammed that she allowed it only to please *me*, but *her* excitement when fucking told me the contrary. She liked it as much as I did, and it became an enduring letch with her.

Whether H°l°n or any other woman — I've known several who liked it — had increased physical pleasure by being fucked under such pudendal condition, it's not possible to say. — With me owing tó the state of my gland, no doubt it did. But imagination is a great factor in human coition, and by its aid, the sexual pleasure is increased to something much higher than mere animalism. It is by the brain that fucking becomes ethereal, divine, it being in the highest state of excitement and activity during this sexual exercise. It is the brain which evokes letches, suggests amatory preliminaries, prolongs and intensifies the pleasure of an act, which mere animals — called "beasts" — begin and finish in a few minutes. Human beings who copulate without thought and rapidly *are like beasts*, for with them it is a mere animal act. — Not so those who delay, prolong, vary, refine, and intensify their pleasures — *therein is their superiority to the beasts* — the animals. What people do in their privacy is their affair alone. A couple or more together, may have pleasure in that which *others* might call *beastly* — although *beasts* do nothing of the sort — but which to them is the highest enjoyment, physical and mental. It is probable that every man and woman, has some letch which they gratify but don't disclose, yet who would nevertheless call it *beastly*, if told that others did it, and would according to the accepted notions — or rather professions — on such matters, call all sexual performance or amusements *beastly*, except quick, animal fucking. But really it is those who copulate without variety, thought, sentiment or soul, who are the *beasts* — because they procreate exactly as *beasts* do, and nothing more. — With animals, fucking is done *without brains* — among the higher organized human beings, fucking is done *with brains* — yet this exercise of the intellect in coition is called *beastly* by the ignorant, who have invented a series of offensive terms, to express their objections. — Their opinion of the sweet congress of man and woman — which is love — is, that it should be a feel, a look, a sniff at the cunt, and a rapid coupling — *very like beasts that ! ! !*

*Letches for spermatized quims. — The French Lapunar. — Selected
amusements. — Six feet high, eight inches pego. — A broken capote.
— A jocular man. — Two using condoms. — Frenchmen's habits. —
Stripping for fucking. — Tonguing with tongue. — Marguerite the
favourite. — One scrubby and big bellied. — A hirsute male. —
Blonde Martha. — Broad handed, cunt frigging. — Against a thigh.
— I, on her, she on me. — Salon des dames. — Martha reappears. —
Fresh, hairy-arsed Carmen. — Her curiosity. — Knows my letch.
— Her enjoyment. — Muscular motions when copulating. — Fat,
tall Egyptienne. — Mignon the little. — Vertical and horizontal. —
H°l°n and her lover. — Four libations without washing. — H°l°n's
lubricious letch.*

After I'd poked H. with her pudenda full of her friend, and
found that she also liked it, all idea of its being nasty vanished, and
altho at times, a dislike arose to it the squeamishness didn't last long
when I had had Sappho and Raffaella. — The desire to fuck directly
after another man continued, not only for increased physical pleas-
ure, but also for the sensuous visions which floated rapidly thro
my brain as I operated, rendering this mode of coition the most
exciting, supremest, and almost killing pleasure. At the lapunar al-
ready named and others, I gratified this letch. — The peep-hole gave
me endless amusement, women were sent to me in another room di-
rectly they had left the male, sometimes on the same evening I saw
four, five, or more, and fucked one or two whose cunts had the most
sperm in them. Of some of these evenings, I retain the narrative,
those telling of anything usual both at the lapunars, and with H's
lover.

At °°°°° and with the intention of going no more to the

lapunar, I nevertheless tho out of health found myself there forty-eight hours afterwards, and in a few minutes was at the peep-hole. Such is my weakness in amorous affairs — such my inability to keep seemingly the firmest resolutions.

After seeing one or two couples enjoying each other in the ordinary way, a big fine Belgian woman whom I knew last autumn and had stroked, came in with a man six feet two or three high. He stripped quite naked and I never saw a finer fellow. He had a dark brown beard, curly hair and cock trimmings, but no hair upon his flesh anywhere. As far as I saw, it looked like that of a woman, my own is not whiter, fairer, or clearer of hair. His prick as he washed it within a yard of my eyes, did not seem proportionate to his size, but no sooner had the Belgian handled it, than it rose proudly to one of the grandest I ever saw, and stood up eight inches from his belly I should say, and longer from the balls side but had a ridiculously small knob. She could only get it half way down her throat at her first amusement, and it looked whilst minetting it as if it must choke her. He wanted to finish there, tho at first he didn't wish that at all, but she knew that I wanted a semenalized quim, for which I paid liberally, refused the libation there and coaxed him to poke her. He would only do so with a capote, and I saw the wetting and fitting it on to his bowsprit. — Then she knelt on the bed with her rump towards me, he at her back to fuck her. I could see the dark haired motte and dark cunt furrow as she posed, till his belly was against it, but almost directly afterwards he turned her on to her back, and himself on to her belly.

It was a fine sight to see him cover her with his grand form, his ample arse jogging, his balls shewing out below his arse cheeks, and every part of their bodies in gentle motion; both silent, tho the brain is so active then, and the tongue quiet usually till the finish. With a soft cry and a sob suddenly given he spent, and soon out came his big prick flopping down. "Ah! the capote has broken." — "So it has," said she, as if surprised, and laying hold of his moist tool near to the root, round which was the capote like a ring of wet skin. — "I must wash" — said he anxiously. — "Have no fear." — "Fetch me soap." — With soap and water he slopped away at his tool uneasily, complaining that the letter — the capote — was bad, and then departed. She kissed his machine before he went, it was hanging flopping, but big still, the little red tip was within a yard of my eye as she kissed it, the whole of his balls and tube in her hands. She only handled and kissed it to show it off to me. I knew that, for it's unusual for a woman to do so such after a fuck. He seemed much pleased with the politeness. She came to me laughing, saying she'd purposely broken the capote to let the sperm into her, because I liked *that*. "Has he not a noble prick, a splendid fellow isn't he? — he is married and timid about gay women" — she remarked. She shewed a well-filled pudenda into which I poured my own sperm. I had only intended to prepare in it for the next woman, but the lubricity and its clip fetched me, and I fetched her. She had unusually large dark nymphæ to her cunt, which is not to my taste, but was handsome faced, breasted, and bummed.

Directly I was alone, again came in another couple. He was a jocular man who repeated his words rapidly and laughingly. "No, no, no, no. — Yes, yes, yes" when he answered the girl. *He* would have a French letter also. — "Why not kiss without," said she. — "Ah, no, no, no, no, — savez vous, c'est l'habitude." — Did he always put a capote on? "Yes, yes, yes." — He was a handsome middle-aged man, only wanting cunt and a spend, cared nothing for the woman, got into and out of the cunt in a business-like way, and never spoke to the girl after he'd fucked her. — He wasn't a quarter of an hour with her. — I had her to chat with me directly after, and she gave me a gamahuche for a few minutes, then I inspected her privates, then off she went. There was of course no spunk in her quim and the sperm letch was on me. I wanted the lubricious feel to my sensitive prick if I fucked.

———————————

Two men, one after the other had used condoms. I have seen during the last few years dozens copulating in the same room, but as far as I can recollect only three used condoms before.

Another thing I note whilst it occurs to me is that nearly all the men are scrupulously clean in their linen, and look as if it was just put on, that *nearly* all divest themselves of much of their clothing, that fully half *strip* nearly to their skin, and not a few till naked all but their socks, before they begin their play. The women of course are invariably naked all but stockings and shoes. It is the costume of that bordello. The men are all gentlemen.

Then in came Marguerite, a nice, handsome well-made, dark-haired creature. She has been long in the house and I have fucked her several times. — No woman has so many friends. Rarely have I been there peeping or waiting, without her coming in to me with a cunt full. A nice young fellow now had her, he was full of sperm, eager for a woman, up her in no time, but talked such a time with her afterwards that I feared all his spunk would be gone, and was angry, for I had a letch for her that night. But her cunt had got lots of sperm in it when she came to me after his departure. I had a prolonged fuck up her with much enjoyment. She is one who gives you her tongue, few of them do, their lips and faces being often painted. It is one of the worst things in a French brothel. Besides, every woman gamahuches and men finish in their mouths, which does not make one anxious to tongue them, and few Frenchmen I notice do. Yet how one misses it. They compare so badly with the fresh-faced, clear-skinned, tongue-sucking, luscious-mouthed Austrians, Hungarians, — and English even — but few of whom will let a man semenalize their mouths, tho not averse to voluptuous play with a man's tool before fucking.

I had that night one or two more sights not worth telling about and having seen six pricks, felt five spermatized cunts, put my prick into four, and spent in two, I went home. Not a bad four hours amusement.

Next night at the peephole. A man who scarcely spoke, but fucked with his trowsers on, was the first. A scrubby young man. The girl grumbled at his present but took no good by it. I didn't care about looking at his sperm for he offended me by his looks and manner. Then came a man full fifty years old, stout, bald headed, and big bellied, who produced a good large stiff-stander. He also knelt the lady on the bed, her bum towards him, then kneeling in her rear, he for a long time contemplated her split and neighbouring charms. I could see fairly well his prick throbbing as he did so, for his shirt was up well. Then into her he thrust it, his shirt dropped and covered his rump, and the play of his buttocks was hidden. He soon gave a quavering half sigh, half groan, and I could see that he drew his prick out to the tip, rested, then drove it up again hard. After once or twice at this movement, he gave a loud baudy scream, and ramming with short thrusts quickly, shouted loudly "ow — ow — ow — ow — howour — ow —" like a dog barking — and wriggling, shoving rapidly, and quivering all over, spent in her. He then bent over her back a long while enjoying her, then carefully pulling his shirt up first, he took his prick in the palm of his hand and backing again, for a long time contemplated her spermatized orifice. She opened her thighs widely to let him see better, turning slightly her rump towards the lights so that I could see the sperm on it. Then bald head departed, she came in, and after I had bathed my doodle in her cunt and brought myself half way to an emission, she stopped me, suggesting my waiting for another woman, which advice I took — had another woman brought to me with a vulva in a most lubricious condition, fucked her, and left.

A few days after I was at the peephole, saw a woman tailed in commonplace fashion, and not worth keeping the narrative of. The next was a novelty.

A fine, fleshy auburn-haired woman came in with a shortish, dark young man. I could see they were acquaintances from the way they kissed. He stripped, and tho well shaped was so hairy about breast, arms and legs, that he was ugly, but he made a wonderful contrast with the large-thighed, lovely white-fleshed woman. I can't recollect her name tho it is only two days since this occurred.

He began pulling her about — then kneeling on the bed between her legs — she on her back, to lick her cunt. Few men at the French baudy houses do much of this, I observe. He licked till she wriggled under it. His bum furrow and balls were black with hair and towards me. Then the two played at sixty nine, his head being then hid from me by her magnificent buttocks which looked like ivory. Then side by side they kissed and he frigged her, slipping a little lower down on the bed to do so. He made her open her thighs as wide as possible, and then with *all* the fingers of his hand he frigged rapidly. I never saw such peculiar frigging, his fingers sometimes closed, sometimes distended, moved over the whole surface of her vulva at the same time. Then he wished her to hold her cunt lips open to let him do it. She only pulled one lip aside. He was on her right side, her white thighs were slightly raised to open them better, and let him operate. When she closed them a little as if fatigued, he pulled them open again, and again all his fingers moved like lightning. — "Oh put it in, put it in," — she said. He took no heed, made no answer that I could hear, soon her belly heaved, her thighs quivered, and with a sighing cry she spent. I felt sure she would, no woman could have stood such long frigging without spending.

His prick as he lay by her had been hidden by her thigh, now he knelt between her legs, with his buttocks on his heels and cock very stiff, looking at her. Then he resumed his position and frigged again till she grumbled. — "No — no" — but he frigged on. He was laying now more on his left side, and I could neither see his left arm nor his prick. Martha (her name I now recollect) resigned herself, and in ten minutes had another crisis. Then he clasped her right thigh closely to him with his right hand, agitating his body slightly, wriggling and half shoving as if fucking, till his head drooped, he let go her thigh, fell back, and both were still, she with her eyes closed and thighs open. In a couple of minutes she got off the bed, putting her hand over her right thigh, for he had spent against it, and held it there till she wiped it with a towel. Then taking up his prick — he had turned on his back now — she skinned and wiped its tip. "You always do it so and you *don't love me*," she said. — Ah! yes he did. — Then he left and she came in to me. "I'm no use, and he never fucks, he always does it the same way, but says he loves me." I threw her on the bed, her cunt was wet with her own spending. "He'd frig for hours if I'd let him. No woman could help spending, I often try not but I *must*, he finds out if I sham, and he's very rich. Then he frigs his cock against my thigh just as you saw him, and not with his own hand." — Then she added, that when his left hand was hidden it was under her bum, and he was fingering her anus, that he kept it there all the time he was frigging her cunt, and also kept gently wriggling his prick against her thigh. — He didn't look about twenty-five years old. — Men have strange fancies. — What delight could he find in rubbing a dry cock against a dry thigh — for he never wetted it, — when a soft cunt was at hand — *I* have frigged between buttocks, and thighs, but always lubricated them first.

She was a splendid creature. I love a woman with large thighs in my arms, as I had her then at the side of the bed, thrust my prick under her auburn-haired motte, and spent in her cunt with rapture. — "I can't understand a man frigging himself *always*," said she — "sometimes of course it's reasonable, but *always*! Ah! my God. — What are women made for. If men do *that* — what's the use of their having cunts?"

She went off, the chambermaid had just adjusted the bed etc. etc., when: "Hush — there is Martha again, shall she come?" — "No — I don't wish to see the same woman twice one night" — which Alexandrine knew. — She stopped her at the door but coming back whispered, "She must come in here, no other room is empty, but you need not have her again." So in Martha came. This time it was another novelty for *she* fucked the man laying over him. — What a size her white arse looked as it rose and fell, shewing his cock stem. — I thought his pego sometimes would come out, till a tightening of her buttocks and her short movements shewed that he'd spent, and she was squeezing his cock with her cunt. She got off of him and went out as if to wash, he meanwhile sat playing with his tool. He wanted it again. — "No, there's someone waiting for me." — He departed quickly then, and she came in to me.

I had had her not twenty minutes before. "*I've* now got foutre, shall I stay?" — "You need not have her unless you like" — said the chambermaid, coming in. "Monsieur (turning to her) never has the same woman twice one evening." — "Have you much spunk?" said I. "Full — look," said she. Her cunt and fingers testified to her truth. — "On to the bed, my dear." — She opened her thighs, there a glut of manhood was in and about her cunt, the oscillation of her buttocks, and the sight of his prick had moved my lust to its depths, the sight of sperm finished me, my prick stood stiff and up into her it went. — The chambermaid said, "You're fortunate Mlle. Martha."

I shut my eyes, and thrust, fancying I saw her on the man. — "Mount me" — I said pulling my prick out." — "Volontiers." — Then the fair-haired, white-arsed bitch covered and fucked me. In the glass on the top of the bed I witnessed her movements — a lovely sight — but it took her long — I had pain as well as pleasure now, hollowed as I spent, and could not move afterwards. I had a splitting in my temples which alarmed me. I've had it at times lately.

My letch for her was strong indeed, for I washed her cunt myself, cleaning every fold and cranny in it. — Many a day is it since I have done such a thing to a strange woman. Then on my back again I put her over me to suck my cock, whilst I fingered her bum and quim, but I didn't spend. — After she had gone, I saw two more couples fucking mother and father fashion, then left.

I had on me one of the lascivious frenzies before alluded to, — tho fatigued could think of nothing else, and wended my way to the bordello a few nights afterwards, having recovered slightly from my exhaustion.

I entered the salon this night. There was a chatter and buzz at once. "It's he! he" — I heard mixed with "Cochon, foutre" and other sympathetic, knowing words. — Many women, I noticed, were anxious to look at me. — With twenty naked beauties before me I was again dazed, could do nothing but look round and round at the dark patches between thighs, scarcely recognizing any woman. "I'll send for a lady," said I, turning to the *sous-maîtresse* and went to my favourite room. When there I ordered ladies to come to me who had just been filled by the males. — Some came, but neither pleased me. — Strangely — how account for it? — I did not desire to see, still less to bathe my penis in their flowing pudendas. — Then I went to my peephole to see if that would rouse my concupiscence.

"Martha est en société," said the chambermaid. — "Will you have her?" I consented but she did not come, had minetted her man, had a clean cunt, and Alexandrine, knowing my taste, had sent her away. Then at the peephole I saw a woman poked. — There was nothing unusual. He was a fine man, who thumbed her cunt whilst she kneeling sideways on the bed pleasured his cock with her lips. — Her rump was nearly towards me, and I could see his thumb up her split, and sometimes up her bumhole. Then he laid her down and finished in regular fashion. — I put my prick into her afterwards but had no desire, no real stiffness, was still indifferent thro past amatory exertions, and after a few thrusts withdrew without emission.

Then I saw two couples at belly to belly grinding, resolved to depart without a spend, was talking with the chambermaid when she went out and returning asked me if I would see Carmen who had just left a gentleman. "Let her come in, I've never seen *her*." — "No — she has only just come to us, she's not been gay before."

In came Carmen, tall and stern faced, looking as if she wanted fattening everywhere to my taste yet was not skinny, she only wanted two stone more flesh. She was dark, had dark eyes and hair, was not handsome. There was a hard look in her face till she said as she threw herself down on the bed, "You like a lady with spunk in her cunt, don't you?" then a soft look of invitation came over her face.

I was struck with the immense hirsuteness of her cunt, the hair being half way up to her navel. It shadowed and filled lower down, so that I couldn't see where the split began, it quite filled the hollow between the cunt lips and the thighs, growing thick and long lower down even, in that part where that hairy ornament usually grows thinner. The cunt region presented in fact the appearance of a frizzy wig, and so hiding the line of parting, that it was barely visible and only for about an inch — I held up her thighs and found the hair thick, tho short, quite round her arse hole, and up to the bum bone. Struck with the density of the curly fuzzy thicket, turning her about so as to see this wonderful hairiness, which more resembled a Negro's head than anything else — only the hair was longer and looser. — At length I said, "You've not been fucked."

She had, and pulling aside the lips, I saw the spermy streak, which was hidden again by the thick hair directly she let go the lips. It then looked as if there were no cunt there at all — hair only.

She began at once questioning. — Why did I like a cunt with *foutre* — was it nicer — how many woman had I seen that night, — had they all been fucked — had I fucked either or put my prick up either? — all was hurried, energetic, spoken in a curious yet lustful manner, not the usual manner of the Paphian.

I told her briefly that I'd not fucked and didn't want to. — "Fuck me — do" — said she energetically — "look, your prick is stiffer, — baisez moi" — all of course was in French. "Come, I want you to do it to me, — do it in the sperm — come — baisez moi — look at the sperm," and she opened the thickly fringed lips again looking at me with eyes which were *fierce* and *lustful* — I think of *that*, now as I recollect their expression, and write.

My prick was beginning to stand, I put her on the bed kneeling, and kneeling in her rear, inserted my penis between the hairy furrow, she impatient, murmuring, — "Do it — do it." — Her buttocks were just the height, her cunt felt tight but lubricious and she began to wriggle at once, turning her head towards the side glass so as to see our movements. For an instant she then frigged herself, left off, gave some shivering jogs with her rump and sighing, her cunt tightened strongly round my prick, soon loosened, she was quiet, and my balls got wet.

"You've spent," said I. — With a cuntal squeeze of my prick she sighed. "Yes go on, fuck on cheri" — perhaps the constricting power of her cunt had stirred my blood, perhaps her discharge had irritated my prick, for I now wanted her, pulled my pego slowly out to see its state, and then had a very long fuck before my sperm came up. It fetched her again, and my prick kept in her without shrinking in an unusual way.

She was so exactly the height, her cunt so well placed, her bum not too big, so that I could have kept my prick in her longer. I felt all round our point of junction and under her cunt, glorying in my dabbling, talking with her, till the chambermaid knocked. — "Mad'lle — Mad'lle Carmen — the gentleman says he will go if you don't go back." — I uncoupled. — "I'll come back again," said she — I followed her to the door, saw her wash her quim at the lavabo, and disappear. I refreshed my article and talked with the chambermaid, who said that Carmen had only been in the house four days, had never been gay before, she believed. One gentleman had called to see her every day, it was he who was with her then. She thought she had been kept, and would prove a salt-cunted, — a hot-arsed one — from what she had seen of her.

I had thought from her manner that she was a fresh hand — would have no other women and about to leave. "I've not paid her," I said. — "Give me her money." — Nearly an hour had gone, I had my hat on, when in Carmen came again — I had told her I wished to see her cunt when washed. — "Shall I wash, or will you have me again now?" — "Ma biche — no more fucking to night" — yet I couldn't resist looking. — "There is foutre now, isn't there?" — There was. "Have you before had a man put into another's leavings in your cunt?" She replied, "Never. Quelque cochonnerie, but it's nice." — To be fucked so now was her letch, I'd inoculated her, she sucked my prick stiff, and was a long time at it. "I can't give you more money." — "Very well, fuck then." — With a long lingering fuck, bum to belly kneeling, we both spent. I waited to see her cunt when washed, — caressed the wonderful growth of hair, then went away. For a night or so I was quiet, and vowed to myself to have no more such larks, yet had not the moral courage to restrain myself from women, and occupied one evening in seeing women washing their cunts before and after. The chambermaid told them that I was looking, and I saw perhaps twenty squatting over the bowl, washing their quims, their piddle rattle out, and the dry rub and scrub afterwards. I only gave a trifle to the chambermaid for this. — I selected one or two women for the size of their backsides and saw them after their exercise with the men, and felt the spermy cunts.

but did no more — a wonderful restraint — then again I stopped away some days from the temple of Venus.

Then very fit I went there and to the peephole. It was so enchanting to see the beautiful female forms twisting lasciviously about the men, enlacing them with arms and legs, their continuous movements, first bum then belly side visible, the flash of the dark mottes and hairy armpits, glimpses of open cunts between distended thighs, the pouting lips with the red stripe between them when their bums were towards me — these sights fascinated me even more than the jogging of their bums, when prick and cunt were joined — the movements of a woman's thighs when a man lays on her belly are not really pretty, and few seemed to fuck poetically and lasciviously at the same time. I saw one or two commonplace fuckings — the huge-arsed Egyptienne was one, whose cunt would now take a soda water bottle up it. She has grown so fat, potbellied, bladder-breasted, shapeless, that I cannot bear her. Then came little Mignon, whom a big fellow tailed almost hiding her as he laid on her. She came to me directly he had gone.

Mignon was a sweet-faced, lightish-brown-haired little creature, about four feet nine inches high, but with the roundness and fullness of form of a Venus. Not a bit of needless fat had she, yet every bone was covered to perfection. She was simply perfect, exquisitely and voluptuously made from neck to ankle, and about eighteen. I longed to fuck her the moment I saw her with the man — and when the lovely cunt, looking in size tho not in fringe that of a girl's of fourteen, with thick sperm just showing outside it between the delicate nymphæ, I put my prick up her at once.

Then with one of my sensual vagaries and changes I pulled it out, made her kneel on the bed with bum low down, and put up her cunt from behind, then gradually made her fall with face and belly flat on to the bed (keeping my prick in her) and pulling up her thighs gradually round my waist, I finished in her so, standing upright at the bed edge, she laying horizontally on the bed, I holding her legs like a wheelbarrow.

I have some recollection of having stroked a woman that way, tho I can't recollect name or occasion now. — Mignon's position seemed when I fucked her a delicious novelty. She was as lithe as a serpent. — When she had washed and came back clean cunted, I examined her beauties, and she repeated the horizontal posture which amused her, but I did not poke her again. She was a great favourite, the chambermaid told me. I did not recollect seeing her before as she usually went to another part of the house. There are two staircases there, and in fact two houses, tho combined.

On returning to England I visited H. and told her all. She wished she'd been with me, always had longed to see a brothel there, would have gone with me there. She seemed excited about the lubricious cunts, yet calling me a beast all the time. I fucked H. within five minutes after I'd entered her house, then laying, telling her these things, she began to frig herself, and almost instantly spent crying out — "spunk," and grasping my prick. — She'd finished so quickly that I believed her emotion a sham, on but feeling her cunt — washed not long before — it satisfied me she'd spent. She then told me that several times when she'd a great letch come on her, and thought about it, that she'd spent involuntarily without touching her cunt. It's not impossible, for in my youth I have spent involuntarily, at the sight of a female whom I wanted — when I was very randy.

One day the following week she'd be alone and would get her "poor friend to come." He was usually smuggled in. "Then you can see him fuck me." — She didn't say what after. "He'll want me, for Mr. Blank has been staying with me, but is going away on Thursday, — you mustn't come to the house till you telegraph to °°° (a female relative). — If Blank's not left town she'll meet you at the end of the street, and you mustn't come." — Such arrangement in fact had existed for some time. — I didn't like it, but would have risked anything to have her.

"You want me to fuck you *after* him" — said I. "I don't, you beast, you shan't do it any more." — "You like me to see his prick and to see you fucked." — She laughed — "I like to know you're looking at us, and that he don't know." — "We men are easily cheated." — "It would take a clever woman to cheat *you*," she replied.

The day came, the coast was clear. In my shirt I stood waiting for my treat, had kissed and gamahuched her, and with difficulty restrained myself from fucking her. Her friend was an hour behind time. H. was fidgety and feared her letter hadn't reached him. A ring followed by a peculiar knock at the street door was heard. —

"It's he," said she smiling baudily. Before that, talking about him she said as if she enjoyed the idea, "Won't he have his cock full, he hasn't fucked for a fortnight." — "Perhaps he has." — "I'll swear he hasn't, he loves me, he'd wait a month for me and would marry me tomorrow, but what's the good, he can't keep himself, his family only allow him a pound a week — he'd wait to have me any length of time, and he cannot afford a woman."

She had thrown a gown over her chemise, so as not to seem too ready — and ran down stairs to open the door to him herself. One of her servants had been sent out, and she had let *me* in herself — much maneuvering was now needed in her domicile. Fear of being caught out in intrigues is one of the miseries of ladies who play these pranks. — Leaning over the banisters I overheard much, he explained his delay, they kissed then. "My friend has just come." — He was in her secrets and knew some one visited her. — "He is in my bedroom — don't make a noise." — "I'll take my boots off." — He did. — "There," said she, "wait till I beckon you, I'll go up and see if his door is closed, he is fearful of Blank coming back."

Upstairs she came, saw me on the landing and nodded. — In I went, closing my door and soon he was in the back bedroom. A few minutes after I was at their door as before. She was exciting him, feeling his prick, both sitting on the bed, his back to the door. Then they nearly stripped. — She said — "Stand up there, let me see it stiff." — He complied like a child, obeyed her always I'd found — lifted his shirt, and I saw his powerful machine standing like a prop. — "You have fucked since you did me last." — "I declare to God I haven't." Then — "Oh let me do it, dear." He went towards her, when a powerful gust of wind (it was a very windy day) blew up the staircase, their door slightly moved, and caught his eye, he came and shut it, I retreated in fear seeing him advance, for had he opened the door he must have caught me. — I had I thought lost the spectacle of his fucking her.

But nothing exceeds the cunning of a Paphian. — Soon I heard her loudly calling out, "Mary, Mary." — Up came the servant, who was told something and went down stairs. It was a dodge to open the door without his noticing it. Cautiously I'd opened mine and peeped. H. was just retiring and winked at me. Her door was now left ajar. — Again and almost directly after, I heard "Ahem," as if clearing her throat — her signal; the next instant, I was at the door.

He was laying on his back, his big prick stiff as a poker shadowing his navel, his left hand feeling her quim as she stood by the bedside and looking up at her affectionately. He thought not of the door, or of any thing else but her cunt.

She handled his prick, then his balls for a minute. "Let's fuck naked" and she threw off her chemise, then he his shirt. She laid down beside him for a second, the next he mounted her, and I heard his sigh of pleasure as his prick went up her sex. Then on he went thrusting. — "Don't hurry," said she — but he fucked hard. — "I must," he sobbed in a gentle voice. — I was mindful of what H. had often said in our conversation, and what I now knew from experience, that a man in the full tide of sexual pleasure thinks of nothing else. — I opened the door slightly, then more, and entered the room as his thrusts grew quicker, saw in H's beautiful face that she was spending, heard, — "Aha — my darling — love — aha" — from him, then both were quiet. — I stood there till H. opened her eyes. Then closing the door ajar and standing with my prick nearly bursting, listened.

"I must go to him [me], he doesn't like to be left long — I'll tell him some excuse and come back soon — put on your shirt, stay here, don't make a noise." — Out she came, shutting the door, smiling at me, holding her cunt as French harlots do — and I suppose all do under similar circumstances — and the next instant was lying on the bedside with thighs wide apart. Her quim overflowing with thick sperm delighted me, the sight made me wild to enter the lubricated sheath, my prick bursting, yet I restrained myself, had sufficient control to do that which whilst waiting I'd resolved. I pulled open the lips, frigged her spermy clitoris, whilst talking baudily. "Did you see his prick?" — "Yes." — "Isn't it a fine one?" — "Yes." — "He never fucked for a fortnight, look what he's spent, how thick it is." — "Wash it and I'll fuck you," said I, not wishing anything of the sort.

I'd caught her. She'd before often said that she let me fuck her thus solely for *my* pleasure. — "No — fuck me — put it in." — "No. — I'm frightened." — "What of? what nonsense — put it up — he's a gentleman." — (He was) — "No, wash — you don't like it so." "Yes I do, fuck me, I like it so, fuck me," said she impatiently. "Get lengthwise on the bed then." She did, I mounted her, my prick plunged up and revelled in the grateful lubricity of her sheath. "Ain't we beasts? — Oh — I'm coming — fuck." — Our tongues joining, stopped further utterance, till my sperm gushed out into cunt. I was as quick as he in spending, certainly his prick hadn't left her cunt seven minutes, before my prick had done its work and quitted her also, tho I lay long up her after my spend.

"Pull it *out* dear, I must go back to him, I told him I would." — "He'll fuck you again." "That's certain." — "Let him fuck in my sperm." — "All right, he'll think it's his own, but I must go downstairs first, don't you come out till you hear me cough." — She went downstairs, and soon returned to his room again. — My door was ajar, again I heard the cough, and looked thro the aperture of the door.

She was just placing herself beside him, he was on his back handling his tool which was half stiff. At once she manipulated it, they kissed and talked. — "What did he say?" — "I told him that my dressmaker was downstairs etc." — "He's easily humbugged." — Both laughed. — "You must be quick, I mustn't keep him longer. Your prick's quite stiff." — He felt her cunt. — "You've not washed." — She said that she'd not had time "but must do so before she went to me." — "Will he do you?" — asked he in his quiet gentlemanly voice — so they talked for five minutes, kissing and dallying. Then her legs were in the air, thighs clasping his, and the rhythmical oscillation of their buttocks began. He was leisurely enjoying a longer job now. Soon as I heard him sigh and saw his thrusts were quicker, I opened the door, knelt at the bed foot, saw his prick moving and balls as they shook with his thrusts. Had I stood upright he'd not have noticed me in his paroxysm of pleasure. — H°l°n did — I heard soft murmurs, saw his buttocks quiver, her eyes close, knew the spends had come, and went back to my room, closing their door ajar.

This back room was only partially furnished — no water was left there with intent, so that he might go to the bedroom below, next the drawing room. She told me this before. Shortly they both went down there — then to the kitchen where she gave him food — tho well dressed he was glad of a meal. Then up she came to me and stood looking at me with voluptuous eyes. — She hadn't washed, shammed that she didn't want it again, but at the sight of her glistening vulva, my prick stood, and with a deliciously slow fuck we spent together again. Four male libations were in her cunt, and she'd spent at each fucking. — Soon after I left.

The conversations I heard and had with her are nearly word for word. — I wrote them down the same evening.

A few days after, I was there then with pleasure in confessing, for — "I have no one to tell anything to but you, and him now," said she. — She told me he had slept with her. "God knows how often I spent, we were both done up. Come on dear, fuck me — I haven't had it since — he's ill. — I'm making him beef tea."

At intervals of a week or two this was repeated — I saw him fuck her, and fucked her directly afterwards. Sometimes only once, sometimes twice, and the fun and room were a little varied at times to avoid surprise. She never afterwards denied her liking for the double libation. — "What beasts we are." — "Not beasts at all dear, and if we are, we like it" — this was said regularly whenever the double fucking came off, but I had her at other times when he was not there. Then I couldn't get her for a long time, and in the summer went abroad.

H°l°n's difficulties. — Poor lover ill. — A little unfledged virgin. — Antecedents and lewedness. — I want her. — H.'s assistance. — Virginity verified. — A ready quim. — Sudden impotence. — Essays and varieties. — Pego potential. — Hymenial rupture. — In an empty house. — A bricklayer's woman. — Pissing on the footway. — Frigging suggested. — The carpenter's bench. — An inconvenient meeting. — Washing in a watercloset basin. — Reminiscences thereon.

Returning home I saw H°l°n. There seemed some confusion in her house, the servants were gone, the female relative and a young girl were now servants. H. was impecunious and I think had had words with her protector. They had lived extravagantly and perhaps he was in difficulties, but she avoided the subject. Her big-pricked lover I saw poking her with the usual sequel twice, then he was ill and ultra-lubricious fucking ceased.

On the last occasion there was a scare. He escaped by a back entrance. H°°° asked me to go quickly, and she had the street watched by the relative before I went out. After that when I visited her she made me fuck her more than ever, more than I wanted, was voluptuous in the highest degree, drained me of sperm. I came to the conclusion that she was short of cock, which pleased me.

Soon after H°°° had a little servant barely fourteen years old, a ragged-headed but not bad-looking lass, short for her age. She'd lightish brown hair and a baudy expression of eye. I did not take notice of her at first, she was such a slovenly, dirty, ragged-headed little bitch, was impudent, disobedient, and chuckled at whatever was said to her as if it were a good joke — H°l°n had the greatest

567

difficulty to make her clean, she bathed her herself and boxed her ears to make her allow her to do so. "She hasn't a bit of hair on her cunt, yet is a randy little devil, and often goes into the watercloset and I know to frig herself," said H. "She looks like it when she comes out." I thought that perhaps H°°° and her lover had played enough pranks before her to make the girl's quim tingle, she being just of an age when sexual heat was getting into her little cunt, and fucking occupy her mind.

H°°° told me that she was one of a large family, that the father and mother quarrelled. The father said he was not sure that the girl was his child. The family, seven in all, slept in one bedroom. — "She's often seen her father and mother fucking I'm sure, tho they may try to hide it. She knows all about it, is a cunning little bitch, when she gets out on an errand she won't come back soon." — She thought the girl was ready for a spree, with any boy or man who wanted to take a liberty with her.

I thought of all this, and that perhaps H. and her protector had been free enough before the girl to teach her something. — She said that he had bathed naked before her, and she had bathed the girl before him. — After having seen the girl two or three times, I thought I should like to twiddle her little cunt a bit. On imparting this to H., she said I might. At the next visit I kissed the girl, gave her a shilling, pinched her bum, and poking at her cunt asked if she'd got any hair there. She giggled and made no reply. — "Why don't you say no, you little fool," said H. who was there. — "No I ain't," said the girl, bursting out laughing. Then I talked baudily, and finished by feeling her bum and belly, and got a finger on the little notch lips. All there was hairless, smooth as ivory, and moist with a fully flavored smell. The smell of a cunt is really nice to me, for I have always smelt my finger whenever it has touched one. I struggled for a look. H. went out of the room to improve my chance, but the lass, after giggling as if the attempt amused her, winced and made a noise, so I desisted. — But I shewed her my cock and gave her sixpence to feel it. The touch of her little hand made it stiff, tho H°°° had not long before taken out its starch. Then I got wild to see the hairless cunt, and hoping to do so, made her feel it more freely and pull the foreskin up and down, which exercise she took to readily, she was delighted and looked quite randy, but

I couldn't get her to let me have a look at her notch. She squirmed and giggled — then. — "Nou — nou — nou" — she cried with nasal vulgarity, and resisting me.

I told H°°° when she came back. The girl grinned, and kept rolling her head about like a Chinese figure as she heard me. "If she'll show me her cunt, I'll give her nice boots and stockings." — "There is a chance for you," said H. Ostentatiously I gave H. the money. "She'll let you next time," said my friend when the girl had left the room. — When two or three days after I went there again — I usually wrote or telegraphed — she had some of the things on, bought with my money. She grabbed at my cock when I showed it as if she was dying for it. I put it against her face, she knelt down and kissed it as I asked her. How she giggled at each of my requests. "I'll put that into your cunt and give you such pleasure soon," said I. "Oho," said she. "Do you know what fucking is?" — With a chuckle she said that her Mrs. had told her, but she knew it I'm sure long before. Then I felt her quim, then smelt my finger, at which she giggled and put her handkerchief into her mouth. I tried to get a glimpse of her privates, H°°° had told me that she'd washed her to make her wholesome for inspection, but the girl turned sulky and wouldn't. I got very randy, for there stood H. in chemise only and looking lovely. — "Show me *your* cunt." On the bed side went she, pulling her chemise up and exposing almost all she had as a woman to show what's kept hidden, opening her thighs wide. — On my knees I pulled her delicious cunt about, smelt, kissed it, and at last licked it till she spent in the sweetest ecstacy. The girl stood in delighted wonderment at the sight of my licking the cunt, and her mistress jogging and wriggling her bum under the titillation. — H°l°n quivers all over under suction and more and more after each spend.

After that the girl answered my questions and did all I told her. — She'd seen her mistress naked when bathing, but never a woman's cunt wide open. — No, she'd never seen that before. — Should she like to have hair on her cunt like her mistress. — "Yeas." — "It will grow quickly when I've fucked you — won't it H°l°n?" — "Certainly." — Then I made her feel her mistress' cunt, and she seemed more delighted with that than feeling my prick — I stood with my pego rigid, close to H°l°n's thighs, once put the girl's hand on to it, — she took it away and put it on to her mistress' motte, looking at the cunt in silent admiration. — "Hasn't she a hand-some cunt?" — "Ho, yeas, hain't it?" — the girl breathed out in a whisper.

After a while. "Show me *your* cunt and I'll give you a shilling." — "Let him, you fool," said H°l°n. — Slowly, thoughtfully, hesita-tingly, down went the girl's bum on the bedside. I threw up her chemise, fell on to my knees, pulled one leg apart, pushed the other, and close to my eyes lay the little hairless belly parting.

It was a lovely little cunt of a most delicate pink color. It didn't look three inches long, was a smaller cunt than I recollect seeing in any girl of her age. Such tiny nymphæ, such a pea-shaped clitoris, and the mouth of the prick sheath closed up, all but a little hole lying low towards her anus, — a hole only large enough to let the tip of my little finger up it. She was as tight a virgin as when she came out of her mother's womb — I examined it, expatiating on its beauty to H°l°n who had already seen it, and who stood by as-sisting me, opening the lips at times herself, and smiling, stooping and feeling my cock, curious apparently to know the effect of the spectacle upon it.

I wiped the little vulva, and then with her permission gama-huched it, but could not make her spend, I think. — Then I gama-huched H°l°n again, and when I had done, telling the lass to do the same, to the astonishment I think of H. she knelt down at once, and eagerly licked her mistress' quim, licked as if she had been used to it, — perhaps she had. — Then sending her out of the room, H°l°n and I had a glorious fuck, never had I spent a more de-licious afternoon.

A virginity was within my reach, in a short time I might take it, and I revelled in the anticipation of splitting the little cartilage, and leaving my sperm in the unpolluted vagina. Soon I went there again, the lass was freer, and stripped at once, I had no difficulty in getting to see it. H. had taught her that obedience was needful. Up went her legs — open her thighs as if she liked the sport. H. had talked to her. Quietly we all then soon got to the frankest obscenity. I licked her little quim, then cautiously she minetted my cock — a mouthful to her — she sucked it so freely that I think she must have been practising on H°l°n's lover, or protector. Then I gamahuched H°l°n till her belly quivered like an aspen leaf and she shrieked out, "Ah! God — fuck — prick — spunk," after I had gamahuched her two or three times, much to the wonder and delight of the little one.

Then the girl licked H.'s cunt, whilst H°°° kissed my prick — suck it she wouldn't — and so we rung the changes till I fucked H°l°n with her bum towards me, the lass standing naked by us, lost in delight and wonderment, putting her hand between my belly and H.'s buttocks, looking up under my balls and doing all I told her. After that H. asked her if she would like to be fucked, at which all laughed together, and all felt each other's privates again, it was suck and lick all round tho H°°° kept her mouth free. Then I said I'd give the girl a sovereign to let me do her. "Oh really, a sovereign?"

Excited by the promise she got on to the bed and I mounted her. — Alas my prick would not get rigid. — Sometimes it got slightly stiff by my frigging and I put it to her cunt, I could get no lodgment, her thighs seeming so small and close that she couldn't open them wide enough to let me. I put her at the side of the bed and pushed my cock against the little notch in vain — my thrusts drove her light little body up on the bed and away from me, as I leant over her and rammed. I was savage with myself and swore that the girl got away purposely. "No, I don't sir," said she quite seriously, "it's you a shovin," then I got more nervous — I and H°°° alternately frigged my cock to a stand, but directly I was on the young one's belly it fell down. After two hours' trial, weary and disgusted I left, yet madly lewed when I smelt the aroma of her cunt on my fingers.

Next day I was there again. She had been well trained, talked baudy, had lost all bashfulness, her mistress had instructed her well I think. She *wanted* to be fucked and said so — I partly stiffened, put her in every position I could think of, licked her and she sucked me but it never got stiff enough to break the virgin barrier.

Then I put my prick into H°°°, the sight of whose sweet, brown, crisply haired plump cunt would stiffen me if I were dying. — Only half the size as it touched the sweet-smelling orifice which I'd first licked, swallowing my saliva, as an aphrodisiac, it began to swell. I squeezed it in, with a delicate heave of her.buttocks it went further, and a grip which her cunt gave as it felt its entry stiffened it a little. I pushed gently in the lubricious channel, and it stiffened more. — "I'm stiff enough dear." — "No, you're not — you can't fuck her, I'm sure." — "I think I can," — and I stopped thrusting. "You can't — fuck — fuck — *me*," and she glued her moist lips to mine. On I went "Push — harder — I'm — com — aharr" — murmured she. Her limbs quieted — her cunt loosened — she had spent. — In a second — "go on" she said. Obeying, I thrust, she moved, she helped me, clipped my pego with a lubricious clip, and my sperm spurted into her. — "You're knocked up, you've been fucking hard somewhere I'm sure," she whispered, — the reverse of truth. — The lass stood looking glum, and scarcely spoke till I was going — then, "Ain't he acomin agin?" quoth she. "Yes, you shall have the sovereign, don't let anyone touch you." — "I won't send her out, but you must fuck her soon," said H°°° to me as we parted.

Almost mad with my failure, instead of resting awhile, I foolishly went there next afternoon, felt my cock every hour in the day to see if it would stiffen and it was not satisfactory, but go I would. H°°° had said all was safe on that day, and a fear lest someone else would fuck the lewed little bitch — for such she was — came over me. — I told H. I was sure I couldn't do it. "Don't be nervous, if you are you won't do it." I looked at the girl, who stripped directly before I'd asked her, and clutched my cock as if eager for it, and at my request gave a chuckle and took it in her mouth. Then I licked the beautiful little quim — gamahuched H°°° — the girl gamahuched her afterwards — we looked at baudy pictures which I'd taken, we drank champagne, I sat her naked bum upon my knee, and she played with my recreant doodle. Then she took it in her mouth again, I sitting naked on the bed to do so, whilst I fingered the cunt of H°°° who laid half naked on the bed beside her to let me. Then I made her sit on the bed and piddle whilst I held the pot, then made H°°° do the same — but all uselessly. Then H°°° turned her bum towards me, the lass had her fingers on H°°°'s quim whilst my finger was up it. — Then I tried to fuck H°°° but couldn't effect an entry — every thing I could think of to excite me I tried, and so did H°°° but my prick got smaller and smaller, till it was nothing but a bit of shrivelled skin.

Then I broke out into a sweat with vexation and disgrace. — H°°° said to the girl that I wasn't well, was nervous, over-excited, but that she'd get her sovereign. — "Let me look at your little cunt again." — The girl quickly jumped on the bed, and opened her thighs like a thorough paced strumpet. "Do you want to be fucked?"

— "Yes I'd like it" — she said. — A voluptuous thrill I had, but all was useless, I cursed and swore, said I had become impotent. H°°° laughed. — "Nonsense, you fucked me three times one evening a week ago, perhaps you've been fucking too much elsewhere," — which wasn't the case. — After about three hours of this, when worried and tired out — almost crying with vexation, — I left H°°° saying I must have her soon or something might prevent me. The girl might be talking. — She might go home perhaps. — A strange revulsion came. "Perhaps I'd better not have her." — "As you like, if *you* don't the butcher will, I caught him kissing her today, she'll have it, so I'll send her away."

Was I spellbound, bewitched? Never in my life before had I more than the most temporary impotency, rarely my pego would not erect itself, even when not a drop of sperm lay waiting in my balls. — I felt now almost mad, for when quite rigid, stiff enough for anything virgin, down drooped my prick directly it touched the delicious little pink, hairless, expectant vulva. The girl was longing for it, dying to let a prick up her — yet I could not pierce her — I could think of nothing else, yet when away from her my prick stood when I thought of its disgrace. The next visit made in a few days, I stripped to my shirt. She also entirely, and laid her little sylphlike frame on the bed without being asked. Never have I seen a girl with such cool and deliberate intention to have her virginity taken. It is incredible almost, and no doubt was due to H°l°n's talk and training.

H°°° sat by the fire reading — she was fatigued with the affair, how lovely she looked in her gauzy chemise, holding a novel in one hand, gently feeling her cunt with the other. She often sits feeling her quim when reading. The fire glowed on her thighs, I could just see sideways the hair of her motte, as I lay on my back licking the little virgin's quim. The lass kneeling over me, sucked my prick as if she loved it, and had practised the art of gamahuching from her infancy, — yet this girl was unfucked and but fourteen years of age. — I pushed up her bum, and I pulled open her little cunt lips — yes she was still intact, unbroken, and again I pulled her bum back to me and licked her cunt. — Slob, blob went her mouth on to my prick as her saliva ran down the stem, and mine ran over my mouth when I squeezed it too closely against her cunt, a delicious baudy preliminary with the fresh little lass. Occasionally I turned my head aside to see. H. feeling her cunt, anon looking at our pranks, then reading a bit.

Suddenly my pego stiffened hornlike — ready — but not of its usual size. When rigid I have at times known it in a similar state, stiff as a poker, but small both in length and thickness — I wanted to fuck her yet singularly had no strong desire for emission. I felt my pego again and tried to bend it but couldn't. "I'll fuck you, dear" I said, got up standing, and quickly put her bum at the bed side. She knew where, for her buttocks had several times lain there for my efforts. — Then I placed the two pillows under her little bum. — I did not feel in a hurry, was singularly calm and collected. "Are you going to fuck?" said H*** I turned my head towards her — her thighs were apart, one hand on her cunt, she had laid down her book and was watching us.

I didn't answer, being absorbed in my work, and in fear of my powers failing me. — I pulled the girl closer to me — her quim was just level with my balls — I was now wonderfully cool and collected, for sperm was not even urging me on — I wanted to deflower her rather than to spend, to do it to her first, and a desire to hurt her in doing it came into my mind. "Come closer, darling" and she did — I put up her legs so that her heels were near my breasts, her thighs against my naked belly, again I felt my prick, still stiff tho small, then holding her legs I lodged my pego in her notch which I had deluged with saliva, and thrust. Push, push — her body went further back on the bed. "Keep your legs up, darling." Furiously I pulled her close to me again, she helped her bum forwards, my prick was still on her notch and now stiffer than ever.

Then thrusting I went as quick as my ballocks would move. She shut her eyes, her mouth opened, her teeth clenched. "Oho, hahoh" came whispering thro her teeth. — "Do I hurt you?" — "Not much" the brave girl whispered. — Thrust. — My prick was going thro something — something tender which gently separated and nipped round my gland — nipped as if something tight were being drawn over it. I knew the sensation — thrust, thrust. — "Oho — ah-ar"— she moaned with a slight shiver. My prick felt suddenly at ease as if in a sheath which clung to it. — "I'm up her" I cried, putting my hand down and feeling the root only of my prick, the rest of it was up her little cunt, my balls covered her arse, her virginity was gone. Oh! the proud delight of that moment as I rested satisfied, feeling round the stem of the invader to be sure there was no mistake, that I was well up that diminutive orifice, which a minute before I could not get my little finger thro. — "I'm up her" I cried. H°l°n came to the bed and seemed surprised, felt my prick stem, and pushing her fingers between our bellies, "She's fucked and no mistake," quoth she, with a lovey baudy smile, then sat on the bed looking on, whilst I went on fucking. Slowly up and down my prick went in the little cunt, so deliciously tight. The girl opened her eyes. "Does it hurt?" — "Not now" — "Is it nice?" — "Yhes!" she whispered. Nature seemed tranquil in me, considering where my prick was. I gloated over the naked body I was in, then at H°'s lovely face and breasts as she sat watching, and she began feeling her own cunt.

Suddenly a throb, a spasm of pleasure shot thru my pego, my prick was swelling more. Another — another throb, the blood was rushing into it, it was full-sized now, the little cunt too tight — I drove it up hard, then pulled it nearly out, then lunged it up again. — "Howooo," moaned the girl. — Now I longed to finish, to fill her cunt with sperm, the heat of lust was strong in me, voluptuous feelings running from brain to ballocks. — "My darling, my spunk's coming — it will spend in your — c — hunt — it's coming. — Aaharr — spunk — fuck" — I cried in delicious pleasure.

She was silent, but her belly winced as I drove hard up her. Then a slight murmur, her eyes closing, a most lovely look came over her face. — "She is spending, look H°l°n." — "Yes she's spending," said H°°°. She breathed hard, her cunt tightened, my prick felt as if it were splitting her, and ramming, shaking her whole body with my thrusts, my prick pulsated and with a final throb gushed out thick spunk into her; then came short movements, wriggles, a gentle churning up and mixing in her cunt *my* spermy fluids with *her* flux and bloody leakings of her torn hymen. — There I stood holding her thighs to me, squeezing my prick up her, looking at her and then at H°l°n, who now on her back on the bed with chemise up, thighs and belly visible, was frigging her cunt vigourously — abandoning herself to unrestrained lust. Satiated tho I was, I put my fingers on to Nell's motte as by her trembling and sweet look I saw that she was spending.

We were all silent, motionless, a lascivious group; my prick then shrinking I held my girl's thighs closer, keeping up her, her little cunt sticking to me like wax. — I could have kept it in her for a week, even had it been no bigger than a gooseberry, so little obstruction did her small buttocks offer, so close her cunt came up to my balls — H°l°n opened her eyes and looked. No woman ever enjoyed a baudy sight or play more than she, and this cunt burglary was a treat to her. — She had never seen a virginity taken in that fashion before, and her behaviour was as much as possible like Sarah F°°z°r's under similar circumstances.

The girl lay in silent enjoyment of a lubricated cunt, and excess of a new pleasure. I wriggled against her, for one cannot keep a prick quite quiet when in a cunt. — She looked at me. — "Do you like fucking?" — "Yeas." — Moisture began oozing from her quim. — "Get up and wash," said H°°° — "She shan't" and I nestled my cock against her closer. — The girl liked it and laid motionless. — "Get up and wash," said H°°° impatiently. — "She shan't." — "You'd better let her. — I saw the wisdom, uncunted, pushed her legs wider apart as I did so, holding them up, and dropped on my knees — saw the little cunt blurred and covered with spunk and streaked with blood — but so little was the blood, that had I not verified the virginity before taking it, I might have doubted its former existence.

Then she washed her lacerated quim. "Throw the water well up," said H. — We were quiet. Fucking and frigging quiets all human beings for a time. Then I put her on the bed, saw the jagged tear my prick had made, and felt it. She winced, said it was sore, I gave her a present and downstairs she went. H. and I chatted about first fuckings and she said we were both beasts. — "Agreed, but we can't help it, we didn't make ourselves." It was one of the most voluptuous incidents of my middle age. — Two or three days afterwards the girl left H°l°n's service.

[As often before said, fucking is always much the same, the preliminaries alone vary. The way H°l°n induced the lass to submit, and frigged herself whilst I took the virginity, is similar to the behaviour of other women in like cases. — Women I think like getting girls fucked, take pleasure in initiating them into love's mysteries, tho there is nothing mysterious about it excepting in the psychology. Madame de Maintenon probably did the same as Sarah F. — Nellie L. — and H°l°n did.]

At about half past eleven on a cold dull morning towards the end of March, passing through a new formed district in the outskirts of the N.W. of London, I turned a corner sharply into new and partially made streets where one or two buildings were already finished ready for letting, and several in the distance building; the remaining land being laid out for letting and enclosed by fencing or hoarding. At the junction of two streets, the hoarding had been canted at the angle, and there squatted a woman on the footway her back against the hoarding, and as I thought at first resting herself, but immediately discovered to be piddling. Her petticoats scarcely covered her knees, I saw the tips of large buttocks, and from the darkness, in the shadow of her petticoats, a strong stream issuing, which spouted out in front of her and splashed audibly.

With lustful delight I walked straight at her, ducking my head as if trying to see her cunt pissing. — As I got close to her the stream ceased, she rose up staring at me, looking surprised and uncomfortable at first, then laughing loudly. — "What do you come this way for, you old bloke," said she. — "Shouldn't I like to feel that cunt," said I. — She laughed heartily. "My old man will feel you damned hard perhaps, you old beast — be off now." — "I'd like to fuck it." — "He'll do that for me at dinner time — you hook it or you'll be sorry enough" — and again she laughed heartily and with lewed look, as if thinking it a good joke. — "Where's your old man?" — "Working there" — and she nodded in the direction of the houses building. "What did yer come a starin at me for, did yer never see it done afore — yer old enough." She had not moved from the spot where she piddled.

She had a big round black hat on with a huge dirty feather in it, a dark dress, a small shawl tied round her chest, a clean white apron, white stockings and thick boots. — She looked like a woman who sold things in the streets from a barrow. — Was she a coster woman — or a labourer's wife or woman — or low whore? All this passed thro my mind rapidly at my first advance. Then I decided from her laughing and general manner that she was a slut if not a regular strumpet. Lust now made me again bolder, for she was tallish, thickly built, dark haired and dark eyed, fresh, healthy looking, and perhaps thirty years old. I had seen just the tip of her buttocks and wanted her. "I'll give you five shillings to feel your cunt and have a look at it" said I boldly. — "Get along with yer, you old bloke, he's a working over there." — "Who?" — "My husband, he'll be out soon to dinner," and she laughed heartily again, as if the whole affair amused her much.

Not a person had passed or was likely to pass thro the half-formed place, excepting work people. — Close by were two houses seemingly finished, the doors wide open. "To let" written on all the windows, there might be or might not be workmen inside. "Come in there and I'll give you ten to have you," said I. — She laughed louder. — "Get along with yer, yer ought to know better, I shall get all I wants at dinner time" and she shook her head. — "Let me do it first." A shake of the head. — "Come." — "What's the time?" — "Half past eleven." — She shook her head again but seemed hesitating — I pulled out the gold, showed it and walking on stopped at the first doorway and beckoned. She peeped round the corner and towards where building was going on — I walked on into the hall of the empty house, heard no sound, no workman was there, and in a minute in she came. — "We must be quick or he'll be out" said she. — "Who?" — "My husband." — "Nonsense, you are not married." — "Yes I am, look" and she showed her hand with a wedding ring. Then I thought it might be true, but felt sure from the way in which she received my advances, that more than one prick had been between her thighs at some time or the other.

We went into the back room, listened and heard no sound. I began feeling her privates. She opened her thighs, I found she'd a heavy arse and thickly haired cunt. — I pulled up her clothes and looked at her massive thighs, to which she rather objected, but I held up her petticoats, pushing her back against a wall, and so for a minute or two I felt and looked at her hairy crack, or rather its beginning, for more was not very visible as she stood.

My pego was standing and I felt awfully lewed on her, yet prudence restrained me. — Who is she, is she wholesome? and such thoughts passed through me whilst I stood reflecting and silent. — Said she, "Make haste, I must go before twelve o'clock — mustn't keep my man waiting." — At that I ceased looking at her thighs and dark haired mount, and laying hold of her round her waist began with the other hand twiddling a fullish clitoris, till she jerked her belly forward a bit. — "Make haste and do it, ain't yer stiff?" — Annoyed at the doubt I told her to see, and unbuttoning my trowsers a bit, let my stiff stander be visible. She laid hold of it at once without my invitation, giving a sort of suppressed "Whew" or whistle and laughing quietly said, "Put it in, be quick." — The handling of my tool gratified me, altho her hand was cold and roughish, and again I pulled up her petticoats, she now helping them up with her unemployed hand, and began again feeling her cunt all about; and so on for a minute, she gently handling my prick, till with a wriggle and a jerk of her belly — that undefinable motion which a woman gives when she's randy, and a man's fingers are on her cunt — she pulled my cock towards her, saying hurriedly, "Now make haste, I must go soon, someone may come, there's carpenters here — don't you see? — Put it in." — She was in greater want of fucking than I was.

Wanting her badly yet fear on me still, "Frig me whilst I feel your cunt." — "I won't, you beast" said she relinquishing my tool. "Do it properly, or not at all," and her petticoats dropped.

I snatched them up again. She aided me opening her thighs for my reception. I was just putting my rod into her, when I fancied that the lips I was opening with my left hand felt unusually wet. — Again fear seized me. — "You're a fine woman and have a nice cunt, but I have had all I want." — Letting go my prick, my coat fell over it and partly it went into my trowsers. I took out half a sovereign from my purse and gave it her. She slipped it into her pocket without thanks, but stood just where she was, eying me. — "Why don't yer do it, what are yer feared on?" — said she. "I'm tired." — "Yer hain't, it hain't that — tired be blowed, what are you feared on? — Do it quick — come on — put it up," and she hitched her clothes up again.

She's got the money and wants fucking, thought I, and my timidity went off. But tho wanting her more than ever I still hesitated, and began to button up my trowsers. She, thinking I was preparing for her bum basting, had planted her back again against the wall, and lifting her clothes up said "Make haste." — "I can't do it there, I don't want it, I only wanted to feel your cunt." — "Do it here, then" said she. In the room was a long workman's bench — some shavings on it. — With a hitch up she sat on it at its end. "You can't lay there." — "Yes, I can" — and back she laid, her legs hanging down over the edge. Excited now beyond all thought of consequences I threw up her clothes, she opened her thighs, for a second I looked at her sex, saw full lips, the red stripe, and thick

dark hair on her motte, got out my pego, and then again hesitated.
I was in one of those nervous moods which I had sometimes on un-
usual occasions.

Seeing that she sat up and caught hold of my prick. — "Come
on, what *are* you afeared for." — "You've got the money" I began.
"Yes and I've got your cock" (with a laugh). "Do you want to be
poked?" — "Yes, be quick." — "Your husband will do it." — "Right
you are, but be quick." — She was too much for me and I put my
prick into her. — She felt the stretch and friction — soon, "aha —
Hoh — Harr" she sighed, her cunt clipped tight and she spent. — I
was not so quick, and her cunt loosened directly — some women's do
— but at length I spent with much delight. She did not uncunt me,
and we stood copulated looking at each other. "You'd best go be-
fore the men's dinner time," at length she said. — Out I pulled it,
she stood up and laughed. "You're a blooming old swell, why did
you say you could not do it, I knowed yer could."

I looked at my watch — it was still nearly ten minutes to
twelve, wiped my prick, went to the water closet and pissed. She
followed. "Are you going to wash your cunt?" — "Yes if there's
water." — There was, and I watched her operations. — "Are you all
right?" said I. "What do yer mean? Oh, I've nothing the matter
with *me*." — "You're not married." — "I am tho." — Then she took
out the half sovereign, spat upon it and put it back into her pocket.
— My lust being over, I noticed what a big, coarse, but healthy
looking bitch she was, felt her hard thighs and buttocks again,
scratched the wig on the motte, and letting her at her request go out
first, soon after went away in another direction.

I had gone some distance, when reflecting on the funny inci-
dent and feeling curious, I walked to that end of the street where
they were building. It was just twelve o'clock and workmen were
coming out. She was standing there and I saw a workman join her.
They were coming my way when, seeing me, she apparently said
something to him, they turned and went off in the opposite direction.
Her eyes opened wide when she saw me — tho a little distance off
I noticed that.

It was a nice morning's adventure. I fancy that she had been
a harlot and had slightly the manners of one. Free and easy as her
virtue seemed, was she the workman's woman, or was she married?
What matters? — I and she enjoyed fucking immensely. I was

amused at her sluicing out her cunt in the watercloset. Several times I have washed my ballocks in one, but never saw a woman do it before. — In empty houses there frequently is no water on. I recollect feeling the cunt of a girl in one, and found no water in the closet to wash fingers in afterwards.

H.'s protector. — His absence. — Her voluptuous needs. — A donkey-prick'd lover. — Caution advised. — Her excuses. — Donkey prick exercising. — The pleasure given by large pricks. — Harry's first sight of a pudenda. — Masturbated by his master. — Protector impecunious. — My visits permitted. — A looking-glass bought. — Miss Def, the ex-harlot. — About Magdalenes. — Foot frigging. — A garden party. — The swing. — A frisky spinster. — Baudy books lent. — Free and easy conversations. — Donkey prick in the garret. — His limp tool. — H.'s anger and objurgations. — She on him. — Energetic buttocks. — They in the best bed room. — The trick with the door. — Mutual pleasure in the lubricated channel. — The aesthetic aspects of fucking.

H°°° had still two servants, but who were changed often now for some reason or another, I guessed to facilitate intrigue. More frequently than otherwise her female relative — the scout — in whom she had great confidence, together with some very young girl and a charwoman, did the work of the house, this looked also suspicious, and the arrangement as if made to favor intrigues. Indeed H. laughingly admitted almost as much. She now was assumed to have quitted gay life for good, and to have consecrated her temple of love to one sole worshipper. I certainly believe that she was inaccessible to men (myself and a lover excepted) was never seen at the haunts of the frail ones, nor at theatres or other places of amusements, and she had cut nearly every Paphian acquaintance of old days. I enquired of women, and at places when they ought to know, but none had seen her. One thought she was ill, most that she was being kept.

H°°° spoke well of her protector. She was proud of his per-

sonal appearance, of his being a gentleman, an Oxford man, well
born and so on, all of which he was. She said she loved him. She
was fond of her home and even of domestic duties. She was a very
active woman, was very clean, and those duties and reading oc-
cupied her. She was very clever, and indeed had most of the qual-
ities which go to make a good wife. She was a gourmet, and most
extravagant in her food, liked cooking it herself, would give five
shillings for a pint of green peas or other choice food, even if she
had to borrow the money to pay for them — but she much preferred
going into debt. This is an illustration of I believe her sole extrav-
agance. She could write well, compose charades, and even write
rhymes which were far from contemptible.

But her nature was luxurious, her sexual force so great that it
conquered. One man could not satisfy her. Altho when with her
protector he fucked her twice daily, and she frigged herself twice
or thrice as well — did it even before his eyes she told me — and I
who saw her weekly fucked her twice or thrice and between our
love exercise often times she frigged herself — no sham, not done
to excite me, there was no object in that — such was her strong
appetite for voluptuous delight, the craving of her flesh. She de-
lighted in baudy books and pictures, and generally in all volup-
tuousness — yet for all this she was not a Messalina quite.

Sometimes now she was left alone for a week or two or longer
by her friend, tho he idolized her, — but he couldn't help his
absence. Then the strong promptings of her carnality placed her in
great temptation. Frigging did not satisfy her, her cunt yearned ir-
resistably for the male. My talk, she averred, so excited her, that
when she thought of that alone it led to her giving way to her
passions. That I don't believe, tho it might have added fuel to the
flames. — She took a fancy after a time to another man. This came
about through going to see a dashing gay woman whom she'd not
seen since she'd been in keeping. The man therefore was a mere
chance acquaintance. He was known in Paphian circles for his
physical perfections, and the desire for his very big prick really
was the reason of her wishing once to see him, and then for a time
her taking to him. But more of this hereafter.

I afterwards witnessed him using his tool. It added greatly to
her pleasure to know that I was a spectator. The deed done, he
gone away, she came to me, her eyes humid with recent pleasure —

still lustful. We fucked, and talked. The idea of my prick being in the avenue his had quitted increased the pleasures of us both when fucking — hers I think more even than mine. Soon after our eroticism entered on even a higher phase of luxuriousness.

When she had thoroughly made the acquaintance of the man with a bigger prick than that of her lover — the biggest she had ever known, she said — she described it rapturously and the delight she felt when it was up her. The gentleman with whom she lived as already said poked her twice daily when there, her poor lover fucked her frequently, I gave her my doodle then once a week, besides gamahuching her which I never failed to do, and in addition to all this she frigged herself nearly every day. — Yet all this did not give her an excess of sexual pleasure, with all her fucking, frigging, and gamahuching, she looked the very picture of health and strength, and had both.

She had met as said this man by chance, was told about him, and it was the idea of his size which affected her sensuous imagination. — He was, she found in the long run, a mean hound, who enjoyed her lovely body yet was often half fucked out before he had her, and scarcely made her the most trifling presents. The size of his prick had made him notorious among gay women, she discovered at last, and he got more cunt than he wanted for nothing. I often advised her to cut him, for she told me all about her affairs with him; not that I preached morality but saw that it was a pity to risk an evidently good chance of being settled comfortably for life. Yet if she wanted another man — if variety was essential, "Have him but beware," I used to say.

I expressed one day a wish to see his pego of which she was always talking. She was proud at that, her eyes glistened voluptuously as she told me of the arrangements for my view. She had long liked telling her letches to me — a willing listener who had no canting objections. — Tho I cautioned her to take care not to be caught by her protector. — She used to reply — "What have I to live for except it. — Philip and I have no society, we can't afford it now — it's a year since I've been to the theatre, — there is nothing but my house, and playing at cards and fucking, to amuse me." — "My darling, fucking is all in life worth living for, but be prudent."

The plan of her house then, owing to the way she and her protector occupied the back bed room, did not favour a secret peep at her with the man, who had become knowing and wary in such matters, by passing most of his time with harlots, and she had a difficult task in humbugging him. It was to come off in the parlour. I at a signal was to go downstairs from her bedroom barefooted, peep thro the parlour door left ajar, was not to make the slightest noise, and retire directly the consummation was effected.

On the day, I was waiting expectant in her bedroom, heard footsteps enter the parlour, went down cautiously to the half landing — heard: — "Ahem" — went lower — heard baudy conversation and then, "It's right up my cunt." Knowing from that that my opportunity had arrived, I pushed the door slightly more open. — She was on the top of him on a sofa, her face hid his from seeing me. — She was kissing him, her chemise was up to her armpits, her bum moved slowly up and down showing a thick prick up her. "It's not stiff," said she angrily. "You've fucked before today." — "I've not fucked since yesterday." — She'd uncunted him as she spoke, and out flopped a huge prick not quite stiff. — There she lay over him thighs wide apart — cunt gaping wide — his prick underneath it. — It was a dodge of hers to gratify my sight, to show me the procreator she was proud of enjoying.

Then she got off, and stood by the side of him, still leaning over and kissing him, to hide his eyes whilst she frigged him. His prick soon stood and a giant it was. She got on to him again, impaled herself, and soon by the short twitching shoves of her buttocks, and the movement of his legs (in trowsers) I saw they were spending. — In a minute his moist tool flopped out of her cunt, and I crept upstairs leaving them still belly to belly on the sofa. She had told him that her sister was in the bed room, to which I soon after heard her coming up, and him going down to the kitchen. Oh the voluptuous delight in her lovely face as she laid on the bedside to let me see her cunt, and the delight she had as my prick glided up it softened by his sperm, and her lewed ecstacy as my sperm mixed with his and hers in spasms of maddening pleasure — for now she delighted in this sort of copulation, said it made her feel as if she were being fucked by both of us at once.

This spectacle was repeated afterwards on a bed in the garret — but after a time she sickened of him and saw him no more. — She however still had her large-pricked poor lover, who one or two years after died, and as I have narrated what I saw and did after him, shall tell no more. She had at various times with string measured the length and circumferences of both of these pricks. The way to get proper measurements was carefully discussed by us. I have the lengths and circumferences of the two pricks, and of Phil's all measured when stiff, round the stem half way down — and from the centre of the tip to where the prick joins the belly.

The biggest of the two pricks did not however nearly come up in size, to that titanic cunt stretcher which Sarah F**z*r enabled me to see thro the peephole at the baudy house some years ago. Tho I had no measure of *that*, it was much larger than any I have ever yet seen — there could be no mistake about it — [I have seen a couple of hundred pricks, just before their owners put them into their women].

This big-pricked man was a coarse looking fellow tho stalwart and handsome. He would stop at the house and feed at her expense, and scarcely give her a present, yet he was not a poor man, but a man of business as she knew, and as I took the trouble to ascertain. H*** told me soon all about him. I was certainly the only confidant she could have in this letch. — He was reckless enough to let a youth from his place of business bring him letters whilst at H.'s and she got acquainted with the lad.

H*** told me one day that she was in bed with big-tool, when the youth (then only sixteen years old) brought him a letter. They both lewed, began chaffing the boy, asked if he'd ever seen a woman naked, and pulled the bed clothes down so as to show her naked to her waist. She permitted, nay liked the lark, and admitted to me she hadn't then seen the prick of a lad of that age, stiff or limp. — "Show her your cock and she'll show you her cunt," said big-tool. The boy, glowing with lust approached the bed. H. opened her thighs invitingly, his master got up and pulled the lad's cock out of his trowsers as stiff as a horn, she opened her thighs wider, the man gave the lad's prick one or two frigs, and the sperm squirted over H.'s thighs. — This, as I happened to be there, was told me the day after it had occurred.

This frigging of the boy led as may be supposed to some erotic episodes. — As a matter of course it stirred H.'s lust, she had never been fucked by one so young, and before long his thin prick and

her cunt were introduced to each other. The narrative of a conse-
quent episode in which I was a participator, as written at the
time, is reserved from the flames.

A little before this H.'s protector was as I'd guessed in money
difficulties. She told him that an old kind friend wanted to visit her,
that money must be got somehow or they must part, and he con-
sented to me — and only me — visiting her. — She had told him I
was too old to poke, and only gamahuched her. Of course I've only
her word for that. I never saw him or he me. He was very unhappy
about it, but sooner than let her again be gay he would consent to
almost anything. — Money and other circumstances, however, pre-
vented my seeing her more frequently, tho I went with greater ease
of mind. She also was not under such anxiety, and we had our
frolics with increased pleasure — for her lascivious delights with me
were greater than ever.

Later on she told me her protector was getting as erotic as I
was, tho he was a very much younger man. My impression is that
she taught him. — Sometimes it was: — "What do you think? Phil
wanted me to do so and so with him?" — or: "We poked in this atti-
tude the other day." — Or: "He likes hearing how formerly I've
been poked," and so on. — Then she and I had great pleasure in
doing the same things together.

One day I wished we had a looking glass to see ourselves in
when fucking. I had told her of the glasses at French houses. — She,
excepting in a cheval glass, had never seen herself reflected in
copulation, and wished she could. — I offered to buy one, but what
would Philip say? "He'd be delighted, we often wish for one when
I tell him I've heard of such things, but he's hard up just now — he
knows you are the only man who visits me." — He didn't know of
her lovers. — Then I paid for a looking glass which she got. It was
nearly as long as her bed, was placed against the wall, the bed
nearly close to it, and henceforth we could see our every movement.

I shall never forget the day the glass came. We put it up to-
gether at the right level, directly we'd done so we rapidly stripped
start naked, mounted the bed, and fucked contemplating ourselves,
and that afternoon not a drop of sperm was left in my balls. I gama-
huched her, and she frigged herself as well, looking in the glass. At
my next visit I heard that Phil had done the same, that night after

night they couldn't sleep for the rutting state the glass put them in, so hung a curtain over the glass when they wished to excite themselves no more. To see H. frigging herself then was indeed a great treat. Her delight was to make me kneel on the bed naked facing the glass, with my stiff one which she held in one hand, whilst she frigged herself with the other, looking in the glass all the time. It was to me a delight — for her form and face were lovely, — to see her in the venereal spasm — an exquisite sight. — Unfortunately however the bed was so placed in the room then, that I could not see either bed or the reflection from the only door available for peeping, hence the fucking exhibitions were always given in other rooms.

Soon after we had the looking glass, a harlot temporarily out of business was often there. She had been a servant, then seduced, then well kept, then general practitioner in copulation, then lodging-house keeper, and was now impecunious. She had been good looking but was to me plain, yet was plumpish and her breast and leg were not uninviting. She had been a sort of go between, scape goat and so on to H°l°n when gay, and of whom she was fond. — H. seemed glad of her, for she was the only Paphian who now visited her, and with whom she could discourse of big pricks, etc., etc.

She (I shall call her Miss Def) was a thorough baudy talker, nothing seemed to please her so much as narrating some meretricious experience, the tricks that she and others had played with men. There was no disguise now before me or between the two women, for that intimacy and confidence which it seems I have the art (unintentionally) of inspiring in gay ladies, had been given me by H°l°n, as far as a woman who has been gay can. But Paphians whether in or out of the calling never tell all to anyone, not even to their lovers. — Does a married woman? These narratives were not inventions got up for my edification, there was no object in doing that. — I never gave Def a farthing — they came out quite naturally in our conversations when sitting together, which naturally turned on fucking.

In that and in amorous reminiscences H. was as much pleased as I was. The Priestesses of Venus, I am convinced, all like their occupation, and to talk over past frolics when they have quitted the life, whatever they may aver to the contrary. — When they are sick and plain in face or form, and unsuccessful, they are repentant and virtuous, are "Magdalenes." Repentance usually pays better *then* than fucking.

I've seen lots of Magdalenes, but never one in good health or who was good looking. — They were failures in their occupation, they wanted face, form, skill, and go, and I guess had ill-fitting cunts, or certainly something wrong in cuntal quarters. So they repented, turned virtuous, were "reclaimed," became Magdalenes and got shelter and money — I dare say when better, or at home in the colonies, they didn't forget they'd got cunts, useful for other things besides pissing.

One afternoon after luncheon, we three had champagne which I had taken there, our talk got smutty. Miss Def shewed her legs which were good, and then her breasts. "Show him your cunt," said H. She did and we talked ourselves into a lewed state, which indeed I always was in directly I set sight on H°'s charms. What led to it was a tale told by Def, about a man in bed between two women all naked, and there not being room, one woman laid across the foot of the bed the feet of the two touching her, and she frigging herself whilst they were fucking. "Let's get on to the bed and do the same," — I suggested.

We all stripped and got on the bed (it was hot weather), Def's cunt was an unusually hairy one, a regular well-fucked, and forty-years-old cunt. — She kissed my prick and H.'s cunt as well, before we laid down. Then our lewedness, and the delicious contact of soft skins, voluptuously suggested all sorts of letches. — Laying on my back feeling H°l°n's cunt, "I'll frig you with my foot," said I to Def. She delighted, let me, and placing my heel against her cunt after she had turned to a convenient position, I pressed and rubbed it there, she clutched my foot round the ankle and guided it, accommodating her cunt so as to get the friction as pleased her. H°l°n half sat up still feeling my prick, and watching this foot frigging. — "Give a poor body a fuck, I haven't had a bit of cock for months," said Def after awhile. "Fuck *me*," said H. impetuously and lying down, for she was hot, and desire sometimes seems to seize her impatiently. Taking my heel from Def's cunt, I mounted my beauty's soft belly and began the exercise with my prick, my toes now downwards naturally.

After a few thrusts. — "Def's frigging herself" said H. — She could see, I laying face downwards could not till I turned my face to the looking glass which I'd bought. — "Go on fucking, I'm looking at Def frigging." — H*l*n's feet and mine were both against the woman's naked body — we could feel the jog of her body as she frigged. "Put my toe in your cunt and frig with it," said I, wanting to feel a cunt with my toe, which I'd never well done before. "Yes, frig with it," said H. with a baudy laugh. — Miss Def caught at my foot quickly without reply, the erotic desire seized her, and I felt my great toe was against the soft slippery surface, could feel distinctly her large clitoris and thick nymphœ, as well as if feeling them with my fingers. H., without letting my prick out of her cunt, managed to twist herself so that she could see that the toe of my right foot was there. "The hair of her cunt's all round your toes — fuck me, — fuck" — said she with delight and energy, getting straight with a sigh of pleasure, moving her backside voluptuously. — I reciprocated, lunged my prick well into her hot avenue, in which it had got a little displaced in her moving to see where my toe was.

Then we fucked on whilst Def frigged, we thought of her whilst our pleasure increased. — "Is your toe on her cunt?" — "Ahaa" — sighed H. — "Yes, I can feel her frigging her cunt with it." — "Ahaa — I'm spending — ahaa — frig *me* — with your toe — some day. — Ahar — won't you? — Ahaa — Aha fuck — bash it up me. — Aharr." — "Spend darling, my spunk's coming. — She's frigging — Ahaa" — and in a baudy delirium our pleasures ended in the ecstacy of the crisis, the woman at the bottom of the bed forgotten. As we ceased fucking Def continued her frig — did what she liked with my foot which she moved on her cunt. — With my other foot I felt her thighs agitated, she sighed, she moaned, my toe and her cunt moved rapidly, and just as we recovered from our pleasures, she gave a sob, a sort of gulp almost as if choking — a most extraordinary noise — and was quiet — my toe still resting on her clitoris, she still holding my foot.

I jumped up as soon as my prick had left H.'s inundated quim, finding my toe moist with Def's effusion. The devil had spent copiously. My getting up roused her, and she felt H.'s overflowing quim. "He's spent a lot, how I'd like a fuck, I haven't had one for an age," quoth she. All three washed, and after a rest I fucked H. again whilst the other handled my balls, delighted with the opportunity of pulling about the testicles, whose juices she so longed to have in her. Then after a glass or two more wine, she asked me to fuck her and H. incited me, — begged me — to "give her a treat" — but I didn't, having no taste for her, and the condition of my toe which I had washed came to my mind and stopped all passion — I have rarely refused a cunt which was new to me; but I did hers.

Early in June, one of the most singular liaisons in my career occurred to me — I have thought other events singular, and perhaps they were as much so but they don't seem like this, for I am at an age which made this unexpected. I don't look my age, I am told, nor do I feel age, and can oftentimes tail an appetizing woman three times in an hour and a half — yet it's nearly forty years since first I fucked a woman.

I was at an afternoon in some grounds near London, and there was a widow with her only daughter who was born in India, her father a colonel. They were in comfortable circumstances, in good society, but there were whispers about the daughter, that her marriage had been broken off mysteriously, that she was a little frisky, had been at a theatre alone with a gentleman, was a bad temper, gave her mother much trouble, — and more obscurely hinted — was fond of a doodle on the sly. I thought nothing about it, it not concerning us, yet it had seemed to me there had been a look in her eye when I conversed with her, which was indicative of desire. I'd found she'd laugh at risky conversation if without frank impropriety, and would egg a man on by questions of assumed ignorance, — then suddenly, "Oh! you're really too bad," and she'd leave — tho her eye gave no signs of her being shocked. Edith H°°r°s°n, — not her name tho phonetically resembling it — knows a lot, some men said, and they suggested the possibility of her having been fucked in India.

She was handsome, well grown, and about seven or eight and twenty, had dark eyes and hair, and a remarkably beautiful foot and ankle, which she displayed as liberally as society permitted. — Tho I didn't then meet her frequently, there was something about her which made my pego tingle when I did. Her eyes used to fix on mine with a stare which gradually softened, and then her face flushed and she turned her eyes away — I thought nothing of that tho at times I wondered if she'd been fucked — dismissing the idea at once.

There had been a cold collation and champagne galore, the company were distributed afterwards, mostly sitting about the grounds, when wanting to piddle, I sought a retired corner and passed a spot where surrounded by shrubs was a swing, and she all alone swinging herself as high as she could. She swung forward just as I approached her, and her white petticoats floating up showed much of her calves. My voluptuous instincts blazed up at the sight of the legs and pretty feet, I bowed my head and tried to look under, involuntarily saying, — "Oh! what a lovely pair, shouldn't I like . . ." — then I broke off recollecting our positions. She tried to stop the swing, I watching till she alighted. All this did not occupy a minute. — She'd taken champagne freely I think — I too much, and with a swelling prick was risky. — She perhaps excited by wine, had at the moment a warmish cunt. — "What would you like?" — said she laughing and looking full at me. — "To have seen a little more." — "Ohoo! oh!" — said she — then both laughed heartily. — "What are you laughing at?" — "At what I should have liked." — "Oh! what a strange man you are, you speak riddles." — "Don't you understand?" — "No." — "You do" — and we looked in each other's eyes again. She looked voluptuous, I fancied.

"You're alone, are you going to run away like Miss °°°°°?" — A lady known to both of us. — "Not with a married man." — "Ah! she *was* foolish, for she might have seen him on the sly," — "Oh! what a horrid suggestion." — "Well — married men are safe flirts, they never tell." — "No, they daren't," said she, and smiled, whilst looking me full in the eyes again, and then colouring up. "I must go to Mamma, she'll wonder where I've been." — "No she won't, she knows, and I guess." — Laughing, off she went, I piddled, and went back to the guests.

Soon after I was walking with her and talking about the young lady, she wasn't surprised, the girl was always flirting with him and had been caught reading objectionable books, and I asked Edith to describe them. — She'd be very sorry to do so. — "Oh — you've seen them then." — No she hadn't, she said in a startled manner, but knew she'd trapped herself — I harped on the subject. "If I lend you a book will you tell me if it's objectionable or not?" She would, and wouldn't tell her mother, nor show it. — "It's all about love — undisguised love — and pictures some might call naughty — objectionable." — "Oh, lend it me." — "I'm frightened — if you're found with it, it will be serious — if not, only you and I will know it, and oldish men know how to hold their tongues." — "Do lend it me — no one shall see it." "It's all about lovers amusing themselves, — but I mustn't lend it you." — "Oh you're joking I know, — but do lend it me." — This is only a summary of a long conversation — for I was cautious, fearing she might shy. Now she was wild to see the book, and must have guessed it was a baudy one. — "I can't send it and can't take it to you" (I didn't visit them). — "I'll meet you out." — She's game thought I, and concluded she'd have her avenue frictionized by the male apparatus. — Then she agreed to meet me two days after, she was going shopping without her mother.

The party was over, her mother had a carriage, and a seat in it was offered me — in the carriage in the dusk I squeezed her hand, she I thought returned it, I pressed my legs against hers and she didn't move hers away — mine were between the two women. — I went on talking to Mamma and taking no notice of the daughter — Mamma asked me in when they alighted, but I declined, and as I handed Edith out pressed her hand saying, "I wish the swing had shown more." — She only said "Thursday" and we parted.

I was at the place, but didn't expect her. — Flirts with their cunts telling them they are neglected — as they do to spinsters approaching thirty — are sometimes after food, champagne, and suggestive gossip, apt to get lustful thrills, and listen to talk, and to say things which next day they regret — I took a *Fanny Hill* with me. — Punctual, there she was, saying she'd not expected *me*. "I've got the book, don't be angry afterwards with me." — "I won't." — "But I want a word with you first, get into a cab, for five minutes, we can't talk in the street." — Into a four wheeler we got, I told her more about the book, avoiding baudy words, that the pictures showed "people making love." She put it into her pocket rapidly, I got a kiss, said "Oh that swing, it's made me want" and we parted naming a day to meet for her to return it. — Afterwards I thought of the risks and wondered at myself — for I'd no defined intentions. The pleasure of lending a real lady a baudy book was my delight — the idea of she and I reading books on sexualities in common — such of course would be the case — delighted me.

She met me and returned the book carefully sealed up. — "What do you think of it?" — "It's disgraceful, you'd no business to lend me such a book." — "You asked me." — "I didn't expect it was one like that. — What must you think of me?" — "Nothing, you've

seen such before." — "I'm sure I haven't." — This sham of hers went
on a little time in the street. — "I won't lend you any others." —
"Oh!" she said eagerly, "have you any more?" — I asked her to
meet me somewhere where we could see them privately, but she
wouldn't answer, I got her into a cab, kissed her, and I tried a feel
unsuccessfully. Would I assure her it was not so improper as the
other — a precious transparent sham. — I told her it was not, but
was baudier. She took it and another day returned it.

I was on reflexion staggered with what had occurred, so un-
looked for, so unpremeditated. The secret baudiness of the affair,
my perpetual wondering whether she'd had the doodle up her,
kept up my excitement and the lady's also, I suppose. She remarked
that she could talk to me as a father, tho few fathers I apprehend
have talked to daughters so. Within a few weeks I'd spoken of the
pleasure of frigging and gamahuching and offered to instruct her.
She said she didn't believe it, but should wait til she was married,
and so on. — She steadily refused to go to a house with me. Then I
left town in the belief that she was a cunning bitch, who'd been
fucked, frigged and gamahuched, was trying to entrap me into
some compromising action, and resolved never to meet her again.
For a couple of months abroad I was nearly chaste, and then re-
turned to London.

When I returned to H°°° I found the poor lover still absent. —
She and her protector had been in the country and *he* was still. —
Donkey prick then frequently had H°l°n, then *he* having also been
away, she ran short of her delight. I hadn't been in the house five
minutes before she said, "Come upstairs" and began undoing her
clothes before she reached the room. Afterwards she named many
times for me to be there, when she could have Priapus also, but
with difficulty arrangements could be made to suit all. "I like to
know you're looking at us." — "Yes and you like me to fuck after
him." — "Yes I do — ain't we beasts?"

The man was cunning and often shut the door. He was whimsi-
cal — wouldn't often undress — and she loving his prick let him
have his way. — One day I was there, he as usual in the kitchen —
for she cooked for him there and from that place he could more eas-
ily escape by a back way. — But the fellow wouldn't come upstairs,
and fucked her on the kitchen table — she was so long away that I
wondered. — When she came up, she had just got him out of the

house, and the sperm was abundant in her quim, tho a quarter of an hour since she'd fucked. She was dressed, and I fucked her from behind against the bed, the only time I think I had then done so on these double fucking occasions — tho I've tailed her in every possible attitude — I delighted usually to see her face as I fucked her whilst we talked. — "Ah! — isn't his prick a big one?" — "Yes I should like to feel it." — "I should like to feel both your pricks at once. — Aha — beast — fuck harder — Ahar." — "His sperm's thick today." — "Yes isn't it lovely, smooth? — ahaa — don't stop — fuck — I'm coming." The angelic smile came over her face, her cunt gripping and we spent together. This is typical. We never fucked without talking about pricks and sperm and making all sorts of lewed suggestions to each other, till pleasure stopped utterances.

There was a garret where sometimes the little servant — when she had one — slept. It contained scarcely any furniture but a bed. One day when there was no fear of surprise, she said she'd make him go up there and get him naked. It was in the afternoon of a warm autumn day, he'd had a feast of rumpsteak and had tippled enough whiskey and water, when I heard him going up the stairs, and in time out I stepped and listened. He was jovial and incautious, yet I was fearful of going up until I heard, "Ahem" — for the carpetless stairs creaked. Then I heard every word as plainly as if I'd been in the room. — He wanted to go to sleep first. — "Fuck and sleep afterwards. — Piss first." — "I don't want" — but I heard the water rattle, and laughter as they got on to the bed, and then, "Ahem."

As I peeped thro the door left ajar — the bed had been cunningly placed so as to prevent his looking at the door — he was lying on his back with shirt on only, she frigging his cock, which was thick but pendant. — "You've fucked before today." — He denied it — was tired. — She angry, was sure he'd been fucking hard the night before, and came used up — she'd had enough of him, he'd been like that often lately, she wasn't going to have his lasts — and so on. — "Suck me." — She wouldn't — he'd better dress and go off to do it, — get another woman. — "Show me your cunt." — Then he frigged himself and got a glorious erection. — "Lie down." — She wouldn't now. "No, stand up naked and let me see it, stand up or you shan't have me." — He drew off his shirt and stood naked with a donkey sized doodle. It was worth seeing, a noble, well proportioned shaft standing out seven or eight inches from the belly, and perhaps nine from his balls, and looking an inch and a half in diameter. It was white skinned, and had a full plum shaped tip of a bright red, it was circled at his belly with a well defined thicket of lightish brown hair, (he was fairish with blue eyes) which didn't creep towards thighs and navel. His ballocks was ponderous. Altogether, it was the biggest prick but one I've ever seen, and the handsomest. The sight of it made my own stiffen voluptuously, and at the same time desire to handle his — I don't wonder at the ladies who are connoisseurs in Priapean tools, admiring his and wishing to enjoy it once, tho certain it is that a pego of average size gives as much sexual pleasure to a woman as the greatest cunt whacker. — A huge stiff prick when a man is standing naked always looks a little ridiculous, so it's strange that my prick should have stood sympathetically at the sight of his.

H*** sat looking at it silently. — Once for an instant she turned her eyes to the door where I was peeping. There was admiration, pride, and lust in her eyes. — The expression of, — "Isn't it a beauty, and it's going up me?" — looking back at it again, her thighs spasmodically closed, then opened, as if a spasm of pleasure was passing through her, and putting her fingers on her cunt she kept them there.

But the prick began to droop. She gave it a violent frig, it then stood stiff, then rapidly fell, and she bullied him — I was pleased to see a man not thirty with his prick not quite ready, as mine has been on one or two occasions, tho I can still fuck her twice in the hour. — After some more angry remarks from her, she threw off her chemise and mounted him, her rump was within six feet of my eyes, and I saw her introduce the prick into her cunt and do the fucking. — His tool kept shrinking — she called him a "used-up beast" told him to go, but wanted the spend, kept reinserting his machine when needful, and fucking energetically. I had a glorious sight of this grand propagator, which she often brought out to the tip and then plunged up her. Then her bum oscillated quickly, her cunt nestled down till his balls were close up to it — she cried out loudly. — "Fuck — spend, Arthur. — Ahaa" — and was quiet.

In a minute. — "You've not spent." — "I was just coming." — "You haven't any spunk in you," and moving her buttocks, out came his prick shining with her spending and stiff enough. — I saw H.'s face, which was lewed. Without a word turning on to him again, up went the long thick gristle into her, and she oscillated her splendid buttocks till she'd spent twice more without his spending once; she after each crisis ballyragging him, he making all sorts of excuses. More than half an hour had she been at the work, and yet went on till at length she got a spend out of him — I never saw her so hot before, her face was moist and scarlet, her eyes humid, with her spending, yet fierce, and as she rolled off she gave his prick a slap. "You've been fucking before today, you liar, get off as fast as you can, you don't bring your fucked out balls into my house again — you won't fuck me again, you mean beast." — All his sins came out, she'd already told me of his meanness.

He made all sorts of excuses but she wasn't pacified. She put on her chemise, came down to my bedroom landing and called out, "Arthur's going, let him out — don't let him go into the kitchen." — He heard this, came down dressed and still excusing himself — she replying to all, — "It's a lie. — It's a lie" — till he was out of the house. Then she came to me and smiled. — "Isn't it a splendid prick?" Then she told me she'd heard the stairs creak, but he'd not noticed it. — "I'm quite wet, I spent three times, he spent at last, the blackguard is fucked out, yet he knew three days ago he was coming — my cunt's wet — won't you have me?" I said no, but was wrought up to the highest pitch of lust, and in half an hour had fucked her twice. She declared donkey prick should never have her again, but I was sure he would. — "He has a noble prick hasn't he?" said she admiringly. — "Yes, but he's a coarse brute, not even handsome, not a gentleman." — "Certainly not a gentleman, but he's a noble prick, all the women want him, he pays none, I'm told." — I fancy Miss Def — now with a house of her own again — was the informant.

I never yet saw a woman fucking a man so plainly, as on that bright afternoon. The beams of the sun at last struck right across her backside, her arsehole, cunt, his prick and balls I saw as plainly as if I had been within a foot of them, and had held a candle to look. — How I longed to feel his tool as she fucked him, and how delighted she would have been. But she was annoyed when afterwards I said, "Your bum furrow is getting brown, H." — "You beast — what if it is, so is yours." — "I know it." — She never could bear to be told about her furrow browning, or later on that hairs were beginning to show round her bum hole, as they do in most women after five and twenty and in southern nations earlier. It detracts from the beauty of the region.

On both occasions, *she* had covered *him*, to prevent him going quickly to the door and his chance of catching me. The next time for some reason of her own — who fathoms a woman's dodges? — she had him in her own bedroom which had now been changed. I waited in the backroom. He was still enough and full, laid on her, half fucked her, and then she made him finish with her rump towards him. H°°° laughed as he got off the bed with his great tool sticking out. Then it disappeared up her, and I thought must have hurt her. The fucking was soon over. How beautiful it was, how exciting it looked! They remained coupled for a minute, then she uncunted him saying, "You lie down, I must go to my sister and will be back in a minute." He threw himself on the bed, giving her rump a slap as they parted and the next second she was with me on my bed. "Don't talk loud, he thinks my sister's here, he's never seen her."

Her eyes shone with voluptuous light and softness. "Hasn't he spent? my cunt's full, hasn't he a lovely prick?" said she sighing and laying down. I looked at it, pulled open the lips, pushed one finger up, then my balls could wait no longer, I had been stiff since I saw his prick, and plunged my pego up her. Ah! my delight — to feel my prick up her and his sperm all round it. — H. put her hand to feel, then clasping my bum, and heaving her arse. — "Ohoo — fuck" she cried and glued her mouth to mine. Furiously our backsides oscillated, far too soon my sperm rose. "Hurt me — shove hard," she whispered, heaving her cunt up, and the next minute both were spending, her ecstacy as great as mine. Then quickly back she went to him, her cunt full as before, her motte and thighs wet with our essence. — "Make him fuck you in it." — "If I can, but he likes it washed before he does me again" were the last words.

She closed their door with a bang, cunningly giving the handle a turn so that it was left ajar, but so close that I could see nothing. To facilitate that a fortnight before she'd cut away, at eye height, a slip off of one edge, and painted it afterwards. We had arranged this together after the manner at the French lapunar. She laid down on the bed for *me* to see *her*, then I for her to see *me*, and we moved her bed a little to give the best view of those upon it, both delighted at the dodge. I couldn't see their heads when they were fucking, but saw all from their breasts downwards. — Now she took the side furthest off, and nearer the fireplace, and he turning to her had his back to me. — "Ahem" — I pushed the door slightly open and saw them both well.

She began frigging *him*, then he felt *her*. "You've not washed." — "No, how could I? — I will." — "My spunk's on your thighs." — "Yes, did you spend?" — "My ballocks were damned full," — said he with a coarse laugh. — Both laughed, and went on talking about some woman who had one of the smallest cunts he'd ever fucked, and about some swell Paphians she had known formerly, whilst she went on frigging him till, "It's stiff, let's do it." — "Wash it." — She got up, and holding the ewer, — "There's no water." — "Ring for Sally and I'll show her my prick" — said he laughing and handling it. — "I shan't — you'd better not — never mind washing" — getting on the bed again and frigging his tool. — In another minute after lewed chat he mounted her, she'd pulled her chemise off and tried to pull off his shirt. Saying it was cold, he refused but tucked. it up to his waist.

They were fucking in an instant. Is the spectacle of even a handsome couple fucking beautiful or not? — Is the sight of a beautiful creature, all modesty and grace — whom one has walked, talked, and danced with, to be admired when on her back, heaving her buttocks up, her thighs high and round the man's whilst under is a thick gristly stem protruding from his belly, and going like a steam piston in and out of a bush of hair round her cunt — is it beautiful? Both rumps jog, and heave, and thrust and meet, till with sighs and murmurs both are quiet. Is it a spectacle beautiful or not? — No. — Yet an entrancing one. — One that no man or woman would hesitate to look at, enjoy, and envy, none whose cunt wouldn't· yearn — whose prick wouldn't stiffen at the sight. — Yet it's not beautiful, tho exciting, stimulating, entrancing to all the senses.

This was really a fine couple I must say, much as I disliked his vulgarity, but to know that that big tube, with its inner tube of discharge, was thrusting up *her* tube, with the intensest pleasure to both, made my prick, without frigging, stand till I heard their murmurs, knew that their pleasure was over.

He rolled off of her, she didn't hurry him. "Get me a glass of whiskey and water." — "I shan't, you've had enough, get it yourself in the· kitchen if you want it, don't make a noise, I don't want my sister to know a man's here." The scout — Mrs. **** — took care the man shouldn't know I was there. Hastily he put on his clothes

and went off. "Hish" said she as he went downstairs and she waited
till he got to the kitchen.

In she came and I looked at her sexual treasure. Sperm is
now to me clean, wholesome. It's the outcome of life — the issue
and cause of the greatest human pleasure to giver and receiver. —
I no longer mind my fingers being in it, but like to feel a cunt which
is lubricated with it. — I opened hers, felt up it, wiped my fingers
on my balls, and on her motte — the salacity of the act delighted me.
"You beast, you," said she but looking pleased with the lascivious
act. Then up into her my prick went, and prick and cunt then rev-
elled in the unction and the thrusts, and the lubricated friction of
our movements, till both sobbed out our joy in the delicious crisis —
her cunt discharged, my balls shot forth their sperm, and we mixed
this essence of male and female life in her sweet channel — oh happy
woman!

Pressing her sweet form to mine, her hand clasping my but-
tocks — in the lubricious conjunction we lay. — Slowly I still kissed
her, our wet lips mingling moistures there as we lay conjoined —
eyes closed — baudily thinking — vague visions of lust dreamily
passing thro our brains. "Aren't we beasts?" — the first words spok-
en. — "Damn it, H°l°n — don't say that again — it's nonsense —
nothing beastly about it — what beast could do or care about doing
what you and I have done? — it's heavenly, divine — don't — I've
often told you you annoy me by saying it." She laughed, her belly
jogged, her cunt moved, and out came my prick, and at once as
many and as much as I could get of my fingers up her cunt I put
there — lewed still.

This again was on a warm autumn afternoon, for it suited us
both to meet at that time — the master of the house was then away.
Soon donkey prick was got out of the house. I dressed, we had tea
and toast, then I licked her cunt till she was exhausted with pleasure,
then left.

My heroic resolution. — The whore and the railway porter. — Against a viaduct. — Michael's prick and Michael using it. — On the early fucking of poor girls. — Another juvenile virgin. — Her antecedents and harlotting sisters. — Her salacity and taste for minetting. — Nervous impotency again. — Virility restored. — Virginity ruptured. — Female pleasures at their first fucking. — On the way virginities are lost and won.

It seems strange to myself, that tho I stopped in the City of **** on my return from the south, I kept away from the lapunar with the peephole — for once I kept to my resolve. — But I am tired, I suppose, of the spectacles which have so much delighted me. — Was this fatigue of travel, satiety — or age?

On my return I saw H, who was delighted, and the first afternoon spent with her in using my tongue, fingers and prick, left her tranquil enough for twenty-four hours at least. — Donkey prick she was getting very weary of, the other lover was still ill, her protector more loving than ever. — "Oh! I'm so glad to see you again and have some one to tell things to." — Tell she did, and I think all about her fuckings, cooking, Donkey prick's meanness, young Harry's lust. &c. — Then for the first time I think she wanted to borrow a trifle which she got as a gift instead of a loan — for she was delightful, with beauty, cleanliness, fine taste, wit and lasciviousness combined. [How rare that combination.]

Towards the end of February, on a dirty but warmish night for that month, I visited an old relative in the suburbs, and went there by a loop line of railway which had not been opened long. I

met there with a little adventure, being I suppose always on the
look out and unable to resist a grope of a warm cunt, whenever I
got the opportunity of groping comfortably.

The station in the suburb led out of a wide long road about
a tenth of a mile from a main metropolitan thoroughfare. On my
return I found I was three-quarters of an hour too early, so loitered
about the road, smoking and thinking, I noticed at length two
women, unmistakably harlots of a middling class. Quite in my youth
I had many times fucked in that very road when there were only
oil lamps there·and against fences enclosing fields and strawberry
grounds. There were more houses about the road now, yet on both
sides of the station road and viaduct, there were still large fields,
and from the road which led up to the station was another — just
before reaching it — which passed *under* the viaduct, connecting
with a farm road and was altogether between fields, and led to a
farm house.

After a time chatting, I gave the women a shilling apiece to
feel their cunts, tho this was in the main road. Then said one, —
"Why don't you have me? Let's go on the other side of the viaduct
and nobody will see us — we are very often done there." There I
went with one, promising another shilling for an uninterrupted
grope, it seemed a pleasant way of passing the time. I soon stood
besides her having passed into the farm road, the night was quite
dark, not a light was in that road, but a little light was shed down
from the station platform above our heads, tho not sufficient to dis-
tinguish features by. Having pulled her petticoats up to her waist,
I felt her bum and belly everywhere. She piddled over my fingers,
felt my tool, and I was satisfied, tho my cock was stiffening as she
left off.

As I first had seen her standing outside the station door, I now
said I wondered they didn't prevent her. She laughed. — They
wouldn't interfere, why should they? — she knew the porters and
they knew her. — "They fuck you?" — "Both on em — I let em — it
keeps them square." — Then I heard that the porters had their pleas-
ure with her up against the viaduct, just where we were standing, —
my fingers still twisting her cunt ringlets. — "I'll give five shillings
to see one fuck you," said I impetuously as the idea came suddenly
on me. "Will you? all right, wait till the next train's gone and I'll

fetch one." "But I'll feel him first." — "Oh. I don't know about that." — "I'll give him half a crown, and it's all in the dark." — It was so dark that I could scarcely see her face. "I'll ask — one I think would, but I don't know about the other — here's the train."

A bell rang, the train moved in and moved off, she went when the passengers had gone off up to the station door, and I standing far off by the archway, after a time saw her talking to a man. Then she came to me. He'd be there as soon as he could, and we were to keep there in the dark. Finding I had ten shillings in silver in my purse, I put it into my greatcoat pocket ready — refusing to pay her beforehand as she asked me — then pulled my coat collar high up round my neck, and put on a comforter to hide my face as much as I could. — We stood talking about the porter and his prick, — which was a good big one she told me, that he was married and was named Michael. — Soon after, a big strongly built male form came under the arch to us. — He was evidently anxious not to be known and said he wouldn't fuck if I didn't go further off. I refused, and tho nervous had screwed up my determination to feel him when fucking her, or wouldn't pay. I told her this when she had come to me, he standing with his face to the viaduct. She, fearing the loss of five shillings, went and persuaded him energetically. "Come along old man, yer didn't mind when the farmer passed the other night," I heard. Then I guessed from her movements she was feeling his cock. He had pulled his cap well over his eyes and kept himself turned towards her, and I kept at the back of *him* not wishing to be known or to know him. In the darkness there was but little probability of future recognition of each other.

All was silent, I approached and supposed he was obdurate spite of her manipulation of his doodle. "Feel my pussy," I guessed by the movement that she'd lifted her clothes, and for a minute again all was quiet. — Then — "There — isn't it stiff — put it in." — I closed on him, — she'd her back against the brick piers. "Let me feel it first, and I'll give you the half crown," I mumbled. "Let him feel it Mick — don't be a fool." — I closed to his back, he'd made no reply — put my hand round and grasped a prick as stiff as a poker, then felt his balls. — She moved her hand away from them to let me — he turned his head sideways from me, whilst I manipulated his prick for a minute in silence. — My own prick then stiffened, throbbed sensuously, I longed to fuck her myself, and next to see him do it. The old letch for a lubricated cunt came thrilling.

"Put it up her" mumbled I, my hand having roved up and down his prick for a minute or so. In a second he was oscillating his rump, was fucking her rapidly, heeding me not now as again going to his side, my hand stole between them till I grasped his balls, and the come and go of his rod in her cunt was perceptible, — then Michael murmured, sighed, and spent. From the moment he began ramming her till he'd spent he seemed to think of nothing, never uttered a sound — tho still he leaned his head over her left shoulder so that I couldn't see his face, — which was just what I wanted.

Ere he'd withdrawn his prick from its cosy lodging, I drew to his back again and put out the half crown, saying so. He took it with his left hand, and the next second suddenly and without turning round to see me — without uttering a word, — ran off quickly under the viaduct, and was out of sight in a second. The woman laughed. — I gave her the five shillings and felt her overflowing lubricious quim. I now was trembling with lust. — "Oh I'd like to fuck you." — "All right, put it in." — "I'm frightened." — "You need not be." — "I'm a married man." — "So is he." — I wonder I restrained myself for my prick was throbbing with lust, but groping the lubricious receptacle, thinking of the solid prick which had spent in it, and God knows what other voluptuous reminiscences, I let her frig me, spent on the ground, and then pissed over my fingers to purify them.

She was squatting, washing her cunt with her own piddle — when "that's your train." — I wouldn't go by it fearing to see the porter, tho I'd never seen his face nor he mine, said I should go by cab and miss the train I'd been waiting for. "I must go," said she, "I nearly always get a friend by this train." — "And you fuck here?" — "Generally — sometimes we go further up the lane, there's a fence all the way to the farm — if you wait here you'll see us at it." We both moved into the station road, I waited by the arch, but she got no friend. Then I led her to a lamp in the main road to see her face, and found her really a good looking young woman. Surprised, I wondered she didn't take men to a house. — "So I do if they'll come, and there is a nice one seven minutes from here, but they're generally in such a hurry."— I was interested, so gave her another half crown for a chat. She'd done well since the station was opened — had two or three men each night there — was rarely, five minutes with any of them — they did her, and often got to the station just as the train stopped there.

One middle-aged man who had had her several times, came usually by the train just come, he waited till all was clear, then rapidly went under the archway, she following him. When he'd fucked her he went off quickly, she never moved off for some minutes, so as to prevent any suspicions about his little game, he'd arranged it so.

Strange desire to see that porter came over me, I checked it for a day or two, but four or five evenings afterwards took a ticket by train to that station and waited there. There were two porters, but I couldn't identify my man, the two being in form so much alike. I kept there wandering about, till the station master asked me why I was waiting — I told him for some one who'd come by next train. Soon after he called a porter, another said. "He wants you Mick," and he I believe whose prick I had felt, came — I stared at *him*, but *he* evidently had no recollection of *me*. He was a fine strapping fellow of about thirty-five. I'd have given a sovereign to have seen and felt his prick again. It delighted me to know that I'd felt it and seen him fucking, and that he hadn't a notion that I had done so.

[I wonder at myself — wonder if many men in this metropolis have had such out of the way letches — and adventures.]

[Then again came the chance of a youthful virginity, and a singular illustration of the effect of nervousness upon me, mentally and physically. So identical were the nervous phenomena, so similar all circumstances attending that defloration to what took placed about six months ago, that the narrative seems even to *me*, like a reproduction of an old event clothed in new language. But it is not so. As each of the two incidents occurred, the same or the next day it was written down. I do not dwell on my nervous sufferings, but they were painfully great, I was a psychological study to myself for some time after the event.

· [All circumstances attending the deflorating this lass are evidence that most poor girls are fucked before they are sixteen. It is immaterial who does it, *but they will be fucked.* — *She* is quite as willing to have it done, as *he* to do it, and probably it is the female who incites the male (unwittingly perhaps) following simply the law of nature — quite as much as the male incites the female to the pleasure. What rot then this talk about male seduction, when it is nature which seduces both. Equally absurd also the sentimental bosh about young virgins being bought and sold. The results to the girl are the same whether she is fucked for money or *love* — or if the term be liked better — for *lust*. A prick up her *she will have* before she's sixteen. She *will* have her sexual pleasure, paid or unpaid for it. The poor alone are philosophical in amatory matters.]

H. was impecunious, and having made money by the lass whose virginity I took last spring, I shall always think put this temptation in my way for further profit. — I found there one day a little servant about fourteen years old, fairly pretty, sprightly and pleasing, and thought I should like to investigate her privates as soon as I set eyes on her. — H. said the lass was daughter of a sea coast man, and had two sisters gay, had been stopping with one in London who had let her see men fuck her. "She won't be long before *she* has it." She had found out that this girl frigged herself. — I suppose all girls of fourteen do — and wanted to be fucked, knew all about it, had said so. — H. and she had already looked at each other's cunts — women like doing that — and she had frigged the girl who was *"virgo intacta"* — warranted. "If *you* don't have her some one will soon, her sister won't let her stop here she'll make money out of her, and if not the girl will let some man fuck her." — "I'll have her" said I, and began courting the lass.

Soon after, H said she'd have nothing to do with it, but still she would not hinder me. I reminded her of what she'd told me. — She replied, that certainly the girl would have a man soon somehow, or somewhere, for she was so lewed and curious, that a little persuasion would get her. — H's change of front, her object in holding back now, was not very clear to me, but felt sure she'd like to see me fuck the lass for baudy pleasure if for nothing else. Telling her so, she laughed and said she should.

That day I kissed the slut, gave her a trifling present, and felt up to her navel. She let me readily, even seemed complimented by my attention. — H. was present. — "There's no hair on your dear little cunt." "Not yet," she replied — I had then one of those long exciting preliminary, baudy, inductive conversations, — so very delicious with an unpoked girl, and equally delicious to her. — "You know what fucking is, don't you my darling?" — "No," said she hanging her head and looking confused — "What a lie," said H. — "You've seen gentlemen doing it to your sister." — "Oh" said the lass. At length she confessed it. Then I felt freely all about her hidden charms, my hands roved up and down, I insinuated a finger between her thighs closed tightly, but it rubbed between the lips of the grove, and brought away the female aroma. Ah me how nice is the smell of cunt, which some fools say isn't nice. — She was sitting on my knee, I wanted to see her naked but that she refused, I pulled up her clothes, she pushed them down, whining. H. winked at me. "Your cunt smells so nice," said I. — "You're a nasty man" she replied, coloring up and looking at H.

"Let me another day, dear." Then as customary, I gave money to buy shoes and stockings. Having felt her till my cock was restive, I began caressing H°°° "Come and look at your mistress' cunt." — H. favored me, for our conversation had made *her* lewed, she turned on to the bed and about, and let me look at her cunt. Then the girl after a little persuasion felt H's cunt. — We had wine, I gamahuched H., the girl got tight with the drink and also gamahuched her, then I again made H. spend and again with my lingual titillation until she was well-nigh exhausted with spending, and then fucked her twice at the side of the bed, letting the girl see my prick go in and out, and I taught her to play with my balls. — Never had a lass seen so much I think in about three hours. We had a deliciously baudy treat, and at the end half screwed, laughingly she admitted that she too should like to be fucked. Odd if she hadn't, for her modesty had gone to the winds, had been going before she came to H. and our talk and acts would have made the coldest virgin randy, and her cunt hot and reeking with lubricious juices. — This girl in whose eyes was lust, who kissed me again and again when I left — tho still resting a look at her privates — was dying to let me, tho I left without doing it.

Next visit, H. told me that since my absence, she had been gamahuched by the lass who loved doing it, and she'd again frigged the lass who was longing to be fucked. — "Give her a sovereign, and she will let you." — So I began kissing and coaxing her, but she had such a bad cold in her head and wanted her pocket handkerchief so often, that she was unpleasant to me, so much so that desire for her was chilled, I never could bear a snotty-nosed female.

I tried to evoke my lust by a frig and other devices uselessly. I thought of my impotence with the former little lass and fear came over me of similar trouble, I fancied my prick shrunk, felt it and whispered to H. "I shall not be able to fuck her I'm sure." — "Nonsense, don't think so — can't you fuck me three times nearly every time you come to see me? — Why can't you fuck her then? — Nonsense — don't think about it" — was H's reply. But it was so — the result of the girl's bad cold in the first place, and then a fearful, ridiculous nervousness, thro thinking about my former frigidity.

Next visit she had neat stockings and shoes on — my gift. — "Let's look at your little cunt, darling." — H. had prepared her for the request, and the girl got slowly on to the bed. "Pull up your clothes," said I, liking to see her do that. — With hesitation slowly up she pulled them, — "Higher darling" but she stopped, and I pulled her chemise up above her navel. I was enraptured with breaking down her modesty, with making a supposed virgin expose herself so much. Then I looked long and lasciviously. She was a nice little creature, not plump but not bony, nor did I feel any prominences as I ran my hand over her from her nascent bubbies to her thighs. Then dropping on my knees by the bedside, I opened wide her thighs and saw the delicate pink grove. All was well washed and sweet — H. took care of that.

I gloated on the pretty cunt. Not a hair discolored the creamy colored lips, nor interfered with the view of the little flaps and clitoris which were just showing. There was the hymen closed all but a little hole, a perforation into which I cautiously inserted my little finger, at which she winced. All was so pink, so rosy, so delicate, that restraining myself no longer and removing my finger, I put my tongue to it; throwing her thighs over my arms and placing my hands under her little bum, I licked her cunt furiously. For so long a time I had licked no cunt excepting those of which the thatch tickled my nose — the well-haired cunt of H.'s mostly — that this was a delicious novelty and the rosy-tinted, sweet virgin quim licking gave me voluptuous delight — H. stood by with her soft baudy eyes enjoying the sight. I licked till my tongue ached, the lass enjoying it, showing no life excepting an occasional twitch of

her thighs, or an involuntary slight heave of her little backside —
I can't say if she spent or not. — She told H. that she did. Then I
left off and gamahuched H. till she was wild with delight, and
sobbed out when spending — as she does also when she's fucking. —
"Fuck — oho — aha — ahar — spunk." — She and I always indulge
thus and stimulate our passion. She pushed me away just as her
salt spendings reached my tongue, she always either clutches or
pushes my head furiously when her spend is on.

Then I laid the lass along the bed, she seeming joyous at it,
and told her that the tongue could not give her the pleasure that a
prick could, and so did H. "Its fifty times greater than sucking or
frigging gives you dear — let me put this into your cunt." — "Shall
I" — said she to H. "Do what you like," was the reply.

I mounted her, but my prick fell flapping against the pretty
cunt. Three minutes before, I was stiff to bursting, now not a bit of
strength was in it. The girl and H. had both felt it stiff as a
ramrod — now it was a bit of pendant gristle. — I rubbed, thrust
and rubbed the tip up against the virgin slit, pinched it and
squeezed it, shook it, but all was useless. — Off I got, placed H.
against the bed with rump towards me, and a few pushes up her
invigorating quim stiffened it enough to have gone thro. a street
door. — With the moisture of her dear cunt on it, again I put it
against the little virgin cunt — Down it then drooped again. I tried
it again but all was useless, then weary and ashamed I gave it up
after half an hour trial. — After some wine and talk I turned H.'s
rump to me, and "a levrette" fucked and spent in her. — No diffi-
culty had I in the lovely avenue of that delicious stimulating crea-
ture.

I had put the lass so that she could see our copulation, see that
I was stiff and had spent. H. then herself fingered the little one's
cunt, and once inserted a tip of a finger. I got the lass to see my
prick as it came out of the gruelly quim, but my cock wouldn't
stand to *her*, and I left annoyed, telling her she'd not get her pres-
ent, till I had left her quim as wet with my spendings as H°l°n's
was. — "Ain't I doing as you told me," said she to H°l°n — in an
anxious tone. — "Certainly, it's not your fault."

"Never mind, he'll do you next time," said H. — but the next
time — a couple of days after — was only a repetition. I could not
fuck her, tho the girl helped me, twisted and turned like an eel,

as I told her. Yet again H. drew out my sperm easily. — What witchery was on me? — I stayed away longer, and when I went felt strong — that I should succeed. There was the little ready lass a virgin still, as closely I investigated and satisfied myself — randy lass tho she was. — We all three stripped and began amorous tricks. — "You'll do her today" said H. feeling my prick. — I put the little one on the side of the bed. — "Should you like to be fucked dear." — "*Oh I should — so — like — to be fucked,*" — said she, emphasising her words just as written. Strong desire was in every word, and in every look of the little dear face — surely never was a young virgin more determined to taste the male — it seems incredible almost as I write it, but such was the result — largely of H.'s teaching — who laughed. "Since you were here she and Phil have been in bed with me, he fucking me — haven't you?" — "Oh yes." — Nothing more was said — the lass kissed my prick — I licked and wetted the virgin quim, there was the unbroken virginity. "Hurrah!" my prick was hot and stiff, I felt her, brought her to the edge of the bed, put her legs up against my chest, and nervously agitated, lodged *my* prick against her notch and pushed. — "Does that hurt you?" — "A little." — I thrust again. — "Oho" — she gently sobbed as another prick thrust told — and she winced and her bum drew back. — A few more short pushes and I felt the barrier give way, felt my prick tearing it open, then in it glided easily up the smooth canal, till her womb stopped it. — Glorying, I felt my prick fully sheathed. "Feel it H°l°n" — I cried. — "I'm up her" — H. felt it. — "She's got it." — The girl put down her hand and felt at my request my prick stem hidden in her cunt. — "Is it nice love?" — "Oh yes," she whispered. — Then taking my time, with long steady thrusts and withdrawals, so that every inch of her vagina could feel the friction, I fucked till at length hot spunk gushed·into her cópiously, and the sweet little lass spent with me. — Long time I kept it up her, triumphing, looking at her contented face, then out came my prick slobbered and blood streaked. — Her cunt was bleeding slightly and letting out my sperm, as she lay still in dreamy voluptuousness, satisfied, bewildered with her new pleasure, her reeking cunt soothed and gratified by my sperm, and so she lay, thighs apart with her legs hanging down seemingly happy, till told to get up and wash. — H°l°n stood looking — speechless.

Never was a virginity at last taken with greater ease or luxury than hers, never was a girl more anxious to lose it. She washed her cunt under H°l°n's directions, and the basin full of water got red. Again I looked at her quim which would not stop bleeding. — "Yes I liked it," said she, and that it was much nicer than frigging herself, that she was glad she had been fucked. She kissed me as if she wished her lips to eat into mine — did the young, hot-cunted loving slut, — whose willingness for fucking was remarkable.

I have often heard women say that until their second or third poke, they had no pleasure with a man, that they believed few if any enjoyed the first. — H°l°n seemed even to have that belief, but her two young ones both spent at their first fuck. I'll swear I have known full grown virgins fetched by my gristly rammer, the first time it was put up them, and that their pleasure followed the slight pain which the splitting gives. I incline to the belief that breaking thro the hymen really gives very little pain. I know as much about it as most men, and am sure that many a virgin spends with her first fuck. — What astonished me was that I had again the same temporary impotency I'd had with the other young servant — one of H°l°n's — some months before. I believe it was thinking of my difficulty with the first one which unmanned me with this girl, and my failing in the first attempt on her — I feared it would be so the moment nervousness set in, and so it was. It was not want of sperm, for I fucked H°l°n easily enough when I couldn't fuck Nancy.

It is needless to tell more about this amour, the only novelty was in opening up her quim to masculine pleasure. She soon left H°l°n and took to whoring with her sister, who had also her cunt plugged before she was fourteen. H°°° was no doubt right when she said that some one was sure to fuck the lass soon. Harlot she wanted to be and was. Whether a girl in her condition of life has it at fourteen, or postpones it till sixteen, the end is the same, she merely has two years more frigging instead of fucking. Physically and morally which is the worst — or best? — Both are natural and according to some notions improper — to talk, think or write about copulation, or to do anything with our genitals is always highly improper to some people. — Yet we were created with cock and cunt, and sperm, for that alone, live indeed for that alone. — All males and females think and talk about it constantly and fuck as much as they can. — "How improper," say some fools and hum-

bugs. This law of nature will make them fuck without permission of
priest, registrar, or law, for the multiplication of the species comes
about by this very improper act, called fucking.

[Thinking over this episode — one day I wrote the following
about "Virginities."

[How much alike is all this amatory work, varying only broadly
in the preliminaries, — less and less in detail as familiarity in-
creases. — How soon the time comes when full opportunity occurs.
— Introduction, civilities, liking, and then desire springs up in the
man or woman, or both. It is contagious. — Then cautious advances
of the man, tentative remarks, almost instinctive at times — at other
times designed. Pride in the man's attentions and flattery soothes the
woman, and the road to surrender is paved. In him now lust rises,
hope springs up, then come warmer and suggestive words. — Were
not man and woman made to give each other pleasure? — how
many give each other pleasure in secret — the world knows nothing
of it, — it's easy enough to accomplish. — Why not we? — to kiss,
to cuddle, how sweet to both — how lovely is the touch of naked
flesh with naked flesh — nice even when palm meets palm but only
to be fully tasted when in bed. — "Let us." — "Oh! fie! — I don't
know what you mean. — Oh! how rude you are" — and she blushes,
tries to look offended, yet half smiles with downcast eyes.

[She likes to hear these hints — suggestions of conjugality and
its pleasure — tho she forbids. Luxurious thoughts now arise, chas-
ing each other thro her brain. Is it more pleasure than frigging
herself, she thinks. — Desires — complicated at first by such
thoughts and fears and prudence, arise. Ah! a thrill passes through
her, starting from her centre of bliss. Again and again that voluptu-
ous thrill, — that half faint feeling as her cunt again sends forth
those carnal waves of desire, desire not precise in its wants but in-
definite, softly languishing. — Lust with its soothing, brain stealing
voluptuous sensations, is working her body and soul for its end, and
she thinks of fucking. They look into each other's eyes, male in-
stinct tells him of *her* carnal wants, and *his* lust burns fiercely.

[Then further talk and broader hints of the sweets of con-
nection — two joined in one. — A pressure of the palms, a kiss, a hug

round the waist — closer together they now, limbs meeting, their
warmth of flesh mingling. Does lustful aroma issue from one or from
both as prick and cunt inflame. — French writers say it does and
steeps the senses, and deadens prudence. — Certainly never does
woman's flesh smell to me so sweetly, so excitingly as now — her
lustful aromas rise from neck, and armpits, from the hair of her
head issues sexual perfume. Then acts follow words. — "Let me. —
What a lovely ankle." — "Oh! take your hand away." — up steals his
hand above the garter and the warm soft flesh of thigh is felt. — Up
starts his prober hard as horn, lustful — heated pulsations moving
it: It nods with lust. — A thrust of hand — a cry. — "Oh — don't."
— A struggle and his fingers touch her clitoris. — "Oh! now. —
Leave off — I'll scream." — But his finger keeps there. — "Ah —
oho — what a shame." — The struggle is over, her voice sinks lower
to a whining murmur — no screech follows the threat. — Both mur-
mur softly now, "let me." — "No." — "I won't hurt you — let me
fuck you." — "No." — His hand goes further back below the clitoris,
touches the portcullis of her womb, and then she struggles hard. —
All useless, maiden.

[The invasion is complete — the titillation tells and enervates.
She has voluptuous delight, mental and physical, in his fingers lay-
ing between the lips of the soft lubricious orifice. Tho with a few
struggles she says, "don't." — Out comes his flaming prick — her
hand feebly refusing at first soon grasps the throbbing rigidity. —
Lust now overwhelms them both — unconscious, blind agents al-
most, working out are they their share in the great scheme of gen-
eration. — Instinct prevails, restless are his fingers till she yields,
falls back, refusing all the time yet helplessly is yielding. Up he lifts
the curtains of her nudity. A kiss on the white soft belly whilst
the aroma of the avenue makes him reel with fierce desire. In a sec-
ond his prick touches it. — Thrust — Thrust, throb — "ahrr — oh
don't — you hurt." — He is full up her, his balls touch her buttocks,
her cunt tightens, then spends from every pore. "Aharr — my dar-
ling," and his sperm jets into her. — Soft broken murmurs die away
into silence, their limbs are still now in the exhaustion of pleasure —
the deed is done — nature is satisfied — the object of creation at-
tained. — Thus are virginities taken. — *Ex uno disce omnes* — vari-
ations in time and according to age, and place, and hour, and op-

portunity—some quicker—some shorter in progress,—but the end the same—always the same.—Nature will have it so.—*Ex uno disce omnes.*—We were fucked for—born to fuck in our turn —to beget others to fuck.—*Ex uno disce omnes.* As in the beginning, now and ever it will be—Fucking.]

A small cunt on the Derby day. — Under a portico at midnight. — The brothel afterwards. — A harlot's history. — On cunts generally. — Nationalities of the women I have fucked. — The beauty of cunts. — Their fucking qualities. — Ignorance on this head. — Ages of the women I have fucked. — How the sight of cunts affects men. — Physiognomy of cunts. — Their classification.

A month or more after I had the little virgin at H.'s, at past midnight of the Derby day when the street was unusually quiet after the day's festivities, I who had supped with friends on our return, walked along *****. A short neat-looking girl approached, evidently not intending to notice me, I was heated with food, wine, and the day's outing, the idea of a free and easy cunt being at hand roused my passions, and I accosted her. "Where are you going, my dear?" "Why home of course." — We stopped, talked, and in a few seconds "Let me feel your cunt and I'll give you a shilling." — She looked up and down the silent street. — "Be quick then." — We turned up a street still quieter, with large handsome houses with porticos, beneath one of which my hand was soon round her bum and a finger — after a general feel over the soft surface of her sexual gap — was up the male receptacle. — After a minute's groping. — "What a tight cunt you've got, how old are you?" I asked. "Turned seventeen."

Then many questions and answers in a quiet tone, whilst still my hand roved about the slippery surface of the red opening, ever and anon a finger gliding in and out of the juicy folds, then frigging the little soft protuberance where the belly divides. — "Why, it's like a girl's of fourteen." — "So they say," — and further answers. — "Some men like it, some don't. — No I haven't had it tonight, worse

615

luck." — Then indignantly. — "A park woman? that I ain't." —
Then I heard she'd been to the races in a chaise with her sister and
husband and his brother, and had had a jolly evening. — The broth-
er was "on night watch for a fortnight and obliged to leave" — "or
he'd have had me — ain't you curious? — No I've just piddled and
can't do it — no I won't try — that will do — oh leave off — I must
get-home."

Her bum waggling, she drew it back and dislodged me, —
"You'll make me want it," said she as my fingers again moved about
her quim. Soon after, — "Let me feel yours?" She felt my trowsers at
the proper spot, I looked up and down the silent street, saw no one
and produced my shaft. "Aha — it's stiff." — I was red hot now by
desire for the little quim, and we felt each other restlessly, until
— "Why don't you have me?" — "Do you want it?" — "I just do —
oh you'll fetch me — don't" — and again she dislodged my fingers
as her bum wagged with lustful thrills.

That brought me to my senses, and tho my pego throbbed I
paid her. — "If I'd had that before I'd have rode home — there —
why don't you do me?" — "We shall be seen." — "We shan't" —
"I've no more money, I've lost all betting." — "So have I — do it —
come close to the door — we shan't be noticed." — "I've no money,
I tell you." — "Never mind — do me." — I thought for a second
hesitating but wanting her badly. — "Here's half a crown. — Now
don't let me if you're not sure you're quite well." — She pocketed
the money. — "I'm all right, I never was ill in my life," — and she
went up another step, and set her back against the side of the porch
which just there was walled. She was short but a willing cock and
cunt will help each other to the great act of nature. — Soon I was
up to my balls in her, and we fucked ourselves into Elysium. — What
a grip her cunt gave as my lubricious emulsion throbbed into it.

There we stood coupled till we heard the heavy footsteps of a
constable in the distance, then uncunting, we walked off laughing
to the main road. "You wanted it." — "I just did." — "If he hadn't
come we'd have done it again." — "Yes, we'll go back," said the
girl. — We stood talking till the policeman appeared and went far
away. Then "Come back," said she. We went to another portico,
I felt her gluey quim, she frigged me — just then a clock struck one.
— "I must go." — "You'll do it in a minute," said the randy-cunted
lass frigging my cock hard — but I was for reasons obliged rapidly

to go, I'd no idea it was so late. Altho I've had no special liking for tight cunts — quite the contrary once — there is no accounting for a letch, and as my prick pistoned her, the sheath had seemed so exquisite in its lubricity, that I asked her to meet me another night. She lived much further off, knew no house there, but she'd be with me. I must pay her. — I didn't much expect she'd keep her word, but gave her five shillings, promising another five if she'd be at a place named. Three days after she came and I had her. She was a slim, well made, fairly good looking young strumpet, and had very clean under linen. Her cunt was slightly fledged, had little lips, scarcely any nymphæ, was lovely to look at and perhaps the tightest cunt I ever had in a girl of her age. I fucked her twice, then frigged her, and sent her away contented. As I felt up her cunt, it seemed as if no prick could get into it — but cunt is a distendible article.

We had champagne, and her tongue loosened. Laughing heartily "I did want it just when you felt me, I'd wanted it all the evening, I've never been felt in the street before. — Toni forgot the time and distance, so went off suddenly or he'd lost his place." — He'd intended to have her but things went wrong, there had been words through drink. "So I was athinking of it when I met *you*." She was fifteen and a half when first fucked for about half a dozen times, then for a year never had it again, then she wouldn't let her mother "keep her under" any longer, and she'd been "regular gay" two months. — "I don't let the people about us know *that*, — when I goes out I never goes near mother." — I got her address, but never used it.

[Then I fell ill, and during that time wrote the following essay on cunts. — I had intended to destroy it, because it is no part of the narrative of my secret life, but reserved it at last.]

In my travels in various parts of the globe, I have never failed to have the women of the various countries passed through, as well as many of the women of the provinces, countries, and nationalities, which in some cases make together what is called an Empire. Thus women of Croatia, Styria and Dalmatia, and those of Vienna and Pesth, altho all belonging to the Austrian empire are of absolutely different physical types. — A Dalcarlian and a woman of Gottenburg differ greatly, yet both are of the Swedish kingdom. — In Great Britain, the English, Irish, Scotch, and Welsh are of different types, and there is even a great difference in face and form between a Yorkshire and Devonshire woman — both English.

I have tasted the sexual treasures of all these fair creatures in their capital cities, and many of their large towns; not only in Europe, but in lands and countries away over many oceans. I have sought abroad variety in races and breeds at the best lapunars, where they keep women of different nationalities to suit the tastes and languages of travellers. Thus I have had women of all parts of the world, and from parts in which I have not set foot. They may differ in face, form, and color, but all fuck much in the same manner, their endearments, tricks and vices are nearly the same, yet I found great charm in the variety, and always voluptuous delight in offering the homage of my priapus to a woman of a type or nationality unknown to me.

Looking thro diaries and memoranda, I find that I have had women of twenty-seven different empires, kingdoms or countries, and eighty or more different nationalities, including every one in Europe except a Laplander. I have stroked Negress, Mulatto, Creole, Indian half breeds, Greek, Armenian, Turk, Egyptian, Hindu, and other hairless-cunted ones, and squaws of the wild American and Canadian races. — I am but ***** years old, and the variety I have had astonishes me. May I live to have further selection, and increase the variety of my charmers.

I have had of course women in most parts of the United Kingdom, but fewer Irish women than others; having generally found them the lowest, baudiest, foulest-tongued, blarneying, lying, cheating, as well as the dirtiest of all the harlots I ever had.

[In the manuscript the names of the various places where I had the women, together with dates were mostly set forth, but to do so here would disclose too much.]

I have probably fucked now — and I have tried carefully to ascertain it — something like twelve hundred women, and have felt the cunts of certainly three hundred others of whom I have seen a hundred and fifty naked. My acquaintance with the others beginning and ending mostly in the streets, with the delicate operation of what is called stink-fingering. Many incidents connected with these fugitive sexual amusements have been briefly described already, and on revision I find but few others worth noticing, tho some of them at the time struck me as novel. I expect that for the most part they were but such, as every man who with an amorous temperament has behaved in his secret life much as I have done, has met with. So to the flames with these short histories of amatory, fingering, &c. &c.

My sense of the beautiful in all things, which makes me now more than ever look to form in a woman more than to face, has shewn to me distinct beauty in some cunts compared with others. For many years — tho perhaps it did not absolutely determine my selection of the woman at first, I still must have been conscious of it — it must in a degree have determined afterwards, whether I had the woman a second night or not (gay women). Altho the reasons why I selected the lady for the second night's amusement are mixed and difficult to analyze, my recollection dwells pleasantly on those women whose cunts pleased me by their look, whilst the externals of those whose slits lacked attraction and looked ugly to me, I think of even now with some dislike. For years past this perception of the physiognomy of cunts has been ripening by experience and reflection, and now when I lift a woman's chemise, my first impulse is to see if her cunt is pretty or not.

I have in fact become a connoisseur in cunts, tho probably my taste in that female article is not that of other men. There are perhaps many who would call those cunts ugly, which I call handsome, and vice versa; just as they might differ from me about what is beautiful in form, face or color of a woman; and even about her style of fucking, her manners, language, or other particulars.

Not only is beauty, or want of beauty, to be seen in the externals of a cunt, but it is to be noticed when the fringed covers are opened. Many a woman looks well enough as she lies on a bed with thighs nearly closed, and the triangle of hair — be its color what it may — shadowing the top of the rift which forms her sex at the bottom of her belly, but whose vulva looks plain enough, seen when the outworks are opened wide, and large nymphæ growing from a clitoris protrude, and the opening to the avenue of love looks large and ragged. — Other cunts with small delicate inner lips, which merge into the general surface before they reach the small looking opening at the lower end, are pretty, and invite the entry of the prick beneath the little nubbly red clitoris. — The charm of color also enters into the effect. The delicate pink coral tint of a very youthful virgin, is much more pleasing than the deep bluish carmine — the color of many matured, well fucked, or well frigged quims, or of those which have let through them several infants.

The saying that every woman is the same in the dark, is the saying of ignorance. It implies that every cunt gives equal pleasure, an error which I think I have exposed before, and combatted with several men. The pleasures which cunts give men in coition vary greatly. Scores of women I never seem to have properly entered or enjoyed. In some my prick seemed lost, in others felt an obstruction. In some it seemed to move irregularly, meeting obstacles here and there, as if the cunt resisted its probing, or when a snug place was found for the tip — wherein lies all male pleasure — at the next thrust it was lost and difficult to find again. Up others my prick has struck their end before half its length was sheathed in it. Sometimes a pretty looking little orifice leads to a capacious tube inside, and is wanting in gentle pressure on the prick when within its folds. I have had some women, up whose cunts I have thrust a finger by the side of my pego when within it, tho it was swollen to full size, and seemed large enough to fill any cunt, and yet the vagina seemed a cavern to it.

There are cunts which fit me to perfection, in which my prick revels in voluptuous delight, from the moment it enters till it leaves it; in which it cannot go wrong, whether lying quiescently within its warm lubricious folds, whether the thrusts be long or short, quick or slow. Such cunts make me feel that I have an angel in my embraces. Others do their work of coition uncomfortably, making me almost glad when the orgasm is over, and leaving me indifferent to the woman when my prick leaves her. What my experience is, must be that of others.

I have either fucked, felt, or seen the cunts of a child in its cradle, and those of females of all ages between six and fifty, have seen them of all sizes and developments, and in color from pale coral to mulberry crimson — I have seen those bare of hair, those with but hairy stubble, those with bushes six inches long, and covering them from bum bone to navel. It might have been expected that I was satiated, that all curiosity, all charm in this female attribute had gone from me.

Nevertheless the sight of this sexual organ pleases me as much as ever, sometimes I think more. Little intrinsic beauty as it may have, little as it may add — artistically considered, — to the beauty of the female form in those parts wherein it is set. — Nay, altho at times I may have thought it ugly in a beautiful woman, it has still a charm, which makes me desire to see the cunt of every young female I meet.

This is the reflex in the brain of the joy that the penetration of the cunt has given me, of the intense mental and physical pleasure of fucking, pleasure which for the time makes the plainest woman adorable, and her cunt a gem which the mines of Golconda cannot match.

There is no more exquisite, voluptuously thrilling sight, than that of a well formed woman sitting or lying down naked, with legs closed, her cunt hidden by the thighs, and only indicated by the shade from the curls of her motte, which thicken near to the top of the temple of Venus as if to hide it. Then as her thighs gently open and the gap in the bottom of her belly opens slightly with them, the swell of the lips show, the delicate clitoris and nymphœ are disclosed, the enticing red tint of the whole surface is seen, and all is fringed with crisp, soft, curly, shiny hair, whilst around all is the smooth ivory flesh of belly and thighs, making it look like a jewel in a case. Man's eyes can never rest on a sweeter picture.

Then as the thighs widen for man's embrace, and the cunt shows itself in all its length and breadth, red and glistening with moisture and lust, all seen but the lower end where lies the entrance for the prick, which is partly closed by the ivory buttocks, and seems of a darker red, by the shade in which it lies, telling of the secrecy and profundity of the tube which the prick is to fathom, and in which it enters, stiffens, throbs, emits, and shrinks out whilst its owner almost faints with the pleasure it receives and gives, is there aught in this wide world which is comparable to a cunt? How can any man cease to have curiosity, desire, and a charm in it?

At such moments my brain whirls with visions of beauty and of pleasure, past, present, and to come. My eyes embrace the whole region from anus to navel, the cunt seems invested with seraphic beauty and its possessor to be an angel. Thus even now I can gaze on cunts with all the joy of my youth, and even tho I have seen fourteen hundred, long to see fourteen hundred more.

Of the physiognomy of cunts, and of their pleasure-giving capa-

bilities, perhaps I know as much as most men. Physiognomically
they may be divided into five classes, but a cunt may partake of the
characteristics of one, two or more, and particularly in respect of
development, of clitoris and nymphæ. I classify them as follows. —
Clean-cut cunts. — Clean-cut with stripes. — Lipped with flappers.
— Skinny lipped. — Full lipped — and Pouters.

Clean-cut cunts. — Are those resembling a cut through an
orange; the flesh on each side is full, thick, swelling up, turning in-
wards slightly, and forming a fattish pad rather than lips, altho a
tendency to the form of lips may be seen. Neither clitoris nor
nymphæ are seen in some, tho in all the flesh seems reddening as
the sides turn inwards and meet, showing the slightest coral stripe,
a mere hint of the red surface inside. This sort of cunt is most beau-
tiful in girls up to about fourteen years of age, just before the hair
begins to grow on them, tho they are to be seen in much older fe-
males. The pads of flesh are firm yet elastic, and that of the motte
— which is full — is equally so. This class of cunt generally alters
by age, but I have seen it in one thirty-five years old. There is
usually ample space between the thighs where there are these
cunts in full grown women, so that a man's hand can lay comfort-
ably between them, and grasp a whole handful of vulva. Perhaps
the bones of the thighs are set widely apart in the pelvis, but I
have seen and felt this width of cunt in short women.

Straight cut cunts with stripes. — These cunts are much like
the former, but the nymphæ are slightly more developed, as well
as the clitoris — not largely, but sufficiently to give a visible red
stripe between and seeming to open the outer lips. Sometimes the
red shows largely only when the thighs are widish apart — in others
it shows even when the thighs are closed. — In some the little
clitoris (not an ugly big one) just protrudes itself under the dark
hair which thickens just about the split, and an inch below it the
nymphæ are lost to view unless the thighs be wide apart. I have
seen this cunt in women up to thirty, and it is to me certainly the
most delicate, most refined, handsomest, and most exciting cunt. I
have nearly always found it in the finest modelled, plump, and
loveliest woman. — It is indeed the only class of cunt which can
be said to be handsome. A cunt is perhaps not a really handsome

object at all, tho sexual instincts make its contemplation exciting
and charming ,to a man.

Lipped cunts with flappers. — These have the lips usually fully
formed, the clitoris sticks out and the nymphæ hang out from it
nearly the whole length of the split down towards the vagina. —
Women towards forty have mostly this cunt, and if they have
fucked or frigged themselves much, the color is of a very dark
pink or carmine. I have seen it in women of nearly a mulberry red.
The nymphæ I have also seen hanging out of or projecting beyond
the lips, from three quarters to an inch and a half in depth, it was
so detestable to me, that it quite spoiled my liking for a really well
made pretty woman of thirty-five whom I once knew. Many French
gay women in the baudy houses get this sort of cunt, I expect thro
excessive venery. They grow thus oftentimes in women if they have
children. — It is a cunt nearly as ugly to me as the pouting cunts.
[Years after writing this I had a girl under sixteen years of age
and looking fourteen, with nymphæ hanging an inch and a half
outside the lips and a quite large clitoris. The nymphæ on one
side was much larger than the other, and her vagina would have
engulphed the prick of a giant. I saw and fucked her a second
time, out of sheer curiosity.]

Skinny lipped cunts. — These may be either with or without the
nymphæ shewing. Poor slim, youngish, half starved women with
thin thighs and miserable rabbit backsides, have this form of cunt.
It is not ugly actually, unless the nymphæ are too obtrusive, which
they frequently are, for many of these poor thin women have had a
child, and you may see the signs of that on their poor flat bellies
lying in a hollow between their ill covered hip bones — [women
with this class of cunt usually sham modestly, put their hands over
their gaps, say they don't like it looked at and giggle in an affected
manner. I suppose they are conscious of the want of beauty in
those parts.]

Full lipped cunts. — These are usually mature, they puff out
like the half of a sausage, then die away into ample flesh on each
side under a fat, fully-haired mons veneris or motte. Women fleshy
and well fed have them, and they look well and handsome between
the large white thighs and the big round buttocks below, between
which they are enclosed and lay. They were the cunts which I
loved most in my youth and long after. Mary, one of my first loves,

and Louisa Fisher had such cunts in perfection. — I expect they are most attractive to quite young men, for they realize the cunts which all boys — as I very well recollect — figure to themselves before they have seen the sex of a woman. The general effect of the cunt is that it is capacious. Women with this class of cunt usually allow them to be looked at and fingered freely, and smile voluptuously at the man whilst the inspection is going on, as if proud of their notches, and they like the men to look at and to appreciate them.

Pouters. — The lips of these cunts are like half thin sausages, and almost seem to hang down from the belly, so that they leave a furrow between the the outer sides of the lips and the inner side of the thighs. It is the ugliest cunt — and is still uglier if the nymphæ show much, as they often do. They look as if the owners were in a consumption. The hair on these cunts I have found often look straggling and thin — or if thickish, the bush is weak, long, and with but little curl in it. — Several times when I have found myself with a woman who had this ugly sort of genital, I have been unable to stroke her. — Pouters, like the thin lipped cunts — usually belong to women, lanky, thin, poor, ill fed and not too young, poor, short, skinny arsed seamstresses, those whose bum bones you can feel. I fancy it is largely through want of nourishment in their case and frequently through ill health. — Middle aged, needy whores — those who wear veils and try to pass themselves off as thirty when they are nearer fifty — have them. — I have in my youth many a time been taken in by them, but never now go after a woman who wears a veil.

All classes of beauty may be found with one or other of the defects, for the variety in combination of outer lips, clitoris, nymphæ, motte, and hair in quantity, size, and shape is infinite. No two cunts are exactly the same in look, hence the charm of variety, and the ever recurrent desire for fresh women by the male. There is always a charm in novelty, it is born with us.

Luck. — Harry masturbated. — An orgy. — Two males and one female. — Bum-fucking intentions. — H. gamahuched by both. — Simultaneous masturbations. — Confession of sodomy. — Anus and pudenda plugged. — Sphincter and thumb. — Fucking cum cocksucking. — H.'s unsated lust. — Champagne and repose. — Amorous exercises resumed. — Baudy ejaculations. — Fucked out. — Voluptuous eyes. — Balls handled. — Prolonged conjunction. — Finger and bumhole. — More repose and more champagne. — Erotic fury. — All exhausted. — Finis. — Reflexions.

In August I went abroad, returning in October. — Beyond a visit to a lapunar, there was nothing worth relating. — Indeed my fidelity was remarkable.

I had been but little to see H**** since the last youthful virginity was taken. Going there towards the middle of October on my return, she had much to tell me. She had quarrelled with the "mean cur" (Donkey prick) yet had not absolutely broken with him. Her other lover was dead. With a little pressure — for she was really longing to tell me — I found she had gratified Harry and herself by letting the lad fuck her, and was frightened of Donkey prick knowing it thro the possible indiscretion of the lad in keeping silence about what he must have been proud of — lucky beggar. — She described his prick to me, compared it with the donkey tool and her protector's, told me laughing how the lad behaved at his first fuck, and whilst we were talking this over, a letter came from Donkey prick which was brought by the lad who was waiting for a reply. With that instantaneous letch, and recklessness of consequences which when they come, come more rapidly than ever, "Show me his prick, let me see him," — I said hastily.

The idea pleased her. "But I don't want him to know *me*." "Keep your hat on." — She would go and see him. I rubbed some black off a stove with my finger, darkened under my eyes, and made my eyebrows also darker and wider with it, put on a skull sleeping cap which I happened by mere chance to have in the pocket of my traveling suit, and also a pair of tinted glass spectacles which I had used on glaciers. Really I scarcely knew myself when I looked in the glass.

She laughed when she saw my disguise. She had written a letter to the Donkey whilst down stairs, and now thought for a minute. Donkey prick was going out of town. — Harry was to take the reply to him at the station, and dare not wait long to fuck her as I now suggested, or he perhaps might lose his place — Donkey prick being a hard master. — "I'll make him show his prick and make it stiff." — "All right." — On the landing she called him up into the bed room. — "Never mind this gentleman." He was scared at seeing me. — Then what followed took place as quickly as I write this narrative of it. — All was unpremeditated by either of us, one letch leads to another, I follow blindly the promptings of instinct when in this concupiscent state.

"How's your prick, Harry?" said she. He seemed perfectly flabbergasted for a moment, looked at me, then at her. — "Is it stiff?" — "No it ain't," said he — shamefaced in manner. "Show it me." — "No" — said he very solemnly and looking but for an instant only at me. "Why? you know I've seen it." — He grinned. "Do" — said I speaking in a husky voice "and I'll give you five shillings." — H**** said. "There, show it, and I'll show you my cunt." — He reflected — "I can't — if I don't catch him before the train, he'll sack me perhaps." — "I'll give you a cab fare and here is five shillings" — shewing it. — H. then without more ado laid hold of him and pulled his prick out, he unresisting. "When did you fuck last?" — "Not since *you*," said the lad getting bolder. — "Have you frigged yourself?" — "No." — "Would you like to see my cunt." — "Oh yes." — She went to the bed and lay down on the edge. — "I'll give you half a sovereign if you'll let me frig you" for that letch now seized me. — "There's luck, Harry." — He never looked at *me*, was engrossed with *her* and made no reply — his prick was not stiff.

H. pulled up her clothes. — At the sight of her lovely cunt quickly up rose his prick erect — a longish but thin article, perhaps to thicken, in a year or two — I seized and felt, then frigged it, he making no resistance and she inciting him. "Let me fuck you — do," — said he piteously, as I found by a certain vibration of his belly that he felt the pleasure. "No. You get the half sovereign." — "Open your thighs wider," said I, "pull open the lips" — for I wanted to make him spend over her cunt. She saw my game. — "Is it nice?" — "Yes" — "Shall you spend," said she. — "Yhes" — and his bum jogged. I felt him coming. "Bend forward, put your prick nearer her cunt." "Oh let's fuck," he cried as his sperm shot over her vulva, and I frigged till not a drop was left in his balls.

He put his hand to feel the lovely receptacle, but she arose and I gave him the money. "You take the letter and be off, or you'll catch it," said she. — In a minute he was out of the room, buttoning up his trowsers as he went. She laughed. "Fuck me, dear," said she going on to the bed, and shewing her mucilaginated vulva. — But I'd fucked her twice and couldn't again then, so without further word she frigged herself. — "Ain't we beasts?" said she as she washed her cunt. "No; I'll gamahuche you." — "Do. I've not been fucked for a week. Phil's away, and I've quarrelled with Donkey" — as we now named him. — "But you've frigged yourself." — "Of course, every night — I sleep by myself and read in bed till tired, then frig myself and go to sleep."

[It was a great piece of luck this to me and the next time I saw H°°° we talked over this masturbating frolic with the lad. She had been fucked by him twice, and the letch gratified, desired no more of him. But his youth and inexperience started in me a wish to see him fucking, to be in the room and then for us all together to do what we liked erotically. Before I left it had all been planned. The baudy episode — tho so long and prolix — is one of the remaining evidences of how this manuscript was originally written. It is too much trouble to abbreviate and I retain it nearly as it was written. It's the narrative of one of those erotic frenzies, which come over women and men when together, and they are heated by wine and lust.]

On the evening about a fortnight after, H. looked lovely in laced chemise, crimson silk stockings, and pretty slippers. — As she threw up her legs shewing her beautifully formed thighs and buttocks, the chestnut curls filling the space between them, relieved by a slight red stripe in the centre, never had I seen a more bewitchingly voluptuous sight. Rapidly my cock stood stiff and nodding, tho I was a little out of condition. — What a lovely odour it had as I gently licked her clitoris for a minute. But we had other fish to fry. "Harry's here," said she. I stripped to my shirt, then he came up, a tall slim youth now just turned seventeen. Quickly *he* too stripped, for he knew the treat in store for him. I laid hold of his long thin tool, which was not stiff, and he seemed nervous.

How strange seems the handling of another's prick tho it's so like one's own. "Show him your cunt." — Back she went on the bed exhibiting her charms. The delicious red gap opened, his prick stiffened at once, and after a feel or two of his rigid gristle, I made him wash it tho already clean as a whistle. — I'd already washed my own. Then a letch came on suddenly, for I had arranged nothing — and taking his prick in my mouth I palated it. What a pleasant sensation is a nice smooth prick moving about one's mouth. No wonder French Paphians say that until a woman has sucked one whilst she's spending under another man's fucking, frigging, or gamahuche, that she has never tasted the supremest voluptuous pleasure. Some however had told me that they liked licking another woman's cunt, whilst a woman gamahuched them, better than sucking a prick in those exciting moments. But erotic tastes of course vary.

I laid him on the side of the bed alternately sucking or frigging him. — H. was lying by his side, and he put his left fingers on her cunt. — I had intended to let him have his full complete pleasure in my mouth, but changed my mind. Then we laid together on the bed — head to tail — making what the French call sixty-nine or *tête-bêche*, and we sucked each other's pricks. — He was pleased with the performance. — H. laying by our side said she should frig herself. Whether she did or not I can't say, being too much engrossed with minetting his doodle. — He did not irruminate me with skill, and after a little time we ceased and his prick drooped.

Then I mounted his belly as he lay on his back, and showed H. how I used to rub pricks with Miss F°°z°r's young man, and putting both pricks together made H. clutch them as well as she could with one hand. — But two ballocks were too large for her hand. — Then came on a desire of long standing, that of feeling the sensation of a prick up my own bumhole. — He consented to operate without hesitation. These erotic tricks will give H. something

new to think of when she frigs herself in the morning — as she
says she usually does before she gets up. Her delight in our per-
formance was immense, she felt us about everywhere, looked every-
where and gave herself gentle frigs at times as well.

His prick was much smaller than mine, and according to H.'s
opinion what would be called a small prick. It was in size like a
longish thin beef sausage, and as I thought just the size for me.
So wetting my bum hole and feeling nervous, I laid down on my
backside on the edge of the bed lifting up my thighs, choosing
that position so as to watch his face whilst he spent. — We could not
manage it that way, I turned my rump round, H. delighted guided
his prick to the orifice, and at one thrust he went half way up. A
revulsion came instantly, "Pull it out," I cried. — Out it came, she
laughed and there it ended. — I did not feel pleased with myself
at all. — What is the good of my philosophy?

H°l°n's fingers had been feeling her own quim, almost the
entire time since we had all been together, and her face now looked
wild with voluptuousness. — She cried out "Fuck me, fuck me" and
threw herself on the edge of the bed, thighs distended, cunt gaping.
But I knew my powers were too small that night to expedite my
pleasure crises, and wished to prolong the erotic excitement, so
would not fuck her nor let him. — But I gamahuched her. Then
he did the same. She lay full length on the bed, he knelt between
her legs, and whilst he plied his tongue upon her vulva, I laid on
my back between her legs and his, and took his prick in my mouth.
I felt her legs trembling and heard her sighs of delight, she was
entering into the erotic amusement with heart and soul, cunt and
bum hole as well, as I knew by her movements, ejaculations, and
then tranquillity. She spent just as a rapid ramming of his prick
between my tongue and palate, told me he was about to spend
also. So I rejected his tool quickly.

With rigid prick and incited by H. he continued licking her
cunt till she spent again. Then I laid them both side by side on the
edge of the bed, he began frigging *her*, and I frigging *him*. — "It's
coming" said he, and at the instant out shot his sperm in four or
five quick spurts, the first going nearly up to his breast. — How the
young beggar's legs quivered as his juice left him. Nelly leant over
and looked as he spent. — His sperm was thinner than it should
have been, tho he said he had neither fucked for a fortnight, nor

frigged himself for a week. I believed he lied. — My sperm would have been at his age thicker after a week's abstinence. The last time he had fucked her before me it was much more and thicker. He reaffirmed that he had not spent for a week, and she declared he had not fucked *her*, so I suppose it was true.

He washed and pissed, again I played with his doodle and questioned him. He had he said buggered a man once, and frigged one. — Now he had a nice young woman, who let him have her for half a crown when he could afford it, but he only earned a pound a week and had to keep herself out of that. His prick was soon stiff again. — He gave her cunt another lick, and then we went to work in the way I had arranged with her when by ourselves. He did not know our game.

H. in our many conversations on erotic whims and fancies, had expressed a great desire to have two pricks up her orifices at the same time. She wanted to know if it were possible, if sexual pleasure was increased by the simultaneous plugging of cunt and bumhole, and wondered if it would increase the pleasure of the man. I had shewn her pictures of the positions in which the three placed themselves for the double coupling, and we arranged to try that evening. He was not now to know what we were at, his inexperience coupled with his excitement at being fucked by a most lovely creature, were calculated to leave him in the dark as to the operations at her back door. But we were obliged to be cautious.

He laid on the bedside his legs hanging down, whilst she standing with legs distended and enclosing his, leant over him — I watched the operation from the floor kneeling, and saw his doodle going up and down her cunt. Then when we knew his pleasure was increasing, I lubricated her bumhole with my spittle, and rising pressed my pego between her buttocks and against his prick, touching it from time to time as she moved her cunt on it. I did this as a blind. Soon after. "Do you feel my prick?" said I. "Yes." — He didn't, for I was then putting my finger against it, but he was too engrossed with his pleasure to notice it. Then she backed her rump artfully, and his prick came out, as she pushed her buttocks towards me, and she kept on talking to him whilst making a show of introducing his pego again to her pudenda.

At the first push my prick failed. It was right in direction — for I had tried the orifice with thumb and finger — all inconvenient nails removed — and, knew the road was clear. — Push — push — push with still failure, and then came nervous fear. There were the loveliest buttocks that belly ever pressed, or balls dangled against, smooth, sweet-smelling flesh, an anus without taint or hair, a sweet cunt and youthful prick, and a woman wanting the supremest voluptuousness. Every erotic incitement to sight, touch, and imagination was there, but all was useless. My nature rebelled. Tho I wanted to do what she and I had talked of and wished for, my recreant prick would not rise to the needful rigidity — the more I strove the less my success.

I was mad not for myself but for *her* disappointment — it was *her* letch. — We had discussed the subject many times, and I longed for her to have sperm shed in her cunt and fundament at the same time. Further trial was useless, his prick was again worked by her, and I knew by her manner that she was near her crisis, when anxious to give her other orifice, the pleasure, kneeling I licked her bum hole then thrust my thumb into it, took his balls in my other hand and thumbuggered her whilst I squeezed his cods. She cried out. "Oh — bugger, fuck," — when madly excited and both spent. Then his prick flopped out.wet and glairy from her cunt into my hand which was still beneath his balls — I arose and so did sweet H. looking with bright voluptuous eyes at me. — He lay still on his back with eyes closed and prick flopping down, with a pearl of spunk on its tip. Then too late my damned, disgraced prick stood stiff like an iron rod, and could have gone into a virgin's arsehole twelve years old, or slipped into H.'s with ease. Sheer nervousness stopped it from doing duty, aided I think by a natural dislike — much as I desired the novelty, — novelty *with* her and *for* her.

The strongest fuckstress, with unlimited capability for sexual pleasure, the most voluptuous woman, the woman with the most thirsty cunt I ever knew, guessed my condition and state of mind. — "*You* fuck me, dear," said she, and falling back on the bed opened her thighs. Her cunt was glistening with what he had left there. — He'd not uncunted two minutes, nor she finished spending four, yet she wanted my prick — either to gratify me or herself.

Randy enough I went near and pulled.open the lips, saw the glistening orifice, pushed fingers up and withdrew them covered with the products of *her* quim and *his* doodle, and looked in her voluptuous eyes. — "Fuck — come on — fuck me." — "You can't want it." — "Yes — do me — do it." — Harry then roused himself, I caught hold of his tool still thickish. "Wash it, piddle, and she'll suck *you* whilst I fuck *her*." — *He* who only had spoken the whole evening in monosyllables, did that quickly. I laid him on the bed and she leant over him standing and bending, laid her face on his belly, her bum towards me. — "Suck his prick dear" — "I shan't." — She wouldn't, entreaty was useless, I could not wait, so opening her lower lips for a final look at the sperm, put my prick up her. — Oh! what a sigh and a wriggle she gave as I drove it hard against her womb. Her liking always was for violent thrusts, she liked her cunt stunned almost. — It gives her the greatest pleasure she often tells me. [When at a future day I dildoed her, she liked it pushed violently up her.]

I husbanded my powers, urged her to gamahuche him, hoping she would. — Her refusals grew less positive, and at last into her mouth went his prick but only for a minute. — "There I've done it," said she. — His doodle had stood, but drooped directly her lips left it.

She'd do it no more, but laying her face on his prick, wriggling her backside, saying, — "Oh fuck me — fuck harder — go on dear." What a fetch she has when she tightens her cunt round my prick and wriggles her lovely bum, it is almost impossible to stop thrusting!

But I would not finish, pulled out my prick and felt with pleasure its now spermy surface. I turned her round on to her back at the edge of the bed, and put him standing between her thighs. Then belly on belly, cock to cunt, all sorts of postures suggested themselves to me whilst they posed so, and I varied them till I could vary no longer.

Then I made him kneel on the bed over her head, his belly towards me. His prick hung down still biggish just over her head, whilst into her cunt I drove again my stiff stander and fucked, bending my head towards him to catch in my mouth his prick. She laid hold of it and held it towards me, I took it into my mouth and fucked her, holding her thighs and sucking him. — The young beggar's prick soon stood again — went half down my throat. — "Is his prick stiff again?" said she, spasmodically. — "Yes" — I mumbled. — "Oh, we're beasts — fuck me, fuck." — But as my pleasure came on her mouth pleased me best, I let go his prick, and sinking over her put my tongue out to meet hers, and with mouths joined we spent. — He had slipped on one side when I relinquished his doodle, and when I raised myself and severed my wet lips from hers — our pleasure over — he was looking at us, and she with closed eyes had found and was clutching his doodle stiff still. What a treat for the young beggar. — Thousands would give a twenty-pound note to have seen and done all this. He had the treat for nothing. — All was her device, her lecherous suggestion.

Then we all washed, drank more champagne, and after a slight rest we both felt Harry's pego. Taking it into my mouth it stiffened. — "Can you fuck again?" — "I'll try," said he.

Ready as if she had not been tailed for a month, her eyes liquid and beaming with voluptuous desire, she turned at once her bum towards him at the side of the bed, and gave him free access. I guided his pego, and the young chap began fucking hard again. — Then I laid myself on the bed, her face now on *my* belly, but spite of all I could say she would not suck *me*. Was she frightened that *he* would tell Donkey prick of her? Annoyed I arose, and slipping my hand under his belly, frigged her little clitoris whilst he was fucking her at her back, I could feel his prick going up and down, in and out her cunt, and felt even his balls — which are small. — From time to time I left my post to view the operators from afar, to see his bum oscillate and her thighs move. — It was a long job for him, but *she* spent soon. — The more she spends, the more violent at times seem her passions. — "Ah — don't stop, Harry — fuck — let your spunk come into my cunt," she cried as she spent. He didn't spend but worked on like a steam engine. — "Spunk — Spunk" — she cried again. Flap, flap went his belly up against her fat buttocks, the sound was almost as if her bum was being slapped by hand. — I thought he'd never spend so long was he in her, till I saw his eyes close. — "Are you coming?" — "Yhes." — "Ahaa — fuck fuck," — she screamed again, her whole frame quivered, then action ceased, she slipped a little forward fatigued, his belly and pego following with her, and there they still were in copulation both silent and exhausted. — Soon after she uncunted him, and without a word turned onto the bed and laid down — I looked at her cunt and squeezed his prick, felt madly lewed but had no cockstand — I dare not excite myself too much now — I was envious, dull at not being able at once to fuck her again.

She lay with eyes brilliant, humid with pleasure and a little blue beneath the lids, and very red in face. She looked at me intently. "Do it again," said she. — "I can't." — "You can, I am sure" — leaning on one elbow she raised her upper knee, her cunt slightly opening, and I felt it. He was washing. — "Put it in for a minute." — "It's not stiff." — Reaching out a hand she gave it a grip. — "You can fuck," said she edging herself to the bedside again and opening her thighs. "Do it this way just as I am lying." — I could not resist and put my pego where she wished it — would do anything to bring my prick to touch her cunt. — It was not three inches long — but directly the tip was on her vulva and she rubbed it there, it began to swell. Stiff, stiffer it grew as she nudged it into her cunt. "It's quite stiff," said she — I feared a relapse and set to work vigorously, sucked her sweet mouth, exhausted it of spittle which I swallowed and then we spent together, *he* now looking on. — It was an exciting but killing fuck to me — my sperm felt like hot lead running from my ballocks, and the knob felt so sore as I spent, that I left off thrusting or wriggling, and finished by her repeating cuntal compressions and grind, in the art of which she is perfect mistress. — When I first knew her and her cunt was smaller, she never exercised that grip even if she had it — now her lovely avenue tho certainly larger to the fingers, is fatter inside, and has a delicious power of compression.

Harry now was silent, and she at last seemed fatigued, yet sitting by his side began again restlessly twiddling his cock. There were evident signs of its swelling — I felt it, but my lust was satisfied and I cared no more about feeling it. We chatted and drank awhile, and then she laid herself along the bed as if going to repose. Not a bit of it — her lust was not sated yet. She put a hand on to his tool and said, "Fuck me, dear." He said he could not. "Try — I'll make you." H.'s eyes when she wants fucking have a voluptuous expression beyond description. — It appeals to my senses irresistibly — It is lewedness itself, and yet without coarseness, and even has softness and innocence so mixed with it, that it gives me the idea of a virgin who is randy and seeking the help of man, without in her innocence quite knowing what she wants, what he will do, and that there is neither shame nor harm in trying to get the article of which she does not know the use. Her voice also is low, soft and melodious — I was sitting when I saw that she was now in furious rut. — I've seen her so before — and she said to the lad "Get on me — lay on me dear." — "I can't do it." — "You shall," said she impetuously. "Lay on my thigh." The slim youth turned at once his belly on to hers. *He* had now no modesty left — we had knocked that out of him quite.

Wildly almost, she pulled his head to hers and kissed him, her eyes closed, her bum jogged, down went one hand between their bellies, a slight movement of *his* buttocks, a hitch of *her* bum, a twist, a jerk, then up go her knees and legs, her backside slips lower down, and by a slight twist she had got his prick into her. Then she gave two sharp heaves, clutched his backside and was quiet — her eyes were closed — I would give much to know what lewed thoughts were passing through her baudy brain just then, a flood of lascivious images I'm sure, whilst her cunt was quietly, gently clipping his doodle. She opened her eyes when I said, — "Fuck her well." — "Fuck dear," said she to him and began gently her share of the exercise. He began also shagging, but quietly. "Is your prick stiff?" said I — "Yhes." — A strong smell of sperm, prick, cunt, and sweat, the aroma of randy human flesh now pervaded the hot room, — the smell of rutting male and female, which stimulated me in an extraordinary way. I got lewed, my prick swelled, and for a moment I wanted to pull him off and fuck her myself, but restrained myself and put my hand under his balls to please my lust that way.

If he was a minute upon her he was forty. — Never have I had such a sight, never assisted at such a long fucking scene. She was beautiful in enjoying herself like a Messalina all the time — I squeezed his balls and gently encouraged him with lewed words, she with loving words till she went off into delirious obscenity. With her fine, strong, lovely shaped legs, thighs, and haunches she clipped him, he couldn't if he would have moved off of her. Every few minutes she kissed him rapturously crying, — "Put out your tongue, dear, kiss — Kiss. — Ahaa — fuck — fuck harder — put your spunk in my cunt." — Then came prolonged loud cries. — "Ahrrr — harre" — and she violently moved her buttocks, her thighs quivered — and after screeching. — "Aharrr" — beginning loud and ending softly, she was quiet and had spent. But a minute after she was ŏscillating her bum as violently as ever, and crying, "Spend Harry, spend — kiss — kiss — put out your tongue — kiss — you've not spent — spend dear, kiss" — and her kisses resounded.

I moved nearer to her, and standing, slid my hand under her raised thighs and gently intruded my middle finger up her bum hole. — Her eyes opened and stared at me baudily. "Further up," sobbed she in a whisper, her bum still moving. Then she outstretched her hand, and grasped my prick, and I bending to her, we kissed wet kisses. His head then was laying over her left shoulder hidden, he was ramming like a steam engine, and neither knew where my finger was, nor thought of aught but her cunt, I guess.

Again he put his mouth to hers, their tongues met, and she still holding my pego, on went the fuck. The ramming indeed had never stopped for an instant. My finger was now well up her bum, his balls knocking against my hand, and each minute her baudy delirium came on. — "Now — spend Harry — spend. — Oh God — fuck — fuck — bugger. — Aharrr — aharrr." — Again a screech, again quietness, and as languidly he thrust again she stimulated him. — "Fuck dear, that's it — your prick's stiff — isn't it?" — "Yhes" — "Your spunk's coming." — "Y — hess." — "Ahaa — spunk — fuck. — Ahharr" — she screeched. The room rang with her deliriously voluptuous cries, and again all was quiet. So now was *he* for he'd spent, and out came my fingers as her sphincter strongly clipped it and *she* spent.

I thought all was over but it was not, her rutting was unabated. "Keep it in dear — you'll spend again" — "I can't" — "Yes, lie still." — Again her thighs clipped his, and her hands clutched his backside. I felt under his balls the genial mucilaginous moisture of their passions oozing. His prick was small and I slid my finger up her cunt besides it. — He never noticed it. "Don't you beast," — said she. — "Give me some champagne." I withdrew my moistened finger, gave her a glass, filled my mouth with some and emptied that into hers. She took it kissing me. She was mad for the male tho she murmured after her habit. — "Ain't we beasts?" — "No love, it's delicious, no beast could do what we do." — He lay now with eyes closed, almost asleep, insensible, half only upon her, his face half buried in the pillow. — She raised her head partially, not disturbing his body, I held up her head, and a full glass of champagne went down her throat. — Then she fell back again and put her hand between their bellies. "Is his prick out?" said I.

No reply made she — I put my hand under his buttocks, touched his prick which was still swollen, found she was introducing it to her quim and it touched my hand in doing it. — I saw that heave, jog and wriggle of her backside, her legs cross his, her hands clamp onto his buttocks, the jog, jog gently of her rump, then knew that again his pendant doodle was well in her lubricious cunt, and that she'd keep it there. — "How wet your cunt is, H°l°n," said I. — "Beast" she softly murmured and began fucking quicker, tho *he* lay quite still. — Her eyes were again closed, her face scarlet. "Feel his balls," said she softly. — "Do you like my doing it?" — "Yes, it will make him stiff — do *that* again." — Her eyes opened on me with a fierce baudiness in them as she said that. — The exquisite voluptuous look, the desire of a virgin was no more there — delirious rutting, obscene wants in their plenitude was in them, the fiercest lust. — Up went my finger in her bum, —. "Aha. — Aha — God" — sobbed she in quick staccato ejaculations. —. "Fuck me dear."

He roused himself at that, grasped her buttocks, thrust for a little time then relaxed his hold and lay lifeless on her. "I can't do it, I'm sure." — "You can, lay still a little." — Still he laid like a log, but not she. — An almost imperceptible movement of her rump and thighs went on, ever and anon her eyes opened on me with a lustful glare, then closed again, and not a word she spoke whilst still her thighs and buttocks heaved. — I knew her cunt was clipping, was nutcracking his tool, — often times I've felt that delicious constriction of her cunt, as in baudy reverie I've laid upon her, half faint with the voluptuous delight of her embrace. — Some minutes ran away like this, whilst I was looking at their nakedness, feeling *his* balls withdrawing my finger from *her*, then gently, soothingly replacing it up her bum, frigging my own prick every now and then — none of us spoke.

Then more quickly came her heaves, he recommenced his thrusts. "Fuck dear, — there — it's stiff. — Ahaa — yes — you'll spend soon." — "Yes" murmured he. — "Yes, — shove hard — give me your spunk." All was so softly murmured and with voices so fatigued, that I could scarcely hear them. Again I took my finger from her bumhole (for the position fatigued my hand), on they went slowly, again he stopped, again went on, each minute quicker, and soon furiously rammed hard whilst she heaved her backside up and down, thumping the bed which creaked and rocked with their boundings, and the champagne glasses on the tray jingled. Up into her bum hole went my finger. "Aharr," she shivered out. — "Bugger — fuck — fuck Harry — quicker — aharr — my God — I shall die — y'r spunk's — com — com — aharr — God — I shall go mad." — "Ohooo" groaned he. Her sphincter tightened and pinched my finger out, another bound up and down, one more scream, then both were squirming, another scream from her, a hard short groan from him, and then she threw her arms back above her head, lay still with eyes closed, mouth wide open, face blood red, and covered with perspiration, her bosom heaving violently.

He rolled half off of her, his prick lay against her thigh dribbling out thin sperm, his face covered with perspiration and again half buried in the pillow and laying nearly a lifeless mass at once he slept. Her thighs were wide apart, no sperm showing: his spend must have been small. Both were fucked out, exhausted with amorous strain.

My strength had been gradually returning, and prick stood like a horn as I felt again his prick, and thrust my fingers up her lubricious cunt. No heed took either of my playing with their genitals. — I forgot the pains in my temples — cared not whether I died or not, so long as I could again penetrate that lovely body, could fuck and spend in that exquisite cunt. Pouring out more champagne I roused her and she drank it at a draught. "Am I not a beast?" said she falling back again. — "No love, and I'll fuck you." — "No, no. You cannot, I'm done and you'd better not." — "I will." Pushing the lad's leg off hers — he fast asleep — and tearing off my shirt, I threw myself upon her naked form and rushed my prick up her. Her cunt seemed large and wet but in a second it tightened on my pego. — Then in short phrases, with baudy ejaculations, both screaming obscenities, we fucked. — "Is my prick larger than his?" — "Ah, yes" — "longer?" — "yes — aha, my God leave off, you'll kill me — I shall go mad." — "Ah, darling — cunt — fuck." — "Aha — prick — fuck me you bugger — spunk in me arsehole fuck — bugger — fuck — fuck." — With screams of mutual pleasure we spent together, then lay embracing, both dozing, prick and cunt joined in the spermy bath.

"Get up love, I want to piddle," said she. I rolled off of her belly. — She rose staggering but smiling, kissed me and looked half ashamed. Her hair was loose, her face blood red and sweaty, her eyes humid with pleasure, and puffy and blue the skin under her eyes. She sat on the pot by the bedside looking at me and I at her, and still with voluptuous thoughts she put up her hand and felt my prick. — "You've fucked me well." — "My God! aren't we three beasts — I'm done for." — "So am I."

I'd fucked her thrice, he thrice. — She spent to each of our sexual spasms and many more times. During their last long belly to belly fucking *she* kept him up to it for *her* whole and sole pleasure, for she was oblivious of *me.* — She must have spent thrice to his once, for her lovely expression of face, her musical cries, her baudy ejaculations during the orgasm — I know them full well by long experience — were not shammed. That would have been needless and impossible. — The tightening of her bum hole on my finger told the same tale, for the sphincter tightens in both man and woman when they spend. — She'd also frigged herself, been gamahuched by both of us, and spent under all. For two hours and a half, out of the four and a half I was with her that night, either finger, tongue, or prick had been at her cunt and for one hour and a half a prick *up* it.

Impossible as it seems even to me as I write it — absurd, almost incredible — she must have spent or experienced some venereal orgasm — something which gave her sexual pleasure, which elicited her cries, sighs, and flesh quiverings, with other evidences of sexual delight, from twelve to twenty times. She may not have spent always, her vaginal juices may have refused to issue, their sources may have been exhausted after a time, yet pleasure she had I am sure. There was no need to sham, why should she, for she gained no more. The amusement was planned by us — so far as such a programme can be, jointly for our joint erotic delight. — Harry was but a cypher tho an active one, a pawn to be moved for our mutual delight, and nothing more — tho of course much to his delight — lucky youth.

I thought of the orgy perpetually until I saw her again three days after. I couldn't get to her before. — She looked smiling and fresh as ever, not a trace of fatigue was on her face, but she admitted that she was quite worn out that night, and had spent as nearly as she could tell, twelve or fifteen times, had laid a bed all next day, drank strong beef tea, and that such another night would almost kill her. — Never had she spent so much, never had had such a night before and should recollect it to the last day of her life. She hadn't seen Harry since and didn't want. — "We mustn't be long, Philip is coming to town tonight and will stop a fortnight, he'll be here in two hours, so get away soon." Her cunt had got its cherry red on it again, its delicate scent filled my nostrils and excited my brain, I gamahuched it, fucked her twice and left. — As I drove off I saw a cab with portmanteaus on the top going in the direction of her house. — Instinct again helped me, and stopping my cab, telling the driver to follow me, I walked slowly back, and when in sight saw the cab stop at what I suppose was her door. — It was, I found afterwards, her protector, and I'd been nearly caught there.

[Lascivious orgies I've had of various sorts — maddening, exciting, all — but for a refined voluptuous evening none ever came up to this. — To the last day of my acquaintance with her I shall recollect it. — We often talked about it together for some years after.

[I altered but very slightly the wording in places of this narrative, omissions were not needed. Would that I could illustrate it by pencil.]

Edith the frisky. — My bedroom. — Exhibition of a stiff prick. — Exhibition of a bleeding cunt. — My regrets. — Next day's amusements. — A week's work. — Departure. — Edith's grief. — Her history partly.

Edith was a complete puzzle to me. Does she fuck or frig herself, or play with women's cunts, has she any cuntal defect? She looks sensuous from eyes to mouth, she'll talk on sexual subjects freely but in a modest sort of way, yet won't let me feel her. Is she gamahuched by women? These thoughts passed thro my mind and that she had Sapphic tastes was my conclusion. Dressing for dinner, I determined on a bold attempt. Our seats were side by side, and when dinner was nearly over, I did what I've done, to half a dozen women, put my hand under the table cloth — which happened to be just long enough to cover it — and pressed her clothes against her belly as near her cunt as I could. She looked at me hard, and just then a gentleman on the other side of her spoke — she replied, and then quietly put her hand down and pushed mine away, without uttering a word, but looking at me intently.

After dinner we sat awhile in the reading room. She made no allusion to what I'd done. "I must go to Mamma." At length she agreed to come to my room. "I'll sit with Mamma a quarter of an hour first." — I got champagne in my room, and in twenty minutes, she was with me. She'd told Mamma she was going to the reading room to chat with some ladies. Then she smiled, looking full in my eyes. I seized and kissed her rapturously praising her beauty, and she permitted it. I scarcely expected her, and had resolved if she came to use no more hints and delicate phrases, but to speak baudily to the utmost of my wants, and of the pleasures of fucking; to get that pleasure if nothing further. It delights me to say the baudiest to a modest or quasi-modest woman. They all like it tho some profess to be shocked.

On a little sofa by the table we sat side by side. She took champagne, tho she rarely drank wine, and I showed the first photo. — "I won't show you any more unless you let me explain." — "I don't want it." — "But I will." — "No." — "He's ready to fuck her, isn't his prick stiff? How I envy them — let us do what they are going to do." She made no reply. — "Have *you* ever been licked so?" said I showing the next. — "Of course not." — But she looked confused, there was something in her manner what made me fancy that *that* was her letch. I went on exhibiting and commenting and explaining in the baudiest words, whilst she kept silence. At length she began to drink champagne as if not conscious of what she was doing, got excited and began to laugh and question. — "Mind, I'm your father" and I kissed her and she kissed me. — "A pretty sort of parent." — "A pretty daughter." — "Look at papa's prick," — said I unable to restrain myself any longer, and pulled it out. "Feel it." — "I'm going to Mamma." — "Feel it." — "I must go to Mamma." She tried to rise, I stooped, fearing to miss my opportunity, and got my hand up her clothes to her motte. "Oh! my God! — leave off," — she squealed out, and our joint movements turned over the slight table with the champagne, the glasses, and photos, on to the floor. I held her tightly, insinuating my fingers between her thighs and begging her to be quiet. "They'll hear in the next room." — She struggled silently. — "Oh, you hurt." — I'd got a finger on to her clitoris.

"You wretch to do that, I wouldn't have believed it." — "I'm madly in love with you. — Look." — Out came my pego. She looked me full in the face as I rose and flourished my erection. Again she rose to go as I showed it. I pushed her down and sat by her side, hugging her, begging, praying, endearing. — "What nonsense, dear." All was now confusion. — "I won't let you out," — and going to the door took the key out. "It's a shame to behave so." — "My love, no one will know but you and I, let me." — She shook her head. — "Well let me gamahuche you." "What's that?" — said she quickly. — "*You* know, lick your cunt to give you pleasure, make you spend with my tongue as *women* do to you." — "They don't, it's a story," said she fiercely. — "Hish dear, be quiet."

Swearing my love, holding her round the waist to me, kissing her and she once or twice kissing me, she pacified, tho still so excited as I'd never before seen her. She helped me to pick up the things, my tumbler and broken glass, wiped some wetted photos, looking at each carefully as she did so without remark; ever and anon staring at me for an instant. What was passing thro her mind? — Again I hugged and kissed. "Why don't you kiss me Edith?" — "There then." The table d'hote was early (for theatre goers) and it was light all this time, but dusk now was coming on. One glass remained in the bottle spite of its tumble. I poured it out into the glass and she drank it off at once. "Have more wine?" — "I don't care," — she replied in a reckless tone. — "Get behind the bed whilst it comes." She did, and I took in the wine without her being seen. Then sitting on the sofa she again looked at the photos rapidly, one after the other. I now pulled down the blind and lighted one candle on the mantel shelf (a feeble light). Again she gulped down champagne, but there was not the slightest signs of her being elevated by it, and we talked whilst still she looked at the photos, and listened to my plain remarks about them. Was she lewed, and controlling her sexual wants?

"Are you going to wait till you're married before you are fucked, dear?" — Nothing now seemed to upset her and she began answering, "I never *shall* be married," laughing cynically. — "Do it without then. — Now don't be foolish, let me feel you." — "I won't." Is she going to yield? passed through my mind as I put my hand down. She barely resisted, but crossed her legs just as my fingers touched the thicket. — "Now don't." — I couldn't get my fingers to her clitoris, her thighs prevented it, but roved my hand over thighs and bum, and up to her navel, feeling ivory smoothness, extolling its beauty, praying her to let me feel the slit. — "No — no — no," — was all she said, as she gently squirmed about on the sofa resisting me.

Pulling her closer to me — kissing her cheek incessantly, or her lips when half turned at times to me, she was quiet and seemed reflecting. — "Open your thighs — do, love." — "I won't."

—"Feel my prick — do." — "I won't. — Ceasing to feel *her*,
pulled it out again and still holding her tightly, placed her han
found it. — "Feel it, Edith dear," and for a minute only she did
I had withdrawn my hand from her thighs to do that, and now
had to get it back. She didn't hinder me, her thighs were no
longer crossed, my fingers went between the soft lips of th
warm nick, settled on her clitoris and there frigged gently. — "Oh
— take your hand away." Again she crossed her thighs imprisoning
my fingers, and stopping the luscious titillation. She'd felt the
pleasure, and knew she was drifting towards the irrevocable, wa
struggling with her sexual desires.

"Let me dear — do." — "Oh you hurt me." — "Now I don't
and won't — I swear I won't." — I fidgeted my hand, her thighs
opened slightly, my finger recommenced its gentle movement on the
bud of love, on the soft pulpy mass of clitoris and nymphæ — which
seemed large and full — till again she sighed. "Aherr — oho —
don't," and her face turned to mine. I put my lips to hers, put
again my prick in her hand, and again got my other hand up her
clothes on to her cunt and frigged away. — "Oho — ah — don't." —
"Feel it — frig *me*, love — let me spend in your hand." — "Aha," —
she sighed. "Let me fuck you dear, I'm dying for you." — She
sighed, she was about to spend, her thighs quivered, when with a
sudden effort she got up, let go my prick and dislodged my fingers
from their warm place. "I must go to Mamma," she said loudly,
almost violently. "You shan't." — "I must." — She moved towards
the door, when catching her round the waist with rapid effort
I pushed her against the bed, lifted her upon it, and threw my-
self beside her, talking voluptuously, swearing I'd have her. She,
now inert, didn't resist. "Let me go for God sake," — was all she
said. "Hish dear, they'll hear you." — Again I was frigging her
and had placed her hand on my prick, when she gave a strange
half cry, half hysterical laugh, she had passed the rubicon, meant
fucking. Who could wonder at it after all she'd seen, heard, and
done on that day — and all she knew?

No more was said. Lust at times works craftily and slowly.
I'd fears that a sudden shock might spoil my chance, but caution
now left me, all was a chaos of loving baudy words and deeds
the sighs of a woman with a sweating cunt, and wanting fucking
her fearing it, of a man reckless with desire and a turgid prick

y kisses grew more rapturous, attempts more bold, her resistance ss and less. "Don't — aha — don't — you'll ruin me. — Don't now," - she sighed as lustful pleasure enervated her, and my fingers oved quickly over clitoris and nymphæ. With a sigh her thighs en opened, resistance ceased. The moment had come, I felt my wer — how the male instinct tells! — Withdrawing my hand om the lovely aperture, tearing open my trowsers, pushing them wn, pulling up my shirt, freeing my prick and balls, rapidly I rned my belly on to hers, grasping a haunch with one hand, inting my prick with the other. — "Let's fuck, darling." Then my et lips met hers, closing her mouth. "Don't — no — for God sake n't," she murmured inarticulately as my tongue forced itself tween her lips, that lovely moist embrace of mouth and mouth. Oh — pray." — Then all words ceased.

Not a movement of legs, arms or buttocks hindered me as our ellies met, and my thighs slid down between hers widening them part, opening the road to the earthly paradise of humanity, she alpitating, with cunt yearning for a prick, subdued, utterly silent ll she felt my fingers opening the way for my entry. "Ho — ho," he cried sharply as roughly in my impatience I lodged my prick nd gave its first pressure at the gate of love.

Then thrusting, — "Ho — you hurt," she gasped. I had not en-ered, a barrier stopped my prick. I felt rapidly round it, was it he wrong path? — No, the tip was in its proper place. Again I hrust. — "Ohoo." — She's virgin, flashed thro my mind — thrust — hrust. "Ho — ho" — thrust, thrust, thrust — I gave rapidly and iolently — with cunt splitting force. "Ohoo," she moaned, as my rick with a plunge filled her cunt, and my balls dangled against er ivory buttocks. A virgin again, by Jove!! And for an instant rested.

Then as the joyous fact entered my mind, wild with delight could not rest an instant in my victory, my prick ready to spend or the last hour, plunged up and down her luscious cunt. — She'll leed — oh joy, that blood — and as that crossed my mind my perm seethed up, my prick felt bursting. — "Fuck — spunk — spend darling, spend," — I sighed, and the essence of life spurted out, topping all utterances in the ineffable pleasure of the jetting, nd my prick lay weltering in an emollient bath, was bathing in er sperm flooded cunt, to which she'd added naught but that

soft moisture which the voluptuous wants and urgings of her na
ture had issued before our bodies were one, before my prick ha
touched the entrance to her shrine. — Pain had stopped her plea
ure, barred her spend, ready as the flood gate of her temple ha
been to open. I'd fucked too quickly, so she'd missed the de
lirious pleasure, the glorious reward of her cuntal pain, of th
sacrifice of her virginity.

I was so astonished at the unexpected virginity, that for
minute or two I didn't speak. She lay inert with clothes up to he
navel, thighs apart, silent, motionless, excepting that she put on
arm across her eyes. Blood was on my prick, and signs of bloo
on one of her thighs, I put my hand broadly over her vulva, an
withdrew it with more sanguinary evidences of virginity that I'v
usually found. "Get up — wash dear, you are bleeding," twice
said before she moved. "I don't care," at length she murmured
a reckless tone, but got up, sat down on the sofa by the sma
table, and buried her head in her hands.

Then came over me a feeling of regret, a feeling similar
that which I had when I fucked my married cousin Hannah — tha
I'd injured her — and felt deeply sorry. But the thing was don
and after all she was as much to blame as me. What other woma
in such social position, had ever entered into such relations wit
a man as she had? — Must she not have expected to be tailed? —
These thoughts comforted me.

She sat so, without moving or replying for some minute
"Your chemise will be stained." — "I don't care." — Then she lifte
her head, looked at me earnestly and said, "I'm ruined," the
washed her cunt. — I put a towel between her thighs and sat dow
by her side again, saying that her "ruin" was nonsense, sayin
what I have to other virgins to comfort them, and absurd as
seems had comforted them. But this liaison was a peculiar one.
Never had I fucked a *lady* virgin before, and old enough to b
her father, and knowing that the consequences might be mo
serious to *her* than to women of a commoner sort, again I fe
very very sorry. Three fourths of the servant class and the cla
below them, have been fucked well before they marry, and y
the couples are content. The lower classes know well that a cu
improves in giving pleasure by practice.

"I must go to Mamma," — said she after listening long, an

almost without reply. That turned the current of my thoughts. She hadn't spent. What if she refused to let me fuck her again, repented and avoided me. "You mustn't yet." "I must, she'll wonder where I am." — "We haven't been an hour and a half together, I want to fuck you again." — She wouldn't — insisted on going. I caught her round the waist, kissed her and she kissed me. "Will you swear you'll come back?" — "Yes — yes, if I can, but I must go to Mamma." — She was so excited and resolute that I let her go.

Wondering if she'd keep her word, I put my room to rights, picked up some fragments of broken glass, let the chambermaid empty the slops. All was done in ten minutes. Then I lighted another candle, and sat down marvelling at the virginity I had found in a manner as unexpected as that of Phoebe's not six months ago, yet such was my luck. During forty years I had never had such two extraordinary chances, and both now came within a short period of each other.

In about twenty minutes in came Edith. "You've kept your word dear." — Then side by side we sat, and first she told me how she had humbugged her mother, but she must go back to her in an hour. Then all was talk of fucking, the photos were seen again, besides a dozen others which I'd reserved. With what sensuous delight she listened whilst I described them in baudiest language. It delighted me to say the words to a *lady*. Soon after in silence we were sitting, kissing, billing and cooing, she looking at times at my prick, I at her thighs, then feeling her still bleeding cunt, she handling my procreator from tip to testicles. What a delicious treat for us both, what voluptuous novelty to her. — Soon uprose my love staff — her bum moved with the sensuous pleasure which my finger generated on her clitoris, and gently I led her willing, ready, dying to be fucked, to the bed.

There she was plastic, silently submitted to be felt and seen — subdued by lust. Never did I enjoy a second fuck more. Not too full or too randy now, I kept my pego quiet up her for a time before I thrust, and we talked in this holy conjunction, she only too pleased to converse. Did it hurt her now — how hurt her before — was it really pain to her? Was the sensation of my quiescent prick nice? and so on. All was about our genitals, and the pleasure they gave mutually to their owners, in the maddening

yet soothing delight of fucking. Then thrusting and kissing her
felt her cunt stiffen round my prick — an exceeding tightness
it. — I knew what that meant, and in a few rapid, long thrust
lungers — hitting the profundity of her sex then nestling it in i
depths — with a long sigh of pleasure the tightness of her cu
ceased, a soft, lubricious, creeping feeling took its place. Edith ha
had her first spend with a prick, ere a throb of pleasure was fe
by me. Resting, I looked at her as with eyes closed and palpitatir
bosom, she lay voluptuously tranquil in dreamy pleasure. Out
pulled my prick from her lubricious sheath, rested, talked lewedl
reinserted it, and fucked till she and I both spent together. The
off she went to her mother, not waiting to purify her cunt. I wei
to bed. A luscious evening — never one more luscious — was ove

Next day as arranged we scarcely spoke in the dining roon
After midday meal we talked in the reading room. — Not a blush -
not a sign of modesty or regret had she, but quite cool, was read
to come to my room whenever I named a time. — A most extrao
dinary creature. — She'd tell her Mamma that she'd walk out wit
some ladies, actually did so, left them, and found her way back t
me. "Let's go into bed together." — "I'm frightened." — "Bot
naked gives the height of pleasure." — "I'm frightened." Yet she
risked being seen entering my room. I partially undressed he
With the coquetry of a woman, she'd the loveliest silk stocking
and boots on, making her legs look exquisite. With what deligh
I twiddled her cunt as we sat on the little sofa, where I had just
glimpse of her garters, and naked thighs, and she bending her heac
could see the florid knob of my piercer which she held in he
hand. — "Let me frig you." She laid her head on my shoulde:
opened her thighs wider, and enjoyed it whilst still holding m
pego, and silently thinking. It was an intense delight to me, exce
ling in its refined sensuality the erotic games with the finest ha:
lots.

Our passions fully roused by the delicate twiddlings and la:
civious talk — she listened but never replied baudily, — "Come t
the bed love." She rose at once with me, I laid her on the bedsid
lifted her petticoats, saw all her charms, kissed belly and thig
and motte, just gave the clitoris one little tickle with my tongu
then lunged my prick up and stood asking her how she liked it. .
cuntal grip replied, and lifting her thighs over my arms, we fucke
with fullest lust and love. My spunk jetted forth as hers was she

to mix with it, and with kisses, and soft dreaming murmurs we stayed in voluptuous silence coupled.

Recovered from our Elysium, still holding her body to mine by her thighs, genitals still joined. "Can you feel my prick in your cunt still?" — "Yes." — And thus we talked, till my scrotum stuck to her lovely buttocks with the mucilaginous overflow from her cunt. Then separating we washed, and at length she consented to my seeing quietly and fully all her secret charms, which in my excitement, in my hurry to enjoy, I'd only momentarily glanced at. First I looked at the seat of the hymen about which recent rupture there could be no doubt, evidences of her virginity were wonderfully evident, and it was sore still she said. How thick the broken membrane seemed to me. That might have been fancy, yet certainly I'd never had a tougher one to get through.

"Show me the photos again." — I did, we looked over and talked about them. — Never have I seen a woman so eager to see baudy pictures, she feasted on them, looked through them again and again. Then she felt my prick and as she did so, I felt her cunt. The soothing influence of my fingers was felt, voluptuous sensations crept through her. Then she sought fuller explanations, turned and looked at me, as I spoke the baudiest words. I told her I'd seen a thousand cunts. — "Oh! impossible." — Her interest became intense in cunts. — "Yes dear, and scarcely one exactly like the other." "Do many show as much as mine?" — She looked confused as she asked and turned her eyes to the photos. "Oh many," — which was a lie. So talking, looking at photos, explaining, telling her I had done all and seen all done which were pictured in the photos, she at last laid her head on my shoulder with a sigh. — She was lewed, ready to receive my prick up her again, and again let me lift up her chemise and admire her beauties. She seemed pleased to let me.

I was surprized to find her so fine a woman, well grown, plump, rather indeed inclining to stoutness. Her breasts were smallish but beautifully shaped, and with lovely pink nipples, larger and more prominent than is usual in virgins. The shape of her thighs was fine, they touched all the way to her knees, and the contour of her haunches was superb. Her little feet looked smaller and prettier when she was naked than when dressed, she was always displaying them enticingly when sitting, and wore shortish petticoats (not then fashionable) I believe to show her feet.

Her cunt and motte, covered with hair of the darkest chestnut — the color of that on her head — was curly, close, and about the silkiest that I ever felt. It curled so round the soft plump lips, that the cleft was in shadow all but where large and thick nymphæ and an unusually large clitoris protruded, forming a bunch which took three fingers to cover. Lower down the nymphae were soon lost in the cleft, and died away into the general surface of her cunt, but the large projection like a big red poppy bud partly opened, was to me very ugly, and spoiled what otherwise would have been a beautiful cunt. Was it always so, or was it the result of frigging herself? I never asked and shall never know — I swore that her cunt was lovely. She looked at me as if she didn't believe my praise. Had she seen other cunts?

I admired all, and indeed was enraptured with her unexpected beauty of form. — "Now you're nearly naked, be quite naked love, let's get into bed and talk." — "I'm frightened." — "Why? Your mother thinks you out — what folly." — I stripped myself and stood close to her, feeling her cunt and lifting up her chemise, she holding my pego. "Let our flesh meet everywhere, take it off, you shall, you must," and I began taking off her chemise spite of her resistance. Then into bed rapidly she got to hide her beautiful nudity, I with her, and after cuddling, kissing, feeling every crank and cranny. — "Your stockings, — I cannot feel your legs," — and in the bed I pulled *those* off. Both naked as we left our mothers' wombs I folded her in my arms. How exquisite is the embrace when man and woman are both naked, how the hands rove from knees to neck, and up and down and round, and into every cranny, armpits, bum furrow and cunt. Then our hands settled on the sacred implements of Venus, tongue played with tongue, all speech was lustful words, till I mounted her and we fucked with prolonged rapture, sank into a sweet sleep and slept too long. "Oh! What will Mamma think!" With one feel up her gluey avenue I let her go. In greatest haste she dressed and left, stopping neither to wash or piddle. What would Mamma have said, had she known the condition of Edith's cunt?

At dinner I was intentionally placed near some friends who had arrived — distance from her we thought might help to lull suspicions if any arose. A chat with her for a minute in the reading room afterwards. — "Have you washed your cunt?" She nodded and smiled, then went to her mother, and at about eight o'clock came to my room again. Again we fucked and she went off in twenty minutes, leaving me a wee bit fatigued with my exercises.

Next morning I reflected — I had come to this city intending to stop two days, had already stopped four, and had deflorated a lady who seemed ready to risk anything to be fucked. I had suggested caution which in a degree she observed, but — "I don't care what becomes of me," — said twice or thrice in a way as if social ruin stared her in the face, I didn't like. I couldn't stop much longer, and didn't want to get home fucked out, poking twice or more day after day is more than I can stand now. So, tho her exquisite signs of sexual delight when I was up her, her burning kisses, voluptuous sighs, her intense lovingness whilst fucking, gave me the most exquisite enjoyment, I resolved to save my strength and health a little, and to leave.

She usually breakfasted with her mother, but next morning appeared early on a terrace overlooking the sea. I determined to tell her I was going but hadn't the heart. She was going out with some ladies and I was to go to see her mother. I did, and found she was getting her leg well, quicker than the doctor had thought. Her brother was coming, etc. etc. This quite suited my intentions, and on leaving whispered "I shall be in my room at half past ten, the door will be open," — intending to inform her. Then I went to breakfast, had my tobacco, went to my room, and there she was.

My intentions vanished directly I saw her, my only thought was of her secret charms. What puts letches into my head I can't tell, but suddenly I wanted to gamahuche her. I had explained to her the meaning of the word the night before, and she'd admitted that her cunt had been licked by her Ayah in India, when she was not fourteen years old. She refused to let me, was in a hurry to dress to go out with some ladies, etc. etc. We were standing close together and I was feeling her cunt. "What have you put those damned drawers on for?" (She'd not had them on before.) "It's coldish this morning." — It was. — "I hate them." — But I felt her quim thro them, not wishing to fuck, hating to be hurried in that delicious friction. — "Let me kiss it." — "No." Yet in a minute she was on the bedside, her bum on my hands, thighs over my arms, my nose buried in her silky motte, my tongue searching for her clitoris between the large nymphæ, and found easily for it was full sized. I kissed her thighs, held them up that my lips might kiss and rub over her satiny buttocks, then her belly, then I nib-

bled at her love bud, licked all over the vulva, shot my tongue
up the avenue, then played it on the clitoris, sucking it in at times,
then nibbling it gently, till I felt her thighs begin to twitch, her
cunt slightly jerk up. Quicker went my tongue. — "Aherr." — "Feel
my head love," at once her hands grasped it, on went my tongue —
"Ahrr — ehha" — her thighs for an instant stiffened, then quivering
relaxed, a flush of cuntal juices met my tongue whilst still it lin-
gered playing gently on her clitoris, giving the fullest pleasure,
letting her lose none. Raising my head, looking at the moistened
vulva, opening its red lips wider, again to see and glory in the cocks-
comb edges of her lost hymen, I rose up. She was lying with eyes
closed enervated by her spend. — Ah the luscious tranquility in
mind and body which a spend gives both man and woman. Then
she quickly got off the bed pushing down her clothes, and for
the first time showed signs of modesty. She looked ashamed and
away from me with flushed face as I said, "That's what gamahuch-
ing is." — "I must go — what will they think of seeing me come out
of your room so often?" (I wondered too, for she hadn't before
seemed to care.) "Shall I buy some more photographs?" — "Oh, do,
do," with vivacity. — "Wash your quim, dear — let *me* wash it." —
Without a word she left the room, chancing whom might be in the
corridor.

All the remainder of the day I did nothing but think of fucking
her, of looking at her lovely thighs and buttocks, at her secret
charms again — and of the position I'd fuck her in. Then I re-
solved to stay a day or two longer, yet knew that I *must* tell her,
and leave at some time. Her manner was quite like one who ex-
pected the liaison to be permanent. What really passed in her mind
about that I know not, for when together, our entire time was em-
ployed in talking about copulation, its preliminaries, and looking
at photographs. Of photos I went out and bought another collec-
tion, met her in the hotel with the ladies she'd been out with, ar-
ranged that she should come to my room as before, soon after table
d'hôte dinner — at which I wasn't to dine — and she was to hum-
bug her mother. I heard that Mamma always asked about me, and
I began to fear suspiciously.

In the evening she came and took care to wait till no one was
about. The door locked, "Have you got any more photos?" were
almost her first words. Producing them we sat down, she looked

them thro with lustful avidity, whilst I had one hand on her thigh. — It seemed to me almost incredible, that such complete familiarity should have come about between us in so short a time, she unmistakably a virgin four days before, — but so it was — I told her I'd fucked a thousand women. "Oh what a story." Her mother had said I was a libertine by the look of my eyes. All this was seen, said and done, in a quarter of an hour, then, — "Let's do it dear." She rose up at once ready for fucking. What woman doesn't when it's a novelty? It happened to be an unusually cold night and I suggested bed. — No she couldn't be away long and feared her mamma sending for her. — But naked we got into bed, and fucked again, laid in each other's arms after feeling and fumbling our gluey genitals till they were dry again. Then I rose on my knees and made her pull my foreskin up and down, and then I put my fingers up her cunt as far as I could — all this with loving amourous talk — till again my prick was up her and again we fucked.

In the interval between our pleasure my leaving occurred to me, yet I postponed telling it. Our talk was so delicious about sexualities, that I hadn't the heart to say what I'd intended. There is no more delicious conversation, than when a man tells to a neophyte all his experience in sexual matters. How Edith's quim heated I could tell by the way she cuddled me, the way she clutched my pego and asked about other women's cunts — very curious about those — and much about harlots and their 'doings; and yet I couldn't get her to utter a baudy word. — She was certainly a curious one.

The rest of the pleasant yet in some respects sad amour, must be shortened. Next day in the morning I asked her to come to my room. — Visitors were out, the chambermaid had done the rooms — there are times when but few are in the corridors — when she came. "Edith dear, "I'm obliged to go to London," — I blurted out determined to get it over. — She stared at me with mouth wide open for an instant, then flopped down heavily on a chair, buried her face in her hands, and burst out into a flood of tears and sobbing. I awaited sadly, soothing as well as I could but could say nothing effectual. — At length she quieted and to some remark of mine, — "I knew it must be, and I've ruined myself," — not that I'd ruined her — I said that that was nonsense, but she repeated it, and that she should never marry now. We talked an hour, she

in much grief, begging me to stop a day or two for she should never
see me again — would I wait till her uncle came? We separated
without fucking.

She however came next evening and we fucked twice. How
she managed to humbug her mother at leaving her alone so much,
is needless to tell. I saw her mother in her room next day, and be-
fore I left am sure she had no suspicions about me. I waited three
days more till her uncle arrived, and we fucked twice every day,
and talked about that operation ad libitum and all appertaining to
it. Then I made her a present of the photos on condition of her
repeating after me the three words, "prick, cunt, fuck" — the only
obscene words I ever heard her say. Yet she'd a hot cunt, was
salacious to her bumhole I am sure. I frigged her once, and gama-
huched her every day after the first, besides fucking her. We part-
ed the last evening in tears. She said she loved me.

In our conversations, she told me she'd had three offers of
marriage *nearly*, but they were broken off, she never knew why.
She declared that no man had ever taken a liberty with her but me
and some school girls, that one or two female Indian servants had
gamahuched her, tho she'd never heard that name for cunt licking
before I had said it — which is possible. — I gathered that she'd a
sister in India and somehow came to the conclusion that both sis-
ters were illigitimate, tho I never heard such a thing hinted of
them. — Was her mother ever married? I wondered. — Certainly
she was a thoroughly well educated lady. The day before I left
Edith her courses came on whilst fucking. I congratulated her on
it, but as before she remarked, she said didn't care what became
of her.

[Three years or so afterwards, I heard she was married to a
very rich man who took her to Brazil, and that is all I know about
her. — It was a singular liaison, and somehow I have always felt
sad when I think of it.]

At the lapunar and peephole. — Alexandrine's advice. — Katie's instruction. — Marguerite's fornication. — Profits and losses. — A hairy arsed harlot. — About the propriety of seeing and feeling other men's pricks. — A double cunted strumpet. — Katie's eventful history. — England again. — Alteration in the arrangement of my narrative. — The philosophy of fucking virgins and juveniles. — H. lost and found. — Mutual friggings in a cab. — The snug accommodation house. — Baudy books and prints. — H.'s pleasure in meeting me. — Minetted by Misses R and Black. — Baudy triads. — A flagellation spectacle. — Three women and self. — An orgy. — Black becomes favourite.

Taking rest tho travelling, I reached the city of pleasure and was welcomed with open arms by Alexandrine, who still retained her post. There was much change in the woman-kind in the bordel since last I was there — a longish time ago — but enough of the old ones left to know me. — "C'est lui," — when I appeared in the salon. Marguerite was there as beautiful as ever, indeed still *more* beautiful in form. A wonder — for there she certainly has been seven years and more and Alexandrine tells me, never has less than five men, and frequently seven, in each twenty-four hours. "She makes much, as much as any three women. — But. Ah! — it all goes outside to some one." — "Un homme?" — "Je le suppose," and she shrugged her shoulders. I fucked Marguerite and told her she'd made a fortune. "But I spend it." — "How then?" — "In pleasure." — "Ah there is *un amant de cœur.*" — "Peut-être," — and she smiled. — She was a lovely creature.

I saw also about a dozen couples fucking, saw the Cyprians before it, enjoined them to shew off the men's pricks well, and was obeyed. The sight or a handsome stiff pego, I sometimes fancy now excites me more than the sight of the more secret female organ. — Why? — Is my desire to see this procreating tool improper or not? Prejudice and education in false principles would make answer. "Yes." — If it be so, then man made in God's own image, is in his nudity a thing to be ashamed of, and his pego obscene, filthy, abominable. Yet the creator has made him with that tool for the great purpose of peopling the world, of creating beings whom he then endows with souls. Strange that it should be thought abominable and immoral for a man to show it, or other men to see and touch it — simply ludicrous. — All males at some time have both exposed their own, and felt other men's pricks — perhaps only boys' pricks — but the act is the same. — Powerful organ which all love and women worship — why art thou called filthy and obscene?

One evening a nearly black haired woman came in to me, with a copious overflowing libation in her quim — fat spunk and lots of it. — I looked, investigated, said she might go, and proffered payment. "Mais baisez moi donc." — "Ah no I want it not." "But you must, you shall, you have not kissed me for three years." I had quite forgotten her, then recollected her hairiness which had displeased me then, and displeased me now. She was one of the hairiest in the region of cunt and bum hole I ever saw. From navel to arsehole, it was black, long, curly, thick, and hid everything. The gap was hidden by it quite, her buttocks were covered with hair up to the bum bones, gradually thinning off to those ossifications, but still black and thick. It must have been an inch long round her anus, and all jet black. It filled the hollow between cunt and thigh. As she knelt, it looked like the arse of a black bear and was ugly, yet such was her almost angry persuasiveness — such the excitement of novelty — that I fucked her, tho against my will as I did it, but I verily believe to her great delight.

"There is a fresh woman and she's two cunts," said Alexandrine to me as I entered one night. "Impossible." — "It's true, she comes from Marseilles and has been stopping at the F°r°y's and now is here." — I asked for Katie, and had a chat with her. — "Yes it is true, and she is in society now." — "Better and better," I said. "Let her come to me after." Awaiting her, I amused myself with Katie, who told me all about the woman till she entered.

I put her on to the bedside quickly. — She had heard of my letch — and opened her thighs. There was much thick sperm outside, what looked like any other cunt, and I said the *two cunts* was a joke. But Katie coming to my aid pulled open the lips, which so far resembled an ordinary quim, but down the centre of the cunt, was a membrane or diaphragm looking like one of the nymphæ, extending from the clitoris to the lower end of the split. The two proper nymphæ were in their place. I put my finger up. — "There is no sperm in there," said Katie, "look here" — and putting the central division on one side, there was the opening with sperm in it. I rapidly looked all over her two quims randy in mind, but was just then not strong, not well, and my prick would not stand. — Katie sucked it to a slight rigidity and I put it with difficulty up the spermy orifice. — It would not remain there, her cunt fell away from me. "There is not much spunk in you," — said I. — "Not much," said the Marseillaise, "it's all run out, but the Monsieur is waiting for me to go back." — So I let her go. She came back soon after with her cunt or cunts washed. — Excited and lusting for her, yet I now couldn't get my prick stiff at all so tried Katie's quim which didn't rise it, and in despair I left the house.

Next day I had the same two women. Kate, because being English she interpreted for me when my French failed me, and I learned all about the double cunted one. I saw her piss, felt one then the other vagina, felt to the top or bottom of each, rubbed the womb entrances, put two fingers, one up each cunt at the same time, and felt and pinched the gristly or fleshy division between the two. Every enquiry I made was answered with frankness. Katie gamahuched me, and so did "*double cunt.*" — All was again useless, I wanted the woman, yet had a dislike to her. So tipping handsomely for the trouble I had given, I departed again with flaccid tool, and without having this time even got the tip up either of the double cunts, or the single cunt, for I tried Katie's — I had done for myself by recent amours I suppose.

The third time I was better, and had had a cock-stand when thinking of the funny fucking apparatus of the Marseillaise. It was in the afternoon after a good luncheon that I went to see her, and had her to myself for a couple of hours.

She was a well grown woman say five feet six high with firm fleshy large buttocks, scarcely any waist, good shoulders, large firm breasts, and full sized thighs. From knees to ankles the legs were

hairy and ugly. She had dark hair on her head, and a slight dark-
ish moustache on her mouth, and dark eyes. Her face had a some-
what sad expression in it. — The hair of her motte had the growth
of a woman of thirty and was very dark. She said she was twenty-
three. — There was scarcely a sign of hair by her anus. Her cunt
may be likened to one of the short leathern purses like a bag,
which opens with a clasp, and shews inside a division or central
pocket, with a pocket on each side of it. The cunt had the central
division only and two pockets only, that is, a cunt — on each side.
The centre division looked like one of the nymphæ, but there were
nymphæ of the ordinary size and usual place, just within the outer
lips — I am certain that a man not knowing of the peculiar physical
conformation of the woman, might have put his prick up one of the
cunts, fucked and finished, without knowing that another cunt was
by the side of his penis — always supposing that he had been lewed
and full of sperm when he began feeling, looking, and fucking. In
brief, in the usual physical condition of a healthy man when want-
ing a woman.

From what she told me on this and another occasion, she did
not seem to have been conscious of her peculiar conformation till
her menses began to show. She had them now from one cunt after
the other — never at the same time from both. Each lasted about
three days — under her true clitoris, but lower down and on either
side of the central division of the two vaginas, were two little piss
ducts, and she pissed first from one and then from the other. —
These piddle openings were not just inside and near to the vaginas
or prick holes as in most women, but higher above them tho both
were hidden partially by the diaphragm dividing the cunts and
by the nymphæ and outer lips. I am sorry I did not see her piss.

She had pleasure she said in fucking, but could not say the
pleasure was more from one cunt than the other. — She seemed
from her description to have had the usual alloverish voluptuous
sensation from both cunts when fucked. She had been in the family
way on her left side womb, and when four months gone and her
belly much swollen, the doctors told her parturition probably
would kill her, and so she procured abortion. — The central division
where it joined the real clitoris, protruded like a *second clitoris,*
the piddle vent holes a little lower down were on each side of it.
She could frig herself to pleasure and a spend on the lower as well

as the upper clitoris. Sometimes one cunt spent, sometimes the other, she didn't know which would spend when she frigged herself.

The doctors said that she had two bladders with two distinct wombs and adjuncts. How they were connected with her breasts for milk, they did not know. They warned her against breeding. — A person, a doctor, had offered her a large sum to go to America to exhibit herself, but she was frightened and refused. She liked whoring in her native land best. The doctors had passed implements and drawn off the water from each of her bladders as an experiment, to settle the point whether she had two bladders or not.

I forgot to ask her about her virginity. She liked fucking she said — and when she frigged either clitoris she .eemed to spend from one cunt or both, she could not control it, *but both cunts did not wet.* — Two friends once had her together. She stood over the one with the shortest prick, and the other pushed up her other quim from her rump side — the one she was on was well up her, but the other got his prick only a little way in, for it was difficult. Both spent up her and she spent — all three nearly at the same time — but she never could tell *which* of her cunts, or if *both* did, but she spent certainly. She was made so lewed when they did it she couldn't tell. Then both fucked her twice again, one after the other, both looking on alternately. "Yes, once in the other's spunk, the other time in different cunts." — "One liked fucking in the foutre?" — "Oui, *like you*," — said she with a smile. — She'd heard of me. — They were Frenchmen. — She was all the evening with them.

I saw her again some months after. She had then gone to another lapunar — all the clients at **** had had her. *She did not take,* few men had her more than once for curiosity. She didn't like them not to fuck her but many did not. — I went thro all the examinations again and heard the same story. — I got my prick first up one cunt then another, but could not spend, and after trying in every attitude came away without spending. — She this time told me that she'd had two virginities, one her lover took — the doctor who examined her subsequently had the second.

I was resolved to fuck her, visited her again, heard all over again and a lot more. My cock stood so I mounted her, I pushed my prick up her left avenue, then exchanged it for the right one. I wanted to compare difference of sensations — if any — and wheth-

er the cunts gave the same sort of feel to my tool as a one cunted
woman gave me — but over-excited again, my tool to my annoy-
ance began to dwindle and came out flabby almost suddenly. —
The abnormal nature of the female's organ in fact gave me a slight
disgust, but really tho curious, there was nothing in the slightest
degree — as I now think of it — disgusting about it. Again by the
help of her fingers and her mouth I rallied, and bringing her to the
side of the bed, I first looked at her quim from behind her bum,
then reversing her and lifting her heavy thighs up, I asked her to
put in my prick for me. — "Which cunt?" — asked she. "Your left,
the side you bred in." She placed it there, up went my prick, and
I left my sperm in the favoured avenue.

Her cunts did not seem as nice and smooth as the ordinary fe-
male article — but somewhat fatigued, not much wanting it, and
over-worked before — for my cock had recently gone into quite a
dozen cunts and mostly smooth with sperm and I had seen thirty
couples copulating — I was rather done up — I'd had difficulty also
in finding where this woman had moved to, so I was not in a good
state for judging, and felt all the time that I was fucking out of
mere curiosity.

A few months after I sought her at the same house. — She'd
left. — Then I asked Alexandrine, who under pledge again (she'd
told me before) gave me another address — but she had left, had
gone abroad they told me. — Perhaps so, and all Europe may see
this lusus naturæ.

[I have always regretted not asking more and precise ques-
tions of this double cunted woman — but the excitement caused
naturally by talking on the subject, and having the cunts at hand
and the naked owner of them there ready and willing to fuck made
me forget asking much which I intended. I should have written
down my questions, and asked them seriatim. — But that might
have scared her, and she would most likely have lied more than
perhaps she did, but as far as I narrate I think it is all true about
her. — I had Katie — the only English woman in the house, — to
interpret and aid me. But above all, Alexandrine, who had been
for a few years my friend, aid, and adviser in erotic business told
me a great deal.

[Katie had a wonderful history. From being an ordinary harlot
there, and first in London, then at Lyons, she married the nephew

of the mistress of the bordel, and was for a time practically mistress of the establishment — and would with her husband have inherited it, with an income as far as I could make out of quite three thousand pounds a year. Good behaviour in her lodgings got her that marriage and that position, prosperity upset her. — She became a drunkard, quarrelled with the women, and caused rows in the house (never permitted in a French "maison de tolerance"), was rejected and dismissed — of course still married — and as far as I could learn, she was afterwards sent to England a confirmed drunkard, her husband keeping her here. — Her name had occurred in the original narrative, but in the abbreviations those incidents had been destroyed — hence the need to preserve this short memoir of her here — an eventful history.]

My narrative is nearly finished, my amatory career ending. My sexual powers lessen tho still strong, but as the urgings of concupiscence are less powerful, opportunities seem not to occur so frequently and my sins against chastity grow fewer. The actors and actresses will henceforth be nameless or named wrongly for they are living and about. — The houses which gave me shelter exist, but must not be named. The amatory episodes were for the most part more briefly written by me than formerly, and need but little abbreviation. Their chronological order will not be quite followed in the interest of all the actors, actresses and self.

[Here is placed a loose paragraph — I fancy I have written a similar one before — but lest not so, it's well to preserve it.]

[How similar for the most part have been my temporary amours. How similar the behaviour of the women who have procured me the virgins. Whether L°°l°e, F°°z°r or others, all were similar. All the virgins were got for money. What pleasure also the Paphians had in enticing the lasses, and for their own lust in seeing the hymens taken — in inducing the girls to fuck. — What complete unanimity in opinion, that their little protegés would soon be fucked by some one if not by me. What tales they told me of the nascent desires, lewed wishes and erotic knowledge and habits of the girls at that early age, and the encouragement they gave to the males — mostly lads a little older than themselves and of the same class. — Verily a gentleman had better fuck them for money, than a butcher boy for nothing. It is the fate of such girls to be fucked young, neither laws social or legal can prevent it. — Given opportunities — who has them like the children of the poor? — and they *will* copulate. It is the law of nature which nothing can thwart. A man need have no "compunctions of conscience" — as it is termed — about having such girls first, for assuredly he will have done no harm, and has only been an agent in the inevitable. The consequences to the female being the same, whoever she may first have been fucked by.

The first week of my return I telegraphed a meeting with H. Getting no reply I went to her house which was empty. I telegraphed the scout, got no response, went there and *she* had flown, but I found that her letters were sent to a neighbouring chandler's shop — I wrote there naming an appointment in the dark near •••• and there found H. waiting. All was changed, she lived in the country, was not sure if she could meet me, but if so at great risk, didn't know when or where but in a week would let me know. We drove through a park which was on the road to her station and felt each other's carnal agents, I besought her to get out and let us fuck against a tree. She was indignant at the proposal, and it ended in our frigging each other in the cab, face to face, kissing and tonguing, to the great injury of her bonnet, and a little soiling of her silk dress and my trowsers. Who would care where sperm fell in such an entrancing ride.

A week after, a place of rendezvous was found, at a convenient snug little house where we met generally. — Before she'd taken anything off but her bonnet and I my hat, we fucked on the bedside with intense mutual delight. Directly I'd uncunted, we both stripped start naked and got into bed, drank champagne there, and fucked and fucked again till my pego would stiffen no longer; fucked four times, a great effort now for me, but not for her. But frigging and gamahuching always satisfied her as a finish — luckily.

Then our meetings were at longer intervals apart, which only made them more delicious. But I alas, am obliged to husband my strength more than formerly, so the long intervals suit me better. When next we met, we found that the mistress of the estab-

lishment had voluptuous photographs, pictures, and engravings by
hundreds, and one or two chests full of the best and baudiest books
in English and French. — We revelled in them that day for all
were placed at our disposal. — We sat feeling each other's genitals
between our fuckings, looking and commenting on the artistic dis-
play of nudities and erotic fancies, and wishing we could partici-
pate in such performances ourselves. They awakened ideas which
had slumbered in me certainly. She said in her also, but she always
declared that I had put desires into her head unknown before.
We were well matched.

Living far off now, without a male or female friend with whom
to talk about sexualities, more than ever now she looked to our
days of meeting, and hours of unrestrained voluptuousness. After
hearing all she had done at home even to domestic details — which
she was fond of telling as showing her domestic comfort, — lust
and love in all its whims and varieties we talked about. "Did you
ever do that?" "Do you recollect when I showed you °°°'s prick?"
— "When did so and so occur?" So ran our talk. How often he'd
fucked her or gamahuched her, how often she'd frigged herself,
the sperm *he* spent, and all the domestic baudy doings were told
me with delight, and similar frankness exacted from me. — Then
came wishes. "Let Mrs °°°°° get us another woman, you fuck *her*
whilst she gamahuches *me*," was a request made whilst after fuck-
ing, we laid reposing in the bed. — I agreed. — "Let her be stout, I'd
like one as stout as Camille," — these are the very words said fun-
nily enough in a half shamed faced way — for absence and the
change in her circumstances, at first seemed to impose some stupid
modesty on her. — But both of us liked to call a spade a spade.

All was accomplished. The abbess as I shall call her, we ascer-
tained would procure us every pleasure, tho only cautiously and
from time to time she disclosed her powers. A very plump and al-
most fat, handsome woman of two and twenty was our first com-
panion. — "Don't let *me* ask her, *you* say that *you* want her to lick
my cunt — I don't want her to think that *I* wish it," — said H. So it
was done, we had champagne, I stripped the plump one, then asked
H. to look at her quim — which she was longing to do — and then
incited her to the gamahuche. Baudy talk and wine raising our
lust made us friends soon, and Miss R. jumped at the idea of gama-
huching the other. Then naked all three (warm weather now),

Looking-glasses arranged so that H. could see all, she laid on the bed-side whilst R. gamahuched her. On the bed by H.'s side I also laid, she frigging me during her pleasure. "Aha — God — lick quicker. — I'm spending," — and she spent nearly pulling my prick off during her first ecstasy.

Pausing for a minute, R. recommenced, for H. likes to continue uninterruptedly at that luscious game, till she has spent at least twice. It was a lovely sight to see H. with her beautiful thighs, and the coral little gash set in the lovely chestnut hair, which R. held open for a minute to admire. Then her mouth set greedily upon it, her hands under H.'s buttocks, the dark hair of R.'s armpits just peeping, her big white buttocks nearly touching her heels. I stooped down this time and peeped along the furrow past the bumhole, and could just see the red end of her cunt with the short crisp hair around it. Then straddling across her waist, my prick laying on her back between her blade bones, I watched the lovely face of H. which in her sexual ecstasy is a lovely sight. "Fuck, her," she cried to me. But I wouldn't. Next minute saw H.'s lovely eyes fixed on mine, whilst with soft cries she spent.

A rest, more champagne, a discourse about the pleasures of woman cunt licking woman and of men doing it, and H. again was on the bed. — "Oh, I'm so lewed I want a fuck so," said R. — "He'll fuck you, won't you?" — I complied. Further back on the bed now the better to reach her cunt with her tongue, with pillows under her head lay H. when R. recommenced her lingual exercise on the sweet and fresh-washed quim. I standing up now at R.'s back. — "Fuck her, and spend when I do," said H. — R.'s bum towards me was almost too fat an one as she bent, so I made her bend lower, and then between the buttock went my prick, dividing two well haired, very fat lips of her sanctum of pleasure. She adjusted her height to the exercise when my tip was well lodged, my balls were soon against the buttocks, every inch of my prick up a cunt deliciously lubricated by its owner's randiness. — "It's up her cunt love," I cried, began fucking and R. began gamahuching. All now was silence but the lap now and then of R.'s tongue on H.'s cunt. "She's coming darling — I shall spend," — I cried at length. — "Oh — God — fuck her, fuck, slap her bum," cried H., writhing and sighing. — My slaps on the fat arse resounded, as R. writhed and shivered with pleasure whilst licking on, and both of us spent as H. spent under the tongue titillation. Then with slobbered prick and wet cunts we got up. Soon after standing by the bedside I fucked H. whilst she frigged Miss R. Never were there three baudy ones together who enjoyed the erotic tricks more than we did.

These delightful voluptuous exercises were repeated with variations on other days. R. sucked my prick and took its libation whilst I was lying full length on the bed, H. kneeling over my head, I licking her clitoris the looking glasses so arranged that H. could see all. Another day I fucked R. whilst she frigged H. Then I put my prick into both women and finished in R.'s cunt, which completed that day's amusement.

Soon afterwards we noticed wales upon R.'s capacious white buttocks. It was from her last whipping she said. That disclosed what in time was sure to have become known to us. That the abbess was an expert in flagellation, that swells both old and young came under her experienced hand. Questioned, the abbess told us all, was indeed proud of her performances, shewed us the varied apparatus with which she either tickled or bled the masculine bums, and women's as well, or superintended men flogging female bums. Such as the fat arsed R.'s were preferred, tho some she said liked younger and thinner buttocks. Some brought and birched a woman whom they liked and fucked, some a special woman to birch them. They all paid very handsomely for bleeding a fair pair of buttocks.

R. told us that flagellation *of her* backside made her lewed an hour after or so. She liked the birch just to hurt slightly the cunt lips. Then if she couldn't get a man, she frigged herself — that some girls said it did not affect them lewedly — others that it did. — We talked quietly with the abbess about this. Both H. and I desired to see the operation, and heard that some men liked to be seen by other men when being flogged. If we would come on a certain day, there would be then a gentleman who had a taste for being made a spectacle, and she would arrange for us to see — for pay of course.

We went on the day but the man didn't appear. Two ladies were ready waiting to flog him. The abbess said it didn't matter, something had detained him, that when he disappointed he always paid the money for all concerned. One of them was dressed as a ballet girl, the other only in chemise, such were his orders. — She in chemise, was a sweet faced, dark haired shortish girl of nineteen, with fine teeth. We asked her to our room to take wine, and it ended in H°°° frigging her and my fucking her, then in my fucking

H., whilst she looked at the other's quim, and we agreed she would
be better for our amorous games than R. — I will call this dark one
"Black." She had one of the most delicate, refined, cock stiffening,
slightly lipped, slightly haired cunts I ever saw: it resembled H.'s
cunt years ago. Black took at once a frantic letch for gamahuching
H. — and who wouldn't? — When *my* mouth covers it, I can scarce-
ly tear it away from it.

At our next visit the flagellation came off. As H., who'd only
her chemise on, and I my shirt and wearing a mask, entered the
room, there was a man kneeling on a large chair at the foot of
the bed, over which he was bending. Over the seat and back of the
chair was a large towel to receive his spendings. He had a woman's
dress on tucked up to his waist, showing his naked rump and thighs,
with his feet in male socks and boots. On his head was a woman's
cap tied carefully round his face to hide whiskers — if he had any
— and he wore a half mask which left his mouth free. — At his back,
standing, was one youngish girl holding a birch and dressed as a
ballet dancer, with petticoats far up above her knees, and showing
naked thighs. Her breasts were naked, hanging over her stays and
showing dark haired armpits. Another tall, well formed, tho thin-
nish female, naked all but boots and stockings, with hair dyed a
bright yellow, whilst her cunt and armpits' fringes were dark brown,
stood also at his back — a bold, insolent looking bitch whom I
one day fucked after she'd gamahuched H. — tho I didn't like
either her face, cunt, form, or manner — but she was new to me.

What he had done with the women before we entered we were
told afterwards by yellow head, was very simple. He'd stripped
both women naked, and saw the one dress herself as ballet girl,
nothing more. Neither had touched his prick nor he their cunts.
When the door was closed after we entered, he whispered to the
abbess that he wanted to see my prick. Determined to go thro the
whole performance, I lifted my shirt and shewed it big but not stiff.
He wanted to feel it but that I refused. "Be a good boy or Miss
Yellow (as I shall call her) will whip you hard," said the abbess.
— "Oh — no — no — pray don't," he whispered in reply. He spoke
always in whispers. Then he said H. was lovely and wanted to see
her cunt, which she refused. He never turned round during this
but remained kneeling. Then after childish talk between him and
the abbess (he always in whispers), "Now she shall whip you, you

naughty boy," said the abbess — and "swish" the rod descended heavily upon his rump.

"Oho — ho — ho," he whispered as he felt the twinge. I moved round to the other side of him where I could see his prick more plainly. It was longish, pendant, and the prepuce covered its tip nearly. — Swish — swish — went the birch, and again he cried in whispers. — "Ho, ho." — H. then moved round to my side to see better. — Yellow head from behind him felt his prick. — The abbess winked at me. — Then he laid his head on the bedstead frame and grasped it with both hands, whilst very leisurely the birch fell on him and he cried. "Ho — ho." — His rump got red and then he cried *aloud*. — "Oh, I can't" — then sunk his voice to a whisper in finishing his sentence. — Yellow head again felt his prick which was stiffer, and *he* sideways felt *her* cunt, but still not looking round.

Then was a rest and a little talk, he still speaking in whispers. The abbess treated him like a child. I felt Yellow head's motte, she looking at H. to see if *she* permitted *me* the license. Yellow head then took up the birch, and H. and I moved to the other side of the bed. Both of us were excited, H.'s face was flushed with lust, I felt her cunt, and she my pego, now stiff. "Look at those two," quoth the abbess. We, and both the women laughed. — The patient had turned his head to look, but could see nothing but us standing. — Swish — swish, fell heavily the rod on his arse, now very red indeed. — "Let me lick her cunt," whispered he, nodding at H. — She refused. — "I'll give her five pounds," he whispered. H. hesitated, but short of money as usual, at length she consented, beside she was lewed to her bum-hole — "I shall spend," she whispered to me as she got on to the bed and saying aloud, "Five pounds, mind." — "He'll pay, he's a gentleman," murmured the abbess.

Then was a spectacle such as I never saw before nor shall again. H. settled on the bed, thighs wide apart, quim gaping, legs over the bed frame, cunt close up to the victim, but too low for his tongue to reach the goal. The abbess, Miss Yellow head and I, pushed pillow after pillow under her lovely bum till it was up to the requisite level, and greedily he began licking it. I moved round him again, looking curiously at his prick which was now stiff. — "Let *him* feel it," he whispered more loudly than usual. I felt and frigged it for a second. Whilst I did so, swish — swish — fell the rod on his rump, which writhed. — "Um — um — hum," — he murmured, his mouth full of H.'s cunt. "Ahrr," sighed H., whose lovely face expressed her pleasure, for she was lewed. Yellow head laid hold of his prick, gave it two or three gentle frigs, and out spurted a shower of semen. Then he was quiet with his mouth full on H.'s open quim, whilst still Yellow head continued frigging his shrinking organ. — "Have you spent?" — said I. "Damn it, I was just coming," said H., jogging her cunt still up against his mouth, wild for her spend. But he was lifeless, all desire to lick her had gone.

At a hint from the abbess we went to our bed-room. — "Fuck me." — On the bed she got, her cunt wet with his saliva, my prick nodding its wants and lust, up I plunged it in her wet cunt, thrust my tongue into her sweet mouth, our salivas poured into each other's, and we spent in rapture, almost before we had began the glorious to and fro of my prick in her lubricious avenue.

Neither of us had seen such a sight before, never had either of us even seen any one flogged, and we talked about it till the abbess came up. The man had left, but only gave three sovereigns for H.'s complaisance. "No doubt she's kept the other two," — said H. afterwards. The young ladies were still below, would we like to have a chat with them? Our passions were well roused, H. at once said "Yes," and up they came. We had champagne, giving the abbess some, then all talked about flagellation. The younger woman showed marks of the birch on her bum, and when the abbess had gone, we heard more about the rich victim, whom both had seen before and who was between fifty and sixty. He always had two women, but not always they two, they'd never known him allow strangers to be present when he was flogged, and he wanted to know if H. would whip him some day. (She never would.) Then we all four stripped, both women gamahuched H. and whilst the younger one was doing *that* I fucked Yellow head, whose cunt I couldn't bear. Then *she* gamahuched H. and I without any effort fucked up the other girl and found *her* cunt delicious. — In the intervals we laid pell mell on the bed together, topsy — turvy, — arsy — versy, and any how and in all sorts of ways, looked at each other's cunts, the two women both sucked my prick to stiffness but no further and Yellow head put her finger up *my* bum as I fucked the younger girl at the bedside feeling H.'s lovely sweet cunt whilst I did so, and as *her* rump was towards me I paid the finger compliment to *her* bum-hole. — We had champagne till all were tight, and gloried in most unrestrained baudiness in act and talk. We all pissed, and I felt their amber streams whilst issuing, and pissed myself against Yellow head's cunt, H. holding the basin. — Then fatigued with lustful exercises — H. excepted — we had strong tea, and went our ways. A veritable orgy, and an extravagantly expensive one.

Now it was very clear and frankly avowed by H., that our meetings were the delight of her life, that tho happy at home they were friendless nearly, and she looked forward to meeting me with the greatest pleasure, not only to tell me all, but to indulge with me in reminiscences, and have baudy afternoons with other women. "And it's your fault, you've told me more than all the men and women together whom I've known." — But there were hindrances. Sometimes two or three weeks intervened between our meetings at the abbess'; tho each meeting brought some baudy novelty.

When next we met we had little Black and not Miss R. for our companion, and Black and I together gave H. her complete dose of pleasure. Two fucks, a frig, and three or four gamahuches, some by me, some by Black, seemed the quantum which she called a jolly baudy afternoon. All were pleased, for B. loved gamahuching H., and being gamahuched by *me,* and tho so young, willingly sucked my pego to its liquid culmination. — H. still refusing to do that, or to touch B.'s quim with her tongue. — What with conversation about fucking in general — of the erotic caprices of men, of money gained and spent, sexual incitements, etc. etc. — in which conversations the abbess joined now at times — we passed most voluptuous afternoons or evenings. — But the cost was heavy — for the abbess' house was quiet and expensive, and champagne and a second gay lady added much to the sum total of the expenses of meeting H.

The abbess was the most kindly woman of her class I ever knew and superior to her business, her house the nicest and quietest.

An idle day in the outer suburbs. — Bread and cheese at the public house. — The showman's daughter Kit. — On the road. — Against a field gatepost. — On straw in a calf shed. — In a barn. — A masturbating miller's boy. — Epitome of voluptuous amusements with H. — A female trio and myself. — Copulation, fornication, irrumination. — Bum-digitation, cunni-tonguing, and cunni-dildoing.

Later on this year came other luck for me. — On a muggy misty morning towards the end of October, I was at a sessions house at the extreme east of London, having to my annoyance been summoned as witness in action of a friend of mine, against a farmer whose cart had damaged his carriage when driving me. On arriving I found to my further annoyance that the trial was postponed. This information sent had never reached me.

It was near a poor village, a couple of miles from the Thames in an agricultural district. Having nothing to do and not having ever seen the neighbourhood, I strolled about, went into the church and so on. Then feeling hungry — having left home early — entered a small public house, in front of which stood three or four showman's vans. Inside at the bar were the showman and wife drinking beer and smoking, and a fine, strapping, light haired florid faced girl of about seventeen — evidently a daughter — together with a much younger girl. I was amused at hearing them talk about a fair they were going to, and of "Jack" whom they were waiting for, who had gone somewhere to buy a donkey. — "I shan't wait much longer, it ought to a bin here afore *us.* — You'd better wait Kit, gie him another hour, and then come on if he don't turn up — leave word, he'll know where to find us to night, *you'll* catch us up before we gets to ***, we'll stop two hours there and grub."

I had ordered bread, and cheese and ale, things sometimes good from a small country brewer even at a village public house, and that food I like. They had also a morning's paper with which and the food I sat in the parlor which was at one end of a long bar counter, a tap room being at the other end. The doors of both were wide open — I'd seated myself there with my back to the street window, to read better, and also because the door being wide open, it amused me to hear the loud chatter of the showman and family, as well as to look at the daughter, whose sturdy legs and well fed, bronzed, but handsome face had made me speculate upon the beauty of her hidden charms. Then my cock began to swell, as she turned towards the mother, stooped, and by her movements I saw plainly she was tying her garters. There was no one to see but me and her parents, so there was no harm. But women of that class think nothing of tying up their garters in public, simply turning away a little from those near them. The exposure of a good leg is to me always exciting, I think of the woman's cunt directly, and did so now.

Whilst eating and reading and every now and then looking along the bar, the showman said again, "Damned if I wastes time any longer, wait for Jack an hour, mind." Then he, wife and child left. "Go and sit down Miss," said the landlord at the bar. The girl moved straight to the parlor. — "Not there," shouted the landlord, "that's the parlor, to the side." But the girl was well in the room as he spoke. — "Never mind, sit down Miss, I'm going directly." — "Thankee sir," and she sat down looking pleased. — The barman came, apologetically to oust her, but I said the girl might remain, that I was going soon, so he departed. In a minute we had commenced talking, soon after she was partaking of bread, cheese and bottled ale which I ordered freely and I was looking at her healthy handsome face, seized with what is sometimes called "a sinful lust of the flesh." My cock rose up prompting me so that I was obliged to push it into a convenient position between my trowsers and belly. — No one came in, for it was not the time of day for parlor customers, who are the *evening* topers in a village.

Was the ale good? "Ain't it just. We drinks fourpenny. —

Dad drinks beer." — She was delighted at talking to a gentleman
and fed herself with freedom and the utter absence of that ill at
ease, which I've so often found with servants whom I have taken
to dine or sup. She told me all about the show, she slept in the
last wagon with her sister. — "Mother and Dad in the other —
It's the biggest." — "And don't brother Jack sleep with you?" —
Her ruddy face grew ruddier, she was confused. — "Course not,
— there ain't no room till we are at fairs." — Then I heard that
Jack wasn't her brother. Another bottle of ale opened her mouth
more, and made me think how I could manage to open her lower
mouth. I heard that Jack was a sort of partner, was her cousin —
looked after the horses — went away the day before to buy a don-
key. They wondered why he hadn't arrived, but sometimes he
was away nearly a week when they'd business. — "Jack's your
sweetheart." — "Well what if he be?" "He sleeps with you when
you're at fairs. — "He don't" — "He does — "He don't" — "He
does." — "Well what if he do, we're agoin to marry and Dad
known on it?" at length she said, bursting out laughing.

Generally if alone with a woman I get some facts from her.
"I wish I was Jack, I'd marry you." — "Oh aint yer a lying stiff,"
said she laughing heartily. "Where's your next fair I'll come and
sleep with you." — "Oh ain't yer a chaffing, I must go." — "No,
give me a kiss." — "Shan't, I must go." — "Damned if I wouldn't
give a sovereign to sleep with you," I blurted out, ready almost to
ravish her. — "No, none a that sir please" as I attempted a feel,
after a kiss which she let me take. Then she gave me a sudden
push — A very strong one — and laughing got to the door. —
"Look," said I, randy mad and pulling out my flaming stiff pegó.
— "Oh — ain't you one." — She walked to the bar, but looked at
my cunt rammer long, and laughed before she went: I felt sure
I'd made her lewed.

Refreshed and meaning to have a look at the country, I
paid and departed, winking at the girl, she smiling in return, in the
way women do when gratified by lewed talk and sight of a stiff
prick. — Every woman is really gratified by a man's desiring to
fuck her, whether the desire be delicately implied, or quite coarse-
ly expressed. — "Good morning Miss," said I most politely. "Good
morning Sir," and I passed out.

I strolled along a country road, flat fields with large ditches and big uncut hedges in each side, enclosing large spaces of naked arable land with occasional pasturage as far as I could see. At long distances apart, was a poor cottage or two together, at places here and there a shabby farm house or barn. Scarcely a laborer on the road and a cart visible about every five minutes. A duller district I have rarely seen, it was dullness itself. Not a breath of wind, made a rustle in tree or hedge, all was silent, mournful, yet the novelty pleased me, and on I strolled smoking, sometimes singing and stopping every now and then. At last I asked of a chance laborer the distance to °°°°.

A quick tramp and heavy footsteps in the distance struck my ear; footsteps as of some one walking much quicker than myself. Nearer and nearer they came and on turning round, there was the showman's daughter.

She smiled all over her face and so did I — "What you, Miss, where's Jack?" were my first words. — "Oh — he ain't turned up." — "You'll have no bedfellow — you'll be cold." — "Shan't," — she replied laughing. — "I'll sleep with you." — "Will you now, ain't yer kind?" with a good humoured sneer. "Yes, and I'll give you a new dress." — "Oh — lor — who'd a thought it?" and she laughed heartily, as I did. There was a joking, yet voluptuous twinkle in her eyes which made me feel sure she felt lewed. — "Yes and would give it to have you ten minutes alone." — "Oh ain't yer generous." — "Yes and I'll give you this for nothing," pointing to my prick — at which she roared. "Don't walk so quick I shall lose that pretty face too soon." — "I must catch em up." — "You'll wear your boots out and it's going to rain. How I wish I were your boots." — "My boots?" looking quite astonished. — "Yes, then I look up and see what I'm dying to see, let me." — "Shan't, you beast" — and again she laughed, repeating "my boots — ha — ha — ha my — boots." — Two or three minutes more baudy chaff, and I'd taken half a dozen kisses.

Chaffing on more broadly still had made her quim tingle, for she now chaffed delicately in return, as we walked slower along looking into each other's faces. — We heard a loud crack of a whip, and a male voice loudly encouraging a horse, the hedges were thick and high with their summer's growth and hindered our seeing. "They're a givin it hot," said she. A field gate was near, we went to it, and saw an excavation in the field, into which ap-

parently a cart had slid and partially the horse which a man was
flogging to make it pull out and which with violent struggles it
did. Standing close together there I put my arm round her
waist, "Adun now," — but she submitted to a dozen kisses and
gave one in return. Then inflamed by hugging her plump form,
I put my hand outside her clothes and tucked them against her
cunt. "I've had it stiff ever since I saw you — let us." — "Adun
now I shan't" — but she didn't move from the gate. The man
and cart had disappeared, the hedge hid us partially, and still
I stood kissing, begging her to let me, she saying "I won't, you
shan't" but not moving. — "I'll give you a couple of sovereigns." I
would have given her more for I was mad with lust. — To that
she made no reply. — Gold, omnipotent Gold!!

Then as I always do, always did — I wonder if .all men do
— pulled out my prick and forced her hand to it. "There's some
one's coming — hide it," — said she scared. Sure enough there was
the tramp of feet and soon a couple of farm laborers came by
us, whilst we stood gazing over the gate, till they were lost in
the distance.

Again I showed it and she modestly shame-facedly felt it but
saying, — "I shan't," — I'd just got my hand between her thighs,
when, "Don't, there's a carriage coming." She was right, and again
my machine was hidden. — An open carriage with ladies in it
rolled past, the only genteel vehicle I'd seen. Again I kissed,
again pulled out my tool. "If you don't let me I shall spend" —
"I won't — we can't here — I shan't." "We can — only let me feel
it nicely darling." Next minute my fingers were on her clitoris. "No
— oho — no, we'll be caught — some one will be a comin by."
— I was frigging her hard, my prick standing out and throbbing,
she dying to be fucked.

Sure now of having her, certain that her cunt was thirsting for
my spunk, quickly I stepped out into the long straight road and
not a soul could be seen. Back instantly. "No one's about." — "I
won't there" — but I pushed her gently without resistance, for she
wanted a fuck — with her back against the gatepost, where the
ground was higher than in the centre of the gateway. She was short-
ish, the hedge grown uncut round the post hid us well — and in a
minute my prick was up her. She was young, strong and lewed,
my ballocks were full, and in three or four minutes her cunt had all

could give. We revelled in the conjunction long afterwards, I holding her round her solid naked buttocks, she tightening me to her my waist after she'd spent. We went on kissing, my cock still lingering in her, till she, "There's a man coming." — We both listened, prick and cunt still joined. — "I think it's Jack — it is. — Oh, don't let him see you." — Out came my prick, down dropped her petticoats, *she* went into the road and walked on, *I* got over the gate and hid behind the hedge, my prick hanging out. I didn't want a scene.

A man passed by with quickish heavy footsteps, then over the gate I got and peeping round the hedge saw him ahead of her, and she squatting and piddling near the ditch. — It wasn't Jack. joined her. — "I *was* in a stew," said she. — "You've washed your cunt." — "I ain't got no water." — "You've piddled, let's feel," — she wouldn't let me. — On we walked talking baudily as I could, delighted in doing so, she listening, at times laughing, for nearly an hour, till in the long distance I saw houses and smoke. — "That's where Dad stops." — "Let's do it again." — "We can't *now*," — said she, looking at me as if she wished we could. More people — all farm people seemingly passed and now appeared to look at us more curiously. It's not often that a gentleman and a sturdy showman's woman are seen walking together along a high road. But I had no tall silk hat on, a hat which declares class more than any other part of a man's habiliments.

We dawdled, I pressed her to fuck. She feared, said it was impossible, and we turned to another field gate. In the field it opened onto there was pasturages and cows about tho not in *that* field. A little way back by a hedge in the field was a wooden shed half open but with a gate, a rough place looking as if built for sheep by laborers, not by carpenters. Thinking it might suit our amatory wants, I got over the gate — for this gate also was locked — and opened the gate of the shed which was fastened by a rough latch. In it was a grindstone and a huge roller. An inner gate shewed straw. I opened that and out rushed a calf nearly knocking me over, which limped far away, for it was lame and quickly went towards a hedge where were cows in a field beyond. It startled me as I opened the door. Seeing that we could fuck there unobserved, I stepped out and beckoned her. With the agility of a boy she climbed the gate, shewing her plump legs and dirty petticoats,

and in a minute was in the shed. Fearing the animal had soile
its bed, I threw down some clean straw which was in a corner in th
entrance division, she laid down at once quite ready, and I thre
up her petticoats — the only thing she objected to and wouldn
have but saw fat thighs, a little light hair on a fat motte, and th
ever adorable split in her belly. Then I pulled open her legs. —
"Now don't do that." — I insisted and felt her cunt still soft an
lubricated with my sperm, and next minute we were fucking, I wit
the pleasure which novelty and a pretty young randy cunt give
me. — "Listen," said she stopping my thrusts and nearly uncuntin
me. But there was no one, we had left the doors open purposely —
I was just spending. "Be quick, I'm so frightened." — "Do yo
want it?" — "Yes, be quick, I'll do it soon" — and in another mi
ute her cunt stood (as some French women say) gave grind an
suction to my prick, out throbbed its mucilage, and her cunt gri
ping exuded its juices. Two minutes after she was back over th
gate, and after having closed the shed door I followed her. —
"Don't let us go to °°°° together," said she. — "Dad's there." —
"All right, here are two sovereigns." She looked at them wistfull
then angrily, — "I know what yer thinks me but I ain't." —
know that but take it." — "Thank you," — taking it she spat on
— "How old are you?" — "Just turned seventeen," she'd said it b
fore. — "How long has Jack fucked you?" — She colored up. —
"Just a year ago on my birthday." "He won't marry you." — "Yes l
will at Christmas, and I hope you ain't filled me." After our fir
coupling she let me say anything baudy, and I revelled in it b
she wasn't a bit baudy herself. — I would feel her cunt again. —
"Don't my thighs are wet." — Then she started off alone.

———————

I loitered till she was well out of sight, then started on to th
village where were the show vans, and Dad smoking a pipe outsi
a public house. He stared at me, as I sat myself besides him aft
ordering a glass of ale. Then I entered into conversation with hi
about shows and fairs. — "Was you the gent at °°°°?" asked h
— I said I was, he took some ale with me, and for three quarters
an hour told me the habits of his class. I saw Kit go in and out
a show dwelling, and into the public house, and once on an op
portunity winked at her, which she returned with a half smile. E

ally the vans with all of them went off. Kit walked by the side of
the second and nodded to me as she left. I wondered if she'd
washed her cunt, whether my sperm had been absorbed into her,
whether I'd *filled* her — A most delicious day I'd spent.

I'd walked seven miles, felt hungry, got some very tough beef
at the public house, felt pleased with my morning's work, then
thought of getting back. The landlord said there was a trap, but a
man looking a compound of potboy, groom, and coachman, said
that it couldn't go. — "As I'm to take M^rs **** to *** station."

The fly — old, dusty, and discolored, was to call at some gen-
tleman's house — I hadn't seen such a house on the road I'd
walked — to a station on a branch line. Time was no object to me,
so said I go by it as far as he could take me, and did at three o'clock.
— "Go along that lane past the mill, turn to your right and straight
on is your station, Sir," said coachman as I got out of the fly. Fol-
lowing his direction I was soon away from the high road, and in a
cart road lane went leisurely along, smoking, thinking much of the
hard rumped, tight cunted lass I'd fucked, till my prick stood
again, and I lapsed into a state of general lewedness.

I've often proved the truth of the adage. "It never rains but it
pours." — After a longish walk between fields I saw sheds and out
buildings, and then a larger sort of shed. — The mist had gone, sky
got cloudy, and rain to sprinkle, and having no umbrella I entered
the shed, and the first thing I saw was a lad not I should say six-
teen years old, white as if from a flour mill — which was the case —
sitting on the ground, half reclining against a heap of matting, and
frigging himself.

I was staggered and could only look. He, so soon as he saw me
began hiding his pego. My erotic tastes then (spite of my two
pudendal amusements) — blazed up again.

It is singular that now the sight of a stiff prick stiffens mine,
and reckless of consequences, not indeed thinking of them, I said
at once with a strong letch, "Go on, I'll give you five shillings to
see you frig yourself." — "I beg yer pardon Sir," said he sheepishly,
and rose up. — "Don't be a fool, I'll give you five shillings," and
took out a handful of silver. — He looked at it and grinned. — I
talked on desirous of seeing his pego, of seeing him frig himself,
erotic wishes flashed thro my brain rapidly, I encouraged him
baudily, the money tempted him. Monosyllabic replies now came

from him. — "Yes." — "No." — "What are you here for?" — "D'y
know master °°° of the mill?" Then after satisfying himself that
was a stranger. — "Gie us the cash first," said he saucily. — "N
not till I've seen you." — "Yer won't tell will yer?" — "No." -
"Look out and tell as if any one be nigh, and ye'll gie it us wor
yer?" — There was no chance of any one being nigh, for now
poured in torrents and thundered, but I looked out. Whilst n
back was turned he produced his prick and began frigging. The
I wanted to do the work. — "There, let *me*, and you shall hav
this," and I showed him a half sovereign. — "Take it." — He did.
fancied he might cheat me but he didn't — I took hold of h
prick and frigged it, talking to him all the time about cunts. — Y
he'd fucked two or three. — "But I cairn't allus get at em." — The
— "Oho — aha — its a comin'" — and out shot surprising jets
thick and thin cunt soothing lubrication. I frigged on till his pri
dwindled, wondering at his boyish strength. He seemed delighte
with the operation. To my questions, "Yes — I does it now ar
agin, It's a half day they've given me today — they are short
water. I said I'd wait here till another chap came." Then as quick
as possible I left him, wondering at my temerity, walked rapid
thro the rain to the station, arrived wet, but glad to catch th
train.

Now for brevity sake I epitomize the narrative of my doin,
with H°°° during this year and years after. At intervals we m
and indulged in every lascivious caprice. I had taken home fro
°°° a fine dildo which squirted liquids, and which it amused h
to be fucked with. Then I fucked her with it, licking her clitor
whilst I did it to her. Then Miss Black licked her clitoris whilst th
dildo was working up H. — Then with the dildo strapped on
her, H. dildoed Black. Then she dildoed Black whilst I fucked h
from behind. Then I fucked the pretty little black cunted la
whilst she gamahuched H. — Another time I dildoed H. whilst la
ing on her back, and B. licked her clitoris, and at the same tin
and unknown to B., — for H. objected to any woman knowing th
I played with her bum hole — put my middle finger up that tig'
anal orifice, and H. spent in ecstacies during the dildo fuckin
finger buggering, and cunt licking. I could feel whilst up her bu
the dildo moving up and down in her cunt, and H. grew a litt
fond of that double insertion. — We kept it to ourselves, tho oft

alking about it when alone, with her never failing remark, "Ain't
ve beasts?" and my reply, "No, beasts don't do that."

After that she dildoed R. who was fattish and big arsed. —
I.'s taste was for fat women to gamahuche her. — Then she frigged
R., whilst standing in the rear I fucked the fat arsed one. Then we
had R. and B. together, and I gamahuched H. whilst she frigged
both women who lay one on each side of her. Then the two quiet
trumpets — they were not street walkers — gamahuched each
other whilst I fucked H. All these pranks were reflected in large
cheval glasses, so that we could see every posture. At intervals of
rest we drank champagne, eat cakes and sandwiches. Every woman
as she pissed I made to mount the bed, and squat over a basin,
whilst I kneeling on the floor in front of her, contemplated the am-
ber jet from the crimson gash. How we laughed one day when B.
et a little fart when piddling, and how annoyed she was, how
modest, how she blushed — harlot tho she was — but it's a fact.

I now gamahuched H. as much as she liked it done to her:
the broad lick of her sweet vulva, the plunge of my tongue up the
soft avenue was delicious to me, but *her* great pleasure was in frig-
ging another woman whilst I was titillating her clitoris with my
tongue. Then I had a whim which she didn't like but to which I
made her yield. I laid on my back on the bed naked, H. naked
knelt over me, a knee on each side of my head, her cunt on my
mouth so that I could lick her clitoris easily, whilst I grasped her
satiny buttocks. Then one of the women — either R. or B. — gama-
huched me and took my libation into her mouth. In the glasses H.
could see all this. I with mouth on her cunt, and head enclosed by
her lovely thighs could not. I could tell always when H. was about
to spend, by the trembling movements of her thighs, and shiver
of her belly and bum, and her cry. "Oh — I'm coming — suck his
prick — spend dear — aha — spunk." — She used these licencious
ejaculations always now. She'd spend twice before I did once for
I'd usually fucked her once before, and was longer in coming than
she with her lustful capabilities. Indeed this double minetting was
usually the termination of the day's amusements, when all three
had been fucked, frigged, or gamahuched.

Of course as said all these amusements were not had on the
same day, this is an epitome of what took place from time to time
during this and a few years after. — Each day's amusement was

noted down by me soon after, but are condensed here. Our mere-
tricious tricks were nearly always played in the afternoon in broa
daylight, beginning soon after luncheon, and in a room on whic
the sun shone brilliantly most of the day; often times on prick an
cunt fell the warm sunbeams. The room was one where none coul
see or hear us, and where the amiable assistants got for us wer
mostly young and handsome, and who could bear any amount
light, any inspection of their secret charms, and who full of h
blood and the voluptuousness of youth, and stimulated by cham
pagne, loved the baudy tricks and spent freely.

And to complete this catalogue of letches, and delights, —
occurred two years later when when I first dildoed H. — I had a
umbrella with a smooth handle of peculiar shape, and H. was de-
lighted to let me fuck her with it till she spent.

Indeed most things that a man, and three women could d
together we did. What was wanting to complete the variety was I
to gamahuche me, but she'd neither do that, nor gamahuche th
other women tho she'd frig them till they could spend no longer. —
In after years once under pressure of circumstances H. took m
libation in her mouth, and once sucked me up to rigidity only.

At a Lancashire seaport. — A millhand. — The last night of har-
lotting. — At the brothel. — Singular beauty. — Singular history.
— Two frisky workwomen. — Caught by a rope. — Lewed talk. —
Lewed wants. — A handy coffee shop. — One pleasured, one
pained. — Another flagellation at the Abbess'. — A straight haired
cunt tonsured. — H.'s letch for novelty. — The barrister gratified.
— Fucking in masks.

In late autumn this year I was at a Lancashire seaport town,
and at about five o'clock one afternoon, wandering about looking at
the shops, noticed a well made, well grown woman, with an abso-
lutely lovely face and marvellously clear complexion — tho perhaps
too white — who was sauntering along doing the same. I stood
close to her whilst she looked at a bonnet shop, but she took no
notice of me. Was she a harlot or not, wandering about alone?
I'd had no sexual desire before, now in a minute it overwhelmed —
desire for her.

She was dressed like a genteel, poorish, middle class woman
excessively plainly, but the dress was worn with such an air of dis-
tinction, that for the moment I chased the idea of her accessibility.
— I followed her a long distance noticing the swing of her
haunches, and the way she placed her pretty feet which were vis-
ible — for her petticoats were short. — Her boots tho neat were
common and thick. She took no notice of passers by, nor they of
her. She cannot be a strumpet thought I, but a handsome offer may
get her if she's poor. — But where take her to? For I knew no place.
Abandoning half formed intentions, yet with a voluptuous pego I
stopped, and just then she turned round and retraced her steps,

meeting me, looking casually at me just as any other woman might. I turned round and followed her, still with undefined intention.

Again she stopped at a shop. I stopped too and remarked that what she was looking at was pretty. She quietly looked at me and agreed that it was. Her manner made me now think she was to be had. She walked on and I did by her side. — "How lovely you are, let me go home with you." — "Ah! No — impossible — good day Sir," and she turned round. Yet there was something in her manner — I knew not what — which faintly bespoke the courtezan.

With hope I turned round also, and walked by her side repeating my wish, asking her to have a glass of wine, and so on. — She begged me to go, was waiting for a friend, it would do her harm if she were seen walking with a gentleman. — Yes, she expected him every minute. — "I wish I were he, I'd give a couple of sovereigns to be half an hour with you." She stopped short at once and looked at me. "A couple of sovereigns! That *would* be a help to us just now." — She said this as if reflecting, as if speaking to herself. — Then again she walked on, I keeping still by her side but keeping silence.

"Don't come with me, I'm expecting my lad." Then she hesitated, then went on. "If he doesn't come by this, he can't come for two hours — tell me the time." — I did. "An he come, we'll be off together at once, if not and ye'll give me two sovereigns, ye may, but I ain't got no lodgings, I've given them up, for I'm off tonight and for good."

Then she said she must wait full ten minutes to make sure, she'd walk up and down, I was to wait at the corner of a street she pointed out, then if her lad hadn't arrived she be with me. — She spoke in broad Lancashire dialect, which I do not attempt to imitate, and which at times I could scarcely understand.

Never did ten minutes seem so long to me. — I counted every minute in a fever of impatience, pictured her secret charms to myself, wondered at split, motte, thighs, whether she'd fuck well, and if she wanted fucking. At times I furtively felt my pego which kept rising and falling with lust, and feared I should not have her, for full ten minutes had passed when she appeared. "Where shall we go?" said I. — "I've no lodgings now and only know a poor place about here." — I would have gone to a pig sty with her, and in five minutes the poor place held us. It was a little obscure house in a court, almost a cottage, with but two rooms for hire, but the bed room was comfortable with a good fire.

"My lad can't be here for two hours and a half now, there be'ant another train yet, and ye'll gie me *two*?" said she the instant the door was closed. — My reply was to produce the coins and put them into her hand. — "It will do us a power of good just now, and ye'll be the last." — "Why?" — "I'm going away to night to be married." — I scarcely heeded what she said being so impatient for my pleasure, and put my hand up her petticoats. She repulsed them, and I thought for the instant she was going to bilk me.

Not the first time that idea has come over me when with a gay woman. "Let's feel it." — "Wait a bit, you shall, don't fear." Composed in manner and as unlike a harlot as possible, she took off bonnet and jacket most carefully and then sat down. "Let's feel your cunt." — "I will." Stooping I pushed my hand up her petticoats, and felt the silky fringed notch. — "Ye're in a hurry" — laughing. "Take your things off and let me see your cunt." — "You shall. — You shall, — never fear — wait a bit." Slowly she took them off — I divested myself of clothing and showed my prick. — "Ohooo," she whispered, and stopped undressing. "Take them off." — "What, all? — There" — and she stood naked.

A more beautifully made woman I never saw, and for a minute was speechless with admiration, then folded her in my arms, kissing, extolling her loveliness, pressing my stiff prick against her belly with mine. — Then, — still both standing — my fingers were titillating her love seat, when quietly her hand stole down and clasped my pego, and so we stood silent, I'd roused her passions. "Let me see it." Without reply, on to the bed she got and laid with thighs apart. A hurried look at the pretty groove, a sniff a kiss on the motte, a finger thrust rapidly up and down the moist avenue. — "Let's fuck" — next minute we were embracing with voluptuous gentle sighs, my prick enclosed in her lubricious cunt and gliding up and down, our bodies one; and ah too soon, came tightening of her cunt around my prick, which throbbed and spent, and we lay quietly in each other's arms in soft repose. Then soon after. "You enjoyed it?" a foolish question but I always put it. — She made no reply, but patted my arse cheeks in an affectionate, coaxing manner.

I uncunted at last and she "It's cold. — Let me put on my chemise." She did, we rose, pissed, washed — the usual routine — then sat by the fire — tho it wasn't very cold weather. — She asked me to give her "a glass." — "What?" "Whiskey." — That was brought. I'd been wearing a cape which now I put over her, and put on my own frock coat over my shirt, then drinking we sat and talked side by side. The ecstatic sexual embrace cools desire, and for a time erotic curiosity is almost dead, but it soon revived in me, and I began twidding her quim. "I ain't in a hurry," said she then, told me her history, partly before, partly after our second embrace, but its told here continuously.

"Yes, a millhand, at a cotton mill." — At seventeen the young master "did me." Her father was an engineer at the mill, found it out soon after, kicked up a row, and a hundred pounds was given *him* as damages, for the damage done to *her* virginity. — The money unsettled him, he drank a bit, she left the mill, worked then steadily at home for a while, and no one entered her preserve, and then, somehow she "longed for a bit," she supposed — and got fucked again. — "Yes, for love only," and then turned harlot. A young man in the mill also a mechanician, knew her history, knew her father, found her out, fucked her harlot wise, fell in love with her, then fucked for love and she also with him. She saved money, and he saved a bit, her father approved and gave up what he'd not spent in liquor, her seducer had promised twenty pounds when they were married, and they were going to marry and open a little shop at °°°° where he'd found work. — He was coming there now to meet her when I had, if he could get away in time, but certainly he would get away in time, but certainly he would come by the next train. Her box was at the station, she'd given up the key of her lodging — that baudy house was the only place she could wait in "till I meet my lad."

"I didn't mean to let you — I've not done it for a week and told him I wouldn't, but money will be so useful to us at a start." — "Oh don't — you'll make me queer." — "Oh, don't talk of *him* — come on and do it then." Lewed she was with my talk, with titillation, and her feel of my shaft, and on the bed again we fucked.

She wanted it more than before, as I guessed by her clasp, the way her tongue met mine, her squeeze of my buttocks, her heaves, quivers and love sighs.

She was only eighteen and a half, yet her form was full and perfect as three and twenty. She'd the loveliest thighs, the sweetest little silky fringed notch, scarcely nymphæ or clitoris — quite a young girl's cunt. — She was proud of her shape and willingly let me see all, delighted with my praise. Her manners were utterly unlike those of a whore. The hair on head and tail was light chestnut, no dark stain was on her bum furrow which was nearly as white as her buttocks, and *they* were ivory. It grew dark soon after I was there and we had candles — for which they charged extra — and I held one to the furrow to inspect her whilst she knelt on the bed. Then after a time unable to tail her a third time, I gave her pleasure with my tongue, and never licked a more delicate clitoris. She'd a face handsome in her bonnet, but it was far more beautiful without it. Her eyes were dark blue. — She hadn't the slightest look or allure of a strumpet.

The whiskey made her talk freely, and we had lots of time. Five shillings was her usual fee. — "For I don't dress like swell ones." — "No, not often ten — I don't like speaking to gents. —I've only been three months at the business and don't like it— nor the gals." "Why did I go to millwork? Father made me so as to look after me, he said, mother didn't want me to go. — You may wait and see me with him but don't come near me, I'm quite sure he'll come for me. — I shan't tell him what I've done tonight, I wouldn't ha' done it but we want money so." I waited in the distance, saw her meet and go towards the station with a decent young man, her lad evidently. — I've met from time to time some interesting harlots and this was one of them, so retain the narrative about her.

Late on a dull, moist, dark night in November, I was passing along a quiet street in a poor neighbourhood, when two women approached me singing and loudly laughing. They held a short rope between them, and as they came near, thinking them a common frolicksome and half screwed couple, I moved to the edge of the footway to let them pass. They larking, lengthened the rope, and caught and entwined me with it just below my hips, laughing heartily at their trick. — "We've caught you young man, what will you stand?" — It was close to a gaslamp, and seeing it was a handsome, bold faced woman who spoke. — "Stand my dear? — It won't stand any more, you've pulled it off with the rope, look for it." — I happened to have a hottish ballocks that night, and baudy replies came naturally — tho far from being young.

At that both laughed so heartily and I as well, and we standing close together — the rope still round me, — made such a noise, that some one on the other side of the way stopped to look at us. — "I can't see it," said the biggest and plump one, who looked about five and twenty. The other a slim, poor looking creature of about eighteen, only giggled, and then became silent. "It's between your thighs perhaps." — "Ho, ho, ho — it ain't *you're* wearing it still." — "He, he, he," giggled the slim one. — "No, between your thighs — let me feel there. — It was stiff and if I find it there I'll give you five shillings, and you shall put it back if you can, I can't go home without it." — "Ho, ho, ho — what?" — "My peg," — and I pushed at her clothes in the region of her cunt. — "Give me the five bob then and you shall." — "Polly — Polly — yer don't know what yer about," said the other remonstrating. — "His peg — ho, ho, ho," laughed the other.

They were game I saw, whores they didn't seem to be, but workers of a poor class and who decidedly had been drinking. That class doesn't mind baudy language, they hear enough of it. — "I call it a peg to ladies, but there's another name." — "Tell us." — "Polly — come along." — "Feel if it's on yer yet. — Ho, ho," and Polly laughed still, as untwining the rope she was putting her hands between the fold of my great coat, when the other pulled them away. "Polly — yer don't know what yer about." — "Shut up," — said Polly. "Come along." — "I shan't." "Let's have a glass of wine and I'll feel if you've got it about *you* my dear," said I. — "*You've* got it right enough." — "Lord, so I have, and it's still stiff." — Then the other — named Sarah — again rebuked the elder, said she should go and was told she might, but, "Don't be a fool, come and have a drink with the gent," — which I'd offered. — "Follow us, there's a nice Pub around the next street," said Polly, who seemed to know the locality.

I was going to the Pub, knowing that Bacchus helps Venus, and thinking I might somehow get into the plump one who'd excited my desires, when it occurred to me as not desirable to be seen by a chance medley of poor people, at a public house in a poor neighbourhood with two common workwomen. I lusted for Polly now, and *because* she was so coarse and common — singular are my letches — and perhaps would have gone to the Pub, sooner than lose the chance of seeing what I knew was a spanking bum. At the street corner was a poor looking coffee shop. "Let's go in here, they'll fetch us all we want," said I. — In we two went, the other loitered outside. — "I'll wait for you." — "Come in, don't be a fool," and in came Sarah.

They'd nothing but tea and coffee, but they fetched us liquor for which they charged highly. They sat at a table in a corner with me, the two drank gin and water, the eldest's tongue ran on incessantly, I chaffing baudily but without frank words, she delighted replying and looking in my eyes lustfully. Then under the table I grasped her large thigh outside her clothes, and nudged her belly. "Now, don't." — "It's there." — "It ain't." — "It is." — "What?" — "Don't, Polly," said the thin one again. — Just then in came one looking like a cabman, who bought a roll and butter, and disappeared with it, but he'd eyed us so the whole time he was there that I felt uncomfortable, and so soon as he had gone, asked if they had a private room.

The mistress said "No," looked at the maid, and they held a conversation in a low tone. Then she said they had no private rooms, but there was one I might have till the house was closed. I accepted it, and we went up a narrow staircase to a bedroom. There the servant, "We don't let rooms, but this is it, five shillings — will you please pay first, Sir?" — I gave it her, the liquor was brought up, but Sarah wouldn't stop when she saw the bed. — "I shan't then — your agoin' on too far — yer don't know what yer adoing." — Down stairs she went, and I was alone with the plump one. — "I'll take her some gin," said she, and pouring out half a tumbler, down she went returning alone, Sarah wouldn't come. "We'd best perhaps go down agin," said Polly thoughtfully.

After seemingly a minute's reflexion, again she said, "Perhaps I'd better go." — "Nonsense, what did you come up here for?" — saying that I locked the door, closed on Polly, pushed her against the bed, and assaulted her privates. She'd so egged me on to baudy

chaff and smutty suggestions, that I'd felt sure of having her, but
as my hand touched her thighs she resisted, pushed down her
clothes, pushed me away stoutly, laughing as if half pleased tho
refusing, and squalling loudly. — "You shan't — don't now — a
joke's a joke — I won't — I'm married." — "You're not — where's
your ring?" — "Pawned." — "I *will* fuck you. "You shan't" and
she scuffled as much as virtuous servants have done whom I've
assailed similarly. I was so annoyed at my hindrance, felt so spite-
ful, that leaving off I angrily said, "You're not married, your linen's
dirty, that's why you won't let me." I didn't mean it, but savagely
wanted to offend her, to say something to annoy, and *that* came
impromptu. I said much of the same sort, but all in the same strain.

"Dirty? Me dirty? Cleaner than you I'll swear. Dirty! I'd wash
my shift to rags rather than be dirty. — You *have* cheek. — Show
me *your* shirt — look." — Saying that she turned up her petticoats
to her garters, and I saw that stockings and all she had on was as
white as could be, tho her ankle jackboots were muddy. — "Your
cunt's dirty then." — "You lie, it ain't." "Let's put this up it,"
pulling out my prick. — "Shan't." — But she looked at my cunt
prodder which was in splendid force. She was lewed before, now
leweder still and she laughed. I closed on her again, got my fingers
on the soft slit with but trifling hindrance, and frigged away at it.
— "Now don't — oh don't." Voluptuous sensations were conquer-
ing for me. — What woman can refuse a prick when the man's
fingers have been in full possession of her cunt a minute? "Feel my
prick." — She slid her hand down to it after twice saying, "Shan't"
and in another minute it was up her cunt, as she lay at the bed-
side on to which I pushed and lifted her. Quiet, absorbed in carnal
pleasure, the delicious crisis came on, and dissolved us, spending
into immobility and silence.

Quietly she lay as holding up her thighs, nestling my pego into
her, we looked into each other's eyes in silence, enjoying the carnal
junction. Fucking is in its essential always the same, the idealities
are everything, therein lays the charm of variety. I felt singular de-
light in fucking this common woman whom I'd only seen half an
hour. — It takes longer to tell than to act. — Who might be mar-
ried or single, or of any occupation, and whose cunt I'd not even
seen. Relinquishing one thigh I pushed her petticoats up, and look-

ing down saw a dark fully haired motte, the hair mingling with mine, and put a finger on to the clitoris — "Isn't fucking lovely?" — "Isn't it?" replied she.

Catching hold of her thigh again, I squeezed my belly well against hers, feeling my pego to be dwindling. "Has your friend been fucked?" "Dunno, but she has got a lover." — "Where's your husband?" — "God knows, on the tramp I suppose." — "You *are* married." — She nodded. "Who fucks you now?" — "No one." — "What a story." — She laughed, and it squeezed my cock out of her. Then we washed in the same basin, there was no towel, so shirt and chemise did duty.

Afterwards — "Show me your cunt." — "All right, I'm clean, — look," — pulling her clothes up to her motte, she let me see, saying how clean her linen was. I saw a cunt fat lipped, and full fledged. "No, I ain't had a child," said she, noticing my investigations. — Another letch came on. "I'd give *you* ten shillings to see your friend's cunt, and *she* ten to show it." — She seemed surprized. — "Will you? Don't think she will." — "Try to get her upstairs." — "I will, but she's a stupid, don't say you've done it to me." — Saying that, she put on her bonnet and went downstairs.

The two had as said "had a drop" before I'd met them. They'd had gin since, Sarah had had a tumbler more than half full to drink whilst down stairs. Opening the door I heard much laughing, and Sarah appeared, pushed up stairs by Polly into the room. No sooner there than I told her I wanted to see her little quim and would give her ten shillings — I'd got their names pat. "Polly says then she'll show me hers."

Tho slightly screwed she refused and there was much talk. — "We ain't whores," said she. — Polly pulled her petticoats up to her garters, and then she pulled out my prick, again fairly stiff. — Both laughed at it. — Polly said, "It's getting late — will yer or won't yer? — I'll show him mine if you'll show him yours." — "Suppose Jack hears on it." — "Jack be blowed, how can he know unless you tells him." — I put on the table the two half sovereigns and they eyed them. — "Will you now? If not we'll go." — "It's agoin' too far," said Sarah — I put the money in my pocket. — "You show him first." — "There, then," said Polly, putting her bum on the bed and exposing her charms. — The other chuckled. — "He, He, He, look at you." — "You've seen it before, come on, show it him." — She went to Sarah and pushed her up chuckling. "He, He, He" but she was yielding, and next minute was laying on the bed, petticoats up to her navel, legs hanging down, her crack just visible, whilst Polly in a similar position but with thighs well apart, lay laughing by her side.

I investigated the cunts of both, but the young one didn't like that. — "You've been fucked," said I. — "I ain't." — "She has," said Polly. — "I ain't been." — "I'll fuck you then." — "No, you shan't." — She roused herself and half got off the bed, I promised not to attempt it and got her to lay down again with cunt showing. "I'll fuck *you* then." — "All right," said Polly. Next second my balls were banging against her buttocks. — "Oh! If Jack ever heard," giggled the slim one. — "Jack be buggered," said Polly, heaving her rump responsively to my thrusts. Silent were all three now as I fucked, feeling Sarah's thin thighs and quim. — "Aha — fuck — cunt," I cried. — "Ahrr — Ahrr," sobbed Polly. — "Oho, you hurt," cried out the slim one. In the paroxysms of pleasure I'd hurt her cunt with my fingers.

"We'd better get home or there'll be a jolly kick up," said the slim one whilst still my prick was in the other's quim. — I was in a hurry also, uncunted, and in five minutes was out of the house, after giving the two half sovereigns. — They were not sisters they said, which was all I could learn, excepting that they'd carried something home between them tied up with the rope, and had had a drop with the money they'd got. I think they were laundresses.

I enjoyed this chance amour immensely, it was so different from the business-like fucking with a harlot, price agreed beforehand. But how strange! As we met as strangers in the street, who could have imagined that they'd show me their cunts, and that one would be fucked twice within an hour. These impromptu amours are delicious.

A long time had passed since we saw the man birched, and H. and I wished to see another. The abbess said she'd try to arrange it, but some of her men strongly objected to be made a show of, tho one or two liked it. She didn't know when the exposants would come, or when we should be there, all was a mere chance, yet it was only on our being all there at the same time that it could come off. Three or four months ran away before it did. There one day, said the abbess, "If you'd like to see a birching to day, there will be a gentleman who likes to be looked at, but when I tell you, you must hold up your chemise and shew him your *twatts*, he'll see it, tho you may think he won't, don't speak a word and leave directly he spends."

H. wouldn't mask herself and went down with a lovely laced chemise only on. — I with a shirt on only but masked. Laying along a sofa, was a fair haired, bearded man whom I judged between thirty five and forty, with his face hidden by both hands. He was laying about three quarters on his belly, so that we could see his prick — which was not stiff — and balls. His shirt was tucked up to above his waist, his trousers pulled down to his knees, and the whole of his backside and thighs were bare. We stood by his side and the abbess began. — Swish. She talked some nonsense to him, about her being the governess and correcting him, to which he made no reply. The swishing went on slowly at about a stroke a minute, gradually his prick elongated and the gland extruded itself completely, as his backside grew redder and redder. Then she struck more quickly. — "Ohoo," — he murmuringly whispered — "Ho — ho — I can't." — Swish. — Swish. — His backside began to oscillate, his prick rubbed between his belly and the soft white sheet which covered the sofa. Then as arranged, H., who stood nearer his head than I did lifted her chemise up to her navel, showing her lovely thighs and chestnut covered motte, she liked shewing it. I saw his fingers open so that he could look thro them at her, yet I couldn't see a bit of his face, he murmured something as if in pleasure, jogged his belly as if fucking, and his prick which I could see well now, shot out a lot of sperm on to the sheet. Then he ceased and laid quiet, she dropped her chemise covering her charms, and we both left. I paid for the sight, and dare say that the victim paid for the sight of H.'s nudity.

Miss R., the fat rumped, had long ceased to be seen, and Miss B. at times could not be had tho both of us liked her, for she was a demon at minetting, and with difficulty could be got away from H.'s quim when once her mouth was on it. She had also as said a lovely cunt in size, shape, color, and growth of fringe. So fucking

her from behind whilst she gamahuched H. gave infinite pleasure
to us all.

The abbess liked to introduce others and no doubt got paid
for it. One day a Miss D°°sy was named. — "Speaks three lan-
guages, has been kept, not long been gay, and now only on the
quiet, quite up to fun." — So we had Miss. D. a tallish, quite fair
haired woman of say eight and twenty, a genteel woman who spoke
French and German as I found, and who really knew much about
Europe. She like all the others took a letch for H. — they all do —
and of course I fucked her whilst minetting H. — the usual formula.
But somehow her cunt didn't fit me at all, and I cared not about
fucking her. Yet we had her several times, she was so conversable,
and talked erotic philosophy in chaste language in the way poor
Camille used, and for some reason or other — who can give rea-
sons for letches tho we try? — the two women used to examine very
curiously each other's cunts — a thing which usually H. did not
care about doing, tho she'd frig any cunt near her when I was
fucking her.

Miss D.'s cuntal fringe was silky but not very curly, and at
half way down the sides of the lips the curls ceased and the hair
became actually straight and long. It continued so nearly round
the division between prick hole and bum hole, and when she
squatted to piddle — of course I made her do that, her cunt looked
— as indeed it did when she stood upright or lay on the bed with
thighs apart, — not unlike the end of a broom. I told her of this,
saying it was ugly. — H. agreed with me.

Miss D. said *she* didn't like it and looked carefully at H.'s one
day — whose lips as they die away towards her bum hole are
slightly covered by the shortest hairs with a charming tendency to
curl — I said that if D.'s were clipped short they would look nicer
to me — tho perhaps not to others, for tastes vary. — It ended in
my artistically trimming Miss D°°sy's straggling cuntal fringe with
the scissors. — Next time seen she was delighted, for the short hairs
had actually curled partially, she examined them with a hand glass
before us, and we without the glass. The beauty of her cunt was
really enhanced by my tonsorial skill, and particularly when she
knelt on the bed and we viewed her quim from behind.

Yet as her cunt after several trials didn't fit me, we discontinued seeing her. She was soon after again kept by a gentleman, the abbess said. — She was a conversable woman, and no doubt her cunt had found a suitable partner. — Some cunts never seem to fit me — others are delicious.

A couple of years nearly had passed since the erotic quartette. We often talked about it and H. wished we could play the same games again, but I had no such intention nor could afford it. I saw however from the tone our conversation often took, that she wanted to have another man. "Shouldn't you like to see me fucked? I should like to feel your prick whilst he fucked me," and so on.

We talked so before the abbess one day, who said "and I know one who is dying to have her." Then it transpired that a frequenter of the house had seen H°°° when going away one day, and had fallen violently in love with her. "Has he a big prick?" asked H. eagerly. The abbess said he had, that he was a gentleman, a barrister, but poor. We talked over this and agreed to have him. He was spoken to, and it was ultimately arranged that we should all be masked, and that he was to fuck H. whilst I was present. The big prick, the prick she'd never seen, made H. ready for anything, and she didn't disguise the pleasure that the novelty would give her.

This took some time to bring about, they never knowing long before hand, when habitues may arrive. One afternoon the abbess said as we entered, "He's coming, I've just got a letter and have sent for a lady for him, he'll consent to masks, or anything else to have your friend." We were a little startled at first. H. said she couldn't till she'd seen what sort of man he was. She wasn't going to let any ugly, old, common man have her.

When he arrived she went down to be introduced him, and came back approving, he was a fine tall handsome man of thirty and wanted to fuck her there and then. Her eyes glistened with lust, she had the exquisitely, voluptuous look in her face which she has when randy. I layed down the conditions. He was to be naked all but his shirt, I to see his prick, and feel it if I liked. — "No," said the abbess, "he won't allow that." — "Then he shan't have her." — Down the abbess went and returning said that I might feel him if I liked. — "Let him come," — said H. impatiently. Up he came with mask on and soon divested himself of his clothes. H. without mask sat on his knee and pulled about a grand, stiff tool,

triumphantly, whilst he fingered her quim. He was well made but
rather hairy on his legs which I didn't like — many men are hairy
legged.

Then she played one or two baudy tricks, and lastly turned
her bum to him whilst he sat on a chair and got his prick up her. I
sitting on a low chair opposite saw it hidden in her cunt, his balls
hanging outside, his hands round her belly, one finger rubbing her
clitoris. — "Aha, go to the bed," murmured he. He didn't attempt
to disguise his voice as I did. To the bed they went where side by
side she fondled his love staff, then he mounted her. — "You shan't
fuck me with that on," said she, and suddenly pulled off his mask
and dropped it on the floor. He cared about nothing now but pos-
sessing her, put his prick in her cunt rapidly, whilst she raised
the thigh nearest the bedside high up, so that I who now ap-
proached the bed could see his prick ramming between her cunt
lips — see the in and out movement, an exciting sight.

He'd given some rapid strokes when I threw up his shirt to
his waist, to see the wag of his buttocks which were white but
nothing remarkably handsome, and I didn't admire a central fur-
row strongly haired up to his backbone, but the come and go of
his priapean shaft pleased me. He gave a sigh of pleasure and then
I laid hold of his testicles. — "Ho," said he with a loud cry, and
with a violent start uncunted. "Don't do that." — "What is it?"
said H., ceasing her bum wagging. — I told. — "Fuck me, put it
in, let him feel them, you will like it." Before she'd said it all,
his glowing tipped machine was again hidden, his balls wagged
more than ever, soon the violent movement of her thighs and but-
tocks heralded her coming joy, and I heard, "Fuck dear — aha —
spunk," and heard his murmurs of love. His ample balls were now
soon steady over her bumhole, and both were quiet. *She* with
closed eyes enjoying the blissful oozings of her cunt, the soothing
influence of spermatic injection, *his* buttocks moving with the
slightest gentlest jogs, rubbing his tender gland within the inner-
most recesses of her sexual treasure, whilst I held his balls, he seem-
ingly unconscious of it.

"Get off," said she. Without a word off he got. There she lay
with overflowing cunt, thighs wide apart, looking lewedly at me
who had withdrawn then to the bed's foot. Holding his tool as he
got off of her, he picked up the mask, put it on, and went to the

washing stand. H. lay with thighs apart and pointing to her cunt. I had had no intention of having her so, had said so, but the sight overwhelmed me. Going to her, she moved herself to the bedside silently, knowing the desires she'd evoked better than I, filled with luxurious desires herself. Next second my pego was engulphed in her lubricious avenue, I rammed like a steam engine, her eyes glared at me with lust, and both spent almost directly, whilst still he was soaping and slopping his privates, never looking round till she'd got off the bed and I stood looking out of the window. I must have spent in a minute, never had I spent more rapidly wrought up by what I had seen. Then I sat down whilst he was pulling on his trowsers.

He said not a word and would I think have left, but H., — "What do you put your things on for, ain't you going to have me again?" "Oh yes, if you will." — Take your trowsers off then and give me a bottle of champagne." He did — we'd been already drinking champagne.

Again we talked and drank. She washed her cunt, again sat on his knee, played with his pego, never ceased handling it, shewing it to me. — "Feel it, isn't it a fine one?" — "No — no," said he sharply — "you said you would let him feel it." I felt modestly the gristly elastic propagator and then he felt mine. They kissed and toyed, his fingers on her cunt. He whispered something. — "Had I fucked her in his sperm?" — she told me afterwards. — She'd answered, "No." — So drinking and talking, at intervals she feeling both our pricks at once, time ran away and his prick grew stiff. Then at her request he took his clothes into another room, remaining in his shirt and socks, and again fucked H., whilst again I held his balls, and then he left. We afterwards enjoyed each others genitals, she had her fourth spend, and with my spunk mingled with his in her cunt, we slept for a few minutes.

The abbess came into us. He was about leaving and had been extolling H.'s charms who wanting to see him before he left, quitted the room and was gone sometime. Returning, "He's fucked you again." — I saw it from the lascivious circles round her eyes and from her manner. "Yes," — said she in a half shamed way, "and he never made me a compliment." — "Did you ask him?" — "No, but he might have done so, he's had me three times." I, half disgusted and a little screwed, — "I'm glad he didn't, am surprised you wish to be treated as a whore. — You wanted a change, a fresh prick, a big one — be content." She was very angry with me for saying "Whore" and I was with her for desiring money. — The old leven was in her still, she wanted her pleasures but to be paid for them. No doubt, the abbess got money tho she said he'd only paid for sending for the other woman and his room.

H. said she believed he'd given the abbess five pounds, and that he might have given *her* half a dozen pairs of gloves. A month afterwards the abbess said he was there and wanted H. but I wouldn't let her, nor did she wish to go, and never saw him afterwards.

"Fuck me," said H. a quarter of an hour after. — "I cannot." — "Try." — "I can't." — She was in full rut, one of her lascivious frenzies was on her — her eyes were voluptuous, were wildly luminous with sexual passion — but oh! So beautiful. — Laying hold of my pego she frigged it but uselessly, then talking all the time about his prick, ever and anon thrusting her tongue into my mouth, lascivious enough to stir a dead man, — she was partly screwed which increased her pecklessness. — "Lick my cunt then." — "Piss then." — "Let me piss in your mouth, I've done so." — "I wouldn't." — "Lick me then." — I began. — "Suck my prick, my darling, till its stiff, and then I'll fuck you." — Voluptuous thrills ran thro me as I tasted the salt of her cunt. "I can't, I don't know how, I never have, but I will kiss it," and she kissed it from bum hole to tip. Then in her raging lust she yielded to my repeated wishes, into that lovely cherry lipped mouth went my prick, whilst with my nose up her vagina, I licked her clitoris as she knelt over me and clasped her ivory buttocks. — It took effect — the gentle rub of her mouth, the smell of her cunt. — "There — it's — stiff — fuck me now." — Agile as a monkey, she got from off my mouth on to her back, and lay with thighs wide apart, shewing the crimson gap. — She had her way. — I fucked her long, long, deliciously, whilst twice she spent to my one libation.

The narrative in its chronological order of events I finish. Many more incidents might have been told of varied delights, of whims and fancies normal and abnormal, yet tho the places, participants and actresses were different, the amatory amusements were similar to others played elsewhere, and their repetition in the narrative would be tedious.

I break with the past, my amatory career is over, my secret life finished. My philosophy remains the same. My deeds leave me no regret — with the exception perhaps of a very few. — Would that I were young enough to continue in the same course — that all might happen to me over again. — But age forbids, duty forbids, affection forbids — Eros adieu.

'J